Studies in Church History

54

(2018)

THE CHURCH AND EMPIRE

THE CHURCH AND EMPIRE

EDITED BY

STEWART J. BROWN
CHARLOTTE METHUEN
ANDREW SPICER

PUBLISHED FOR
THE ECCLESIASTICAL HISTORY SOCIETY
BY
CAMBRIDGE UNIVERSITY PRESS
2018

Published by Cambridge University Press
on behalf of the Ecclesiastical History Society
University Printing House, Cambridge CB2 8BS, United Kingdom

First published 2018

ISBN 9781108473798

ISSN 0424–2084

SUBSCRIPTIONS: *Studies in Church History* is an annual subscription
journal (ISSN 0424–2084). The 2018 subscription price (excluding VAT),
which includes print and electronic access, is £105 (US $169 in the USA,
Canada and Mexico) for institutions and £58 (US $93 in the USA, Canada
and Mexico) for individuals ordering direct from the Press and certifying that
the volume is for their personal use. An electronic-only subscription is also
available to institutions at £82 (US $130 in the USA, Canada and Mexico).
Special arrangements exist for members of the Ecclesiastical History Society.

Previous volumes are available online at www.cambridge.org/StudCH

Printed in the United Kingdom by Bell & Bain Ltd
A catalogue record for this publication is available from the British Library

Contents

Preface   ix

List of Contributors   xi

List of Abbreviations   xiii

List of Illustrations   xvi

Introduction   1
    Stewart J. Brown

Towards a Spiritual Empire: Christian Exegesis of the   16
Universal Census at the Time of Jesus's Birth
    Tiziana Faitini

The 'Servant of God': Divine Favour and Instrumentality   31
under Constantine, 318–25
    Andrew J. Pottenger

Imperium and the City of God: Augustine on Church and   46
Empire
    Gillian Clark

The Popes as Rulers of Rome in the Aftermath of Empire,   71
476–769
    Rosamond McKitterick

Empire, Ethnic Election and Exegesis in the *Opus Caroli*   96
(*Libri Carolini*) (*President's Prize*)
    Conor O'Brien

Super gentes et regna: Papal 'Empire' in the Later Eleventh and   109
Twelfth Centuries
    Benedict G. E. Wiedemann

Emperor and Church in the Last Centuries of Byzantium   123
    Ruth Macrides

Contents

An English Bishop Afloat in an Irish See: John Bale, Bishop   144
of Ossory, 1552–3
     Stephen N. Tong

Roman *Imperium* and the Restoration Church   159
     Jacqueline Rose

The Episcopal Church, the Roman Empire and the Royal   176
Supremacy in Restoration Scotland
     Andrew Carter

Concepts of Mission in Scottish Presbyterianism: The   190
SSPCK, the Highlands and Britain's American Colonies,
1709–40
     Clare Loughlin

Christianity and Empire: The Catholic Mission in Late   208
Imperial China
     R. Po-Chia Hsia

Providential Empire? The Established Church of England   225
and the Nineteenth-Century British Empire in India
(*Presidential Address*)
     Stewart J. Brown

Special Worship in the British Empire: From the Seventeenth   260
to the Twentieth Centuries
     Joseph Hardwick and Philip Williamson

Queen Adelaide and the Extension of Anglicanism in Malta   281
     Nicholas Dixon

Claiming the Land: The Church Missionary Society and   296
Architecture in the Arctic (*Kennedy Prize*)
     Emily Turner

Anglican Emigrant Chaplaincy in the British Empire and   314
Beyond, *c.*1840–1900
     Rowan Strong

Contents

Sisters and Brothers Abroad: Gender, Race, Empire and   328
Anglican Missionary Reformism in Hawai'i and the Pacific,
1858–75
    Steven S. Maughan

Ultramontane Efforts in the Ottoman Empire during the   345
1860s and 1870s
    Maryam Kartashyan

'*Britishers* and Protestants': Protestantism and Imperial British   359
Identities in Britain, Canada and Australia from the 1880s to
the 1920s
    Géraldine Vaughan

Englishness, Empire and Nostalgia: A Heterodox Religious   374
Community's Appeal in the Inter-War Years
    Jane Shaw

A Triangular Conflict: The Nyasaland Protectorate and Two   393
Missions, 1915–33
    David Thompson

Social Anglicanism and Empire: C. F. Andrews's Christian   407
Socialism
    Philip Lockley

Preface

The theme of *Studies in Church History* 54 is 'The Church and Empire'. This volume presents a selection of peer-reviewed articles derived from the wide variety of communications offered to the Ecclesiastical History Society's Summer Conference and Winter Meeting 2016–17. These meetings took place under the presidency of Stewart J. Brown at the University of Edinburgh in July 2016 and at Magdalene College, Cambridge, in January 2017.

We thank Professor Brown for suggesting the theme, 'The Church and Empire', which proved thought-provoking and stimulating, attracting record numbers of participants and communications. We would also like to thank him for his leadership of the society as president for 2016–17. Without those who prepared and presented papers, chaired sessions, participated in discussions and offered their time and expertise as peer reviewers, neither the conferences nor this volume would have been possible. We are grateful to them all. Dr Tim Grass has once again provided unstinting support in the editorial process: we thank him for all his work on this volume, and on so many other aspects of the society's business, and the Ecclesiastical History Society for funding his post.

The Summer Conference and Winter Meeting were successfully organized by the society's outgoing conference secretary, Professor Michael Walsh, and his successor, Dr David Hart, supported by the conference teams at the University of Edinburgh and Magdalene College, Cambridge. They worked together with the society's secretary, Dr Gareth Atkins, to whom we are particularly grateful for arranging the Winter Meeting venue.

The Ecclesiastical History Society supports two prizes for essays accepted for publication in *Studies in Church History*. The Kennedy Prize, for the best essay by a postgraduate student, has this year been awarded to Emily Turner for her article, 'Claiming the Land: The Church Missionary Society and Architecture in the Arctic'. The President's Prize, for the best article by an early career scholar, is being presented for the first time. It has been won by Dr Conor O'Brien, for his article, 'Empire, Ethnic Election and Exegesis in the

Opus Caroli (*Libri Carolini*)'. We extend our congratulations to them both.

Charlotte Methuen
University of Glasgow

Andrew Spicer
Oxford Brookes University

Contributors

Stewart J. Brown
>Professor of Ecclesiastical History, University of Edinburgh

Andrew Carter
>Postgraduate student, University of St Andrews

Gillian Clark
>Professor Emerita of Ancient History, University of Bristol

Nicholas Dixon
>Postgraduate student, Pembroke College, Cambridge

Tiziana Faitini
>School of International Studies, Trento

Joseph Hardwick
>Senior Lecturer in British History, Northumbria University

R. Po-Chia Hsia
>Edwin Erle Sparks Professor of History, Pennsylvania State University

Mariam Kartashyan
>Postdoctoral researcher and Assistant, Department for Old Catholic Theology, University of Bern

Philip Lockley
>Curate, St Clement's Church, Oxford

Clare Loughlin
>Postgraduate student, University of Edinburgh

Ruth Macrides
>Reader in Byzantine Studies, University of Birmingham

Steven S. Maughan
>Bernie McCain Chair in the Humanities and Professor of History, The College of Idaho

Contributors

Rosamond McKitterick
> Professor of Medieval History and Director of Research, Faculty of History, University of Cambridge

Conor O'Brien
> Junior Research Fellow in History, Churchill College, Cambridge

Andrew J. Pottenger
> Postgraduate student, University of Manchester

Jacqueline Rose
> Lecturer in History, University of St Andrews

Jane Shaw
> Professor of Religious Studies, Stanford University

Rowan Strong
> Professor of Church History, Murdoch University

David M. Thompson
> Emeritus Professor of Modern Church History, University of Cambridge

Stephen Tong
> Postgraduate student, University of Cambridge

Emily Turner
> Postgraduate student, University of Edinburgh

Géraldine Vaughan
> Lecturer in Modern British History, Université de Rouen

Benedict G. E. Wiedemann
> Postgraduate student, University College London

Philip Williamson
> Professor of Modern British History, Durham University

Abbreviations

AH	*Archivium Hibernicum* (1911–)
AHP	*Archivum historiae pontificiae* (1963–)
AHR	*American Historical Review* (1895–)
ASV	Archivio Segreto Vaticano
BCH	*British Catholic History* (2015–)
BL	British Library
Bodl.	Bodleian Library
CChr.COGD	Corpus Christianorum Conciliorum Oecumenicorum Generaliumque Decreta (Turnhout, 2006–)
CChr.SL	Corpus Christianorum, series Latina (Turnhout, 1953–)
CERS	Church of England Record Society
CHC	*Cambridge History of Christianity*, 9 vols (Cambridge, 2005–9)
ChH	*Church History* (1932–)
CSPD	*Calendar of State Papers, Domestic*
CUL	Cambridge University Library
DOP	*Dumbarton Oaks Papers* (1941–)
EHR	*English Historical Review* (1886–)
EME	*Early Medieval Europe* (1992–)
ET	English translation
FC	Fathers of the Church
HistJ	*Historical Journal* (1958–)
HR	*Historical Research* (1986–)
IBMR	*International Bulletin of Missionary Research* (1977–2015); *International Bulletin of Mission Research* (2016–)
IKZ	*Internationale Kirchliche Zeitschrift* (1911–)
InR	*Innes Review* (1950–)
JAH	*Journal of African History* (1960–)
JBS	*Journal of British Studies* (1961–)
JEH	*Journal of Ecclesiastical History* (1950–)
JICH	*Journal of Imperial and Commonwealth History* (1972–)
JRH	*Journal of Religious History* (1960–)
JRS	*Journal of Roman Studies* (1911–)
JThS	*Journal of Theological Studies* (1899–)

LCL	Loeb Classical Library
LPL	Lambeth Palace Library
MGH	Monumenta Germaniae Historica inde ab a. *c.*500 usque ad a. 1500, ed. G. H. Pertz et al. (Hanover, Berlin, etc., 1826–)
MGH Conc.	Monumenta Germaniae Historica, Concilia (1893–)
MGH Const.	MGH Constitutiones et acta publica imperatorum et regum (1893–)
MGH DD	Monumenta Germaniae Historica, Diplomata regum et imperatorum Germaniae (1879–)
MGH Epp.	Monumenta Germaniae Historica, Epistolae (1887–)
MGH Fontes iuris	Monumenta Germaniae Historica, Fontes iuris Germanici antiqui in usum scholarum separatism editi (1869–)
MGH Poetae	Monumenta Germaniae Historica, Poetae Latini mediii aevi (1978–)
MGH SRG i.u.s.	Monumenta Germaniae Historica, Scriptores rerum Germanicarum in usum scholarum seperatum editi (1871–)
MGH SRM	Monumenta Germaniae Historica, Scriptores rerum Merovingicarum, 7 vols (1884–1951)
MGH SS	Monumenta Germaniae Historica, Scriptores (in folio) (1826–)
n.d.	no date
NLS	National Library of Scotland
n.pl.	no place
NRS	National Records of Scotland
n.s.	new series
ODCC	*Oxford Dictionary of the Christian Church*, ed. F. L. Cross, with E. A. Livingstone, 3rd edn (Oxford, 1997; 3rd edn revised 2005)
ODNB	*Oxford Dictionary of National Biography*, ed. H. C. G. Matthew and Brian Harrison (Oxford, 2004)
OED	*Oxford English Dictionary*
OHA	*Oxford History of Anglicanism*, 5 vols (Oxford, 2017)
P&P	*Past and Present* (1952–)

PHS	*Proceedings of the Huguenot Society of Great Britain and Ireland* (1885–2012)
PL	Patrologia Latina, ed. J.-P. Migne, 217 vols + 4 index vols (Paris, 1844–65)
PO	Patrologia Orientalis, ed. R. Graffin and F. Nau (Paris, 1907–)
RQ	*Renaissance Quarterly* (1967–)
SCH	Studies in Church History
s.n.	*sub nomine* ('under the name')
SOAS	School of Oriental and African Studies
Speculum	*Speculum: A Journal of Medieval Studies* (1925–)
s.v.	*sub verbo* ('under the word')
TNA	The National Archives
TTH	Translated Texts for Historians
UL	University Library

Jacqueline Rose, 'Roman *Imperium* and the Restoration Church'

Fig. 1. The Emperors Constantine and Julian, representing faith and apostasy. Engraved title page of William Gouge, *The Whole-Armor of God* (London, 1619), Cambridge University Library, shelfmark Syn.7.61.110. Reproduced by kind permission of the Syndics of Cambridge University Library.   163

Joseph Hardwick and Philip Williamson, 'Special Worship in the British Empire: From the Seventeenth to the Twentieth Centuries'

Fig. 1. Proclamation for a thanksgiving day by Benning Wentworth, governor of New Hampshire, 28 February 1760, containing the English proclamation of 23 October 1759 for the military victories in Canada. Library of Congress, Printed Ephemera Collection, portfolio 87, folder 9. Reproduced by permission of the Library of Congress.   265

Fig. 2. Proclamation for the day of thanksgiving for the peace treaty of Versailles, 1919, to be observed throughout the empire, as printed in *The South Australian Government Gazette*, 4 July 1919. Reproduced by permission of the Government of South Australia.   270

Emily Turner, 'Claiming the Land: The Church Missionary Society and Architecture in the Arctic'

Fig. 1. St. Thomas's Church, Moose Factory, 1856–64, completed 1884. Author's photograph.   307

Fig. 2. Plan of Fort Norman, Mackenzie River, Northwest Territories, [1898]. Winnipeg, Hudson's Bay Company Archives, G.1/315.   308

Fig. 3. Hay River, late nineteenth century. Toronto, Anglican Church of Canada General Synod Archives, P7559–73.   309

Fig. 4. Church of Our Lady of Good Hope, Fort Good Hope, 1865–85. Author's photograph.   312

Introduction

The theme of this fifty-fourth volume of *Studies in Church History* is 'The Church and Empire', and the twenty-three articles included here explore the complex and ever-evolving relationship of ecclesiastical and imperial power within a range of historical contexts. The articles represent plenary addresses and a selection of the communications presented at two highly successful Ecclesiastical History Society conferences during my presidential year – a Summer Conference held at the University of Edinburgh in July 2016 and a Winter Meeting held at Magdalene College, Cambridge, in January 2017. Both conferences attracted a large number of speakers and participants from across the world, and reflected the considerable scholarly interest in questions concerning the relations of Church and empire. These questions include the extent to which Christianity in the Western world became linked to the political power of large imperial states, the nature and extent of the connection of Christianity to the expansion of Western imperialism in the early modern and modern periods, and the manner in which the Church often came into conflict with imperial power, especially when Christians insisted on the spiritual independence of the Church and on maintaining an independent Christian moral witness against the wars of conquest, cruelty, racism, oppression and arrogance of power that too often have been associated with imperial rule.

From its beginnings, the Christian Church has had a close, often symbiotic relationship with imperial power. Christianity emerged as a religion within the Roman empire; its founder suffered the Roman death of crucifixion within a Roman province by the act of a Roman governor. Early Christians experienced sporadic but brutal persecution and executions at the hands of imperial Roman officials, because they would not sacrifice to the imperial gods and insisted on the exclusive claims of their religion. Yet the early spread of Christianity was also assisted by Roman roads and sea routes, by Roman urban centres and by the *Pax Romana* prevailing across the Mediterranean world. And in time, persecution ceased and the empire became largely Christian. In 313 CE the Roman emperor Constantine granted Christianity toleration and protection under Roman law, and promoted unity among Christians, most notably by the First Council of Nicaea in 325. By the Edict of Thessalonica in 380, the emperor Theodosius I made the Christianity of the Nicene Creed the only officially legitimate religion in the Roman empire. Now it was pagans and other non-Christians who experienced persecution. Increasingly the institutions of the Church grew to resemble those of the empire, examples being the liturgical dress and hierarchical organization of its clergy, the use of the basilica form in Christian places of worship and the claims to universal spiritual authority made by the bishops of Rome. In the teachings of the Church, the institutions of both Church and Roman empire came to be portrayed as divinely sanctioned and part of the providential plan for humankind.

The Western Roman empire collapsed in the later fifth century under pressure from northern invaders, but the Western Church survived amid warfare and social dislocation. The popes in Rome now began emulating the style of the Roman emperors, while the clergy helped preserve Roman learning and culture, keeping alive memories of the Roman empire. The ideal of the Roman empire was revived in ninth-century Europe with the Carolingian empire: the Carolingians embraced the alliance of Church and empire and portrayed themselves as promoting the true universal Christianity, and they had a significant role in the Christianization of Europe. The Carolingian empire soon weakened but it was revived in the tenth century, and by the thirteenth century it was being called, significantly, the Holy Roman Empire. Alongside the Holy Roman Empire, other empires emerged in the West, including the Anglo-Norman, Genoese and Venetian empires; they too viewed themselves as Christian empires, looking to the ancient Roman model of the unity of Church and empire.

In Asia Minor and the Balkans, the Eastern Roman or Byzantine empire, with its great capital of Constantinople, survived until the fifteenth century. The Byzantine alliance of Church and empire was expressed in the lavish ceremonial of the imperial court and the rich decoration of its churches. The Byzantine, or Eastern Orthodox, Church gradually diverged in theology and worship from the Roman Catholic Church in the West, and the division became formal and permanent with the Great Schism of 1054. The Byzantine empire collapsed with the fall of Constantinople to the Islamic Turks in 1453. But then the emerging Muscovite empire in the north, which had embraced Eastern Orthodoxy, gradually developed its claim to be the true successor to the ancient Roman empire. Its capital of Moscow became the 'third Rome', rising up after the fall first of ancient Rome and then of Constantinople. The Muscovite, or Russian, empire expressed the union of Orthodox Church and empire in the person of the tsar, or 'Holy Father', spreading Orthodox Christianity across northern and central Asia, until the Russian Revolution of 1917.

In medieval Europe, reconceptualizations of the political-theological ideal of the papacy led to tensions over the proper form to be taken by relations between the Church and the successor states of the Roman *imperium*, especially the states comprising the Holy Roman Empire. These reconceptualizations of papal empire included the ideas that the pope in Rome, as the vicar of Christ, was the *dominus mundi*, or the one supreme authority over the world, and had the authority to appoint and depose emperors and kings. But against this conception of papal empire there were conflicting notions of 'regnal imperialism', by which each monarch acted as an 'emperor', in the manner of the Roman emperor Constantine, within their own kingdoms, and exercised a degree of authority over the Church within their territories in the interest of Church unity. The Investiture Controversy of the late eleventh and early twelfth centuries was one expression of these tensions between *dominus mundi* and regnal imperialism, and it weakened earlier medieval efforts to unite papacy and imperial rule. The sixteenth-century Reformation further shattered the older unity of Church and empire. At the beginning of the English Reformation, King Henry VIII famously based his claim to royal supremacy over the Church on the grounds that 'this realm of England is an empire', relying on conceptions of *imperium* that reflected those of Constantine and the fourth-century Roman empire. In the German context, princes, dukes and other civic authorities increasingly claimed the authority of both emperor and pope. The Reformation, and especially the wars that followed it, would lead to the policy within the diverse territories of the Holy Roman Empire of *cuius regio, eius religio*, by which the ruler of each territory would determine the religion of that territory, a policy that would largely endure into the nineteenth century.

The beginnings of the era of European discovery and colonization from the sixteenth century brought new conceptions of the alliance of Church and empire, now focused on territorial expansion rather than constitutional relations. The churches, both Catholic and Protestant, became associated with European expansion in the Americas, Asia and later Africa, and the formation of the Spanish, Portuguese,

Dutch, French and British empires. For many Christians, the territorial expansion of the European empires was part of the divine plan for the spread of Christianity. God, they believed, now worked through empires for the Christianization of the non-Western world, just as God had worked through the ancient Roman empire for the Christianization of the Western world. Missionaries often followed in the wake of conquest; the Bible often followed the flag. The Spanish conquest and destruction of the Aztec and Inca empires in the New World was followed by priests who baptized the surviving populations and subsequently organized them into dioceses and parishes of the Catholic Church. Clergy accompanied colonial settlers in the extraordinary migration of European peoples to the new settlement colonies in the Americas, South Africa, Australia and New Zealand. Missionaries, supported by churches and voluntary Christian societies at home, worked for the conversion of the subject peoples of the empires, and viewed missionary outreach as the providential purpose of empire. But the connection of the Bible and the flag was always an ambiguous one. Many missionaries came to see themselves not only as preachers of the gospel but also as protectors of the original inhabitants against enslavement, abuse and exploitation. In their role as protectors, they sometimes appealed for justice to the Christian imperial authorities in Europe. The sixteenth-century Spanish Dominican Bartolomé de las Casas appealed successfully to the Spanish emperor to extend legal protection to the indigenous peoples in the Spanish territories in the Americas. In the late eighteenth and early nineteenth centuries, Protestant Christians took a leading role in ending legal slavery within the British empire, which convinced many that their empire had a providential purpose in spreading not only Christianity but also freedom to the wider world. But missionaries could also be outspoken critics of empires, who could denounce conquest and exploitation, and who could believe themselves called by God to be defenders of the human rights and dignity of the subject peoples. The ever-changing relations of Christianity and imperialism, of glory and power, of Church and empire, have had a profound influence on the development of the Christian religion.

The Content and Structure of the Volume

The twenty-three articles in this volume have been organized in a chronological order. They fall into five loosely defined periods:

Antiquity and Late Antiquity, medieval Europe, the early modern world, the nineteenth century and the period leading into the twentieth century. The individual articles were not commissioned by the editors and they do not represent an attempt to provide comprehensive coverage of the theme of Church and empire through the centuries. Rather, they form a collection of discrete case studies illustrating different aspects of the volume's theme. A preponderance of the articles deals with the British empire, which reflects the preponderance of communications offered at the two conferences and also points to the growing scholarly interest in the religious aspects of British imperialism. But this said, the articles do cover a wide range of topics in the global history of Christianity.

ANTIQUITY AND LATE ANTIQUITY

The first three articles explore the relations of Church and empire in Antiquity and Late Antiquity. Tiziana Faitini's article, 'Towards a Spiritual Empire: Christian Exegesis of the Universal Census at the Time of Jesus's Birth', considers the depiction in the Gospel of Luke of the Roman census at the time of Christ's birth, and then proceeds to discuss interpretations of the census by three Church Fathers, Origen, Ambrose of Milan and Orosius, and their reception and adaptation by medieval commentators. For these interpreters, the census was symbolic of Christ's offer of eternal life to all inhabitants of the world, while it also, especially for Orosius, represented Christ's endorsement of the Roman empire as integral to the divine plan for propagating the gospel. Andrew J. Pottenger, in '"The Servant of God": Divine Favour and Instrumentality under Constantine, 318–25', offers an assessment of the motivations behind Constantine's efforts as emperor to promote unity within the Church. Constantine, Pottenger argues, genuinely believed that God's favour both to his reign and to the empire was directly connected to God's expectation of proper order and discipline within the Church. Division among Christians risked incurring divine punishment, while unity in the Church would bring the divine favour upon which Constantine believed 'his life, power and the public welfare depended'.

In '*Imperium* and the City of God: Augustine on Church and Empire', Gillian Clark provides a fresh reading of Augustine's *City of God*. In that work, she maintains, Augustine was not, as many have held, offering a contrast of 'the Church as the city of God and the empire as the earthly city'. Rather, for Augustine everything that was, was ordained of God, and this included empires. He believed both that imperial rule was necessary for the right ordering of the world, and that imperial power intrinsically was neither good nor bad. The crucial opposition in Augustine's *City of God* was not between Church and empire, but between those who worshipped the true God and those who did not. Whether a person was mainly a citizen of the city of God or of the earthly city depended on that individual's response to the love of God. The Roman empire, for Augustine, existed by God's will and could be inhabited by citizens of the city of God.

MEDIEVAL EUROPE

The next four articles explore aspects of Church and empire in medieval Europe. Rosamond McKitterick's article, 'The Popes as Rulers of Rome in the Aftermath of Empire, 476–769', shows how, after the last Roman emperor was deposed in 476, the papacy deliberately wove aspects of Roman imperial rule into its spiritual *imperium*. For her evidence, she draws upon the *Liber pontificalis*, a collection of 112 biographies of the popes from St Peter in the first century to Pope Stephen V at the end of the ninth century. The text, which was written over a considerable period of time, reveals for McKitterick much about the 'ideological position adopted by the papacy in the new political configuration of the former Western Roman empire'. It highlights both the antiquity of the Catholic Church in Rome and the role of the bishops of Rome in shaping the ecclesiastical structures, doctrinal beliefs and patterns of worship for the whole Catholic Church. In the later biographies, moreover, the *Liber pontificalis* provides descriptions of the decoration, liturgical treasures and architecture of the ecclesiastical buildings erected by the popes; it shows the new Christian basilicas, resembling imperial *aulae* or assembly halls and built in expensive marble or stone, to be potent examples of imperial emulation. 'The authors of the *Liber pontificalis*', McKitterick concludes, 'created a powerful picture of the popes … as the rulers of Rome and of the Church.'

In his article, 'Empire, Ethnic Election and Exegesis in the *Opus Caroli* (*Libri Carolini*)' (which was awarded the society's President's Prize for the best article by an early career scholar), Conor O'Brien shows how catholicity and Roman *imperium* were jointly revived by the Carolingian dynasty. Drawing on the massive eighth-century theological treatise, *Opus Caroli*, which was written at the command of Charlemagne and directed against the 'heresies' of the Byzantine empire, O'Brien argues that the Frankish Carolingians based their claim to be the heirs of the Christian Roman empire not on divine election but rather on their defence of Christian universalism and the true catholic Church. They, and not the Byzantines, were the true successors of the Roman empire because they actively represented 'the universal Christian standards which the Greeks had failed to meet'. Benedict Wiedemann's article, '*Super gentes et regna*: Papal "Empire" in the Later Eleventh and Twelfth Centuries', considers the changing nature of the papal *imperium* in medieval Europe during the period of the Investiture Controversy. Devoting particular attention to the cases of the Norman states in southern Italy and the kingdom of Aragon, Wiedemann shows that notions of the pope's temporal authority, including the idea that kings accepted their kingdoms from the pope, were fading by the twelfth century. It was becoming clear that the papal 'empire', whatever the nature of its spiritual power, did not include temporal power over kings and emperors.

In her consideration of 'Emperor and Church in the Last Centuries of Byzantium', Ruth Macrides explores the relationship of Church and emperor in the final centuries of the Byzantine empire, giving particular attention to the role of ceremonial at the imperial court, including ritual and ceremonial dress, as expressive of the relationship between the patriarch of Constantinople and the emperor. She discerns considerable continuities in the relationship of emperor and Church throughout her period, and she does not find evidence that the Church was growing in power and influence relative to the emperor (as some have argued) or that the patriarch was exercising ecclesiastical power over the whole of the Eastern Church. Her assessment also indicates that there were more continuities between the Byzantine and Ottoman empires in the relationship of Church and ruler than previously thought.

THE EARLY MODERN WORLD

The five articles in this section explore themes of Church and empire in the early modern period, with the first four focusing on the English, Irish and Scottish churches. In 'An English Bishop Afloat in an Irish See: John Bale, Bishop of Ossory, 1552–3', Stephen Tong makes effective use of the *Vocacyon*, an early example of English auto-biography, to explore the life of the English cleric, John Bale, and his brief and turbulent tenure as the Protestant bishop of Ossory in Ireland. Tong argues that the Edwardian church in Ireland had a double purpose of winning converts to Protestantism and extending Tudor imperial authority in the island. It pursued this second purpose by aligning the Irish church with the English church and spreading the English language through sermons and the use of the Book of Common Prayer.

In 'Roman *Imperium* and the Restoration Church', Jacqueline Rose shows how authors in later Stuart England used examples from the fourth-century Roman empire in interpreting their own English *imperium*. More particularly, she considers how amid the political tensions of the 1680s some English Protestant authors drew comparisons between the Roman emperor Julian the Apostate (361–3), who had sought to restore paganism in the Roman empire, and James, duke of York, who many feared would, on coming to the throne, seek to restore Catholicism in the English *imperium*. These comparisons contributed in turn to discussions of how Christians should respond to an 'apostate' ruler, including the nature and extent of Christian passive obedience due to the ruler whom God placed on the throne. Andrew Carter explores a related theme in his 'The Episcopal Church, the Roman Empire and the Royal Supremacy in Restoration Scotland', noting how defenders of the established episcopal church in Restoration Scotland during the 1660s and 1670s appealed to the example of the Church in the ancient Roman empire. Scottish episcopalians, Carter maintains, drew on the model of ancient Rome in three ways: to demonstrate early Christian passive obedience to the emperor, to show that the doctrine of royal supremacy was rooted in the reign of Constantine, and to highlight the role of the *imperium* in preserving the unity of the Church against faction, enthusiasm and heterodoxy.

In the next article, Clare Loughlin directs attention to Scotland and Scottish Presbyterianism within the expanding early eighteenth-century British empire. 'Concepts of Mission in Scottish Presbyterianism: The SSPCK, the Highlands and Britain's American Colonies, 1709–40' considers the mission work of the Society in Scotland for Propagating Christian Knowledge (SSPCK), first in the Scottish highlands and islands, and then from 1729 in the British colonies in North America. While previous scholars have emphasized the 'civilizing' aspirations of the SSPCK, Loughlin highlights the fundamental importance of the Christianizing mission in the society's work. For the SSPCK, she argues, the expanding British empire had a providential purpose, which was to facilitate the spread of Christianity to all peoples. By sharing in this divine design for empire, Presbyterian Scotland could recover a sense of itself as a nation chosen by God at the Reformation and brought into union with England by divine plan.

In 'Christianity and Empire: The Catholic Mission in Late Imperial China', Ronnie Po-Chia Hsia, a historian of the European Reformations and biographer of the Jesuit missionary Matteo Ricci, continues the exploration of missions and empire with a wide-ranging discussion of the history of missions in imperial China. He compares and contrasts two periods in the history of Christian missions in China. The first was the period of the early Catholic, especially Jesuit, missions in China from the late sixteenth to the early eighteenth centuries. These early Catholic missionaries, he notes, were not supported by Western military power, their mission was characterized by respect for Chinese civilization and they endeavoured to accommodate Christianity to Chinese culture. As a result, they had considerable success – until the papacy in Rome condemned their policy of accommodation in the early eighteenth century, leading an outraged Chinese emperor to expel the missionaries. Hsia's second phase of Christian missionary activity began in the early nineteenth century, and was associated with the military aggression of Western imperial powers, especially Britain and France. This connection between Christian missions and Western imperialism, as Hsia shows, was in stark contrast to the early modern Catholic missions, and would have highly damaging effects for Christianity in twentieth-century China.

THE NINETEENTH CENTURY

The next group of articles explores the relations of Church and empire in the global context during the nineteenth century, considering the complex interactions of missions, mass migrations of people, settlement colonies and Western imperial dominion over the vast populations in Asia and Africa. 'Providential Empire? The Established Church of England and the Nineteenth-Century British Empire in India' is based on my own presidential address as a historian of modern Britain and the British empire. It explores the idea, prevalent in Britain, that Britain's imperial control of India, the 'crown jewel' of the nineteenth-century British empire, was part of the providential plan for the spread of Christianity to Asia, and that India would be Christianized through the alliance of Church and empire as represented by an established Anglican Church in India. This idea inspired considerable effort and it had some success. But it did not lead even remotely to the Christianization of the whole of India, and failure raised troubling questions for many Anglicans about the alliance of Church and empire, and the providential purpose of empires. The failure also drew some Anglicans to new interpretations of the providential purpose, including the idea that the divine purpose of the British empire might be to facilitate dialogue and cross-fertilization between the religions of the West and the East.

In 'Special Worship in the British Empire: From the Seventeenth to the Twentieth Centuries', Joseph Hardwick and Philip Williamson consider the role of special days of worship, which were proclaimed at times of crisis by the British crown and later by colonial governments, in promoting a sense of unity across the British empire. These special days of worship revealed much about British attitudes towards divine providence, collective sin and special repentance. The records of how people responded to these special days over the course of time also reflected the changing attitudes concerning divine providence and the higher purposes of empire. As the authors argue, the continuing practice of proclaiming special days of worship suggests that 'the sense of a unified and righteous empire under God remained strong' well into the twentieth century.

In 'Queen Adelaide and the Extension of Anglicanism in Malta', Nicholas Dixon explores the fascinating early history of the grandiose neo-classical St Paul's Church, known as 'Queen Adelaide's Church', in Valletta, Malta. Dixon shows how this Anglican church, consecrated in 1844, was part of the larger movement for the extension of Anglicanism in the Mediterranean world, a movement that also found expression in the consecration of the first bishop of Gibraltar in 1842. Malta, many hoped, would become a centre of Anglican missionary activity at a time when imperial Britain had a major presence in the Mediterranean. However, the Catholic Maltese disliked having this large Protestant church with its spire of over sixty metres towering over their city, and the church did not fulfil its larger missionary aspirations; it became mainly a church for Malta's English-speaking Protestant community. Emily Turner's article, 'Claiming the Land: The Church Missionary Society and Architecture in the Arctic', was awarded the Kennedy Prize for the best article by a postgraduate student. It explores the Anglican missions in the forbidding landscape of the Canadian Arctic, and in particular their use of architecture to bring Christianity and civilization to the limits of the habitable earth. The Canadian Arctic, Turner shows, captured the imagination of the mission-supporting public in Britain, and in 1820 the Church Missionary Society (CMS) began establishing mission stations, often adjacent to the trading posts of the Hudson's Bay Company. Turner gives particular attention to the buildings of the CMS mission stations, including the use of the Gothic style and the ideal of settled villages, with the church and school at the centre, as means of transforming the Arctic land and peoples, and integrating them into the Protestant empire.

Rowan Strong, in his article, 'Anglican Emigrant Chaplaincy and the British Empire and Beyond, c.1840–1900', discusses Anglican efforts to provide emigrants with chaplaincy services on the long voyages to their new homes in the settlement colonies and beyond. The aim of this emigrant chaplaincy, he argues, was less about spreading a British Christian culture to the British empire, and more about promoting the preaching, discipline and pastoral work of the Anglican Church in the new settlements. This commitment to the church was the primary concern in emigrant chaplaincy when it began in the 1840s, and it remained the primary concern in the 1880s and 1890s, despite the rising popularity of imperialism. Indeed, he concludes, imperialist attitudes were relatively scarce in the Anglican emigrant chaplaincy networks. In 'Sisters and Brothers Abroad: Gender, Race, Empire and Anglican Missionary Reformism in Hawai'i and the Pacific, 1858–75', Steven Maughan considers the work of the English Anglo-Catholics, especially the Anglican sisters of the Society of the Most Holy Trinity, in the Hawaiian archipelago during the period when both Britain and the United States were demonstrating imperialist ambitions for the islands. While they disliked the austerities of American evangelicalism and the ambitions of American imperialists, the Anglo-Catholic missionaries in Hawaii were not much interested in supporting British imperial designs; far more important for them were the enculturation of Christianity and the spiritual mission of the Anglican Church in the islands.

In her article, 'Ultramontane Efforts in the Ottoman Empire during the 1860s and 1870s', Mariam Kartashyan directs attention to a complex episode that involved the Armenian Catholic patriarchate, the papacy, the Ottoman empire and the Western imperial powers. It began in the later 1860s, when the more assertive papacy of Pius IX, with its ultramontane commitments, moved to increase its authority over the Armenian Catholic Church in matters of doctrine, ritual and ecclesiastical appointment. Although in union with Rome since 1742, the Armenian Catholics had long enjoyed considerable autonomy as well as certain protections granted by the Ottoman government. Now the papacy acted to enhance its power in the East by restricting the traditional ecclesiastical rights of the Armenian Catholic Church. This resulted in considerable Armenian Catholic discontent and resistance, while the Ottoman regime also opposed the ultramontane policies of the papacy. The Western imperial powers, however, agreed to support the papal actions, and the Armenian Catholic Church and the Ottoman empire were forced to acquiesce in the enhanced papal power and authority.

Into the Twentieth Century

The final group of articles consider the connections of Protestantism and the British empire in the late nineteenth and twentieth centuries. In '"Britishers and Protestants": Protestantism and Imperial British Identities in Britain, Canada and Australia from the 1880s to the 1920s', Géraldine Vaughan notes how Protestant associations, including the Imperial Protestant Federation (1898) and the Orange Lodges, sought to preserve what they defined as the Protestant identity of the British empire. For them, this Protestant imperial identity represented progress and freedom. However, it was now under threat as a result of large-scale Catholic migration from Ireland and Europe into the British settlement colonies, with the Catholic migrants being seen as characterized by disloyalty, superstition and papal tyranny. The advocates of imperial Protestantism, Vaughan further observes, were not a small fringe; by 1906, the Imperial Protestant Federation alone claimed some 1.6 million members across the British empire. Continuing twentieth-century belief in a Protestant, providential British empire receives further attention in 'Englishness, Empire and Nostalgia: A Heterodox Religious Community's

Appeal in the Inter-War Years'. Here Jane Shaw explores the Panacea Society, a Protestant millenarian group based in England, which established networks of believers throughout the British empire. Shaw considers the Panacea Society's beliefs and activities between 1919 and 1939, including their links with the early nineteenth-century prophetic movement of Joanna Southcott, their sense of Britain being at the centre of the world and their distinctive healing ministry. However, by the end of the 1930s, both imperial Protestantism and the Panacea Society were waning, reflecting declining belief in a providential British empire.

The final two articles in this volume focus on twentieth-century Christian missionary critics of empire. In 'A Triangular Conflict: The Nyasaland Protectorate and Two Missions, 1915–33', David Thompson directs his attention to the complex relations of missions, empire and liberation movements in early twentieth-century central Africa. Thompson explores the problems that arose from Britain's expulsion of all missionaries from its Nyasaland protectorate in the aftermath of the rising for independence led by John Chilembwe in 1915. While the colonial administrators suspected most missionaries of being overly sympathetic to African aspirations, they viewed the missionaries of the Churches of Christ, with their ideas of racial equality through education, as especially dangerous. The main Presbyterian missions encouraged government distrust of the Churches of Christ, whose missionaries were not readmitted to Nyasaland until 1928. By then, Africans were increasingly taking over the leadership of the Churches of Christ and embracing these churches, accelerating the very process of African empowerment which the colonial administrators had sought to curtail. In the closing article of this volume, Philip Lockley considers an Anglican missionary whose Christian social values led him to identify with the subject peoples of empire and become an uncompromising critic of imperialism. In 'Social Anglicanism and Empire: C. F. Andrews's Christian Socialism', Lockley discusses the early career of Andrews, who first came to India in 1904, aged thirty-three, as a Church of England missionary, and soon became the friend of Mahatma Gandhi and supporter of Indian independence. For Lockley, the vital defining influence in Andrews's life was the Christian socialism he had espoused in England during the 1890s, including an emphasis on Christ's incarnation as representing the unity of humankind and the Church's special mission to the poor. Andrews's Christian socialist commitments, as

Lockley shows, were developed through settlement work in deprived areas of London, and then taken with him to India, where he embraced a global perspective on social justice, a critique of empire and a lifelong effort to disentangle the historic links between Church and empire.

***

As the wide-ranging articles in this volume indicate, relations between the Church and imperial power have had a vital role in shaping the global history of Christianity. The Church emerged within the Roman empire, and as it developed its larger mission to the world the Church often mirrored the forms of imperial rule. Both Church and empire claimed to embody universal truths and values, both claimed to unite peoples of different racial, ethnic and national identities into a larger whole, and both claimed to represent 'civilization'. The Church could view empires as forming part of the providential plan for humankind, facilitating the spread of the gospel through networks of communication, the maintenance of internal peace and order, the promotion of common languages, and legal protections for churches and missionaries. Empires could view churches as valuable allies in imperial rule, teaching their adherents the virtues of passive obedience and non-resistance, and uniting populations around a common faith.

But empires were also based on power, conquest and the subjugation of other peoples; they could turn regions into deserts and call it peace, and they could derive wealth from tribute, exploitation and slavery. What they called civilization often meant oppression to subject peoples. An underlying question that informs many of the articles collected here is the extent to which the Church could preserve its independent spiritual witness while in alliance with imperial power. The Church should recognize only the headship of Christ and it was called by its founder to special concern for the poor and oppressed of the world. Yet the temptation to compromise some of its fundamental principles in order to secure the benefits of alliance with imperial power, including state support for its pastoral work and missionary outreach, could be very great indeed. It is apparent from these articles that many Christians, in their commitment to church principles, were prepared to distance themselves from, or even challenge, imperial power structures. Other Christians, however, viewed imperial power as divinely ordained. Moreover, even when churches believed that they preserved their independent Christian witness while in alliance with empire, for subject peoples the churches could nonetheless appear as supporters of imperial dominance. How the Church can and should relate to secular power remains an enduring question even in our arguably post-imperial age.

Stewart J. Brown

Towards a Spiritual Empire: Christian Exegesis of the Universal Census at the Time of Jesus's Birth

Tiziana Faitini*
Trento

This article focuses on the exegetical interpretation of Luke's narrative of the census (or registration) carried out at the time of Jesus's birth (Luke 2: 1–5). After some brief remarks on the juridical institution of the census (the so-called professio census*) in ancient Rome, a selection of the exegetical interpretations of this pericope developed by various ancient and medieval authors is presented. Origen, Ambrose, Orosius, Bede and Bonaventure are discussed, among others. A number of medieval authors, including Dante Alighieri and Bartolus of Saxoferrato, are also considered. The analysis argues, on the one hand, that a spiritualization of the institution of the census occurred and led to the spiritual empire of Christ being seen as replacing the temporal empire of Augustus; on the other, that reference to this institution was used to legitimize political authority in the eyes of believers. This interpretative tradition is thus shown to offer a vivid example of the close intertwining of theological and juridical concepts and practices which has characterized the relationship between the Church and empire from the former's very beginning.*

This article analyses from a theologico-political perspective a selection of the ancient and medieval exegetical interpretations of Luke's description of the census carried out at the time of Jesus's birth (Luke 2: 1–5). A clear understanding of this interpretative tradition can best be gained by careful consideration of certain formal and juridical aspects of the Roman census, the so-called *professio census*, upon which these authors elaborate, and the article begins with a brief description of these.[1] It then considers the spiritualization of the census: as the spiritual empire of Christ replaced the temporal empire

* School of International Studies, via T. Gar 14, 38122 Trento, Italy. E-mail: tizianafaitini@yahoo.it.

I am very grateful to the editors and the anonymous reviewers for their constructive and valuable suggestions.

[1] For the profound theological and juridical influence of this tradition, see Tiziana Faitini, 'The Latin Roots of the "Profession": Metamorphoses of the Concept in Law and Theology from Ancient Rome to the Middle Ages', *History of Political Thought* 38 (2017),

Studies in Church History 54 (2018) 16–30
doi: 10.1017/stc.2017.2

© Ecclesiastical History Society 2018

of Augustus, the Roman census was Christianized and imbued with redemptive meaning by Christian exegetes. This development has previously been observed, but only incidentally; the process is here explored in greater depth.[2] Alongside this spiritualization, however, from the time of Orosius on, many commentators understood Jesus's participation in the census as a legitimation of believers' obedience to political authority. This political reading of Luke's pericope can also be discerned in medieval political and juridical texts. The analysis offered here thus provides us with a vivid example of the close, reciprocal intertwining of theological and juridical concepts and practices which has characterized the relationship between the Church and empire since the foundation of the Church.[3]

The *Professio Census* and its Presence in Luke's Gospel

The biblical account of the universal census, or registration, ordered by Caesar Augustus and held at the time of Christ's birth, is well known. The first lines of the second chapter of Luke's Gospel read as follows:

> And it came to pass, that in those days there went out a decree from Caesar Augustus, that the whole world should be enrolled (*ut describeretur universus orbis*). This enrolling (*descriptio*) was first made by Cyrinus, the governor of Syria. And all went to be enrolled (*ut profiterentur*), every one into their own city. And Joseph also went up from Galilee, out of the city of Nazareth into Judea, to the city of David, which is called Bethlehem: because he was of the house and

---

603–22. It is on this basis that the act which marks the beginning of a person's life as a member of a religious order is termed religious 'profession'.

[2] See Ilona Opelt, 'Augustustheologie und Augustustypologie', *Jahrbuch für Antike und Christentum* 4 (1961), 44–57, at 46, who referred to a 'Christianisierung des Römischen Census', mentioning Origen, Ambrose, Orosius and Gregory the Great.

[3] For an introduction to the extensive bibliography on political theology and the historical intertwining of theology and politics, see Henning Ottmann, 'Politische Theologie als Begriffsgeschichte', in Volker Gerhardt, ed., *Der Begriff der Politik. Bedingungen und Gründe politischen Handelns* (Stuttgart, 1990), 169–88; Michele Nicoletti and Luigi Sartori, *Teologia politica* (Bologna, 1991); Robert Hepp, 'Theologie, politische', in Joachim Ritter, ed., *Historisches Wörterbuch der Philosophie*, 13 vols (Basel, 1998), 10: 1105–12; Christian Meier, 'Was ist politische Theologie?', in Jan Assmann, ed., *Politische Theologie zwischen Ägypten und Israel* (Munich, 1995), 3–18; Peter Scott and William T. Cavanaugh, eds, *The Blackwell Companion to Political Theology* (Malden, MA, 2004).

family of David. He went to be enrolled (*ut profiteretur*) with Mary his espoused wife, who was expecting a child.[4]

In the Vulgate version of this passage, given in brackets, the words *describo / descriptio* and *profiteor* are all used to translate the Greek *apographesthai / apographē*, a technical term rendering the Latin *censum profiteri* or *professio census*, the institution of the census under Roman law.[5]

According to tradition, the census was introduced in Rome by Servius Tullius in the sixth century BCE. Held regularly during the Roman Republic, it consisted of an official declaration by the *pater familias* of his family and property, made on oath before designated officials, roughly every five years. From the middle of the fifth century BCE, oversight over the procedure was assigned to the magistracy of the *censores*. Their task was to count all citizens and divide them, according to their rank and wealth, into the various classes of the Centuriate order. From the end of the following century, the process involved identifying citizens as members of a particular tribe, which replaced both the *curiae* and family membership in the definition of citizenship. This designation served as the framework for the collection of taxes, for military conscription and for eligibility to vote in the assembly of the *comitia tributa*.[6]

---

[4] Luke 2: 1–5 (Douay-Rheims version, slightly modified). For the Vulgate, the *Biblia Sacra iuxta Vulgatam versionem*, ed. Robert Weber and Roger Gryson (Stuttgart, 2007), is used. There are a number of problems with the historical identification of the census spoken of by Luke; for useful references, see Paul W. Barnett, '*Apographe* and *apographesthai* in Luke 2, 1–5', *Expository Times* 85 (1973–4), 377–80.

[5] For the Greek text, see *Novum Testamentum Graece*, ed. Eberhard Nestle, Kurt Aland et al., 28th edn (Stuttgart, 2012). In the New Testament the Greek term *apographēs* also appears in Acts 5: 37, which speaks of the prophet Judas the Galilean and emphasizes that he was born during the census (probably also that mentioned by Luke), and in Heb. 12: 23, which the Vulgate translates as *ecclesiam primitivorum qui conscripti sunt in caelis*. *Apographesthai / apographē* generally means 'to enter in a list / list or register', and often refers to the declaration of property or persons liable to taxation, and to the Roman census in particular. For the use of these terms in the New Testament and in early Christian literature and further details of the technical, fiscal meaning of *apographē*, see F. Blass and A. Debrunner, *A Greek Grammar of the New Testament and other Early Christian Literature*, transl. Robert W. Funk (Chicago, IL, and London, 1961), *s.v.* 'apographē', §5.3, 5; Geoffrey W. H. Lampe, ed., *A Patristic Greek Lexicon* (Oxford, 1976), 190, *s.vv.* 'apographē / apographomai'; Joseph A. Fitzmyer, *The Gospel according to Luke*, 2 vols, Anchor Bible 28–28A (New York, 1981), 1: 405.

[6] See Elio Lo Cascio, 'Il *census* a Roma e la sua evoluzione dall'età «serviane» alla prima età imperiale', *Mélanges de l'École française de Rome* 113 (2001), 565–603. With important modifications, the census was to last throughout the imperial era, as attested by article

As scholars have clarified, the census focused on the valuation of property, but as a consequence it was also crucial to the definition of citizenship, and thus key to the political, military and fiscal organization of the Roman *res publica*.[7]   Moreover, the census had a moral and religious significance. It was associated with the so-called *regimen morum* (intended to ensure that citizens behaved in accordance with their *dignitas*), and ended in a purification ceremony (*lustrum*). This ceremony served as a ritual refounding of the city, attesting to the fact that citizen rolls did not include anyone unworthy and so providing the city with divine protection.[8]   The act of declaration made in front of censors implied submission to, and inclusion within, a political, moral, military and fiscal order: the definition of each person's civic and social identity and their holding of citizenship were contingent upon this act.

THE EXEGETICAL TRADITION: FROM ORIGEN TO BEDE

The lengthy exegetical elaboration on Luke's pericope, to which we now turn, sheds light on what may be called a theological translation of this specific juridical institution, and, from a general point of view, on the intertwining between theological and juridical conceptualizations.[9]

The first noteworthy explanation of this passage was provided by Origen of Alexandria in his *Homilies on Luke*, and has survived only in Jerome's translation. In most early Christian texts, with the partial exception of Hippolytus of Rome,[10] the census ordered by Augustus

---

50.15 (*De censibus*) of the *Digesta*, a compendium of juristic writings on Roman law compiled by order of Justinian in the sixth century, and by some provisions collected on the initiative of the same emperor in the *Codex Iustiniani* (e.g. C. 4.47.3, C. 8.53.7–8). On the tasks of the *censores*, see Michel Humm, 'I fondamenti della Repubblica romana. Istituzioni, diritto, religione', in Alessandro Barbero, ed., *Storia d'Europa e del Mediterraneo*, 15 vols (Rome, 2008), 5: 467–520, at 489–91.

[7] See Michel Humm, 'Il *regimen morum* dei censori e le identità dei cittadini', in Alessandro Corbino, Michel Humbert and Giovanni Negri, eds, *Homo, caput, persona. La costruzione giuridica dell'identità nell'esperienza romana* (Pavia, 2010), 283–314, at 311–12.

[8] See Humm, 'I fondamenti della Repubblica romana', 491.

[9] For the broader historical perspective of this analysis, see *Politica e religione. Annuario di teologia politica / Yearbook of Political Theology: Censo, ceto, professione. Il censimento come problema teologico-politico* (Brescia, 2015); Tiziana Faitini, *Il lavoro come professione. Una storia della professionalità tra etica e politica* (Rome, 2016).

[10] In his *Commentary on Daniel* 4.9.2–3, Hippolytus contrasts the Roman empire and the heavenly kingdom, thus giving the census a significantly different interpretation from

is mentioned to give historical, objective evidence of the time and the place of Jesus's nativity,[11] but Origen elaborated on Luke's passage, drawing out its spiritual meaning. He defined the first universal census – that is, that during which Jesus was born – as a sacrament (*sacramentum*), that is, in terms of the military oath taken by men enlisting as soldiers in Rome.[12] Origen also observed that it was theologically necessary for Christ to be 'recorded in the census of the whole world' (*in totius orbis professione*), so that he in turn 'could enrol those from the whole world with himself "in the book of the living"' described in Revelation.[13] Here, Origen drew an implicit parallel between the census and the last judgement, and this would become a *topos* from Gregory the Great onwards.[14] The formal act

---

that of the tradition I outline. He observes that when the Romans flourished, Jesus, through the apostles, summoned all nations and made a nation of Christians with a new name in their hearts. His kingdom 'is counterfeited by that which rules according to the operation of Satan, but similarly this kingdom also collects those born from all nations and prepares those who are called Romans for war. And on account of this also the first census happened under Augustus ... so that the men of this world, being registered in the earthly kingdom, were called Romans, but those who believe in the heavenly kingdom were named Christians': ET Thomas C. Schmidt, *Hippolytus of Rome: Commentary on Daniel* (2010), 125–6, online at: <https://web.archive.org/web/20101207125246/http://www.chronicon.net/chroniconfiles/Hippolytus%20Commentary%20on%20Daniel%20by%20TC%20Schmidt.pdf>, accessed 2 May 2017.

[11] See, for instance, Justin Martyr, *Dialogue with Trypho* 78.4; Tertullian, *Against Marcion* 4.7.7, 4.19.10, 4.36.8–9. Clement of Alexandria mentions the census in his chronology of the world: *Stromata* 1.21.145.1. I checked all the references to Luke 2: 1–5 in texts from the first to the third century collected by the expanded *Biblia patristica*, most of which are only cursory; the *Biblia patristica* is online at: <http://www.biblindex.org>, accessed 2 May 2017.

[12] The military metaphor is of Pauline origin, and had been widely used since the time of the early martyr acts: see the classic study by Adolf Harnack, Militia Christi: *The Christian Religion and the Military in the First Three Centuries*, transl. David McInnes Grade (Philadelphia, PA, 1982); and, for a broader recent overview, Katherine Allen Smith, *War and the Making of Medieval Monastic Culture* (Woodbridge, 2011), 71–111.

[13] Origen, *Homélies sur saint Luc*, ed. Henri Crouzel, François Fournier and Pierre Perichon (Paris, 1998), 196 (homily 11); ET *Homilies on Luke*, transl. Joseph T. Lienhard, FC 94 (Washington DC, 2009), 47.

[14] 'Why was it that the world was being enrolled (*describitur*) just before the Lord's birth except to show that he was coming as man to enroll his elect in eternity (*quia ille veniebat in carne, qui electos suos ascriberet in aeternitate*)? On the other hand, it is said of the condemned by the prophet: "May they be blotted out of the book of the living, and not be enrolled with the righteous (Ps 69: 28)"': Gregory the Great, *Forty Gospel Homilies*, transl. David Hurst (Kalamazoo, MI, 1990), 51; Latin text in Gregorius Magnus, *Homiliae in evangelia* 7.2.4–6 (CChr.SL 141, 54). Part of this passage (*quia ... aeternitate*) is included in the *Glossa ordinaria* on Luke's verses, although it is ascribed to Bede the Venerable: see the marginal gloss 'Exiit edictum a ce[sare] aug[usto]', on Luke 2: 1, in *Biblia Latina cum*

of the census is being interpreted in a spiritual sense, and the census is Christianized and imbued with sacred and redemptive meaning; nevertheless, Origen's reference to eternal life and to the heavenly citizenry reveals his understanding of the legal significance of the census in Roman law.

No relevant comments on this passage can be found in the writings of Eusebius of Caesarea.[15] However, towards the end of the fourth century Ambrose of Milan wrote extensively on it in his *Exposition of the Gospel of Luke*, which would have considerable later influence. The *Exposition* was in fact one of the main sources for the readings of these verses from the gospel in the *Glossa ordinaria*, where Ambrose's reading was combined with Bede's *Exposition of the Gospel of Luke*, which will be touched upon later.[16] Moreover, the commentary of

---

Glossa ordinaria, ed. Karlfried Froehlich and Margaret T. Gibson (facsimile reprint of the *editio princeps* of Adolph Rusch of Strasbourg, 1480/1; Turnhout, 1992). For similar interpretations, see Hugh of St Cher, *Hugonis cardinalis opera omnia in universum Vetus, et Novum Testamentum*, 8 vols (Venice, 1703), 8: fol. 143ʳ; Albert the Great, *Enarrationes in primam partem Evangelii Lucae*, in *Opera omnia*, ed. S. Borgnet, 38 vols (Paris, 1890–9), 22: 190 (2.1).

[15] Eusebius mentions the census when dealing with the context and chronological aspects of the nativity, e.g. *Ecclesiastical History* 1.5.2–6; *Questions on the Gospel* 1.12. In the surviving parts of his *Commentary on Luke*, no significant elements are present; the text is corrupted and never quoted by other Church Fathers: David S. Wallace-Hadrill, 'Eusebius of Caesarea's Commentary on Luke: Its Origin and Early History', *HThR* 67 (1974), 55–63.

[16] From a theologico-political perspective, the long marginal gloss on Luke 2: 1 in *Biblia Latina cum Glossa ordinaria*, 'Exiit edictum a ce[sare] aug[usto]', is noteworthy, particularly as far as this passage is concerned: 'In quo nomen augusti vere impletur qui suos augere sufficiens – censoribus suae professionis non pecuniae: sed fidei oblatione signare praecepit: quia dum professio secularis obstenditur, spiritalis impletur. Abolito autem censu synagogae vetusto novus census ecclesiae paratur, qui tormenta non exigit: sed aufert; qui non uno numismate: sed una signatur fide' ('In it the name of Augustus, that is, he who can make his [subjects] grow, was fulfilled. The censors of this enrolment are ordered to mark the subjects not with a monetary payment, but with their offering of faith; while the secular census is appointed, the spiritual is fulfilled. When the old census of the synagogue was abolished, a new census of the Church was prepared which did not require torments, but abolished them, and is sealed not by money, but by faith alone'). The whole gloss is ascribed to Bede but, as pointed out in n. 14, this ascription must be partially corrected. The first part of the quotation (*In quo ... praecepit*) summarizes a passage from Bede's *Exposition* (see n. 27 below); from *quia* to *aufert*, the gloss comes from Ambrose's *Exposition* (see n. 20 below). I have not precisely identified the last part (*qui non ... fide*), which is thematically close to the subsequent lines in Ambrose's *Exposition*, referring to a census in which 'faith alone seals each' (see n. 21 below).

the bishop of Milan is widely used in Thomas Aquinas's *Catena aurea* on this pericope.[17]

Notwithstanding Ambrose's reliance on Origen's reading,[18] the originality of his contribution is undoubted. His experience as a *iudex* before becoming a bishop may well explain the freshness of his interpretation, which takes into account the juridical aspects of the census and translates them into spiritual terms. This also exemplifies the fact that his juridical knowledge makes him a key figure in any historical attempt to probe the constant interchange between theological and juridical conceptualizations in the Western tradition.[19]

Ambrose here shifts the legal, earthly connotation of the *census* onto a spiritual plane, making of it a 'spiritual census' (*professio spiritalis*). Indeed, he writes:

> … while the secular census is appointed, the spiritual is fulfilled, to be told, not to the king of the lands, but to the king of heaven. The profession of faith is a census of minds; for when the old census of the synagogue was abolished, a new census of the Church was prepared which did not require torments, but abolished them.[20]

Through the profession of faith, souls are registered, and the secular census, whether Roman or Jewish, is replaced with that of the religious community. This census is to be declared to the king of heaven; it is not material or social circumstances that are to be accounted for,

---

[17] Thomas Aquinas, *Catena aurea in quatuor evangelia*, ed. Angelico Guarienti, 2 vols (Turin, 1953), 2: 29–30 ('In Lucam' 2.1).

[18] On the close connection between the *lectiones* of Ambrose and Origen, see 'Introduzione', in Ambrose, *Opera omnia / Opera esegetiche*, 11–12: *Esposizione del Vangelo secondo Luca*, ed. Giovanni Coppa, 2 vols (Rome, 1978), 1: 9–63, at 32–5; Celestino Corsato, *La* Expositio Evangelii secundum Lucam *di sant'Ambrogio. Ermeneutica, simbologia, fonti* (Rome, 1993), 183–91.

[19] For a description of how Ambrose uses Roman law, both in his borrowing of terminology and in his theological reinterpretation of resolutions codified in the imperial *leges*, see Jean Gaudemet, 'Droit séculier et droit de l'église chez Ambroise', in Giuseppe Lazzati, ed., *Ambrosius episcopus. Atti del Congresso internazionale di studi ambrosiani nel 16. centenario della elevazione di sant'Ambrogio alla cattedra episcopale*, 2 vols (Milan, 1976), 1: 286–315, at 287–300; see also Brunella Moroni, 'Lessico teologico per un destinatario imperiale. Terminologia giuridico-amministrativa e cerimoniale di corte nel *De fide* di Sant'Ambrogio', in Luigi F. Pizzolato and Marco Rizzi, eds, *Nec timeo mori. Atti del Congresso internazionale di studi ambrosiani nel XVI centenario della morte di sant'Ambrogio* (Milan, 1998), 341–63, at 343–5.

[20] Ambrose of Milan, *Exposition of the Holy Gospel according to Saint Luke*, transl. Theodosia Tomkinson (Etna, CA, 1998), 50 (2.36; ET slightly modified); Latin text from CChrSL 14 in Ambrose, *Esposizione*, 1: 176.

but the deepest corners of the mind. In this registration 'dimensions, not of lands, but of minds and spirits are assessed', because 'faith alone seals each'.[21]

What Ambrose described was a more universal census than that imposed by Augustus. Everybody, notwithstanding their nationality or their age, was involved:

> None is exempt from this census, because every age is liable to serve Christ … . Then, that ye may know that the census is not of Augustus, but of Christ, the whole world is bidden to enrol. When Christ is born, all confess Him; when the world is included, all are tested.[22]

A census with such universal reach (*professione totius orbis*), concluded Ambrose, could be mandated only by a lord who has 'power (*imperium*) over the whole world'.[23] In his reading, the birth of Christ heralded the beginning of a movement of spiritualization and universalization, which led from the secular census to the spiritual one, and which substituted the power of Augustus with that of Christ. The analogy between the king of heaven (*rex caeli*) and the king of the lands (*rex terrarum*) recalls the relationship between what Augustine will call the two cities, although Ambrose does not make this explicit;[24] Augustine, however, did not comment on the universal census mentioned by Luke, either in *City of God* or elsewhere.

An in-depth discussion of this analogy with regard to the verses in question – and thus an explicitly political interpretation of them, implicitly aimed at the justification of Roman authority – can be found in the work of Augustine's student Orosius, who is key to understanding the developing relationship between Church and empire. In the *History against the Pagans*, Orosius highlighted the synchronicity of Christ's birth and Augustus's peaceful reign, developing a 'theology of Augustus' and associating the Christianization of the figure of the emperor with the Romanization of the figure of Christ.[25] In arguing this, Orosius suggested that the coincidence of Jesus's birth with

---

[21] Ambrose, *Exposition*, 50 (2.36); see also ibid. 51 (2.38).

[22] Ibid. 50 (2.37).

[23] Ibid.; Latin text in Ambrose, *Esposizione*, 1: 178. This passage is included in the marginal gloss 'Universus orbis' on Luke 2: 1 in *Biblia Latina cum Glossa ordinaria*.

[24] For references to Ambrose's distinction between the two orders, divine and civil, and the superiority of the former, see Gaudemet, 'Droit séculier', 304–6.

[25] On the 'theology of Augustus' elaborated in book 6 of the *History against the Pagans*, see Erik Peterson, *Der Monotheismus als politisches Problem. Ein Beitrag zur Geschichte der politischen Theologie im Imperium Romanum* (Leipzig, 1935); Opelt, 'Augustustheologie'.

the census demonstrated that he had chosen to be a Roman citizen: 'of this city [i.e. Rome], when he came, he especially wished to be entitled to be called a Roman citizen by the declaration made in the Roman census list'.[26] For Orosius, the unification of the *orbis Romanum* under Augustus was part of God's plan for the propagation of the gospel, and he presented the emperor as the forerunner of Christ, who in turn endorsed Rome as his fatherland, thus offering a justification of imperial power.

We turn now to the other important source for the *Glossa ordinaria* on this passage, the Venerable Bede. Both in his *Exposition of the Gospel of Luke* and in one of his homilies on the gospels, composed for Christmas, Bede dealt with the beginning of the second chapter of Luke and interwove all the elements analysed so far: he read the pericope in a spiritual sense (as had Origen and Ambrose) while also stressing its political and historical meaning (as did Orosius) and making the analogy between the city of God and the city of men very explicit. According to the Anglo-Saxon theologian's *Exposition*, the imperial decree was an earthly forerunner of the decree enforced by Christ the King, which announced universal salvation:

> A decree went out from Caesar Augustus that all the world should be enrolled, because a decree from Christ the King (*Regis Christi*) was impending, thanks to which all the world was to attain salvation. And making the name of Augustus perfectly fulfilled – that is, wanting to make his [subjects] grow and being himself able to do so – he ordered the censors of his enrolment to mark the subjects, not with a monetary payment, but with their offering of faith (*censoribus suae professionis non ablatione pecuniae subiectos sed fidei oblatione signare praecipit*).[27]

Bede's homily is even clearer. The enrolment of the world 'recalled as having been done by an earthly king' (*a terreno rege*) also designates

---

See also Hans-Werner Goetz, *Die Geschichtstheologie des Orosius* (Darmstadt, 1980), 71–88; and, for a recent critical reading of the Eusebianism of Orosius, Peter Van Nuffelen, *Orosius and the Rhetoric of History* (Oxford, 2012), 191–7.

[26] '[D]icendus civis Romanus census professione Romani': Paulus Orosius, *Seven Books of History against the Pagans*, transl. Roy J. Deferrari, FC 50 (Washington DC, 1964), 281–2 (6.22), ET modified; Latin text in Orosius, *Le storie contro i pagani*, ed. Adolf Lippold, 2 vols (Milan, 2001), 2: 234.

[27] Bede, 'In Lucae evangelium expositio', in *Bedae Opera. Pars 2: Opera exegetica*, 3: *In Lucae evangelium expositio. In Marci evangelium expositio*, CChr.SL 120, 45–6 (my translation).

'the works of the heavenly king' (*caelestis opera regis*).[28] The true fatherland of the Christian is the Church, and, to an even greater extent, the heavenly Church. The census proclaimed by Augustus must thus be carried out spiritually in obedience to the king of heaven:

> The fact that all were going, in response to the edict of Augustus, each to report to his own city, [betokens what] we must do spiritually as a service to our king (*in nostri regis est nobis servitio spiritaliter agendum*). Indeed, our city is the holy church, which is in part still journeying away from the Lord on earth, and in part already reigns with the Lord in heaven.[29]

The tax ('*debitum censum*') which 'is due to the king who has been born' attests to a spiritual debt which has to be paid by complying 'with divine commands in the unity of the Church now present' and 'by the tireless course of good works'.[30] Bede adds that as Christians, we ought to represent Christ's image 'on the same denarius of our good way of life' (*bonae nostrae conversationis*): just as, in the case of the coin of Augustus, the currency of payment is legal tender when stamped with the head of the ruler, so too, a Christian's way of life must be hallmarked by the image and name of Christ, and by obedience to his commands.[31] The evangelic exhortation to 'render to Caesar things which are Caesar's' is only implicitly evoked in these lines, while it is explicitly referred to (in the version given by Matthew 22: 21) in the *Exposition*.[32]

---

[28] Bede, *Homilies on the Gospel. Book One: Advent to Lent*, transl. Lawrence T. Martin and David Hurst (Kalamazoo, MI, 1991), 54 (1.6); Latin text in Bede, 'Homiliarum Evangelii libri II', *Bedae Opera. Pars 3/4: Opera Homiletica. Opera Rhythmica*, CChr.SL 122, 37–45, at 38 (1.6).

[29] Ibid. 54 (1.6); Latin text 38 (1.6).

[30] Ibid. See also Bede, 'In Lucae evangelium expositio', CChr.SL 120, 46.

[31] 'In the act of reporting in the census one gave a denarius, which had the weight of ten *nummi*, and which bore the image and the name of Caesar. We also must imitate this spiritually, for we pay a denarius to our king (*regi nostro*) when we busy ourselves with fulfilling the ten commands of his law, and written on this denarius we bear the name of this same king of ours when we remember in all our acts that we are called "Christians" from "Christ", and take care to keep inviolate in us the dignity of his name. We also ought to represent his image in the same denarius of our good way of life, which is what he himself taught when he said, "Be holy because I the God your Lord am holy"': CChr.SL 122, 38–9 (1.6); Bede, *Homilies*, 54 (1.6).

[32] See Bede, 'In Lucae evangelium expositio', CChr.SL 120, 46–7. The passage is also summarized in the marginal gloss 'Cyrino' on Luke 2: 2 in *Biblia Latina cum Glossa ordinaria*.

Bede's exegesis asserts that the heavenly kingdom is based on an economy of salvation: moral conduct becomes the currency of that kingdom, and is exchanged in the circulation of credit and debt which began with the coming of the Redeemer, who gave himself for human sins. This offers a further example of the widespread use made by Christian commentators of a pre-existent economic and legal lexicon. At the same time, these readings also made a decisive contribution to the evolution of such a lexicon.[33]

Bede's focus thus far had been on spiritual exegesis, and in particular the debt which has to be paid in the spiritual realm by Christians through their moral actions. At the same time, in his exploration of the historical, literal sense of the biblical text, Bede's homily also highlighted the secular debt that needs to be paid on earth, to the Roman empire:

> He himself did not disdain to commit himself to servitude (*inpendere servitium*) to one who was unaware of true charity. Here also by his example he pointed out in advance what the prince of the apostles was afterwards to teach in words, 'Be subject (*subditi estote*) to every human creature for God's sake, whether to the king as sovereign, or to the leaders as sent by him (1 Pet. 2: 13–14)'.[34]

Jesus himself, in undergoing the earthly census, confirmed the legitimacy of that debt, thus confirming that Christian believers were to be subject to the authority of earthly, political institutions.

SOME THIRTEENTH- AND FOURTEENTH-CENTURY INTERPRETATIONS: EXEGESIS AND BEYOND

Bede introduced a direct connection with the theme of obedience to established temporal power, which had only been hinted at by Orosius but which frequently recurred in subsequent exegeses on these verses. No significant explorations of this text have been found in

---

[33] For useful insights into the economy of salvation defined within Christendom, and its importance for the elaboration of economic rationality and the economic lexicon, see Giovanni Todeschini, *Il prezzo della salvezza. Lessici medievali del pensiero economico* (Rome, 1994); Peter Brown, *Through the Eye of a Needle: Wealth, the Fall of Rome, and the Making of Christianity in the West* (Princeton, NJ, 2012); Valentina Toneatto, *Les Banquiers du Seigneur* (Rennes, 2012); Paolo Evangelisti, *Il pensiero economico nel Medioevo* (Rome, 2016).

[34] CChr.SL 122, 40 (1.6); Bede, *Homilies*, 57 (1.6).

any Carolingian commentaries on Luke's Gospel, but the theme appears to have been much developed in the thirteenth and fourteenth centuries, a period during which commentaries on Luke's Gospel proliferated.[35] While a complete survey of these is not within the scope of this article, a few representative examples will illustrate the political reading of the pericope in medieval exegetical, political and juridical texts.

In the thirteenth century, Hugh of St Cher defined the census as 'the exhibition of subjection' (*subiectionis exhibitio*).[36] Albert the Great, in addition to drawing the usual analogy between the earthly census (*descriptio orbis*) and the last judgement, i.e. the enrolment in eternal life (*descriptio in aeternitate*), referred to Matthew 22: 21 and the well-known exhortation to render 'to Caesar the things that are Caesar's', as Bede had done earlier.[37] Bonaventure of Bagnoregio also offered some very explicit remarks on this question. In his *Commentary on the Gospel of Luke*,[38] he quoted Bede, emphasizing that Jesus was included in the census in order to comply with all higher authorities, thus making clear, in Bonaventure's reading, that 'human authority is similar to divine' and that 'the command of rulers is not to be contemned in any way'.[39] The power of Augustus, who mandated a universal census at a time of universal peace, prefigured the authority of Christ, whilst at the same time retaining its temporal significance. In registering themselves, Joseph and Mary obeyed this power:

> [they] did the will of the king, and no one did otherwise. And thus they made themselves subject to the king in registering (*subiectionem*

---

[35] For the Carolingian era, I checked Christianus Druthmarus Stabulensis, *Expositio in Lucam Evangelistam*, PL 106, cols 1503–14; Walafridus Strabo Fuldensis, *Expositio in Quatuor Evangelia. In Lucam*, PL 114, cols 893–904; Sedulius Scotus, *In argumentum secundum Lucam expositiuncula*, PL 103, cols 285–90. A list of medieval commentaries on Luke's Gospel is given by Barbara Faes de Mottoni, 'Introduzione', in *Sancti Bonaventurae Commentarius in Evangelium S. Lucae*, ed. eadem, 4 vols (Rome, 1999–2012), 1: 7–26, at 19–20; this includes more than twenty commentaries written in the thirteenth century.
[36] *Hugonis cardinalis opera omnia*, 8: fol. 139ᵛ.
[37] Albertus Magnus, *Enarrationes*, 190 (2.1); see also Alberto Colli, 'Considerazioni sul censimento di Cesare Augusto nelle esegesi di Ugo di St. Cher e Alberto il Grande', in *Censo, ceto, professione*, 121–40.
[38] Bonaventure, *Works*, 8/1: *St Bonaventure's Commentary on the Gospel of Luke: Ch. 1–8*, ed. Robert J. Karris (New York, 2001); the Latin text is in *Sancti Bonaventurae Commentarius*, ed. Faes de Mottoni.
[39] *St Bonaventure's Commentary*, ed. Karris, 143 (8); Bede is quoted at ibid. 138 (4).

habebant ad regem in professione), in acknowledgment of his authority, and made peace with one another through tranquil and just living together, according to what Romans 13: 7–8 has: 'Render to all whatever is their due. Tribute to whom tribute is due' … . To register that they are subject to Roman rule, and this by undergoing the census. And this was just, as Matthew 22: 21 has: 'Render to Caesar the things that are Caesar's, and to God the things that are God's'. … Through her obedience she [Mary] would give us an example of how to obey all higher authority, in accordance with what we read in 1 Peter 2: 13–14.[40]

The link between census and obedience could not be more explicit, and is stressed by Bonaventure's references to a number of biblical passages typically quoted by Christian authors in regard to political subjection (Matt. 22: 21, Rom 13: 7–8, 1 Pet. 2: 13–14).[41] Similarly, a canon collected in the *Liber Extra*, the important collection of decretals promulgated by Gregory IX in 1234, clearly defines the *praestatio tributi* as *probatio subiectionis*.[42] For these thirteenth-century authors, the census signalled subjection to a king, whether earthly or celestial: it was an act of inclusion – whether political, theological, or both – which signalled admission to an established, peaceful order. However, it was also required in order to be included among the worthy citizens and the redeemed, that is, necessary for salvation, earthly or celestial.

This observation does not apply only to exegetical scholarship. In his *De monarchia*, Dante Alighieri also referred to Jesus's compliance with the imperial edict concerning the census, which he saw as legitimizing the jurisdiction of the Roman empire and consequently the validity and the independence of temporal power in general.[43]

---

[40] Ibid. 139–40 (5; translation slightly modified); Latin text in *Sancti Bonaventurae Commentarius*, ed. Faes de Mottoni, 1: 168 (5).

[41] On the exegesis of these passages, in the framework of a discussion of Christian thought on political subjection, see Marco Rizzi, *Cesare e Dio. Potere secolare e potere spirituale in Occidente* (Bologna, 2009), which, however, never mentions Luke 2: 1–5.

[42] *Liber Extra*, 10.3.39.2. See Peter Landau, 'Die Verteilung kirchlicher Abgaben im klassischen kanonischen Recht', in Franck Roumy et al., eds, *Der Einfluss der Kanonistik auf die europäische Rechtskultur. 5: Das Recht der Wirtschaft* (Köln, 2016), 223–42.

[43] 'Christ chose to be born of the Virgin Mary under an edict authorized by Rome. … Christ so chose in order that the son of God, being made man, might be enrolled (*conscriberetur*) as a man in that unique census (*descriptione*) of the human race. And by this action he approved the edict. … Therefore Christ by his actions gave us cause to believe that the edict was just that Augustus, exercising the authority of the Romans, had issued.

Similarly, some jurists referred to Luke's narrative when requiring the fulfilment of political, and in particular fiscal, obligations: in the thirteenth century, Rolandus de Luca, for example, repeatedly mentioned this narrative when commenting on questions relating to taxation.[44] Luke's pericope was also invoked to confirm the legitimacy and supremacy of the emperor's authority over local kings and princes, as in Bartolus of Saxoferrato's commentary on the *Digesta*, written in the first half of the fourteenth century,[45] and in Bartolomeus of Novara's commentary on the *Institutiones*, published later in the fourteenth century, under the better-known name of Baldus de Ubaldi.[46] Bartolus, perhaps the most important Italian jurist of his time, dealt at length with the *lex* 'Hostes', and, in defining the concepts of enemy and empire, noted:

> And if someone argues that the emperor is not the lord (*dominus*) and the king of all the world, they are heretics, as they speak against the decisions of the Church, against the holy Gospel which says: 'a decree went out from Emperor Augustus that all the world should be registered' … . In this way, even Christ acknowledged the emperor as lord.[47]

And since to issue an edict justly implies having the jurisdiction (*iurisdictio*) to do so, it is necessary that one who approves a just edict also approves the jurisdiction of the one who issued it': Dante, *Monarchia*, transl. Richard Kay (Toronto, ON, 1998), 183–5 (2.10.6, 8); Latin text ibid.

[44] See Sara Menzinger, *Verso la costruzione di un diritto pubblico cittadino*, in Emanuele Conte and Sara Menzinger, eds, *La* Summa Trium Librorum *di Rolando da Lucca (1195–1234). Fisco, politica, scientia iuris*, Ricerche dell'Istituto Storico Germanico di Roma 8 (Rome, 2012), cxxv–ccxviii, at clvi.

[45] Bartolus of Saxoferrato, *Super digesto novo* (Basel, 1563). On the use of theological sources made by Bartolus, see Diego Quaglioni, 'Diritto e teologia nel «Tractatus testimoniorum» bartoliano', in idem, *'Civilis sapientia'. Dottrine giuridiche e dottrine politiche fra Medioevo e Età moderna* (Rimini, 1989), 107–25. The important anonymous treatise *Questiones de iuris subtilitatibus*, written in the twelfth century, had mentioned the census ordered by Augustus and taken a similar position: see Magnus Ryan, 'Political Thought', in David Johnston, ed., *The Cambridge Companion to Roman Law* (Cambridge, 2015), 423–51, at 428–9.

[46] Baldus de Ubaldis, *Commentaria ad quatuor Institutionum libros* (Lyon, 1585), fol. 10^v (on.1.12.5). The text was probably quite well known; it was printed at the beginning of the modern era under the name of Baldus, who was Bartolus's pupil and an important scholar of his time. On the true identity of the author of this commentary, see Domenico Maffei, 'Bartolomeo da Novara autore della *Lectura Institutionum* attribuita a Baldo degli Ubaldi?', *Rivista di storia del diritto italiano* 63 (1990), 5–22.

[47] Bartolus of Saxoferrato, *Super digesto novo*, D.49.15.24; my translation.

Bartolus's interpretation is striking for its explicit claim, argued on the basis of Luke's account of the census, that Christian doctrine demands that Christians should recognize the emperor's authority.

Conclusion

It is apparent from the exegetical tradition outlined here that the Roman juridical institution of the *professio census* became a theoretical tool through which Christian theologians could conceptualize the economy of salvation. It was used to describe the individual Christian's admission to eternal life, foreshadowing the last judgement, to explain why each Christian is indebted to Christ, and to show how this debt must be paid. A spiritualization of the institution of the census occurred, in which the spiritual empire of Christ was seen as replacing the temporal empire of Augustus. However, this passage and its account of Christ's involvement in the census, a juridical institution, also allowed theologians to acknowledge the authority of Roman emperors and to justify Christian acceptance of, and subjection to, political authority. Luke's pericope should indeed find its place alongside other better-known biblical references used for this purpose (e.g. Matt. 22: 21; Rom. 13: 7–8; 1 Pet. 2: 13–14). The census depicted in Luke's Gospel is therefore a perfect example of the close overlap between theological and juridical concepts and practices which has been a key feature in defining the relationship between the Church and empire in the European tradition.

The 'Servant of God': Divine Favour and Instrumentality under Constantine, 318–25

Andrew J. Pottenger*

University of Manchester

This article focuses on the doctrine of divine favour and instrumentality as viewed from the emperor's own perspective, in relation to the early development of the 'Arian controversy' as far as the Council of Nicaea. While modern writers have focused on explicit statements by Constantine to suggest that unity was the emperor's highest priority, this article reveals a pattern by which he sought to manage divine favour and argues that doing so effectively was of primary importance to him. Such a shift in understanding the emperor's priorities adds to the range of explanations for his later apparent inconsistencies as the actual achievement of unity continually eluded him.

Securing divine favour was a significant theme in ancient Roman historical writing.[1] From an early date, successful Roman generals such as Scipio Africanus, Marius, Sulla, Pompey and Julius Caesar claimed divine favour in their military efforts.[2] Emperors such as Augustus, Trajan and Marcus Aurelius likewise expressed gratitude to divine patrons for granting them protection and success.[3] By the late third

* Nazarene Theological College, Dene Rd, Didsbury, Manchester, M20 2GU. E-mail: ajpott@hotmail.com.

  This article is based on a chapter from my doctoral thesis, which examines (from Constantine's point of view) the early stages in his interventions aimed at helping Christians resolve internal conflicts due to schism and heresy. I wish to thank the editorial team, along with Andrew Fear, Geordan Hammond and Svetlana Khobnya, for their valuable input.

[1] For examples of this theme from the later Republic through to Constantine's reign, see the references in nn. 2, 3 below and Lactantius, *On the Deaths of the Persecutors* 48.2–12; Eusebius, *Ecclesiastical History* 10.5.4–24, 10.6.1–5, 10.7.1–2; idem, *Life of Constantine* 2.24–42, 2.46.1–3, 2.48–60, 2.64–72, 3.12.1–5, 3.17–20.2, 3.30–32.2; Optatus of Milevis, *Against the Donatists*, Appendices 3, 5–7, 9.

[2] Livy, *History of Rome* 26.44–5; Plutarch, 'Marius' 17–22, 'Sulla' 6.1–5, 29.6, and 'Pompey' 68.2, in *Parallel Lives of Famous Greeks and Romans*; Appian, *The Civil Wars* 2.68.

[3] Augustus Caesar, *Acts of the Deified Augustus* 21, 24; Suetonius, 'Augustus' 29, in *Lives of the Twelve Caesars*; Cassius Dio, *History of Rome* 68.25.5, 72.8–9; Anon., *The Augustan History* 24.4.

Studies in Church History 54 (2018) 31–45   © Ecclesiastical History Society 2018
doi: 10.1017/stc.2017.3

century, Roman emperors increasingly publicized close links with certain gods and continued seeking their aid to restore an empire in crisis.[4] For example, Aurelian (270–5) paid respects to the Syrian sun god following victory over Queen Zenobia of Palmyra at the Battle of Emesa in 273. Returning to Rome, he built a temple and dedicated it to the 'unconquerable sun' (*sol invictus*).[5] The imperial tetrarchy from which Constantine (306–37) emerged had been based on an emperor's personal association with divinity, the original two *Augusti* – Diocletian and Maximian – being identified with Jupiter and Hercules respectively.[6] Ruling the empire as a Christian following his famous victory over Maxentius at the Milvian Bridge outside Rome on 28 October 312, Constantine ever afterwards sought to ally himself with the 'supreme god', whom he soon identified with the God worshipped by Christians.[7] Thus, like his predecessors, Constantine was also concerned to remain on good terms with divinity by expressing gratitude as a beneficiary of divine assistance.[8]

[4] For an overview of the 'third-century crisis', see John Drinkwater, 'Maximinus to Diocletian and the "Crisis"', in Alan Bowman, Averil Cameron and Peter Garnsey, eds, *Cambridge Ancient History*, 12: *The Crisis of Empire, A.D. 193–337*, 2nd edn (Cambridge, 2005), 28–66; see also Lukas de Blois, 'The Crisis of the Third Century A.D. in the Roman Empire: A Modern Myth?', in idem and J. Rich, eds, *The Transformation of Economic Life under the Roman Empire* (Amsterdam, 2002), 204–17.

[5] Anon., 'Aurelian' 25.1–6, in *Augustan History*; Eutropius, *An Abbreviated History of Rome* 9.15.1; Sextus Aurelius Victor, *Book on the Caesars* 35.7.

[6] For example, *The Latin Panegyrics* 10.4.1–2, 10.11.6, 8.4.1–2, 7.8.1–3 (*In Praise of Later Roman Emperors: The* Panegyrici Latini, ed. and transl. C. E. V. Nixon and Barbara Saylor Rodgers [Berkeley, CA, 1994], 59–60, 71, 113–14, 200–1); cf. Sextus Aurelius Victor, *Caesars* 39; Eutropius, *Abbreviated History* 9.26.

[7] For views on Constantine's 'conversion', traditionally associated with this battle, see Timothy Barnes, *Constantine and Eusebius* (Cambridge, 1981), 34–53; T. G. Elliott, 'Constantine's Conversion: Do we really need it?', *Phoenix* 41 (1987), 420–38; Harold A. Drake, *Constantine and the Bishops: The Politics of Intolerance* (Baltimore, MD, 2002), 154–91. On the development of Constantine's religious beliefs, see Tarmo Toom, 'Constantine's *Summus Deus* and the Nicene *Unus Deus*: Imperial Agenda and Ecclesiastical Conviction', *Vox Patrum* 34 (2014), 103–22; Mark Edwards, *Religions of the Constantinian Empire* (Oxford, 2015), 179–99.

[8] Further background on Roman concepts of patronage can be found in John Nicols, *Civic Patronage in the Roman Empire* (Leiden, 2014); Brenda Longfellow, *Roman Imperialism and Civic Patronage: Form, Meaning, and Ideology in Monumental Fountain Complexes* (Cambridge, 2011); Kate Cooper and Julia Hillner, eds, *Religion, Dynasty and Patronage in Early Christian Rome, 300–900* (Cambridge, 2007). Constantine referred twice in his *Oration to the Assembly of the Saints* to an exchange of benefits and gratitude between God and his worshippers. In the first instance, he claimed it would be absurd for human beings to offer gratitude in exchange for benefits given to each other while failing to respond gratefully to God for his aid: *Oration* 23. The second example ended

Despite the long tradition of imperial appeals to divine aid, some scholars prefer to focus on more 'secular' aspects of Constantine's reign.[9] Yet the emperor's public and private religious opinions continue to excite interest. For example, Jonathan Bardill holds that Constantine genuinely believed and presented himself as a Christian by late summer 314.[10] However, his emphasis on Constantine's 'ambiguity' downplays the emperor's sense of divine mission.[11] Klaus Girardet also opposes any dismissal of Constantine's early and genuine Christian conversion, outlining what he believes are explicit examples of the emperor's authentic faith from several imperial documents dated between 312 and 314.[12] His reading of Constantine's early statements pertaining to Christianity rules out ambiguity altogether by overemphasizing their possible Christian meaning for the emperor himself.[13]

By contrast, this article will not argue for a particular position regarding the extent to which Constantine's conversion may or may not have been authentic. I have instead assumed a sociological

his speech on a similar note, as he attributed the benefits of salvation and public welfare to Christ, whose continuing help is sought through prayer and worship: ibid. 26.

[9] For example, see Noel Lenski, 'Introduction', in idem, ed., *The Cambridge Companion to the Age of Constantine* (Cambridge, 2006), 1–13, at 10; Raymond Van Dam, *The Roman Revolution of Constantine* (Cambridge, 2007), 10–11; David S. Potter, *Constantine the Emperor* (Oxford, 2013), 3–4.

[10] Jonathan Bardill, *Constantine: Divine Emperor of the Christian Golden Age* (Cambridge, 2013), 273.

[11] Ibid. 1, 271–5, 280–4, 290–9. For Constantine's sense of divine mission, see Eusebius, *Ecclesiastical History* 10.7.1–2; Optatus, *Life* 2.28.1–29.3, 2.55.1–56.2, 2.64–7, 4.9.

[12] Klaus Girardet, 'Ein spätantiker "Sonnenkönig" als Christ', *Göttinger Forum für Altertumswissenschaft* 16 (2013), 371–81. Girardet relies heavily on Constantine's *Oration*, to which he assigns an earlier date than most scholars: 16 April 314. For varying views on dating, see Harold Drake, 'Suggestions of Date in Constantine's Oration to the Saints', *American Journal of Philology* 106 (1985), 335–49; Robin Lane Fox, *Pagans and Christians in the Mediterranean World from the Second Century A.D. to the Conversion of Constantine* (New York, 2006), 642–4, 777–8; Timothy Barnes, 'Constantine's Speech to the Assembly of the Saints: Place and Date of Delivery', *JThS* 52 (2001), 26–36; *Constantine and Christendom*, transl. Mark J. Edwards, TTH 39 (Liverpool, 2003), ix–xxix. The difficulty in dating the *Oration* contributes enormously to the challenge of attempting to draw out information concerning what Constantine believed at any point during his religious development. For this reason, it is referred to sparingly in this article.

[13] Girardet includes the legions' prayer that Eusebius attributed to Constantine (see Eusebius, *Life* 4.20.1) and one of two imperial letters from Constantine to Anulinus, proconsul of Africa: Eusebius, *Ecclesiastical History* 10.7.1–2. In both instances, Girardet too easily follows Eusebius's commentary: cf. ibid. 10.1.2, 10.8.1; idem, *Life* 4.19–20.2. He also appears to confuse Eusebius's words with the prayer's text: Girardet, 'Ein spätantiker "Sonnenkönig" als Christ', 374, 380.

view of conversion as a process, so that Constantine's ambiguity is understood in terms of religious development.[14] Shortly after his victory over Maxentius, the emperor identified the god from whom he had sought aid in that battle with the God of Christians. His religious allegiance seemingly confirmed by defeating Licinius in 324, the emperor actively increased his understanding of Christianity's view of God until his death in 337. Out of gratitude for such assistance from his divine patron, he consistently sought to protect and support Christianity without alienating the majority of the empire's population. However, internal church disputes created difficulties for Constantine by forcing him to choose which competing institutional and theological version of Christianity to support. As the emperor himself was keenly aware, this had direct implications for his ability to maintain the divine favour on which (according to imperial tradition) he believed that his power depended.

This article argues from the imperial documents preserved by Optatus of Milevis and Eusebius of Caesarea that Constantine's primary concern was to preserve divine blessing by working as the 'servant of God' to restore unity among his worshippers.[15] The emperor's pattern of attempting to maintain and restore divine favour when he perceived it to be endangered will be defined through a brief examination of his involvement with the Donatist schism. This pattern, which has not received prior analysis and which thus forms the article's main contribution, remained consistent when Constantine subsequently intervened in the conflict involving Alexander and Arius. Finally, the emperor's self-described role as the 'servant of God' will

---

[14] I follow Drake's suggestion that conversion (as experienced rather than recalled) involves 'a number of progressive awakenings'. I also accept Drake's argument that the real question is not whether or not Constantine was a genuine Christian, but rather what kind of Christian he became: see Drake, *Constantine*, 188 n. 53, 200–1. For further reading about sociological perspectives on conversion, see Keith A. Roberts, *Religion in Sociological Perspective* (Homewood, IL, 1984), 134–81; Rodney Stark, *The Rise of Christianity* (New York, 1996), 13–20.

[15] For helpful summaries of scholarship on the authenticity and reliability of the documents attached to the work by Optatus, see W. H. C. Frend, *The Donatist Church: A Movement of Protest in Roman North Africa* (Oxford, 1952), xi–xv; Optatus, *Against the Donatists*, transl. Mark J. Edwards, TTH 27 (Liverpool, 1997), xxvi–xxxi. See also n. 26 below for particular difficulties in relation to the letter to 'Aelafius' in Optatus, *Against the Donatists*, App. 3. Concerning imperial documents contained in Eusebius's *Life of Constantine*, see Friedhelm Winkelmann, 'Zur Geschichte des Authentizitätsproblems der Vita Constantini', *Klio* 40 (1962), 187–243; 'Introduction', in Eusebius, *Life of Constantine*, transl. Averil Cameron and Stuart G. Hall (Oxford, 1999), 16–21.

be discussed in terms of his attempts to restore divine favour during the early stages of that particular ecclesiastical conflict.

MANAGING DIVINE FAVOUR: CONSTANTINE AND THE DONATIST SCHISM

Having defeated Maxentius in 312, Constantine assumed control of Italy and Africa, in addition to the territories of Britain, Spain and Gaul inherited from his father six years earlier.[16] In February 313, Constantine and his Eastern colleague Licinius (who would soon defeat his rival in the East, Maximinus Daia) met at Milan to arrange the terms of their mutual support.[17] Maintaining divine favour was the primary principle behind the rescript issued in the names of both emperors and traditionally known as the 'Edict of Milan'.[18] Liberty in religion was granted so that 'whatever divinity there is in the seat of heaven' might be favourably disposed.[19] Having announced his religious policy in agreement with Licinius, Constantine proceeded to implement restitution toward Christians as a display of continuing gratitude for divine favour – whoever that divinity might be. By pursuing an agreed policy of restitution toward Christians at the imperial treasury's expense, Licinius and Constantine hoped to ensure that there would be no grounds for recrimination against Christians when others were legally bound to surrender any property obtained through confiscation during the persecutions.[20] Likewise, repeatedly emphasizing that liberty was granted 'both to Christians and to all men', the two emperors implied that no Christian could expect to be justified or excused in seeking vengeance against their persecutors.[21] Thus all worshippers of the 'supreme divinity' (*summa*

---

[16] Eutropius, *Abbreviated History* 10.1; Sextus Aurelius Victor, *Caesars* 40; Lactantius, *Deaths of Persecutors* 43–4; Eusebius, *Life* 1.19–22, 1.25–41.

[17] Lactantius, *Deaths of Persecutors* 48.1–12; Eusebius, *Ecclesiastical History* 10.5.1–14.

[18] On the traditional title for this document, see Milton V. Anastos, 'The Edict of Milan (313): A Defence of its Traditional Authorship and Designation', *Revue des études byzantines* 25 (1967), 13–41; Timothy Barnes, 'Constantine after Seventeen Hundred Years: The *Cambridge Companion*, the York Exhibition, and a Recent Biography', *International Journal of the Classical Tradition* 14 (2007), 185–220. For convenience, the term 'Edict of Milan' will be used in quotation marks.

[19] '[Q]uo quicquid [est] divinitatis in sede caelesti': Lactantius, *Deaths of Persecutors* 48.2. The Latin text and its quoted translation are from *Lactantius: De mortibus persecutorum*, transl. J. L. Creed, Oxford Early Christian Texts (Oxford, 1984).

[20] Lactantius, *Deaths of Persecutors* 48.2; Eusebius, *Ecclesiastical History* 10.5.2–4.

[21] Lactantius, *Deaths of Persecutors* 48.2–6.

divinitas) received imperial protection, thereby assuring continuing divine favour.[22] Overall, however, this document clearly favoured Christianity without contradicting the agreed policy of embracing all forms of religion.[23] Such restitution as it extended to Christians easily grew to include bestowing actual benefits upon them.[24]

However, competing churches presided over by rival bishops in North Africa complicated Constantine's display of granting such benefits.[25] He perceived that the deep breach among Christians threatened the continuity of divine favour.[26] Acting on the expectation that such internal ecclesiastical disputes ought to be resolved by the bishops themselves, Constantine summoned a hearing of bishops assembled in Rome to make 'the most careful investigation' so that a 'just decision' could be made.[27] When that decision went against the party opposing Caecilian, they appealed to Constantine, who agreed to broaden representation of both sides at a council to be held at Arles in August 314.[28] Caecilian's opponents again lost the episcopal decision and petitioned Constantine further. Writing to the 'catholic' party in North Africa after Arles, Constantine expressed consternation at the continuing appeals by the Donatists for imperial intervention: 'They demand my judgment when I myself await the judgment of Christ. For I tell you ... that the judgment of priests should be regarded as if God himself were in the judge's seat'.[29] In a letter

---

[22] Ibid. 48.3.

[23] Ibid. 48.2–3, 6–12; cf. Timothy Barnes, *Constantine: Dynasty, Power, and Religion in the Later Roman Empire* (Malden, MA, 2014), 93–7.

[24] Eusebius, *Ecclesiastical History* 10.6.1–5; Lane Fox, *Pagans and Christians*, 610, 624–33; *Against the Donatists*, transl. Edwards, xiv; see also n. 18 above.

[25] Eusebius, *Ecclesiastical History* 10.5.20, 10.6.1–7.2.

[26] Ibid. 10.5.18, 10.7.1; Optatus, *Against the Donatists*, App. 3. The latter reference is a letter of Constantine to 'Aelafius', supposedly a *vicarius* of Africa during the spring of 314. The difficulties surrounding his name and position among the known *vicarii* of Africa contribute to doubts concerning this document's authenticity: A. H. M. Jones, J. R. Martindale and J. Morris, *The Prosopography of the Later Roman Empire*, 3 vols (Cambridge, 1971–92), 1: 16; Timothy Barnes, *The New Empire of Diocletian and Constantine* (Cambridge, 1982), 145 n. 18; Simon Corcoran, *The Empire of the Tetrarchs: Imperial Pronouncements and Government, A.D. 284–324* (Oxford, 1996), 329–31; *Against the Donatists*, transl. Edwards, 181 n. 1. Concerning the authenticity of Optatus's Appendix 3, which has been questioned because of the difficulties of identifying its addressee, see Frend, *Donatist Church*, xi–xv; *Against the Donatists*, transl. Edwards, xxviii.

[27] Eusebius, *Ecclesiastical History* 10.5.20; Optatus, *Against the Donatists*, App. 3; cf. Eusebius, *Ecclesiastical History* 7.30.18–19.

[28] Optatus, *Against the Donatists* 1.22; David S. Potter, *The Roman Empire at Bay: A.D. 180–395* (London, 2008), 407.

[29] Optatus, *Against the Donatists*, App. 5 (transl. Edwards, 190).

releasing Christian clergy in communion with Caecilian from civic obligations, Constantine linked the basis for this immunity to a principle of divine reciprocity: violations of proper worship 'brought great dangers on public affairs' while its 'lawful restoration and preservation' guaranteed continuing divine favour.[30]

Thus a pattern for imperial management of divine favour was established. The policies of liberty and restitution in the 'Edict of Milan' attempted to inaugurate the shared *imperium* of Constantine and Licinius on positive terms with divinity. However, the schism among Christians in North Africa disturbed the proper order and discipline of divine worship and therefore endangered the continuity of God's favour. Constantine worked with both sides in the North African dispute in order to avoid further disruption to the continuance of divine blessing towards the whole empire.

DIVINE FAVOUR ENDANGERED: EARLY INTERVENTION IN THE 'ARIAN CONTROVERSY'[31]

A similar pattern emerged following Constantine's final victory over Licinius in 324. Again, imperial policies concerning religion were announced in Constantine's newly won territories, policies intended to maintain the divine blessing that he believed had aided him against his enemy. Again, Constantine learned of conflict among the worshippers of his God and believed such discord endangered the continuance of divine blessing on the empire and upon himself. Again, he acted according to his keenly felt obligation as emperor to restore unity for the sake of continuing divine favour.

According to traditionally accepted dating, the theological conflict associated with the name of Arius began in Alexandria during 318, when the presbyter came into open disagreement with his bishop, Alexander.[32] Over the next six years, partisans on both sides cast their nets ever wider throughout the empire in search of support for

[30] Eusebius, *Ecclesiastical History* 10.7.1–2 (*The Ecclesiastical History of Eusebius of Caesarea*, transl. J. E. L. Oulton and H. J. Lawlor, LCL 265, 2 vols [Cambridge, 1980], 463–5).
[31] On the term 'Arian controversy', see R. P. C. Hanson, *The Search for the Christian Doctrine of God: The Arian Controversy, A.D. 318–381* (Edinburgh, 1988), xvii–xxi. For convenience, I have used it in a general and purely descriptive sense.
[32] For different views on when the dispute began, see Barnes, *Constantine and Eusebius*, 205–7; Hanson, *Search*, 129–38; John Behr, *The Nicene Faith*, 1: *True God of True God* (Crestwood, NJ, 2004), 62–6; David M. Gwynn, *The Eusebians: The Polemic of*

their respective viewpoints.[33] The conflict intensified to the point that from 321 Licinius apparently saw fit to ban all episcopal gatherings.[34] This action restrained ecclesiastical conflict in the East for a time, but it also allowed Constantine and his supporters to number Licinius among the persecuting emperors.[35] Licinius's defeat in autumn 324 enabled these Eastern bishops to renew their assemblies, and Christian division in these regions again burst into the open.[36] Only around this time, while formulating policy for his new Eastern subjects, did Constantine claim to have learned of the specific dispute involving Alexander and Arius.[37] Having ostensibly hoped to enlist Eastern clergy in resolving the ongoing Donatist dispute in the West, the news reaching Constantine's ears was that Christians were even more divided in the East.[38] Quarrels over the relationship of Jesus the Son to God the Father coincided with the Melitian schism.[39] This dispute was of a similar nature to the Donatist conflict, and like the current theological disturbance was centred in Egypt. Finally, some variance between Christians in both halves of the empire over celebrating Easter led Constantine to seek the establishment of a uniform practice.[40]

Upon being informed of such multiple levels of division, the emperor sent a letter to those most directly involved in the widespread theological disturbance: Alexander and Arius.[41] The letter is usually

Athanasius of Alexandria and the Construction of the 'Arian Controversy' (Oxford, 2007), 59–69.

[33] Eusebius, *Life* 2.61–2; Socrates of Constantinople, *Ecclesiastical History* 1.5. For a discussion of the chronological arrangement of the ancient evidence, see Rowan Williams, *Arius: Heresy and Tradition*, 2nd edn (London, 2001), 48–61.

[34] Eusebius, *Life* 1.51.1; Socrates, *Ecclesiastical History* 1.3; Sozomen, *Ecclesiastical History* 1.2; Barnes, *Constantine and Eusebius*, 206; Hanson, *Search*, 131; Williams, *Arius*, 49; Gwynn, *Eusebians*, 60–1.

[35] Eusebius, *Life* 1.49.1, 1.51.1–2; Socrates, *Ecclesiastical History* 1.3.

[36] Hanson, *Search*, 134–6; Gwynn, *Eusebians*, 61.

[37] Eusebius, *Life* 2.65.1–2, 2.68.1.

[38] Ibid. 2.66–68.1.

[39] J. G. G. Norman, 'Melitian Schisms', in J. D. Douglas, ed., *The New International Dictionary of the Christian Church* (Exeter, 1978), 647–8; Michael P. McHugh, 'Melitius of Lycopolis', in Everett Ferguson, ed., *Encyclopedia of Early Christianity*, 2nd edn (New York, 1999), 745.

[40] Eusebius, *Life* 2.61.2–62, 3.4.1–5.2, 3.16.1–19.3.

[41] Ibid. 2.64–72; Paul Parvis, 'Constantine's Letter to Arius and Alexander?', *Studia Patristica* 39 (2006), 89–95. Parvis draws on arguments by B. H. Warmington and Stuart Hall suggesting that this document was addressed to the synod at Antioch in 325 rather than to Alexander and Arius as individuals. He argues that an official other than

invoked in discussions of Constantine's interest in ecclesiastical unity, for reasons that are obvious from the text itself.[42] However, it is also significant in revealing a clear link in the emperor's mind between ecclesiastical unity and divine favour.[43] Constantine opened the letter by invoking his God as witness to his activity according to a two-part approach involving the religious and political unification of the provinces. Uniting the provinces in a consistent view of God involved rational persuasion, while achieving political unity had demonstrably required the power of military force.[44] Unity among God's worshippers, according to Constantine, would of itself have a positive impact on the corporate well-being of his subjects.[45] The emperor also claimed to have suffered what he called a 'deadly wound' specifically in relation to the conflict between these two men and their respective partisans.[46] There was probably more to that comment than an exaggerated expression of disappointment. It also described Constantine's sense of danger as he feared divine vengeance. He already believed that disunity among the Christians of North Africa risked

---

Ossius of Cordoba presented the letter, and that the central issue was a disputed episcopal succession. While a fully developed argument opposing Parvis, Warmington and Hall lies outside the purpose of this essay, the following points are offered here in response: the letter may not be addressed to Alexander and Arius as individuals, but I suggest these named persons in addition to their respective supporters are the intended recipients; the suggestion that the issue centred on episcopal succession rather than theology can be dismissed on that basis as well as from the letter's text (for which see, for example, Eusebius, *Life* 2.69, 2.71.2–7); it remains reasonable to follow Socrates's identification of the person entrusted with the letter as Ossius (Socrates, *Ecclesiastical History* 1.7), since the bishop is named earlier and functions in a similar capacity as imperial representative to the churches in Constantine's letter to Caecilian (Eusebius, *Ecclesiastical History* 10.6.2); this does not mean Ossius embarked on his mission alone and it is reasonable to accept the participation of someone like Marianus the notary: Parvis, 'Constantine's Letter?', 92.

[42] Øyvind Norderval, 'The Emperor Constantine and Arius: Unity in the Church and Unity in the Empire' *Studia Theologica* 42 (1988), 113–50, at 118–20; Drake, *Constantine*, 240–2; Bardill, *Constantine*, 291–3.

[43] Constantine explicitly invoked divine support in addressing ecclesiastical discord: Eusebius, *Life* 2.68.2–3. Other scholars observe the same link, but not necessarily in relation to this letter; moreover, no known analysis emphasizes the specific issue of divine favour in relation to Constantine's approach to ecclesiastical unity: see, for instance, Drake, *Constantine*, 320; Paul Stephenson, *Constantine: Unconquered Emperor, Christian Victor* (London, 2009), 305–6; Maijastina Kahlos, *Forbearance and Compulsion: The Rhetoric of Religious Tolerance and Intolerance in Late Antiquity* (London, 2009), 62–4.

[44] Eusebius, *Life* 2.65.1–2.

[45] Ibid. 2.65.2.

[46] Ibid. 2.68.1.

provoking God's wrath.[47] Combined with the news of multiple divisions affecting his new Eastern provinces, it is not difficult to believe that Constantine felt quite threatened.

Yet he did not long dwell on these negative aspects in this letter, proceeding quickly to describe his attempts to investigate the causes behind the disturbance originating among Alexandrian Christians.[48] According to the emperor's understanding, 'the cause was exposed as extremely trivial and unworthy of so much controversy'.[49] The conflict's 'small and utterly trivial' nature was repeatedly emphasized throughout the rest of this letter.[50] This is an interesting remark by an emperor who clearly treated ecclesiastical division as a serious threat, and we shall return to it in due course. Some modern writers have pointed to such terminology as evidence that Constantine failed to grasp the debate's real theological significance or that he valued unity over doctrine.[51] It is also often assumed that Constantine must also have pursued unity above every other concern. Explicit statements by the emperor would appear to be irrefutable evidence of this. For

[47] Eusebius, *Ecclesiastical History* 10.5.18, 10.17.1. This is not to ignore the more explicitly political dangers Constantine faced. For example, keeping the city of Rome supplied with oil, grain and corn was of vital importance for holding on to power, while the continuity of such provision was believed to depend on divine favour: see Athanasius, *Apology Against the Arians* 18; *Theodosian Code* 14.24–5 (ET *The Theodosian Code and Novels and the Sirmondian Constitutions*, transl. Clyde Pharr [Clark, NJ, 2001; first publ. 1952]); Timothy Barnes, *Athanasius and Constantius: Theology and Politics in the Constantinian Empire* (Cambridge, 1993), 178–9; Christoph Auffarth, 'With the Grain came the Gods from the Orient to Rome: The Example of Serapis and some Systematic Reflections', in Peter Wick and Volker Rabens, eds, *Religions and Trade: Religious Formation, Transformation and Cross-Cultural Exchange between East and West* (Boston, MA, 2014), 19–44, at 32.
[48] Eusebius, *Life* 2.68.2–3.
[49] Ibid. 2.68.2.
[50] Ibid. 2.68.2–3, 2.71.1, 3.
[51] Norderval, 'Constantine and Arius', 115, 118–21; Drake, *Constantine*, 238–44; A. H. M. Jones, *The Later Roman Empire, 284–602: A Social, Economic and Administrative Survey*, 2 vols (Oxford, 1973), 1: 86; Stephenson, *Constantine*, 265–6. However, Edwards describes a Constantine who was perhaps more in tune with the theological issues at stake than it might seem: Edwards, 'Why did Constantine Label Arius a Porphyrian?', *L'Antiquité classique* 82 (2013), 239–47, at 243–7. Additionally, it is unfair to criticize Constantine for failing to comprehend more fully a theological debate that was still developing and which taxed the greatest theological minds during and after his lifetime. Rather than showing a lack of interest, Eusebius claimed that Constantine engaged with doctrinal questions and enjoyed opportunities to declaim to the court on the meaning of various biblical passages: Eusebius, *Life of Constantine* 4.29. The emperor's *Oration* reveals the truth of Eusebius's words, although Constantine's Christological assertions in this speech provoke scholarly debate concerning its date and the extent of his 'Arian' theology.

example, at the beginning of the letter to Alexander and Arius, Constantine wrote that his 'first concern was that the attitude toward the divinity of all the provinces should be united in one consistent view'.[52] Second, in the same passage of the letter, he spoke of uniting the provinces in terms evoking traditional imperial language regarding the 'restoration' of the republic. Regarding the emperor's earlier mentioned means of 'healing' the empire of its 'wounds' through reason and force, the concern in both cases was clearly for unity. The emperor himself seemed to emphasize this particular point: 'I knew that if I were to establish a general concord among the servants of God in accordance with my prayers, the course of public affairs would also enjoy the change consonant with the pious desires of all'.[53] At the risk of stating the obvious, it appears to be this very concept of unity that was chiefly endangered by division among Christians in the East, where the disputants addressed by Constantine in this letter were a significant factor.

Unity was unquestionably of great importance to the emperor. In terms of imperial politics, this, too, risks stating the obvious. After all, it is inconceivable that any Roman emperor would have long tolerated (or survived) a state of affairs in which any kind of disturbance spread without interference. Therefore, the answer to why Constantine highly valued unity may appear so evident as to need little further analysis. Yet an implicit concern for maintaining divine favour shows through in the emperor's words. As he believed division among God's worshippers risked divine punishment, so he was likewise convinced that restoring unity thereby renewed divine favour. It was not unity for its own sake but the restoration of divine favour brought about by means of unity that he hoped would bring back a 'quiet life' of 'peaceful days and undisturbed nights'.[54] This is not to suggest that Constantine's motives were purely religious, or that the emperor's management of divine aid did not serve his political interests. But there is no reason to think that Constantine did not genuinely believe in the necessity of divine favour, or that he used religious language solely for political purposes. Although the emperor's explicit statements about unity did not refer to seeking God's support in every case, it can be suggested that divine favour was so evident a

---

[52] Ibid. 2.65.1.
[53] Ibid. 2.65.1–2 (transl. Cameron and Hall, 116).
[54] Ibid. 2.72.1 (transl. Cameron and Hall, 119).

primary motivating factor that he simply did not need to say it at all times. Roman emperors relied no more exclusively on political unity for holding on to power than their generals depended only on the coordinated movements of the legions for success on the battlefield: the continuing favour of the right god(s) was as essential in governing as in warfare. Constantine's words and actions favouring Christianity indicated his desire to maintain the pleasure of the 'supreme God' by expressing gratitude for the benefits received in battle, in the hope they would continue in the form of peaceful and prosperous government. Divine favour was a decisive and even, as this article argues, a primary factor.

RESTORING DIVINE FAVOUR: DIVINE INSTRUMENTALITY AND THE 'SERVANT OF GOD'

According to Eusebius, Constantine viewed his task of overcoming division among Eastern Christians in terms of another war in which he must prove victorious.[55] In order to 'march against' the invisible enemy who disturbed the peace of the Church, Eusebius wrote that Constantine mobilized a 'legion of God' by forming a broadly representative episcopal council on a hitherto unknown scale.[56] As in any military conflict, it required careful tactical planning on the emperor's part. First, he changed the originally announced location from Ancyra to Nicaea. His stated justification for the change need not be entirely ignored, but most scholars believe Constantine had other motives.[57] If Barnes is correct and the bishops gathered in Alexandria were initially responsible for announcing the great council in Ancyra, Constantine's changing of the venue ensured a less partisan result by removing the gathering from under the authority of Marcellus, a vocal opponent of Arius. But even if Hanson's assertion that Constantine himself initially suggested Ancyra is accurate, the change to Nicaea (as Barnes speculated) may have helped the emperor stay near Nicomedia at a time of increasing uncertainty due to political fallout from Licinius's defeat.[58] Such language evoking

---

[55] Ibid. 3.5.3–6.1.
[56] Ibid. 3.6–9 (transl. Cameron and Hall, 123–4).
[57] Alastair H. B. Logan, 'Marcellus of Ancyra and the Councils of A.D. 325: Antioch, Ancyra, Nicaea', *JThS* 43 (1992), 428–46, at 429–36; Norderval, 'Constantine and Arius', 123; Barnes, *Constantine*, 121; Drake, *Constantine*, 251–2.
[58] Barnes, *Constantine and Eusebius*, 214–15; Hanson, *Search*, 152–3.

'spiritual warfare' could very well have occurred to the mind of the emperor himself, and may have held particular appeal to one who was familiar with the New Testament.[59]   Eusebius paraphrased a speech apparently delivered by Constantine at the council's opening in which military metaphors dominated.[60]   Though Eusebius acknowledged that he had not recorded Constantine's exact words, such symbolic language could have been used by an emperor as easily as any bishop.[61] Regarding division in the Church as 'graver than any war or fierce battle', the emperor prayed for the same divine help that had given him victories in battle to grant the Church 'healing through [his] own instrumentality'.[62] Having therefore assembled such a 'legion of God' at Nicaea, Constantine then declared that unity was the desired result of their forthcoming deliberations. That would be pleasing to God and gratifying to the emperor.[63]   In other words, while unity was foremost on the emperor's agenda for the council the achievement of harmony among God's worshippers continued to serve the purpose of restoring divine favour.

Such effective managing of divine aid was the emperor's chief religious duty as the 'servant of God'. He had referred to himself this way once in a letter to the 'catholic' bishops after the council of Arles (314).[64]   Ten years later, 'service' came to epitomize Constantine's view of his role in relation to ecclesiastical affairs. Although the exact phrase 'servant of God' occurred only twice in his preserved correspondence after 324, references abound to his 'service', 'obedient service' and 'service to the supreme God', as well as self-description in relation to other bishops and even lay Christians as their 'fellow-servant'.[65] The biblical resonance of such servant language invited

---

[59] For example, Eph. 6: 10–17. On military metaphors in the New Testament, see Thomas R. Yoder Neufeld, *Jesus and the Subversion of Violence: Wrestling with the New Testament Evidence* (London, 2011), 122–49.

[60] The speech is preserved in paraphrased form in Eusebius, *Life* 3.12.1–5.

[61] Eusebius's acknowledgement appears prior to the speech itself: ibid. 3.11.

[62] Ibid. 3.12.3 (transl. Cameron and Hall, 126).

[63] Ibid. 3.12.5 (transl. Cameron and Hall, 126).

[64] Optatus, *Against the Donatists*, App. 5 (transl. Edwards, 189).

[65] Eusebius, *Life* 2.29.3, 2.31.2. References include: τὴν ἐμὴν ὑπηρεσίαν (ibid. 2.28.2), θεραπείαν τῇ παρ' ἐμοῦ παιδευόμενον ὑπουργίᾳ (ibid.), τῷ θεράποντι τοῦ θεοῦ (2.29.3), οἳ θεοῦ θεράποντες (2.31.2), τῷ μεγίστῳ διακονεῖται θεῷ (2.38), ἡμετέρᾳ δ' ὑπηρεσίᾳ (2.46.2), σοῦ θεράποντος (2.55.1), τοῦ μεγάλου θεοῦ θεράποντας (2.71.2), συνθεραπόντων (2.72.1), συνθεράπων (3.17.2). For the Greek text, see Friedhelm Winkelmann, ed., *Eusebius Werke*, 1.1. *Über das Leben des Kaisers Konstantins* (Berlin, 1975).

Andrew J. Pottenger

comparison with Moses and Paul.[66] Moses's status as ancient Israel's leader in political and military as well as religious matters makes this the most likely comparison in relation to a Roman emperor. This would also seem clear from Eusebius's explicit drawing of parallels between Moses and Constantine in several descriptions of the emperor.[67] Examination of the Greek words used in relation to Moses and Paul confirms these assumptions. Paul opened his letters to the Romans and to a protégé named Titus by describing himself as a 'servant of God', using the term δοῦλος, while Moses was referred to in the Septuagint as θεραπεία.[68] The former word could be more accurately rendered 'slave', emphasizing the apostle's servile status in relation to his God. However, θεραπεία is a more active term for 'service', and its range of meanings encompasses a sense of usefulness with religious or medicinal overtones.[69] In contrast with the more static meaning of δοῦλος, the emphasis of θεραπεία is on attending to what needs to be done. Thus, in his role as 'servant of God', Constantine claimed to be God's instrument for accomplishing the divine will on earth. This was not merely a divine legitimation of power under a single exclusive and omnipotent God. While an emperor would not think of abasing himself to the status of a mere slave, he would want to be seen as a useful instrument for 'curing' whatever ills he perceived were being suffered prior to or during his reign.

Conclusion

Divine favour was long believed crucial to a successful imperial reign. Constantine believed, in accordance with a version of this tradition modified to integrate his new religious identification, that the God whom Christians worshipped was the 'supreme God' whose power worked on his behalf in battle against the supernatural powers called upon by Maxentius and Licinius. Convinced that he had received divine aid in defeating these rivals, Constantine's primary concern as

[66] Cf. Ex. 14: 31; Num. 1: 7–8; Rom. 1: 1; Titus 1: 1. For Drake's argument that Constantine styled himself after Paul by appealing to the title 'man of God', see H. A. Drake, 'The Emperor as a "Man of God": The Impact of Constantine the Great's Conversion on Roman Ideas of Kingship', *Historia* 35 (2016) [online journal], at: <https://doi.org/10.1590/1980-436920160000000083>, accessed 13 April 2017.
[67] Eusebius, *Life* 1.12, 1.19, 1.38–9.
[68] See n. 66 above.
[69] Henry George Liddell and Robert Scott, *A Greek-English Lexicon* (Oxford, 1976), 792–3.

44

the 'servant of God' was the successful management of divine favour upon which he believed his life and power and the public welfare depended. Ecclesiastical unity, while undoubtedly of great importance to the emperor, served that end rather than being itself his chief objective. Constantine's view was that continuity of God's favour rested on proper worship, which he believed required general harmony among Christians and the performance of Christian rites according to standard ecclesiastical order as determined by a majority of bishops assembled in a council. When he learned of divisions between varying parties of Christians, he worked actively with ecclesiastical leaders as their 'fellow-servant' to create space in which matters could be investigated and unity restored as the disputing factions worked out their own decisions.

However, ecclesiastical leaders did not achieve the emperor's hopes for a united Christian Church within the Roman Empire. Far from realizing unanimity, Nicaea's definition of the 'consubstantial' relation of the Father and the Son raised as many questions as it managed to answer.[70] Although Constantine continued to hold the episcopacy in high regard and wished to work with the bishops in bringing about the desired unity among Christians, not every bishop was as willing to work with the emperor.[71] For Constantine, continuing divine favour depended on the restoration of ecclesiastical unity. But because orthodox doctrine was of great importance to the bishops, divine favour and instrumentality alone proved insufficient as a doctrine of power guiding a Christian emperor in relation to the ecclesiastical hierarchy.

[70] Socrates, *Ecclesiastical History* 1.14 (for Eusebius's letter defending and qualifying his acceptance of Nicene terminology), 23, 26–7, 36. Apart from the existing political conflicts among Church leaders, much controversy continued over the term ὁμοούσιος and its precise meaning in the Nicene definition, given its non-biblical origin and prior connotations of Sabellian heresy.

[71] Drake highlights the notion of competing 'agendas and priorities that clouded relations between Constantine and the bishops'. His work also emphasizes the variety of contending purposes among the bishops themselves: see Drake, *Constantine*, 30–1, 235–71, with reference to the Arian controversy.

Imperium and the City of God: Augustine on Church and Empire

Gillian Clark[*]

University of Bristol

In early fifth-century Roman Africa, Augustine faced pagan opponents who thought that the Roman empire was at risk because Christian emperors banned the worship of its gods, and that Christian ethics were no way to run an empire. He also faced Christian opponents who held that theirs was the true Church, and that the Roman empire was the oppressive power of Babylon. For Augustine, Church and empire consist of people. Everyone belongs either to the heavenly city, the community of all who love God even to disregard of themselves, or to the earthly city, the community of all who love themselves even to disregard of God. The two cities are intermixed until the final judgement shows that some who share Christian sacraments belong to the earthly city, and some officers of empire belong to the heavenly city. Empire manifests the earthly city's desire to dominate, but imperium, *the acknowledged right to give orders, is necessary to avoid permanent conflict. Empire, like everything else, is given or permitted by God, for purposes we do not know.*

[Volusianus] says, moreover, that Christ's preaching and teaching are wholly incompatible with our traditions of government, in that (as many people say) it is agreed that Christ taught that we ought to return no one evil for evil, and to offer the other cheek to someone who hits us, and to give our cloak to someone who insists on taking our tunic, and to go twice the distance with someone who requisitions our service. All these, he affirms, are contrary to our traditions of government. For who would endure to have something taken from him by an enemy, or would not wish to repay evil, by right of war, to the raider of a Roman province? Your Reverence understands what could be said about the rest. He thinks that all these concerns can be added to the question at issue, in that under Christian emperors, who strongly maintain the Christian religion, it is evident (even

* 49 Bellevue Crescent, Bristol, BS8 4TF. E-mail: Gillian.clark@bris.ac.uk.

Studies in Church History 54 (2018) 46–70   © Ecclesiastical History Society 2018
doi: 10.1017/stc.2017.4

if he himself is silent on this) that such great evils have befallen the commonwealth.[1]

This is part of a letter sent in 411/12 by Marcellinus, a Christian imperial officer, to Augustine, bishop of Hippo Regius on the north African coast. They had met in Carthage, the capital city of Roman Africa, where Marcellinus was on a special mission from the imperial court to resolve a century-old dispute between two churches, each claiming to be the true and universal Church because the other had betrayed the faith.[2] Each also accused the other of appropriating church property and imperial funds, and of endangering public order. Some Christians had lobbied for the application of imperial laws against heretics; others argued that the Church should not call in the empire to settle disagreements, and each side claimed that the other had been the first to do this.[3]

In 411 Marcellinus chaired the Conference of Carthage, a meeting of rival bishops, in which Augustine was prominent.[4] Also in Carthage, for a different reason, were several members of the traditional Roman elite, who had property in Africa but usually lived in the city of Rome or on their estates in Italy. Among them was the influential senator Volusianus, a former proconsul of Africa.[5] His concerns about Christianity and empire, passed on in the letter of Marcellinus, were shared by many others who had made the short sea-crossing from Italy to Africa as refugees from a war-band of Goths. In August 410 these Goths, led by Alaric, shocked the Roman world by sacking the city of Rome. The city was no longer

[1] Augustine, *Ep.* 136.2. All translations are my own. 'Our traditions of government' is one possible translation of *reipublicae mores,* but both Latin words have a wide range. *Mores,* 'the way things are done', covers both 'custom' and 'morality'. *Res publica,* often translated 'commonwealth', means literally 'common concerns', hence 'government', or 'the country' in the political sense: see further Malcolm Schofield, 'Cicero's definition of *res publica*', in J. G. F. Powell, ed., *Cicero the Philosopher* (Oxford, 1995), 63–83.
[2] Marcellinus was *tribunus et notarius*: see A. H. M. Jones, *The Later Roman Empire, 284–602: A Social, Economic and Administrative Survey,* 3 vols (Oxford, 1964), 2: 572–5, on this status; and Brent Shaw, *Sacred Violence: African Christians and Sectarian Hatred in the Age of Augustine* (Cambridge, 2011), 496–505, on the use of *tribuni et notarii* in African disputes where local officials were reluctant to intervene.
[3] On the dispute, usually called the 'Donatist controversy', see Richard Miles, ed., *The Donatist Schism: Controversy and Contexts* (Liverpool, 2016).
[4] On the conference, see Neil McLynn, 'The Conference of Carthage Reconsidered', ibid. 220–48.
[5] For historical reasons, the district around Carthage was called *Africa proconsularis* and its governor held the prestigious title 'proconsul'.

the centre of government. Its inland site on the Italian peninsula, some distance from an adequate harbour and on a river which was liable to flood, was not the best base for meeting the challenges of the fifth-century world; in 410 the Western imperial court was based at Ravenna and the Eastern imperial court at Constantinople. But 'Rome' still signified the empire as well as the city, and the city was still the historic and symbolic capital of empire.

Marcellinus, Augustine and Volusianus exemplify a range of relationships between Church and empire in the early fifth century. Marcellinus, sent by a Christian emperor to resolve a dispute among churches, evidently did not see a conflict between his own Christian commitment and his role as an imperial civil servant. Augustine, a priest, then a bishop of the minority church in Roman Africa since the early 390s, did see a conflict, for himself if not for others. In his earlier career as a teacher of rhetoric, a skill which was essential for any public role, he had risen to be the publicly funded professor of rhetoric at Milan, where the Western imperial court was then in residence; he had hoped for a post in the imperial service, perhaps in the lowest rank of provincial governors.[6] His duties included speeches in praise of a boy emperor, and he later wrote that he and his audience knew that what he said was false.[7] Augustine had renounced this career for a life of prayer and study, and returned from Italy to his homeland in Africa, but after he was ordained he had to engage with imperial officers. Bishops in Late Antiquity were expected to intercede with local officials, and if necessary with the imperial court, both for the enforcement of imperial law against offenders and for mercy in punishing them. Volusianus, the third person in this exchange, was not Christian, but that was not an obstacle to holding senior offices in the service of Christian emperors. His status as a Roman aristocrat allowed him to voice his objections to Christian teaching, if not in public speeches, at least in conversations and letter-exchanges which were not intended to be private. His mother was Christian, and Augustine wrote to him offering to discuss any difficulties he found in Christian Scripture and belief. Volusianus responded politely but without commitment, preferring to converse about literature and philosophy.[8]

[6] Augustine, *Confessiones* 6.11.19.
[7] Ibid. 6.6.9.
[8] Augustine, *Ep.* 132, 135, 137; on this exchange, see Éric Rebillard, *Christians and their Many Identities in Late Antiquity: North Africa 200–450 CE* (Ithaca, NY, 2012), 81–2.

Marcellinus was sufficiently impressed by Augustine to ask him (rather than the bishop of Carthage, Aurelius) for an effective response to the views expressed by Volusianus. His letter, with Augustine's reply, survived in Augustine's correspondence to illustrate both the context in which Augustine began work on *City of God* and the questions which prompted him to do so. As Marcellinus said, Volusianus raised some objections which had been answered many times: that magicians achieved greater miracles than those ascribed to Christ, and that, even if the incarnation could be explained, it was inexplicable that God should have changed his mind about sacrifice between the Old Testament and the New.[9] But some of the questions Volusianus asked or implied were specifically about empire. Is Christian teaching incompatible with running an empire? Was Christianity to blame for the troubles of the Roman empire, and in particular for the sack of Rome by a band of barbarians, two decades after a Christian emperor banned public and private worship of the gods who had given empire to Rome?

The emperor Theodosius I banned pagan worship in 391, the year Augustine became a priest. This was the culmination of dramatic change, in the years which are now called the fourth century, in the relationship of Church and empire.[10] For the first three centuries Christians had been at risk of trial and execution by imperial officers, because some Romans saw Christians as terror suspects deluded by a false religion, or held that Christians posed a threat because they would not sacrifice to the gods of Rome and would not obey the authorities when told to do so. Some Christians therefore saw Rome as a new Babylon, the oppressive and idolatrous empire which held God's people captive. Some Christians died as martyrs; some tried to explain that Christianity was no threat but fulfilled Roman ideals; many were more pluralist than their leaders wished. Persecution of Christians was usually local and short-lived, but the fourth century began with a sustained attempt by the emperor Diocletian to ensure that his subjects were united in sacrificing to the gods of Rome. For most people this was not a problem, because local gods were identified with Roman gods, and educated people could understand all these gods as expressions or aspects of the universal divine power.

---

[9] Augustine, *Ep.* 136.3.
[10] There are many fuller accounts of this development. For a brief account, with further bibliography, see Gillian Clark, *Christianity and Roman Society* (Cambridge, 2004).

The religion of the Jews was protected by Roman law, and they would have offered sacrifice for the well-being of the empire if their Temple had not been destroyed; some Roman intellectuals equated the God of the Jews with Jupiter.[11] But Christians were taught that Christ's sacrifice was once for all, and that the gods of Rome were man-made idols or malign demons. For those who would not recant or compromise, Diocletian's attempt was the 'Great Persecution'. Africa suffered less than some parts of the eastern Mediterranean, but different responses among Christians had led to the schism which still confronted Marcellinus a century later.

Persecution failed, and after the victory of Constantine, the first emperor who openly supported Christianity, only one emperor was openly not Christian. This was Julian, known to Christians as 'the Apostate', who dismissed Christians as 'Galilaeans' from the backwoods of an obscure province, in contrast with the great religious tradition of the Mediterranean and Near Eastern world. He did not persecute, but he did try to revive the traditional religion, especially the practice of blood sacrifice. Julian's reign lasted eighteen months, and when he died on a disastrous expedition against the rival power of Persia, his last words (so later historians claimed) were *Vicisti, Galilaee*: 'you win, Galilean'. Some fourth-century emperors tolerated the traditional religion and kept their distance from church concerns, others became involved because of their own strong views; some Christians thought that theology and ecclesiastical politics were not the emperor's business, especially if they differed from him. Imperial officials, so far as the evidence goes, were appointed because of their connections and their competence, without any preference for Christians. That did not change when, almost a century after Diocletian, the committed Christian Theodosius I, who ruled both the Eastern and the Western parts of the empire, felt able to ban all public and private worship of the gods of Rome.[12]

Understandably, some Christians saw in this remarkable sequence the triumph of Christianity. Among them was Eusebius, the founder of ecclesiastical history, who lived through the transformation. His beloved teacher Pamphilus died a martyr in the Great Persecution, but Eusebius was among the bishops who in 325 were summoned by Constantine to the Council of Nicaea and invited to dine in the

---

[11] Augustine, *De consensu evangelistarum* 1.22.30.
[12] The relevant laws are excerpted in *Codex Theodosianus* 16.10.10–11 (391/2).

imperial palace, where troops with drawn swords formed a guard of honour, not an execution squad.[13] Augustine sometimes shared this amazed delight. In a work written around 400 he quoted the prophet Jeremiah: 'the nations will come to you from the ends of the earth, and will say "Our fathers held falsehood, futility which profited them nothing; shall a man make himself gods, and they are no gods?"' It is happening now, said Augustine, they are coming to Christ and breaking their images.[14] But Augustine was not triumphalist, because he knew all too well that banning pagan cult did not make the Roman empire Christian.

Roman Africa extended along the northern seaboard to the west of Egypt and Libya. On its inland borders were people who had not yet heard the gospel.[15] Even where the gospel was regularly preached, towns were full of temples and statues of the gods, which were legally protected as heritage, and traditional festivals of the gods continued as local holidays. Most officials chose not to notice that some pagan practice continued. Augustine said that many people were still pagan in their hearts, and few were more than one generation away from paganism. Some had no interest in Christian teachings, many delayed making the commitment of baptism, and even baptized Christians compromised. A man would accept an invitation to dinner in the temple complex, in a room adorned with images of gods, rather than offend the powerful person who had invited him; a woman with a sick child would use any amulet on offer.[16] So the empire was not Christian; nor was there a united Church, for throughout the empire there were disagreements about theology, authority and claims to primacy. This was especially clear in Africa. Augustine's congregation in Hippo could hear from their basilica the distinctive songs of the rival 'Donatist' congregation, whose members argued that Augustine and his fellow bishops were in a line of succession from those who had betrayed the faith, so were not validly ordained and could not validly

---

[13] Eusebius, *De vita Constantini* 3.15. For arguments that Eusebius was nevertheless not a triumphal optimist, see Aaron P. Johnson, *Eusebius* (London, 2014); Hazel Johannessen, *The Demonic in the Political Thought of Eusebius of Caesarea* (Oxford, 2016). On Eusebius in comparison with Augustine, see Peter Van Nuffelen, *Orosius and the Rhetoric of Empire* (Oxford, 2012), 186–206.

[14] Jer. 16: 19–20; Augustine, *De consensu evangelistarum* 1.26.40.

[15] Augustine, *Ep.* 199.12.46; this letter to Bishop Hesychius is mentioned at *De civitate Dei* 20.5.

[16] Éric Rebillard, 'Religious Sociology: Being Christian in the Time of Augustine', in Mark Vessey, ed., *A Companion to Augustine* (Chichester, 2012), 40–53.

baptize, consecrate the eucharist or ordain other clergy.[17] Yet, as Augustine said in a sermon, 'we are brothers, we call upon one God, we believe in one Christ, we hear one gospel, we sing one psalm, we reply with one Amen, we shout one Alleluia, we celebrate one Easter'.[18] Augustine used scriptural language about 'the Church' as the body of Christ and the bride of Christ; he contrasted 'the Church' with 'the synagogue' which failed to go beyond the Old Testament; he praised the emperor Theodosius for aiding 'the Church' in her struggle with heretics and pagans. But he also consistently said that we are the Church.[19] In this life 'the Church' is not an entity: it is people.

Augustine knew that the Roman empire was not Christian, but when the Goths sacked the city of Rome, the easy explanation was 'Christian times'. Uneducated people, but also others who knew better, declared that the gods who made the Roman empire great were offended by neglect and had withdrawn their protection from Christian emperors and their subjects.[20] Present-day historians prefer to think in terms of misunderstandings and inconsistent policies in the relationship of Roman officials with the people they called 'barbarians'.[21] On the northern frontiers of the empire there were always challenges, and in the later fourth century pressure on Roman territory increased because these northern peoples, who were usually identified as Goths, themselves came under pressure from other groups moving west from central Asia. Sometimes barbarians were encouraged to settle on Roman territory as a border defence force against further immigration. Their warrior culture and their tradition of personal loyalty to a leader made them useful recruits to the Roman army, and some who were especially tall and imposing even served as imperial bodyguards. Many were Christian. But sometimes mismanaged immigration led to conflict, and although it was assumed that disciplined Roman troops would defeat savage barbarians, this

[17] For the arguments, see Mark Edwards, 'The Donatist Schism and Theology', in Miles, ed., *Donatist Schism*, 101–19; and for their effect on Augustine's understanding of the Church, Alexander Evers, 'Augustine on the Church (Against the Donatists)', in Vessey, ed., *Companion to Augustine*, 375–85.
[18] Augustine, *Enarrationes in Psalmos* 54.16.
[19] See further Tarsicius van Bavel, 'Church', in Allan D. Fitzgerald, ed., *Augustine through the Ages: An Encyclopedia* (Grand Rapids, MI., 1999), 172–3.
[20] Augustine, *De civitate Dei* 1.33; on 'Christian times', see R. A. Markus, *Saeculum: History and Society in the Theology of St Augustine*, 2nd edn (Cambridge, 1988), 22–44.
[21] Peter Heather, *Empires and Barbarians: The Fall of Rome and the Birth of Europe* (Oxford, 2010).

did not always happen. In 378 the emperor Valens, and two-thirds of his troops, died in defeat at Adrianople in northern Greece.

It was difficult to have a consistent policy, because the 'barbarians' were not all Goths, and even among those who were, shifting alliances and changing demands were usual. In the two years of uneasy negotiation before the attack on Rome in August 410, Alaric led his war-band around Italy, asking at different times for status as a Roman commander, for land where his people could settle, for a guaranteed supply of corn and for treasure. He did not try to occupy and hold the city, or to destroy it and massacre the inhabitants; he allowed some people to take sanctuary in churches and shrines; and he withdrew after three days. It could have been much worse. But Rome was the symbolic capital of empire, and for Christians it was the city of Peter and Paul, of churches and martyr-shrines.[22]

Until recent years, this trauma was understood through the words of Jerome, who, far away in his monastery in Bethlehem, heard the terrible news in letters from friends. Rome was the city of his schooldays and the scene of successes in his early career. In the preface to his long-delayed commentary on Ezekiel, he wrote that he could scarcely finish his work for grief. He invoked Vergil on the fall of Troy, its streets piled with corpses, and the Psalms on the fall of Jerusalem: their blood is poured out like water and there is no one to bury them. The brightest light in the world has gone out, said Jerome; the empire is beheaded, the world perished in one city.[23] Historians and archaeologists now think that Jerome overstated the case, and that Augustine (who showed no personal attachment to the city of Rome) was right when he told his congregation to keep those three dreadful days in perspective.[24] Rome, Augustine said, had suffered far worse before Christian times, from invasion, civil war and natural disasters, and had not now been annihilated like Sodom and Gomorrah. Cities are built of stone and timber, and they fall, but Rome is people, Rome is the Romans. What matters, always, is how each person responds to God's judgement and God's mercy.[25]

The world continued much as before, the assault was brief, and casualty figures were relatively low. The city of Rome was no longer

---

[22] See the review-discussion by Peter Van Nuffelen, 'Not Much Happened: 410 and All That', *JRS* 105 (2015), 322–9.

[23] Jerome, *In Ezechielem*, prologue.

[24] Van Nuffelen, 'Not Much Happened'.

[25] Augustine, *Sermones* 81.9.

a centre of government; some emperors never went there. But these calm reflections were not obvious at the time. Latin-speaking school-boys were brought up on classical texts, from more than four centuries earlier, in which Rome meant the empire as well as the city. The *Aeneid* of Vergil was a core text of the late antique curriculum, so every educated person knew how Jupiter, king of the gods, declared that he gave Rome empire without end, without boundaries of space or time: *imperium sine fine dedi.*[26] Augustine remarked in a sermon that many people had also read about the visit of Aeneas to the underworld, or had seen stage adaptations.[27] Perhaps these performances included Anchises, father of Aeneas, showing him a vision of Rome's future glory and declaring Rome's mission statement: other nations may excel in the arts and sciences, but:

> You, Roman, remember to rule the peoples with your empire
> (These will be your arts) and to impose the custom of peace,
> To spare the subject and fight down the proud.[28]

> *Tu regere imperio populos, Romane, memento*
> *(hae tibi erunt artes), pacisque imponere morem,*
> *parcere subiectis et debellare superbos.*

Christians too could be impressed by the extent of the empire in which they lived, and could see it as part of the true God's plan for the growth of the Church. Christ, they said, was born at the time when Rome's first emperor, Augustus, imposed peace on the known world; monarchy and monotheism went together; and peace allowed the gospel to spread in the common languages of Greek and Latin.[29]

The exceptional range of the Roman empire was made visible in the *Chronological Tables* of Eusebius. Augustine had a copy of Jerome's Latin translation and update.[30] The codex, the spine-hinged book, was in the early fourth century a relatively new form of technology, and Eusebius made impressive use of it to set out kingdoms in

---

[26] Vergil, *Aeneid* 1.278–9. On late antique education, see Robert Kaster, *Guardians of Language: The Grammarian and Society in Late Antiquity* (Berkeley, CA, 1988).

[27] Augustine, *Sermones* 241.5.

[28] Vergil, *Aeneid* 6.851–3.

[29] For example, Orosius, *Historiae adversus paganos* 6.1.5-8; see Van Nuffelen, *Orosius*, 194–7.

[30] Augustine's friend Alypius asked Paulinus in 394 to lend the *Chronicle* for copying; Augustine first cited it in *Quaestiones in Exodum* 2.47, begun in 419 at the earliest, and mentioned the 'chronicle of Eusebius and Jerome' in *De civitate Dei* 18.31.

parallel columns, from the earliest known until his own time. Sometimes there were as many as nine columns, which required a double-page spread, but gradually they merged or disappeared until only Rome was left.[31] This was inaccurate, because Persia had made a comeback as the rival great power east of the Euphrates. But even those Romans who knew, as Augustine did, that Persian rule continued, were unlikely to know the extent of the insecure Persian empire.[32] The late Roman empire extended from Scotland to the Sudan and from Spain to Syria. There was free movement of people within it, because this was an empire of cities and their local territories, not of nation states or ethnic groups, and all freeborn inhabitants of the Roman empire were Roman citizens. The historian Orosius, himself a refugee from barbarian threats to Spain, wrote that refugees found their country and their laws wherever they went.[33] In the years when he taught rhetoric, Augustine could cross the Mediterranean from North Africa to Italy as an economic migrant in search of better students, because language, culture and system of government were the same. He knew people who, like Jerome, moved to or from the eastern Mediterranean, where Greek was the common language, but Latin was still the language of law and systems of government and education were still the same.

So empire mattered, and Augustine understood why Marcellinus wanted an effective reply to Volusianus. He responded to the request with a long letter which could be read aloud and circulated, and ended by asking Marcellinus to tell him of any further objections, so that he could offer a further reply in a letter or a treatise.[34] If that is what Marcellinus expected, it would be misleading to say that what he got was *City of God*, because he did not survive to read even the opening books: he was executed in 413, soon after Augustine started work, on a false charge of supporting rebellion. But in the preface to *City of God* Augustine addressed his 'dearest son Marcellinus', saying that he undertook this great and demanding work to defend the city of God against its enemies who prefer their own gods to its founder. This declaration shows that *City of God* is not primarily a book about

---

[31] Anthony Grafton and Megan Williams, *Christianity and the Transformation of the Book* (Cambridge MA, 2006); Alden A. Mosshammer, *The Chronicle of Eusebius and Greek Chronographic Tradition* (Lewisburg, PA, 1979).
[32] For Persian rule, see Augustine, *De civitate Dei* 4.7.
[33] Orosius, *Historiae adversus paganos* 5.2.1.
[34] Augustine, *Ep.* 138.

empire: it is a book about worshipping the true God. That is confirmed by the plan which Augustine summarized at the end of book 1; he did not then expect it to take some thirteen years to complete, delayed because there was always another deadline.[35]

According to this summary, the city of God and the earthly city are intermixed in this age, until they are pulled apart in the final judgement. Augustine's task is to explain the origin, course and due ends of these two cities, so that the glory of the city of God will shine more brightly by comparison. But first there is more to say in answer to those who blame the disasters of the Roman commonwealth on Christianity, which forbids sacrifice to their gods. Augustine will therefore set out the moral and physical evils which affected Rome before Christianity; he will show what Roman qualities were helped by the true God who enlarged their empire, whereas their gods were no help at all; and he will argue against those who say that their gods are to be worshipped, not for blessings in this life, but for benefits after death. He duly followed this plan in twenty-two books, the equivalent of chapters in a present-day academic work. The first ten books rebut the enemies of the city of God: books 1–5 argue against worshipping many gods for benefits in this life, books 6–10 against worshipping many gods for blessings after death. In these ten books Augustine says little about the city of God.[36] Then twelve books deal with the origins, course and ends of the two cities, four books for each. The opening section of *City of God*, books 1–5, includes some forceful comments about empire, which is a supposed benefit of worshipping the gods of Rome, but thereafter the Roman empire almost disappears from view until book 18, when it reappears in a rapid survey of the history of the earthly city.

Nonetheless, new readers of *City of God* could easily conclude that the Roman empire is the earthly city opposed to the Church. The preface begins with the words 'the most glorious city of God', *gloriosissimam civitatem Dei*. Augustine assumed that his readers knew what this meant, and did not define the two cities, heavenly and earthly, which he then contrasted. It was for him a familiar motif. He had used the theme of two cities, symbolized by Jerusalem and Babylon, since the first work he had written as a priest two decades

[35] For the topics to be covered, see Augustine, *De civitate Dei* 1.35–6; for urgent matters intervening, idem, *Retractationes* 2.69.
[36] Augustine, *De civitate Dei* 1.35, 5.16.

earlier; it recurs in his preaching; and he included a clear account in his advice to an anxious deacon on what to say to a catechism class:

> There Jerusalem was founded, that most renowned city of God, which serves as a sign of the free city which is called the heavenly Jerusalem; this is a Hebrew word which is translated 'vision of peace'. Its citizens are all the sanctified people who were and are and shall be, and all sanctified spirits, including those who in the highest heavens obey God with devotion. The king of this city is the Lord Jesus Christ. ... This city was taken captive, and much of it was led away to Babylon. Just as Jerusalem signifies the city and society of the holy, so Babylon signifies the city and society of the wicked, for it is said to be translated 'confusion'. We have spoken earlier of these two cities, which from the beginning of the human race to the end of the age proceed intermixed through changing times, and will be separated in the last judgement.[37]

The best-known definition of the two cities appears much later in *City of God*, in the conclusion to the four books on the origins of the two cities to which all rational beings, angels and humans, belong. Two loves made two cities: the city of God is the community of all who love God even to disregard of themselves; the earthly city is the community of all who love themselves even to disregard of God. The earthly city glories in itself and is dominated by the lust for domination; the heavenly city glories in God and its citizens serve each other, those in charge by advising and their subordinates by obeying.[38]

Commentators import Augustine's later explanation in discussing the start of book 1, but without it *City of God* seems to say at the outset that the city of God is the Church and the earthly city is the Roman empire. Resisting the proud and giving grace to the humble, he argued, belongs to God alone; but human pride wants to claim it, and delights to hear, in praise of itself, 'To spare the subject and fight down the proud': this is a very familiar quotation from Vergil's mission statement for the Roman empire.[39] So Augustine must also speak of the earthly city which has entire nations as its slaves, but is itself dominated by the lust for domination. From the earthly city

---

[37] Augustine, *De catechizandis rudibus* 31–2; for the theme in Augustine's writings, see further Gerard O'Daly, *Augustine's City of God: A Reader's Guide* (Oxford, 1999), 62–6.
[38] Augustine, *De civitate Dei* 14.28. Augustine borrowed the phrase *libido dominandi* from the historian Sallust, another author well known to Latin-speaking schoolboys: Sallust, *Catilinae coniuratio* 2.2, cited by Augustine, *De civitate Dei* 3.14.
[39] Vergil, *Aeneid* 6.853.

come the enemies of the city of God. Some will see the error of their ways and become adequate citizens. Others are full of hatred, even though they survived to attack the city of God only because they took refuge in its holy places: they sought asylum in churches and martyr-shrines which the barbarians respected.

From the contrast between the Bible and Vergil, and from the allusion to people taking refuge in churches when the barbarians sacked Rome, it seems obvious that the Church is the city of God and the Roman empire is the earthly city. But at the end of book 1 Augustine made an important addition. He called the city of God *peregrina civitas*, and both these words need consideration. *Civitas* is conventionally translated 'city', but this could be misleading. *Civitas* is the community of *cives*, citizens, who live in a city or in its territory.[40] *Peregrina* is conventionally translated 'pilgrim', but that is also misleading. Pilgrimage to a shrine or a saint or the Holy Land was a new development in Augustine's lifetime and, like many of his contemporaries, he was not in favour. In the classical Latin he was trained to write, *peregrinatio* is travelling or living away from home, by choice or as an exile, and a *peregrinus* is a traveller or a resident foreigner: that is, someone who lives in a city, has protection from its laws, but is not one of its citizens.[41] So *peregrina civitas* is a conscious paradox. It expresses the situation of Christians in this life: they are the part of the city of God which is away from its everlasting home in heaven and is a resident foreigner in the earthly city. At the end of book 1, Augustine warned this *peregrina civitas* to remember that some of its future citizens are hidden among its enemies, and that 'it has with it some of those enemies, joined in communion of the sacraments, who will not be with it in the eternal destiny of the saints' unless they change; and he repeated what he had said in earlier writings, that 'the two cities are intertwined and intermingled in this age, until they are pulled apart at the final judgement'.[42]

So there is not a simple opposition of the Church as the city of God and the empire as the earthly city. The difference between them

---

[40] See further Catherine Conybeare, 'The City of Augustine: On the Interpretation of *civitas*', in Carol Harrison, Caroline Humfress and Isabella Sandwell, eds, *Being Christian in Late Antiquity: A Festschrift for Gillian Clark* (Oxford, 2010), 139–55.
[41] Discussed further in Gillian Clark, 'Pilgrims and Foreigners: Augustine on Travelling Home', in Linda Ellis and Frank Kidner, eds, *Travel, Communication and Geography in Late Antiquity* (Aldershot, 2004), 149–58.
[42] Augustine, *De civitate Dei* 1.35.

is in what they want, and what the cities want is what their individual citizens want. Just as Rome is the Romans, so the city of God and the earthly city are their citizens. Someone who is formally a member of the Church, as a baptized Christian or even as a member of the clergy, may be a citizen of the earthly city, because he wants to dominate and possess and be praised. An imperial official may be a citizen of the city of God, because he wants God to be praised, and wants to serve and protect the people over whom he has the authority which Romans traditionally called *imperium*. This is not the same as the domination sought by the earthly city. *Imperium* is conventionally translated 'empire', but its basic meaning is the acknowledged right *imperare*, to give orders. Specifically, *imperium* was the power conferred on a military or civil commander who had responsibility for imposing and maintaining peace, and who could therefore give orders to kill. *Imperium* came to mean also the territory in which that right was acknowledged, so that *imperium Romanum* means the Roman empire.

Augustine's account of humanity shows why there must be *imperium* in the sense of 'acknowledged right to give orders'. In *City of God*, the definition of the two cities comes at the end of the four books on their origins, in which Augustine interpreted the creation narrative in Genesis as showing how some angels, and the first humans, turned from God to themselves, thus forming the earthly or impious city. He could give no explanation for this turn, because it did not make sense.[43] But its consequence is that all humans inherit from their common ancestor the tendency to want their own way, not God's. Everyone wants to be the master, *dominus*, and that means permanent conflict at all levels of society, household and city and world, unless there is agreement on giving and obeying orders: *imperandi oboediendique*. This agreement is needed also in the *peregrina civitas*, the part of the city of God which in this mortal life is a resident foreigner in the earthly city.[44] God created humans as naturally social beings who are also linked by common ancestry; Eve was made from Adam, not created together with Adam, so that all would have the same ancestor.[45] Humans were meant to cooperate in natural

[43] Discussed further in Gillian Clark, 'Deficient Causes: Augustine on Creation and Angels', in Anna Marmodoro and Brian Prince, eds, *Causation and Creation in Late Antiquity* (Cambridge, 2015), 220–36.
[44] Augustine, *De civitate Dei* 19.17.
[45] Ibid. 12.22; 19.5.

hierarchy, the stronger in reason guiding the weaker, who would willingly follow their guidance. This manifestly does not happen.

Augustine set out the need for *imperium* in book 19, the first of his last four books on the 'ends' of the two cities. 'Ends' (*fines*) has a double sense: what will happen to them and what is the final good for which they pursue all other goods. Book 19 is now the most widely read book of *City of God*, and is often used in debates on political theory. Are there ways of ordering society so as to maximize human flourishing and to minimize crime and conflict, or does human nature make this an unrealistic aim, so that the most any government can do is to 'impose the custom of peace', as in Vergil's mission statement for Rome?[46] Augustine was not interested in political theory, but in the response of individual human beings to God's love. His views on the use of force are set out in letters to imperial officials, the individuals who had responsibility for law enforcement in specific cases.[47] Latin does not have a word for 'the state' as distinct from the people. The *res publica* was managed by officials appointed by the emperor; they implemented imperial policy if they knew what it was, but information took time to circulate and requests for guidance could not have an immediate response, so officials often had to make their own decisions. Augustine understood the difficulty in individual cases of establishing the truth as a judge, and of giving orders as a judge or a military commander which would cause the taking of human life.[48] He is often credited with establishing the principles of just war, but in fact he accepted the standard Roman view expressed by Cicero: wars of aggression are unjust, but (as Volusianus said) Roman officers have a duty to defend the people and their allies against aggression. When he wrote to officials, Augustine urged them to act not from anger but from the wish to protect, and to show mercy wherever possible.[49]

---

[46] On 'Augustinian realism', see Eugene TeSelle, *Living in Two Cities: Augustinian Trajectories in Political Thought* (Scranton, PA, 1998).

[47] E. M. Atkins and R. J. Dodaro, eds, *Augustine: Political Writings*, Cambridge Texts in the History of Political Thought (Cambridge, 2001), xvii–xxv. Shaw, *Sacred Violence*, 496–505, discusses transient local governors, whose term of office usually ran from April to April, and who were unlikely to know much about Africa.

[48] Augustine, *De civitate Dei* 19.6. For Augustine's own experience, see Neil McLynn, 'Administrator: Augustine in his Diocese', in Vessey, ed., *Companion to Augustine*, 310–22.

[49] Robert Markus, 'Saint Augustine's Views on the "Just War"', in W. J. Sheils, ed., *The Church and War*, SCH 20 (Oxford, 1983), 1–13.

In the great tradition of Roman self-criticism, a speaker in Cicero's philosophical dialogue *De re publica*, 'On the Commonwealth', observed that by defending their allies the Romans have conquered the world.[50] Augustine read, or re-read, this dialogue in the years when he began work on *City of God*.[51] Much of it is now lost, and Augustine is an important source of fragments, but he is not a source for Cicero on forms of government: monarchy, aristocracy, democracy, the mixed constitution. This lack of interest in political theory is not peculiar to Augustine. In his time there was no live debate on forms of government because there was in practice no alternative to monarchy. Regime change meant only the substitution of one ruler for another. For Augustine, *regnum*, 'kingship', was not an accusation of tyranny, as it was for Cicero; he knew why the old Romans rejected *regnum*, but he used the word without comment as a synonym for 'empire'.[52] Someone (not necessarily one person) has to rule, and everyone benefits when good people rule as far and wide as possible. But Augustine asked: 'In relation to this mortal life, which is led and finished in a few days, what does it matter under whose orders a man lives, who is so soon to die, provided those who give the orders do not compel people to unjust or impious acts?'[53]

Augustine knew that a comment he had made in one context could be read differently in relation to a later debate; his *Retractationes*, the annotated list of his writings which he compiled late in his life, included some corrections of possible misunderstandings. This particular question, taken out of context, could be used to argue for passive obedience: all rulers, good or bad, have power by God's will or permission, so a Christian should not try to change the system but should obey the ruler, taking bad rule as moral training or as deserved punishment; if obedience conflicts with moral and religious duty, the Christian should embrace martyrdom. In context, Augustine's question is an argument against imperialism. What, in practice, does it matter who conquers and who is conquered? In the Roman empire, Augustine pointed out, taxes, laws and education are the

---

[50] Cicero, *De re publica* 3.35, cited by the grammarian Nonius Marcellus, *De compendiosa doctrina* 3.800.
[51] Margaret Atkins, 'Old Philosophy and New Power: Cicero in Fifth-Century North Africa', in Gillian Clark and Tessa Rajak, eds, *Philosophy and Power in the Graeco-Roman World* (Oxford, 2002), 251–69.
[52] Augustine, *De civitate Dei* 5.12.
[53] Ibid. 5.17.

same for the Romans and for the peoples they conquered, and there are Roman senators who have never seen Rome.[54] For readers in our post-colonial times, it is worth remembering that though Rome first acquired territory in Africa by victory over Carthage in the mid-second century BCE, Roman Africa in the early centuries CE was not controlled and exploited by a colonial power. There were great estates whose owners lived elsewhere, but Africa was a prosperous part of the empire, exporting grain and olive oil, and from it came teachers of rhetoric, advocates, civil servants and even emperors.

In Roman tradition, there was an obvious answer to the question 'what does it matter who conquers and who is conquered?' Victory brings glory; Augustine lived in the Roman, not the Carthaginian, empire. He observed that the old Romans were eager for their country's glory, thinking it glorious to dominate and rule but inglorious to serve, and that the desire for glory kept other desires in check.[55] But was the glory worth it? Augustine did not argue that the Roman empire brought the blessings of civilization, for Egypt and the Near East and Greece were much older civilizations, and had also been part of Rome's empire for many centuries. He did recognize some advantages of empire. The *imperiosa civitas*, the city that gives orders, imposed a common language, so that there is an abundance of interpreters. Human beings, Augustine thought, cannot get on if they cannot talk to each other, to the point that a man would rather be with his own dog than with another human whose language he does not speak.[56] Augustine especially recognized the value of peace, maintained by the threat, and if necessary the use, of force. In Cicero's dialogue *De re publica*, he observed, one speaker argues the case that injustice is necessary for government: it is unjust for some people to serve others, but Rome could not otherwise rule its provinces. Another speaker counters that it is just, because for 'such people' slavery is beneficial: unprincipled people lose their freedom to do wrong, so they are better off when subjected.[57] Augustine could see in his work as a bishop the benefits of limiting the freedom of the wicked, and one of the most poignant examples concerns unlawful servitude. He explained it, a year or so after he wrote book 19, in a letter to his

[54] Ibid.
[55] Ibid. 5.12.
[56] Ibid. 19.7.
[57] Ibid. 21.

long-standing friend and fellow bishop Alypius, a former legal adviser who went on several diplomatic missions to the imperial court.[58]

Slave traders operating in Africa were shipping overseas people they had bought as slaves. Almost all of these people were freeborn Romans, but once separated from their families and communities, it was much more difficult for them to be reclaimed. Only a few had been sold by their parents, and even then they were bought and marketed as slaves, whereas Roman law allowed only the sale of twenty-five years of labour. The traders hardly ever bought genuine slaves from their owners, and because there was a market, raiders in rural areas were kidnapping and selling free people. The emperor Honorius had addressed to the prefect Hadrianus a law which could be invoked to free the victims, but it condemned the traders to flogging with lead-weighted ropes, which was likely to kill them.[59] Augustine wanted Alypius to lobby for the law to be reissued, but with a reduced punishment. The proper authorities must decide how to apply the law:

> Many people are ransomed from barbarians, but those who are transported to overseas provinces have no access to ransom. Barbarians are resisted when Roman soldiers are successfully deployed to rescue Romans held captive by barbarians. But who resists these traders not in animals but in people, not in barbarians but in Roman provincials? They have spread everywhere, so that for the price they offer people are brought to them everywhere and from everywhere, seized by force or trapped by deception. Who resists them in the name of Roman freedom, not common but individual freedom?[60]

Members of Augustine's congregation at Hippo had rescued a hundred and twenty people who were about to be shipped abroad, but the traders sought to repossess them, and had powerful patrons who were already causing trouble. It was Roman rule, administered by Roman officials according to Roman law, which would safeguard the freedom of Roman citizens.

---

[58] Augustine, *Ep.* 10*, probably written in 428. I thank the peer reviewer who suggested this example.
[59] Hadrianus was prefect of Italy and Africa in 401–5 and again in 413–14: A. H. M. Jones, J. R. Martindale and J. Morris, eds, *The Prosopography of the Later Roman Empire*, 3 vols (Cambridge, 1971–92), 1: 406 (Hadrianus 2).
[60] Augustine, *Ep.* 10*.6.

Augustine acknowledged that imperfect human peace is very different from heavenly peace, but recognized that everyone benefits from it, and 'the *civitas peregrina*, the heavenly city while it lives away from home, makes use of the various instruments for human peace'.[61] Human peace and common language are valuable achievements – but at what a cost in blood![62] Because of the human drive to dominate, there has to be *imperium* in the sense of 'acknowledged right to give orders'. But there does not have to be *imperium* in the sense of 'extensive territory in which the right to give orders is acknowledged'. Empire in this sense manifests the domination and possessiveness which characterize the earthly city. At the start of his rapid survey of its history, in book 18, Augustine explained that human society has the double bond of common human nature and common ancestry, but conflict arises as people pursue their own interests; the stronger oppress the weaker, and empires result because the weaker prefer subjection to death.[63] In the opening books of *City of God* he showed how empires begin with injustice and expand by war. Augustine cited a summary of 'foreign' history (that is, history other than Greek and Roman) for the claim that at first, kingdoms were small and peaceful, their frontiers were protected but not extended, and kings ruled because their people acknowledged their wisdom.[64] The first empire, the Assyrian, began when King Ninus made the first war of aggression against inoffensive neighbours. That empire extended far and wide, like the Roman empire, and lasted longer than the Roman empire had yet lasted in Augustine's time.[65] Augustine thought that Babylon, the symbol of the earthly city, was the capital of Assyria, and he characterized Rome as a second, Western, Babylon, in the extent and duration of its empire.[66] He exploited Roman authorities to show that Rome was founded in fratricide and in wars with kindred peoples, and that it always manifested injustice and conflict. Rome's empire expanded in reaction to foreign injustice; perhaps, Augustine suggested, the Romans who deified so many abstracts, such as Victory

[61] Augustine, *De civitate Dei* 19.26.
[62] Ibid. 7.
[63] Ibid. 18.2.
[64] Ibid. 4.6.
[65] Ibid.
[66] Ibid. 16.17, 18.2.

and Fortune, should also deify Foreign Iniquity and worship her as the goddess who gave them empire.[67]

Empires depend on war and on someone's injustice. Volusianus argued that Christian ethics were not compatible with Roman traditions of government, because unjust demands must be resisted, in person or by right of war when a Roman province is raided. Augustine found a more fundamental challenge to Roman traditions in Cicero's dialogue *De re publica*. The character Philus, reluctantly but forcefully arguing the case for injustice, says that 'He extended the frontiers of empire' is engraved on the monuments of Rome's greatest commanders, but how could that be done without taking something from someone else?[68] Philus concludes that nations, like individuals, prefer to rule unjustly than to be enslaved justly, and to take things from other people rather than have things taken from them.[69] Augustine, as always, insisted on thinking of empire in terms of individuals, not of nations:

> What is the reason, where is the sense, in wanting to be famous for the extent and greatness of empire? You cannot demonstrate the happiness of people who live always among the disasters of war, in blood which is human whether shed by fellow citizens or by enemies, in fearful darkness and bloodstained cruelty. Their happiness is like the fragile brilliance of glass, which prompts greater fear that it will suddenly shatter. To judge this more readily, let us not be carried away by empty pomposity, or blunt the edge of our attention with lofty-sounding names for things, when we hear 'peoples, kingdoms, provinces'. Let us posit two people, for the individual is the basic unit of city and kingdom, however extensive its occupation of land.[70]

One of the two people is rich and famous, with great estates, but constantly stressed and suspicious; the other is moderately prosperous but has enough for his needs, and is beloved by his family, on excellent terms with his kin and neighbours and friends, dutiful, kind, healthy, frugal, decent and with a quiet conscience. Augustine asked his readers which they would choose to be. Moving up the scale from individual to group, he challenged them to find a difference

---

[67] For fratricide, see ibid. 3.6; wars for territory, ibid. 3.10; wars with kindred peoples, ibid. 3.14; foreign injustice, ibid. 4.15.
[68] Cicero, *De re publica* 3.24.
[69] Ibid. 3.26–7.
[70] Augustine, *De civitate Dei* 4.3.

between empire and highway robbery: 'Take away justice, and what are kingdoms but large-scale gangs (*magna latrocinia*)? For what are gangs but small kingdoms? This too is a band of people, ruled by the orders of a leader, held together by a bond of society, its loot shared out by agreed law.'[71] The gang has a social contract, but that is not enough for justice. Augustine borrowed from Cicero the pirate's answer to Alexander the Great, who had asked what he thought he was doing infesting the sea: 'The same as you do infesting the world, but because I do it in a little boat I am called *latro*, and because you do it with a big fleet you are called *imperator*.'[72] *Latrones* are not ordinary thieves, but outlaws, armed robbers who operate as part of a group. Those in authority may impose the name on people who consider themselves to be freedom fighters, but even so, *latrones* use force to take what they want. On the first ever war of aggression, Augustine commented: 'to wage war on neighbours, and advance from there to more wars, to crush and subject, from sheer desire for rule, peoples who offered no provocation – what is this but *latrocinium* on a grand scale?'[73]

Empires depend on war and injustice, but victory in war and advancement of empire gave glory, and the desire for glory had its uses. Vergil presented Rome's empire as the reward of piety and virtue, and as he moved towards the end of his first five books, Augustine acknowledged the moral qualities for which the true God saw fit to enlarge it:

> When the kingdoms of the East had long been famous, God decided that there should also be a Western kingdom, later in time but more famous in extent and greatness of empire; and to repress the grievous suffering of many peoples, he granted it especially to men who, for the sake of honour, praise and glory, were concerned for the homeland in which they sought glory, and did not hesitate to put its security before their own, holding in check, for this one vice, namely the love of praise, desire for money and many other vices.[74]

Such people, Augustine said, can be a moral example to Christians, but they were motivated not by love of God and neighbour, but by

---

[71] Ibid. 4.4.
[72] Ibid.
[73] Ibid. 4.6
[74] Ibid. 5.13.

concern for their own reputation. So they were citizens of the earthly city, and as Jesus said of people who give alms conspicuously, they have their reward already: they are remembered and praised:

> They disregarded their private property for the sake of common property, that is, for the commonwealth and its treasury; they resisted avarice; they gave impartial advice to their fatherland; they were not guilty of crimes as defined by their laws, or of lust. By all these arts they strove, on the apparently true way, for honours and *imperium* and glory. They were honoured by almost all peoples; they imposed the laws of their *imperium* on many peoples; today they are glorious in literature and history among almost all peoples. They have no grounds for complaint against the justice of the supreme and true God: they have their reward.[75]

Augustine concluded: 'I absolutely do not see what difference it makes to security and morality, which give people authentic dignity, that some conquered and some were conquered ... Take away boasting, and what are people but people?'[76] Victory, glory, rule without limits of space and time, all the lofty claims of empire are dismissed.

City of God is not primarily a book about empire: it is a book about worshipping the true God. Augustine's opponents claimed that empire was owed to the gods of Rome; he was certain that empire, like everything else, happens by the will or permission of God, who for his own inscrutable reasons gives power to good and to bad rulers.[77] Can God's purpose for the Roman empire be discerned in divinely inspired Scripture? According to the *Chronological Tables* of Eusebius there were 2,242 years of biblical history, from Adam to Abraham, before any other Greek or non-Greek history was known; so when Augustine discussed the course of the two cities in books 15–18 of *City of God*, the Bible was for this period his source not only for the history of the people of God, but also for the history of the earthly city which began with Cain. At the start of book 18 Augustine acknowledged that from the time of Abraham he had continued to discuss the history of the people of God, and must therefore expound the history of the earthly city, at least as much as seemed sufficient for comparison.[78] From the *Chronological Tables* he could

---

[75] Ibid. 5.15; see Matt. 6: 2.
[76] Ibid. 5.17.
[77] Ibid. 4.33, 5.21.
[78] Ibid. 18.1.

see that at the start of the Assyrian empire, Abraham was promised that all nations descended from him should be blessed; and that at the start of 'the Western Babylon' in whose rule Christ was to come and fulfil those promises, there appeared prophets whose message was not just for the people of Israel, but for the future benefit of the Gentiles.[79] These were the Old Testament prophets who were interpreted as foretelling Christ.

Augustine said, in very Roman language, that 'Rome was founded as a kind of second Babylon, like a daughter of the first Babylon, through which it pleased God to subject the world and pacify it far and wide in one society of commonwealth and laws.'[80] He commented that subjecting the world was a harder task for Rome than it had been for Assyria, because Rome was surrounded by well-trained warlike peoples. But he said nothing else on what it meant to be a second Babylon. He did not argue that Rome was an oppressive empire like Babylon, as some of his Donatist opponents maintained; or that Rome would inevitably fall as Babylon had fallen; or that Rome was transformed by the birth of Christ and by the achievement of peace under Rome's first emperor.[81] In Augustine's brief narrative, civil wars bring Augustus to power, Christ is born while Augustus has *imperium*, then Augustus fights more wars.[82] The successors of Augustus continued to fight wars. In 412, just before Augustine started work on *City of God*, he preached on Psalm 46, which includes the prophecy about God 'making wars cease even to the ends of the earth'. This, he said, we do not yet see fulfilled.[83] In *City of God* he had very little to say about Rome and its emperors after the coming of Christ, except when, in the conclusion of the first five books, he gave a few examples to illustrate his general argument about imperial power. *Felix*, 'fortunate', was one of the conventional titles of a Roman emperor. Christian emperors, Augustine said, are called fortunate not because they are victorious or because their long

[79] Ibid. 18.27.
[80] '[C]ondita est civitas Romana velut altera Babylon et velut prioris filia Babylonis per quam Deo placuit orbem debellare terrarum et in unam societatem rei publicae legumque perductum longe lateque pacare': ibid. 18.22.
[81] Discussed further in Gillian Clark, 'Fragile Brilliance: Augustine, Decadence, and "Other Antiquity"', in Marco Formisano and Therese Fuhrer, eds, *Décadence: 'Decline and Fall' or 'Other Antiquity'?* (Heidelberg, 2014), 35–52.
[82] Augustine, *De civitate Dei* 3.30; contrast Orosius, *historiae adversus paganos* 6.20.
[83] Psa. 46: 9, Augustine, *Enarrationes in Psalmos* 71.10–11; see also Markus, *Saeculum*, 52.

and tranquil reign ends in peaceful succession, but because they rule with justice and mercy, making their own power subject to God. If Christian emperors were always successful, we might conclude that God is to be worshipped for benefits in this life. But God allocates imperial power to good and to bad; for emperors as for everyone else, what matters is the relationship of the individual to God.[84]

For Augustine, the Roman empire was the current manifestation of the earthly city which is symbolized by Babylon. But *imperium* is necessary, and power is not in itself either bad or good; the question is whether the holder of earthly power worships the true God, rather than loving inferior earthly power.[85] It is possible to serve, or to be, a ruler of Babylon and still to be a citizen of the city of God. Augustine argued that Rome had never been a *res publica* according to Cicero's definition, that is, a community united by agreement on *ius* (which covers both positive law and a sense of justice) and by common interest, because from the outset there was injustice and conflict, and because there can be no true *res publica* where the true God is not worshipped. Justice requires that everyone should have his due, and it cannot be just, either to people or to God, to remove people from God's service. But Augustine did not suggest that there could be a true Christian commonwealth, united in agreement on *ius* and common interest, in an empire or in a church where the true God is worshipped, and where there is justice because all receive their due. Only the city of God, the community of angels and humans who love God, could be called such a true *res publica*.[86] The city of God is also the true Church. But the Church in this world is made up of people, just as Rome is the Romans, and only some of them are citizens of the city of God.

As Augustine's reputation grew, to make him the most influential theologian of Western European Christianity, many people sought to co-opt him in support of their own ideas, including their ideas about a Christian commonwealth.[87] He was often quoted selectively and out of context, sometimes by readers who had read only excerpts, or

---

[84] Augustine, *De civitate Dei* 5.24–6.
[85] Ibid. 12.8, 5.26.
[86] Ibid. 2.21.
[87] Matthew Kempshall, '*De re publica* in Medieval and Renaissance Thought', in John North and Jonathan Powell, eds, *Cicero's Republic* (London, 2001), 99–135, discusses medieval and early modern attempts to argue for a church-guided state.

who did not have full texts.[88] Those who argued that the temporal power of empire should be guided or judged or validated by the spiritual power of the Church did not take into account Augustine's belief that in this world the two cities are mixed: temporal rulers and their servants may be citizens of the city of God, office-holders in the Church may be citizens of the earthly city. His own advice in *City of God* remains a protection: do not be misled by big words, by abstracts and entities such as Church and empire, but think about the people. What matters, always, is individual citizenship in one of the two cities, and that depends on the response of an individual human being to the love of God.

---

[88] Bonnie Kent, 'Reinventing Augustine's Ethics: The Afterlife of *City of God*', in James Wetzel, ed., *Augustine's City of God: A Critical Guide* (Cambridge, 2012), 225–44.

The Popes as Rulers of Rome in the Aftermath of Empire, 476–769

Rosamond McKitterick*

Sidney Sussex College, University of Cambridge

This article explores the degree to which the rule and style of the bishops of Rome after the deposition of the last Roman emperor in the West in 476 had any imperial elements, in the light of the evidence contained within the Liber pontificalis. *Papal rule in Rome was cast as a replacement of imperial rule in religious matters, an opportunity for the bishop to assume political responsibility and also a deliberate emulation of imperial behaviour. This is manifest above all in the textual record in the* Liber pontificalis *of the papal embellishment of Rome, and in the physical evidence of the extant basilicas of the city. The deliberately imperial elements of papal self-presentation and the importance of Rome's primacy, apostolic succession and orthodoxy, all articulated so emphatically within the* Liber pontificalis, *indicate the multitude of strands by which the papacy wove the fabric of its own* imperium *or power.*

The bishop of Rome in the year 476 was Simplicius. When in that same year the military leader Odoacer deposed Romulus Augustulus, the sixteen-year-old puppet emperor of the West who had reigned for a mere ten months, Simplicius had already been bishop for eight years; he held the see for a further seven years thereafter. Simplicius's biography in the text known as the *Liber pontificalis*, first compiled in the 530s, records that it was he who dedicated the church of San Stefano Rotondo on the Caelian hill, as well as some other churches, and that he instituted the 'weekly turns' (i.e. regular liturgical observance) at the basilicas of Saint Peter, San Paolo fuori le Mura and San Lorenzo fuori le mura. On receiving a report from Acacius, bishop of Constantinople, that Peter, bishop of Alexandria, was a 'Eutychian heretic', and given that the church of Rome was the 'first apostolic see', Simplicius condemned Peter, 'awaiting the time of his repentance'. In addition to gifts of gold and silver to Roman churches,

* Sidney Sussex College, Cambridge, CB2 3HU. E-mail: rdm21@cam.ac.uk

Studies in Church History 54 (2018) 71–95   © Ecclesiastical History Society 2018
doi: 10.1017/stc.2017.5

Simplicius also ordained fifty-eight priests and eleven deacons and consecrated eighty-eight bishops; he was buried in St Peter's.[1]

There is not a whisper in this Life concerning imperial politics in Italy, not even in the form of a dating clause, still less of the event in 476 regarded as so momentous as to be dubbed subsequently, however misleadingly, as the 'Fall of Rome'. Simplicius's successor Felix III, moreover, who held the see between 483 and 492, is simply described, in a matter of fact statement, as 'bishop in the time of King Odoacer until the time of king Theodoric'.[2] This is the only allusion to Odoacer's period of rule, Theodoric the Ostrogoth's ruthless takeover as ruler of Italy and recognition by the Eastern emperor Zeno, and Odoacer's assassination at a 'reconciliation banquet' held by Theodoric in Ravenna in 493.[3]

Such a lack of comment on the part of the narrator(s) of Pope Simplicius's life might be regarded as similar to the lack of immediate recognition among contemporaries of the significance of Christopher Columbus's first voyage and his discovery of the New World. In manuscript additions made in Deventer for the years from 1482 to 1513, for example, at the end of a composite volume from the Florencehuis comprising the 1483 edition of Eusebius-Jerome's Chronicle and the 1513 edition of the Chronicle of Sigebert of Gembloux (Athenaeum Bibliotheek 111.E.13), 1492 is recorded as the year the Jews were expelled from Spain. Even though Columbus's letter of 1493 about his achievement was printed and reprinted widely throughout Europe, it was many years before the full significance of his discovery began to be extrapolated.[4]

---

[1] 'Eodem tempore fuit ecclesia, hoc est prima sedis apostolica, executrix'; 'expectans tempus paenitentiae': *Liber pontificalis*, ed. Louis Duchesne, *Le* Liber pontificalis. *Texte, introduction et commentaire*, 2 vols (Paris, 1886, 1892), 1: 249 [hereafter: *LP*]. For convenience I also provide page references to the easily accessible and excellent translation by Raymond Davis, *The Book of Pontiffs (*Liber pontificalis*): The Ancient Biographies of the First Ninety Roman Bishops to AD 715*, TTH 6, 3rd edn (Liverpool, 2010), 40.

[2] '[H]ic fuit temporibus Odoacris regis usque ad tempora Theodorici regis': *LP* 1: 252 (Davis, *Pontiffs*, 40).

[3] Numerous modern narrative accounts and studies of these events exist, from the classic Thomas Hodgkin, *Italy and her Invaders*, 3: *The Ostrogothic Invasion* (London, 1896), to the essays in *Teodorico il Grande e i Goti d'Italia*, Atti del XIII Congresso internazionale di Studio sull'Alto Medioevo, Milan, 2–6 novembre 1992 (Spoleto, 1993). Still a useful account is Peter Llewellyn, *Rome in the Dark Ages*, 2nd edn (London, 1993); and a stimulating interpretation is offered by Patrick Amory, *People and Identity in Ostrogothic Italy, 489–554* (Cambridge, 1997). Odoacer's period of rule remains relatively neglected.

[4] See the summary of the many editions and translations in Thomas R. Adams, 'Review: A. Payne (ed.), *The Spanish Letter of Columbus. A Facsimile of the Original Edition*

Nevertheless, the lack of reaction by the authors of the *Liber pontificalis* to the events in Ravenna in 476 acts as a warning not to assume that the Byzantine historians' representation in the sixth century of the 'fall of Rome',[5] still less what subsequent ideologues and imperial and papal apologists made of the relationship between Church and empire, whether in the West or in the East, are the only ways to understand the transformations of the fifth, sixth and seventh centuries. Contemporaries, whether of the 'deposition of the last Roman emperor in the West' or of the 'discovery of the New World by Christopher Columbus' apparently did not attach the same significance to these events as more recent commentators have done. Even acknowledging this, however, the *Liber pontificalis* author deliberately constructed the history of the early popes with a very specific agenda and audience in mind, as will become clear in what follows. The interpretations of the significance of the conquest of the Lombard kingdom and coronation of Charlemagne as 'emperor of the Romans', or the issues raised by the Investiture Controversy concerning the right of rulers to confer the symbols of office on bishops or abbots, are yet further extrapolations, too often understood in the terms set by nineteenth- and twentieth- (even twenty-first-) century historians rather than those of contemporaries.[6] The silence about Odoacer's deposition of Romulus in the *Liber pontificalis*, therefore, is a prompt to look further at the relationship between the bishop of Rome and the Roman emperors, whether of the West or in the Eastern portion that became known in due course as the Byzantine empire. Further, the degree to which the rule, or even the style, of the bishops in Rome had any imperial elements should

---

published by Bernard Quaritch in 1891 (London, 2006)', *Book Collector*, Autumn 2007, 441–3.

[5] Brian Croke, 'A.D. 476: The Manufacture of a Turning Point', *Chiron* 13 (1983), 81–119.

[6] From a vast literature, the following provides both a useful synthesis and a new appraisal: Mayke de Jong, 'The Empire that was always Decaying: The Carolingians (800–888)', *Medieval Worlds* 2 (2015), 6–25 [online journal], at: <https://doi.org/10.1553/medievalworlds_no2_2015s6>, last accessed 20 January 2017; see also Laury Sarti, 'Frankish Romanness and Charlemagne's Empire', *Speculum* 91 (2016), 1040–58. The classic account remains Peter Classen, *Karl der Großen, das Papsttum und Byzanz. Die Begründung des karolingischer Kaisertums*, ed. Horst Fuhrmann and Claudia Märtl (Sigmaringen, 1985). For new perspectives on the Central Middle Ages, see John Eldevik, *Episcopal Power and Ecclesiastical Reform in the German Empire: Tithes, Lordship and Community, 950–1150* (Cambridge, 2012); John S. Ott, *Bishops, Authority and Community in North-West Europe, c.1050–1150* (Cambridge, 2015).

be explored.[7]   Above all, we need to look at the aftermath of 476 from the perspective of the bishops of Rome. What will emerge is an enriched and rather different understanding of the complex early history of the papacy, which has tended to offer too simplistic an emphasis on apostolic primacy and the cult of St Peter.

Let me start, therefore, with the *Liber pontificalis* itself. The title is an eighteenth-century one; early medieval manuscripts, such as Paris, BnF lat. 13729, from the early ninth century, refer to it as *Liber episcopalis* or *acta* or *gesta pontificum urbis Romae*.[8]   The narrative is improbably credited to Pope Damasus, writing at the prompting of Jerome, in two prefaces at the beginning of the text and present in all the earliest complete manuscripts, though none of these is earlier than the late eighth century.[9]

The distinctive narrative structure of the *Liber pontificalis* takes the form of serial biographies from St Peter in the first century to Pope Stephen V at the end of the ninth century, 112 Lives in all, numbered in sequence in most of the earliest manuscripts. The biographies were written piecemeal, the first stage of which is usually dated *c.*535 (the exact date is disputed) and contains the biographies of the fifty-nine or sixty popes from Peter to either Agapitus or Silverius.[10]   Although the sixth-century portion drew on contemporary knowledge, the biographies covering the centuries before that appear to have been based on earlier and ever scrappier information,

[7] I am, of course, not the first to explore this aspect: see in particular Mark Humphries, 'From Emperor to Pope? Ceremonial, Space, and Authority at Rome from Constantine to Gregory the Great', in Kate Cooper and Julia Hillner, eds, *Religion, Dynasty and Patronage in Early Christian Rome, 300–900* (Cambridge, 2007), 21–58; idem, 'Valentinian III and the City of Rome (425–455): Patronage, Politics, Power', in Lucy Grig and Gavin Kelly, eds, *Two Romes: Rome and Constantinople in Late Antiquity* (Cambridge, 2012), 161–82.
[8] Giovanni Vignoli, *Liber pontificalis seu De Gestis romanorum pontificum quem cum cod. MSS Vaticanis aliisque sumo studio et labore conlatum emendavit*, 3 vols (Rome 1724–55); cf. the rival edition by Francesco Bianchini, repr. in PL 127, 128.
[9] Emmanuel Schelstrate, *Antiquitas ecclesiae dissertationibus monumentis ac notis*, 2 vols (Rome, 1692), 1: 369–75, was apparently the first to refute this. The attribution of the text to Anastasius Bibliothecarius in the later ninth century has taken rather longer to be discarded: but see Klaus Herbers, 'Agir et écrire. Les Actes des papes du IXe siècle et le *Liber pontificalis*', and François Bougard, 'Composition, diffusion et réception des parties tardives du *Liber pontificalis* romain (VIIIe–IXe siècles)', in François Bougard and Michel Sot, eds, *Liber, gesta, histoire. Écrire l'histoire des évêques et des papes de l'antiquité au XXe siècle* (Turnhout, 2009), 109–24, 127–52. See also the comments on the eighteenth-century editions in Carmen Vircillo Franklin, 'Reading the Popes: The *Liber Pontificalis* and its Editors', *Speculum* 92 (2017), 607–29.
[10] Herman Geertman, 'La Genesi del *Liber pontificalis* romano. Un Processo di organizzazione della Memoria', in Bougard and Sot, eds, *Liber, gesta, histoire*, 37–107.

such as martyr *acta*, the papal letter and estate registers, the Liberian catalogue with consular dates framing the list of the popes included in the Calendar of 354,[11] extant inscriptions and the like,[12] mostly dating from the third and fourth centuries onwards. Subsequent sections of the *Liber pontificalis* were added in the seventh century (Lives 60–71) and thereafter on a mostly Life-by-Life basis to the end of the ninth century (Lives 72–112). This can be schematized in a way that reflects the indications of the phases of manuscript transmission, as follows:

LP I (1st redaction – surmised from the existence of early Epitomes F and K),[13] *c.*530: Lives 1–56, Peter to Felix IV (d. 530)

LP I (2nd redaction), *c.*535: Lives 1–59/60, Peter to Agapitus (d. 536) / Silverius (d. 537)

LP IIA: Lives 60–71, Silverius to Boniface V (d. 625)

LP IIB: Lives 72–8, Honorius to Eugene I (d. 657)

LP IIC: Lives 79–81, 82–90, Adeodatus to Agatho, Leo II to Constantine I (d. 715)

LP III: Eighth-century Lives 91 (2 versions), 92, 93, 94 (three versions), 95, 96, 97.1–44, 97.45 to end, Gregory II to Hadrian I (d. 795)

LP IV: Ninth-century Lives 98–112, Leo III, Eugenius to Stephen V (d. 891)[14]

The dating of the first section of the *Liber pontificalis* is hugely significant, for the text was produced in the course of the Ostrogothic wars, when the Emperor Justinian deployed armies, led by his generals, first Belisarius and then Narses, in an attempt to reverse two centuries of political development and 'reconquer' Italy, by then

---

[11] *LP* 1: 1–12; see also Michele Renée Salzman, *On Roman Time: The Codex Calendar of 354 and the Rhythms of Urban Life in Late Antiquity* (Berkeley, CA, 1990).

[12] See the useful summary in Davis, *Pontiffs*, xx–xxxiv.

[13] On Epitomes F and K, see *LP* 1: xlvix–lvii, but this element of the *Liber pontificalis*'s redaction is open to challenge: see Geertman, 'La genesi del *Liber pontificalis* romano'; Andrea Antonio Verardi, 'La genesi del *Liber Pontificalis* alla luce delle vicende della città di Roma tra la fine del V e gli inizi del VI secolo. Una proposta', *Rivista di storia del cristianesimo* 10 (2013), 7–28; Rosamond McKitterick, 'Perceptions of Rome and the Papacy in Late Merovingian Francia: The Cononian recension', in Stefan Esders et al., eds, *East and West in the Early Middle Ages: The Merovingian Kingdoms in Mediterranean Perspective* (Cambridge, forthcoming).

[14] Reproduced from Rosamond McKitterick, 'The Papacy and Byzantium in the Seventh- and Early Eighth-Century Sections of the *Liber pontificalis*', *Papers of the British School at Rome* 84 (2016), 241–73, at 248.

ruled by the Ostrogothic kings, and bring it under the direct rule of the emperor based in Constantinople. The decision to compile the biographies of the first fifty-nine (or sixty) bishops of Rome from Peter to Agapitus (or Silverius), moreover, was apparently taken by officials within the papal administration. The author or authors had access to the papal registers and the documents relating to church estates and property in the *vestiarium* as well as the other chronological lists and historical narratives mentioned earlier. The context is the moment when Italy was not only suffering the consequences of the advances of the armies of Justinian led by Belisarius, but the Christians of Rome had also recently experienced the schism with Byzantium known as the Acacian schism, as well as the tensions usually assumed between Catholic and Arian in Italy itself as a consequence of Ostrogothic rule.[15] The text was precipitated by more than local schism or Roman propaganda wars, although, as I have argued elsewhere, it can indeed be considered as contributing to a wider argument in the first few decades of the sixth century, conducted in the form of historical texts, in which the perception of the imperial past was transformed by the popes themselves.[16] Both the text's format and its content, therefore, need to be read in the light of the political crisis of the 530s. The *Liber pontificalis* is potentially a key piece of evidence for the consolidation of the ideological position adopted by the papacy in the new political configuration of the former Western Roman empire. This involved far more than Rome's primacy and the pope's role as St Peter's successor, crucial elements though these were. Rather than a reiteration of the various statements in papal letters and decretals more usually brought to a discussion of the popes within the post-Roman empire, therefore,[17] it is the *Liber pontificalis* and its

---

[15] Useful background in Jonathan J. Arnold, M. Shane Bjornlie and Kristina Sessa, eds, *A Companion to Ostrogothic Italy* (Leiden, 2016).

[16] Rosamond McKitterick, 'Roman Texts and Roman History in the Early Middle Ages', in Claudia Bolgia, Rosamond McKitterick and John Osborne, eds, *Rome across Time and Space: Cultural Transmission and the Exchange of Ideas c.400–1400* (Cambridge, 2011), 19–34. For schism, see K. Blair-Dixon, 'Memory and Authority in Sixth-Century Rome: The *Liber pontificalis* and the *Collectio Avellana*', in Cooper and Hillner, eds, *Religion, Dynasty and Patronage*, 59–76; cf. also Davis, *Pontiffs*, x–xii; Thomas F. X. Noble, 'A New Look at the *Liber pontificalis*', *AHP* 23 (1985), 347–58; Deborah Mauskopf Deliyannis, 'The Roman *Liber pontificalis*, Papal Primacy, and the Acacian Schism', *Viator* 45 (2014), 1–16.

[17] For the conventional approach, see Walter Ullmann, *Gelasius I. (492–496). Das Papsttum an der Wende der Spätantike zum Mittelalter*, Päpste und Papsttum 18 (Stuttgart,

implications, somewhat overlooked hitherto,[18] that I propose to explore further in this article.

Of crucial importance to the theme of Church and empire, first of all, is the way the *Liber pontificalis* recast the genre of imperial serial biography, with all the ideological implications such a historiographical choice implies. The closest parallels to the papal biographies are the imperial biographical narratives of Suetonius, (pseudo)-Aurelius Victor and the *Historia Augusta*, rather than Old Testament kings, martyrs or saints, as can be seen from the schematic comparison on the next page.[19]

There are, first of all, consistent structural parallels between late antique imperial biographical narratives and the *Liber pontificalis* in the formulaic presentation of information about the subject's name, origin, parentage and career before and after elevation to the imperial or papal throne, including details about disputed elections and rival candidates, challenges to his authority, public works, patronage, buildings and religious observance, his length of reign, death and burial, even if the length accorded each topic varies considerably. I shall return below to the significance of the buildings as a way of establishing a physical presence and lasting memory.

Secondly, the authors portray the relations between the popes and the emperors in a manner that highlights the pre-eminence of the

---

1981); idem, *The Growth of Papal Government in the Middle Ages: A Study in the Ideological Relation of Clerical to Lay Power* (London, 1970); but for refreshing new assessments of these same letters, see Bronwen Neil and Pauline Allen, ed. and transl., *The Letters of Gelasius I (492–496): Pastor and Micro-Manager of the Church of Rome* (Turnhout, 2014). Some new perspectives are to be found in Philippe Blaudeau, 'Narrating Papal Authority (440–530): The Adaptation of the *Liber Pontificalis* to the Apostolic See's developing Claims', in Geoffrey D. Dunn, ed., *The Bishop of Rome in Late Antiquity* (Farnham, 2015), 127–40.

[18] A notable exception is Blaudeau, 'Narrating Papal Authority'; Blaudeau covers some of the same ground that I do here, albeit from a complementary perspective and with different emphases.

[19] Rosamond McKitterick, 'La place du *Liber Pontificalis* dans les genres historiographiques du haut moyen âge', in Bougard and Sot, eds, *Liber, gesta, histoire*, 23–36; for a more extended argument than the short summary here concerning the model provided by Roman imperial biographies, see McKitterick, 'Roman Texts and Roman History'. On Roman martyr narratives, see Clare Pilsworth, 'Dating the Gesta *martyrum*: A Manuscript-based Approach', in Kate Cooper, ed., *The Roman Martyrs and the Politics of Memory*, special issue of *EME* 9 (2000), 271–324; Marios Costambeys, 'Review Article: Property, Ideology and the Territorial Power of the Papacy in the Early Middle Ages', ibid. 367–96; Marianne Sághy, 'The Bishop of Rome and the Martyrs', in Dunn, ed., *Bishop of Rome*, 37–56.

Table 1. Serial Biography: Structural Models

Imperial Lives in Suetonius, *Lives of XII Caesars*; *Historia Augusta*; Eutropius, *Breviarium*; *Kaisergeschichte*; Aurelius Victor, *De Caesaribus*	Papal lives in *Liber pontificalis*
Emperor's name and origin	Pope's name and origin
Life before he became emperor	Career before he became pope
Process of becoming emperor, including disputes and rivals	Election as pope, including disputes and rivals
Career as emperor: includes rebellions, legislation, public works, buildings, patronage, religious observance	Career as pope: includes challenges to authority, legislation, public works, buildings, patronage, religious observance
Death and burial	Death and burial
Length of reign	Length of reign

bishop in Rome. This takes a number of forms. It is particularly apparent in the representation of the early Christian community in Rome as a small and vulnerable group, sometimes tolerated and sometimes persecuted, led by a 'monarch bishop'.[20] In contrast to other texts relating to the many Christian groups in Rome before the early fourth century, the *Liber pontificalis* gives only a slight indication of underlying divisions and divided loyalties or any of the tensions within the Christian communities of Rome discussed by Allen Brent.[21] The theologian Hippolytus (170–235), for example, is only mentioned as a priest who accompanied Bishop Pontian (pope 230–5) into exile. The challenge presented by the rigorist Novatian (200–58), author of letters to Cyprian of Carthage and to Bishops Fabian (236–50) and Cornelius (251–3) (Lives 21 and 22) in the middle of the third century, is subordinated to the curious story in the life of Bishop Cornelius about the translation of the bodies of Saints Peter

---

[20] For a fuller commentary on this portion of the *Liber pontificalis*, see Rosamond McKitterick, 'The *Liber pontificalis* and the Transformation of Rome from Pagan to Christian City in the Early Middle Ages', in Maijastina Kahlos, Katja Ritari and Jan Stenger, eds, *Being Pagan, Being Christian in Late Antiquity and the Early Middle Ages* (Helsinki, forthcoming), on which I draw here.

[21] Allen Brent, *Hippolytus and the Roman Church in the Third Century: Communities in Tension before the Emergence of a Monarch Bishop*, Supplements to Vigiliae Christianae 31 (Leiden 1995); see also John Curran, *Pagan City and Christian Capital: Rome in the Fourth Century* (Oxford, 2000); James A. Papandrea, *Novatian of Rome and the Culmination of Pre-Nicene Orthodoxy* (Princeton, NJ, 2011).

and Paul from the Via Appia to new resting places on the sites of their respective executions.[22]

The bishop of Rome is presented, moreover, as the principal creator of the institutional structure, administration, clerical office and liturgy, not merely for Rome but for the whole Church by the beginning of the fourth century. The text thus affirms the antiquity of the church in Rome and the apostolic underpinning of all its arrangements long before the conversion of Constantine and formal legal recognition of Christianity within the Roman empire.

The insistent catalogue of steadfast bishops killed for their faith by the pagan emperors before Constantine also underpins the bishops' role. Only with the appearance in the narrative of Constantine are the emperors cast in a more favourable light, but even then the author(s) of the *Liber pontificalis* contrive to indicate that it is the bishop who is masterminding the affairs of the Church and in Rome. According to Life 34, Silvester (315–35) not only baptized the emperor Constantine, but is also credited with convening the synod of Nicaea, as well as a synod in Rome at which many provisions for clerical organization and behaviour were made.[23]

The provision of a chronological framework by reference to the reign of emperors in the *Liber pontificalis* might be thought significant. They are noted up to Life 37 of Liberius while the *Liber pontificalis* was still able to follow the Liberian catalogue.[24] Thus Julius (Life 36) was 'bishop in the time of Constantine'. But this seems to be a simple chronological device used while it was available from an already existing list. After Liberius, the next regnal year dating point offered is not until that of Odoacer and Theodoric for Felix III already referred to. For the rest of the period of Ostrogothic rule, dating clauses were inserted as follows:

Life 51: Gelasius I, in the time of Theodoric and the emperor Zeno.
Life 52: Anastasius, bishop in the time of King Theodoric.

---

[22] *LP* 1: 150; see, for example, Henneke Gülzow, *Cyprian und Novatian. Der Briefwechsel zwischen den Gemeinden in Rom und Karthago zur Zeit der Verfolgung des Kaisers Decius* (Tübingen, 1975).

[23] 'Hic fecit constitutum de omne ecclesia. Etiam huius temporibus factum est concilium in Nicea Bithynia et congregati sunt CCCXVIII episcopi catholici': *LP* 1: 171 (Davis, *Pontiffs*, 14).

[24] Also in Life 48, Hilarus issued a decree 'in the consulship of Basiliscus and Hermenericus' (*consulatu Basilisco Hermenerico*): *LP* 1: 242 (Davis, *Pontiffs*, 37), a phrase which seems to have been extracted from the document referred to.

Life 53: Symmachus, bishop in the time of King Theodoric and the emperor Anastasius.

Life 54: Hormisdas, bishop in the time of King Theodoric and the emperor Anastasius from the consulship of Senator to that of Symmachus and Boethius.

Life 55: John I, bishop from the consulship of Maximus to that of Olybrius in the time of Theodoric and the Christian emperor Justin.

Life 56: Felix IV, bishop in the time of King Theodoric and of the emperor Justin from 12 July in the consulship of Maburtius to 12 October in that of Lampadius and Orestes.

Life 57: Boniface II, bishop in the time of the heretic king Athalaric and of the emperor Justin.

Life 58: John II, bishop in the time of king Athalaric and the emperor Justinian.[25]

These too can be regarded as a simple means of adding some chronological precision rather than offering statements about political affiliations or sympathies. It may be significant that it is only during the Ostrogothic period that the secular rulers are particularly acknowledged. Thereafter there are no regnal years of any secular rulers added, except for insertions in a couple of Carolingian manuscripts for the eighth-century lives which again simply seem to be insertions by scribes to provide more precise chronological landmarks.

Rather more substantial narrative strategies to represent relations between the bishops of Rome and the emperors while still in the West either report imperial interference in Roman affairs or concern doctrinal dispute. Thus Julius, Liberius and Felix II were exiled in turn by Constantine II and Constantius, the heretic sons of Constantine. Damasus was noted in passing as being bishop in the time of Julian. The interference of the Emperors Valentinian III and Honorius and the Empress Placidia in the disputed election of Boniface and Eulalius in 418 resulted in the success of the candidate preferred by the imperial family, but the biography of Boniface made it clear that Eulalius, consecrated in the Constantinian basilica, was favoured by the clergy and people of Rome. Valentinian III intervened again when Sixtus III was arraigned by the aristocrat Bassus, a descendant of the famous fourth-century Christian prefect of the city of Rome, Junius Bassus, by ordering that a synod be convened to consider

[25] *LP* 1: 255, 258, 260, 269, 275, 279, 281, 285 (Davis, *Pontiffs*, 40, 41, 42, 45, 48, 49, 50).

the charge. Sixtus was declared innocent and Bassus condemned, though the synod conceded that he was not to be denied the last rites. Valentinian and Placidia were indignant about this concession, condemned Bassus themselves and confiscated his estates, though they were 'merged with the catholic church'; Sixtus nevertheless saw to it that Bassus's body, on the latter's death soon afterwards, was buried in the family tomb chamber in St Peter's basilica, and Sixtus 'saw to the wrapping of his body with linens and spices with his own hands'.[26] Only in the notorious case of Vigilius's elevation as a hoped-for puppet pope by Justinian, however, does the *Liber pontificalis* retrospectively record direct secular intervention to impose an imperial candidate.[27] The *Liber pontificalis* does not record Felix IV as Theodoric's appointee, or John II as Athalaric's.

The episodes concerning the papal standoffs with the Christian emperors on matters of doctrine during the Acacian schism and Three Chapters dispute and prolonged papal resistance to Monophysite and Monothelite interpretations of the Trinity, culminating in the Lateran Council of 649, in addition to persecution and punishment by heretic emperors, are numerous but consistent. These doctrinal controversies have been exhaustively addressed by scholars over the past few decades, so I offer only a sample here.[28] The *Liber pontificalis*'s entry for Leo I is happy to record that the synod of Chalcedon was gathered in the Emperor Marcian's presence, but it is the statement of Chalcedonian orthodoxy in the *Tome* of Leo and Leo's

---

[26] '[O]mnia praedia facultatum eius ecclesiae catholicae sociavit … cum linteaminibus et aromatibus, manibus suis tractans': *LP* 1: 232 (Davis, *Pontiffs*, 34).

[27] For Felix IV, see Louis Duchesne, 'La Succession du pape Félix IV', *Mélanges d'archéologie et d'histoire de l'École française de Rome* 3 (1883), 239–66. For a judicious appraisal of Vigilius's actions, see Claire Sotinel, 'Autorité pontificale et pouvoir impérial sous le règne de Justinien. Le Pape Vigile', *Mélanges de l'Ecole française de Rome. Antiquité* 104 (1992), 439–63; eadem, 'Mémoire perdue ou mémoire manipulée. Le *Liber pontificalis* et la controverse des Trois Chapîtres', in eadem and Maurice Sartre, eds, *L'Usage du passé entre antiquité tardive et haut moyen âge* (Rennes, 2008), 59–76; ET in Claire Sotinel, *Church and Society in Late Antique Italy and Beyond* (Farnham, 2010), chs 1, 3. See also eadem, 'Emperors and Popes in the Sixth Century: The Western View', in Michael Maas, ed., *The Cambridge Companion to the Age of Justinian* (Cambridge, 2005), 267–90.

[28] See, for example, Patrick T. R. Gray, 'The Legacy of Chalcedon: Christological Problems and their Significance', in Maas, ed., *Companion to Justinian*, 215–39; Celia Chazelle and Catherine Cubitt, eds, *The Crisis of the Oikoumene: The Three Chapters and the Failed Quest for Unity in the Sixth-Century Mediterranean* (Turnhout, 2007), especially Richard Price, 'The Three Chapters and the Council of Chalcedon', 17–37; idem, with Philip Booth and Catherine Cubitt, *The Acts of the Lateran Synod of 649* (Liverpool, 2014).

authority which is emphasized. The 'pious emperor Marcian and the empress Pulcheria' even 'laid their royal majesty aside and expounded their faith in the sight of the holy bishops' and insisted on a written version being sent to Pope Leo.[29] Leo's famous embassy to the Huns, moreover, is introduced with the statement that he did it '[f]or the sake of the Roman name' without reference to the emperor.[30] Leo's successor Hilarus (461–8) confirmed the statements of faith from the three synods of Nicaea, Ephesus and Chalcedon and Leo's *Tome*, condemned the teaching of Eutyches and Nestorius, and asserted 'the dominion and preeminence of the holy, catholic and apostolic see'.[31]

The *Liber pontificalis* offers a steady narrative of the Acacian schism. It starts with the condemnation of Peter of Alexandria (who was suspected of Eutychianism) mentioned in the life of Simplicius, the condemnation of Acacius and Peter by Felix III/IV (483–92) and the excommunication of the Roman legate Misenus for accepting Byzantine bribes, the restoration of Misenus by Pope Gelasius I, Gelasius's offer of refuge to the Catholic rival John, bishop of Alexandria, and Gelasius's subsequent condemnation of Acacius and Peter once more and his composition of five books against Nestorius and Eutyches.[32] Anastasius (496–8) earned a thoroughly negative portrait in the *Liber pontificalis*, even though he was buried in St Peter's basilica along with his predecessors. Because he had 'wanted secretly to reinstate Acacius' and had failed to 'consult the priests bishops and clerics of the whole catholic church', he was 'struck down by God's will'.[33] Hormisdas (514–23), on the other hand, made such a determined effort to assert the orthodox position maintained in Rome that the enraged the emperor vigorously protested: 'It is our wish to give orders, not to take them', only to be struck down by a divine thunderbolt.[34]

It was King Theodoric, not the emperor, who was asked to adjudicate in the disputed election between Laurentius and Symmachus, but Theodoric's relationship with the bishops of Rome is

---

[29] '[D]eposita regia maiestate, fidem suum exposuerunt ante conspectum sanctorum episcoporum': Life 47.3–4, *LP* 1: 238 (Davis, *Pontiffs*, 36–7).

[30] 'Hic propter nomen Romanum': *LP* 1: 239 (Davis, *Pontiffs*, 37).

[31] '[E]t confirmans dominationem et principatum sancta sedis catholicae et apostolicae': *LP* 1: 242 (Davis, *Pontiffs*, 37).

[32] *LP* 1: 255 (Davis, *Pontiffs*, 41–2).

[33] '[Q]ui voluit occulte revocare Acacium ... sine consilio presbiterorum vel episcoporum vel clericorum cunctae ecclesiae catholicae ... qui nutu divino percussus est': Life 52 (496–8), *LP* 1: 258 (Davis, *Pontiffs*, 42).

[34] 'Nos iubere volumus, non uobis iuberi': Life 54, *LP* 1: 270 (Davis, *Pontiffs*, 46).

inconsistent and needs fuller analysis than can be attempted here.[35] It was Theodoric whose advice Hormisdas sought in order finally to effect a reconciliation with the new Emperor Justin and restore 'unity with the apostolic see'.[36] The account of Theodoric's treatment of Pope John I (523–6), by contrast, adds a perplexingly sour note to the presentation of a mostly cooperative working relationship between the bishops of Rome and the Ostrogothic kings as rulers of distinct domains.[37]

Thereafter the *Liber pontificalis* reiterates the zeal, even anxiety, with which the emperors reassure the pope of their orthodoxy, reinforced in the life of John II (533–5) by splendid gifts of gold and silver vessels and purple-dyed cloth by the Emperor Justinian to St Peter. This first section of the *Liber pontificalis* culminates in the trouncing by Pope Agapitus of both the Emperor Justinian and the Patriarch Anthemius of Constantinople in argument, and his affirmation of the two natures in one Christ. The emperor then 'abased himself before the apostolic see, prostrating himself before the blessed pope Agapitus'.[38]

The seventh- and early eighth-century sections of the *Liber pontificalis* further enhanced and reinforced the popes' theological and political relationship with the Byzantine emperor, and represent the Roman perception of occasional and irritating imperial intervention in Roman affairs. Not least in relation to a pope's candidature and election and the announcement sent as a courtesy to Constantinople, the Roman perception articulated in the *Liber pontificalis* was that imperial intervention in Roman affairs was not necessary to validate or legitimate the pope's position. I have further suggested, in a recent article on the papacy and Byzantium in the seventh and early eighth centuries, that the composition of the *Liber pontificalis* was resumed in the seventh century in order both to provide a historical record

---

[35] But see the interesting suggestions offered by Patrick Amory, *People and Identity in Ostrogothic Italy, 489–554* (Cambridge, 1997), 195–235.

[36] '[A]d unitatem sedis apostolicae': Life 54.8, *LP* 1: 270 (Davis, *Pontiffs*, 47).

[37] Life 55, *LP* 1: 275–6 (Davis, *Pontiffs*, 48–9); see Thomas F. X. Noble, 'Theodoric and the Papacy', in *Teodorico il Grande e i Goti d'Italia, Atti de XIII congresso internazionale di studi sull'alto Medioevo Milan 1990* (Spoleto, 1993), 395–429. For more recent discussion, see K. Sessa, 'The Roman Church and its Bishops', R. Lizzi Testa, 'Bishops, Ecclesiastical Institutions and the Ostrogothic Regime', in Arnold, Bjornlie and Sessa, eds, *Companion to Ostrogothic Italy*, 435–50 (especially 441–2), 451–79.

[38] '[H]umiliavit se sedi apostolicae et adoravit beatissimum Agapitum papam': *LP* 1: 288 (Davis, *Pontiffs*, 52).

of the popes' confrontations with Byzantium and the patriarch of Constantinople in doctrinal matters and to affirm the papal position in relation to Monothelitism.[39] The *Liber pontificalis* became, in the first and second continuations (Lives 60–71, from Silverius to Boniface V, and Lives 72–90, from Honorius to Constantine I), therefore, an essentially political argument articulated in the form of historical narrative. In so doing, the second and third generations of *Liber pontificalis* authors maintained the very particular agenda of their predecessors, and represented the pope as upholder of the orthodox Christian faith, the leader of the Church, the ruler of Rome and a rival to Byzantium. The second continuation culminates in another papal visit to Constantinople, where Pope Constantine I celebrated mass, after 'the Christian Augustus, crown on head, had prostrated himself and kissed the feet of the pontiff'.[40]

In the form in which it was circulated in the seventh and eighth centuries,[41] the *Liber pontificalis* became a powerful and influential text for Frankish, English and even Byzantine knowledge and understanding of the popes and of their championing of orthodox doctrine, especially of the papal leadership in insisting on Chalcedonian Christological orthodoxy and the principal decisions of the councils of the Lateran in 649 and Constantinople in 680/1.[42] That knowledge and understanding also underpinned the separate lives of the eighth-century popes of the 'third continuation' (Lives 91–6 from Gregory II to Stephen III), up to the eve of Charlemagne's conquest of the Lombard kingdom.[43] While still *sacellarius* and a deacon, for example, Pope Gregory II (715–31) had accompanied Pope Constantine I to Constantinople. After he became pope he headed the opposition to remnants of imperial taxation in Italy and opposed the new ideas

[39] Rosamond McKitterick, 'The Papacy and Byzantium in the Seventh- and Early Eighth-Century Sections of the *Liber pontificalis*', *Papers of the British School at Rome* 84 (2016), 241–74. On the doctrinal issues, see M. Jankowiak, 'The Invention of Dyothelitism', *Studia Patristica* 63 (2013), 335–42; Price, *Lateran Council of 649*.

[40] 'Augustus christianissimus cum regno in capite sese prostravit et pedes osculans pontificis': *LP* 1: 391 (Davis, *Pontiffs*, 88–9). On the imperial 'renewing of the church's privileges' (*omnia privilegia ecclesiae renovavit*) during this same visit, see my comments in 'Papacy and Byzantium', 264–5.

[41] For preliminary comments on this, see ibid. 268–72.

[42] See Michael T. G. Humphreys, *Law, Power, and Imperial Ideology in the Iconoclast Era, c.650–850* (Oxford, 2015).

[43] See Clemens Gantner, *Freunde Roms und Völker der Finsternis. Die päpstlichen Konstruktion von Anderen im 8. und 9. Jahrhundert* (Vienna, Cologne and Weimar, 2014), 60–138.

about iconoclasm emanating from the Byzantine empire, as did his successor Gregory III (731–41): this holy man sent 'written warnings, with the authority of the holy see's teaching, for them to change their minds and quit their error'.[44] Gregory III's messenger George was too frightened to deliver them and when he was allowed by the pope to try again, the imperial authorities in Sicily detained the luckless George en route and prevented subsequent messengers from delivering their messages as well. Having made the point about the emperor's intransigence, the author of Life 92 says no more about the pope's contact with Constantinople. Life 93 on Zacharias (741–52) records only the sending of the 'usual' profession of orthodox faith to Constantinople. Life 94 of Stephen II (752–7) simply mentions the attempts by imperial envoys to prevent the pope's envoys reaching the Frankish ruler Pippin. His brother Pope Paul I (757–67), however, was rather more active in reaction to the iconoclast council of Hieria. He is credited with sending envoys frequently to the emperors in Constantinople, exhorting them 'to restore and establish in their erstwhile veneration the sacred images of our Lord God and Saviour Jesus Christ, his holy mother, the blessed apostles, and all the saints, prophets, martyrs and confessors'.[45] On the fourth day of the synod of Rome in 769 recorded in Life 96 of Stephen III, the Roman attitude to Byzantium and its affairs appears to be neatly summarized in the comment that they 'disallowed and anathematized the execrable synod recently held in the districts of Greece for the removal of these sacred images'.[46]

From these examples, the portrayal in the *Liber pontificalis* of the bishop of Rome in relation to the secular rulers usually assumed to be in political control of Rome is particularly striking. A

[44] '[U]t ab hoc resipiscerent ac se removerent errore, commonitoria scripta vigore apostolicae sedis institutionis'; ET Raymond Davis, *The Lives of the Eighth-Century Popes (Liber pontificalis)*, TTH 13, 2nd edn (Liverpool, 2007), 19.
[45] '[P]ro restitundis confirmandisque in pristino venerationis statu sacratissimis imaginibus domini Dei et salvatoris nostri Iesu Christi, santaeque eius genetricis atque beatorum apostolorum omniumque sanctorum, prophetarum, martyrum et confessorum': *LP* 1: 464 (Davis, *Eighth-Century Popes*, 82).
[46] '[C]onfundentes atque anathematizantes execrabilem illam synodum quae in Grecie partibus nuper facta est pro deponendis ipsis sacris imaginibus': Life 96.23, *LP* 1: 477 (Davis, *Eighth-Century Popes*, 100). For subsequent developments, see Thomas F. X. Noble, *Images, Iconoclasm, and the Carolingians* (Philadelphia, PA, 2009); on *Greci*, see Clemens Gantner, 'The Label "Greeks" in the Papal Diplomatic Repertoire in the Eighth Century', in Walter Pohl and Gerda Heydemann, eds, *Strategies of Identification: Ethnicity and Religion in Early Medieval Europe* (Turnhout, 2013), 303–49.

comparison with the formulation of the history of the Coptic patriarchs of Alexandria in the seventh century is instructive. The *History of the Patriarchs* is thought to have been compiled first of all in the context of the Arab incursions into Egypt for the benefit of the vulnerable Christian community, to aid them to forge communal bonds. It survives in an eleventh-century Arabic version of the text. The history of a community within the jurisdiction of the bishop of Alexandria is achieved by focusing on the bishop, whom the authors clearly wished to be seen as the leader.[47] In the case of both the *Liber pontificalis* and the *History of the Patriarchs*, that leadership in its turn was given a long pedigree in the text, not just by claiming a direct line of apostolic succession from St Peter and St Mark respectively. In Rome's case this leadership was not only of the many Christian religious communities of Rome but extended to the entire Christian Church. Its representation, moreover, was cast not only as a replacement of imperial rule in religious matters and as the opportunity for the bishop to assume political responsibility in Rome and its territories as well, but also as a deliberate emulation of imperial behaviour.

This is manifest above all in the record included in the *Liber pontificalis* of the papal embellishment of Rome. The *Liber pontificalis* is famous, from the Life of Silvester onwards, for the lists and lavish descriptions of buildings dedicated, constructed, repaired and decorated and filled with gifts of gold, silver and bronze furnishings, lights, liturgical vessels and silk hangings, initially by Constantine and his immediate successors, but with Mark's founding of two basilicas in 336, almost exclusively by the popes.[48]

---

[47] I am grateful to Christian Sahner for bringing the *History of the Patriarchs* to my attention: see Basil Evetts, ed., *History of the Patriarchs of the Coptic Church of Alexandria I–IV*, PO 2, 4, 21, 50, also available online at Roger Pearse's invaluable Tertullian project website: <http://www.tertullian.org>, last accessed 20 January 2017; Johannes Den Heijer, 'Coptic Historiography in the Fatimid, Ayyubid and Early Mamluk Periods', *Medieval Encounters* 2 (1996), 67–98; Johananes Den Heijer, *Mawhūb ibn Manṣūr ibn Mufarriğ et l'historiographie copto-arabe. Étude sur la composition de l'Histoire des Patriarches d'Alexandrie*, Corpus Scriptorum Christianorum Orientalium Subsidia 83 (Louvain, 1989).

[48] The literature on these is too great to be listed here. Davis, *Pontiffs*, xxvii–xlv, offers a convenient summary of the early papal endowments. I offer some preliminary remarks about the Constantinian basilica, in particular in 'The Constantinian Basilica in the Early Medieval *Liber pontificalis*', in Lex Bosman, Robert Haynes and Paolo Liverani, eds, *The Lateran, Rome*, British School at Rome Monographs (Cambridge, forthcoming). For articles on many aspects of both decoration and buildings, see the indispensable Federico Guidobaldi and Alessandra Guiglia Guidobaldi, eds, *Ecclesiae Urbis. Atti del congreso*

This textual replacement of emperors with popes as patrons and benefactors in the *Liber pontificalis* is reflected in the architectural styles of Rome's churches as well as the materials from which they were constructed and embellished. Just as the text offers imperial parallels which are then developed in a distinctively papal context and manner, so too in the material evidence their (self-)presentation develops in distinctively complex ways. I can only touch on this issue here, for I intend to develop it more fully elsewhere. Massive Christian basilicas resembling imperial *aulae* or assembly halls, and built with expensive marble and stone, *opus sectile* pavements and revetted walls, mosaics and frescos, ornamented in decorative schemes similar those of imperial temples and palaces, offer visual physical evidence of imperial emulation. How deliberate this was has become a matter of debate. In particular, the use of late antique *spolia* in these buildings has prompted a range of interpretations, from assigning it momentous symbolic significance to treating the reuse of older Roman building materials as a practical expedient. These extremes are not necessarily mutually exclusive, for in many instances it can be demonstrated that there is meaning to be perceived in such reuse, though of course contemporary – as distinct from our own – perceptions may well need to be distinguished.[49] In an exposition that has precipitated considerable constructive as well as critical debate, for example, Maria Fabricius Hansen has suggested with reference to the Lateran baptistery, endowed by Constantine and built early in the fourth century but remodelled under Sixtus III (432–44), that the Christians borrowed imperial 'badges of grandeur and rank' in using purple porphyry stone, as well as recycling *spolia* from imperial buildings. She has drawn attention in particular

---

internazionale di studi sulle chiese di Roma IV–X secolo, Studi di antichità cristiana 59 (Vatican City, 2002); Herman Geertman, *More veterum. Il* Liber Pontificalis *e gli edifici ecclesiastici di Roma nella tarda antichità e nell'alto medioevo*, Archaeologica Traiectina 10 (Groningen, 1975). For more recent studies, see Eric Thunø, *The Apse Mosaic in Early Medieval Rome: Time, Network, and Repetition* (Cambridge, 2015); Cecilia Proverbio, *I cicli affrescati paleocristiani di San Pietro in Vaticano e San Paolo fuori le mura*, Bibliothèque de l'antiquité tardive 33 (Turnhout, 2017).

[49] See especially the Introduction by the editors, 'On the Reuse of Antiquity: The Perspectives of the Archaeologist and of the Historian', Arnold Esch, 'Reading *spolia* in Late Antique and Contemporary Perception', and Paolo Liverani, 'The Reuse of Older Elements in the Architecture of Fourth- and Fifth-Century Rome: A Contribution to the Evaluation of *spolia*', in Richard Brilliant and Dale Kinney, eds, *Reuse Value: Spolia and Appropriation in Art and Architecture from Constantine to Sherrie Levine* (Farnham, 2011), 1–52.

to the massive porphyry exterior columns of the narthex of the baptistery with composite second-century capitals and white marble first-century bases. The capitals may have been transferred from the Temple of Venus Genetrix in the Forum of Caesar. Hansen has further suggested that the builders 'may have wished to make the point that the principles of renewal and procreation embodied in Venus Genetrix were now replaced by baptism'. The building's entablature, very like that of the temple of Hadrian, and the ornamented marble *opus sectile* revetment may be further deliberately Christianizing elements of the decorative styles of imperial buildings now translated into the decoration of Christian holy places.[50] Although partly remodelled under Pope Urban VIII (1623–44), the columns of the baptistery are also of imperial purple porphyry, as are the doorways to the chapels built by Pope Hilarus (461–8), to which were added magnificent bronze doors, with his responsibility clearly indicated on the lintel.[51] The implications of Hansen's arguments for a broader aesthetic interest in recontextualizing aspects of the imperial past in Late Antiquity and the Early Middle Ages merit further exploration and testing that are not possible in this article.

Many of the foundations credited to Constantine, most notably St Peter's basilica, afterwards became recipients of papal munificence, and popes sometimes persuaded later emperors to make generous offerings. Thus, at Sixtus III's request, the Emperor Valentinian III presented an elaborate gold sculpture to St Peter's *confessio*. He also replaced the silver *fastigium* (quite what this was is still disputed)

---

[50] Maria Fabricius Hansen, *The Spolia Churches of Rome: Recycling Antiquity in the Middle Ages* (Aarhus, 2015), 88–92, with colour illustrations, is a useful summary of the ideas expounded in eadem, *The Eloquence of Appropriation: Prolegomena to an Understanding of* Spolia *in Early Christian Rome* (Rome, 2003). For discussion, see in particular Dale Kinney, 'Instances of Appropriation in Late Roman and Early Christian Art', *Essays in Medieval Studies* 28 (2012), 1–22 [online journal], at: <https://doi.org/10.1353/ems.2012.0005> or <http://muse.jhu.edu/article/507995>, last accessed 20 January 2017; and the comments by Elizabeth Marlowe in 'CAA Reviews', online at: <http://www.caareviews.org CrossRef DOI: 10.3202/caa.reviews.2004.69>, last accessed 20 January 2017. For detailed observations on the fabric and archaeology of the Lateran with rather different interpretations from those offered by Hansen, see Olaf Brandt and Federico Guidobaldi, 'Il Battistero lateranense. Nuove interpretazioni delle fasi strutturali', *Rivista di archeologia cristiana* 84 (2008), 189–282.

[51] Handy details of all these churches and their inscriptions are given in Matilda Webb, *The Churches and Catacombs of Early Christian Rome: A Comprehensive Guide* (Brighton, 2001); for illustrations, see Hugo Brandenburg, *Die Frühchristlichen Kirchen Roms vom 4. bis zum 7. Jahrhundert. Der Beginn der abendländischen Kirchenbaukunst* (Milan and Regensburg, 2004), 37–52.

originally donated by the Emperor Constantine to the Constantinian basilica or Lateran.[52]   At St Peter's, the Emperor Honorius constructed a family mausoleum at the beginning of the fifth century, close to the basilica and the saint's shrine. Leo I, who also appears to have commissioned the extensive narrative cycle of biblical scenes in the nave and the representations of Peter and Paul on either side of the triumphal arch, was the first pope actually to be buried in Old St Peter's, as if to outdo the imperial claim to proximity to the saint, and thus inaugurated a papal necropolis intimately associated with the shrine of the apostle St Peter.[53]   In the middle of the eighth century Stephen II and his brother Pope Paul I appropriated Honorius's mausoleum and consecrated it as a chapel dedicated to the newly discovered and translated saint, Petronilla.[54]

In some cases, indeed, known imperial endowments, such as the Empress Eudoxia's foundation of S. Petro in Vincoli at the end of the fourth century,[55] the construction of San Paolo fuori le mura under the Emperors Valentinian II (375–92), Theodosius I (378–95) and Arcadius (395–408), completed under the Emperor Honorius (395–432), or the donation of the triumphal arch at San Paolo by the Empress Galla Placidia, recorded in contemporary inscriptions, are simply not mentioned in the *Liber pontificalis*. The church of San Paolo itself, however, was in any case more or less claimed by Pope Siricius with the mounting of two inscriptions to record that the building was directed by Flavius Filippus and built in the time of *Siricius episcopus tota mente devotus* ('the bishop Siricius [to Christ] with all the devotion').[56] The inscriptions concerning the completion of the basilica make it clear that the emperors are serving the saint: 'Theodosius began and Honorius finished this hall made sacrosanct by the body of Paul, teacher of the world'. The tribute to Galla Placidia cleverly shifts the attention to Pope Leo (440–61): 'Placida's

---

[52] *LP* 1: 233 (Davis, *Pontiffs*, 35).

[53] Rosamond McKitterick, 'The Representation of Old Saint Peter's Basilica in the *Liber Pontificalis*', in eadem et al., eds, *Old Saint Peter's, Rome*, British School at Rome Studies (Cambridge, 2013), 95–118.

[54] Meaghan McEvoy, 'Late Roman Imperial Christianity and the City of Rome in the Fifth Century', ibid. 119–36; Caroline Goodson, 'To be the Daughter of Saint Peter: S. Petronilla and Forging the Franco-Papal Alliance', in Veronica West-Harling, ed., *Three Empires, Three Cities: Identity, Material Culture and Legitimacy in Venice, Ravenna and Rome, 750–1000* (Turnhout, 2015), 159–82.

[55] Davis, *Pontiffs*, xxxix.

[56] Webb, *Churches and Catacombs*, 210.

devoted heart is delighted that all the dignity of her father's work shines resplendent through the zeal of Pope Leo'.[57]

San Paolo became an even more flamboyant assertion of papal rule, self-advertisement and what appears to be deliberate emulation of the imperial images and portraits customarily on public display in late antique Rome.[58] The fourth-century building contained large roundels depicting the popes in succession from St Peter to Laurentius, originally above the arches on the south and north sides of the nave. The installation, if not first commissioning, of these portraits has been credited to Pope Leo but they were probably then augmented by the anti-pope Laurentius up to Laurentius himself as part of his attempt to consolidate his election as pope in rivalry to Pope Symmachus.[59] This first set is usually dated on stylistic grounds to c.500. They were then continued in the Middle Ages but quite how far is not clear, for many of these portraits were destroyed in the catastrophic fire of 1823. Some survive in the Lapidary Museum at San Paolo, but a record of the first series in the form of watercolour reproductions in reduced format was also made in 1634 by Antonio Eclissi.[60] Old St Peter's had a similar set of portraits, all destroyed by the sixteenth- and seventeenth-century Roman equivalents of the 1960s town planners in Britain when they pulled down the old basilica.[61] This series was allegedly created during the reign of Bishop

---

[57] 'THEODOSIUS COEPIT PERFECIT HONORIUS AULUM DOCTORIS MUNDI SACRATAM CORPORE PAULI'; 'PLACIDAE PIA MENS OPERIS DECUS OMNE PATERNI GAUDET PONTIFICIS STUDIO SPLENDERE LEONIS'; ET ibid. 212. For an illustration of the arch and inscriptions, and two of the extant fresco portraits, see Brandenburg, *Die frühchristlichen Kirchen*, 127–9.

[58] Meriwether Stuart, 'How were Imperial Portraits Distributed throughout the Roman Empire?', *American Journal of Archaeology* 43 (1939), 601–17; see also Robert Coates-Stephens, 'The Reuse of Statuary in Late Antique Rome and the End of the Statue Habit', in Franz Alto Bauer and Christian Witschel, eds, *Statuen in der Spätantike* (Wiesbaden, 2007), 171–88.

[59] See my discussion with reference to the earlier literature: Rosamond McKitterick, 'Narrative Strategies in the *Liber pontificalis*: St Paul and San Paolo fuori le mura', *Rivista di storia del cristianesimo* 10 (2013), 115–30; see also the classic study by Lucien de Bruyne, *L'antica serie di ritratti papali della basilica di S. Paolo fuori le mura*, Studi di antichità cristiana 7 (Rome, 1934).

[60] Now Vatican City, BAV, Barberini MS lat. 4407.

[61] For a scholarly reconstruction of elements of the old basilica, see McKitterick et al., eds, *Old St Peter's, Rome*.

Liberius (d. 354) and they were described by Giacomo Grimaldi in 1619.[62]

The representation of the popes in mosaics in some of the churches they endowed, moreover, differs from representations of imperial apotheoses in that the popes are depicted in the company of, and usually even in intimate proximity to, Christ, Mary the Virgin and the saints, and are portrayed as donors. Pope Felix IV (526–30), for example, added a mosaic to the apse of the hall of the 'Temple of Romulus', converted it into a church and dedicated it to the twin martyr 'medical' saints, Cosmas and Damian, announcing to all who saw the mosaic: 'Felix has made to the Lord this offering, worthy of the Lord's servant, that he may be granted life in the airy vault of heaven'.[63] The glorious apse mosaic, today visible at eye level in the upper church because of the seventeenth-century rebuilding, depicts Felix offering a model of his church to Christ, the apostles Paul and Peter and the two saints Cosmas and Damian.[64]

As part of the extraordinary efforts the popes dedicated to the promotion of martyr cults in Rome,[65] Pelagius II (579–90) created a gallery basilica over the tomb of the martyr Lawrence (d. 258) on the Via Tiburtina. The mosaic on the triumphal arch which divides the sixth-century basilica from the thirteenth-century extension created under Honorius III (1216–27), sets Pelagius, holding a model of his church as donor, in the company of Christ, the apostles Peter and Paul and the martyrs Lawrence, Hippolytus and Stephen. An inscription, once probably in the apse, records the decision made by Pelagius to create the shrine for Lawrence.[66]

---

[62] BAV, Barberini Lat. 2733; published as Giacomo Grimaldi, *Descrizione della basilica antica di S. Pietro in Vaticano: Il codice Barberini 2733, Biblioteca apostolica Vaticana*, ed. Reto Niggl (Vatican City, 1972), 138–57 and figs 52–8; Proverbio, *I cicli affrescati palaeocristiani*, ch. 2.

[63] 'OPTULIT HOC DNO FELIX ANTISTITE DIGNUM MUNUS UT AETHERIA VIVAT IN ARCE POLI'.

[64] See *LP* 1: 279 (Davis, *Pontiffs*, 49). The portrait of Felix is a seventeenth-century reconstruction; see Webb, *Churches and Catacombs*, 126–9, including the inscription and translation. For illustrations, see Brandenburg, *Die frühchristlichem Kirchen*, 223; and the important new interpretations of the Felix portrait as well as other papal representations in Thunø, *Apse Mosaic*.

[65] See Cooper, ed., *Roman Martyrs*, 273–396.

[66] *LP* 1: 309 (Davis, *Pontiffs*, 59). For details of the inscriptions and building, see Webb, *Churches and Catacombs*, 240–5; for illustrations, see Brandenburg, *Die frühchristlichen Kirchen*, 236–7.

A model of his church of Santa Agnese fuori le mura, perhaps in emulation of his predecessor, Pelagius II, was presented by Pope Honorius (625–38) to St Agnes in the mosaic recording his replacement of the church built by Pope Symmachus (498–514), who is also portrayed in the apse mosaic. The inscription evokes the gold and purple of the *tesserae*, and ends as follows: 'what all can see in a single upward glance are the sacred offerings dedicated by Honorius. His portrait is identified by robes and by the building. Wearing a radiant heart, he radiates in appearance also'.[67]

In the seventh-century chapel added to the Constantinian Baptistery at the Lateran by Pope John IV 640–2), mosaics commissioned by his successor Theodore (642–9) depict Christ, the two Saints John (the Baptist and the Evangelist), the Virgin Mary, St Paul, the martyr Venantius, Pope John IV holding a model of his chapel, St Peter, Pope Theodore I and another martyr, presumably among those whose remains John IV had had brought along with those of Venantius from Dalmatia. The apse inscription records John's gift: 'John bishop by God's consecration, made devout prayers to the martyrs for the Lord Christ'.[68]

The self-advertisement of Pope John VII (705–7) seemed rather extreme to the author of his Life in the *Liber pontificalis*, for he commented in the account of John's munificence, especially the paintings commissioned for the church of Santa Maria Antiqua, that the bishop 'provided images in various churches; whoever wants to know what he looked like will find his face depicted on them'.[69] The portrait of John VII still extant in the Vatican Treasury was once part of a larger mosaic depicting him with the Virgin.[70] It was John, moreover, who

---

[67] 'SURSUM VERSA NUTU QUOD CUNCTIS CERNITUR UNO PRAESUL HONORIUS HAEC VOTA DICATA DEDIT VESTIBUS ET FACTIS SIGNATUR ILLIUS ORA LUCET ET ASPECTUM LUCIDA CORDA GERENS': *LP* 1: 323 (Davis, *Pontiffs*, 62). For details and the inscription, see Webb, *Churches and Catacombs*, 246–8; for illustrations, see Brandenburg, *Die frühchristlichen Kirchen*, 244–6, who identifies the second episcopal figure as Pope Gregory I (590–604).

[68] 'MARTYRIBUS XPI DNI [*Christi domini*] VOTA JOHANNES REDDIDIT ANTISTES SANCTIFICANTE DEO': *LP* 1: 330 (Davis, *Pontiffs*, 64); see Webb, *Churches and Catacombs*, 47–8. For illustrations, see Brandenburg, *Die frühchristlichen Kirchen*, 53.

[69] 'Fecit vero et imagines per diversas ecclesias quas, quicumque nosse desiderat in eis eius vultum depictum repperiet': *LP* 1: 385 (Davis, *Pontiffs*, 86).

[70] See Antonella Ballardini and Paola Pogliani, 'A Reconstruction of the Oratory of John VII (705–7)', in McKitterick et al., eds, *Old St Peter's, Rome*, 190–213; and the illustration

appropriated the structures above the church on the Palatine hill, possibly hitherto used by secular officials, to build an *episcopium*.[71]

Most spectacularly of all, Paschal I (817–24)'s basilica of Santa Prassede, with its apse, triumphal arch and the mosaics of the chapel Paschal dedicated to St Zeno as a memorial for his mother '*episcopa* Theodora', is a dramatic indication of the continuation of the papal display established by his predecessors. Paschal had himself portrayed with a square nimbus and holding a model of his church and flanking the saints Praxedis and Pudenziana, Zeno, and Christ at his Second Coming. Paschal added his distinctive monogram to the decorative scheme. The inscriptions, set out in gold glass *tesserae* on blue, reiterate the announcement of Paschal's gift: that he was the 'alumnus' of the apostolic seat. The verse at the entrance to the chapel states: 'Ornament shines in the hall, the work of the prelate Paschal, because he made devout prayers and was earnest in paying this due to the Lord'.[72] Paschal's portrait is also to be seen in the apse mosaics of Santa Maria in Domnica and Santa Cecilia in Trastevere.[73] Paschal may have derived the idea for the flamboyant location at least of his monogram from the inscription 'Sixtus the bishop to the People of God' that Sixtus III (432–40) placed at the centre of the triumphal arch in his church of Santa Maria Maggiore.[74]

By 500 there were twenty-seven churches inside the walls of Rome and seven major basilicas outside the walls, including St Peter's

---

of John VII's mosaic in Maria Andoloro, ed., *Santa Maria Antiqua tra Roma e Bisanzio* (Rome, 2016), 249, and discussion, 250–9.

[71] See Andrea Augenti, 'Continuity and Discontinuity of a Seat of Power: The Palatine Hill from the Fifth to the Tenth Century', in Julia M. H. Smith, ed., *Early Medieval Rome and the Christian West: Essays in Honour of Donald A. Bullough* (Leiden, 2000), 43–54.

[72] 'PASCHALIS PRAESULIS OPUS DECOR FULGIT IN AULA QUOD PIA OPTULIT VOTA STUDUIT REDDERE D[omin]O'.

[73] *Liber pontificalis*, Life 100.9, *LP* 2: 54; ET Raymond Davis, *The Lives of the Ninth-Century Popes (*Liber pontificalis*): The Ancient Biographies of Ten Popes from A.D. 817–891*, TTH 20 (Liverpool, 1995), 10–11. For details of the church and the inscription, see Webb, *Churches and Catacombs*, 68–71; for full discussion, see Caroline J. Goodson, *The Rome of Paschal I: Papal Power, Urban Renovation, Church Rebuilding and Relic Translation, 817–824* (Cambridge 2010). On the significance of the square nimbus, see John Osborne, 'The Portrait of Pope Leo IV in San Clemente, Rome: A Re-Examination of the so-called "Square" Nimbus in Medieval Art', *Papers of the British School at Rome* 47 (1979), 58–65.

[74] 'XYSTUS EPISCOPUS PLEBI DEI': Webb, *Churches and Catacombs*, 64, for the inscription; see also the virtual tour, online at: <http://www.vatican.va/various/basiliche/sm_maggiore/index_en.html>, last accessed 20 January 2017.

and San Paolo fuori le Mura.[75]   Between Simplicius in the later
fifth century and Theodore in the middle of the seventh, many
more popes are credited in the *Liber pontificalis* with endowing and
embellishing churches, both within Rome and in outlying districts.
They are presented as continuing an imperial tradition of display and
religious devotion.

The *Liber pontificalis* rarely mentions churches built or paid for
by ordinary citizens or clergy of Rome.   A notable exception is
Santa Sabina, for in the Life of Sixtus III the patronage of Peter the
priest for the construction of the fifth-century basilica of St Sabina
on the Aventine hill is confirmed by the spectacular contemporary
inscription still in this church recording his endowment, in which
Peter refers to the time when 'Celestinus held the highest apostolic
throne and shone forth gloriously as the foremost bishop of the whole
world'.[76]   The widow Vestina, moreover, in the time of Pope Innocent (402–17) left her jewellery to fund the building of basilicas (St
Gervasius and Protasius),[77] the handmaid Demetrias gave land for
the building of St Stephen's basilica, the *matronae* Priscilla and Lucina who gave land for cemeteries; the latter also made her own house
into a *titulus*.[78]

This has not been the place to offer a detailed challenge to the
assumptions concerning the pope's relationship to the Byzantine empire, especially in the aftermath of the Ostrogothic wars.   Instead, I
have argued that this Roman narrative challenges the usual assumptions about the consequences both of the deposition of the last Roman emperor in the West and of Justinian's military campaigns in Ostrogothic Italy.   The authors of the *Liber pontificalis* created a powerful
picture of the popes and a coherent articulation of their ideological
and practical position, especially within the city of Rome itself, as the

[75] See the useful maps in Richard Krautheimer, *Rome: Profile of a City, 312–1308*
(Princeton, NJ, 1980), 32, 51, 74. For full documentation, see idem, Spencer Corbett
and Wolfgang Frankl, *Corpus Basilicarum Christianarum Romae. Le basiliche cristiane
antiche di Roma (sec. IV–IX) / The Early Christian Basilicas of Rome (IV–IX cent.)*, 5 vols,
Monumenti dell'antichità cristiana 2nd ser. 2 (Vatican City, 1937–77).
[76] 'Culmen apostolicum cum caelestinus haberet. Primus et in tot fulgeret episcopus
orbe': Life 46.9, *LP* 1: 235 (Davis, *Pontiffs*, 38); see Webb, *Churches and Catacombs*, 173;
for an illustration of figures of *ecclesia* and *synagoga*, see Brandenburg, *Die frühchristlichen
Kirchen*, 174.
[77] *LP* 1: 220 (Davis, *Pontiffs*, 32).
[78] *LP* 1: 150, 164, 238 (Davis, *Pontiffs*, 9, 13, 38–9). On Lucina, see Kate Cooper, 'The
Martyr, the *Matrona* and the Bishop: The Matron Lucina and the Politics of Martyr Cult
in Fifth- and Sixth-Century Rome', *EME* 8 (1999), 297–318.

rulers of Rome and of the Church. It is no accident that it was most probably during the pontificate of Pope Paul I (757–67) that the notorious claims in the document known as the *Constitutum Constantini* or Donation of Constantine were forged. There are close textual parallels with many details, especially the gifts of Constantine listed in the Life of Silvester. Most obviously, however, the ideological position adopted in the *Constitutum* and the *Liber pontificalis* is very similar, as the most striking sentences from the *Constitutum* demonstrate:

> This sacred church as we determine is to be named, honoured, venerated and proclaimed as the head and summit of all the churches throughout the whole world, just as we have determined through our other imperial decrees.

and further:

> ... the city of Rome and all the provinces of the whole of Italy and the western regions, their districts and cities, we grant and relinquish to that aforesaid pontiff of ours Silvester the universal pope; these ... are to be administered by his power and authority and that of the pontiffs who shall succeed him, and we grant that they shall remain under the jurisdiction of the sacred church of Rome.[79]

Charlemagne's conquest of the Lombard kingdom and the creation of an entirely different political configuration in the West certainly had long-term consequences for the papacy itself, but the deliberately imperial elements of papal self-presentation, quite apart from the importance of Rome's primacy, apostolic succession and orthodoxy articulated so emphatically within the *Liber pontificalis*, indicate the multitude of strands by which the papacy wove the fabric of its own *imperium* or power, an *imperium* like no other because of the apostolic claims to succession from Christ's disciple St Peter.

[79] '[Q]uam sacrosanctam ecclesiam caput et verticem omnium ecclesiarum in universo orbe terrarum dici, coli, venerari et praedicari sancimus, sicut per alia nostra imperialia decreta statuimus'; 'quamque Romae urbis et omnes Italiae seu occidentalium regionum provincias, loca et civitates saepefato beatissimo pontifici, patri nostro Silvestro, universali papae, contradentes atque relinquentes eius vel successorum ipsius pontificum potestati ... disponenda atque iuri sanctae Romanae ecclesiae concedimus permanenda': MGH Fontes iuris 10, 84, 93–4; ET M. Edwards, *Constantine and Christendom: The Oration to the Saints; The Greek and Latin Accounts of the Discovery of the Cross; The Edict of Constantine to Pope Silvester*, TTH 39 (Liverpool, 2003), 107, 113. For a useful survey of recent interpretations, albeit offering a later date for the composition of the text than I favour here, see Caroline J. Goodson and Janet L. Nelson, 'Review Article: The Roman Contexts of the "Donation of Constantine"', *EME* 18 (2010), 446–67.

Empire, Ethnic Election and Exegesis in the *Opus Caroli (Libri Carolini)*

Conor O'Brien*

Churchill College, Cambridge

Modern historians have long argued that the early medieval Franks thought themselves to be the chosen people or new Israel, especially as they gained a great empire under the Carolingian dynasty in the late eighth century. The Opus Caroli of Bishop Theodulf of Orléans has often been cited as one of the clearest expressions of this self-conception as God's elect. A massive work attacking the legitimacy of the Byzantine empire in the context of the iconoclasm dispute during the early 790s, it does indeed contest the Byzantine claim to be the Christian empire. But Theodulf's repeated statement that 'We are the spiritual Israel' is best understood not as an assertion of ethnic election, but as a reference to the Christian tradition of Scripture exegesis which should (he argues) underpin both the Frankish and the Byzantine understanding of images. The Carolingian claim to empire rested on the Frankish championing of the universal Church, and its traditions of orthodoxy and correct biblical interpretation.

'We, who are the spiritual Israel': thus spoke the imperious voice attributed to Charlemagne, the king of the Franks, in a massive theological treatise, the *Opus Caroli*, fulminating against the (as it saw them) heretical rulers of Byzantium.[1] Imperious, and perhaps even proto-imperial, for within less than a decade of those words being written Charlemagne had been crowned emperor in Rome. The *Opus Caroli* systematically attacked the acts of the second council of Nicaea (787) as having embraced the worship of images and condemned its convenors, the Empress Irene and her son Constantine VI, as unworthy of their position, claiming that their arrogance constituted blasphemy and their practices idolatry, and that their empire was the

* Churchill College, Storey's Way, Cambridge, CB3 0DS. E-mail: cpo32@cam.ac.uk.
  I am grateful to the Master and Fellows of Churchill College, Cambridge, for electing me to the research fellowship which made this work possible. Thanks are also due to Zachary Giuliano and to the anonymous readers for their detailed suggestions.

[1] '[N]os, qui spiritalis Israel sumus': *Opus Caroli regis contra synodum* [hereafter: *OC*] 1.17 (MGH Conc. 2 Suppl. 1, 183). All translations are my own.

Studies in Church History 54 (2018) 96–108   © Ecclesiastical History Society 2018
doi: 10.1017/stc.2017.6

spiritual descendant of pagan Babylon.[2] Unsurprisingly, then, recent studies of the *Opus Caroli* (previously known as the *Libri Carolini*) have presented it as the ideological preparation for the transformation of the kingdom of the Franks into an empire, seeking to replace the Greek empire with the 'new Israel' of the Franks.[3]

This reading of the *Opus* as celebrating the ethnic election of the Franks and their status as a chosen people is widespread in scholarship; the statement 'we, who are the spiritual Israel' is almost universally accepted as meaning that the Franks are the new Israel.[4] I know of only one explicit rejection of this interpretation, in a French doctoral thesis published in 2007.[5] This article, however, argues that the *Opus Caroli* presents Charlemagne as the pre-eminent ruler of the Christian world, not through the election of the Franks, but through his constant attention to Christian universality and orthodoxy. In the early ninth century, the Carolingians drew increasingly on an ideology of Christian empire by associating themselves with the promotion of orthodox religion in all places and amongst all peoples;[6] the

[2] *OC* 1.1–3, 3.15 (MGH Conc. 2 Suppl. 1, 105–24, 399–407). Ann Freeman argued that the *Opus Caroli* misrepresented the Nicene council, due to a poor Latin translation of its acts: 'Carolingian Orthodoxy and the Fate of the *Libri Carolini*', *Viator* 16 (1985), 65–108. Recent research has contested this, however, suggesting that the *Opus* displays a good understanding of the Greek arguments: Hans-Georg Thümmel, 'Die fränkische Reaktion auf das 2. Nicaenum 787 in den *Libri Carolini*', in Rainer Berndt, ed., *Das frankfurter Konzil von 794. Kristallisationspunkt karolingischer Kultur* (Mainz, 1997), 965–80; Thomas F. X. Noble, *Images, Iconoclasm, and the Carolingians* (Philadelphia, PA, 2009), 181–3.
[3] Noble, *Images*, chs 4–5; idem, 'Tradition and Learning in Search of Ideology: The *Libri Carolini*', in Richard Sullivan, ed., *'The Gentle Voices of Teachers': Aspects of Learning in the Carolingian Age* (Columbus, OH, 1995), 227–60; Kristina Mitalaité, *Philosophie et théologie de l'image dans les* Libri Carolini (Paris, 2007), 51. But contrast Alberto Ricciardi, 'Prima dell'impero. Antagonismo Franco-Bizantino, identità politiche e ideologia dal mito delle origini Troiane all'*Opus Caroli regis contra Synodum* (*Libri Carolini*)', *Rivista Storica Italiana* 125 (2013), 643–80.
[4] Elisabeth Dahlhaus-Berg, *Nova Antiquitas et Antiqua Novitas. Typologische Exegese und isidorianisches Geschichtsbild bei Theodulf von Orléans* (Cologne, 1975), 196; Celia Chazelle, 'Matter, Spirit, and Image in the *Libri Carolini*', *Recherches Augustiniennes* 21 (1986), 163–84, at 184; Noble, 'Tradition and Learning', 239–40, 249; Karl F. Morrison, 'Anthropology and the Use of Religious Images in the *Opus Caroli Regis* (*Libri Carolini*)', in Jeffrey F. Hamburger and Anne-Marie Bouché, eds, *The Mind's Eye: Art and Theological Argument in the Middle Ages* (Princeton, NJ, 2006), 32–45, at 36.
[5] Mitalaité, *Philosophie et théologie*, 411. Ricciardi, 'Antagonismo Franco-Bizantino', 667–8, does not address the phrase, but the implications of his argument are that he would reject it as a claim for Frankish election.
[6] For example, Jonathan P. Conant, 'Louis the Pious and the Contours of Empire', *EME* 22 (2014), 336–60, especially 357–9; Mayke de Jong, 'The Empire that was Always

Opus Caroli already encouraged such an imperial vision of Charlemagne's power in the 790s. In it the 'spiritual Israel' represented the community of all orthodox Christians.

That the Franks under Charlemagne and his Carolingian predecessors considered themselves a chosen people, the new Israel, was simply accepted for much of the twentieth century.[7] After all, Charlemagne's grandfather Charles Martel had been compared to Joshua for defending the faith from heathens, while his father Pippin was remembered as having been anointed king of the Franks on the model of the Old Testament monarchs, and the great Charles himself was nicknamed David by his court intellectuals.[8] However, in 2000 Mary Garrison published an important article arguing that the Frankish identification with Israel had been exaggerated, coming later and more slowly than traditionally thought.[9] Subsequent work has questioned the old assumption that the Carolingian Franks considered themselves to be the chosen people;[10] many scholars now argue that, while earlier in the eighth century the Carolingians utilized ideas of Frankish ethnic and religious superiority to strengthen their position as they seized power, Charlemagne's reign, with its vast expansion of Carolingian territories into a multi-ethnic empire, saw a shift to a rhetoric which drew on a Christian ideology and which was intended

---

Decaying: The Carolingians (800–888)', *Medieval Worlds* 2 (2015), 6–25, especially 14–15 [online journal], at: <https://www.medievalworlds.net/0xc1aa5576_0x00329658.pdf>, last accessed 12 December 2017.

[7] For example, Ernst Kantorowicz, *Laudes Regiae: A Study in Liturgical Acclamations and Medieval Ruler Worship* (Berkeley, CA, 1946), 56–9; Eugen Ewig, 'Zum christlichen Königsgedanken im Frühmittelalter', in Hartmut Atsma, ed., *Spätantikes und fränkisches Gallien. Gesammelte Schriften (1952–1973)*, 3 vols (Munich, 1976), 1: 3–71, at 41–5; Janet L. Nelson, 'The Lord's Anointed and the People's Choice: Carolingian Royal Ritual', in David Cannadine and Simon Prince, eds, *Rituals of Royalty: Power and Ceremonial in Traditional Societies* (Cambridge, 1987), 137–80, reprinted in eadem, *The Frankish World, 750–900* (London, 1996), 99–131.

[8] Continuation of Fredegar, *Historia vel gesta Francorum* 20 (MGH SRM 2, 177); *Royal Frankish Annals, s.a.* 750 (MGH SRG i.u.s. 6, 8, 10); Alcuin, *Epistola* 41 (MGH Epp. 4, 84).

[9] Mary Garrison, 'The Franks as the New Israel: Education for an Identity from Pippin to Charlemagne', in Yitzhak Hen and Matthew Innes, eds, *The Uses of the Past in Early Medieval Europe* (Cambridge, 2000), 114–61.

[10] Mayke de Jong, 'The State of the Church: *Ecclesia* and Early Medieval State Formation', in Walter Pohl and Veronika Wieser, eds, *Der frühmittelalterliche Staat – europäische Perspektiven* (Vienna, 2009), 241–54, at 250–1; Gerda Heydemann and Walter Pohl, 'The Rhetoric of Election – 1 Peter 2.9 and the Franks', in Doreen van Espelo et al., eds, *Religious Franks: Religion and Power in the Frankish Kingdoms. Studies in Honour of Mayke de Jong* (Manchester, 2016), 13–31.

'to meld together and unite diverse communities'.[11] The rulers of the Frankish empire saw themselves as having a special relationship with God, but increasingly grounded this in a (universal) Christian, rather than Frankish, identity. In the context of this scholarship we should nuance older ideas that the *Opus Caroli* asserted a Frankish identification with the new Israel.

Such interpretations of the *Opus* certainly sit uneasily with the recognition, now established beyond all reasonable doubt, that its author was not a Frank at all. The text as it stands was primarily the work of one man: the Spanish-born Visigoth, Theodulf, later archbishop of Orléans.[12] Theodulf worked on behalf of Charlemagne, in whose voice the text speaks; the king's circle of theologians and advisers seem initially to have mapped out Theodulf's programme of writing, and his text ended up being read and approved by Charlemagne, whose comments appear as marginal glosses in the original manuscript surviving in the Vatican.[13] While the impact of the *Opus Caroli* remains unclear, that it represented a grand politico-ideological statement arising from Carolingian elite discussion, as Thomas Noble argued, seems very likely.[14] It reflected not just the genuine horror felt by devout Carolingians at what they read in the acts of the second Nicene council, but also some of the ideology of Charlemagne's regime in the years leading up to the king's imperial coronation on Christmas Day 800.

While for much of the 780s relations between the Byzantine empire and the Franks had been good, they soured violently at the end of that decade. That development provides the context for the savagery with which the Empress Irene and her son, the Emperor Constantine,

---

[11] Quotation from Matthew Innes, '"Immune from Heresy": Defining the Boundaries of Carolingian Christianity', in Paul Fouracre and David Ganz, eds, *Frankland: The Franks and the World of the Early Middle Ages. Essays in Honour of Dame Jinty Nelson* (Manchester, 2008), 101–25, at 124. See also De Jong, 'State of the Church', 248–51; Helmut Reimitz, *History, Frankish Identity and the Framing of Western Ethnicity, 550–850* (Cambridge, 2015), 295–422, 451–5.

[12] Ann Freeman, *Theodulf of Orléans: Charlemagne's Spokesman against the Second Council of Nicaea* (Aldershot, 2003).

[13] Janet L. Nelson, 'The Voice of Charlemagne', in Richard Gameson and Henrietta Leyser, eds, *Belief and Culture in the Middle Ages: Studies Presented to Henry Mayr-Harting* (Oxford, 2001), 76–88, at 77.

[14] Noble, 'Tradition and Learning', 232, 249–50. Freeman argued that Charlemagne discontinued the project when faced with papal support for Nicaea II: 'Carolingian Orthodoxy'. More recently, Noble has proposed that Rome and the Franks agreed to disagree: *Images*, 172–8.

were denied the status of true Christian rulers in the *Opus Caroli*.[15] Moreover, in the early 790s, as Theodulf worked on countering the decisions of the Eastern council, Charlemagne moved to contest the Byzantine imperial claims that they defended orthodoxy and the universal Church. In 794 he held a church council at Frankfurt which dealt both with the question of the Eastern attitudes to images and with the adoptionist heresy which the court theologians had identified as recently emerging in Spain.[16] Whether Charlemagne intended Frankfurt, which brought together 'all the bishops of the kingdom of the Franks, or of Italy, Aquitaine and Provence',[17] to be an ecumenical council remains unclear, but that was certainly how it was remembered: as a direct rejection of Nicaea II's claims to universal jurisdiction.[18] The *Opus Caroli* denied the Greeks any right to claim that Nicaea was an ecumenical council, and proposed a new basis upon which a council could be deemed universal, probably with preparations for Frankfurt in mind.[19] It also highlighted the multi-ethnic nature of Charlemagne's empire, and his work and that of his predecessors in spreading Roman Christianity to new peoples: 'not only the provinces of all Gaul and Germany and Italy, but even the Saxons and certain peoples of the northern region are recognized as converting to the beginnings of the true faith through us'.[20] Theodulf's text should therefore be read as part of a wider move towards claiming that

[15] Michael McCormick, 'Western Approaches (700–900)', in Jonathan Shepard, ed., *The Cambridge History of the Byzantine Empire, c.500–1492* (Cambridge, 2009), 395–432, at 414–17; Leslie Brubaker and John Haldon, *Byzantium in the Iconoclast Era, c.680–850* (Cambridge, 2011), 258–9. For the circumstances of Irene and Constantine's reign in relation to the council of Nicaea, see ibid. 260–76.

[16] John C. Cavadini, *The Last Christology of the West: Adoptionism in Spain and Gaul, 785–820* (Philadelphia, PA, 1993); Florence Close, *Uniformiser la foi pour unifier l'Empire. Contribution à l'histoire de la pensée politico-théologique de Charlemagne* (Brussels, 2011).

[17] 'Coniungentibus … cunctis regni Francorum seu Italiae, Aquitaniae, Provintiae episcopis ac sacerdotibus synodali concilio': *Capitulare Francofurtense* 1 (MGH Conc. 2.i, 165).

[18] Marie-France Auzépy, 'Francfort et Nicée II', in Berndt, ed., *Das frankfurter Konzil*, 279–300, at 289–90; Close, *Uniformiser la foi*, 126–9; Noble, *Images*, 169–72, 178–80; *Royal Frankish Annals* (and their ninth-century reworking), *s.a.* 794 (MGH SRG i.u.s. 6, 94–5); *Annals of Lorsch*, *s.a.* 794 (MGH SS 1, 35–6).

[19] *OC* 3.11, 4.13, 4.28 (MGH Conc. 2 Suppl. 1, 376–8, 515–22, 557–8); Close, *Uniformiser la foi*, 144–9.

[20] 'Quod non solum omnium Galliarum provinciae et Germania sive Italia, sed etiam Saxones et quaedam aquilonalis plagae gentes per nos … ad verę fidei rudimenta conversae facere noscuntur': *OC* 1.6 (MGH Conc. 2 Suppl. 1, 136).

the Frankish empire was now the true Christian empire, successor to that which had overseen the earlier ecumenical councils, marked with the clear signs of catholic imperialism: orthodoxy and universality.[21]

But did being the new Israel contribute to becoming the new empire? The most recent major study of the *Opus Caroli* in English has no doubt about this: Noble understands Theodulf's message to be that 'Charlemagne is like David, and the Franks are a new chosen people';[22] the 'Franks were the direct heirs of Israel'.[23] In arguing against this interpretation of the *Opus*, I structure my response around a new reading of the text's mention of the 'spiritual Israel'. I maintain that the phrase does not evidence Frankish belief in their election: firstly, because there is little reason to suppose that the 'we' in question refers to the Franks; secondly, because the language appears in a commentary on Christian exegesis, emphasizing separation from the Old Testament and the Jewish past; and thirdly, because 'spiritual Israel' is a patristic term for the universal Church of all peoples.

A contrast between 'us' and 'them' appears frequently in the *Opus Caroli*, meaning that scholars often portray the work as presenting a sharp distinction between good Franks and bad Greeks,[24] but the Franks themselves are never mentioned in the *Opus Caroli*. The only appearance of the word *Franci* comes at the very start of the work in the title given to Charlemagne: 'by the will of God, King of the Franks, ruling Gaul, Germany and Italy, and their neighbouring provinces'.[25]   The *Opus*'s targets are occasionally referred to as 'Greeks' (*Gręci*) or 'Easterners' (*Orientales*), but Theodulf only once presented the theological debate as a contest between East and West, in his preface.[26]   He much preferred to associate his opponents, rather than the 'we' of the text, with ethnic or geographic

---

[21] Dahlhaus-Berg, *Nova Antiquitas*, 200–1; Auzépy, 'Francfort et Nicée II', 299–300.
[22] Noble, *Images*, 209.
[23] Ibid. 234.
[24] Chazelle, 'Matter, Spirit, and Image', 176; Noble, 'Tradition and Learning', 241–4; Morrison, 'Anthropology', 33–4.
[25] 'NUTU DEI REGIS FRANCORUM, GALLIAS, GERMANIAM ITALIAMQUE SIVE HARUM FINITIMAS PROVINTIAS … REGENTIS': *OC* preface (MGH Conc. 2 Suppl. 1, 97). This was not the standard form of Charlemagne's title in the early 790s, which was usually 'king of the Franks and Lombards, and patrician of the Romans'.
[26] 'Contra cuius errores ideo scribere conpulsi sumus, ut … inertem vel potius inermem orientali de parte venientem hostem occidua in parte per nos favente Deo adlata sanctorum patrum sententia feriat' ('Against whose errors therefore we are compelled to write, so that … the opinion of the holy fathers, conveyed (with God's support) through us in

identities.[27] In doing so, he implied that the 'church of one region' had heretically sought 'to anathematize the churches of the whole world'.[28] Theodulf often contrasted 'us' with 'them'[29] (or even 'you'[30]) in purely religious terms, usually referring to the incorrect Byzantines as 'those who adore images', on the basic principle that the *Opus* spoke for orthodox Christians against a group of heretics who talked 'irrationally and most stupidly' (restraint not being a feature of Theodulf's argumentative style).[31]

However, on some occasions the first person plural seems to include the Byzantines who venerate icons. Thus, when Theodulf condemned Irene and Constantine for declaring that God 'co-reigns with us', he picked up their 'us' and spoke in terms of all humans: 'when our being is so different from God's being, and our living so different from his living, and our reigning so different from his reigning, the madness of those who … say that they even co-reign with God ought to be more a source of grief than amazement'.[32] Theodulf moved on to the imperial use of the adjective 'divine' in Byzantium, which he saw as a pagan tradition; he declared: 'We … who both follow Truth and were redeemed by that Truth, just as we spurn the lie of the pagan gods, we ought to spurn pagan words.'[33] The phrase 'we ought' suggests that Theodulf was here lecturing the Byzantines on how all Christians should behave.[34] Theodulf's

---

the Western region, may strike the incompetent, or rather unarmed, enemy coming from the Eastern region'): *OC* preface (MGH Conc. 2 Suppl. 1, 101). Probably this represents the royal 'we' of Charlemagne's voice, used also elsewhere: *OC* 1.6, 4.3 (MGH Conc. 2 Suppl. 1, 136, 494–5).

[27] For Easterners, see *OC* preface, 1.6 (MGH Conc. 2 Suppl. 1, 98–9, 132); Theodulf described the priest John, the representative of the Eastern patriarchs, as 'legatus Orientalium' throughout the *Opus*, which may have been understood in this sense. For Greeks, see *OC* 3.11, 4.18, 4.23 (MGH Conc. 2 Suppl. 1, 375, 532, 546).

[28] '[U]nius partis ecclesia … totius mundi ecclesias conetur anathematizare': *OC* 3.11 (MGH Conc. 2 Suppl. 1, 376).

[29] *OC* 2.9, 2.31, 3.18 (MGH Conc. 2 Suppl. 1, 253, 325, 420).

[30] *OC* 2.30 (MGH Conc. 2 Suppl. 1, 317).

[31] For example, 'ut illi stultissime et inrationabiliter dicunt': *OC* 1.16 (MGH Conc. 2 Suppl. 1, 175).

[32] 'Cum ergo nostrum esse tantum distet a Dei esse et nostrum vivere ab eius vivere et nostrum regnare ab eius regnare, dolenda potius quam admiranda est illorum vęcordia, qui … Deum sibi conregnare etiam dicunt': *OC* 1.1 (MGH Conc. 2 Suppl. 1, 105).

[33] 'Nos … qui et Veritatis sectatores et ab ipsa Veritate redempti sumus, sicut sprevimus gentilium deorum mendacium, spernere debemus gentilia vocabula': *OC* 1.3 (MGH Conc. 2 Suppl. 1, 124).

[34] Cf. Lawrence Nees, *A Tainted Mantle: Hercules and the Classical Tradition at the Carolingian Court* (Philadelphia, PA, 1991), 118.

first person plural also included we 'who come to the faith after the Lord's incarnation', we 'who do not assert those things which were prophesied concerning the coming of Christ and the calling of the Gentiles to be future, but ... believe them to be past', and we 'who worship the one and only God';[35] in other words, 'we' in the *Opus Caroli* often simply means Christians, particularly the Gentiles, who came to the faith only after Christ's incarnation.[36]

That Christian identity proved important in the specific contexts in which Theodulf declared that 'we' are 'the spiritual Israel'. The bishops at Nicaea II had argued that the pictures of the saints encourage Christians to imitate the saints' way of life just as Moses had blue fringes added to the clothing of the Hebrews to remind them to obey God's commands. The *Opus Caroli* offered a different interpretation, explaining that Moses made the blue fringes:

> ... either in order to distinguish the people of Israel, so that [the fringes] might be a sign on clothing, just like circumcision was a sign on the body; or so that we, who are the spiritual Israel, might have a just and holy way of life as a garment, the extremities of which garment ought to be decorated with fringes, since our life ought to be instructed by the testimonies of holy Scripture.[37]

Two chapters later Theodulf addressed the Byzantine assertion that just as the Jews had been given the two cherubim which decorated the Ark of the Covenant, 'so the cross and images of the saints ... are given to us Christians to ... adore'.[38] He mocked the suggestion that 'those who followed the shadow of the Law' (i.e. the Hebrews) should have honoured divinely sanctioned sculptures, whereas 'we who follow the truth, which is Christ', would adore earthly objects

---

[35] '[N]obis, qui post incarnationem dominicam ad fidem venimus' (a quotation from Bede, *De Templo* 1 [CChr.SL 119A, 183]); 'Nos vero, qui ea, quae de Christi adventu et vocatione gentium prophetata sunt, non ut futura autumamus, sed ut prẹterita devota mente tenemus et credimus'; 'nos, qui uni et soli Deo ... servimus': *OC* 1.20, 2.11, 3.18 (MGH Conc. 2 Suppl. 1, 202, 257, 420).

[36] See also *OC* 3.15 (MGH Conc. 2 Suppl. 1, 405–6).

[37] '[S]ive *ad dinoscendum populum Israel*, ut essent signum in *veste*, sicut *circumcisio signum in corpore*, sive ut nos, qui spiritalis Israel sumus, habeamus pro indumento iustitiam et sanctam conversationem, huius indumenti extremitas fimbriis iacinctinis sit ornata, quatenus vita nostra sanctarum Scripturarum sit testimoniis erudita': *OC* 1.17 (MGH Conc. 2 Suppl. 1, 183); text in italics is from Jerome, *Commentarii in Matheum* 4 (CChr.SL 77, 211).

[38] '[S]ic nobis christianis donata est crux et sanctorum imagines ad ... adorandum': *OC* 1.19 (MGH Conc. 2 Suppl. 1, 192). Theodulf directly quotes the Latin translation of the Nicene acts available to him.

made by any craftsman.[39] Here, Theodulf was clearly picking up the contrast between Jews and 'us Christians' made in the Nicene acts in order to run with it to his rhetorical climax:

> We who do not follow the death-dealing letter but the life-giving spirit, who are not the carnal but the spiritual Israel, who having scorned visible things, contemplate the invisible, we give thanks to have received from the Lord not only mysteries greater than images, which lack all mystery, but greater and more lofty signs of mysteries than those same tables [of the Law] or the two cherubim. For clearly the tables and the two cherubim provided patterns of future things, and while the Jews had the things carnally which were hidden prefigurations in typological figures of future things, we hold spiritually in truth those things which were prefigured by those models or carnal prefigurations.[40]

When seen in their context, these claims that 'we' are 'the spiritual Israel' therefore have much more to do with exegesis than with ethnic election. In both cases Theodulf contested the Byzantine understanding of the Old Testament, suggesting that the Nicene fathers had missed the spiritual meaning of the objects in ancient Jewish cult; the Greeks ignored the fact that the Christian fulfilment of the Jewish material lies in the spirit, and not in a continuing veneration of matter, especially since this is now without the divine imprimatur which was given to the cherubim upon Mount Sinai. Exegesis forms a major theme in the *Opus Caroli*, as many scholars have already noted,[41] and the first two books of the work deal mostly with the council of Nicaea's second-rate understanding of Scripture. They make the point repeatedly that the Greeks failed to recognize that the Old Testament finds fulfilment in Christ's incarnation and therefore

---

[39] '[I]llos, qui umbram legis sequebantur, habuisse foederis tabulas continentes legis decalogum, nos, qui veritatem, quae Christus est, sequimur, habere opera quorumlibet artificum': *OC* 1.19 (MGH Conc. 2 Suppl. 1, 192–3).

[40] 'Nos enim, qui non sequimur litteram mortificantem, sed spiritum vivificantem, qui non carnalis, sed spiritalis Israhel sumus, qui spretis visibilibus invisibilia contemplamur, non solum imaginibus maiora mysteria, quae omni mysterio carent, sed ipsis tabulis seu duobus cherubim maiora et eminentiora mysteriorum insignia a Domino accepisse nos gratulamur. Cum videlicet tabulae et duo cherubim exemplaria fuerint futurorum, et cum Iudęi habuerint carnaliter res, quae typicis opertę figuris praefigurationes fuerint futurorum, nos habemus in veritate spiritaliter ea, quae illis exemplaribus sive pręfigurationibus carnalibus pręfigurabantur': *OC* 1.19 (MGH Conc. 2 Suppl. 1, 193).

[41] Dahlhaus-Berg, *Nova Antiquitas*, 191–5; Celia Chazelle, 'Images, Scripture, the Church, and the Libri Carolini', *Proceedings of the PMR Conference* 16–17 (1992–3), 53–76, at 59–61; Noble, *Images*, 187–91; Mitalaité, *Philosophie et théologie*, 410–13.

must be understood spiritually. For Theodulf, the ability to distinguish good exegesis from bad exegesis divided the Byzantines from 'us', clearly right-thinking Christians 'who with God's help understand the prophecy of the Psalms spiritually', and 'who, following the Apostle, understand the Law to be spiritual'.[42]

Such a spiritual understanding of the Old Testament as prefiguring the redeeming actions of Christ and their effects on the lives of believers constituted nothing more, of course, than the approach to Scripture bequeathed to the Middle Ages by the Church Fathers. For the Fathers this Christian exegesis stood sharply apart from an imaginary 'Jewish' understanding of the Bible.[43] Consequently, the purpose of Theodulf's explanations that the spiritual Israel ought to read Scripture spiritually was to suggest continuity, not between the Franks and Israel, but between the bishops of the second council of Nicaea and the Jews.[44] Theodulf borrowed his claim that we 'do not follow the death-dealing letter but the life-giving spirit' from Jerome, who differentiated Christian from Jewish interpretations of the prophets with these words.[45] The *Opus Caroli* therefore reminds the Byzantines that 'we Christians' should not understand things in a Jewish and earthly manner, but suggests that the Greeks were doing just that. In this context, 'we are not the carnal, but the spiritual Israel' asserted distance from, as much as continuity with, the Hebrew past.

The reference to the spiritual Israel was not, therefore, to the Franks as a chosen people, but simply to Christians, all of whom, both Franks and Greeks, ought to read the Bible spiritually. The phrase 'spiritual Israel' appears frequently in patristic and early medieval theology, almost always referring to the Christian people throughout the world. Jerome differentiated the carnal from the spiritual Israel to make the kind of Pauline point which underpins

---

[42] 'Nos autem, qui opitulante Deo psalmorum prophetiam spiritaliter ... intelligimus'; 'nos, qui secundum Apostolum legem spiritalem esse scimus': *OC* 1.30, 2.9 (MGH Conc. 2 Suppl. 1, 231, 253).

[43] R. A. Markus, 'The Jew as a Hermeneutic Device: The Inner Life of a Gregorian Topos', in John C. Cavadini, ed., *Gregory the Great: A Symposium* (London, 1995), 1–15; Paula Fredriksen, *Augustine and the Jews: A Christian Defense of Jews and Judaism* (New York, 2008), 73–8.

[44] The Nicene bishops are compared to Pharisees at *OC* 1.17 (MGH Conc. 2 Suppl. 1, 184).

[45] 'Nos enim, qui non sequimur litteram mortificantem, sed spiritum vivificantem': *OC* 1.19 (MGH Conc. 2 Suppl. 1, 193); 'Nos autem qui non sequimur occidentem litteram, sed spiritum uiuificantem': Jerome, *Commentarii in prophetas minores: In Sophoniam* 3 (CChr.SL 76A, 700); a borrowing not noted by the excellent MGH edition.

Theodulf's use of the terms in relation to matter versus spirit.[46] Bede (d. 735) emphasized Christian universality; the phrase 'spiritual Israel' could refer to 'the Christian people', 'the Catholic, that is universal, Church' or simply the people 'who will be saved in Christ from all the nations of the earth'.[47] The clearest patristic use of the phrase comes in Augustine's *De doctrina christiana*, where he explained that in the Bible the species could sometimes refer to the genus, that is that a scriptural mention of a single city, nation or human could signify all cities, nations or humanity.[48] One must differentiate between those occasions when the species represents the genus and those when it does not, that is, between the passages in which Scripture is speaking of the spiritual Israel and those which refer to the carnal:

> Thus, the spiritual Israel consists, not of one nation, but of all the nations which were promised to the fathers in their seed, which is Christ. This spiritual Israel, therefore, is distinguished from the carnal Israel which is of one nation, by novelty of grace, not by nobility of homeland, in mind, not in nation.[49]

Theodulf knew his Augustine well and *De doctrina christiana* has been identified as an important source for the *Opus Caroli*.[50] Augustine's affirmation that members of the spiritual Israel are not distinguished by ethnic descent even finds an echo in a hymn written by Theodulf for Palm Sunday, in which the Christian boys processing compare themselves to the Jews who gathered on the original Palm Sunday: 'The glory of noble blood made them Hebrews; / behold, the godly crossing over makes us Hebrews.'[51] The patristic meaning

---

[46] Jerome, *Commentarii in Esaiam* 6.15.1 (CChr.SL 73, 254).

[47] '[S]piritalis Israhel, id est populi christiani': Bede, *Homeliae evangelii* 1.17 (CChr.SL 122, 124); 'catholica, id est universalis, ecclesia spiritalis uidelicet Israhel': idem, *In primam partem Samuhelis* 1 (CChr.SL 119, 38–9); 'illa propagationem carnalis Israhel ista spiritalis significat … qui de uniuersis cognationibus terrae in Christo saluator': idem, *In Genesim* 3 (CChr.SL 118A, 169).

[48] Augustine, *De doctrina christiana* 3.34.47 (CChr.SL 32, 106–7).

[49] 'Sic fit Israhel spiritalis non unius gentis, sed omnium, quae promissae sunt patribus in eorum semine, quod est Christus. Hic ergo Israhel spiritalis ab illo Israhele carnali, qui est unius gentis, nouitate gratiae, non nobilitate patriae, et mente, non gente distinguitur': Augustine, *De doctrina christiana* 3.34.48–9 (CChr.SL 32, 109).

[50] Celia Chazelle, '"Not in Painting but in Writing": Augustine and the Supremacy of the Word in the *Libri Carolini*', in Edward English, ed., *Reading and Wisdom: The* De doctrina Christiana *of Augustine in the Middle Ages* (Notre Dame, IN, 1995), 1–22. Theodulf also knew the writings of Jerome and Bede well.

[51] 'Fecerat Hebraeos hos gloria sanguinis alti: / Nos facit Hebraeos transitus ecce pius': Theodulf, *Carmina* 69 (MGH Poetae 1, 558). The *transitus* is presumably both the

of the phrase 'spiritual Israel' matches the significance of its uses in the *Opus Caroli* as explored above. This is unsurprising, considering the depth of Theodulf's patristic knowledge displayed throughout the treatise.

'Spiritual Israel', thus, does not claim for the Franks the status of the chosen people as the successors of Old Testament Israel. Indeed, such an interpretation of Theodulf's words hardly makes sense when 'we' appears in many contexts in the *Opus* but never refers explicitly to the Frankish people, when the phrase has a long patristic history, certainly known to Theodulf, in which it signified the universal Christian people, and when it appears in the context of discussions concerning correct Christian exegesis which emphasize the difference, and not the sameness, of the old and new dispensations. Through a case-study analysis of this one phrase we can, therefore, question the reading of the *Opus Caroli* as presenting the Franks as a chosen people. Instead, the Carolingians grounded their claims to superiority over the Byzantines in the universal Christian standards which the Greeks had failed to meet. The *Opus Caroli* does slip into a kind of Western parochialism on occasion, in its clear preference for evidence from the Latin Fathers and its emphasis on the special status of the Roman Church (without any acknowledgement that the papacy's support for the doctrines of Nicaea II established their orthodoxy).[52] Nonetheless, my analysis reveals the importance of universalism to the assault on Byzantine legitimacy at Charlemagne's court in the early 790s.[53]

This makes sense against the background of wider changes in the politicized use of identity in the Carolingian world, and Theodulf's work may be best understood as part of the shift within Carolingian ideology from a close identification with the Frankish *gens* towards universalizing claims to Christian empire, claims which are echoed in other theological arguments emerging from Charlemagne's circle in the early 790s. When the Frankish bishops rebuked their Spanish colleagues for embracing adoptionism, they presented themselves as

---

Christian's crossing from earthly to heavenly things mentioned next in the poem and Christ's crossing over in death on the cross; it also hints at the crossing from species to genus, a movement Augustine expressed using *transire*: *De doctrina christiana* 3.34.48–9 (CChr.SL 32, 107, 109).

[52] *OC* 1.6, 2.17 (MGH Conc. 2 Suppl. 1, 132–5, 267); Close, *Uniformiser la foi*, 147–50.

[53] See Thomas F. X. Noble, 'Review Article: From the *Libri Carolini* to the *Opus Caroli Regis*', *Journal of Medieval Latin* 9 (1999), 131–47, at 138.

'all the bishops of Germany, Gaul and Aquitaine' speaking with the 'entire clergy of the Catholic peace' to defend the universal Church from the errors of peripheral Christians;[54] the contemporaneous Carolingian assault on Byzantine error rested upon the same ideological foundations. The 794 Council of Frankfurt showed Charlemagne as he wished to be seen: defending 'everywhere' and 'in all things … the orthodox faith, both handed down by apostolic teachers and preserved by the universal Church'.[55] Charlemagne was not an ecumenist, pushing a neutral Christian identity. Such claims to care for the universal Church were just as self-interested and self-important as claims to be the new Israel would have been – but they were different claims.

Theodulf in the *Opus Caroli*, with hyperbolic literalism, revealed how the Greeks had lost sight of the universal Church. The acts of Nicaea II anathematized anyone who 'does not instruct the entire people beloved by Christ to adore images', revealing that the Byzantines had forgotten that the Christian people was a vast group spread throughout the whole world, and that it was therefore impossible for any one person to instruct all Christians in their entirety.[56] 'Almost the entire world is filled with Christ's people', Theodulf declared, in words which received Charlemagne's enthusiastic approbation when the *Opus Caroli* was read out at court. His approval is noted in the margin of the manuscript preserved in the Vatican.[57] The Franks presented themselves as deserving the leadership of the Christian empire, but they did not need to be the chosen people or a new Israel for that; they just needed to speak up for all those things the Eastern emperors had forgotten: the orthodox faith, correct interpretation of Scripture and the universal Church.

---

[54] 'Sancta synodus et venerabiles in Christo patres cum omnibus episcopis Germaniae, Galliae et Aequitaniae et toto catholicae pacis clero praesulibus Hispaniae': the Frankish bishops to the bishops of Spain (MGH Conc. 2.i, 143).

[55] 'Hanc igitur fidem orthodoxam et ab apostolicis traditam doctoribus et ab universali servatam ecclesia nos … ubique in omnibus servare et praedicare profitemur': Charlemagne to the bishops of Spain (MGH Conc. 2.i, 158). On these letters (both of which Alcuin probably wrote), see Close, *Uniformiser la foi*, 115–19; Owen M. Phelan, *The Formation of Christian Europe: The Carolingians, Baptism, and the* Imperium Christianum (Oxford, 2014), 53–6.

[56] 'Anathematizat enim, "qui non instruunt omnem Christo dilectum populum adorare imagines"': *OC* 3.7 (MGH Conc. 2 Suppl. 1, 368).

[57] '[V]idelicet pene totus mundus Christi populo plenus sit': *OC* 3.7 (MGH Conc. 2 Suppl. 1, 368); the marginal note reads 'summe': 'excellently [said]'.

Super gentes et regna: Papal 'Empire' in the Later Eleventh and Twelfth Centuries

Benedict G. E. Wiedemann*

University College London

Papal relations with monarchs in the later eleventh and twelfth centuries have often been characterized as 'feudal', as indicative of some sort of papal dominium mundi, *or as an effort to advance papal 'empire' over the kingdoms of Christendom. More recent scholarship has drawn a distinction between 'protection' and 'feudal' relationships with kings. However, the supposed distinction between the papacy's temporal overlordship of rulers and its spiritual protection may have obscured more than it has revealed. It was only after the disputes over lay investiture of bishops in the period 1078–1122 that a distinctive protective relationship began to emerge. Previously, rulers had been willing to 'accept their kingdom from the pope's hand' or to participate in ceremonies of investiture. In the twelfth century these relationships became more codified and any suggestion that the papacy actually gave kingdoms to kings faded. Thus, the nature of papal 'empire' – or, at least, temporal authority over kings – changed markedly during this period.*

The imperial ambitions of the eleventh-, twelfth- and thirteenth-century popes are well known. Pope Gregory VII (1073–85) wrote in his *Dictatus papae* that only the pope had the right to use the imperial insignia.[1] The popes who followed Gregory VII continued to 'imperialize' the papacy: Bernard of Clairvaux would accuse his protégé, Eugenius III (1145–53), of being 'the heir not of Peter, but of Constantine'.[2] One collection of essays about Innocent III

---

* 7 Lenton Road, The Park, Nottingham; NG7 1DP. E-mail: benedict.wiedemann.09@ucl.ac.uk.

[1] *Das Register Gregors VII.*, ed. Erich Caspar, 2 vols (Berlin, 1920–3), 1: 201–8 (no. 2.55a) [hereafter: *Greg. Reg.*].

[2] Ian S. Robinson, *The Papacy, 1073–1198: Continuity and Innovation* (Cambridge, 1990), 18–26; cf. the recent critique by Dale Kinney, 'Patronage of Art and Architecture', in John Doran and Damian J. Smith, eds, *Pope Innocent II (1130–43): The World vs the City* (London, 2016), 352–88.

Studies in Church History 54 (2018) 109–122   © Ecclesiastical History Society 2018
doi: 10.1017/stc.2017.7

(1198–1216) even posed the question as to whether he was 'Vicar of Christ or Lord of the World?'[3]

If we accept this narrative of imperialization – and there have been criticisms of it – then we must ask further questions: what exactly was the nature of papal *imperium* over the kings of Christian Europe? What, in the later eleventh and twelfth centuries, was the 'constitutional' position of secular rulers vis-à-vis the pope?

The stock answer has been feudalism. The great twentieth-century historian of the medieval papacy, Walter Ullmann, claimed that, in the late eleventh and early twelfth centuries, the newly active Roman papacy sought to bring the monarchs of Europe under their 'feudal lordship':

> … the king … had to surrender his land into full papal ownership … and receive … it back as a fief, so that he became legally an usufructuary. In recognition of his usufruct and of the Petrine protection the king … undertook to render certain services, be they in the form of an annual money payment – *census* or tribute – or in the form of military duties.[4]

Essentially, a king would genuinely give his kingdom to the pope so that the pope became the actual owner of the kingdom.

The two best-known cases of this so-called papal feudal overlordship were the Norman states in southern Italy and the kingdom of Aragon. The German medievalist Johannes Fried, however, made a strong argument in 1980 that the kingdom of Aragon was under papal protection, akin to monasteries which were placed under the protection of St Peter, and argued that such a position granted the papacy no real rights of ownership. It gave the papacy the right to receive an annual payment (the *census*) but the papacy's authority over the kingdom was limited to that payment; it was not evidence of genuine ownership. Fried contrasted this explicitly with the relationship between the papacy and the Normans in southern Italy, where (he thought) the papacy genuinely owned the Norman lands, and

---

[3] James Powell, ed., *Innocent III: Vicar of Christ or Lord of the World?*, 2nd edn (Washington DC, 1994).
[4] Walter Ullmann, *The Growth of Papal Government in the Middle Ages: A Study in the Ideological Relation of Clerical to Lay Power*, 2nd edn (London, 1962), 333; others of this opinion are cited in Robinson, *Papacy*, 302–3.

granted them to the Normans under some form of revocable tenure.[5] Fried, like Ullmann, still believed that the Norman states were under papal feudal lordship. Since Fried's book, little attention has been paid to papal dominion over kings from a comparative perspective. Alfons Becker, following Fried's work, suggested a vague third category between feudal overlordship and protection: 'fidélités non vassaliques'. However, he followed Fried in believing that a distinction between overlordship (as in Sicily and Southern Italy) and protection (as in Aragon) existed in the eleventh century.[6]

In the most recent contribution to the question of papal 'feudal lordship', Stefan Weinfurter identified a change in papal-royal relations in the first half of the twelfth century. He argued that the papacy adopted some feudal terminology and rituals to structure its relations with rulers around and after 1120 (although 'feudal bonds' were never the basis of papal authority).[7] Weinfurter interpreted the ceremony of homage as an intrinsically feudal ritual and regarded its performance in papal-royal relations after 1120 as evidence of the invasion of 'feudal ideas' into the curia.[8] However, the performance of the homage ritual does not allow us to be certain about the nature of papal dominion. Homage is a ritual with a wide range of uses and interpretations which cannot be reduced simply to 'feudal'.[9] The approach adopted here will be to look to ideas about investiture and coronation.

This article will focus on the terminology used in letters between popes and secular rulers during the late eleventh and twelfth centuries; and on what that terminology tells us about how papal-royal relations were conceived. The question is basic: did secular rulers really see themselves as receiving their lands from the pope? What was

[5] Johannes Fried, *Der päpstliche Schutz für Laienfürsten. Die politische Geschichte des päpstlichen Schutzprivilegs für Laien (11.–13. Jahrhundert)* (Heidelberg, 1980), 53–87.
[6] Alfons Becker, 'Politique féodale de la papauté à l'égard des rois et des princes (XIᵉ–XIIᵉ siècles)', in *Chiesa e mondo feudale nei secoli X–XII. Atti della dodicesima Settimana internazionale di studio. Mendola 24–28 Agosto 1992* (Milan, 1995), 411–46, at 419–23, 433–5.
[7] Stefan Weinfurter, 'Die Päpste als "Lehnsherren" von Königen und Kaisern im 11. und 12. Jahrhundert?', in Karl-Heinz Spieß, ed., *Ausbildung und Verbreitung des Lehnswesens im Reich und in Italien im 12. und 13. Jahrhundert* (Ostfildern, 2013), 17–40, at 26–7, 40; my thanks to Michael Schwab for bringing this work to my attention.
[8] Ibid. 25–6.
[9] Paul Hyams, 'Homage and Feudalism: A Judicious Separation', in Natalie Fryde, Pierre Monnet and Otto-Gerhard Oexle, eds, *Die Gegenwart des Feudalismus* (Göttingen, 2002), 13–50.

the nature of papal *imperium* over the monarchs of Europe? I will
argue that in the later eleventh and early twelfth centuries there was
not yet any clear distinction between so-called protection, of the type
which Fried saw between the papacy and Aragon, and the language
used to describe the relationship between the Normans in Sicily and
the pope, which Fried, Weinfurter and many others have called 'feudal overlordship'. Further, the language used to describe the bonds
between popes and both Aragonese and Norman rulers was similar to
that used to describe (and indeed condemn) lay investiture, the practice whereby it was monarchs rather than archbishops or the pope
who ceremonially appointed bishops and abbots. It was around the
1120s to 1150s that this 'language of investiture' ceased to be used
to describe papal-royal relations and it seems likely that this was an
unintended consequence of the end of lay investiture of bishops between *c.*1078 and 1122. Once we have recognized the similarities
between lay investiture and the bonds between pope and kings, it is
possible to determine a new interpretation of how papal *imperium*
over kings was understood, and how it changed.

Aragon, the Normans and the 'language of investiture'

From the early eleventh century, groups of Normans fought as merce-
naries in Southern Italy and eventually sought to take over the coun-
ties and principalities of Southern Italy for themselves. To legitimize their usurpations of these territories, some Norman rulers sought
papal approval. Although they were initially rebuffed, in 1059 an
alliance was formed between the pope and the two most powerful
Norman rulers in the south of Italy. These two potentates, the duke
of Apulia and the prince of Capua, swore oaths to the pope, undertook to give a specified annual payment to him and promised to help
him retain the Roman papacy if necessary.[10] Importantly, however,
we know that the duke of Apulia and the prince of Capua were 'invested' with their lands by the pope. We know this not merely from
chronicle sources, but from the texts of the oaths themselves which
the Norman prince and duke swore, and which were kept by the papal court: in the eleventh century all such oaths end with the Norman
saying: 'I will observe this fidelity to your successors … who … will

[10] Donald Matthew, *The Norman Kingdom of Sicily* (Cambridge, 1992), 9–32.

confirm the investiture' (*investitura*).[11] From the register of Gregory VII, we even have the text of such an investiture; it simply states: 'I, Pope Gregory, invest (*investio*) you, Duke Robert, with the land which my predecessors conceded to you.'[12] Clearly therefore, in the eleventh century, the pope ceremonially invested the Norman rulers.

The kings of Aragon, during the same period, also initiated a special relationship with the papal court. Exactly when this relationship began is difficult to know but it might stem from 1068 when the king, Sancho Ramirez, went on a pilgrimage to Rome. By 1089 the king had established an annual payment to Rome, as he told Pope Urban II in a letter, and as the pope accepted in his reply to Sancho.[13] It is difficult to know whether Sancho was seeking papal legitimation for his rule over the nascent kingdom of Aragon, as the Normans were for their rule over Sicily and Southern Italy. By contrast with the Normans, there is no evidence that Sancho participated in an investiture ceremony, nor was the term 'investiture' used in the letters between Sancho and the pope. However, a papal privilege of 1089 for the royal monastic foundation of Montearagon, and for Sancho himself, claimed the king's successors should 'accept that kingdom from our hand or from the hand of our successors'.[14] In 1095, Sancho's son, Peter I, told Urban II in a letter that he had 'placed himself under your lordship'.[15] And again, also in 1095, in another privilege for the king, which gave the king freedom from excommunication unless it was pronounced by the pope, Urban II told Peter that 'all your successors should accept that kingdom from our hand or the hand of our successors'.[16] Thus, it appears at first glance that my

---

[11] 'Hanc fidelitatem observabo tuis successoribus ... qui ... firmaverunt investituram': *Das Papsttum und die süditalienischen Normannenstaaten, 1053–1212*, ed. Josef Deér (Göttingen, 1969), 17–18, 21–2, 23, 31, 32 (nos. IV/2; VII/1; VIII/1; IX/18a–b).

[12] Vatican City, ASV, Registrum Vaticanum 2, fols 194ʳ⁻ᵛ; *Greg. Reg.*, 2: 515–16 (no. 8.1b); ET *The Register of Pope Gregory VII 1073–1085: An English Translation*, transl. Herbert Edward John Cowdrey (Oxford, 2002), 365.

[13] Robert Somerville and Stephan Kuttner, *Pope Urban II, the 'Collectio Britannica', and the Council of Melfi (1089)* (Oxford, 1996), 97–9, 155–62 (nos 27a, 41a).

[14] '[O]mnes eius successores regnum illud de manu nostra nostrorumve successorum accipiant': Fried, *Der päpstlicher Schutz*, 327–8 (no. 1).

[15] Paul Kehr, *Das Papsttum und die Königreiche Navarra und Aragon bis zur Mitte des XII Jahrhunderts* (Berlin, 1928), 55–7 (no. 1).

[16] '[O]mnes tui successores regnum illud de manu nostra nostrorumve successorum accipiant': *Innocentii III Romani Pontificis regestorum sive epistolarum liber decimus sextus*, PL 216, cols 888–9 (no. 87). This privilege is known only from a *de verbo ad verbum* reissue for King Peter II in 1213.

suggestion – that the terminology used for the Normans and for the Aragonese was the same – must be wrong. The Normans were invested (*investitura*) while the Aragonese were told to 'receive the kingdom' from the pope's hand. But if we turn to the language being used to condemn lay investiture at this time, we can see that in fact investiture and 'accepting something from the hand' are closely connected.

In 1078, a council of Gregory VII declared: 'it is forbidden that anyone should accept investiture of churches from the hand of laymen';[17] in 1089: 'No-one should dare to take investiture of abbey or bishopric or any ecclesiastical dignity from a lay hand';[18] in 1114: 'we forbid that anyone should accept investiture of any ecclesiastical dignity from the hand of the emperor, or a king, or prince or any lay person'.[19] The principle that one accepted (*accipio*) investiture (*investitura*) from the hand (*a / de manu*) of a layman was prohibited by these decrees. The similarities between such language and the Norman and Aragonese terminology are clear: the Aragonese kings were supposed to accept (*accipio*) their kingdom from the hand (*de manu*) of the pontiff; the Norman dukes, on the other hand, received investiture (*investitura*) of their lands. Despite the apparent difference between the Aragonese and Norman kings, the language used in both cases to describe their position vis-à-vis the pope had something fundamental in common: both drew on the terminology used to describe lay investiture.

Significantly, this language of investiture vanished in the twelfth century. The eleventh-century oaths sworn to the pope by the Normans had ended 'I will observe this fidelity to your successors ... who ... will have confirmed the investiture'. However, later twelfth-century oaths from the Norman rulers to the pope – otherwise identical – excised the word *investitura* from this sentence: simply promising: 'I will observe this fidelity to your successors ... who ... will

---

[17] 'Ut contradicatur, ne aliquis accipiat investituram ecclesiarum de manu laicorum': *Greg. Reg.*, 2: 401 (no. 6.5b).
[18] '[N]ullus in clericali ordine constitutus, nullus monachus, episcopatus aut abbatie aut cuiuslibet ecclesiastice dignitatis investituram de manu laici suscipere audeat': Somerville and Kuttner, *Urban II*, 254.
[19] '[I]nterdicimus ne quis investituram episcopatus abbatie, vel cuiuslibet ecclesiastice dignitatis a manu imperatoris, regis, principis, vel cuiuslibet laice persone accipiat': Robert Somerville, 'The Council of Beauvais, 1114', *Traditio* 24 (1968), 493–503, at 503, reprinted in idem, *Papacy, Councils and Canon Law in the 11th–12th Centuries* (Aldershot, 1990), X.

have confirmed what was conceded to me in your privilege'.[20] At the beginning of the papal schism of 1130–8, one of the two elected popes, Anacletus II, elevated the Sicilian count-duke, Roger II, into a king. The 1130 privilege granting Roger the royal title made no mention of *investitura*, however. It allowed Roger to be crowned and anointed by an archbishop of his choosing, but there was no mention of a ceremony of *investitura* performed by the pope.[21] Roger's actual coronation in 1130 was apparently conducted by a cardinal sent by Anacletus, rather than an archbishop, but the lack of any mention of *investitura* in Anacletus's privilege still indicates that this was a coronation ceremony rather than an investiture.[22] Although Anacletus II's side were the losers in the schism, the 'winning' pope, Innocent II, eventually confirmed Roger's kingship in 1139. Because of Roger's support for the antipope Anacletus, Innocent was not initially disposed to look kindly on Roger and indeed led an army against him. Unfortunately for Innocent, Roger was able to defeat the papal army and capture the pope. Once in Norman hands, Innocent proved unsurprisingly willing to confirm Roger's kingship, in essentially the same words as Anacletus.[23] The privilege of 1139, like that of 1130 and the later treaty of 1156 between the Norman kingdom of Sicily and the papacy, made no mention of any sort of ceremonial *investitura* by the pope.[24] The Sicilian king was given the privilege of being crowned and anointed by an archbishop instead.

---

[20] 1188 (William II), 1192 (Tancred): MGH Const. 1, 591–3 (nos 415–16). The 1212 oath of Frederick II also leaves out any mention of investiture in the final clause: MGH Const. 2, 542 (no. 411). So does the 1198 oath of Queen Constance: MGH DD 11.iii, 203–5 (no. 65).

[21] Hartmut Hoffman, 'Langobarden, Normannen, Päpste. Zum Legitimationsproblem in Unteritalien', *Quellen und Forschungen aus italienischen Archiven und Bibliotheken* 58 (1978), 137–80, at 173–6 (no. 1); *Roger II and the Creation of the Kingdom of Sicily*, transl. Graham Loud (Manchester, 2012), 304–6.

[22] *Roger II*, transl. Loud, 184–5.

[23] Graham Loud, *The Latin Church in Norman Italy* (Cambridge, 2007), 151–6.

[24] Hoffman, 'Langobarden, Normannen, Päpste', 176–8 (no. 2); MGH Const. 1, 588–91 (nos 413–14; ET *Roger II*, transl. Loud, 310–12); *The History of the Tyrants of Sicily by 'Hugo Falcandus' 1154–69*, ed. and transl. Graham Loud and Thomas Wiedemann (Manchester, 1998), 248–52. Romuald's chronicle refers to investiture in 1156; however, even if this is accurate (investiture was not mentioned in the texts of the 1130 and 1139 privileges or in the 1156 privilege and treaty), it is clear that it was no longer considered important: MGH SS 19, 429. Even Paul Kehr, who believed in the existence of a feudal relationship, accepted that papal investiture ceased by 1156: Paul Kehr, *Die Belehnungen der süditalienischen Normannenfürsten durch die Päpste 1059–1192* (Berlin, 1934), 52.

The papal-Aragonese relationship also changed in the twelfth century. It finally adopted the terminology of papal *protectio*, the protection afforded to abbeys and churches by St Peter and the pope. Fried thought that *protectio* had been the keyword from the start, but I would suggest that this development was subsequent to the investiture contest, the conflict between *c.*1078 and 1122 over whether laymen could ceremonially invest bishops and abbots with their offices. This *protectio* gave the papacy a limited right: the right to an annual payment. The king of Aragon was not dependent on papal approval for his rule. There would be, in the twelfth century, no more discussions of the Aragonese kings receiving their kingdoms 'from the pope's hand', instead the kingdom would be 'under ours and St Peter's protection': the exact formulation used for protected monasteries.[25] The first use of this formula to describe the king of Aragon appeared in a letter of protection for the boy-king Alfonso II in 1163.[26] This letter, from Pope Alexander III, was also the first indication that the Aragonese were supporting him, rather than his opponent, in the papal schism which had begun in 1159. Perhaps under such circumstances, the papal court had no interest in arguing for a more extreme interpretation of papal-Aragonese relations.

The terminology used to conceptualize papal *imperium* changed during the twelfth century: the language of investiture, by which the pope had conferred government on the rulers of Aragon and Norman Sicily, vanished. Why did this common language of investiture disappear from papal-royal relations at this time? The likely impetus comes from the changes resulting from the conflict between kingdom and priesthood about *inter alia* lay investiture of bishops.

UNINTENDED CONSEQUENCES: THE END OF LAY INVESTITURE OF
BISHOPS AND PAPAL INVESTITURE OF KINGS

The solution to the dispute over lay investitures was for bishops to be invested with the *regalia*, the property granted to the bishopric, by

---

[25] *Papsturkunden in Spanien. Vorarbeiten zur Hispania Pontificia*, 2: *Navarra und Aragon*, ed. Paul Kehr (repr. Göttingen, 1970), 338–41, 341–3, 362–3, 364–6, 369–70, 370–2, 382–6, 404–7, 412–14, 416–18, 422–8, 441–7, 455–7, 468–72, 480–6, 495–7, 518–21, 524-6 (nos 43–4, 59, 61, 64–5, 72, 86, 93, 95–6, 100–1, 111–12, 122, 133, 141–3, 150, 172–3, 177).

[26] *Papsturkunden in Spanien. Vorarbeiten zur Hispania Pontificia*, 1: *Katalanien*, ed. Paul Kehr (Berlin, 1926), 392–3 (no. 107).

the secular rulers and to be consecrated and given the *spiritualia* by their ecclesiastical superior. Kings and emperors had often invested bishops with their bishoprics and drawn little explicit distinction between the property, which was the king's to give, and the sacral character. Such vagueness over whether laymen could give spiritual authority stretched even to the highest honours. In the mid-eleventh century, Emperor Henry III deposed and appointed several popes: even the Roman clergy acknowledged, at least in practice, that the emperor could do this.[27] Such authority apparently extended as far as actually investing the pope.[28] By the 1070s and 1080s, however, the *patricius Romanorum*, the legal justification which Henry IV adduced for imperial oversight of papal elections, was being challenged and dismissed by the Roman Church.[29] From at least 1078 clerical reformers insisted that, since a layman could not consecrate a clergyman, no layman could play any part in the appointment of bishops generally. One counter position to this, articulated by 1100, was that when a king invested a bishop he did not grant him sacral power but only the lands and rents of the bishopric. This counter position did not challenge the argument of the reformers that a king had no capability to invest a bishop with his sacred authority; only a clergyman could do that. Eventually compromises were reached in the early twelfth century, most famously at Worms in 1122, whereby kings invested bishops with their *regalia* and the pope or the appropriate clerical superior invested them with the *spiritualia*, the sacred and spiritual power of a bishop or abbot.[30] This compromise

---

[27] Guido Martin, 'Der salische Herrscher als *Patricius Romanorum*. Zur Einflußnahme Heinrichs III. und Heinrichs IV. auf die Besetzung der *Cathedra Petri*', *Frühmittelalterliche Studien* 28 (1994), 257–95, at 267–9, 294; Mary Stroll, *Popes and Antipopes: The Politics of Eleventh-Century Church Reform* (Leiden, 2012), 16.

[28] A number of sources specify that Cadalus-Honorius II was actually 'invested' (*investiri*) with the papacy by the emperor or his mother in 1061, 'as is the custom': ibid. 139 n. 26; or that he 'accepted the pontifical insignia through the hand' (*accipiens … per manum*) of the monarchs: ibid. 139–40, nn. 27, 30. Note again the interchangeability of 'investiture' and receiving something *a* / *de* / *per manu* / *manum*.

[29] *The Papal Reform of the Eleventh Century: Lives of Pope Leo IX and Pope Gregory VII*, transl. Ian S. Robinson (Manchester, 2004), 5–6, 56–8, 187–8, 209–10; Stroll, *Popes and Antipopes*, 20.

[30] For the thought behind lay investiture, see Stanley Chodorow, 'Paschal II, Henry V, and the Origins of the Crisis of 1111', in James Ross Sweeney and Stanley Chodorow, eds, *Popes, Teachers, and Canon Law in the Middle Ages* (Ithaca, NY, 1989), 3–25, at 7–9, 14–15, 18; idem, 'Ecclesiastical Politics and the Ending of the Investiture Contest: The Papal Election of 1119 and the Negotiations of Mouzon', *Speculum* 46 (1971), 613–40,

accepted that kings could not give clergymen their sacred power, but did allow them to give temporal goods. It was therefore predicated on a degree of possession: the *rex* could invest with the *regalia* – that is, with what pertained to the king.

Once one accepts that position, the idea of 'investiture' took on an extra level of meaning such as to render papal 'investiture' of a king unacceptable. The language of investiture as it was crystallized by the concordat of Worms raised the question: how could the pope invest any ruler with his land unless it was the pope's to give away? Before the investiture contest, no-one was too worried about what allowing kings to invest bishops, or popes to invest princes, might actually *mean*.[31] Prior to the conflict, bishops had been invested by kings even though a king had no power to give a clergyman his sacral authority; likewise, the kings of Aragon were perfectly willing to admit that they received their kingdom from the hand of the pope, while the Normans certainly took part in ceremonies of investiture. What is common here, before the investiture dispute, is a lack of concern with the possible connotations: neither the Aragonese nor the Normans distinguished clearly between the general approval of their rule which they wanted from the papacy and any suggestion that this implied that the pope was actually *giving* the land to a ruler.

The 1076 coronation of the king of Croatia and Dalmatia provides confirmation that in the eleventh century papal investiture of kings did not presuppose temporal authority, but was simply indistinct from spiritual approval. The king, Demetrius Zvonimir, announced to all that he had been 'invested and constituted king, through banner, sword, sceptre and crown' by Gregory VII's legate. The legate and pope must have concurred with this account, since Demetrius's document recounting it was incorporated into Cardinal Deusdedit's

---

at 621–2; Gerd Tellenbach, *The Church in Western Europe from the Tenth to the Early Twelfth Century*, transl. Timothy Reuter (Cambridge, 1993), 266–86; Uta-Renate Blumenthal, *The Investiture Controversy: Church and Monarchy from the Ninth to the Twelfth Century* (Philadelphia, PA, 1988), 163–73; eadem, 'Patrimonia and Regalia in 1111', in *Law, Church, and Society: Essays in Honor of Stephan Kuttner*, ed. K. Pennington and R. Somerville (Philadelphia, PA, 1977), 9–22, reprinted in Uta-Renate Blumenthal, *Papal Reform and Canon Law in the 11th and 12th Centuries* (Aldershot, 1998), IX; H. E. John Cowdrey, *Pope Gregory VII, 1073–1085* (Oxford, 1998), 546–50; Joseph Canning, *A History of Medieval Political Thought, 300–1450* (London, 1996), 82–110, especially 106–7.
[31] For similar observations, see Charles West, *Reframing the Feudal Revolution: Political and Social Revolution between Marne and Moselle, c.800–c.1100* (Cambridge, 2013), 213–21.

collection of canons in the later twelfth century.[32] And what exactly did 'being invested through a crown' imply, other than a coronation ceremony? This account of the Croatian ceremony drew no distinction at all between what we might assume to be a 'feudal' investiture with a banner or a sceptre and what we might think of as a 'spiritual' ceremony of coronation. Any distinction between being invested with land by a superior (who has some right to give that land away) and simply being recognized and approved by God (and his representative) was absent or unclear in 1076.

When the distinction between temporal *regalia* given by the secular superior and spiritualties conferred by the ecclesiastical superior was accepted for episcopal investiture, it had a knock-on effect on papal relations with rulers. Investiture was now something that a king did to 'his' bishops to give them their *regalia*. After the 1130s the Norman kings received the spiritual endorsement they wanted from being crowned and anointed; investiture was no longer equivalent to coronation. The Norman king did not need a ceremonial investiture which might have confused his temporal and spiritual legitimacy. The first appearance of coronation was in the antipope Anacletus's 1130 grant of the royal title to Roger of Sicily, only eight years after the concordat of Worms.[33] Papal investiture had ceased to be of any importance, probably because no-one saw the papacy as giving the actual territory, which is what investiture would have implied after the concordat.

From the 1130s onwards papal relationships with secular powers would move further away from the forms employed in the eleventh century. By the middle of the twelfth century, Aragon was, as Fried argued, a papal protectorate, where the papacy held limited rights only. In the eleventh century, the emperors had argued that they could intervene in papal elections generally through their authority as *patricius*, and had invested popes; in the 1150s, however, Frederick I judged that he could intervene in a papal election because he as emperor was the ultimate source of the pope's *regalia*: the temporal power of the pope in the city of Rome.[34] The emperor's justification

---

[32] 'Ego Demetrius … a te … Gebizo ex apostolice sedis legatione … potestatem optinens … per vexillum, ensem, sceptrum et coronam investitus atque constitutus rex': *Die Kanonessammlung des Kardinals Deusdedit*, ed. Victor Welf von Glanvell (Paderborn, 1905), 383–4.

[33] Hoffman, 'Langobarden, Normannen, Päpste', 173–8.

[34] John B. Freed, *Frederick Barbarossa: The Prince and the Myth* (New Haven, CT, 2016), 254–5.

was now couched solely in temporal terms: it was now dependent on a clear differentiation between the spiritual and temporal powers of the pope, and where those powers came from.

The focus here has been on southern Italy and Aragon because, apart from being the best studied relationships with the papacy, they are also the best documented. Other supposed 'feudal' relationships are often so poorly recorded that little can be said definitively. The evidence adduced to prove, for example, that Gregory VII sought lordship over Brittany or England is fairly ambiguous.[35] We should be wary of building arguments from such meagre evidence.

Gregory VII's letters to King Solomon of Hungary in October 1074 have been read as showing that papal temporal authority over that kingdom was conceived as distinct from papal power over kings generally: Hungary was a papal fief and therefore the pope held temporal power over its king. Writing to Solomon, Gregory expressed grave disquiet that the king had accepted his kingdom as a *beneficium* from the Emperor Henry IV, for the sceptre of Hungary was a *beneficium* of apostolic, not royal, authority. That kingdom had been 'offered and handed over to blessed Peter by King Stephen [the first king] with all his right and power'.[36] This latter phrase again invites comparison with the kingdom of Aragon which, according to King Sancho in 1088, had been 'handed over into the power of God and St Peter'.[37]

Solomon's dealings with the Emperor Henry IV were prompted by the opposition to the Hungarian king, in the preceding years, from his cousin, Duke Gesa.[38] It therefore seems likely that Gregory's criticism of Solomon's association with Henry was prompted by complaints from Gesa and was not entirely initiated by Gregory: Gesa had been in communication with Gregory for months before

---

[35] Brittany: *Sancti Gregorii VII Pontificis Romani operum pars secunda*, PL 148, cols 684–5 (no. 37); Cowdrey, *Gregory VII*, 645. England: *Greg. Reg.*, 2: 499–502 (no. 7.23); *Epistolae diversorum ad Gregorium VII*, PL 148, col. 748 (no. 11); Zachary Nugent Brooke, 'Pope Gregory VII's Demand for Fealty from William the Conqueror', *EHR* 26 (1911), 225–38; idem, *The English Church and the Papacy: From the Conquest to the Reign of King John*, new edn (Cambridge, 1989), 140–3; Cowdrey, *Gregory VII*, 463, 646–7.

[36] '[E]ius regnum a rege Teutonicorum in beneficium, sicut audivimus, suscepisti ... sceptrum regni ... apostolice, non regie magestatis beneficium recognoscas ... [regnum Ungarie] a rege Stephano olim beato Petro cum omni iure et potestate sua oblatum et devote traditum': *Greg. Reg.* 1: 144–6 (no. 2.13; ET *Register of Pope Gregory*, transl. Cowdrey, 108).

[37] Somerville and Kuttner, *Urban II*, 97–9.

[38] Cowdrey, *Gregory VII*, 444–6.

this.[39] Solomon had looked for help from the emperor; Gesa had thus countered by calling on the pope for support.

It is the use of *beneficium* in Gregory's letter which has caused some confusion, because, as well as simply meaning 'gift', *beneficium* could also be a technical term denoting a conditional grant of land (i.e. a fief).[40] But Cowdrey, the doyen of Gregorian studies, noticed the flexibility of the term. In his translation of Pope Gregory's register, the first use of *beneficium* was translated as 'fief' ('you received this kingdom as a fief'); while the second use was translated as 'gift' ('the sceptre of the kingdom … [is] a gift of apostolic, not of royal, sovereignty').[41] In his biography of Gregory, however, Cowdrey translated both uses of *beneficium* in this letter as 'gift'.[42] I do not think that we should here read *beneficium* as a semi-technical term, like 'fief', denoting a unique papal temporal authority over Hungary. Rather, it should be understood as an assertion of papal power over kings generally: all kingdoms were, in the end, gifts from God. Confirmation of this interpretation comes from a letter of Gregory to Duke Gesa of March 1075. Here 'the kingdom of Hungary, *just as other most famous kingdoms* [my emphasis], should be … subject to no king of another kingdom save to the … Roman Church'.[43] Gregory did not see Hungary as distinctly under the temporal power of the pope; instead, all kings were under some form of papal authority which did not explicitly distinguish between sacral and temporal.

CONCLUSION

It was not until the first half of the twelfth century that investiture or 'accepting land from the hand' of someone began to signify that the person who performed the investiture actually owned the thing they were giving away. With the end of the dispute over lay investiture

---

[39] Gregory's earliest surviving communication with a Hungarian was with Gesa, in March 1074: *Greg. Reg.*, 1: 85–6 (no. 1.58).

[40] As, for example, Weinfurter, 'Die Päpste als "Lehnsherren"', 23–4; although he only discusses the first use of it in the letter, and not Gregory's claim that the sceptre was a papal *beneficium*.

[41] *Register of Pope Gregory*, transl. Cowdrey, 108.

[42] Cowdrey, *Gregory VII*, 444.

[43] *Greg. Reg.*, 1: 218–19 (no. 2.63; ET *Register of Pope Gregory*, transl. Cowdrey, 157). Gregory did, in 1074, list points when, he thought, previous Hungarian kings had acknowledged that the pope was the source of royal power, but there is no reason to think that these constituted a basis for a distinct papal temporal lordship over Hungary.

(1122) it was recognized that a king could invest a bishop only with the *regalia*, with what pertained to the king. Now it was clear: how could a pope invest a king with a kingdom, or how could a king 'accept' it from a clergyman, unless the pope actually possessed it, unless it was really his to give away? Previously this had not been such an issue: kings had given away bishoprics, both spiritually and temporally, despite having no sacral legitimacy to do so. The coronation of the king of Croatia-Dalmatia did not distinguish between investiture and coronation. But the kings of Aragon and of Sicily were beginning to do so after the 1120s. Investiture of the Norman rulers of Sicily declined after 1122; the Aragonese kings did not 'accept the kingdom from the hand' of the pope in the twelfth century, and after *c.*1150 the Aragonese-papal relationship clearly came under the rubric of protection.

Papal authority – papal *imperium* – over monarchs does not fit neatly into distinct categories before the mid-twelfth century. We cannot simply say that Gregory VII and his successors believed the pope was the temporal governor of all kings, because it is not clear what the distinction between temporal superiority and spiritual leadership was. By the beginning of the thirteenth century, the distinction between the spiritual power (which the popes had over all kings) and temporal power (which they did not) was explicit: Innocent III, accepting the surrender of the kingdoms of England and Ireland to the papacy in 1213–14, told King John when returning them to him as a fief (*feudum*) that 'those provinces which from of old have had the Holy Roman Church as their proper teacher in spiritual matters should now in temporal things also have her as their special lord'.[44] The two – spiritual magistracy and temporal lordship – were distinguished and did not automatically go together. But to categorize the earlier royal-papal relationships in the eleventh and early twelfth centuries either as 'feudal' or 'protective' is to put the cart before the horse. These types of relationship were only defined after the end of the investiture contest. The old language of investiture, in which popes had indivisibly invested kings with both spiritual and temporal authority, was no longer acceptable. Papal *imperium* had moved on to new ground.

[44] *Selected Letters of Pope Innocent III concerning England (1198–1216)*, ed. and transl. C. R. Cheney and W. H. Semple (London, 1953), 177–83 (no. 67).

Emperor and Church in the Last Centuries of Byzantium

Ruth Macrides*

University of Birmingham

This study discusses relations between the Church and the emperor in the last two centuries of the Byzantine empire's existence, in the Palaiologan period (thirteenth to fifteenth centuries). It questions the accepted view that the Church rose in importance and status as imperial power and authority declined. According to this view, expressed by Steven Runciman and accepted by historians since, a strong Church was the legacy of the Byzantine empire to the Ottomans. In this article the ceremonies of the late Byzantine court, as represented by the mid-fourteenth-century text of Pseudo-Kodinos, are examined for indications of continuity in the emperor's dominant role in the Church in this later period. Gilbert Dagron's contrary perspective is considered. It is then argued that the writings of two late Byzantine churchmen, Symeon of Thessalonike and Makarios of Antioch, who insist on a lesser role for the emperor in the selection and the making of a patriarch, provide evidence for the contemporary performance of the promotion of a patriarch as described by Pseudo-Kodinos. While the two churchmen tried to show that the emperor was subject to the Church, practice shows something different.

It is a commonplace in the modern historiographical literature on late Byzantium that the Church rose in prestige and power in the last centuries of the empire, the thirteenth to fifteenth centuries, just as imperial power and authority declined. According to this view, if, at the beginning of the empire's life in the fourth to sixth centuries, the term caesaropapism could be applied to Church-state relations or the Church could be described as a department of state, by late Byzantium a dramatic reversal had occurred.[1] In his book on the Orthodox Church under Ottoman rule, *The Great Church in*

* Centre for Byzantine, Ottoman and Modern Greek, University of Birmingham, Edgbaston, Birmingham B15 2TT. E-mail: R.J.MACRIDES@bham.ac.uk.
[1] For the history of this term, see Gilbert Dagron, *Emperor and Priest: The Imperial Office in Byzantium*, transl. Jean Birrell (Cambridge, 2003), 282–312; see also a reconsideration of 'the problem of caesaropapism' in Deno J. Geanakoplos, *Byzantine East and Latin West:*

Studies in Church History 54 (2018) 123–143   © Ecclesiastical History Society 2018
doi: 10.1017/stc.2017.8

Captivity, Steven Runciman, writing in the 1960s, expressed the situation as follows:

> The recovery of the capital [in 1261] in the long run benefited the Patriarch more than the Emperor, re-establishing him as unquestioned head of a hierarchy whose sees stretched from the Adriatic to Russia and the Caucasus, while soon the Imperial territory began to shrink. The growing impoverishment of the Empire damaged the Emperor more than the Patriarch. For reasons of economy the Palace ceremonies were curtailed and simplified. The Emperor began to lose his aura of mystery and splendour.[2]

In Runciman's view, a strong Church was the legacy of the Byzantine empire to the Ottomans. All those writing about the Church before and since Runciman have come to a similar conclusion.[3]

In discussions of the change in status of Church and emperor under the Palaiologoi, the last dynasty to rule the empire, the ceremonial of the court which was mentioned by Runciman is rarely examined, while the Church's growth in 'institutional strength, judicial powers and ideological claims' is more often asserted and discussed.[4] This article will re-examine this question and the arguments put forward by those who adopt the view of an empowered Church and a diminished imperial office in the years that saw two attempts at the union

---

Two Worlds of Christendom in the Middle Ages and Renaissance, Studies in Ecclesiastical and Cultural History (Oxford, 1966), 55–83.

[2] Steven Runciman, *The Great Church in Captivity: A Study of the Patriarchate of Constantinople from the Eve of the Turkish Conquest to the Greek War of Independence* (Cambridge, 1968), 66–7.

[3] George Ostrogorsky, *History of the Byzantine State*, transl. Joan Hussey, 2nd edn (Oxford, 1968), 486–7; Donald M. Nicol, *Church and Society in the Last Centuries of Byzantium* (Cambridge, 1979), 28–30; Michael Angold, *Church and Society in Byzantium under the Comneni 1081–1261* (Cambridge, 1995), 562–3; Dimiter G. Angelov, *Imperial Ideology and Political Thought in Byzantium, 1204–1330* (Cambridge, 2007), 351–416; idem, ed., *Church and Society in Late Byzantium* (Kalamazoo, MI, 2009), 1–7; Tom Papademetriou, 'The Turkish Conquests and Decline of the Church reconsidered', in Angelov, ed., *Church and Society*, 183–200, at 184–5; Ekaterini Mitsiou, 'Interaktion zwischen Kaiser und Patriarch im Spiegel des Patriarchatsregisters von Konstantinopel', in Michael Grünbart, Lutz Rickelt and Martin M. Vučetić, eds, *Zwei Sonnen am Goldenen Horn? Kaiserliche und patriarchale Macht im byzantinischen Mittelalter. Akten der internationalen Tagung vom 3. bis 5. November 2010*, part 1 (Berlin, 2011), 79–96.

[4] See Angelov, *Imperial Ideology*, who puts the case for the Church in these terms.

of the Eastern and Western Churches in 1274 and 1439, two civil wars and Turkish conquests of Byzantine lands.[5]

Whoever seeks to determine the relationship between emperor and Church in Byzantium will obtain little help from Byzantine formulations. Only once was an attempt made, in the ninth century, in the reign of Basil I, in a law book in the composition of which the patriarch Photios played a part. Two sections entitled 'On the Emperor' and 'On the Patriarch' describe the spheres of influence and authority of these two powers. The emperor, called a 'lawful dominion', is concerned with the physical wellbeing of the people, while the patriarch, 'a living icon of Christ', cares for their spiritual wellbeing. The legal activities and capacities of emperor and patriarch are clearly demarcated. The emperor must maintain and preserve Holy Scripture, the pronouncements of the seven ecumenical councils and also Roman law. He is not to promulgate any law that transgresses the canons. The patriarch alone, however, interprets the canons of the holy fathers and synods.[6]

This attempt to delineate two powers with separate spheres of influence and distinct functions was short-lived. Thirty years after this law code was issued, a revision was promulgated. Just as it is no surprise that the remarkable formulation of the separate spheres of the two powers was the work of a patriarch, it is equally clear that its undoing was the work of an emperor, none other than a student of Photios, Leo VI. The desire of this emperor to expunge the problematic statements and thus to limit the Church's influence can be understood both in the light of his personal animosity towards Photios and with regard to the opposition he had experienced from the Church over his fourth marriage.[7] Never again was a demarcation of imperial and patriarchal functions and competences undertaken.

---

[5] For a survey of the events of the Palaiologan period, see Donald M. Nicol, *The Last Centuries of Byzantium, 1261–1453*, 2nd edn (Cambridge, 1993).

[6] Ioannes Zepos and Panagiotes Zepos, *Jus Graecoromanum*, 2 vols, 2nd edn (Aalen, 1962) 2: 240–3. See Andreas Schminck, *Studien zu mittelbyzantinischen Rechtsbüchern* (Frankfurt am Main, 1986), 12–15, 62–107, for his revision of the legislation of the Macedonian emperors and his renaming of the text previously known as the *Epanagoge* as the *Eisagoge*.

[7] Andreas Schminck, '*Rota tu volubilis*. Kaisermacht und Patriarchenmacht in Mosaiken', in Ludwig Burgmann, Marie-Theres Fögen and Andreas Schminck, eds, *Cupido legum* (Frankfurt am Main, 1985), 211–34.

Instead, we find sporadic attempts to identify and define imperial rights, but on the level of personal opinion.[8]

A neglected source that can be used to gauge relations between emperor and Church is ceremonial. Until now, only Runciman has mentioned imperial ceremonial in this context. However, for the Byzantines, ceremonial held a constitutional significance, as is evident from the Greek word for ceremony, *katastasis*, literally meaning 'state'.[9] In the absence of a definition on paper of the prerogatives and limits of the emperor's power and his role in the Church, we can look for a definition through performance.

Runciman saw an impoverishment of the emperor's ceremonial as an effect of the impoverishment of empire but he did not indicate the sources from which he drew this conclusion. In fact, the only text he could have had in mind is the mid-fourteenth-century ceremonial book known by its anonymous author's name, Pseudo-Kodinos.[10] The first thing that should be said about this text is the contrast it presents with the much earlier and better-known tenth-century *Book of Ceremonies*. Just a glance at the two is enough to convince historians of a cutting back in later ceremonial. Pseudo-Kodinos is a much shorter work and describes ceremonies for a different palace, not the Great Palace in the south-east corner of the city but another, the Blachernai, in the north-west, diametrically opposite, approximately five kilometres away. The Palaiologan emperors lived in that palace permanently from the time of the return to Constantinople after its reconquest from the Latins in 1261.[11] The significance of this new venue for the ceremonial routine of the court is great. First of all, for

---

[8] For this and other aspects of Church-state relations, see Ruth Macrides, 'Nomos and Kanon on Paper and in Court', in Rosemary Morris, ed., *Church and People in Byzantium* (Birmingham, 1990), 61–86, reprinted in Ruth J. Macrides, *Kinship and Justice in Byzantium, 11th–15th Centuries* (Aldershot, 1999), VI.

[9] Paul Magdalino, *The Empire of Manuel I Komnenos 1143–1180* (Cambridge, 1993), 237–8.

[10] Runciman would have used the edition of I. Bekker (Bonn, 1843), since that of Jean Verpeaux, *Pseudo-Kodinos, Traité des Offices* (Paris, 1966), appeared too close in time to the publication of *The Great Church in Captivity*. In this article, all references to the text will be from the edition, translation and study by Ruth Macrides, J. A. Munitiz and Dimiter Angelov, *Pseudo-Kodinos and the Constantinopolitan Court: Offices and Ceremonies*, Birmingham Byzantine and Ottoman Studies 15 (Farnham, 2013).

[11] For a reconstruction of the palace complex based on a reading of Pseudo-Kodinos, see Ruth Macrides, 'The Citadel of Byzantine Constantinople', in Scott Redford and Nina Ergin, eds, *Cities and Citadels in Turkey: From the Iron Age to the Seljuks*, Ancient Near Eastern Studies Supplement 40 (Louvain, 2013), 277–304.

the first time since the foundation of the city by Constantine, emperor and patriarch were not neighbours. Hagia Sophia, the Great Church, where the patriarch had his apartments, was no longer a few minutes' walk from the palace. A patriarch who wanted to speak with the emperor would have to board a ship and sail up the Golden Horn or go on horseback through the city. Furthermore, the emperor no longer had the use of the hippodrome, a huge space for self-display connected to the Great Palace.[12]

All these changes since the tenth century might signify to some an impoverishment, a loss of splendour for the imperial office. Certainly the scale is different, the court is smaller and the palace is centralized around a courtyard. The Blachernai, unlike the Great Palace, was not a sprawling complex of buildings covering a vast area.[13] Many material changes and developments had taken place since the days of the tenth-century empire; but do these changes signify a loss in imperial stature?

One of those who thinks they do is Gilbert Dagron, who in various publications concerned with the tenth-century *Book of Ceremonies* and in his book *Emperor and Priest* has made passing comments about late Byzantine imperial stature based on the protocols of Pseudo-Kodinos. Several passages arrested Dagron's attention. Their topics range from the symbolism attached to the imperial costume to the formula of words used by the emperor when he promoted a patriarch. I shall deal with each in turn.

Pseudo-Kodinos gives his fullest discussion of imperial attire in his protocol for Christmas, when the emperor appeared on a tall platform in the courtyard of the palace in a ceremony called *prokypsis*. Included in his description of the ceremony is an enumeration of the items of clothing and insignia an emperor might wear and bear, together with an interpretation of the significance of these items. He informs his readers:

> The emperor wears whichever of these headdresses and garments he wishes. However, he always carries the cross in his right hand and a silk cloth similar to a scroll, tied with a handkerchief, in his left hand. This silk cloth contains earth and is called *akakia*. By carrying the

---

[12] Paul Magdalino, 'Court and Capital in Byzantium', in Jeroen Duindam, Tülay Artan and Metin Kunt, eds, *Royal Courts in Dynastic States and Empires: A Global Perspective* (Leiden, 2011), 131–44.
[13] See n. 11 above; Macrides, Munitiz and Angelov, *Pseudo-Kodinos*, 367–78.

cross the emperor shows his faith in Christ; by the crown he shows his office; by the belt, he shows that he is a soldier; by his black *sakkos*, the mystery of the imperial office; by the earth which, as we said, is called *akakia*, that he is humble, as he is mortal and that he is not to be proud or arrogant because the imperial office is so exalted; by the handkerchief, the inconstancy of his office and that it passes from one person to another.[14]

Interpretations of the emperor's clothing can be found also in earlier ceremonial books, the *Kletorologion* of Philotheos (899), a text laying out the seating arrangements at banquets, and the *Book of Ceremonies*. Yet there is a difference. While the two earlier ceremonial books assign a religious symbolism to the garments and insights, Pseudo-Kodinos associates the same items with attributes of the imperial office, imperial virtues, such as advice literature to the emperor (sometimes referred to as a 'Mirror of Princes') might endorse. For him, the belt shows that the emperor is a soldier; for Philotheos, it signifies the winding cloth of Christ.[15] Pseudo-Kodinos describes the *akakia* as similar to a scroll, tied with a handkerchief and filled with earth. He is the first to state that the *akakia* contains earth (χῶμα). For Pseudo-Kodinos, the earth signifies the humble and mortal nature of the emperor. Philotheos makes an indirect reference to the earth in the cloth, interpreting its significance in a divergent way from Pseudo-Kodinos. For Philotheos, the *akakia* represents the resurrection and victory over man's earthly essence.[16]

Dagron sees in these differences of interpretation a 'reflection of the evolution of the imperial institution whose claims to sacredness and quasi-sacerdotal charisma were increasingly officially and effectively challenged by the Church'.[17] Yet before such a conclusion can be drawn, the context of the statements made on the imperial costume should be considered. In the work of Philotheos and in the *Book of Ceremonies* the interpretation of the emperor's clothing is embedded in the protocols for the Easter ceremonies, where references

[14] Ibid. 138–41.
[15] Philotheos, *Kletorologion*, in Nicolas Oikonomides, ed., *Les Listes de préséance byzantines des IXᵉ et Xᵉ siècles* (Paris, 1972), 201 ll. 12–13.
[16] Ibid., ll. 15–16.
[17] Gilbert Dagron, 'From the *mappa* to the *akakia*: Symbolic Drift', in Hagit Amirav and Bas ter Haar Romeny, eds, *From Rome to Constantinople: Studies in Honour of Averil Cameron* (Louvain and Paris, 2007), 203–20, at 217, 219.

to the resurrection can be expected.[18] Pseudo-Kodinos's discussion is found in a much more mundane place – the emperor's wardrobe and the items of clothing he keeps in it. Pseudo-Kodinos inserts this list in his protocol for the *prokypsis* ceremony, the Christmas appearance of the emperor, like a radio or television presenter who fills in time during the intermission at a concert or other performance. While the emperor is changing his costume behind the curtains, Pseudo-Kodinos runs through the items kept in the imperial wardrobe, explaining the significance of each.[19]

Furthermore, Pseudo-Kodinos's connection of the *akakia* with the mortality of the emperor relates to a tradition preserved in Arab authors going back to the late ninth century. Harun-ibn-Yahya describes a procession he witnessed in Constantinople in which the emperor holds in his hand a box of gold containing earth. The official who walks behind him says to him in Greek, 'Remember death'. Al-Bakri, writing in the late eleventh century, gives a similar account.[20] Pseudo-Kodinos, then, transmits a different but coexisting tradition concerning the earth in the *akakia*.

Pseudo-Kodinos's explanation of the significance of individual items of the emperor's attire cannot be interpreted, as Dagron does, as evidence of the emperor's loss of sacrality, especially since Dagron has left an item out of consideration, the *lampas* or large candle carried in front of the emperor on the major feast days. It is also held in front of the enthroned emperor in his reception hall.[21] The *lampas* is described in the twelfth-century canonical commentaries of Theodore Balsamon, who says that it was decorated with two wreaths signifying the emperor's responsibility for the bodies and souls of his subjects.[22]

---

[18] *De cerimoniis aulae Byzantinae*, ed. J. J. Reiske, 2 vols (Bonn 1829–30), 1: 637–9; ET Ann Moffatt and Maxeme Tall, *The Book of Ceremonies: With the Greek Edition of the* Corpus Scriptorum Historiae Byzantinae (*Bonn, 1829*), 2 vols (Canberra, 2012), 2: 367–9; Dagron, 'From the *mappa* to the *akakia*', 209–10.

[19] Macrides, Munitiz and Angelov, *Pseudo-Kodinos*, 134 l. 5 and n. 347, 140 l. 12.

[20] Aleksandr Vasiliev, 'Harun-ibn-Yahya and his Description of Constantinople', *Seminarium Kondakovianum* 5 (1932), 149–63, at 159; for al-Bakri, see David Wasserstein, 'Byzantium and al-Andalus', *Mediterranean Historical Review* 2 (1987), 76–101, at 92.

[21] Macrides, Munitiz and Angelov, *Pseudo-Kodinos*, 118 ll. 1–2, 120 ll. 6–7, 121 n. 297.

[22] Theodore Balsamon, 'On Patriarchal Privileges', in G. A. Rhalles and M. Potles, Σύνταγμα τῶν θείων καὶ ἱερῶν κανόνων, 6 vols (Athens, 1966; first publ. 1852–59), 4: 545; see Maria Parani, '"Rise like the sun, the God-inspired kingship": Light-Symbolism and the Uses of Artificial Lighting in Middle and Late Byzantine Imperial Ceremonial', in Alexei Lidov, ed., *Light and Fire in the Sacred Space* (Moscow, 2013), 159–84 and fig. 2.

This item is the last one discussed by Pseudo-Kodinos in his list of articles of clothing and imperial attributes. Of it, Pseudo-Kodinos says, 'They carry [it] in front of him because of the words of the Lord, "Let your light so shine before men, that they may see your good works and glorify your Father which is in heaven"' (Matt. 5: 16).[23]

On Palm Sunday the candle leads the way along an elevated outdoor walkway that connects the palace to the church. Emperor and clergymen walk along the path strewn with myrtle and laurel leaves. The emperor is in full regalia. The leader of the procession holds the candle of the emperor. He ascends the walkway chanting the hymn attributed to the ninth-century emperor Theophilos, 'Go out nations, go out people and behold today the king of the heavens'. At this point Pseudo-Kodinos explains that the gospel book that joins the procession is a representation of Christ. But it is not the gospel book that follows the holder of the candle: it is the emperor. It is with him that the words of the hymn are associated: 'behold today the king of the heavens'.[24] The sacred connotations traditionally associated with imperial power appear to have survived into the fourteenth century.

Another case for Dagron of diminution of the emperor's prestige is the ceremony of the *prokypsis* mentioned earlier. The origins of the ceremony can be traced to the twelfth century and the reign of Manuel I Komnenos.[25] In the fourteenth century it is performed twice a year, at Christmas and Epiphany, on an elevated platform in the courtyard of the palace.[26] Curtains part to reveal the emperor from the knees up, framed by the columns of the structure and its balustrade. Singers chant verses appropriate to the feast day and instruments sound – trumpets, bugles, kettle drums and flutes.[27]

The *prokypsis* display of the emperor has characteristics similar to his appearance at the hippodrome. Both were imperial manifestations from a height in a structure connected to the palace. The emperor's box at the hippodrome, his *kathisma*, was actually part of the palace at the top of a spiral staircase or ramp. The emperor in his box was seen from a distance by the people of the city. He was framed

---

[23] Macrides, Munitiz and Angelov, *Pseudo-Kodinos*, 140 ll. 8–11.
[24] Ibid. 172 ll. 1–19.
[25] Michael Jeffreys, 'The Comnenian Prokypsis', *Parergon* n.s. 5 (1987), 38–53; Magdalino, *Empire*, 240.
[26] Macrides, Munitiz and Angelov, *Pseudo-Kodinos*, 403–4.
[27] Ibid. 140 l. 12 – 146 l. 6.

by the columns of the box and balustrade and surrounded by members of his court. The crowds chanted 'Rise' (*Anateilon*), inviting the emperor to appear before the start of the races. The emperor's emergence in the *kathisma* was thus compared to the rising of the sun on the horizon.[28]

In his discussion of imperial appearances at the hippodrome based on the *Book of Ceremonies*, Dagron makes a passing reference to the *prokypsis*. He asserts that the magnificence of the imperial emergence in the hippodrome has deteriorated to become a banal appearance on the *prokypsis* platform. He compares the latter to the appearance of a speaker behind the podium, hardly spectacular or grand.[29] If, however, the hippodrome emperor was invited by chanting crowds to rise like the sun, the *prokypsis* emperor actually appeared in a sudden burst of light accompanied by fanfare. On two of the darkest afternoons of the winter months, an immobile illuminated emperor emerged from the frame of the *prokypsis* structure as if from the frame of an icon. As Kantorowicz remarked, the emperor on the *prokypsis* 'stages' Christ.[30] The verses written for the Christmas and Epiphany *prokypseis* celebrate the emperor as imitating 'Him who was born in a cave. Like Christ he emerges from the darkness of the *prokypsis* with light shining on him and from him. He brings light to his subjects but fire to his enemies. As Christ came to earth on Christmas day, the emperor ascends to heaven'.[31] The elevation of the emperor high above his subjects, on a tall platform supported by columns, is also suggestive of a stylite saint's posture and position. Although saints who stood on pillars were no longer a part of the fourteenth-century cityscape, the spectators of this ceremony could not but be reminded of them.[32] The emperor's sacrality is intact.

---

[28] Gilbert Dagron et al., 'L'Organisation et le déroulement des courses d'après le *Livre des cérémonies*', *Travaux et Mémoires* 13 (2000), 3–180, at 123 and nn. 94, 95; Macrides, Munitiz and Angelov, *Pseudo-Kodinos*, 407–8.

[29] Gilbert Dagron, 'Trônes pour un empereur', in Anna Avramea, Angeliki Laiou and Evangelos Chrysos, eds, *Byzantium, State and Society: In Memory of Nikos Oikonomides* (Athens, 2003), 179–203, at 184–5. The *prokypsis* did not, as Dagron claims, take place inside, in churches, but rather always outside, on a platform specially built for the purpose.

[30] Ernst H. Kantorowicz, 'Oriens Augusti – lever du roi', *DOP* 17 (1963) 117–77, at 151.

[31] See the *prokypsis* poems by Manuel Holobolos, in Jean François Boissonade, *Anecdota graeca e codicibus regiis*, 5 vols (Hildesheim, 1962; first publ. Paris, 1829–33), 5: 159–82.

[32] One of the last references to stylite saints in Constantinople, to my knowledge, is Robert of Clari's mention in the early thirteenth century: 'And on each of these columns

Further observations on the emperor's diminished standing are made with regard to his liturgical privileges, which included the right to enter the sanctuary and cense the altar table and clergy there. Pseudo-Kodinos comments: 'It was an old custom at this vesper service, for the emperor to enter the holy sanctuary and to cense the holy altar table and to give the clerics a gift of 100 pounds of gold from the *vestiarion*. Now this does not take place.'[33] Those who believe in a weaker emperor and a stronger Church claim that the emperor was no longer 'permitted' to enter the sanctuary. Pseudo-Kodinos's statement gives no indication of the reason for this change. It is not clear why this old Easter custom attested in the tenth-century *Book of Ceremonies*[34] no longer took place in Pseudo-Kodinos's time, but it is certain that the emperor did not have 100 pounds of gold to give to the Church in the fourteenth century. In the early eleventh century the emperor raised the value of his gift to Hagia Sophia from 100 pounds to 180 pounds of gold.[35] In 1143 the emperor gave 200 pounds of silver coins,[36] while at the end of the thirteenth century he gave 1000 *hyperpyra* or 14 pounds of gold.[37] Large gifts to the Great Church (Hagia Sophia) were a thing of the past in the fourteenth century.

The *Book of Ceremonies* gives a number of occasions, the major feast days, when the emperor entered the sanctuary and censed the altar table.[38] Apart from Pseudo-Kodinos's explicit reference to the discontinuation of this tradition on Easter Day, there is no evidence that all the other occasions for the emperor's entrance into the

---

lived a hermit, in tiny huts which were there': Robert of Clari, *La Conquête de Constantinople*, ed. Peter Noble (Edinburgh, 2005), 109 (§92).

[33] Macrides, Munitiz and Angelov, *Pseudo-Kodinos*, 186 ll. 19–22, 187 n. 534.

[34] *De cerimoniis*, ed. Reiske, 1: 34 ll. 2–5 (Moffatt and Tall, *Book of Ceremonies*, 1: 34).

[35] Ioannis Skylitzes, *Synopsis historiarum*, ed. Hans Thurn (Berlin and New York, 1973), 375; Franz Dölger, *Regesten der Kaiserurkunden des oströmischen Reiches, von 565–1453*, 2: *Regesten von 1025–1204*, rev. ed. Peter Wirth (Munich, 1995), 3–4 (no. 831).

[36] *Nicetae Choniatae Historia*, ed. J.-L. van Dieten, Corpus Fontium Historiae Byzantinae 11 (Berlin and New York, 1975), 49 ll. 35–7.

[37] George Pachymeres, *Relations historiques*, ed. Albert Failler, transl. Vitalien Laurent, 5 vols (Paris, 1984–2000), 4: 31; Kostis Smyrlis, 'Priesthood and Empire: Ecclesiastical Wealth and Privilege under the Early Palaiologoi', in Christian Gastgeber et al., eds, *The Patriarchate of Constantinople in Context and Comparison* (Vienna, 2017), 95–103; Michael F. Hendy, *Studies in the Byzantine Monetary Economy c.300–1450* (Cambridge, 1985), 198–201.

[38] See the discussion by George P. Majeska, 'The Emperor in his Church: Imperial Ritual in the Church of St Sophia', in Henry Maguire, ed., *Byzantine Court Culture from 829 to 1204* (Washington DC, 1997), 1–11.

sanctuary mentioned in the *Book of Ceremonies* were likewise elimi-
nated by the fourteenth century. The protocols in Pseudo-Kodinos
are far fewer and far less detailed than those in the *Book of Ceremonies*,
a fact that has occasioned many arguments *ex silentio*.[39] It is clear,
however, that on their coronation day, emperors entered the sanctuary and censed the altar table. This was the case both in the tenth and
the fourteenth centuries, but there was a significant addition after the
time of the *Book of Ceremonies*: Pseudo-Kodinos describes the emperor on his coronation day receiving communion in the sanctuary
and in the manner of the clergy.[40]

By the fourteenth century the liturgy had become an integral part
of the coronation ritual. Pseudo-Kodinos describes the emperor just
before the Great Entrance, putting on a golden mantle and holding
the cross in one hand and a staff in the other: 'He occupies then the
ecclesiastical rank that they call *depotatos*'.[41]

> Holding then both of these things, namely the cross and the staff
> [*narthex*] he leads the entire Entrance. All the axe-bearing Varangians
> and young armed noblemen, about a hundred in number, follow along
> with him on both sides. They accompany on either side ... near the
> emperor. Immediately after him come the deacons and priests carrying
> other holy vessels and also the holy things themselves.[42]

Symeon, archbishop of Thessalonike (1416/17–29), explains that the
staff of the *depotatos* is soft and light. It is used to maintain good order
in church.[43] Indeed, the emperor at the head of the Great Entrance
procession, surrounded by a large bodyguard, can be seen to clear the
way in the nave. He opens the way for the holy gifts.[44]

Dagron sees in the emperor's status as *depotatos* a 'breathtaking
fall', a 'downgrading' of the emperor's position.[45] Indeed, *depotatos*

---

[39] For a discussion of this point, see Macrides, Munitiz and Angelov, *Pseudo-Kodinos*,
445–8.
[40] Ibid. 232 ll. 18–22, 233 n. 678. In the tenth century the emperor received communion at a small table outside the sanctuary: Majeska, 'The Emperor in his Church',
4.
[41] Macrides, Munitiz and Angelov, *Pseudo-Kodinos*, 228 ll. 4–5, 229 n. 664.
[42] Ibid. 228 l. 5 – 230 l. 6.
[43] Symeon of Thessalonike, *Opera omnia*, PL 155, cols 352C–D.
[44] Robert Taft, 'The Byzantine Imperial Communion Ritual', in Pamela Armstrong, ed.,
Ritual and Art: Byzantine Essays for Christopher Walter (London, 2006), 1–26, at 4–5.
[45] Dagron, *Emperor and Priest*, 280–1, 288.

is a very low title in the Church hierarchy.[46] A tenth-century miracle collection refers to a son of a high official who was cured of a fever at the shrine of the Virgin at Pege, in Constantinople. In thanks for his cure, he served as *depotatos* at the church of the Virgin, leading the procession at the time of the holy eucharist.[47] In the miracle collection, as in Pseudo-Kodinos, the function of the title-holder is to lead the Great Entrance procession.

In the discussion of the *depotatos* title it is assumed that the emperor relinquished or was forced to relinquish a much more potent title, that of the difficult-to-translate *epistemonarches*, 'chief scholar' or 'chief scientific expert'. It is a title associated with twelfth- and thirteenth-century emperors, and especially Manuel I Komnenos, a high-profile emperor if ever there was one.[48] It is used always in connection with the emperor's involvement in church affairs, his interrogation of a patriarch in a synodal gathering, or the synod's consultation with him on a matter of canon law. The last emperor to refer to himself with this designation is Michael VIII Palaiologos who in 1270 instructs the patriarch to give the deacon Theodore Skoutariotes a rank in the hierarchy equivalent to that of *dikaiophylax*, keeper of the law, which the emperor had bestowed on him.[49]

Epistemonarches, however, like *depotatos,* is a minor ecclesiastical position low in the hierarchy. The *epistemonarches* is in charge of discipline in the monastery; until the twelfth century the word is found exclusively in monastic foundation charters where it refers to the duty of the monk *epistemonarches* to keep order at meal times and during chanting.[50] Thus it is similar to *depotatos* in its low rank and its function of maintaining order. But there is one large difference between them. No emperor ever referred to himself as a *depotatos*, whereas emperor and Church applied *epistemonarches* to the emperor, 'a convenient and ambiguous label, a screen which avoided the

---

[46] On the *depotatos* (δηπότατος), see Jean Darrouzès, *Recherches sur les ΟΦΦΙΚΙΑ de l'église byzantine* (Paris, 1970), 215–16, 272–3, 552, 569.

[47] 'Anonymous Miracles of the Pege', in *Miracle Tales from Byzantium*, transl. Alice-Mary Talbot and Scott F. Johnson (Cambridge, MA, and London, 2012), 280–1 (ch. 55).

[48] Angold, *Church and Society*, 99, 100, 102, 530, 546–62; Dagron, *Emperor and Priest*, 253–5. For Manuel I as *epistemonarches*, see Magdalino, *Empire*, 277, 280–1; Angelov, *Imperial Ideology*, 359–60.

[49] For Michael VIII, see Pachymeres, *Relations historiques*, ed. Failler, transl. Laurent, 1: 341 ll. 17–20 (his right as *epistemonarches* to convene a synod to depose the patriarch Arsenios); Zepos and Zepos, *Jus Graecoromanum*, 1: 503 (*prostagma* of 1270 appointing Skoutariotes as *dikaiophylax*).

[50] Macrides, 'Nomos and Kanon', 63 and n. 7.

necessity of justifying more or less recognised rights'.[51] When it suited them, patriarchs would acknowledge the emperor's right to intervene in ecclesiastical affairs by reference to their epistemonarchic competence. Thus, the patriarch Athanasios (1289–93, 1303–9), an ascetic and staunch supporter of the 'liberty of the Church', called on the emperor Andronikos II to expel provincial bishops residing in Constantinople and to put on trial the metropolitan of Cyzicus who was accused of simony. In doing so he made reference to the emperor's epistemonarchic rights.[52] Makarios, metropolitan of Ankyra (1397–1405), attacked the involvement of the emperor in ecclesiastical administration in a treatise on canon law, but referred to his epistemonarchic right in an anti-Latin treatise.[53] These examples indicate that the designations attached to emperors at different times are more indicative of the particular circumstances in which they are used than of the emperor's status.

Finally, Dagron draws attention to the form of words used by the emperor at the ceremony for the promotion of the patriarch. He finds significant the fact that in the *Book of Ceremonies* it is divine grace and the royal office, the *basileia*, that promote the candidate to the position of patriarch, while in Pseudo-Kodinos it is the Holy Trinity alone.[54] But if we look at the protocol for the promotion of a patriarch other striking aspects emerge.

In Pseudo-Kodinos's compilation, the protocol for the promotion of a patriarch[55] follows that for the three highest dignitaries after

---

[51] Dagron, *Emperor and Priest*, 255.

[52] *The Correspondence of Athanasius I, Patriarch of Constantinople*, ed. and transl. Alice-Mary Maffry Talbot, Dumbarton Oaks Texts 3 (Washington DC, 1975), 182 (no. 61), 248 (no. 95). Angelov, who argues for the Church's ascendancy in the Palaiologan period, explains the patriarch's behaviour thus: 'In making these concessions Athanasios proved to be a realist': *Imperial Ideology*, 394.

[53] Dositheos, *Tomos katallages* (Iaşi, 1692), 194–5; new edn by Christos Triantafyllopoulos, 'An Annotated Critical Edition of the Treatise *Against the Errors of the Latins* by Makarios, Metropolitan of Ankyra (1397–1405)', 2 vols (PhD thesis, Royal Holloway, University of London, 2009), 2: 111 ll. 17–18: 'it was given to him by Christ to be *epistemonarches* and *dephensor* of the Church'.

[54] Gilbert Dagron, 'Empires royaux, royautés impériales', in Rainer Maria Kiesow, Regina Ogorek and Spiros Simitis, eds, *Summa. Dieter Simon zum 70. Geburtstag* (Frankfurt am Main, 2005), 81–97, at 92; *De cerimoniis*, ed. Reiske, 1: 565 ll. 1–3 (Moffatt and Tall, *Book of Ceremonies*, 2: 565); Macrides, Munitiz and Angelov, *Pseudo-Kodinos*, 254 ll. 5–8.

[55] The protocol for the patriarchal promotion has been studied by Marie-Hélène Blanchet, 'L'Élection du patriarche à Byzance à la fin du Moyen Âge (XIVᵉ–XVᵉ siècles)', in Corinne Péneau, ed., *Élections et pouvoirs politiques du VIIᵉ au XVIIᵉ siècle* (Paris,

emperor – despot, *sebastokrator* and caesar – and presents a number of parallels with the third of these. The same word 'promotion' (*problesis*) designates the elevation of the highest dignitaries and that of the patriarch.[56] All these promotions take place in a hall of the palace.[57] The emperor wears his crown, which signifies his most formal dress.[58] The patriarch-to-be, called the 'candidate-patriarch',[59] is escorted by a high court official when he steps forward to receive his ensign of office, the staff, from the emperor.[60] The patriarch leaves the palace on horseback, mounting his horse in the palace courtyard, a privilege given only to members of the imperial family and highest dignitaries,[61] and returns to Hagia Sophia accompanied by court officials.[62]

These elements of the patriarch's promotion which are also found in the ceremonial of a dignitary's promotion raise questions about the status of the patriarch. He is both above the highest dignitaries and equal to them. This ambiguity is demonstrated by Pseudo-Kodinos when he explains why the despot, *sebastokrator* and caesar are not present for the patriarchal promotion. It is 'inappropriate' for them to stand while the patriarch sits; nor can they sit while he stands.[63]

Other elements in the protocol further illustrate the patriarch's status vis-à-vis the emperor. Both the emperor and the patriarch sit on thrones that have been prepared for the occasion. However, the two thrones are not side-by-side on the same level. Not only is the emperor's throne raised up on a platform but it is also higher than his usual throne. His throne is like the one used at the emperor's coronation; it is 'four or even five steps high'.[64] By contrast, the throne of the patriarch rests on the floor and is thus much lower than the emperor's, which it faces.[65] To receive his staff of office the patriarch has to 'mount' the platform where the emperor stands.

2006), 63–78; Renauld Rochette, 'Le Ciel et le sang. Le Pouvoir impérial à Byzance à l'époque des Paléologues (1261–1453)' (doctoral thesis, Université Paris I, 2009). See also below, 137–9.

[56] Macrides, Munitiz and Angelov, *Pseudo-Kodinos*, 244 l. 1, 248 l. 1, 250 l. 1.

[57] The *triklinos*: ibid. 244 l. 3, 250 l. 18.

[58] Ibid. 252 l. 3, 253 n. 742.

[59] Ibid. 252 l. 7.

[60] Ibid. 254 ll. 1–4.

[61] Ibid. 257 n. 759, 389.

[62] Ibid. 254 l. 14.

[63] Ibid. 252 l. 11.

[64] Ibid. 250 l. 19 – 252 l. 1, 253 n. 740.

[65] Ibid. 252 ll. 5–8.

He 'again descends'.[66] On the other hand, unlike the despot, the patriarch does not kiss the foot of the emperor after his promotion, a sign of his submission and gratitude, but rather blesses him.[67]

If these outward gestures and material conditions on the occasion of the promotion provide a mixed response to the question of the patriarch's status, the protocol leaves no room for doubt when it describes the way a patriarch-elect becomes patriarch. It is the emperor who creates the patriarch. Until his promotion in the palace he is a patriarch-elect. When the emperor pronounces the words, 'The Holy Trinity … promotes you archbishop of Constantinople, New Rome and ecumenical patriarch', the patriarch is made.[68] This formulation is similar to that used in the 'little consecration' by which a bishop is ordained and, as Pseudo-Kodinos says, in the case of the patriarch the emperor's promotion takes the place of that consecration.[69] Indeed, the whole process of choosing a new patriarch is initiated by an imperial order.[70] The synod cannot meet without this imperative of the emperor and, as is well known, the emperor has the right to reject the candidates put forward by the synod.

Yet it could be asked how we can know that these protocols reflect the practice of the time and are not merely projecting a procedure that was never carried out as described. The answer is that numerous examples of patriarchal elections from different times attest to aspects of the election, while the specifics of the ceremony as Pseudo-Kodinos describes it are corroborated by two fourteenth- and fifteenth-century churchmen whose writings attempt to reduce the significance of the emperor's role in the making of a patriarch. Symeon of Thessalonike is the more consistent and polemical of the two. He explains how patriarchs are made:

> The emperor serves [the decisions] of the synod, for he was established as the anointed of the Lord, defender (*dephensor*) and servant of the Church, and promised this when he was anointed … . They talk nonsense, those who, innovating and struck by malice, say that the emperor makes the patriarch. For, as explained, it is in no way the

---

[66] Ibid. 254 ll. 9–11.
[67] Ibid. 254 ll. 10–11.
[68] Ibid. 254 ll. 5–8.
[69] Ibid. 256 ll. 13–16.
[70] K. N. Sathas, Μεσαιωνικὴ Βιβλιοθήκη, 7 vols (Athens, 1972; first publ. Venice and Paris, 1872–94), 6: 653 ll. 3–20 (no. 19); *De cerimoniis*, ed. Reiske, 1: 564; Rochette, 'Le Ciel et le sang', 393.

emperor but the synod that effects it and the emperor, being pious, simply serves. It is not only because he is protector (*ekdikos*) and emperor anointed by the Church but so that he might, by assisting and serving, cherish and maintain secure [the decisions] of the Church. ... If the one elected is not a priest, he is made priest before he accepts the summons. Then something else happens before ordination; it is called 'promotion'. It is a declaration of agreement from the very mouth of the emperor and [a mark of] honour to the Church that he cherishes the one chosen by her and voted by her, accepted to be the shepherd of the Church and in the name of the Holy Trinity which gave him the imperial majesty, he considers him archbishop of Constantinople, New Rome and ecumenical patriarch. He does not make him patriarch, he confers nothing on him but rather he expresses his agreement and assists in the deed.[71]

Symeon's insistence that the emperor carries out the decisions of the Church as its helper and servant – the verbs 'to serve', 'to assist' and the noun 'servant' appear no fewer than five times in the statements cited above – betrays the importance of the emperor's role in the making of a patriarch, from start to finish. His statements likewise show that the question, who makes a patriarch, was controversial in his time. He engages in a polemic with anonymous opponents, addressing the issues raised by those who 'talk nonsense, those who ... say that the emperor makes the patriarch'. Symeon emphasizes that at every stage of the procedure the emperor is serving the Church, honouring and not 'ruling' it.[72] According to him, as protector of the Church the emperor has permission from on high and from the holy fathers to bring together the holy synod to elect a candidate. When the candidate is elected, the summons brought to him by a high-ranking member of the court, in the name of the emperor, states that it is from the emperor and the holy great synod, 'bearing witness that the emperor makes known the [decision] of the synod not from himself but with the synod. He serves only'.[73] With respect to the emperor's investiture of the patriarch-elect with his staff (*dikanikion*), Symeon declares that the emperor gives 'nothing'.[74]

---

[71] Symeon of Thessalonike, PL 155, cols 437C–444D, at 440B–441A. For a discussion of the statements of Symeon and Makarios, see Blanchet, 'L'Élection', 63–78.
[72] PL 155, col 441C.
[73] Ibid., col. 440C.
[74] Ibid., col. 441B.

In similar fashion, Makarios of Ankyra plays down the emperor's part in the making of a patriarch. He stresses that 'the patriarch is called patriarch before the imperial promotion'. According to him, the promotion in the palace – the venue was not mentioned by Symeon – takes place only for the sake of 'honour'; it has no foundation in civil or canon law.[75] Makarios is, however, less insistent, less polemical. He is also a less consistent writer than Symeon on the subject of the emperor's authority in church matters. His views are contradictory, as can be seen from his use of *epistemonarches* to refer to the emperor in an anti-Latin treatise, discussed above.[76]

Despite the protests of Symeon and Makarios, it remains the case until the end of the Byzantine empire that the process of electing a new patriarch is put in motion only by an imperial order (*prostagma*), that the emperor can reject the candidate elected by the synod and put his own candidate in place, and that the patriarch-elect goes to the palace to be promoted and invested by the emperor. Concerning this last point, Symeon says as much.[77]

Now, as then, the procedure for the election and installation of a patriarch is open to rival interpretations. Bréhier saw in the texts under discussion an evolution in the election procedure that corresponded to a weakening of imperial power.[78] Laurent rejected the idea of an effective change and stated that if there was change it was only 'on the polemical plane, in the thought of two theoreticians carried along by circumstances to fight for the independence of the church, reduced every day more and more'.[79] Blanchet, the latest to analyse the writings of the churchmen, agrees that 'it is difficult to conclude that there was any historical transformation'.[80] She does, however, point out that both Symeon and Makarios directly and indirectly express the view that a patriarch-elect who is a bishop has

[75] For the text, see Vitalien Laurent, 'Le Rituel de l'investiture du patriarche byzantin au début du XVᵉ siècle', *Bulletin de la section historique de l'Académie roumaine* 28 (1947), 218–32, at 231–2.

[76] See above, 135; Angelov, *Imperial Ideology*, 372.

[77] PL 155, cols 441A–C.

[78] L. Bréhier, 'L'Investiture des patriarches à Constantinople au moyen âge', in *Miscellanea Giovanni Mercati*, 3: *Letteratura e storia bizantina*, Studi e testi 123 (Vatican City, 1946), 368–72.

[79] '[S]ur le plan polémique, dans la pensée de deux théoriciens portés par les événements à lutter pour l'indépendance chaque jour plus réduite de l'Église': Laurent, 'Le Rituel', 225.

[80] '[I]l est bien difficile de conclure à une quelconque transformation historique': Blanchet, 'L'Élection', 72.

no need of the 'little consecration'[81] which the emperor's promotion replaces, according to Pseudo-Kodinos.[82] Yet, even in this case, the patriarch-elect must go to the palace and be promoted by the emperor.

The reverse situation of that described by these two late churchmen is indicated by a late fourteenth-century patriarchal document which states that the emperor may employ metropolitans as if they were his *douloi*, 'servants'.[83] In letters addressed to a crowned emperor a metropolitan must refer to himself as the emperor's *doulos kai euchetes*, 'servant and the one who prays for your mighty and holy imperial majesty', a formula close to the one used by lay servants of the emperor.[84] In the fifteenth century the use of the formula was extended to include all clerics. Sylvester Syropoulos, in his account of the council at Ferrara-Florence, where a union of the Churches was agreed in 1438–9, protested, saying that it was not acceptable for the Church to be put to the service of the emperor.[85] In these later centuries churchmen were often among the ambassadors who were sent abroad;[86] churchmen also acted as the emperor's go-between or mediator (*mesazon*) in public affairs, whereas earlier this role was always assigned to a layman.[87] Historians have seen these examples as signs of the growing importance of the Church. They can, however,

---

[81] PL 155, col. 441B; Makarios of Ankyra, ed. Laurent, 'Le Rituel', 232; Blanchet, 'L'Élection', 74–5.

[82] See above, 137.

[83] Jean Darrouzès, '*Ekthésis néa*. Manuel des *pittakia* du XIVe siècle', *Revue des études byzantines* 27 (1969), 5–127, at 55; Vitalien Laurent, 'Les Droits de l'empereur en matière ecclésiastique. L'accord de 1380/82', *Revue des études byzantines* 13 (1955), 5–20, at 16 (§6). For a recent re-examination of this text in which the 'rights' are considered in their historical context, see Petre Guran, 'Patriarche hésychaste et empereur latinophrone. L'Accord de 1380 sur les droits impériaux en matière ecclésiastique', *Revue des études sudest européennes* 39 (2001), 53–62; see also Rochette, 'Le Ciel et le sang', 395–8, who also interprets the synodal act of 1380 as the emperor's reinforcement of his hold over the Church.

[84] Darrouzès, 'Ekthésis néa', 55 (no. 39).

[85] Vitalien Laurent, ed., *Les 'Mémoires' du grand ecclésiastique de l'église de Constantinople Sylvestre Syropoulos sur le concile de Florence (1438–1439)* (Paris, 1971), 104–5 (§4); Rochette, 'Le Ciel et le sang', 397.

[86] Nicholas Oikonomides, 'Byzantine Diplomacy, A.D. 1204–1453: Means and Ends', in Jonathan Shepard and Simon Franklin, eds, *Byzantine Diplomacy* (Aldershot, 1992), , at 80–1; Stavroula Andriopoulou, 'Diplomatic Communication between Byzantium and the West under the later Palaiologoi (1354–1453)' (PhD thesis, University of Birmingham, 2010), 121–32, 358.

[87] The example of the metropolitan of Philadelphia, Phokas, who acted as *mesazon* for John III Vatatzes in the mid-thirteenth century, is cited by Angold as evidence of the Church's dominant position: *Church and Society*, 563. Phokas is, however, the only

be read as signs of the emperor's use of churchmen as his *douloi*.[88] Vitalien Laurent, an Augustinian Assumptionist and editor of these late patriarchal texts, was so revolted by the language of *douleia* (servitude), which he translated as 'slavery' (*l'esclavage*), that he looked upon the Ottoman conquest of the empire as a time of liberation for the Church.[89]

Another factor that has been adduced as evidence of the Church's rising power and prestige is the expansion of its judicial competence. The patriarchal court in Constantinople, whose register has survived for the years from 1315 to 1402,[90] passed judgment not only on cases within its recognized jurisdiction, marriage and inheritance law,[91] but also beyond. For modern historians, the register provides proof of the Church's newly acquired judicial powers. Yet it needs to be considered that the apparent widening of the court's jurisdiction may be due to the fact that in the same period (1394–1402), the imperial court was absent from the capital or not functioning because of the Turkish siege of the city and the dispute between John VII and Manuel II.[92]

The evidence presented above, the ceremonial protocol, the patriarchal document and the writings of the churchmen, admits of a reading that differs from the conventional one. The history of the Church under the Palaiologan emperors in the thirteenth to fifteenth

---

example he cites of a churchman in this position. For Phokas, see Ruth Macrides, *George Akropolites: The History* (Oxford, 2007), 266 n. 24.

[88] A similar example is the establishment of mixed courts of laymen and churchmen established by Andronikos III (1328–41), the so-called 'universal judges' (*katholikoi kritai*). It has been held as significant that churchmen were appointed to serve in these courts next to laymen. Again, the appointment of a bishop to each court of universal judges can be seen as a use of churchmen by the emperor as his 'servants': see Alexander P. Kazhdan et al., eds, *The Oxford Dictionary of Byzantium*, 3 vols (Oxford, 1991), 2: 1158, *s.v.* 'kritai katholikoi'.

[89] Laurent, 'Les Droits', 10–12; Rochette, 'Le Ciel', 397 and n. 345.

[90] Franz Miklosich and Ioseph Müller, eds, *Acta et diplomata graeca medii aevi sacra et profana*, 6 vols (Vienna, 1860–90); new edition with German translation in *Das Register des Patriarchats von Konstantinopel*, 1, ed. Herbert Hunger and Otto Kresten (Vienna, 1981), for 1315–31; 2, ed. Herbert Hunger et al. (Vienna, 1995), for 1337–50; 3, ed. Johannes Koder, Martin Hinterberger and Otto Kresten (Vienna, 2001), for 1350–63.

[91] Ruth Macrides, 'Dowry and Inheritance in the Late Period: Some Cases from the Patriarchal Register', in Dieter Simon, ed., *Eherecht und Familiengut in Antike und Mittelalter* (Munich, 1992), 89–98, reprinted in Macrides, *Kinship and Justice*, V.

[92] Argued by Eleftheria Papagianni, 'Πατριαρχικὸ καὶ αὐτοκρατορικὸ δικαστήριο ἐπὶ Ματθαίου Α΄: Μία σχέση ἀνταγωνισμοῦ', in Theodora Antonopoulou, Sofia Kotzabassi and Marina Loukaki, eds, *Myriobiblos: Essays on Byzantine Literature and Culture* (Boston, MA, Berlin and Munich, 2015), 253–60.

centuries shows that the ascendancy of the emperor over the Church remained strong. The descriptions of imperial debilitation in the last centuries of the empire would seem to have more to do with modern historians' knowledge of shrinking territory and diminished resources than with the actual state of the emperor's office. Pero Tafur, a Spanish traveller who visited Constantinople in 1437, in the reign of John VIII, remarked, 'The emperor's state is as splendid as ever, for nothing is omitted from the ancient ceremonies but, properly regarded, he is like a Bishop without a See'.[93]

What is new in the Palaiologan period is the existence of churchmen who contested loudly the ascendancy of imperial power. In their discussions of ceremonial, Symeon of Thessalonike and Makarios of Ankyra tried to show that the emperor was subject to the Church, while practice shows the opposite.[94] It is their writings that have been adopted by historians to form a picture of the rising Church.

The confident claims made by these churchmen have to do, to some extent, with the sins of the founder of the dynasty, Michael VIII, who usurped power from the young heir to the throne John IV and had him blinded, and who deposed the patriarch Arsenios who had excommunicated him.[95] The so-called Arsenite schism damaged the emperor beyond his death and produced literature that proclaimed the anointer to be superior to the anointed.[96] The lasting effects of this schism in the Church elevated defiance of the Palaiolo-

[93] Pero Tafur, *Travels and Adventures, 1435–1439*, ed. and transl. Malcolm Letts (London, 1926), 145; for his description of the monuments he saw and conversations he had, see ibid. 117–25, 138–48.

[94] For example, the 'groom service' of the emperor for the patriarch, which Symeon of Thessalonike describes but is not otherwise attested: see the comment of Lutz Rickelt, 'Die Exkommunikation Michaels VIII. Palaiologos durch den Patriarchen Arsenios', in Grünbart, Rickelt and Vučetić, eds, *Zwei Sonnen* 1, 97–125, at 104: 'bleibt es fraglich, ob Symeon ein tatsächliche Zeremoniell niedergeschrieben hat'.

[95] On Arsenios and the Arsenite schism, see Ruth Macrides, 'Saints and Sainthood in the Early Palaiologan Period', in Sergei Hackel, ed., *The Byzantine Saint* (Birmingham, 1981), 67–87, especially 73–9, with the older bibliography; Ionut-Alexandru Tudorie, 'Le Schisme Arsénite (1265–1310). Entre AKRIBEIA et OIKONOMIA', *Zbornik Radova* 48 (2011), 133–75; Rickelt, 'Die Exkommunikation Michaels VIII.'; Dimiter G. Angelov, 'The Confession of Michael VIII Palaiologos and King David', *Jahrbuch der Österreichischen Byzantinistik* 56 (2006), 193–204.

[96] 'The anointer is greater than the anointed, the one who blesses greater than the blessed one … . It is all necessary that the emperor, blessed and anointed, should be under the patriarch, as he is in need of grace': Macrides, 'Saints and Sainthood', 78. This statement was first made in the anonymous '*Logos* for St Arsenios, patriarch of Constantinople' in Patmos, cod. Pat. 366, fol. 434ʳ, published by Panagiotis G. Nikolopoulos,

gan emperors to the level of a virtue. A further damaging act of two Palaiologan emperors, the union of the Churches declared by Michael VIII in 1274 and John VIII in 1439 but never accepted, contributed to divisions and gave the Church the moral upper hand.[97] Relations between Church and emperor, not only in the last centuries but also earlier, depended on the personalities and circumstances of the moment. It was these factors that determined who took the lead.

If Runciman's picture of the late Byzantine Church has continued to find acceptance in the literature on Palaiologan Byzantium, his perception of the Church's position under Ottoman rule has been criticized and overturned. The idea that ecclesiastical power was centralized in the patriarchate of Constantinople and that the patriarch had centralized control over the Eastern patriarchates has been shown to be false.[98] It has been shown too that the patriarch in Constantinople was not leader of the whole Orthodox community; he was not 'an ethnarch, the ruler of a millet', as Runciman stated.[99] Runciman 'merged the nineteenth-century ideology of the Patriarchate of Constantinople and Ottoman millet system theory and back-projected this view to the whole Ottoman period'.[100] Given this revision of the Constantinopolitan patriarchate's position under Ottoman rule, it is time to have another look at Byzantium's legacy to the Ottomans. The interpretation of the late Byzantine sources presented here suggests that there was more continuity from the Byzantine empire to Ottoman rule as regards Church-ruler relations than was previously thought.[101]

Ἀνέκδοτος λόγος εἰς Ἀρσένιον Αὐτωρειανόν πατριάρχην Κωσταντινουπόλεως', Ἐπετηρὶς Ἑταιρείας Βυζαντινῶν Σπουδῶν 45 (1981–2), 406–61, at 461.

[97] See the comments of Angelov, *Imperial Ideology*, 414.

[98] Hasan Çolak, *The Orthodox Church in the Early Modern Middle East: Relations between the Ottoman Central Administration and the Patriarchates of Antioch, Jerusalem and Alexandria* (Ankara, 2015).

[99] Runciman, *Great Church*, 171–2; idem, '"Rum Millet": The Orthodox Communities under the Ottoman Sultans', in John J. Yiannias, ed., *The Byzantine Tradition after the Fall of Constantinople* (Charlottesville, NC, and London, 1991), 1–15.

[100] Çolak, *Orthodox Church*, 239; Tom Papademetriou, *Render unto the Sultan: Power, Authority, and the Greek Orthodox Church in the Early Ottoman Centuries* (Oxford, 2015), reviews the older literature.

[101] It should be noted that the revisionists of Runciman's views all accept his and others' perception of a strong Church under the late Byzantine emperors.

An English Bishop Afloat in an Irish See:
John Bale, Bishop of Ossory, 1552–3

Stephen Tong*

University of Cambridge

The Reformation in Ireland has traditionally been seen as an unmitigated failure. This article contributes to current scholarship that is challenging this perception by conceiving the sixteenth-century Irish Church as part of the English Church. It does so by examining the episcopal career of John Bale, bishop of Ossory, County Kilkenny, 1552–3. Bale wrote an account of his Irish experience, known as the Vocacyon, *soon after fleeing his diocese upon the accession of Queen Mary to the English throne and the subsequent restoration of Roman Catholicism. The article considers Bale's episcopal career as an expression of the relationship between Church and state in mid-Tudor England and Ireland. It will be shown that ecclesiastical reform in Ireland was complemented by political subjugation, and vice versa. Having been appointed by Edward VI, Bale upheld the royal supremacy as justification for implementing ecclesiastical reform. The combination of preaching the gospel and enforcing the 1552 Prayer Book was, for Bale, the best method of evangelism. The double effect was to win converts and align the Irish Church with the English form of worship. Hence English reformers exploited the political dominance of England to export their evangelical faith into Ireland.*

The Irish Reformation has traditionally been seen as an unmitigated failure. It has generally been assumed that the inability of Protestantism to take deep root in early modern Ireland was always a foregone conclusion, despite the repeated efforts of English reformers to spread their religion into this corner of the Tudor empire.[1] This

* 20 Reynolds St, Pymble, NSW 2073, Australia. E-mail: stephen.n.tong@gmail.com.
  I would like to thank Jane Dawson, Ashley Null, Jacqueline Rose and Alexandra Walsham for their helpful and encouraging feedback on previous drafts of this article.
[1] For an introduction to this discussion, see Brendan Bradshaw, 'Sword, Word and Strategy in the Reformation of Ireland', *HistJ* 21 (1978), 475–502; Nicholas Canny, 'Why the Reformation Failed in Ireland: Une Question mal posée', *JEH* 30 (1979), 423–50; K. S. Bottigheimer, 'The Failure of the Reformation in Ireland: Une Question bien posée', *JEH* 36 (1985), 196–207; idem and B. Bradshaw, 'Revisionism and the Irish Reformation: A

Studies in Church History 54 (2018) 144–158
doi: 10.1017/stc.2017.9

© Ecclesiastical History Society 2018

is perhaps symptomatic of the historiographical trend to isolate Ireland from England in studies of the period.[2]   Henry Jefferies has recently challenged these models by conceiving the sixteenth-century Irish Church as existing under the umbrella of the English Church.[3] By following Jefferies's lead, this article seeks to understand the Irish Reformation from a contemporary English perspective, namely the autobiographical account given by John Bale in *The Vocacyon of Johan Bale to the bishoprick of Ossorie in Irelande his persecusions in y̓ same & final delyueraunce* (1553).[4] It will be argued that the appointment of English ministers to Irish bishoprics was consistent with efforts to expand the burgeoning Tudor 'empire' through an extension of the English state's religious policy.

The *Vocacyon* tells John Bale's story of being appointed to the bishopric of Ossory, County Kilkenny, by Edward VI; his struggle to make headway against a bloc of conservative clergy; his escape from murderous mobs upon the accession of Mary; and his high-sea adventures involving pirates en route to a safe refuge on the Continent.[5] Due to the specific dates given in the text, it is likely that Bale worked from a diary to compose the *Vocacyon* almost immediately after arriving on the Continent.[6] This 'factual' quality has led it to be described as one of the earliest examples of autobiography in the English language.[7]

Debate', *JEH* 51 (2000), 581–92; H. A. Jefferies, 'The Early Tudor Reformation in the Irish Pale', *JEH* 52 (2001), 34–62.

[2] For the Edwardian Reformation in England, see Diarmaid MacCulloch, *Tudor Church Militant: Edward VI and the Protestant Reformation* (London, 1999); Catharine Davies, *A Religion of the Word: The Defence of the Reformation in the Reign of Edward VI* (Manchester, 2002).

[3] Henry Jefferies, *The Irish Church and the Tudor Reformations* (Dublin, 2010), especially 101–3; idem, 'The Marian Restoration in Ireland', *BCH* 33 (2016), 12–31; see also Brendan Bradshaw, 'The Edwardian Reformation in Ireland, 1547–53', *AH* 34 (1977), 83–99; James Murray, *Enforcing the English Reformation in Ireland: Clerical Resistance and Political Conflict in the Diocese of Dublin, 1534–1590* (Cambridge, 2009).

[4] John Bale, *The Vocacyon of Johan Bale to the Bishoprick of Ossorie in Irelande his Persecusions in ye same & final Delyueraunce* ([Wesel]?, 1553). The critical modern edition of the text is *The Vocacyon of Johan Bale*, ed. P. Happé and J. N. King (New York, 1990).

[5] Ibid.; see also Felicity Heal, *Reformation in Britain and Ireland* (Oxford, 2003), 1–12. For biographical details of Bale, see Leslie P. Fairfield, *John Bale: Mythmaker for the English Reformation* (West Lafayette, IN, 1976); Peter Happé, *John Bale* (New York, 1996), 1–25.

[6] See Bale, *Vocacyon*, ed. Happé and King, 12–13, 17–18.

[7] Leslie P. Fairfield, '*The Vocacyon of Johan Bale* and early English Autobiography', *RQ* 24 (1971), 327–40, at 327; see also Meredith Anne Skura, *Tudor Autobiography: Listening for Inwardness* (Chicago, IL, 2008), ch. 3.

Bale's narrative, however, must be treated with caution. The *Vocacyon* is a carefully constructed piece of self-representation in which Bale offers his own theological interpretation of very recent events with a specific pastoral objective in mind. Written for a beleaguered community of English evangelicals in the nascent stages of their continental exile under Mary, it was a 'homily to true believers' designed to encourage them to persevere in the face of acute persecution.[8]

This work has long attracted attention from literary scholars interested in early modern conceptions of nationality.[9] Likewise, historians have turned to the *Vocacyon* for insights into the prevailing religious conditions of mid-Tudor Ireland.[10] However, previous evaluations of the *Vocacyon* have too readily taken Bale at face value.[11] There is another aspect that is often overlooked, even in Steven Ellis's important essay on Bale's episcopal career: many academics have failed to appreciate that Bale saw himself as an agent of the English crown.[12] This article explores the extent to which Bale's self-conscious English identity affected his attitude to his episcopal office. His ministry as a bishop in Ireland will be contextualized within the wider English movement of religious reform during the reign of Edward VI (1547–53), in an attempt to throw new light on the imperial designs of the English government in this period, when the Edwardian Reformation was at its apogee.[13]

Little is known about Bale's appointment to the vacant see of Ossory in August 1552 apart from the account that we are given in the *Vocacyon*. Thus it remains unclear why he was chosen to fill this role at this particular moment. Bale was well qualified as a known

---

[8] Steven Ellis, 'John Bale, Bishop of Ossory, 1552–3', *Journal of the Butler Society* 2 (1984), 286.
[9] Fairfield, '*Vocacyon* and Autobiography'; John N. King, *English Reformation Literature: The Tudor Origins of the Protestant Tradition* (Princeton, NJ, 1982), 56–76; Andrew Hadfield, 'Translating the Reformation: John Bale's Irish *Vocacyon*', in B. Bradshaw, A. Hadfield and W. Maley, eds, *Representing Ireland: Literature and the Origins of the Conflict, 1534–1660* (Cambridge, 1993), 43–59; Stewart Mottram, *Empire and Nation in Early English Renaissance Literature* (Woodbridge, 2008), 11–34.
[10] See nn. 1, 3 above.
[11] For example, Katherine Walsh, 'Deliberate Provocation or Reforming Zeal? John Bale as First Church of Ireland Bishop of Ossory (1552/53–1563)', in Vincent Carey and Ute Lotz-Heumann, eds, *Taking Sides? Colonial and Confessional Mentalities in Early Modern Ireland* (Dublin, 2003), 42–60.
[12] Ellis, 'John Bale', 283–93.
[13] For the Edwardian Reformation at this period, see MacCulloch, *Tudor Church Militant*, 126.

evangelical and author of the first full commentary in English on the book of Revelation, *The Image of Bothe Churches* (*c*.1545), which viewed history through an apocalyptic lens, and significantly shaped the way mid-Tudor reformers conceived their times as a spiritual contest between members of the true and false Churches.[14] Yet despite this, his own romanticized account of being 'called in a manner from deathe to this office' by the king during his royal progress through Winchester gives the impression that the establishment had previously overlooked Bale for ecclesiastical preferment.[15] Indeed, upon his return to England from a self-imposed exile during the 1540s in the wake of the fall of his former patron Thomas Cromwell and in reaction to the Act of Six Articles, Bale was only able to secure the rather minor post of rector of Bishopstoke, Hampshire, on 26 June 1551, before being promoted to vicar of Swaffham soon after, both thanks to his friend John Ponet, bishop of Winchester.[16]

A possible reason for Bale's ministerial obscurity is that Sir William Paget, an influential member of the Privy Council, was ill disposed toward him. In 1547, Bale had criticized Paget for trying to force the Protestant martyr, Anne Askew, to recant before her execution and accused him of defending transubstantiation.[17] When Bale returned to England in 1548, Paget was still in a powerful political position, and was therefore 'well placed to block Bale from

---

[14] John Bale, *The Image of Bothe Churches* (Antwerp, *c*.1545); see also *John Bale's* The Image of Both Churches, ed. Gretchen E. Minton (Dordrecht, 2013), 1–34; Katharine Firth, *The Apocalyptic Tradition in Reformation Britain, 1530–1645* (Oxford, 1979), 32–68; Catharine Davies, '"Poor Persecuted Little Flock" or "Commonwealth of Christians"? Edwardian Protestant Concepts of the Church', in Peter Lake and Maria Dowling, eds, *Protestantism and the National Church in Sixteenth-Century England* (London, 1987), 78–102.

[15] Bale, *Vocacyon*, sigs B8–C1, at C1. The king's direct involvement in Bale's appointment is consonant with the view that Edward began to take greater control of government from 1550 onwards, especially in regard to religious policy, despite still being a minor. See W. K. Jordan, *Edward VI, The Threshold of Power: The Dominance of the Duke of Northumberland* (London, 1970), 367–8; Jennifer Loach, *Edward VI*, ed. George Bernard and Penry Williams (New Haven, CT, and London, 1999), 130–4.

[16] For details, see John N. King, 'Bale, John (1495–1563)', *ODNB*, online edn (October 2009), at: <http://www.oxforddnb.com/view/article/1175>, accessed 31 October 2017.

[17] John Bale, *The Lattre Examinacyon of Anne Askewe latelye martyred in Smythfelde, by the Wycked Synagoge of Antichrist, with the Elucydacyon of Iohan Bale* ([Wesel]?, 1547), sigs C4ᵛ–7ᵛ.

advancement'.[18] It may be significant that Bale's appointment to Ossory occurred while Paget was disgraced and faced charges of corruption (he received a full pardon in December 1552, and was reinstated to the council the following February).

Other records corroborate the view that Bale had been overlooked by the Edwardian regime. When Archbishop Cranmer wrote to William Cecil on 25 August 1552, he suggested four men for the primacy of Ireland, that is, as archbishop of Armagh; Bale was not on the list.[19] One of Cranmer's recommendations was Hugh Goodacre, who was to join Bale in Dublin for their joint consecration service the following March.[20] Although Cranmer had not considered Bale to fill the important see of Armagh, it is certainly possible that John Ponet had had a hand in the promotions of both Bale and Goodacre: Bale was a prebendary at Winchester, and Goodacre was Ponet's chaplain. Ponet's signature topped the list of signatures on the letter that bestowed the bishopric of Ossory upon Bale, dated 26 August 1552.[21]

Until this point, Bale's name had also been absent from any discussions regarding vacant sees emanating from Ireland. Ossory had been vacant since the death of Milo Baron in 1550, despite proposals of qualified candidates by two successive Lords Deputy of Ireland to the Privy Council in London. In October 1550, Sir Anthony St Leger recommended his own chaplain, Patrick Walsh, for the position.[22] Six months later, St Leger's newly arrived replacement, Sir James Croft, complained to William Cecil about the 'neglicence of the Bysshopes and other spyrituall mynistres', and called for 'some

---

[18] Bale, *Vocacyon*, ed. Happé and King, 6; see also Sybil M. Jack, 'Paget, William, first Baron Paget (1505/6–1563)', *ODNB*, online edn (January 2008), at: <http://www.oxforddnb.com/view/article/21121>, accessed 31 October 2017.

[19] Thomas Cranmer, *Miscellaneous Writings and Letters of Thomas Cranmer*, ed. J. E. Cox (Cambridge, 1846), 438. Armagh had been vacant since the Roman Catholic George Dowdall had fled to the Continent in 1551 on the grounds that 'he would never be bishop where the holy Mass (as he called it) was abolished': *Original Letters and Papers in Illustration of the History of the Church in Ireland during the Reigns of Edward VI, Mary and Elizabeth*, ed. E. P. Shirley (London, 1851), 58; see also Jefferies, *Irish Church*, 93–8. W. K. Jordan suggests that William Turner had been offered the see of Ossory, but had 'declined because of his ignorance of the language': Jordan, *Threshold of Power*, 368.

[20] Ibid. Note that Cranmer refers to Goodacre as 'Whitacre'; see also Bale, *Vocacyon*, sigs C2–C2^v. For Goodacre, see Henry Jefferies, 'Goodacre, Hugh (d. 1553)', *ODNB*, online edn (2004), at: <http://www.oxforddnb.com/view/article/10947>, accessed 31 October 2017.

[21] A full copy of the letter is found in Bale, *Vocacyon*, sigs B8^v–C1.

[22] Walsh was later made dean of Waterford: *Original Letters*, ed. Shirley, 41–2, 47–8.

lerned men' to be sent over to reform the Irish Church.[23] A short while after this, Croft wrote to John Dudley, the Lord President of the council, and suggested Thomas Leverous to fill one of the vacant sees – Armagh, Cassell or Ossory. According to Croft's commendation, Leverous was a highly suitable and qualified candidate since he was able to preach in both English and Irish.[24] However, these requests fell on deaf ears. The dismissal – or ignoring – of the suggestions for episcopal promotion made by local authorities indicates that the Edwardian administration treated ecclesiastical reform in Ireland as a matter for the English authorities, and the Irish Church as part of the English establishment.

Other bishoprics in England had only been offered to trusted evangelicals.[25] Ireland was no different. The council had made it clear to Croft that 'the [financial] fruicts of the busshoprick' are not meet for any man 'but a good mynister and a preacher of the worde of God'.[26] In other words, the administration would only appoint a trusted political ally who would also be willing and able to administer the type of reform that matched the evangelical mould being promoted elsewhere in the Tudor 'empire'. Bale certainly fitted that bill. Having trained as a Carmelite friar, he converted in the early 1530s and soon made a name for himself as a political dramatist and a writer with a 'brass-knuckled polemical style'.[27] But as already noted, he had been overlooked for ecclesiastical promotion until this point in time.

Whatever the political reasons for Bale's appointment, he portrayed it as a providential act. Bale framed his 'vocacion to the bishoprick of Ossorie in Ireland' as a matter of divine 'election' facilitated by his earthly king.[28] In doing so, he unashamedly associated himself with the apostle Paul.[29] Just as Christ had appointed Paul apostle to the Gentiles, so Edward had appointed Bale as his ambassador and advocate to tame the 'wild Irish' through religious reform.[30] The

---

[23] Ibid. 63.

[24] Ibid. 61–2.

[25] Barret L. Beer, 'Episcopacy and Reform in Mid-Tudor England', *Albion* 23 (1991), 231–52.

[26] *Original Letters*, ed. Shirley, 52–3.

[27] Elizabeth Evenden and Thomas S. Freeman, *Religion and the Book in Early Modern England: The Making of John Foxe's 'Book of Martyrs'* (Cambridge, 2011), 38–79, at 38.

[28] Bale, *Vocacyon*, sig. C1.

[29] Cf. Acts 9; for a contrasting discussion, see Skura, *Tudor Autobiography*, 55–60.

[30] Bale, *Vocacyon*, sig. F7.

letter of appointment carried the king's authority, and Bale under-stood it as a directive to establish English order in Ireland.[31] Within days of his arrival to Ireland, Bale noted that 'heathnysh behavers' (i.e. traditional practices associated with the mass) went unchecked be-cause 'Christe had there no Bishop, neyther yet the Kynges Majestie of Englande any faithful officer of the mayer'.[32] Soon after, Bale's dis-gust was compounded when he discovered that it was considered 'an honour in this lande to have a spirituall man as a bishop, an Abbot, a Monke, a Fryre, or a Prest' as father. Thus he resolved 'to refourme it [i.e. the Irish Church] ... by our preachinges [so that] the popes superstitions wolde diminishe & true Christen religion increase'.[33] There was little doubt in Bale's mind that he was being sent as a missionary bishop, ordained by God and commissioned by Edward to help establish the English Church in Ireland.

Throughout his ministry, Bale applied the concept of empire to describe his work, seeking to exploit England's imperial prerogative and impose evangelical doctrine and practice upon his diocese by constantly invoking the royal supremacy.[34] Reflecting on his time as bishop of Ossory, Bale claimed to have 'mayntened the politicall ordre by [preaching evangelical] doctrine, & [thus] moved the com-mens always to obeye their magistrates'.[35] Despite fleeing Henry's regime in the 1540s, Bale referred to Henry in the *Vocacyon* as 'that noble prince' who completed 'that wonderfull wurke of God ... an overthrowe [of] the great Golias of Rome'.[36] The royal supremacy continued to affect modes of thinking within the fledgling communi-ties of exiled evangelicals even as Henry VIII's elder daughter sought to dismantle it. Other Marian exiles would soon challenge this view: most prominently, Bale's close friend and mentor, John Ponet, would go on to write the first defence of regicide in his treatise, *Politike Power* (1556).[37] Bale never followed Ponet's lead in this regard,

[31] Ibid. sig. C1.
[32] Ibid. sigs C1ᵛ–C2.
[33] Ibid. sigs C2–C2ᵛ.
[34] See comments regarding the contemporary use of 'empire' by J. R. Tanner, *Tudor Con-stitutional Documents A.D. 1485–1603 with an Historical Commentary* (Bath, 1922), 40; G. R. Elton, *The Tudor Constitution: Documents and Commentary* (Cambridge, 1960), 332; Mottram, *Empire and Nation*, 11–34.
[35] Bale, *Vocacyon*, sig. C4ᵛ.
[36] Ibid. sig. B7ᵛ.
[37] [John Ponet], *A Shorte Treatise of Politike Power, and of the True Obedience which Sub-jects Owe to Kynges and other Civile Governours, with an Exhortation to all True Naturall*

however.[38] Indeed, the picture Bale gives of his time in Ireland is quite the opposite. He had, in his view, leveraged the political hegemony of the English Church afforded by the Tudor empire to pursue his goal of reforming his remote diocese in south-eastern Ireland. Although Bale crossed the Irish Sea, he understood his ministry as falling under English legal jurisdiction, both civil and ecclesiastical.

Bale's view was not out of step with the prevailing culture of obedience throughout the Tudor century.[39] Nor was it a novel way of conceiving the reach and influence of the English crown in Ireland. The various acts of parliament that established the royal supremacy refashioned Henry VIII's position and title as combined ruler over Church and state with imperial terminology. According to the Act in Restraint of Appeals (1533), 'this Realme of Englond' was 'an Impire', and Henry was declared the 'Supreme heede and King having the Dignitie and Roiall Estate of the Imperiall Crown' over 'a Body politike compacte of all sortes and degrees of people', including those living in areas outside England, such as the Irish Pale and Calais.[40]

This imperial concept was reinforced with ecclesiastical overtones during Edward's reign. The royal proclamation of July 1547 that ordered the *Book of Homilies* to be read out in every parish referred to the ecclesiastical institution as 'this Church of England *and* Ireland'. Edward VI was called the 'supreme head immediately under God of the spirituality and temporality of the same church'.[41] By the end of the reign, Edward was being hailed as 'king of England, France and Irelande defendoure of the faith: and of the church of Englande and also of Ireland in earthe the Supreme head' in the official

---

Englishe Men ([Strasbourg], 1556); see also Stephen Alford, *Kingship and Politics in the Reign of Edward VI* (Cambridge, 2002), 176–9; Mark Earngey, 'New Light on the Life and Theology of Bishop John Ponet (1514–1556)' (MPhil thesis, Oxford University, 2016), 41–3.

[38] Walsh points out that in contrast to other Marian exiles, Bale was a first-generation reformer. This may help to explain the variance between Bale and Ponet on the royal supremacy: Walsh, 'Deliberate Provocation', 47.

[39] Hadfield argues that the Old English in the Pale generally considered themselves as under the jurisdiction of the English crown: Hadfield, 'Translating the Reformation', 43–4; see also Ryan Reeves, *English Evangelicals and Tudor Obedience, c.1527–1570* (Leiden, 2014), especially ch. 3; Stephen Chavura, *Tudor Protestant Political Thought, 1547–1603* (Leiden, 2011), especially ch. 5.

[40] 24 Hen. VIII c. 12, in *Statutes of the Realm* 3 (London, 1963), 427.

[41] *Tudor Royal Proclamations, 1: The Early Tudors, 1485–1553*, ed. Paul L. Hughes and James F. Larkin (New Haven, CT, 1964), 403 (no. 287); emphasis added.

catechism.[42] Thus in both a civic and ecclesiastical sense, mid-Tudor reformers saw Ireland and its Church as falling under the dominion of the English crown. In theory, then, the Edwardian Church, as an institution of the Tudor empire, extended beyond the geographic borders of England and incorporated the dioceses of Ireland. On this basis, the ecclesiastical institution could be used as a political instrument to enhance the colonial reach of the Tudor crown.

From an ecclesiastical perspective, the diocese of Dublin (if not the entire Irish Church) had long been seen as the handmaid of the English Church.[43] Edward's reign saw a continuation of this relationship. In 1547 George Browne, archbishop of Dublin (1536–54), proposed a scheme for the endowment of a university in his diocese to advance 'the unspeakeable reformacōn of that realme … [and to increase] the obedience of [the king's] Lawes' there.[44] This was not mere lip service to the new evangelical king. Under Henry VIII, Browne had shown an inclination to support the Reformation in his diocese. In a letter written to Henry's chief minister, Thomas Cromwell, in 1538, the archbishop of Dublin made a particular point of mentioning his personal involvement in deleting 'out of the canon of the masse or other bookes the name of the Busshop of rome'.[45] Under Edward, Browne also promoted the ministry of Walter Palatyne, a Scotsman who preached in Dublin against the pope, 'the masse and other ceremonies'.[46] In 1548 Christopher Bodkin, archbishop of Tuam (1536–72), wrote from beyond the Pale in County Galway to render his 'diligent service' to Edward Bellingham, the Lord Deputy at the time. Bodkin had noted that due to a 'lack of regemen & Justice', his county 'nydyth reformacōn more than eūr'.[47] These examples demonstrate that well before Bale was considered for the see of Ossory, existing bishops were making some attempt to reform their Irish sees in accordance with the new ecclesiastical outlook of the Edwardian regime.[48] Political weight was added to this movement with the 1549 Act of Uniformity, which Bellingham

---

[42] *Short Catechism* (London, 1553), sig. A2. For a full discussion of catechisms, see Ian Green, *The Christian's ABC: Catechisms and Catechizing in England* c.1530–1740 (Oxford, 1996), 46–92, especially 59–62.
[43] Murray, *Enforcing the Tudor Reformation*, 20–47.
[44] *Original Letters*, ed. Shirley, 11.
[45] London, LPL, MS 602, fol. 104ᵛ.
[46] *Original Letters*, ed. Shirley, 19–21, at 19.
[47] Ibid. 17.
[48] For other examples, see ibid. 22–5, 28–35.

actively enforced.[49] Moreover, as Jefferies argues, although the act did not explicitly mention Ireland, it was imposed upon the anglophone parishes of the Pale 'with the acquiescence of the local secular elite'.[50] Such moves emphasized to the local population the extension of England's political, and thereby ecclesiastical, authority over Ireland.

Changes to public worship furthered the Edwardian regime's process of annexing the Irish Church to itself. In 1551, the 1549 edition of the Book of Common Prayer became the first book printed in Ireland. Royal instructions to the Lord Deputy made it clear that the new English liturgy was to become the standard form of public worship in Ireland.[51] Church services were to be conducted 'in the englishe tongue in all places'. The only exception allowed was where a majority did not understand English, in which case the liturgy was to be 'translated truly into the Irish tongue, unto such tyme as the people maye be brought to understand the englishe'.[52] This was, as Cummings comments, 'an exemplary moment of colonization'.[53] A population that had showed no previous signs of welcoming reform was now impelled to pray for deliverance from 'the tyranny of the bishop of Rome and all his detestable enormities' in English.[54] Initially, however, the Edwardian Reformation in Ireland was in practice aimed at, and intended for, those who understood English. An abridged Irish-Gaelic translation of the 1559 Prayer Book was not produced until 1608, while the complete liturgy only appeared in 1712.[55] As a point of comparison, Thomas Gualtier made a French translation of the 1552 Prayer Book for use in the Channel Islands and the French Stranger Church in December 1552, although no translation of any edition of the Prayer Book into Manx

---

[49] Ibid. 32–3.
[50] Jefferies, *Irish Church*, 93.
[51] *Original Letters*, ed. Shirley, 39–41.
[52] Ibid. 40.
[53] *The Books of Common Prayer: The Texts of 1549, 1559, and 1662*, ed. Brian Cummings (Oxford, 2011), xlvii.
[54] A prayer from the Litany, *The Boke of Common Praier* (Dublin, 1551), sig. O5. This copy is housed in Trinity College Library, Dublin; a digitized version is available online at: <http://digitalcollections.tcd.ie/home/index.php?DRIS_ID=BOCP1551_001>.
[55] David N. Griffiths, 'Prayer-Book Translations in the Nineteenth Century', *The Library*, 6th ser. 4 (1984), 1–24, at 11; Griffiths lists all translations of Prayer Books before 1900 in an appendix: ibid. 20–4. See also idem, 'The French Translations of the English Book of Common Prayer', *PHS* 22 (1970–6), 90–114, idem, 'The Early Translations of the Book of Common Prayer', *The Library* 6th ser. 3 (1981), 1–16.

was made until 1610, nor published until 1765.[56] At the same time, William Salesbury was translating sections of the 1549 Prayer Book into Welsh, although this was not published until 1567.[57] No Latin version of the 1552 Prayer Book was ever produced, nor did the 1559 edition appear in French.[58]

Forcing the Irish Church to adopt English as its official language of prayer and worship was a powerful means of enveloping it into the English Reformation. As Felicity Heal has demonstrated, 'authority … was clearly on the side of the dominant tongue'.[59] Although Cranmer encouraged reformers in Ireland to learn Irish Gaelic in order to be better equipped to reach local communities, there is no evidence to suggest that Bale ever entertained this possibility.[60] This limited Bale's reach to those within the Pale. His inability to engage with the Gaelic population was also partly a function of the politico-cultural divisions within sixteenth-century Ireland. As Ellis points out, imposing religious reform upon the Gaelic communities required a 'political conquest' via military means.[61] Bale was surely not ignorant of these circumstances. He delineated the population between native-born Irish and those of English birth.[62] Yet Bale's decision to conduct his ministry according to the doctrines and rites established by English law reflected his political and religious allegiance to the Edwardian establishment, and mirrored the official relationship of Church and state between England and Ireland.

The most obvious example of this in the *Vocacyon* is Bale's description of his consecration. The service became a flashpoint because the dean of Christ Church Cathedral in Dublin, Thomas Lockwood, or, as Bale calls him, 'Blockhead', tried to prevent the use of the revised Ordinal of 1552 in consecrating the bishops elect,

[56] Ibid. 23; Griffiths, 'Early Translations', 7. See also Diarmaid MacCulloch, 'The Importance of Jan Laski in the English Reformation', in Christoph Strohm, ed., *Johannes a Lasco (1499–1560). Polnischer Baron, Humanist und europäischer Reformator*, Spätmittelalter und Reformation n.s. 14 (Tübingen, 2000), 325–46, at 336; Jennifer Loach, '"A Close League with the King of France": Lady Jane Grey's Proclamation in French and its Part in a planned Betrayal', *PHS* 25 (1989–93), 234–41, at 235.
[57] Felicity Heal, 'Mediating the Word: Language and Dialects in the British and Irish Reformations', *JEH* 56 (2005), 261–86.
[58] Griffiths, 'French Translations', 93.
[59] Heal, 'Mediating the Word', 265.
[60] Cranmer to Cecil, *Miscellaneous Writings*, ed. Cox, 438; see also Jefferies, *Irish Church*, 98–9.
[61] Ellis, 'John Bale', 284.
[62] Bale, *Vocacyon*, especially sigs F3–8.

Bale and Goodacre.[63]   Although the 1549 Prayer Book had been printed in Ireland in 1551, it did not contain the reformed Ordinal of 1550, which was subsequently revised and incorporated into the 1552 Prayer Book.[64] This variation of Prayer Book editions between England and Ireland highlights the differing pace of official reform across the Tudor empire, from its centre in London to the farthest outposts in the English Pale of Ireland.   While the English Church accelerated its reform programme under the protectorship of John Dudley, duke of Northumberland, the Irish Church lagged behind.[65] Lockwood understood this. Thus

> ... he wolde in no wise permyt yᵉ obseruacion to be done after yᵉ boke of consecratinge bishoppes wᶜ was last set fourth in Englāde by acte of parlement alleginge yᵗ it wolde be both an occasiō of tumulte and also that it was not as yet consented to by acte of their parlemēt in Irelande.[66]

This standoff between Bale and Lockwood was not just about which edition of the Prayer Book was to be used in Ireland, nor was it about retaining traditional forms of ceremonial as embodied in the 1549 Prayer Book.   At a deeper level, it was a disagreement over which parliament had authority in Ireland, and by implication, the freedom which the Irish Church had from the English Church in matters of doctrine and worship.

Ironically, had Bale been familiar with the Irish Prayer Book of 1551, he could have invoked it to counter Lockwood's argument. The 'Prayer for the Lord Deputy' was an additional prayer for the Irish edition that for obvious reasons was not in the English equivalent of 1549.   By using it, Irish congregations besought God to 'lighten the herte of thy seruaunt [i.e. the Lord Deputy], now gouernour ouer this realme under our most dread and soueraigne Lord, Edward the sixt', so that he might set the example of living in 'due obedience to their kyng'.[67] This prayer reveals one way that liturgy

---

[63] Ibid. sigs C2–C3ᵛ. The presiding bishop was 'George the archebishop of Dublyne', who had 'Thomas the bisshop of Kyldare & Vrbane yᵉ bishop of Duno assisinge him': ibid., sig C2ᵛ.

[64] *The Boke of Common Praier* (Dublin, 1551).

[65] Ellis, 'John Bale', 285; MacCulloch, *Tudor Church Militant*, 52–6.

[66] Bale, *Vocacyon*, sigs C2ᵛ–C3. Constitutionally, Lockwood was right; I thank Paul Cavill for pointing this out to me.

[67] *The Boke of Common Praier* (Dublin, 1551), sig. S4ᵛ.

was used to establish a clear political hierarchy of England over Ireland. The implication was that every Irish resident who prayed it was an English subject.

The impasse over Bale's consecration was eventually broken by his forceful will and obstinate obedience to English law. He was adamant that the more conspicuously evangelical Prayer Book of 1552 was to be used in all of Edward's domains: 'If Englande and Ireland be under one kinge they are both bounde to the obedience of one lawe under him'. Clearly Bale saw Ossory as a diocese of the wider Edwardian Church, not as a separate entity. Furthermore, the soon-to-be consecrated bishop asserted that once he set foot in Ossory 'I wolde execute nothinge for my part there but accordinge to the rules of that lattre boke [i.e. the 1552 Prayer Book]'.[68] This was more than a matter of political principle; it was an issue of godliness. Bale argued that 'true obedience to Gods most holy wurde' involved obeying 'the commaundement of your christen Kynge'. Hence Bale 'requryed [all prebendaries and priests in Kilkenny] to observe and folowe that only boke of commen prayer whych the kynge & hys counsel that yeare put fourth by acte of parlement'.[69] Thus the Prayer Book became a signal of Tudor imperial domination in the diocese of Ossory at least. The liturgical reform enforced by Bale throughout his diocese serves to highlight again that the Edwardian Reformation was advanced in Ireland on the back of political might. Paradoxically, it would be political forces that undid Bale's Irish mission too.

The abrupt change in monarchs in July 1553, from the evangelical Edward to the Roman Catholic Mary, drastically altered the ecclesiastical circumstances throughout the Tudor empire. The local Irish clergy acted quickly to restore traditional religion.[70] Bale was hounded from his episcopal see by mutinous clergy who looked to the new monarch for religious leadership, and he fled Ossory in search of a safe refuge on the Continent.[71] The Marian exile reminds us that, for many mid-Tudor evangelicals, the Edwardian Reformation remained unfinished business. That was how Bale felt about his time in Ireland.

[68] Bale, *Vocacyon*, sig. C3.
[69] Ibid., sig. D5ᵛ.
[70] Ibid., sigs C8–D4.
[71] Bale first intended to travel to Scotland, but pirates intervened, and he ended up on the Continent: ibid., sigs D8ᵛ–F2ᵛ.

When Bale was writing the *Vocacyon*, the outcome of the Reformation in Ireland was far from a foregone conclusion.[72] According
to Bale, a 'great nombre' of people had been won over to his brand of
Protestantism. This did not stop a band of 'cruell murtherers' from
killing five of Bale's household servants in August 1553, however. In
response, the local mayor, Robert Shea, deployed a retinue of a hundred horsemen and three hundred foot soldiers to deliver Bale from
the imminent threat to his life. The many 'yonge men' in this co-
terie carried their bishop to safety that night while 'syngynge psalms
and other godly songes'.[73] Bale recorded that they were welcomed
to Kilkenny by the townsfolk lining the streets with 'candels lyght
in their hādes [and] shoughting out prayses to God for deliuerynge
me'.[74] These positive remarks suggest that Bale believed (or wished to
believe) that he had made some inroads into the hearts and minds of
his Irish flock. Beyond the *Vocacyon*, however, there is little evidence
to suggest that the doctrinal aspects of the Edwardian Reformation
had developed any deep roots within the Irish population by the end
of 1553.[75] Both Ellis and Jefferies point to the lack of evangelical
preachers as a key reason for the shallow acceptance of reform in
sixteenth-century Ireland.[76] Walsh points the finger directly at Bale,
arguing that his 'insensitivity … and lack of pragmatism guaranteed
that he was doomed to failure'.[77] From Bale's perspective, his attempt
to import the Reformation into Ireland did not fail on account of inadequate strategy. Rather, it was explained as God's providential punishment of the Tudor 'empire' for not having embraced 'the heavenly
doctryne' of justification by grace through faith in Christ alone.[78]

Bale may have lost his Irish battle, but he was confident of God's
ultimate victory in the spiritual war in which the mid-Tudor 'empire'
was embroiled. This was the broader point of the *Vocacyon*. Bale
manipulated his personal experience in Ireland to provide an example
for other exile congregations to mimic. Continued use of the Prayer
Book would give these new congregations 'the face of an English

---

[72] See Bradshaw, 'Edwardian Reformation', 95–6; Jefferies, *Irish Church*, 104–21.
[73] Bale, *Vocacyon*, sig. D4ᵛ.
[74] Ibid., sig. D5.
[75] Jefferies, *Irish Church*, 101–3.
[76] Ibid; Ellis, 'John Bale', 291–2.
[77] Walsh, 'Deliberate Provocation', 59.
[78] Bale, *Vocacyon*, sig. F2ᵛ.

churche' as it had done for Bale in Ossory.[79]   This proved to be tendentious for some exiles, as the unsavoury affair of the so-called 'Troubles at Frankfurt' (1554–5) demonstrated.[80]   But as an initial response to the Marian restoration, the *Vocacyon* must be read as an attempt to conceive the fellowship of believers associated with the Edwardian Reformation as belonging to a unified Church of the Tudor 'empire'. This applied as much to evangelicals in England as it did to those in Ireland and those exiled on the Continent.

Bale's Irish mission stands as an instructive episode within the wider story of the evangelical movement of the sixteenth-century English Church. His episcopal career was an expression of the overlapping interests of Church and state in the Tudor 'empire' under Edward VI. Ecclesiastical reform in Ireland was complemented by political subjugation, and vice versa. While Bale sought to conform the doctrine and practice of the Irish Church to its English counterpart, the political dominance of England was reinforced through the use of the English liturgy. In this way, Bale was simultaneously his king's ambassador and the mouthpiece of his sovereign Lord.

---

[79] *A Brief Discourse of the Troubles begun at Frankfort, in the Year 1554, about the Book of Common Prayer and Ceremonies*, ed. John Petheram (London, 1846), fol. xxxviii.
[80] Timothy Duguid, 'The 'Troubles' at Frankfurt: A New Chronology', *Reformation & Renaissance Review* 14 (2012), 243–68; Karl Gunther, *Reformation Unbound: Protestant Visions of Reform in England, 1525–1590* (Cambridge, 2014), 158–88; Jane Dawson, *John Knox* (New Haven, CT, 2015), 90–108.

Roman *Imperium* and the Restoration Church

Jacqueline Rose*

University of St Andrews

This article examines the late-seventeenth-century Church of England's understanding of rulers' ecclesiastical imperium *through analysing a pamphlet debate about Julian the Apostate and Church-state relations in the fourth-century Roman empire. In 1682 an Anglican cleric, Samuel Johnson, printed an account of Julian's reign that argued that the primitive Christians had resisted the emperor's persecutory policies and that Johnson's contemporaries should adopt the same stance towards the Catholic heir presumptive, James, duke of York. Surveying the reaction to Johnson, this article probes the ability of Anglican royalists to map fourth-century Roman onto seventeenth-century English* imperium, *their assertions about how Christians should respond to an apostate monarch, and whether these authors fulfilled such claims when James came to the throne. It also considers their negotiation of the question of whether miracles existed in the fourth-century imperial Church. It concludes that, despite Rome's territorial dimensions,* imperium *remained a fundamentally legal-constitutional concept in this period, and that the debate over Julian highlights the fundamentally tense and ambivalent relationship between Church and empire.*

'[God], who gave [power] to the Christian Constantine also gave it to the apostate Julian'

Augustine of Hippo, *The City of God* 5.21.

The Emperor Constantine's conversion to Christianity marked a seismic shift in the relationship between Church and empire. Whatever the ambiguities of his 'conversion',[1] down the centuries Constantine became the poster boy for Christian *imperium*. Nowhere was this image more apparent than in the intensely magisterial reformation

* School of History, St Katharine's Lodge, The Scores, St Andrews, KY16 9BA. E-mail: jer9@st-andrews.ac.uk.
[1] Raymond Van Dam, 'The Many Conversions of the Emperor Constantine', in Kenneth Mills and Anthony Grafton, eds, *Conversion in Late Antiquity and the Early Middle Ages* (Rochester, NY, 2003), 127–51.

Studies in Church History 54 (2018) 159–175   © Ecclesiastical History Society 2018
doi: 10.1017/stc.2017.10

begun by Henry VIII in the 1530s that made him and his successors supreme heads or governors of the English Church. Parliament's declaration that the realm of England was an 'empire' blended older understandings of this term as a sovereign and independent jurisdiction owning no superior under God with Henry's new claims to such supreme authority in ecclesiastical as well as temporal matters. The threefold meaning of *imperium* in Tudor England – sovereign independence, ecclesiastical supremacy and territorial extension – was well served by Constantine and his fourth-century Roman empire, references to which echoed in the visual, aural and textual propaganda of the Reformation Church of England.

Yet this long-established celebratory sense of the partnership of Church and empire was increasingly subverted in the later seventeenth century by an emerging discourse that identified the fourth century as the point where the two powers became entangled, and thereby corrupted. The poet Andrew Marvell complained that the 'unnatural Copulation of Ecclesiastical and Temporal' had introduced worldly ambition into the Church, giving bishops the unchristian power (and incentive) to persecute which they exercised to the full in Marvell's own day by vigorous prosecution of Protestant Dissenters.[2] Unlike their anticlerical successors of the early Enlightenment, men like Marvell did not complain about Constantine's Council of Nicaea (325) establishing the orthodox belief in the Trinity; their focus was rather on the ecclesiological consequences of an imperial and therefore imperious Church, which seemed to constitute an episcopal *imperium in imperio* – a state within a state. In the early 1680s, an anonymous author described how Christianity's establishment had subverted the Church's original apostolic democracy, spawning first bishops, then patriarchs, then popes.[3]

That this author referenced not only Constantine but also Julian the Apostate signalled a shift towards awareness of Constantine's fourth-century successors and their far from orthodox religious policies. This article analyses the 1680s controversy surrounding Julian, emperor from 361–3, an argument that at the time constituted a

---

[2] Andrew Marvell, *The Rehearsal Transpros'd and the Rehearsal Transpros'd the Second Part*, ed. D. I. B. Smith (Oxford, 1971), 238. On this tradition, see also William Poole, 'John Milton and the Beard-Hater: Encounters with Julian the Apostate', *Seventeenth Century* 31 (2016), 161–89.
[3] 'Philaretus Anthropopolita', *Some Seasonable Remarks upon the Deplorable Fall of the Emperour Julian* (London, 1681).

high-profile political and ecclesiastical debate, but which has been largely neglected by modern scholars.[4] Yet the Julian dispute high-lights a number of important themes in the relationship between Church and empire. Complementing recent work on the learned patristic scholarship of the Restoration Church of England,[5] this article demonstrates anew how the history of Christian Rome provided a powerful weapon in political debate. An understanding of the quarrel highlights a relatively neglected aspect of 1680s succession politics and the way in which the campaign to exclude a Catholic heir to the throne was pursued and refuted through investigation of the interstices of law and religious politics in the later Roman empire. Most significantly for this volume, it uses the 1680s controversy to probe empire in a dual sense: both the Restoration's understanding of Christian Rome and the nature of *imperium* in the latter stages of England's 'long Reformation'. After a brief outline of the crucial events in Julian's life and of the Restoration quarrel, it will consider what empire meant to later Stuart authors and the difficulties they encountered in mapping fourth-century Roman onto seventeenth-century English *imperium*; the arguments over how the fourth-century Church had, and therefore how the seventeenth-century Church should, respond to apostate monarchs; the difficulties of putting this theory into practice; and, finally, how Protestant authors navigated accounts of miracles occurring in the era of an imperial Church. This will show the continuing strength of a legal-constitutional rather than territorial conception of empire and some of the inherent problems that empire posed for the Church.

Long held in suspicion (and nearly murdered) by Constantine's successor Constantius, Julian had a Christian upbringing and converted to paganism *c*.351, although he carefully concealed his new faith. Dispatched as Caesar to defend the empire in Gaul in 356, Julian was proclaimed Augustus by the army (perhaps with a little encouragement) in Paris in 360. Constantius's death the following year en route to fight his rival left Julian unopposed; overtly declaring his paganism, he returned in triumph to the East. As Restoration authors recognized, Julian's 'persecution' was of a subtle kind. He slandered the 'Galileans', prosecuted them for secular offences and

---

[4] It is mentioned briefly by Poole, 'Milton and the Beard-Hater', 172, see also 167–8; but otherwise the essential article is that by Melinda Zook (n. 9 below).
[5] Jean-Louis Quantin, *The Church of England and Christian Antiquity* (Oxford, 2009).

failed to punish mobs who attacked them, thus denying them martyrdom. To divide his Christian opponents, he declared toleration
and invited back the Catholic bishops removed by Arians under Constantius. Exactly how the Christians had responded to this was examined through consideration of certain crucial episodes: Julian giving
a donative to his army if they threw frankincense on the fire, money
which they rejected with horror when they realized it had led them
into pagan worship; the scorn showed to him by those who laughed
at his beard, especially in Antioch, when the ascetic emperor refused
to attend the theatres and chariot races.[6] Even more contentious
were the fire that had thwarted Julian's attempt to rebuild the Jewish Temple in Jerusalem, whether the Christian soldier Valentinian
had hit an officer when obliged to attend pagan worship, whether a
bishop had kicked the emperor, and whether the javelin that killed
Julian during his expedition against the Persians had been thrown
by a Christian. Unlike the designer of an engraved frontispiece of
1619 (fig. 1), Restoration authors never cited the emperor's supposed
dying remark that the 'Galilean' (Christ) had triumphed.[7] Although
eschewing numismatic material, they were not confessionally narrow-
minded, drawing on the pagan Ammianus Marcellinus as well as the
Cappadocian Gregory of Nazianzus, on the pagan Zosimus as well as
the Christians Socrates and Sozumen, and they were aware of Julian's
response to the Antiochians, the *Misopogon*.[8]

In 1682, attention to Julian was galvanized by a book entitled
Julian the Apostate, written by Samuel Johnson, vicar of Corringham
in Essex. Johnson made two crucial claims. First, he drew a parallel
between the pagan apostate emperor and the heir presumptive to
the English throne, James, duke of York, who had converted to
Catholicism. James, Johnson suggested, had dissembled his faith,
and could not be trusted to tolerate Protestants, for all Catholic
monarchs were obliged to extirpate heretics on pain of deposition.
Such fears of a Catholic successor – another Mary Tudor – had
resulted in attempts between 1679 and 1681 to exclude James from

[6] G. W. Bowersock, *Julian the Apostate* (London, 1978); Maud W. Gleason, 'Festive
Satire: Julian's *Misopogon* and the New Year at Antioch', *JRS* 76 (1986), 106–19.
[7] It is a later addition to Theodoret's ecclesiastical history: *ODCC, s.n.* 'Julian the Apostate'.
[8] On the plentiful sources for the reign, see Bowersock, *Julian*, ch. 1; on the early modern
tradition, see Poole, 'Milton and the Beard-Hater'. John Bennet, *Constantius the Apostate*
(London, 1683), included a list of sources.

Figure 1. (Colour online) The Emperors Constantine and Julian, representing faith and apostasy. Engraved title page of William Gouge, *The Whole-Armor of God* (London, 1619), Cambridge University Library, shelfmark Syn.7.61.110. Reproduced by kind permission of the Syndics of Cambridge University Library.

the line of succession. Second, Johnson argued that the primitive Christians had not quietly submitted to Julian, but slandered him, and mocked his beard so much that he wished he had never come to power. They were entirely justified in defying him, because (unlike Christians in earlier persecutions) they had the laws of the empire on their side. Johnson conceded that they had not attacked his person, but that was simply because they lacked strength and arms for physical resistance. In Johnson's eyes, that mysterious javelin was undoubtedly thrown by a Christian.[9] This was the model of behaviour Johnson intimated that his contemporaries should follow under a popish successor, suggestions for which he was tried for seditious libel, fined five hundred marks, had his book burned by Oxford University and was denounced in sermons by leading clerics at Oxford. The royalist antiquarian Anthony Wood decried Johnson's 'Fanatical piece' for offering 'plausible pleas to justifie, & specious persuasions to encourage people to rebellion & resistance & ... with the utmost strength of arms to vigorously oppose' any Catholic king.[10] A barrage of Anglican royalist criticism attacked Johnson's account of the primitive Christians.

It is important to recognize just how subversive Johnson's account was of a crucial facet of the Restoration Church of England's identity. That church turned to the first centuries of Christianity in claiming to recover pure Christian doctrine from corrupt Romish accretions, to demonstrate an early church government that was episcopal, not presbyterian or papal, and, with Constantine, to evidence the royal supremacy. The primitive Christian political theology of passive obedience (not obeying a sinful order, but submitting to the punishment incurred thereby) was also cited by the Anglican Church to separate herself from Presbyterian and Catholic resistance theory. Thus, while Johnson accused the Church of England of popery in supporting a Catholic successor, he was himself frequently indicted for propagating popish resistance theory. A flourishing Restoration line of argument held that popes had been the first Christians who rebelled against emperors and that denial of passive obedience was therefore popish. Had not Cardinal Bellarmine held the primitive Christians to be too weak to resist? Johnson's *Julian* attacked a sermon that was preached on the fast day for the martyr king, Charles I, by George Hickes, an expert exponent of such histories of seditious

---

[9] Samuel Johnson, *Julian the Apostate* (London, 1682). Johnson's career is surveyed in Melinda Zook, 'Early Whig Ideology, Ancient Constitutionalism, and the Reverend Samuel Johnson', *JBS* 32 (1993), 139–65; but beyond listing the responses and correctly identifying George Hickes's *Jovian* (London, 1683) as pre-eminent, she does not discuss the debate in detail.

[10] Oxford, Bodl., MS Wood F.47, fol. 407ʳ (the note 'AA34' referred to in Anthony Wood, *Life and Times*, ed. Andrew Clark, 5 vols [Oxford, 1891–1900], 3: 18–19); see also MS Wood F.47, fol. 629ʳ; ibid., fol. 627ᵛ is the note 'FF43' referred to in Wood's *Life*.

ideas.[11] That an Anglican clergyman had denounced passive obedience in a book about an apostate emperor led to an obvious response: who was the greater apostate?[12] One of the first notices of *Julian*, by the Tory poet Nahum Tate in May 1682, called on its readers to 'See how th'apostate plies his trait'rous text, / The Gospel wrack'd, and church-historians vex'd'.[13]

Beneath the invective, there was nonetheless a serious engagement with the nature of *imperium* in both Rome and England, and discussion of the extent to which laws of inheritance, political authority and royal ecclesiastical power were the same in both polities. Anglican royalists had to tread a fine line between endorsing English monarchs' *imperium* and distinguishing it from that of Rome. England, Hickes insisted, was a '*perfect Sovereignty* or Empire' and the king a '*Compleat, Imperial,* and *Independent Soveraign*', citing in support of this Reformation statutes such as the Henrician Act in Restraint of Appeals and the Elizabethan Act of Supremacy. Imperial power was subject only to divine and natural law, although it could be restricted in its exercise by human law, that is, by self-limitation, in the same way that an omnipotent God governed by truth and justice. English kings were therefore the fount of all jurisdiction, the only wielders of the sword, accountable solely to God, and to be obeyed by these 'Laws Imperial' even when they violated the '*Political* Laws' that protected the liberties and property of their subjects. Despite conflating passive obedience and non-resistance, and arguing that English kings were only morally bound to govern well, Hickes insisted that they did not exercise tyranny, which 'differs almost as much from an absolute Civil Monarchy, as an absolute Civil Monarchy doth from a limited Civil Monarchy'.[14] The Catholic Edward Meredith outlined how

---

[11] Edward Pelling, *The Apostate Protestant* (London, 1685), 42; Hickes, *Jovian*, 238; idem, *A Sermon Preached ... at Bow Church on the 30th of January* (London, 1682); see Jacqueline Rose, 'Robert Brady's Intellectual History and Royalist Antipopery in Restoration England', *EHR* 122 (2007), 1287–1317.

[12] Hickes, *Jovian*, 83, 208; John Northleigh, *The Triumph of our Monarchy* (London, 1685), 15; Anon., *The Life of Boetius Recommended to the Author of the Life of Julian* (London, 1683), 31–2; Thomas Long, *A Vindication of the Primitive Christians* (London, 1683), sig. B3ʳ, p. 386; John Dryden and Nahum Tate, *The Second Part of Absalom and Achitophel*, in George deForest Lord, ed., *Poems on Affairs of State*, 7 vols (New Haven, CT, 1963–75), 3: ll. 352–99.

[13] Nahum Tate, 'Old England', in Lord, ed., *Poems*, 3: ll. 21–2.

[14] Hickes, *Jovian*, 204–17, 239–40, 243–4, 269, 193.

despotic power (to which submission was owed) was softened by the addition of law into the authority to which obedience was due.[15]

Yet this model of *imperium*, which often echoed that of Roman law, had for Hickes to be qualitatively different from the power of fourth-century rulers to change the empire's religion. The Christians under Julian had not been illegally persecuted, he argued, for they were condemned by a despotic emperor whose power was *un*like that of a self-limiting English imperial monarch. In Rome, the pleasure of the emperor was an unwritten law, and that pleasure ran against Christians in Julian's time. Constantine could not have changed the imperial religion to Christianity if he did not have such power. Julian could therefore, unfortunately, change it back again.[16] By contrast, John Dowell argued that the maxim *quod principi placuit, legis habet vigorem* (the will of the prince has the force of law) did not apply in England, where monarchs could not change the established religion without parliamentary consent. How could one use 'an example of *Julian*, whose power was absolute and arbitrary, to justify any thing in *England*, where the Power is limited and divided'?[17] Thus, while Dowell and Hickes both sought to protect the English Church from magisterial whim, they inadvertently described royal power quite differently. Thomas Long solved the problem another way, explaining that an absolute and arbitrary power was necessary for Constantine to have created a Christian empire, but not exploring what that meant for England.[18]

The Anglican royalist arguments about fourth-century temporal and ecclesiastical *imperium* thus each worked well on their own terms, but caused problems when their proponents tried to apply both simultaneously. The difficulties of upholding a strongly royalist account of temporal power while denying that this would allow James to change the Church meant it was safer to fall back on asserting that James would find it impossible to re-establish Catholicism in England, even if he was legally empowered so to do.[19] Johnson and his supporters mocked their opponents' contradictions, treating Hickes's division of the imperial and political laws and his assertion of

[15] Edward Meredith, *Some Remarques upon a Late Popular Piece of Nonsense* (London, 1682), 4.
[16] Hickes, *Jovian*, 85–6, 90–1; Bennet, *Constantius*, 40–2.
[17] John Dowell, *The Triumph of Christianity* (London, 1683), 159–61, 164–5, 176.
[18] Long, *Vindication*, 173, 296–8.
[19] Meredith, *Remarques*, 27–32; Northleigh, *Triumph*, 456–8, 450.

imperial law limited in its exercise as absurd. Quoting the fifteenth-century lawyer Sir John Fortescue's description of England as a 'regal and political' dominion, Johnson rejected absolute, arbitrary, boundless power as a form of Turkish slavery.[20] However, even when arguing that English kings, governing by law, were more powerful than those with five times their lands, Johnson said little about the territorial dimensions of the Roman empire. Instead, he and his supporters parsed the Henrician statutes that declared an English 'empire' to show that they asserted one free from *foreign* interference. The Act of Appeals' claims about an imperial crown and the 'plenary, whole, and Entire' power of the king excluded *papal* meddling; the Act for Exoneration from Exactions paid to the See of Rome declared the realm's freedom from subjection but denied the authority of human laws not made by 'THE PEOPLE OF THIS YOUR REALM ... BY THEIR OWN CONSENT' in parliament. That both sides cited Reformation statutes exposed the contradiction at the heart of the Henrician legislation between an imperial crown / realm and a monarchical emperor.[21]

Having dissected the imperial power of the ruler, writers then turned to their second theme, the Church's reaction to an *imperium* abused by a pagan or apostate emperor. All agreed that the first- and second-century Christians had suffered persecution without actively resisting, exemplified by the Theban Legion, who had refused to sacrifice and had been slaughtered, despite clearly having the ability to resist. As is well known, the early modern Church of England presented herself as staunchly maintaining passive obedience. Her clergy constantly cited Romans 13, the Pauline injunction to obey earthly powers, praised the passive obedience of their primitive Christian counterparts who 'outdid themselves' in submitting to their monarchs: 'their Passive Obedience was their glory, and their Blood watered the Church of Christ',[22] and reasserted that 'prayers and tears' were the proper response to tyranny and persecution. Yet

---

[20] Johnson, *Julian's Arts*, 170, iii, 84, 164–5, 170–86; Robert Howard, *A Letter to Mr Samuel Johnson* (London, 1692), 4.

[21] Johnson, *Julian's Arts*, 188–90, 197; Anon., *Letter of Remarkes*, 9–11; the latter was attributed to William Atwood by William Hopkins, *Animadversions on Mr Johnson's Answer to Jovian* (London, 1681), sigs a2ʳ⁻ᵛ, and to the Earl of Anglesey by Anthony A. Wood, *Athenae Oxonienses: An Exact History of all the Writers and Bishops who have had their Education in the University of Oxford*, ed. Philip Bliss, 4 vols, 3rd edn (London, 1813–20), 4: col. 185.

[22] Samuel Parker, *Religion and Loyalty*, 2 vols (London, 1684–5), 1: 142–3 (§19); Dowell, *Triumph*, 163.

prayers in particular proved contentious. What the debate over Johnson's *Julian* demonstrated – more than many other occasions on which the church emphasized her loyalty – was a detailed discussion of what actually constituted passive obedience versus active resistance. Were certain deeds – kicking the emperor, striking his officer – resistance? Above all, were words resistance?

That Julian's Christian subjects had forcefully asserted his error, and defiantly prayed and sung psalms about idolaters, was not in question. Johnson and his supporters argued that such invective amounted to resistance: 'active Tongue-Assault'.[23] Anglican royalists had three answers. First, they argued that the words of a tiny minority, even if they did go too far, did not outweigh the obedience of the vast majority, particularly that of the army.[24] Second, they toned down any slanders by reinterpreting the words used: thus they argued that 'confound' in Psalm 71 did not mean 'destroy', and that Gregory of Nazianzus's invective was not a plain representation of historical fact but full of amplifications (rhetorical devices used to exaggerate crimes).[25] Likewise, they claimed that the governor of Berea who had rebuked his son in front of the emperor for turning pagan had done so respectfully, while Marius, bishop of Chalcedon, 'reflected not on his *Person*, but his *Paganism*'.[26] Such language was therefore no more violent than the critiques of the Arian Constantius, who was a worse persecutor than Julian had been, and was still obeyed.[27] Similar strategies were used to refute the idea that Gregory (or his father) had kicked Julian. Hickes denied that 'kicking' could be the correct translation – could an aged and infirm bishop really have managed it? Even if so, it was but 'one Eccentrick Example in 360 years'.[28]

[23] Sir Robert Howard, *The History of the Reigns of Edward and Richard II* (London, 1690), preface, xi; Anon., *The Account of the Life of Julian the Apostate Vindicated* (London, 1682), 32.
[24] Bennet, *Constantius*, 15–17; Long, *Vindication*, ch. 3. On the army, see Hickes, *Jovian*, 170–2; Pelling, *Apostate Protestant*, 42–3; Parker, *Religion and Loyalty*, 2: 2.
[25] Hopkins, *Animadversions*, 16; Hickes, *Jovian*, 127; Bennet, *Constantius*, sig. [A6]ʳ; Long, *Vindication*, 8, 63.
[26] Long, *Vindication*, 74. Hickes dismissed Marius as an Arian: *Jovian*, 107–9.
[27] Bennet, *Constantius*; Long, *Vindication*, sig. B3ᵛ; Dowell, *Triumph*, 167; Hickes, *Jovian*, 162.
[28] Hickes, *Jovian*, 115–21, sig. A8ᵛ; Hopkins, *Animadversions*, 107–9; Long, *Vindication*, 78–81; cf. Bennet, *Constantius*, 24.

Third, after diminishing the invective, it was redescribed as the necessary duty of Christians to an erring ruler: that is, as admonition or counsel. Passive obedience should not constitute silent acceptance of error but was compatible with fulsome critiques of paganism (or popery). A civil resolution to defend one's faith might be appreciated, not punished.[29] Hickes said his fellow clergy thought it their 'Duty ... to tell not only a Popish Prince, but a Popish King to his Face, did he openly profess the Popish Religion, that he was an *Idolater*, a *Bread-worshipper*, a *Goddess-worshipper*, a *Creature-worshipper*, an *Image-worshipper*, a *Wafer-worshipper*'. Hickes labelled this freedom of rebuke '*Confessorian Parrhesia*', *parrhesia* being the classical figure of freedom of speech that introduced advisory discourses. This 'Liberty of Speech', of which there were 'Examples ... in most Persecutions', stretched back to opposition to Nebuchadnezzar, establishing an admonitory tradition of those who, 'inspired with Zeal and Courage, used ordinarily to shew it in *the Freedom of their Speech* before Kings, and Governours'.[30] Such zealous linguistic admonition – preaching *memento mori*, threatening divine wrath – was martyr-like courting of persecution, but not physical resistance; criticizing imperial sins, not kicking the emperor's shins.

Vigorous counsel thus seemed to be the way to blend deference to imperial authority and royal supremacy with an upright defence of the Church. In arguing that two independent civil and ecclesiastical powers could coexist, Samuel Parker stated that passive obedience made Christians the best subjects, while a Christian emperor, governing rightly, would not meddle with but protect the Church.[31] Parker contrasted the bold and brave, yet civil, admonitions of orthodox bishops with the flattery of the Arian clergy who monopolized access to Constantius and misled him. There was an implicit hope here that an apostate emperor (read: Catholic monarch) might be nudged back into good behaviour by counsel, obviating the need for resistance. This bears an ironic relationship to a classical tradition in which Julian's actions were held to have been mitigated by the good counsel of *pagan* philosophers.[32]

[29] Parker, *Religion and Loyalty*, 2: 29.
[30] Hickes, *Jovian*, 96, 106–7 (the reference to opposition to Nebuchadnezzar is to Dan. 3: 16–18); David Colclough, *Freedom of Speech in Early Stuart England* (Cambridge, 2005), ch. 1.
[31] Parker, *Religion and Loyalty*, especially vol. 1, pt I.
[32] Peter Brown, *Power and Persuasion in Late Antiquity* (Madison, WI, 1992), 67–8.

What made these late Restoration writers so sensitive to the question of whether words constituted rebellion? First, they were highly sensitive to the effectiveness of preaching. Anglican royalists frequently denounced the Civil War Presbyterians and Independents who had incited rebellion and regicide. Long even compared primitive Christian orations on passive obedience to a mock speech, drawn from Johnson's *Julian*, encouraging the army to resist.[33] Meanwhile, those on Johnson's side crossly denounced the power of the pulpit in fostering obedience. Second, the fears and jealousies aroused by the rhetoric of Charles I as a popish king, which had done so much to contribute to distrust and civil war, seemed to be revived by the wild rumours of the Popish Plot and Exclusion Crisis. While an early Restoration statute had banned calling the king a papist,[34] in late 1683, renewed judicial endorsement was given to the equation of words and resistance, when Lord Chief Justice Jeffreys used Algernon Sidney's republican *Discourses* as the second witness needed to convict him of treason, for '*scribere est agere*': to write is to act.

The British Julian's accession to the throne in 1685 tested assertions about practising passive obedience. James II ironically proved to out-Julian Julian, not overtly attacking the Church of England or forcing conversions, but instead undermining its privileged position by offering toleration to Dissenters and Catholics and prosecuting its criticisms of his co-religionists. Even his attack on Anglicans' monopoly of university positions could be equated to Julian's suppression of Christian tutoring.[35] Under James, Johnson carried his theory of resistance into practice, circulating seditious material within the army, for which he was fined, pilloried and defrocked.[36] By contrast, John Northleigh's attack on Johnson and those who 'Burlesque the very Bible, traduce the Doctrines of all Primitive Christianity' was dedicated to James II.[37] Indeed, as late as February 1688 Northleigh was offering support for James's policies in a pamphlet, twenty thousand copies of which were printed with royal

---

[33] Long, *Vindication*, 158–64.

[34] 13 Car. II c.1.

[35] In the 1650s, John Evelyn stated that Oliver Cromwell 'imitated the *Apostate Julian*' when the Protector banned Anglicans from teaching: John Evelyn, *Diary*, ed. Esmond S. de Beer, 6 vols (Oxford, 1955), 3: 163.

[36] Ri. Morley Registratius and J. Wickham Legg, 'The Degradation in 1686 of the Rev. Samuel Johnson', *EHR* 29 (1914), 723–42.

[37] Northleigh, *Triumph*, sig. C3ʳ.

financial support.[38] Samuel Parker would also demonstrate complicity in royal policies, taking up the mastership of Magdalen College, Oxford (where the Catholic Meredith was appointed to a fellowship) after a battle between James and the fellows over the king's Catholic nominee.

But the usual Anglican response was rather more complicated. Most refused to support active resistance to James, but many churchmen vehemently criticized royal policies and refused to cooperate with them.[39] Hickes is again the most prominent example. He attended James's coronation, although he failed to obtain a pardon for his brother's involvement in the Monmouth rebellion. He preached against royal policies, printed a substantial critique of Catholicism in 1687, and proclaimed that if the bishop of Worcester died, then as dean (a position to which he was appointed in August 1683, clearly as a reward for *Jovian*) he would not summon the chapter, thus preventing the king from forcing any Catholic bishop on them.[40] Yet Hickes was soon to be reminded of the dangers that adherence to passive obedience might pose to his church. In April 1688, Daniel Kenrick, a local minister, used an assize sermon on Romans 13 in Worcester Cathedral to defend the royal policy of a 'lasting Indulgence' (statutory toleration of Dissenters and Catholics) by arguing for absolute obedience on the model of Christ, the apostles and the primitive Christians. This was more than coincidental. While not attacking his dean by name, his target was clearly evident in his claim that passive obedience was not practised by those who criticized the king and prayed against him with 'bitter Words … as disobedient, as … a Javelin' and his insistence that none were to use 'Confessorian Boldness' to call the king an idolater or 'impiously' describe him as a 'Wafer-worshipper'.[41] Hickes nevertheless had good reasons to think his conduct a perfect example of passive obedience: criticizing James's religion, but refusing to swear the oath of allegiance to William and Mary in 1689, and even refusing to leave his deanery when deposed

---

[38] Andrew M. Coleby, 'Northleigh, John (1656/7–1705)', *ODNB*, online edn (2004), at: <http://www.oxforddnb.com/view/article/20331>, accessed 26 May 2016.

[39] Mark Goldie, 'The Political Thought of the Anglican Revolution', in R. A. Beddard, ed., *The Revolutions of 1688* (Oxford, 1991), 102–36.

[40] Theodor Harmsen, 'Hickes, George (1642–1715)', *ODNB*, online edn (January 2008), at: <http://www.oxforddnb.com/view/article/13203>, accessed 26 May 2016; George Hickes, *An Apologetical Vindication of the Church of England* (London, 1687).

[41] Daniel Kenrick, *A Sermon Preached at the Cathedral-Church of Worcester at the Lent-Assize, April 7th 1688* (London, 1688), 9, [20–1], 29.

as a nonjuror, pinning up a proclamation of his rights, for which he was outlawed in 1691.[42]

The *Julian* debate had a post-revolutionary coda. The events of James II's reign proved, for Johnson and his supporters, how dangerous a Catholic king might be; and, for their opponents, how effective the practice of passive obedience was. In 1689 Johnson therefore printed a renewed attack on imperial sovereignty, timely in the wake of a deposition that, try as it might, could not quite deny that it had removed a king, while Sir Robert Howard praised Johnson, 'one of the greatest Persons of the Nation', both in parliament and in print.[43] Howard pointed out the contradictory behaviour of the Church under James, using Hickes's conduct to impugn Anglican loyalty. This was criticized by a correspondent of Hickes in 1691, who argued that passive obedience had thwarted James; Howard responded the following year, asserting that passive obedience would never have saved the country from James's tyranny.[44]

While the utility of Julian for discussions of *imperium* and obedience seemed to be exhausted by 1692, one further dimension of his reign deserves notice as an example of how fourth-century Rome was used by the Church of England in her confessional battles. The Anglican claim that the age of miracles had ceased was tested by the accounts in their sources of visions and, above all, by the events that thwarted the endeavour to refound the Temple: fireballs from the ground, an earthquake and a 'miraculous Light in the Heavens, which appeared in the form of a Cross, and powdered the Garments not only of Christians, but Pagans, with Crosses'.[45] While Johnson had mentioned the episode to demonstrate that divine intervention was necessary because Christians lacked the strength to resist the emperor, most of his opponents did not interrogate it. Long cited it briefly, although he did not explicitly refute it in the way in which he denied visions of Julian's death.[46] But one author, John Dowell, did unambiguously endorse both the story of the Temple and the accounts of miracles and signs. Sometimes he described events as

---

[42] 'Hickes', *ODNB*.
[43] Johnson, *Julian's Arts* (printed in 1683 but hidden from the government: see *CSPD, Jan.-Aug. 1683*, 336); Anchitell Grey, *Debates of the Honourable House of Commons*, 10 vols (London, 1763), 9: 288–9; Howard, *History*, preface.
[44] Hopkins, *Animadversions*, 6–7, 77, 101; Howard, *Letter*.
[45] Dowell, *Triumph*, 66.
[46] Long, *Vindication*, 365, 112.

providentially determined: God misleading emperors into making
bad decisions, treatments well within the realm of Calvinist orthodoxy.[47]   He recounted the sticky ends of Julian's evil pagan coun-
sellors, especially that of his uncle and namesake, another apostate,
whose blood and excrement spouted from his mouth; but even this
was not so very different from Protestant martyrologists' descriptions
of the deaths of persecutors.[48]   Yet Dowell went further, describing
the young man who appeared to wipe Theodorus's brow when he
was racked.[49]   He defended the 'Revelations' and 'Visions' that ge-
ographically distant Christians had had of Julian's death. This went
beyond the extraordinary and preternatural operations of Providence
that signalled God's judgement and slipped into the realm of *miracula*. For Dowell, although miracles were 'not so frequent as they were
in Apostolical times, yet they never ceased in the Church of God'. He
saw in Julian's reign a chance not only to refute the political theology
of the apostate Johnson, but also to fight a wider campaign against
the philosophers like Thomas Hobbes and Benedict Spinoza who denied miracles. Perhaps not coincidentally, his book was printed in the
same year as Charles Blount's epitome of these radical philosophers
in his *Miracles no Violations of the Laws of Nature* (London, 1683).
Tellingly, Dowell condemned the bad Christians who denied their
faith under Julian as Hobbist Nicodemites.[50]

Comparing Dowell's discussion to that of William Warburton
seventy years later demonstrates the changing ways in which Anglicans defended the possibility of miracles in the fourth century.
Warburton's work exemplifies the shift towards what Jane Shaw has
called evidentialist cases for miracles that eschewed both Catholic and
Dissenting credulity about their frequency while avoiding the critical
stance about post-biblical *miracula* that had opened a door to free-

---

[47] Dowell, *Triumph*, 25, 98, 90–6; cf. Augustine, *City of God* 5.21.
[48] Dowell, *Triumph*, 47–9.
[49] Ibid. 43–4; compare his earlier critical stance in *The Clergies Honour* (London, 1681),
60–1. Ironically, the episode had been cited by Johnson (*Julian*, 47–8) and his supporters
(Anon., *Account of the Life*, 29); cf. Meredith, *Remarques*, 23. It comes from Tyrannius
Rufinus's continuation of Eusebius's *Ecclesiastical History*, 1.36: Tyrannii Rufini, *Opera
Omnia*, PL 21, col. 504.
[50] Dowell, *Triumph*, 101–17, 122–3; see also his *The Leviathan Heretical* (Oxford, 1683).
By defending, in *Leviathan*, ch. 42, Naaman's concealing his true belief and bowing to
the idol in the house of Rimmon (2 Kings 5: 17–19), Hobbes endorsed the idea that one
could legitimately hide one's faith. Nicodemus was the disciple who came to Jesus in the
night (John 3: 2); Nicodemism, a timid or hidden Christianity.

thinkers and sceptics.[51]   Where Dowell cited the Fathers, Warburton rejected Conyers Middleton's attack on post-apostolic miracles by comparing different sources, admitting that patristic narratives took liberties with chronology, and separating the phenomena God had caused from their natural effects. Thus Warburton claimed the fire that erupted from the ground could not have occurred naturally where the Temple was located, but that the crosses on people's clothes derived from the phosphate thrown up settling on the warp and weft of linen. The idea that miracles must have ceased in the fourth century because God would not have approved of (by intervening to defend) a Church corrupted by imperial power and popery had, by this period, become more important than showing that the primitive Christians had obeyed Julian.[52]

The Christian Roman empire thus proved a fruitful, if also highly problematic, source for early modern English Protestants. The nature of the Church-state relationship lay at the heart of the debate over Johnson's *Julian*, and it stimulated discussion not merely of Constantine but of a whole range of fourth-century emperors and events. These figures and occurrences could be invoked by defenders of the Restoration Church and monarchy, but they also needed to be controlled, for elements of them were always liable to be appropriated by the opponents of Anglican royalism. As late as the 1680s, therefore, the correct interpretation of the early Christian empire was vital to establish in order to defend a particular view about the identity of the Church of England.

In one sense, the timing of the *Julian* debate made it one of the last episodes in the history of a particular interpretation of *imperium*. Although the 1680s were an age of expansion, the territorial dimensions of the fourth-century empire went almost unnoticed. Sovereignty, civil and ecclesiastical, was the primary focus of the argument and the foremost meaning of empire; yet within a few decades empire's principal import would be a territorial one. The transition between these two meanings of empire, legal-constitutional and territorial, requires further study. But in another sense the Restoration debate highlights

[51] Jane Shaw, *Miracles in Enlightenment England* (New Haven, CT, 2006), 2–3, chs. 2, 7; see also Alexandra Walsham, 'Miracles in Post-Reformation England', in Kate Cooper and Jeremy Gregory, eds, *Signs, Wonders, Miracles: Representations of Divine Power in the Life of the Church*, SCH 41 (Woodbridge, 2005), 273–306, especially 286–7.
[52] William Warburton, *Julian, or a Discourse concerning the Earthquake and Firey Eruption*, 2nd edn (London, 1751).

a more transhistorical phenomenon: the inherently tense relationship
between Church and empire. It provoked some of the most fulsome
defences of and sharpest thoughts about passive obedience produced
by the Restoration Church of England, but also hinted at the ways
in which her clergy would respond critically to an apostate king who
(in their eyes) abused his ecclesiastical *imperium*. When, in 1686, an
Anglican preacher celebrated the first anniversary of James II's coronation by declaring that his Catholic king was 'not a Nero, but a
Constantine the Great to us',[53] he tactfully avoided any mention of
Julian. Some of his congregation may not have felt quite so sanguine,
as they braced themselves to implement the passive obedience that
would eventually destroy the British Julian's *imperium*.

---

[53] Thomas Cartwright, *A Sermon Preached upon the Anniversary Solemnity of the Happy
Inauguration of our Dread Soveraign Lord King James II: In the Collegiate Church of Ripon,
February the 6th. 1685/6* (London, 1686), 15.

The Episcopal Church, the Roman Empire and the Royal Supremacy in Restoration Scotland

Andrew Carter*
University of St Andrews

The churchmen who adhered to the established Church in Scotland during the years from 1661 to 1689, the last period in which it had bishops, have been overlooked by historians in favour of laymen and presbyterian dissenters. This article breaks new ground by examining the episcopalian clergy's attitude to the royal supremacy. To do so, it explores how Scottish episcopalians used the early Church under the Roman empire to illustrate their ideal relationship between Church and monarch. Three phases are evident in their approach. First, it was argued that conformists were, like early Christians, living in proper obedience, while presbyterians were seeking to create a separate jurisdiction in conflict with the king's. Later, Bishop Andrew Honeyman of Orkney tried to put some limitations on the royal supremacy over the Church, arguing that church courts had an independent power of discipline. This became politically unacceptable after the 1669 Act of Supremacy gave the king complete power over the Church, and, in the final phase, the history of the early Church was used to undermine the power of the church courts. The Church under the Roman empire, much like the royal supremacy itself, changed from an instrument to encourage conformity to a means of delegitimizing any clerical opposition to royal policy.

James Sharp, archbishop of St Andrews, spent 28 October 1669 in a succession of arguments over the extent of the royal supremacy over the Church. He said 'wild things' to the earl of Tweeddale in the morning, had a 'sound bout' with the earl of Lauderdale after lunch, was 'towzled' in a committee by a number of nobles, and went another round with Lauderdale in the evening. The clash was unusual because Sharp and Lauderdale, the king's Scottish secretary and now commissioner to parliament, had been close allies while the Restoration settlement was shaped in Scotland during the years from 1660 to

* Flat 6, 23 Parson's Green Terrace, Edinburgh, EH8 7AG. E-mail: apc6@standrews.ac.uk.

Studies in Church History 54 (2018) 176–189   © Ecclesiastical History Society 2018
doi: 10.1017/stc.2017.11

1663. Both formerly leading presbyterians, they had helped shepherd the Church of Scotland through the transition back to episcopacy under a ruling monarch after twenty-three years of presbyterianism established in defiance of royal control. Now, however, Lauderdale was pushing for a new Act of Supremacy, to which Sharp and his fellow bishops objected strenuously. While Sharp's opposition was eventually worn down, Lauderdale 'found the old Spirit of Presbitry did remaine with some of the Bishops (soe unwilling are Church-men, by what name or title soever they are dignified to part with power)', and rushed the act through parliament before they could organize any opposition.[1] This apparent divergence between bishops and statesmen over the supremacy has usually been seen as a proxy struggle over the government's newly tolerant religious policy, or as a matter of power politics, with little attention being given to the un-derlying intellectual issues for the churchmen. This article explores how episcopalian attitudes to the royal supremacy changed during the 1660s and 1670s by examining the different ways clerical writers used the Church under the Roman empire in their arguments.

Our knowledge of the intellectual and religious culture of Restora-tion Scotland has advanced considerably in recent years. Where once it was believed to be populated with corrupt and persecuting politicians and bloody-minded religious fanatics, now historians see that Restoration Scotland had its share of political thinkers engaged in lively public debate, as well as base violence. Clare Jackson has shown that the governing royalists were engaged in a deliberate and sophisticated project of restoring order after the civil wars, at the centre of which was the uncompromising assertion of royal power over all other sources of authority.[2] Alasdair Raffe has shown how, from a kernel of disagreement over the decision to restore bishops in the Church of Scotland in 1661, the differences between religious conformists and nonconformists grew as they repeatedly argued and sought to distinguish themselves from each other, until presbyterians and episcopalians had developed quite separate religious cultures.[3]

[1] Osmund Airy, ed., *The Lauderdale Papers*, 3 vols (London, 1884–5), 2: 151–3, 263.
[2] Clare Jackson, *Restoration Scotland, 1660–1690: Royalist Politics, Religion and Ideas* (Woodbridge, 2003); eadem, 'Buchanan in Hell: Sir James Turner's Civil War Royalism', in Caroline Erskine and Roger Mason, eds, *George Buchanan: Political Thought in Early Modern Britain and Europe* (Farnham, 2012), 205–28.
[3] Alasdair Raffe, *Culture of Controversy: Religious Arguments in Scotland, 1660–1714* (Woodbridge, 2012); idem, 'Presbyterians and Episcopalians: The Formation of Con-fessional Cultures in Scotland, 1660–1715', *EHR* 125 (2010), 570–98.

Political and constitutional thought on the presbyterian side of the divide has been explored by Caroline Erskine, but the political thought of the episcopalian clergy has not yet received much dedicated attention.[4] Conformist ministers and bishops have been seen, by default, as rather unimaginative royal yes-men: so-called Erastians who accepted complete royal control of the Church.[5] As we shall see, however, what drove Sharp and his fellow bishops to oppose the Act of Supremacy was a theory of the royal supremacy which limited the king's powers over the Church. That their opposition was something of a surprise to Lauderdale is due to the fact that episcopalians talked about the royal supremacy in very different ways during the course of the period.

Uncovering the pattern of this change is hampered by the relative lack of episcopalian material, which is no small reason for the neglect. Raffe has noted that episcopalians put considerably fewer works into print during the period, a weakness which contributed to episcopacy's ultimate failure.[6] Nor did they benefit from such a dedicated antiquarian in the early eighteenth century as Robert Wodrow, who made it his life's work to preserve vast quantities of manuscript material relating to Restoration presbyterians.[7] Given the uneven extent of source material, a good way to recover episcopalian attitudes and track how they changed is to follow one type of argument over time. Alongside Scripture and the works of Protestant divines, ministers regularly looked for precedent in the Christian Church during its first four or five centuries of existence under the Roman empire. The 'primitive Church' was taken to be a purer, uncorrupted form of Christianity. This is useful for our purposes, since the idea that the early Church had been governed by bishops became increasingly important for Scottish episcopalians as time went on.[8] As well

[4] Caroline Erskine, 'The Political Thought of the Restoration Covenanters', in Sharon Adams and Julian Goodacre, eds, *Scotland in the Age of Two Revolutions* (Woodbridge, 2014), 155–72.
[5] However, episcopalian thought earlier in the century has received attention in David Mullan, *Episcopacy in Scotland: The History of an Idea, 1560–1630* (Edinburgh, 1986).
[6] Alasdair Raffe, 'The Restoration, the Revolution and the Failure of Episcopacy in Scotland', in Tim Harris and Stephen Taylor, eds, *The Final Crisis of the Stuart Monarchy: The Revolutions of 1688–91 in their British, Atlantic and European Context* (Woodbridge, 2013), 87–108, at 102–7.
[7] Some episcopalian manuscripts were preserved by Wodrow, such as Edinburgh, NLS, MS Wodrow Quarto C, fols 270–4, 'Some Positions relating to Publick Worship'.
[8] Raffe, 'Presbyterians and Episcopalians', 575–7.

as ecclesiology, clergy also considered the early Church's relationship with the Roman empire, and the implications this had for the Scottish Church's relationship with the crown. They thought the Scottish monarch's authority was of the same kind as that of the Roman emperor. Antiquity thus provided a model, not just for a better Church, but for better Church-state relations. It therefore offered an ideal standard by which to judge the relationship between the Scottish Church and the royal supremacy.

Although the overall thrust of episcopalian references to the Roman empire was to argue that a Christian's duty was to obey their sovereign, the precise emphasis shifted over time. The period can be divided into three phases. In the first, immediately after the Restoration, churchmen used early Christian obedience to pagan emperors to defend Charles's temporal authority in the face of those who (quite rightly) doubted his commitment to covenanted presbyterianism. Then, later in the 1660s, they encouraged conformity to the Restoration settlement, by showing that it had been established by a legitimate use of the royal supremacy in the tradition of Constantine. Finally, after the 1669 Act of Supremacy had given Charles sweeping ecclesiastical powers, the ancient Church was used to justify complete royal control over the Church, in order to stop resistance from presbyterians and episcopalians alike.

Initially, though, we need to note that episcopalian thought was rooted in mid-century presbyterianism in two ways. First, most of the episcopalian clergy had been presbyterians prior to the Restoration, and they retained some of the basic assumptions. Presbyterians had long been committed to a 'two kingdoms' theory of Church-state relations, in which the Church was to have absolute control over spiritual matters without interference from the civil magistrate. As we shall see, episcopalians continued to defend the idea of a spiritual sphere with inherent legitimacy, distinct from the monarch. When Lauderdale complained about the 'old Spirit of Presbitry' in recalcitrant bishops, he was describing their intellectual history as well as making a dismissive joke.

Secondly, episcopalian thought, and indeed the episcopal settlement itself, developed in reaction to the radical constitutional theories associated with presbyterianism. Although under the 'two kingdoms' theory ministers were not meant to act directly in secular politics, they were nonetheless thought to have the liberty to criticize the government publicly when they deemed it to be behaving contrary to God's law. Combined with a willingness to sanction resistance to monarchs who overstepped their bounds, this meant in theory that the king had no influence upon the Church but the Church could demand that an ungodly king be resisted.[9] When this theory had been put into practice in a rising against Charles I, the Scottish episcopate had been abolished. The General Assembly of the Church at Glasgow in 1638 declared episcopacy inconsistent with the National Covenant, an oath required by all ministers which was supplemented by the more overtly anti-episcopal Solemn League and Covenant in 1643, both sworn in defiance of the king. (These covenants were the grounds on which almost a third of Scottish ministers refused to conform after 1662).[10] This link between presbyterianism and a contractual theory of monarchy explained why royalists favoured an episcopal settlement in the early 1660s. Thomas Sydserf, the last surviving pre-Restoration bishop, wrote a memorandum for Charles II in the summer of 1660 in which his main argument was that 'Presbyterian government as it is in this age professed and exercised in Scotland, is directly inconsistent with Kingly power, even as Soveraignetie be established by the Lawes of Scotland'.[11] Charles needed little persuasion after his brief but bruising time in Scotland in the early 1650s, and he ordered the restitution of bishops in August 1661, noting presbyterianism's 'unsuitableness ... to our monarchical estate'.[12] From its roots, episcopacy in Restoration Scotland was linked to obedience to the monarch.

The first task for royalist churchmen at the Restoration was to push back against the covenanting resistance theories which had predominated in the 1640s and 1650s. They started doing this in the summer of 1660, immediately after the king had returned but before episcopacy was restored, through a series of sermons given in celebration of Charles's restoration. At this point the Church was bitterly divided. On one side were a radical minority faction, known as

[9] David Mullan, *Scottish Puritanism, 1590–1638* (Oxford, 2000), 259–60.
[10] Ian B. Cowan, *The Scottish Covenanters, 1660–88* (London, 1676), 45–63.
[11] Oxford, Bodl., MS Clarendon 75, 'Information for his Sacrid Ma[tie] in order to the setling of the Church of Scotland', fol. 427[r].
[12] Robert Wodrow, *The History of the Sufferings of the Church of Scotland*, 6 vols (Glasgow, 1828), 1: 230; *Records of the Privy Council of Scotland*, 3rd ser., ed. P. Hume Brown et al., 16 vols (Edinburgh, 1908–70), 1: 31; 'Records of the Parliaments of Scotland to 1707', 1662/5/9, 'Act for the restitution and reestablishment of the antient government of the church by archbishops and bishops', 27 May 1662, online at: <http://www.rps.ac.uk>, accessed 6 November 2017.

the Protesters, who had opposed Charles II during his time in Scotland for being insufficiently committed to presbyterianism. In the early 1650s they had pushed the Church into declaring that Charles could only be permitted to exercise power if he was bound by the covenants, and they continued to suggest that an ungodly magistrate should be actively resisted. On the other were the moderate faction, the Resolutioners, who had supported Charles and most of whom later conformed to the episcopal settlement.[13] The surviving printed Restoration sermons come from moderate Resolutioner ministers from a number of towns, all of whom later conformed to episcopacy, and some of whom became bishops. The key purpose of these sermons was to counter the Protesters' position that the obedience due to a king was linked to his being an orthodox Christian, and not merely orthodox but Protestant, and not merely protestant but presbyterian, and not merely presbyterian but presbyterian according to the covenants sworn in the 1640s.[14]

The Resolutioner preachers asserted that Charles's authority was supreme, and could not be challenged. As the minister of Linlithgow (and later bishop of Dunblane), James Ramsay argued, since the king's authority was direct from God, 'he is [ac]countable to none else but to God only'.[15] A subject's duty, as several preachers emphasized, was obedience rather than judgement or reproof.[16] John Menzies, professor of Divinity at Marischal College, Aberdeen, himself formerly a Protester, undercut any claims radicals might make to be defending Protestant orthodoxy by citing 'the testimony of judicious Calvine' on the duty of obedience to the magistrate.[17] To soothe any worries, the Resolutioners played up the benefits to the Church of a king who could act as a 'nursing father', ending the Cromwellian toleration of errors, healing splits in the Church and

[13] Kyle David Holfelder, 'Factionalism in the Kirk during the Cromwellian Invasion and Occupation of Scotland: The Protestor-Resolutioner Controversy' (PhD thesis, University of Edinburgh, 1999).

[14] James Ramsay, *Moses Returned from Midian* (Edinburgh, 1660); John Menzies, *Britannia Rediviva* (Aberdeen, 1660); Matthias Symson, *Mephibosheth; or, The Lively Picture of a Loyal Subject* (Edinburgh, 1660); Robert Lawrie, *God Save the King: or, the Loyal and Joyfull Acclamation of Subjects to their King* (Edinburgh, 1660); Alexander Scroggie, *Mirabilia Dei, or Britania Gaudio Exultans* (Edinburgh 1660); John Paterson, *Post Nubila Phoebus, or A Sermon of Thanksgiving* (Aberdeen, 1660).

[15] Ramsay, *Moses Returned*, 10.

[16] Ibid. 14–16; Paterson, *Post Nubila Phoebus*, 4–5, 16-20; Symson, *Mephibosheth*, 13–16.

[17] Menzies, *Britannia Rediviva*, 'Epistle Dedicatory', 2.

supporting the spread of the gospel.[18] Crucially, these arguments referred to Charles's temporal authority. At this point, the clergy who were shortly to conform to episcopacy were simply aiming to disassociate the Scottish Church from radical resistance theories, part of the same backlash which would lead to the return of bishops. For now, these ministers did not have anything controversial to say about royal power over the Church.

Most of the supporting examples given in the sermons themselves were biblical. However, when the sermons came to be printed, and so made available to a wider (and better educated) reading public than the initial hearers, John Menzies and Alexander Scroggie both added dedications that discussed classical precedents. Menzies opened his argument with the ringing declaration that 'Loyaltie was the glory of the Primitive Christians, Confessours & Martyrs, both under the heathen Persecutions, & afterwards under Hereticall Emperours'. Reusing material from a previous series of public divinity lectures in which he had given 'pregnant instances of primitive Loyalty', he focused on the presence of Christians in the armies of heathen and Arian emperors: soldiers of the Emperor Julian (who was guilty of 'grosse heathenism') had declared themselves to be long-standing Christians after Julian's death, providing an example of 'a Christian Army, which retained their allegeance under the Worst of Princes, under that Heathenish Apostate Iulian'. Similarly, the orthodox Christian commanders under the Arian Valens told the emperor of his errors 'with such humble freedom as became Loyall Subjects' but 'abstained from all violence, and contained themselves within the bounds of Loyall freedom of admonition'. Menzies cited the opinion of Valentinian II, also Arian, that St Ambrose 'had such influence upon his Army, that if he would have given a word to the Souldiers, they would have seised on the Emperour and laid him fast', but Ambrose's true Christian loyalty prevented this. Lastly, he cited the third-century writer Tertullian to argue that, under persecution, Christians had refrained from avenging themselves even though they were numerous enough to do so.[19] As he had noted in the body of his sermon, since ancient Christians had obeyed a pagan emperor,

---

[18] Symson, *Mephibosheth*, 7, 21–2; Ramsay, *Moses Returned*, 12–13; Lawrie, *God Save the King*, 5, 7; Scroggie, *Mirabilia Dei*, 10.

[19] Menzies, *Britannia Rediviva*, 'Epistle Dedicatory'.

Scotland should consider itself blessed that its sovereign was at least Protestant.[20]

The Aberdeen minister Alexander Scroggie brought together several other examples in his dedicatory epistle to show 'the heroick Loyalty of the holy Fathers, Commanders and Christians in primitive times'. To the obedience of Julian the Apostate's soldiers and the non-resistance witnessed by Tertullian, he added a quotation from Cyprian: 'We do not resist … although our numbers be great; if we would be revenged, we could not want force'. This non-resistance was illustrated with the legend of the 6,666 soldiers of the Theban Legion who reputedly suffered martyrdom under Emperor Maximian rather than resist him. Scroggie turned this against Protesters in the Church by noting: 'If others should not resist, far lesse [should] Ministers who should be Paterns [do so]'.[21] By appealing to the precedent of the Church in supposedly purer times, these ministers were able to present resistance theories as modern innovations which should be dispensed with. But although they were amplifying royal power to discredit presbyterian political theories, they were not yet challenging presbyterian ideas about royal power over the Church.

This same set of stories was repeated by later writers in the 1660s and 1670s, once bishops were re-established, to support much the same argument: the authority of the monarch and the law should be obeyed meekly and without resistance; this included the laws underpinning the return of bishops.[22] However, other ancient examples were also cited to address much more specific aspects of the Restoration settlement dealing with the royal supremacy, marking a second phase in how the early Church was used. Rather than acknowledging the temporal authority of pagan emperors, episcopalians now looked at the Church under Christian emperors.

The leading episcopalian apologist of the 1660s was Andrew Honeyman, bishop of Orkney, who in 1668 and 1669 wrote lengthy replies to the notorious presbyterian pamphlet, *Naphtali*. He used Tertullian, Cyprian and the Theban Legion to argue that episcopalian conformists were following in the footsteps of the early Christians by

---

[20] Ibid. 13–14.

[21] Scroggie, *Mirabilia Dei*, 'Epistle Dedicatory', fols 2^v–3^r.

[22] [Andrew Honeyman], *A Survey of the Insolent and Infamous Libel, Entituled Naphtali, &c.* …, Part 1 (n.pl., 1668), 38–42; Gilbert Burnet, *A Vindication of the Authority, Constitution, and Laws of the Church and State of Scotland* (Glasgow, 1673), 53–68; [James Gordon], *The Reformed Bishop: Or, XIX Articles* (n.pl., 1679), 92–3.

obeying the king and his laws, while nonconformists were betraying that tradition by refusing to submit to Charles's just authority.[23] However, he also used the Church under the Roman empire to address a controversy over the king's power relating to church courts. While bishops were being restored in 1661 and 1662, the king had banned church courts from meeting, for fear that they would petition against the change. Honeyman himself had been on the receiving end of an earlier form of this policy, having been deeply suspicious of bishops. He drew up just such an anti-episcopal petition for the synod of Fife before the synod was dramatically dismissed by the earl of Rothes.[24]

It is worth noting that church courts were much more important in Scotland than in England: kirk sessions in each parish, local presbyteries and provincial synods were fundamental to how the Scottish Church functioned. Their suspension, albeit temporary, was deeply traumatic. It was an affront to 'two kingdoms' theorists, who saw it as an unwarranted incursion by the king into the spiritual sphere. When church courts met again under bishops, they did so with royal permission, which presbyterian nonconformists thought showed them to be invalid: true church courts met under a warrant derived from Christ himself, without reference to the civil magistrate.[25] Even those like Honeyman who ultimately reconciled themselves with the new order were proud of the independence of synods and presbyteries from secular interference: one of the factors which persuaded Honeyman that the Restoration Scottish Church was legitimate was that, unlike the Church of England, its disciplinary courts remained under clerical control, and had not become dominated by lay lawyers and officials.[26]

Honeyman was writing to win over moderate presbyterians, who on the one hand were unwilling to defy the Church established by law, but on the other did not want to abandon the presbyterian

---

[23] [Honeyman], *Survey of Naphtali*, 1: 38–42.

[24] Gilbert Burnet, *Bishop Burnet's History of his own Time*, 6 vols (Edinburgh, 1833), 1: 218; William Row, *The Life of Mr Robert Blair, Minister of St Andrews, containing his Autobiography from 1593 to 1636 with Supplement to his Life and Continuation of the History of the Times to 1680*, ed. Thomas M'Crie (Edinburgh, 1848), 382.

[25] Raffe, 'Restoration, Revolution', 92–3.

[26] [Andrew Honeyman], *The Seasonable Case of Submission to the Church-Government, as now Re-established by Law, Briefly Stated and Determined* (Edinburgh, 1662), 29–30.

principles they had held during the 1640s and 1650s.[27] He there-fore had to strike a subtle balance between a king who did not have total power over the Church but could not be resisted, and a Church which retained some inherent power but not so much that it became dangerously independent of the king. To negotiate this tricky subject, he turned to the position of church councils under Christian Roman emperors in the fourth and fifth centuries. Practice in this period showed that all ecumenical councils were 'convocated by emperors', and Honeyman argued that imperial laws were what allowed lesser synods and courts to meet. He underscored this by appealing to the presence of emperors or their commissioners at church councils, in particular Constantine at the Council of Nicaea in 325 and Marcian at Chalcedon in 451.[28] Since Christian emperors had had the power to convene synods and councils, Honeyman thought the Scottish crown retained the same right. Indeed, he went further, and argued that even pagan and persecuting emperors like Nero and Tiberius had theoretically had that right, but had disqualified themselves by their actions; the claims of a supportive Protestant monarch like Charles II were therefore unimpeachable.[29]

However, there were limits to what Honeyman would allow the king. His general principle was that although the king gave the Church permission to exercise its function, it ultimately derived the authority for that function from an inherent spiritual power, granted by Christ, with which the king could not interfere. It was an accepted part of the royal supremacy in England that, although the king could direct the Church in external matters, matters like ordination and the administration of sacraments were beyond his reach, and reserved to clerics.[30] Honeyman tried to extend this to in-clude church discipline. Discipline was much more important within the Scottish Church, both practically and theoretically: kirk sessions kept a stern watch within each parish, and the public repentance and shaming of sinners was a regular part of weekly worship. Scottish presbyterians had also long held that discipline as administered by

---

[27] [Andrew Honeyman], *Survey of Naphtali*, Part 2 (Edinburgh, 1669), 'To the Reader', fols 1ᵛ–2ʳ.
[28] Ibid. 82, 84–5.
[29] Ibid. 59.
[30] Ibid. 96–8; for English views, see Jacqueline Rose, *Godly Kingship in Restoration England: The Politics of the Royal Supremacy, 1660–1688* (Cambridge, 2011), 143–4, 154–62, 225–7.

sessions, presbyteries and synods was one of the Church's divinely ordained functions. In its 1560 Confession, the Scottish Church had made a rare departure from Calvin and made ecclesiastical discipline a mark of the true Church. This was still the standard position a century later: Bishop Honeyman's brother, James, included discipline among the signs of the true Church in a set of theses presented to his local presbytery in 1665.[31] Even while arguing for royal supremacy over Church courts, Andrew Honeyman therefore tried to carve out some protection for them. For instance, he would not directly defend Charles's dissolution of presbyterian synods. He noted that the king had the right to dismiss 'a heretical or seditious meeting, calling themselves a Synod ... as some of the antient Emperors have done with Pseudo-synods'. Although he strongly implied that any court which opposed royal policy would find itself in this category, he did not allow the king to dissolve a properly constituted, well-behaved meeting of ministers. Even the power of the ancient emperors was not arbitrary.[32]

More significantly, Honeyman also denied that the king could interfere with the sentences and censures passed by church courts, be it public repentance or excommunication. Although he could investigate the process and ensure that church courts were not abusing their powers, the judgments themselves could not be overturned. Only in the case of a church court's corruption or misconduct could the king step in. Honeyman illustrated this with St Paul's own appeal to Caesar, which he attributed to a desire to avoid the corrupt court of the Jewish priests.[33]

This careful limitation of the king's influence over church censures might seem to be a pedantic point of little practical significance, but a few months after Honeyman wrote, in 1669, it provoked a direct clash with royal policy which dramatically altered the balance of power between Church and state in Scotland. In an attempt to deal with numerous vacant parishes and widespread nonconformity, the government determined on a policy of indulgence, licensing deposed presbyterian ministers to preach in vacant parishes. Bishops

[31] Edinburgh, NRS, CH2/157/1, Minutes of the presbytery of Fordoun, 1662–1685, 28; *The Works of John Knox*, ed. David Laing, 6 vols (Edinburgh, 1895), 2: 110; see also Ivo Macnaughton Clark, *A History of Church Discipline in Scotland* (Aberdeen, 1929), 56–84.
[32] [Honeyman], *Survey of Naphtali*, 2: 92–3.
[33] Ibid. 103–7.

and other conformist churchmen were greatly disturbed by this circumventing of their authority. In particular, they were affronted that some of the deposed ministers who were to be indulged had been deposed and censured by synods: that is, the king was to give preaching licenses to those whom church courts had directly forbidden to preach. The episcopalian synod of Glasgow passed a remonstrance condemning this as a humiliation which would fatally undermine their authority.[34]

The government responded ruthlessly to this defiance. The 1669 parliament passed an Act of Supremacy to remove any legal doubt about the king's ability to grant indulgences, prompting the rows between Archbishop Sharp and Lauderdale noted earlier. The king was declared to have 'supreme authority and supremacy over all persons and all causes ecclesiastical', and to have the power to make act and edicts about any churchman 'and concerning all ecclesiastical meetings and matters to be proposed and determined in them'.[35] As a warning to the Church, Charles used the powers gained from this act to force the resignation of Alexander Burnet, who had made repeated legal objections to the policy of indulgence, as archbishop of Glasgow. The other bishops were cowed, and the indulgences continued to be granted to censured ministers.[36] Despite Honeyman's earlier attempts to persuade presbyterians that the king could not and would not ride roughshod over church courts, the crown had done precisely that.

The defence of the new form of royal supremacy was left to Gilbert Burnet, one of the government's favourite churchmen in the early 1670s and, after the 1688 Revolution, the Williamite bishop of Salisbury. This marked the third stage in how the ancient Church was used. Burnet had to remove any claim that synods or presbyteries might make to an inherent power independent of the king, and to do so he too turned to the Church under the Roman empire. His 1673 *Vindication of the Authority, Constitution and Laws of the Church and State of Scotland* was written in the form of a dialogue. It is a testament to the emphasis placed on examples from the ancient Church that the episcopalian character was named Philarchaues, 'lover of

---

[34] Julia Buckroyd, *Church and State in Scotland, 1660–81* (Edinburgh, 1980), 75–84.

[35] 'Records of the Parliaments of Scotland to 1707', 1669/10/13, 'Act asserting his majesty's supremacy over all persons and in all causes ecclesiastical', online at: <http://www.rps.ac.uk>, accessed 8 September 2016.

[36] Buckroyd, *Church and State*, 85–105.

antiquity', while another participant, Polyhistor, a historian, was largely included as a conduit for lengthy discussions of the early Church.[37] Indeed, Burnet used Polyhistor to advertise his own forth-coming *Observations on the First and Second Canons, commonly as-cribed to the Apostles*, in which he compiled the opinions of a num-ber of early Christian writers on the offices of bishops, presbyters and deacons, and which was published the same year as a sort of aficionado's appendix to his dialogue.[38]

Burnet argued that the king as civil magistrate had entire power over synods 'for there can be but one Supream; and two Coordinat Powers are a Chymaera'.[39] That is, even the very limited indepen-dence Honeyman had tried to establish was too close to the inevitable chaos of presbyterian polity. While Honeyman had defended 'godly discipline' as a part of the clergy's inherent prerogative, Burnet denied that it could be, arguing that 'till a divine Command be produced for Synods or Discipline, it cannot be lawfully gone about without or against [the king's] authority'.[40] The Church might claim a power of discipline (and count it as one of the marks of a true Church), but this had 'no positive warrant from scripture'.[41] The crux of his argument against church courts having any independent authority was based on their history under the Roman empire. In Burnet's telling, it was only towards the end of the second century that churchmen began to associate together in provincial synods based upon the borders of imperial provinces – a 'mould from the division of the Empire', as he put it. Since this development came long after the apostles, and was based upon secular considerations, Burnet felt it showed that synods and presbyteries 'can be derived from no divine Original, and so were, as to their particular form, but of human Constitution'.[42] Since the constitution was human and changeable, it ought to be determined by the laws of the civil magistrate. Burnet further justified this close secular oversight by pointing to the Church of Antioch's appeal to the pagan emperor Aurelian in a dispute over church property, and the imperial nomination of bishops after the Council of Laodicea in

---

[37] Burnet, *Vindication*, 'The Collocutors'.
[38] Ibid. 358–9; [Gilbert Burnet], *Observations on the First and Second of the Canons, commonly ascribed to the Holy Apostles* (Glasgow, 1673).
[39] Burnet, *Vindication*, 202.
[40] Ibid. 219–20.
[41] Ibid. 331.
[42] Ibid. 196, cf. 307–8.

364.[43] Thus, although church courts could indeed dole out godly discipline, their ability to do so was based not on some intrinsic spiritual power, as Honeyman had maintained, but on the laws laid down by the civil magistrate. Just as the early Church under imperial power had been moulded by civil demarcations and considerations, so now in the Restoration the Church could not claim any prerogative that threatened the king's authority.

In conclusion, Scottish episcopalians had a more varied approach to the royal supremacy than has previously been thought. They initially turned to the Church's relationship with the Roman empire in order to persuade presbyterians to abandon nonconformity and doctrines of resistance. Andrew Honeyman had used the emperors' convocation of church councils to justify the specific features of the Restoration royal supremacy as it related to church courts. Nonetheless, he tried to demarcate a special role for church courts as instruments of discipline independent of the king. By citing ancient precedent, he hoped to reassure moderate presbyterians that the king's actions were no threat to the power of the Church. After the clash over Indulgences and the 1669 Act of Supremacy, however, this limited conception of the supremacy became impolitic. Gilbert Burnet's use of ancient exempla was therefore markedly different from that of his predecessors. Previous authors, including Honeyman, had turned to the ancient Church to illustrate what they saw as eternal Christian truths, which they hoped presbyterians might respect. Burnet used it to show how dramatically the Church had changed over time, particularly with regard to its institutional structures, something he catalogued at length in his linked *Observations*.[44] From this he denied the legitimacy of any church discipline distinct from secular laws, a radical shift which would be disputed not only by presbyterians but also by moderate episcopalians like Bishop Honeyman. The Church under the Roman empire, much like the royal supremacy itself, had changed from an instrument to encourage conformity to a means of delegitimizing any clerical opposition to royal policy, even from within the established Church.

---

[43] Ibid. 208–9.
[44] See, for instance, his discussion of obsolete offices: Burnet, *Observations*, 107–20.

Concepts of Mission in Scottish Presbyterianism: The SSPCK, the Highlands and Britain's American Colonies, 1709–40

Clare Loughlin*

University of Edinburgh

This article examines the Society in Scotland for Propagating Christian Knowledge (SSPCK) and its missions in the Highlands and Britain's American colonies. Constituted in 1709 and operating as an auxiliary arm of the Church of Scotland, the SSPCK aimed to extend Christianity in 'Popish and Infidel parts of the world'. It founded numerous Highland charity schools, and from 1729 sponsored missions to Native Americans in New England and Georgia. Missions were increasingly important in British overseas expansion; consequently, historians have viewed the society as a civilizing agency, which deployed religious instruction to assimilate 'savage' heathens into the fold of Britain's empire. This article suggests that the SSPCK was equally concerned with Christianization: missionaries focused on spiritual edification for the salvation of souls, indicating a disjuncture between the society's objectives and the priorities of imperial expansion. It also challenges the parity assumed by historians between the SSPCK's domestic and foreign missions, arguing that the society increasingly prioritized colonial endeavours in an attempt to recover providential favour. In doing so, it sheds new light on Scottish ideas of mission during the first half of the eighteenth century, and reassesses the Scottish Church's role in Britain's emerging empire.

The Society in Scotland for Propagating Christian Knowledge (SSPCK) was the first organization in Scotland dedicated to missionary activity. Constituted by royal charter in 1709, the SSPCK grew out of a number of smaller societies for the reformation of manners that had proliferated across Edinburgh and the Lowlands during the 1690s, all dedicated to improving national morality, piety and

* 19/1 Spottiswoode Rd, Edinburgh, EH9 1BJ. E-mail: s0803325@sms.ed.ac.uk.
  For their advice during the preparation of this article I am especially grateful to Alasdair Raffe, Alexander Murdoch and Gabriel Glickman. This research was supported by the Wolfson Foundation.

Studies in Church History 54 (2018) 190–207   © Ecclesiastical History Society 2018
doi: 10.1017/stc.2017.12

virtue.[1] Operating as an auxiliary arm of the Church of Scotland, which had been re-established as Presbyterian in 1690, the society founded charity schools across the Highlands to instruct children 'in the principles of the Christian reformed Protestant religion', part of a wider arsenal of efforts to eradicate Catholicism from the region.[2] But the SSPCK's foundation charter also expressed broader ambitions: to spread Christianity across 'Popish and Infidel parts of the world'.[3] In pursuit of this aim, from 1729 the society sponsored three ministers to convert Native Americans in New England, and in 1735 financed a separate mission to Native Americans and emigrant Highlanders in Georgia.[4]

The SSPCK's domestic and foreign initiatives emerged at a time when missions were becoming increasingly important to British overseas expansion. Widespread conviction that the extension of Protestantism was the nation's safeguard drove much of the growth in eighteenth-century British missions, giving the empire a moral foundation and protecting it against the encroachments of foreign Catholic powers.[5] Consequently, historians have interpreted the SSPCK primarily as a civilizing agency: it deployed religious instruction as part of a broader campaign of cultural assimilation, designed to strengthen loyalty to Britain at home and overseas.[6] Yet this was not the sole aim of its work. The SSPCK also promoted an agenda of Christianization, cultivating religious knowledge and piety for the salvation of souls. It was an agenda that paralleled, and often outstripped, political and civil objectives, but which has received little attention. This article remedies that neglect by re-examining the relationship between the SSPCK's Highland and American missions.

---

[1] Donald E. Meek, 'Scottish Highlanders, North American Indians and the SSPCK: Some Cultural Perspectives', *RSCHS* 23 (1989), 378–96, at 382.
[2] Edinburgh, NRS, SSPCK General Meeting Minutes [hereafter: GMM], GD95/1/1, 31; Clotilde Prunier, *Anti-Catholic Strategies in Eighteenth-Century Scotland* (Frankfurt-am-Main, 2004), 131–6.
[3] NRS, GMM, GD95/1/1, 32.
[4] John A. Grigg, '"How This Shall Be Brought About": The Development of the SSPCK's American Policy', *Itinerario* 32 (2008), 43–60.
[5] Andrew Porter, *Religion versus Empire? British Protestant Missionaries and Overseas Expansion, 1700–1914* (Manchester, 2004), 7; Laura M. Stevens, 'The Souls of Highlanders, the Salvation of Indians: Scottish Mission and Eighteenth-Century British Empire', in Joel W. Martin and Mark A. Nicholas, eds, *Native Americans, Christianity, and the Reshaping of the American Religious Landscape* (Chapel Hill, NC, 2010), 179–201, at 185–8.
[6] Meek, 'Highlanders', 384.

Hitherto, Christianization has occupied a limited position in the history of eighteenth-century Scottish missions. Donald Meek's assertion that the SSPCK's objectives shifted 'from civilization to salvation' only in the later eighteenth century has proved highly influential.[7] Scholars have connected Christianization exclusively with the rise of evangelicalism – that activist Protestant movement which rejected the scepticism of earlier generations about the possibility of conversion by human agency, and which imparted knowledge of Scripture to inspire a profound, individual conversion experience.[8] A crucial turning point in this process was the 'Great Awakening'.[9] For Andrew Porter, the religious revivals that blossomed across the British Atlantic world in the 1740s occasioned a fundamental change in the society's priorities: convinced that the revivals signified the approaching millennium, its focus shifted from cultural assimilation to securing conversions and inculcating piety in anticipation of the Second Coming.[10] The transatlantic evangelical network that developed through the revivals included many SSPCK members; in 1749 the American minister Jonathan Edwards published posthumously the diaries of David Brainerd, perhaps the society's most famous colonial missionary, in an attempt to inspire a new awakening.[11] Yet closer examination of the SSPCK's records and publications calls into question this emphasis on the role played by evangelicalism. As we shall see, the society's commitment to Christianizing ideals long predated the revivals, and was present from the beginning in its Highland schools. As for millennial expectations, these were not exclusively an evangelical concern either. Recent research has challenged the dominance of evangelicalism in the SSPCK after 1750.[12] Closer scrutiny of the connections between Christianization and evangelicalism during the first half of the eighteenth century thus prompts a

[7] Ibid. 396.
[8] Ian Maxwell, 'Civilization or Christianity? The Scottish Debate on Mission Methods', in Brian Stanley, ed., *Christian Missions and the Enlightenment* (Richmond, VA, 2001), 123–41, at 124; Jeffrey Stephen, *Defending the Revolution: The Church of Scotland 1689–1716* (Farnham, 2013), 258–9.
[9] Donald E. Meek, 'Protestant Missions and the Evangelization of the Scottish Highlands, 1700–1850', *IBMR* 21 (1997), 67–71, at 68.
[10] Porter, *Religion versus Empire*, 32–6; Stevens, 'Souls of Highlanders', 187.
[11] George M. Marsden, *Jonathan Edwards: A Life* (New Haven, CT, and London, 2003), 320–30.
[12] Rusty Roberson, 'Scottish Missions and Religious Enlightenment in Colonial America: The SSPCK in Transatlantic Context' (PhD thesis, University of Edinburgh, 2012), 225–58.

192

reassessment of Scottish ideas of mission, and of the relationship between the Scottish Church and Britain's eighteenth-century empire.

This article outlines firstly the SSPCK's activities in the Highlands from 1709 until 1729. It demonstrates the centrality of Christianization in the society's schools, and suggests that its religious instruction was emphatically Presbyterian, weaving together individual conversions with the extension of the Church of Scotland's influence through the region. It then explores the SSPCK's expansion to New England and Georgia. The society was praised for bolstering Britain's imperial security; the Highland colony in Georgia in particular was perceived as an essential strategic block against Spanish incursions.[13] Yet this was not the main objective of its endeavours. The society used colonial expansion to further its own agenda of spreading Reformed Christianity, articulating a distinctly Scottish vision for mission. However, this vision became more important in America than it did in the Highlands. The tendency to present the SSPCK's domestic and foreign missions as twin pillars of a civilizing scheme has overlooked the fact that the society's activism against Highland Catholics waned in the 1730s, with greater attention being devoted to the colonies. The final part of this article suggests that this shift in priorities was entwined with growing anxiety that Scotland had lost providential favour. Linda Colley has argued that the connection between Protestantism and imperial expansion in the eighteenth century was overwhelmingly positive: flourishing missionary organizations confirmed for contemporaries Britain's place among elect nations.[14] The SSPCK's response to the imperial venture suggests that, in Scotland, the relationship between Church and empire was more problematic.

HIGHLAND MISSIONS, 1709–29

The SSPCK's ambitions to extend Christianity across 'Popish and Infidel parts of the world' first found expression in the Highlands. The region was widely regarded as the equivalent of a foreign mission field, in desperate need of receiving true religion and the rule of law.[15] Presbyterianism had only a marginal presence in the Highlands in 1690; most inhabitants adhered either to Episcopalianism or

[13] Ibid. 97.
[14] Linda Colley, *Britons: Forging the Nation 1707–1837* (London, 1992), 19–54.
[15] Meek, 'Highlanders', 378.

Catholicism, a considerable challenge to the re-established Church's authority. The deposition of James VII in 1689 had occasioned renewed efforts to counter the perceived 'increase of popery' in Highland parishes.[16] The SSPCK had a vital role to play in extending Presbyterianism's foothold. Operating through an Edinburgh-based committee of directors and a subcommittee, both composed of clergy and laity, the society collected donations in Scotland and England to fund Highland schools and schoolmasters to supplement existing parish schools.[17] Besides giving a basic grounding in writing, arithmetic and church music, its schoolmasters taught pupils 'to read the Holy Scriptures, and other good and pious books'; they were also obliged to 'catechise their scholars at least twice a week' and 'pray publickly with them twice a day'.[18] The SSPCK's schools provided a vital bulwark against Catholicism. Schoolmasters were selected according to their ability to engage in the 'popish controversie' and expose Rome's errors, thereby preventing apostasies and, it was hoped, reclaiming Catholics from superstition.[19] In this the tract *A Protestant's Resolution, shewing his Reasons why he will not be a Papist* proved particularly useful: the society's subcommittee noted in 1728 that 'the papists in the north hav[e] found, That their interests hath suffered' through its distribution.[20]

While its schools were open to all, 'Popish as weil as Protestant of all denominations', the society was uncompromising in the Presbyterian nature of its education.[21] Schoolmasters had to subscribe the Westminster Confession and be approved by local presbyteries, which automatically excluded Episcopalians.[22] In some ways this confessional emphasis is surprising. The society had been established jointly between Presbyterians and Episcopalians; the Episcopal minister James Kirkwood was instrumental in its formation.[23] Yet willingness to extend membership to non-Presbyterians did not dilute the religious education offered in SSPCK schools. Schoolmasters were obliged to teach all children the Shorter Catechism and secure their

[16] Prunier, *Strategies*, 22.
[17] Nathan P. Gray, '"A publick benefite to the nation": The Charitable and Religious Origins of the SSPCK, 1690–1715' (PhD thesis, University of Glasgow, 2011), 130–1.
[18] NRS, GMM, GD95/1/1, 31.
[19] Prunier, *Strategies*, 131.
[20] NRS, SSPCK Committee Meeting Minutes [hereafter: CMM], GD95/2/4, 193.
[21] NRS, GMM, GD95/1/1, 31.
[22] Gray, 'Charitable and Religious Origins', 184.
[23] Ibid. 101.

pupils' attendance at Presbyterian ordinances.[24] Such policies often proved difficult to implement in practice; nevertheless, the under-lying principles of Presbyterian education remained central to the society.[25] And although loyal Episcopalians were acknowledged to be useful against rival Catholic missionaries, cooperation between the two confessions was limited: in 1711, John Clow refused to set-tle as schoolmaster in the parish of Blair Atholl because its minister was Episcopalian.[26] For the SSPCK, educational initiatives were en-twined with entrenching the Church of Scotland's authority in the Highlands.

Presbyterianism was viewed by many as the means to secure loy-alty among the Highlanders, who were thought to be Jacobites.[27] In 1726, the SSPCK established a school in the heavily nonjuring parish of Lochalsh in direct response to 'the violent opposition given by the enemies of the present establishment' which was reported there by the presbytery of Gairloch.[28] More broadly, the society's apparent antipa-thy towards Gaelic, coupled with its designs to introduce industry among the Highlanders, seemingly reinforced the connections be-tween education and civilization.[29] In 1723, the SSPCK proclaimed that industry was essential for 'civilizing that rude, ignorant and de-luded People, who are now hurtful to the Commonwealth'.[30] Pro-posals followed in 1729 that 'any who please may erect manufacto-ries near their charity schools', aligning education with economic im-provement.[31] Yet such commitments were conveyed predominantly in public petitions aimed at securing financial support from central

---

[24] NRS, GMM, GD95/1/1, 135–8; for Episcopalian reactions to this policy, see Stephen, *Defending the Revolution*, 261.
[25] On the difficulties schoolmasters faced in securing children's attendance at Presbyte-rian services, see Clotilde Prunier, '"They must have their children educated some way": The Education of Catholics in Eighteenth-Century Scotland', *InR* 60 (2009), 22–40, at 29–33.
[26] Gray, 'Charitable and Religious Origins', 179.
[27] Prunier, *Strategies*, 22–3.
[28] NRS, Presbytery of Gairloch Minutes, CH2/567/1, 8–9.
[29] C. W. J. Withers, 'Education and Anglicization: The Policy of the SSPCK towards the Education of the Highlander, 1709–1825', *Journal of Scottish Studies* 26 (1982), 37–56. See Gray, 'Charitable and Religious Origins', 11–13, for a critique of the SSPCK as an anti-Gaelic organization.
[30] *Memorial concerning the State of the Highlands and Islands of Scotland* (London, 1723), 1.
[31] NRS, CMM, GD95/2/4, 241; Prunier, *Strategies*, 21.

government or the general public.[32] Schoolmasters showed no inclination to set up industrial schools, and while the society enshrined a commitment to teaching 'Husbandry, House Wifery, Trades and Manufacture' in 1737, no steps were taken to establish such schools until 1754.[33] Beyond the rhetoric of its official publications, the SSPCK's civilizing policies lacked definition and drive.

Closer examination of the SSPCK's records reveals a striking emphasis on using education to cultivate piety and devotion. In 1729, for instance, the society ordered the erection of 'Petty Itinerant Charity Schools' to supplement its existing fixed establishments, 'finding from their patent that the main design of their erection was the further promoting of Christian Knowledge, and the Increase of piety and virtue' against 'Error, Idolatry, Superstition and Ignorance'.[34] The importance of inculcating religious knowledge for its own sake was reflected in the accompanying demand for

> Itinerant Teachers, who understand the principles of our holy religion, and can teach children to read, tho they do neither write a fair hand themselves, nor understand Arithmetick … there is a good number of pious young men that have been at their own charity schools, abundantly qualified … for teaching these petty Itinerant schools …[35]

Schoolmasters were also charged with the spiritual edification of the wider population. A report of the death of Alexander Fraser in the parish of Abertarff in 1720 noted that 'he not only had a flourishing school, but on the Lords day kept diets for prayer reading and catechising which were punctually attended by the Countrey people not excluding the papists themselves'.[36] Donald McQueen, minister of Sleat in Skye, similarly confirmed in 1727 that the local schoolmaster 'reads, prays and sings Psalms with the people on the Lord's day in [my] absence, and in his spare hours catechises the people'.[37] In tandem with these efforts, the society also sought to improve religious knowledge in areas entirely free from Catholic or Jacobite influence.

[32] For example, *An Account of the Rise, Constitution and Management of the Society in Scotland for Propagating Christian Knowledge* (Edinburgh, 1720), 7.
[33] NRS, Presbytery of Mull Minutes, CH2/273/1, 17; NRS, GMM, GD95/1/4, 57; John MacInnes, *The Evangelical Movement in the Highlands of Scotland, 1688 to 1800* (Aberdeen, 1951), 251.
[34] NRS, GMM, GD95/1/3, 147.
[35] Ibid.
[36] NRS, GMM, GD95/1/2, 111.
[37] NRS, CMM, GD95/2/4, 91–2.

Its first school was established in 1710 on the nominally Presbyterian island of St Kilda. A 1729 visitation reported that the minister-schoolmaster there, Alexander Buchan, 'determined to know nothing among them but Jesus Christ and him crucified', with the pleasing result that 'as to Christian Knowledge, they are not inferior to their Equals in our bounds, so they far exceed them in piety'.[38] Far from being subverted to the causes of political stability and cultural assimilation, Christianization assumed an importance in its own right in the SSPCK's Highland missions. These priorities would later come to the fore when the society became involved in the imperial project.

COLONIAL EXPANSION: NEW ENGLAND AND GEORGIA

By 1729 the SSPCK was running seventy-eight schools across the Highlands, although its success in converting large numbers of Catholics was mixed at best.[39] During its early years of operation, expansion to other 'Popish and Infidel parts of the world' had been given little practical thought. This changed in 1717, when Daniel Williams, a Presbyterian minister in London, left the SSPCK a substantial bequest to 'maintain a competent number of well qualify'd Ministers in Infidel Foreign Countries' to bring heathens 'to the Knowledge of Christ Jesus'.[40] Williams left £100 for this purpose, along with the revenues from his estate at Catworth, near Cambridge. However, this would only be made available after the society had sponsored at least three ministers overseas for one year at their own expense.[41] This prompted the SSPCK to consider seriously the prospect of overseas missions, although its immediate reaction was unfavourable.[42] In 1722 it attempted, unsuccessfully, to modify Williams's legacy in favour of the Highlands, claiming that 'the Great Ignorance that prevails' in those 'vast and desolate bounds necessarily requires a greater number of schools than [we] have been yet able to support'.[43]

---

[38] NRS, Royal Bounty Committee Register, CH1/5/51, 338–40.
[39] *The State of the Society in Scotland for Propagating Christian Knowledge* (Edinburgh, 1729), 27–33; Prunier, *Strategies*, 139.
[40] *A True Copy of the Last Will and Testament of the Late Reverend Daniel Williams, DD* (London, 1717), 16–18.
[41] Roberson, 'Scottish Missions', 65.
[42] William Kellaway, *The New England Company, 1649–1776: Missionary Society to the American Indians* (London, 1961), 186.
[43] NRS, CMM, GD95/2/3, 149.

After more than a decade of wrangling about the terms of the bequest, in 1729 the SSPCK announced New England as its mission field. Williams had not specified a particular country, but America was an obvious choice: English missionary organizations were already operating there, albeit focused more on the white colonial population, and the existing church structures would provide the support needed for missionaries to function effectively.[44] A board of correspondents was established in Boston in 1730, authorized to recruit three ministers to go among Native Americans 'to endeavour their conversion to God in Christ'.[45] By late 1732 these missionaries were in place, based at separate forts close to indigenous settlements in the Massachusetts borderlands.[46] In 1735 the society additionally agreed to sponsor a Gaelic-speaking Presbyterian minister, John McLeod, to minister the Gospel among Native Americans and emigrant Highlanders in the new settlement of Darien, Georgia.[47]

The decision to embark on colonial missions immediately elevated the SSPCK's work from national to imperial significance. Like its English counterparts, the society was lauded at home for its role in strengthening the empire through the extension of Protestantism.[48] Its presence in Georgia in particular was viewed as an essential means of entrenching British influence in the region. Georgia's trustees had specifically requested Highland emigrants for the colony, playing on their distinctive martial culture to garner native support for Britain over Spanish colonists.[49] John McLeod's dual ministry to Highlanders and Native Americans was a crucial element in forging this alliance.[50] The attempted integration of so-called 'alien' cultures was underlined by the society's instruction to missionaries to teach Native Americans 'to understand and speak the English language', thus incorporating them within the fold of the empire and fostering loyalty towards Britain over the rival territorial claims of Spain and New France.[51]

At first glance, then, the SSPCK's provision of colonial missionaries suggests that the society was lending the imperial venture spiritual

[44] Grigg, 'SSPCK's American Policy', 47–8.
[45] NRS, GMM, GD95/1/3, 201.
[46] Roberson, 'Scottish Missions', 93.
[47] NRS, CMM, GD95/2/5, 252.
[48] Stevens, 'Souls of Highlanders', 186.
[49] Alexander Murdoch, *Scotland and America, c.1600–c.1800* (Basingstoke, 2010), 111.
[50] Roberson, 'Scottish Missions', 97–8.
[51] NRS, GMM, GD95/1/3, 214.

authority, facilitating the extension of Protestantism as a means of strengthening the ties between Britain and its colonies, and enhancing Scotland's status in the empire in the process.[52] This should not, however, obscure the equally forceful Christianizing agenda underpinning the SSPCK's work; indeed, the society's approach to colonial missions indicates that its aims and strategies were more likely to be in tension with the political necessities involved in imperial expansion than to endorse them wholeheartedly. This quickly became apparent in the continuing confessional emphasis of the SSPCK's missions. Britain's government pragmatically viewed most branches of Protestantism as co-defenders against the international Catholic threat; contemporary commentators noted that English colonial missions possessed an ecumenical flavour far less likely in a domestic context.[53] Yet the society participated little in this irenic missionary tradition, and often acted in outright opposition to it.[54] Its intended colonial outpost was Presbyterian Pennsylvania; only when the synod of Philadelphia proved noncommittal about the project did the SSPCK look to other colonies for a missionary base.[55] New England was the second most preferable location, as its Congregationalists were 'nearest to the Church of Scotland in Religious matters'.[56] As with the society's Highland schools, Reformed religion infused its missions in New England and Georgia. Outlining 'the lamentable circumstances' in America 'for want of the Light of the Blessed Gospel', the society commissioned its missionaries to impart:

> The Christian Reformed Protestant religion; and in order thereunto, not only to preach and catechise, But also ... teaching the foresaid heathens, To read the holy Scriptures of the Old and New Testaments, and other good and pious books ... to direct them how to pray, and to carry on as becometh the Gospel ... .[57]

Missionaries were instructed to 'use your best endeavours to confirm such [i.e. Native Americans] in the truth of our holy religion,

---

[52] Stevens, 'Souls of Highlanders', 193.

[53] Grigg, 'SSPCK's American Policy', 44; Stevens, 'Souls of Highlanders', 184.

[54] For instances of confessional conflict between the SSPCK and other missionary organizations, see Kellaway, *New England Company*, 187.

[55] NRS, CMM, GD95/2/4, 303–4. In 1730 the Philadelphia synod declared its enthusiasm for the project, but by this point the SSPCK had settled on New England: NRS, GMM, GD95/1/3, 206–8.

[56] NRS, GMM, GD95/1/3, 198.

[57] Ibid. 213–14.

and engage them to persevere therein', administering 'the seals of the Covenant of Grace' to them 'when you judge them fit to receive ... the same', and were further exhorted to 'Let the Glory of God, and salvation of precious souls be your chief motive, you are employed upon a very Important and Glorious work'.[58] Reports from the colonies emphasized the spiritual progress being made. A letter from the society's Boston correspondents in 1733 confirmed that the missionaries 'daily converse[d] with the Indians' and were 'sometimes Invited to pray and keep Sabbath with them', expressing hopes that they would soon 'clearly see the way of their Salvation'.[59] The centrality of spiritual edification to the SSPCK's missions was underlined in 1737, when the society dismissed its New England ministers: all three had refused to live within indigenous communities, but instead had acted primarily as military chaplains in their respective forts.[60] It was not enough simply to maintain a peripheral presence alongside native settlements or establish cordial relations with individual Native Americans. The successful spread of the gospel depended upon missionaries who 'undertake to live and inhabit with the Indians ... and thereby have access to instruct them in principles of the Christian religion'.[61] The society's colonial missions were a vehicle to extend Reformed Christianity's reach, transplanting the methods of evangelization that it had deployed in the Highlands. Civilization, so central to imperial ambitions, was a distinctly secondary objective.

PRESBYTERIAN FRAGMENTATION, PROVIDENCE AND THE CONVERSION OF THE WORLD TO CHRIST

The importance of Christianization to Scottish missions found expression in the SSPCK's rhetoric about its progress at home and abroad. It portrayed colonial expansion as part of its plan to 'advanc[e] the Knowledge of Christ, in Places needing the Means thereof', saving the souls of Highlanders and Native Americans alike, whose ignorance rendered their conversion so necessary.[62] Parallels between the two fields were repeatedly reinforced in the society's

[58] Ibid. 214.
[59] Ibid. 373–4.
[60] NRS, GMM, GD95/1/4, 57; Grigg, 'SSPCK's American Policy', 52.
[61] NRS, GMM, GD95/1/4, 57.
[62] 'Act in favour of the Society in Scotland for Propagating Christian Knowledge', in *The Principal Acts of the General Assembly of the Church of Scotland* (Edinburgh, 1729), 9.

publications. Preaching at its annual meeting in 1730, the minister John Matthison spoke of:

> Vast numbers of mankind sitting in Darkness, and in the region of the shadow of death, living in the utmost Barbarity, and stupid Ignorance, not only in foreign parts, but even at home in the remote Highlands and Islands of Scotland. Our Bowels should yearn towards these miserable Creatures … we should contribute our utmost Endeavours to deliver those precious Souls that are perishing for lack of Knowledge.[63]

However, the parity presented between domestic and foreign missions was not reflected in practice. From the later 1720s the SSPCK, and indeed the wider church, had expressed doubts about the viability of converting large numbers of Highland Catholics. As the 1730s progressed, schools were removed from heavily Catholic parishes and resettled in areas 'safe' from 'popish' incursions, to the chagrin of ministers struggling against Catholic populations.[64] While it never abandoned the Catholic Highlands entirely, the society claimed that its reformation was largely accomplished, thereby allowing advancement to other fields of endeavour.[65] 'The Society have extended their Views and Care even to foreign parts', the minister William Hamilton proclaimed in 1732; 'this they have done, after having erected great Numbers of Schools in our own Highlands and Islands'.[66]

This change of direction did not go unnoticed. 'Our Society ought certainly to keep at Home, till the Means of Instructing their own Inhabitants and Countrymen be put upon a solid lasting way', argued the anonymous author of *The Highland Complaint* in 1737. This pamphlet denounced the SSPCK's decision 'to take in the whole habitable World' before the Highlands were fully reformed, a step which the author claimed 'has proven fatal to our Reformation'.[67] Responding to this accusation, the society somewhat defensively explained that it 'endeavoured to chuse such places as missionaries had

---

[63] John Matthison, *The Necessity of Divine Revelation and Knowledge thereof in Order to Salvation* (Edinburgh, 1730), 21.

[64] For example, NRS, CH1/2/73, fol. 336, Donald McLeod to the Royal Bounty Committee, 6 March 1736.

[65] *A Short State of the Society in Scotland for Propagating Christian Knowledge* (Edinburgh, 1732), 27.

[66] William Hamilton, *The Truth and Excellency of the Christian Religion* (Edinburgh, 1732), 31.

[67] *The Highland Complaint, Transmitted by a Gentleman of that Country to his Friend at Edinburgh* (Edinburgh, 1737), 18–22.

most encouragement in'.[68] The SSPCK's enthusiasm for 'preaching the Glorious Gospel of Christ for the Instruction and conversion of the poor Indians' far outweighed the actual numbers of missionaries in the colonies, which were destined to remain small due to financial constraints.[69] Nevertheless, in terms of converting 'heathen' souls, its gaze had turned decisively towards America, eclipsing the reclaiming of the Highlands from 'popery'.

Several motivations informed the SSPCK's shift in priority, not least the prospect of material benefits. Its directors noted in 1735 that sponsoring a minister in Georgia 'may be followed with new donations', further raising the society's profile at home and overseas.[70] Historians have also suggested that the SSPCK, unable to make significant headway in the Highlands, increasingly viewed Native Americans as more capable of receiving Christianity.[71] William Hamilton expressed such sentiments when, in a possible rebuke to Highland Catholic hostility, he argued that the plight of Native Americans 'calls the louder for a remedy, in as much as we find … that these poor Souls, destitute of the Means of Knowledge, are not filled with those Prejudices against the Gospel'.[72] Yet the SSPCK experienced multiple difficulties in America too, not least as a result of questionable missionary zeal. The setback caused by the society's dismissal of its New England missionaries was compounded by a series of disastrous events in Georgia. Over half of the colony's Highland population was killed in the 1740 siege of St Augustine, Spanish Florida; McLeod left Darien the following year, complaining of inadequate conditions and insufficient pay, and the society's efforts ceased in the American South.[73] The SSPCK was subsequently reluctant to sponsor emigrant schemes elsewhere, declining, for instance, to supply a minister for Highlanders in North Carolina.[74] However, there was no suggestion of paring back the quest for Native American conversions. Indeed, the society appointed a second board of correspondents in

[68] NRS, GD95/10/144B, Letter to Highland presbyteries concerning new parishes, 1737.
[69] NRS, GMM, GD95/1/4, 17.
[70] NRS, GMM, GD95/1/3, 452.
[71] Murdoch, *Scotland and America*, 113.
[72] Hamilton, *Truth and Excellency*, 28.
[73] Roberson, 'Scottish Missions', 98–9.
[74] Murdoch, *Scotland and America*, 113.

1738 for missions in New York, New Jersey and Pennsylvania along-side those in New England.[75]

The SSPCK's increased enthusiasm for colonial missions becomes clearer when we consider the wider theological context in which the society existed. Scottish Presbyterians were acutely aware of the millenarian implications of missionary work. Belief that the widespread conversion of heathens signalled the approaching millennium became prevalent after 1700.[76] Robert Millar, minister of Paisley, exemplified this view in *The History of the Propagation of Christianity, and Overthrow of Paganism*. Published in 1723 and dedicated to the SSPCK, Millar stressed the necessity of new missions 'to promote Christianity among heathens' and expressed his 'sincere Concern for the Success of this important Affair'.[77] Such influences prompted much speculation within the society about the divine implications of its work. The minister James Smith observed in a 1733 sermon to the SSPCK that:

> The Endeavours of the Society here have been remarkably blessed of God, not only for spreading the Knowledge of the Gospel in the remote and barbarous Places of our own Country, but are beginning to take place in *America* also. What promising Appearances are these? ... What if this be the dawning of these happy Times, When the Earth shall be full of the Knowledge of the Lord? [78]

Smith's sermon highlighted the ideological significance of America in millennial expectations. The religious significance of the New World had long occupied a place in European thought; but for Scottish Presbyterians, the disastrous Darien expedition in the 1690s had occasioned profound anxieties that Scotland had lost divine favour.[79] These fears were compounded in 1733 when long-simmering theological and doctrinal disputes erupted, and four ministers seceded from the Church of Scotland.[80] Confronted with the visible fragmentation of Scottish Presbyterianism, providential favour was in

---

[75] NRS, GMM, GD95/1/4, 86–7.
[76] James A. De Jong, *As the Waters cover the Sea: Millennial Expectations in the Rise of Anglo-American Missions 1640–1810* (London, 1970), 113.
[77] Robert Millar, *The History of the Propagation of Christianity, and Overthrow of Paganism*, 2 vols (Edinburgh, 1723), 2: 523–4.
[78] James Smith, *The Misery of Ignorant and Unconverted Sinners* (Edinburgh, 1733), 22.
[79] Murdoch, *Scotland and America*, 126.
[80] Ibid. 132–3.

grave doubt. And though the colonies were far from immune to theo-logical rifts, Scots perceived blossoming Protestant piety in America, enhanced by events such as the awakening at Northampton, Mas-sachusetts, in 1734–5.[81]

Against this background of Presbyterian dismay at the fractured state of the Church, the SSPCK's determined involvement in con-verting Native Americans was not so much a triumphal expression of an elect nation winning souls for Britain and Providence, but rather an anxious desire to secure Scotland's place in what it believed to be the site of the world's spiritual renewal. While it refused to ex-pand elsewhere, for instance rejecting overtures in 1742 to send mis-sionaries to East India, the society repeatedly stressed that American missions would encourage Providence to favour it and the Church.[82] 'Nothing [is] more likely to draw down a Blessing from Heaven', it proclaimed upon announcing the New England scheme.[83] 'Our En-couragement otherwise to promote this good Design is great', agreed James Smith; 'the Blessing of God seems visibly to accompany the pious Design of propagating the Gospel'.[84] The society's colonial missions were motivated increasingly by objectives distinct from the standard rhetoric of Christian conversion and territorial expansion. The conversion of heathens would not only save souls; it would se-cure divine favour towards the SSPCK and Scotland as the instigators of missionary activity.

Such opinions were not confined to the evangelical wing of Scot-tish Presbyterianism. Certainly, prominent evangelicals seized on the millenarian implications of America: in 1741 the minister Alexander Webster entreated the society to 'scatter the mist of Barbarity and Ignorance' to facilitate 'the happy Time' of Christ's coming.[85] How-ever, this position was equally advocated by more moderate members of the SSPCK. John Gowdie's sermon to the society in 1735, for in-stance, devoted considerable attention to the conversion of the world to Christ and the paramount importance of the SSPCK's endeavours in divine plans. Failure to support this work, he warned, would pro-voke 'the dishonour of God, the reproach of our holy religion and

[81] Marsden, *Jonathan Edwards*, 178.
[82] Roberson, 'Scottish Missions', 109.
[83] NRS, GMM, GD95/1/3, 197.
[84] Smith, *Unconverted Sinners*, 22.
[85] Alexander Webster, *Supernatural Revelation the only Sure Hope of Sinners* (Edinburgh, 1741), 49.

the ruin of … precious souls'.[86] The society was united in the belief that colonial missions were vital for regenerating Scottish Presbyterianism's status as divinely favoured. The empire provided the crucial framework for this to occur, but also awakened serious doubts within the society as to Scotland's place among the elect. In this environment, the more prosaic reality of extirpating Highland Catholicism took second place.

CONCLUSION

The SSPCK's activities in 'Popish and Infidel parts of the world' offer multiple insights into Scottish ideas of mission in the eighteenth century. At a time when missions were regarded primarily as a means of civilizing savage heathens, the society articulated a distinct concept of mission, in which Christianization and the salvation of souls sat alongside civil and political goals, and in many respects superseded these secular aims. Through its endeavours in the Highlands and America, it established a blueprint for conversion based on spiritual edification which future generations of missionaries would replicate. The SSPCK's legacy was particularly evident in India; the missions of Alexander Duff in Calcutta in the 1830s and William Miller in Madras in the 1860s demonstrated that education, piety and conversion had become firmly interwoven in the imperial context.[87]

That the SSPCK placed such emphasis on Christianization before the outpouring of religious revivalism began is particularly significant. While the society became increasingly evangelical in the 1740s, this did not occasion a fundamental shift in its missionary objectives; the need to impart religious knowledge and inculcate piety to save souls had been the central objective of its Highland charity schools from their inception. The revivals may have enhanced the importance of these aims, but did not stimulate their creation. Consequently, we should be wary of ascribing civil and religious goals to particular wings or factions within Scottish Presbyterianism. Future research should explore how the society's priorities of civilization and Christianization interacted as the century progressed, both in the Highlands and overseas.

[86] John Gowdie, *The Propagation of Christianity and the Blessed Effects thereof* (Edinburgh, 1735), 25–6.
[87] Andrew F. Walls, *The Missionary Movement in Christian History: Studies in the Transmission of Faith* (Edinburgh, 1996), 203–4.

More broadly, examining the SSPCK's missions compels us to question the relationship between Scottish Presbyterianism and Britain's emerging empire. The society's missionaries certainly sought to inculcate loyalty through religious education and to establish a level of political stability in peripheral territories. In 1740 the society proclaimed that its work had contributed to 'the lasting and increasing Interest of the British Empire'.[88] However, its missions embraced a much more ambitious remit than providing a buffer against Jacobite insurrectionists or the encroachments of foreign powers. From the beginning, the SSPCK's colonial missions were an extension of its evangelizing agenda that had first found expression in the Highlands. But the way in which the society pursued its objectives at home and abroad shows that its attempts to claim souls for Christ were bound up with deeper questions about the Scottish Church's spiritual authority. In the Highlands the society sought to extend and entrench Presbyterianism's influence by pursuing a strictly Reformed educational programme, rather than seeking ecumenical cooperation. This approach also underpinned its work in New England and Georgia, going against the grain of increasing confessional collaboration that characterized English missions. For the SSPCK, participation in the imperial venture did not mean subsuming Scotland's own religious ambitions in favour of the wider political needs of an expanding empire.

Underlying anxiety about the Scottish Church's status as divinely favoured led to the gradual growth of a conviction within the society that its greatest impact could be made in the colonies, rather than in the Highlands. The SSPCK's growing enthusiasm for colonial missions at the expense of reclaiming Highland Catholics as the 1730s wore on stemmed from considerable disquiet that Scotland had lost divine favour. Introducing Native Americans to Christianity was an important goal in its own right, but by doing so the society was attempting to give Scottish Presbyterianism an active role in the site of the world's spiritual renewal. This indicates a fundamentally more complex relationship between the Scottish Church and Britain's empire than we might expect. Colonial expansion provided multiple opportunities for more sustained, successful missionary endeavours than had been previously possible. Yet far from viewing missions

---

[88] *A Succinct View of the Society in Scotland for Propagating Christian Knowledge* (Edinburgh, [1740?]), 4.

as a reflection of the superiority of an elect nation, the SSPCK's relationship with Britain's American colonies was decidedly ambiguous, exposing the fragility of Scottish religious confidence, rather than confirming it. Further research is needed to trace how these attitudes developed over time. But during this formative period of Scottish missionary endeavour, Britain's expanding empire provoked profound anxiety, uncertainty and doubt about Scotland's place within the divine schemes of Providence.

Christianity and Empire: The Catholic Mission in Late Imperial China

R. Po-chia Hsia*

Pennsylvania State University

*Reflecting on the theme of 'Empire and Christianity', this article com-
pares two periods in the Catholic mission to China. The first period,
between 1583 and 1800, was characterized by the accommodation of
European missionaries to the laws, culture and customs of the Chinese
empire during the Ming and Qing dynasties. The work of the Jesuits, in
particular, demonstrated a method of evangelization in which Christian
teachings could be accommodated to the political realities of Late Imperial
China as exemplified by the work of Matteo Ricci, Ferdinand Verbiest,
Tomas Pereira, Joachim Gerbillon and many generations of Jesuits and
missionaries of other religious orders. The Chinese Rites Controversy, however, disrupted this accommodation between Christianity and empire in
China. Despite tacit toleration in the capital, Christianity was outlawed
after 1705. After the suppression of the Society of Jesus in 1773, Catholicism in China became increasingly indigenized. In 1842, after the defeat
of the Qing empire by the British in the First Opium War, the prohibition of Christianity was lifted. Both Catholic and Protestant missionaries
entered China, backed by Western diplomatic and military power. This
led to the confrontation between China and Christianity, culminating in
the 1900 Boxer Uprising. A concerted effort to indigenize Christianity in
the early twentieth century ultimately failed, resulting in the separation of
Christianity in China from global Christianity after 1950.*

Eric Liddell (1902–45), an alumnus of the University of Edinburgh
and a missionary in China, is seen by many in contemporary China
as a good missionary, having served there during the Second World
War and dying of illness in a Japanese civilian camp just before liberation.[1] The Protestant Liddell is thus a counterpart to Frédéric

* Department of History, 108 Weaver, Penn State, University Park, PA 16802, USA.
E-mail: rxh46@psu.edu.
[1] A brief biography is available on the website of the Eric Liddell Centre, online at: <https://www.ericliddell.org/about-us/eric-liddell/biography/>, last accessed 14
November 2017; see also Ellen Caughey, *Eric Liddell: Olympian and Missionary* (Ul-
richsville, OH, 2000).

Studies in Church History 54 (2018) 208–224   © Ecclesiastical History Society 2018
doi: 10.1017/stc.2018.1

Vincent Lebbe (1877–1940). Lebbe, a Belgian Lazarist missionary, had sided with Chinese Catholics against a French-dominated
ecclesiastical establishment in Late Imperial and Republican China,
championing a vision of Christianity free of imperialist and colonial-
ist encrustations. Lebbe eventually adopted Chinese citizenship and
also died during the Second World War.[2] Liddell and Lebbe were
among a minority of Western missionaries in China who were deeply
troubled by the intertwining of Western imperialism and Christianity and sought a *modus vivendi* with rising Chinese nationalism and
anti-imperialism. From the mid-nineteenth century, Christianity had
gradually become juxtaposed but opposed to Chinese civilization, as
Protestant Britain and Catholic France defeated the Qing empire in
the two Opium Wars (1839–42 and 1858–60), and forced China to
sign unequal treaties, the terms of which included the lifting of the
ban on Christian evangelization. 'Jesus Christ flew to China on the
back of gun shells, whereas the Buddha rode on a white elephant'
was the laconic comment of Chiang Monlin, the first minister of education in the government of the Republic of China.[3] But there had
been a time when Christian missionaries had accommodated to the
laws and culture of Late Imperial China, and the story of evangelization might have had a different outcome. This article will explore the
theme of 'Church and Empire' by studying two periods of Christian
evangelization and analysing the ways in which the culture of empires, both Chinese and Western, changed the course of the history
of Christianity. The story began with the Jesuit mission some two
hundred and fifty years before the first Opium War.

THE CATHOLIC MISSION TO LATE IMPERIAL CHINA

In 1692, the Emperor Kangxi (reigned 1651–1722) issued a decree
for his European servants, the Jesuit scientists and musicians serving him at court. He decreed that their religion was good and that

---

[2] For a succinct biography of Lebbe, see Hao Fang, *Zhongguo Tianzhujiao renwuchuan*,
3 vols (Beijing, 1988), 3: 314–21; for a more detailed account and for the historical
context, see Ernest P. Young, *Ecclesiastical Colony: China's Catholic Church and the French
Religious Protectorate* (Oxford, 2013).
[3] '如來佛是騎著白象來到中國的, 耶穌基督卻是騎在炮彈上飛過來的': 蒋梦
麟 [Jiang Menglin], 《西潮·新潮》 [*Xichao / Xinchao*] (Hunan, 2000), 13. For an
English translation, see Chiang Monlin, *Tides from the West: A Chinese Autobiography*
(New Haven, CT, 1947), 4. Chiang studied with John Dewey at Columbia University
and was president of Peking University between 1919 and 1927.

his subjects should not be impeded from worshipping in Christian churches. This was the much vaunted edict of toleration celebrated in the West.[4] Among the services recently rendered by the Jesuits to the Qing empire was the work of the Portuguese Tomas Pereira (1645–1708) and the Frenchman Jean-François Gerbillon (1654–1707), who together accompanied a Manchu army to the Amur River, where they confronted the Russian garrison at Nerchinsk and forced it to negotiate a treaty, formally demarcating the frontier between the two empires and ending Russian incursions into Manchuria. Since the Russian and Manchu parties shared no common language other than Latin, this first diplomatic success was a credit to Jesuit ingenuity.[5] Earlier in Kangxi's reign, the Belgian Jesuit Ferdinand Verbiest (1623–88) had served as director of the bureau of astronomy, succeeding the German Jesuit Adam Schall von Bell (1592–1666), who had served Kangxi's father, the emperor Shunzhi.[6] To his councillors, Kangxi explained: 'What I am doing now, I do for the love of them, without any concern for others. I am so convinced of their attachment and their loyalty, that even if Europe took arms against me, I shall not cease to enjoy the same goodness they have shown me.'[7]

The Jesuits would indeed remain loyal to the Qing empire. But those who had belonged to the order before its suppression were all dead by the time that Europeans came to take arms against the great-great-grandson of Kangxi in the First Opium War. What went wrong? Or, to state the question a better way: how did the harmonious relationship between Christian mission and Chinese empire in the seventeenth century end up in a confrontation between civilizations in the late nineteenth century?

Originating in the second half of the sixteenth century, the mission to China was the longest and most persistent Catholic endeavour in

[4] See my 'Christianité et tolérance dans l'Empire chinois', in Guy Saupin, Rémy Fabre and Marcel Launay, eds, *La Tolérance. Colloque international de Nantes, mai 1998. Quatrième centenaire de l'édit de Nantes* (Rennes, 1999), 445–50.

[5] See *The Jesuits and the Sino-Russian Treaty of Nerchinsk (1689): The Diary of Thomas Pereira*, ed. Joseph S. Sebes, Bibliotheca Instituti Historici Societatis Iesu 18 (Rome, 1961).

[6] For Jesuit astronomers in the service of China, see Noël Golvers, *Ferdinand Verbiest S.J. (1623–1688) and the Chinese Heaven* (Leuven, 2003), 15–25.

[7] Charles le Gobien, *Histoire de l'édit de l'empereur de la Chine, en faveur de la religion chrestienne. Avec un Eclaircissement sur les honneurs que les Chinois rendent à Confucius et aux morts* (Paris, 1698), 173.

the early modern world beyond the colonial territories of the Iberian empires. Between the 1580s and 1800, about a thousand missionaries, European and Chinese, worked in this new territory for evangelism; at the mission's height, it ministered to as many as three hundred thousand converts.[8] Unlike neighbouring Japan, where the mission experienced first spectacular growth and then savage persecution, Catholicism in China progressed slowly but established communities of the faithful that persisted into modern times, despite sporadic and short periods of persecutions. Unlike those in the New World, missionaries arrived in China without soldiers and officials of Western colonizing powers. More so than elsewhere, European missionaries encountered and accommodated themselves to a civilization that was alien, alluring and challenging. The tensions between religions which characterized the Catholic missions in the Ottoman and Persian empires and the aggressive spirit toward Hinduism and Islam in South Asia were altogether less pronounced in Late Imperial China, where state ideology was not determined by allegiance to a single religion.[9] In the following pages, we will examine the history of the mission, its personnel, methods and converts, and we will study Catholicism's relationship with the religions of China.[10]

Although the first Catholic clergy arrived in China aboard Portuguese ships in the opening decades of the sixteenth century, there are no records of evangelization among the coastal and maritime Chinese populations; this was because the Portuguese came as pirates and traders. The first to try to evangelize was Francis Xavier, the apostle of Asia and the first Jesuit missionary in East Asia, but he died in 1552 on the island of Shangchuan, off the Guangdong coast, before he could embark on his planned China mission. Only after the establishment of a permanent Portuguese base in Macao around 1555,

---

[8] For numbers of missionaries and converts in Ming and Qing China, see Nicolas Standaert, ed., *Handbook of Christianity in China*, 1: *635–1800* (Leiden, 2001); for a succinct narrative, see R. Po-chia Hsia, 'Imperial China and the Christian Mission', in idem, ed., *A Companion to Early Modern Catholic Global Missions* (Leiden, 2018), 344–66.

[9] See R. Po-chia Hsia, 'Catholic Global Missions and the Expansion of Europe', ibid. 1–16.

[10] In addition to the titles cited above, for some of the best scholarship on the Christian mission in Late Imperial China, see Eugenio Menegon, *Ancestors, Virgins, and Friars: Christianity as a Local Religion in Late Imperial China* (Cambridge, MA, 2009); Liam M. Brockey, *Journey to the East: The Jesuit Mission to China, 1579–1724* (Cambridge, MA, 2007).

a grant from Chinese officials, was the foundation laid for future Catholic missions.

Accompanying merchants to trade fairs in Guangzhou, Catholic chaplains from Macao first observed the religious customs of Ming China. Despite several attempts to establish a mission in the province, undertaken in the 1570s by Portuguese Jesuits from Macao and Spanish mendicants from the Philippines, the first success was achieved only in 1582/3 by an Italian Jesuit, Michele Ruggieri, who had prepared for the mission by three years of intensive study of Chinese language and culture in Macao. However, one of his Jesuit companions, Matteo Ricci (1552–1610), would eclipse him in fame and importance after Ruggieri's return to Italy in 1587.[11]

The most famous of all the China missionaries, Ricci's success rested on his approach. Whereas the first Jesuits dressed as Buddhist monks and made few converts, he assumed the persona of a Western scholar immersed in the study of classical Chinese learning and attracted the attention of the Chinese elites, the mandarins and literati who owed their careers and reputations precisely to such learning. Aside from his charisma, remarked on by many Chinese scholars, Ricci created a brilliant persona with his scientific, technical and geographical knowledge, reinforced by a collection of Western scientific instruments, maps and curiosities. After a modest beginning, Ricci's career took off in 1594. By the time of his death in 1610, he had climbed to the apex of Ming society and reached the imperial capital in Beijing. Jesuit residences had been established in four cities and converts numbered more than a thousand, compared to a few score in the first decade.

Between 1610 and 1644, the mission reached new heights of success. It saw the fastest percentile increase of conversions in the entire history of Christianity in China (albeit the absolute numbers remained modest and were indeed miniscule relative to the total population); it attracted converts from the highest echelons of Late Ming society, among them the highest ranking mandarins and members of the imperial family, and an even broader circle of elite admirers and supporters; it consolidated a successful cultural policy of evangelization, using Western science and the humanities

---

[11] See R. Po-chia Hsia, *A Jesuit in the Forbidden City: Matteo Ricci 1552–1610* (Oxford, 2010); idem, *Matteo Ricci and the Catholic Mission to China: A Short History with Documents* (Indianapolis, IN and Cambridge, MA, 2016).

as handmaidens to the queen, theology; it spread to most of the provinces of the country, setting up residences and building churches; and through an energetic programme of composing and publishing Chinese-language Christian literature, ranging from liturgical to literary and scientific works, it achieved a high degree of cultural accommodation and domestication. While in the beginning it was the exclusive domain of the Society of Jesus, after the 1630s the China mission opened up to mendicant friars from the Spanish Philippines, as maritime trade intensified between Fujian and Luzon.

Yet the cataclysm of the mid-seventeenth century almost shattered this Christian edifice. Famine, rebellion and invasion brought death and destruction: peasant rebels overthrew Ming rule (1368–1644), Manchu troops invaded China, and the country was plunged into two decades of war and disorder. Entire Christian communities perished. Two Christian centres survived: Portuguese Macao and Beijing. A haven from warfare, Macao continued to serve as a base for sending personnel and supplies inland. For more than a decade, the Jesuits and Portuguese supported the resistance regime of the southern Ming. Three dowagers and empresses of the Yongli court in southern China converted to Catholicism, as did a number of leading courtiers and the heir apparent of the Emperor Yongli, a boy baptized as Constantine. But when the Manchu Qing forces crushed the Yongli regime in the 1650s, the only remaining hope for converting China lay in Beijing.

In the imperial capital, the Catholic mission survived thanks to the work of Jesuit scientists at the imperial court. Appreciated for their astronomical knowledge, the Catholic mission survived the rebel conquest and the Manchu takeover. Confirmed as superior and director of the Imperial Observatory, the German Jesuit Adam Schall became a confidant and father figure for the much younger Qing Emperor Shunzhi (reigned 1638–61). With political patronage established in Beijing, the Catholic mission rapidly reoriented itself to serve the Qing regime, focusing now on obtaining patronage from the Manchu ruling class rather than on the Han Chinese literati and mandarin elites, as had been the case under the Ming dynasty.

Imperial patronage proved fickle and almost fatal. The death of the emperor Shunzhi in 1661 unleashed a crisis. Blamed for selecting unpropitious dates for burials in the imperial court, the Jesuits, without patronage, were open to attack by their enemies, the xenophobic Confucian scholar Yang Guangxien and Muslim astronomers at court. Placed under house arrest, Schall died before he was put on trial; Christian missionaries were rounded up in the whole country and sent to Guangzhou, in preparation for their expulsion. In this moment of crisis, science saved the day. The Belgian Jesuit Ferdinand Verbiest in Beijing demonstrated his superior astronomical and mathematical knowledge in predicting an eclipse and convinced the young Emperor Kangxi that Christian missionaries were innocent of the charges levied against them. The order of expulsion was rescinded, Verbiest was reinstated in the Imperial Observatory, and Christianity survived this crisis and entered a golden age in Imperial China.[12]

The period from 1665 to 1705 represented a prosperous time for the Catholic mission. An energetic and intelligent ruler, the young Kangxi developed an immense curiosity for Western learning, especially in mathematics, and a great respect and affection for Western missionaries, who served as tutors in his private study and at court as astronomers and painters, becoming loyal servants to an imperial master. In return, he bestowed gifts and favours on the missionaries and, as noted above, issued an edict in 1692 explicitly allowing his subjects to practise this Western religion.

With imperial patronage and favour, the Catholic mission prospered. New missionaries arrived, including French Jesuits sent by Louis XIV in 1684; they became embroiled in a jurisdictional dispute with the Portuguese fathers already entrenched in China. In time, the society sanctioned two separate Jesuit missions, one under Portuguese, the other under French, direction. However, this internal tension was overshadowed by a far sharper confrontation that would eventually have negative repercussions for the entire mission, the Chinese Rites Controversy.[13]

The origins of this confrontation went back to the first Spanish mendicant friars who had evangelized in the 1630s and 1640s. Having arrived from Mexico and the Philippines, territories won to the Church by Spanish arms, the friars had developed a different vision

[12] See Golvers, *Verbiest*.
[13] An older, still useful work gives an overview of the Rites Controversy: George Minamiki, *The Chinese Rites Controversy from its Beginning to Modern Times* (Chicago, IL, 1985). More recent studies have focused on specific aspects of the controversy and explored new sources: see, for example, Nicolas Standaert, ed., *Chinese Voices in the Rites Controversy: Travelling Books, Community Networks, Intercultural Arguments*, Bibliotheca Instituti Historici Societatis Iesu 75 (Rome, 2012).

of evangelization, one based on the superiority of Christian civilization to all others and on the unique value of Spanish experiences. In
China, the friars questioned the Jesuits' policy of accommodation to
Chinese customs, a policy first established by Ricci and confirmed by
subsequent generations of Jesuit missionaries, particularly pertaining
to the rituals performed in honour of ancestors and the great Chinese sage, Confucius. Whereas the Jesuits defined these as civic rituals, matters indifferent to Christian doctrine, the friars attacked these
practices as religious superstitions. Both sides sent representatives to
argue their case in Rome. The dispute led to a war of words that
engrossed public opinion in Europe and energized opposition to the
Society of Jesus.

The Jesuit missionary strategy of harmonizing Confucianism with
Christianity emerged from two considerations.[14] First, for Ricci,
the originator of this strategy, Confucian culture had equalled the
achievements of Greco-Roman civilization; since the latter had served
as the foundation for the evangelization of the West, Confucianism as
seen by the Jesuits could serve a similar function. Secondly, among all
the religions of China, Ricci had identified Buddhism, the most popular religion, as the hypothetical enemy of Christianization, despite
several expressions of friendship by Buddhist monks during the early
years of the Jesuit mission. Provoked by Jesuit animosity, Christian-
Buddhist polemic flared up in the early decades of the seventeenth
century, although it died down after the first two generation of Jesuit
missionaries had passed from the scene.

More in the manner of religious polemic than interfaith dialogue,
Catholic missionaries in Late Imperial China showed little or no curiosity about Chinese religions, except for the sole surviving Jewish
community in Kaifeng. Apart from one religious debate in the 1640s
between the Jesuit Nicolas Longobardo and some Muslim leaders,
Christian missionaries had few if any dealings with the numerous
Chinese Muslim communities, nor did they show any further interest in Buddhism or Daoism.[15] Moreover, Christianity proved

[14] The best introduction is still the older work by Paul A. Rule, *K'ung-tzu or Confucius?
The Jesuit Interpretation of Confucianism* (Sydney, 1986). More recent scholarship has focused on studying the Jesuit 'translations' of Confucian classics: see Thierry Meynard, ed.,
Confucius Sinarum Philosophus *(1687): The First Translation of the Confucian Classics*,
Monumenta Historica Societatis Iesu [hereafter: MHSI] n.s. 6 (Rome, 2011).
[15] For Christian encounters with Islam in China, see R. Po-chia Hsia, 'Christian Conversion in Late Ming China: Niccolo Longobardo and Shandong', *Medieval History Journal*

215

attractive to some adherents of popular religions and banned sects in seventeenth- and eighteenth-century China, an association that brought with it negative political connotations that the missionaries were at pain to disclaim.

Even while the Catholic mission was entering its golden age under the reign of Kangxi, the Jesuits were losing the war in the field of papal politics and public opinion in Europe. In 1704, the papacy condemned certain Chinese rituals in honour of ancestors and Confucius as idolatrous and forbade converts to participate in them. A papal legate, Charles Thomas Maillard de Tournon (1668–1710), was dispatched to proclaim the papal decree in China and present the case to the imperial court. Ill-advised and prepared, the Tournon legation was a disaster.[16] Irked by Western pronouncements on Chinese rituals, the Emperor Kangxi dismissed the papal legate, who eventually died of an illness in Macao, virtually under house arrest by the hostile Portuguese, who were strong supporters of the Jesuits. Nonetheless, and despite the overwhelming opposition of Chinese converts, the papal bull condemning Chinese rituals was publicized in 1705 and all missionaries were enjoined to enforce its stipulations.

It was a watershed. Hitherto represented as a synthesis between East and West and harmonious with Confucian learning, Christianity was now perceived by many as alien, aggressive and anti-Chinese. While Chinese Christians reluctantly abided by the new stipulations, numbers of conversions dropped, especially among the literati elites. The most severe blow came from the emperor, who withdrew his patronage. Kangxi proclaimed Christianity a superstitious and troublesome religion, and while he continued to allow its practice by his Western servants at court, he forbade adherence to Christianity among his own subjects. All Western missionaries had either to swear that they would not leave China and that they would adhere to the ways of Father Ricci, or else to leave the country. The split in the

---

12 (2009), 275–301; idem, 天主教与明末社会: 崇祯朝龙华民山东传教的几个问题 ['Tianzhu jiao yu Mingmo shehui'], 历史研究 [*Lishi yanjiu*], 2009 no. 2, 51–67. For Christianity and Buddhism, see idem, 'The Jesuit Encounter with Buddhism in Ming China', in M. Antoni Üçerler, ed., *Christianity and Cultures: Japan and China in Comparison 1543–1644* (Rome, 2009), 19–44.

[16] See Kilian Stumpf, *The* Acta Pekinensia *or Historical Records of the Maillard de Tournon Legation*, 1: *December 1705–August 1706*, ed. Paul Rule and Claudia von Collani, MHSI n.s. 9 (Rome and Macau, 2015).

mission was great: the Dominicans, the Augustinians and the priests of the Paris Foreign Missions (Société des Missions étrangères de Paris) refused to accept the conditions and left; the Franciscans were divided in their allegiance; but the great majority of Jesuits accepted Kangxi's conditions. With the exception of Beijing, after 1707 Christianity was outlawed in the Qing empire.

Despite the ban, Christian communities continued. Some churches were seized and converted into schools, and Western missionaries in the provinces went into hiding, but religious life continued for the most part, tolerated by local officials. Kangxi died in 1722, and the succession struggle unleashed another crisis. The new Emperor Yongzhen (reigned 1722–35) prevailed against a brother who was supported by a powerful Manchu noble family, the Sunu, many of whom were Christian converts; the intrigue of a Portuguese Jesuit exacerbated matters. The Sunus were losers in the political struggle and were exiled, but they were celebrated as Christian martyrs in Jesuit letters. The Jesuit, João Mourão, was executed, a death remembered largely with embarrassed silence in missionary records. Still, Christian communities remained largely undisturbed, and laws decreed were not always vigorously enforced. However, two decades later the zeal of a governor in Fujian would change all this.

In 1746, the discovery of a covert Spanish missionary in Fujian unleashed a manhunt. In the end, five Dominican friars and more than a dozen Chinese catechists and Christian leaders were arrested. Interpreting the anti-Christian law rigorously (the death penalty had not been stipulated in the original ban), the governor quietly executed the missionaries in prison before the Jesuits in Beijing could intervene to secure an imperial pardon. Two years later, it was the turn of the Jesuits to suffer martyrdom when a dispute between two Christians in Suzhou led to the denunciation, arrest and quick executions of two of their number. These cases had some aspects in common: both were zealously prosecuted by anti-Christian provincial mandarins, who interpreted and executed the law rigorously; and in both cases, the missionaries at the imperial court tried and failed to secure an imperial pardon. Nonetheless, these instances of persecution did not reflect a new hostility on the part of the Emperor Qianlong (reigned 1735–96), grandson of Kangxi, who enjoyed the service of Western missionary painters and musicians at court. Rather, a combination of local circumstances and indifference at court sealed the fate of the missionaries. In 1752, officials in Hubei province initiated another hunt for Christians, alarmed by a mistaken notion that a local rebellion was in collusion with Christianity. This time the emperor intervened, instructing his mandarins that the two had nothing to do with one another.[17]

Officially banned by the Qing state, the Christian mission continued to be sustained by the two poles of Beijing and Macao. In the imperial capital, worshippers openly attended mass at all four Christian churches, a practice tolerated by Qianlong in reward for the service of his Western missionaries. To the best of their abilities, these missionary courtiers exercised discretion in extending protection to missionaries and converts in the provinces, while Macao served as the rear base. Couriers from the internal mission travelled to the Portuguese enclave carrying letters and reports, and returned to the interior conveying monies, letters and supplies, and escorting missionaries newly arrived from Europe and travelling in disguise.

In 1784, authorities intercepted one of these runs. The emperor was stunned. Enraged that Christianity continued to thrive almost eight decades after being declared illegal by his grandfather, Qianlong ordered an anti-Christian campaign in all provinces of the realm. The 1784–5 persecutions represented the gravest crisis of the mission: scores of Western missionaries and Chinese priests were arrested, some died in prison, and hundreds of converts were punished, by exile, prison and caning.[18] Moreover, the persecutions came at a time when the mission had lost any effective lobby and protection in the imperial capital. Still, the Christian communities survived, left alone again after this tempest, as the Qing state turned to face graver challenges from Muslim and White Lotus rebellions.

Meanwhile, the Society of Jesus had been suppressed in Europe in 1773. In China, the former Jesuits lived in Beijing under imperial protection while Lazarist missionaries took over their churches.[19]

---

[17] For these persecutions in the mid-eighteenth century, see R. Po-chia Hsia, *Noble Patronage and Jesuit Missions: Maria Theresia von Fugger-Wellenburg (1690–1762) and Jesuit Missionaries in China and Vietnam*, MHSI n.s. 2 (Rome, 2006), 57–61, 81–9.

[18] The standard work by Bernard Willeke, *Imperial Government and Catholic Missions in China during the Years 1784–85* (St Bonaventure, NY, 1948), must be supplemented with more recent documentary publications: Number One Historical Archive, 清中前期西洋天主教在華活動檔案史料 [*Qing zhong qian qi xiyang Tianzhujiao zai Hua huodong dangan shiliao*], 4 vols (Beijing, 2003).

[19] See R. Po-chia Hsia, 'The End of the Jesuit Mission in China', in Jeffrey D. Burson and Jonathan Wright, eds, *The Jesuit Suppression in Global Context: Causes, Events, and Consequences* (Cambridge, 2015), 100–16.

Between the 1770s and 1840, with only a handful of Western missionaries in the country, the proportion of Chinese clergy increased and most Christian communities were guided by strong local lay leadership. Despite persecutions, Christianity survived in China.[20] The history of the Catholic mission shows that the Jesuit accommodation to Chinese culture and imperial institutions was a proven formula of success. Its unravelling resulted not from Chinese opposition but from differences within the missionary enterprise. Despite its complexity and multi-dimensionality, the Chinese Rites Controversy was essentially a quarrel between religious orders and missionary methods. The fact that the Jesuits were the losing party implied a negative turn for evangelization in China. Nevertheless, a small but vibrant Chinese Christian community survived into the early nineteenth century, when imperial laws of prohibition were no longer rigorously applied. However, in that century, hostility toward this Western religion would flare up within a few decades, when Western missionaries again entered China, this time backed by diplomacy and military force.

WESTERN IMPERIALISM AND THE CHRISTIAN MISSION

In the earliest years of the nineteenth century, the first Protestant missionary, the Englishman Robert Morrison (1782–1834), arrived in China and initiated a century of Protestant evangelization supported by Protestant mission societies in Europe and North America.[21] Morrison preached the gospel surreptitiously while working for the British East India Company, but after the prohibition against Christian evangelization was lifted in 1842, following the defeat of the Qing empire by Britain in the First Opium War, later missionaries could preach the gospel openly. This new wave of Christianity came into China along with Western gunboats and strong-arm diplomacy, and it brought about a direct confrontation between Chinese culture and Western Christianity.

Britain and France were jointly victorious over the Chinese empire in the Second Opium War, and both Catholic and Protestant

[20] For this understudied period in the history of Chinese Christianity, see Xiaojuan Huang, 'Christian Communities and Alternative Devotions in China 1780–1860' (PhD dissertation, Princeton University, 2006).
[21] See Christopher A. Daily, *Robert Morrison and the Protestant Plan for China* (Hong Kong, 2013).

Christianity benefited. There was an explosive growth in the number of Protestant missionaries in China, from about a hundred in 1871 to about 2,800 by the 1890s, of whom about half were British.[22] The earliest Christian church built in China after the Opium Wars was the Catholic Sacred Heart Cathedral in Guangzhou, the capital of Guangdong province, the region where Anglo-Chinese conflict first broke out. Constructed rapidly between 1861 and 1863 by the Paris Foreign Missions, Sacred Heart Cathedral, called by locals 'Stone Chamber' on account of its material, dominated the skyline with its neo-Gothic spire. Architecturally and artistically at odds with the surrounding neighbourhood of single- or two-storied Chinese houses, this cathedral occupied the site of the former residence of the viceroy of Guangdong and Guangxi provinces. Its neo-Gothic silhouette symbolized Christian triumph over a pagan city with numerous Buddhist and Daoist temples, all built in seemingly similar Chinese styles. The first parcels of the ground on which it was built had been acquired by Christians during the Anglo-French occupation of the city; subsequent lots were purchased in part by third parties (usually Chinese Christians) because many neighbours refused to sell to foreigners. The Sacred Heart Cathedral became the centre of the diocese of Guangdong, assigned to the Paris Foreign Missions in a Catholic ecclesiastical division of mission territories in China, in which Italian Franciscans, French Jesuits, German Societas Verbum Dei priests and Spanish Dominicans were each assigned 'spheres of evangelization', much in the way that the Western powers (and later Japan) had carved out for themselves 'spheres of influence' in a tottering Qing empire and a divided Chinese republic.[23]

Just ten years after the Treaty of Tianjin (ratified in 1860) that ended the Second Opium War, the conflict between China and the West became conflated with the tension between Chinese and Christian civilizations. In 1870, a crowd gathered outside the French convent in Tianjin, one of the so-called 'treaty-ports' opened to Western settlement, as required by the Western powers in the treaties of 1842 and 1860. The French nuns had taken in and baptized abandoned infants, most of whom survived only for a short time. Wild dogs had dug out the small shallow graves where these unfortunate baby girls

[22] Andrew Porter, *Religion versus Empire? British Protestant Missionaries and Overseas Expansion, 1700–1914* (Manchester, 2004), 207.
[23] See Hongyan Xiang, 'Land, Church, and Power: French Catholic Mission in Guangzhou, 1840–1930' (PhD dissertation, Pennsylvania State University, 2014).

were buried. Soon rumours set the city afire with tales of Christian cruelty and murder. Since France had assumed the role of protector of all Catholic missions in China, the unequal treaties also demanded diplomatic recognition and protection for all ecclesiastical personnel. The French consul in Tianxin rushed to the convent. Faced by an angry mob, he panicked and fired into it. The violence that followed resulted in the deaths of the French consul and dozens of foreigners and Chinese Christians. French diplomatic remonstrance resulted in arrests and executions of rioters, which further exacerbated the hostility toward Christianity.[24]

Tianjin was the first major *jiao an* (literally 'religious case') that involved diplomatic wrangling between the Qing imperial government and Western powers. After Tianjin, there was a rising tide of anti-Christian cases. Many had small beginnings. Disputes between neighbours, one Christian and the other non-Christian; disagreements over properties formerly owned by the Catholic Church and reclaimed after 1860; resentment by local mandarins over the diplomatic privileges enjoyed by foreign missionaries: all these and many more similar situations would lead to larger conflagrations. Resentment of Westerners incited violence against missionaries, which triggered diplomatic pressure and governmental repression, leading to more resentment and hatred: thus went the vicious cycle. Anti-Christian violence reached a crescendo in the closing years of the nineteenth century with the murder of two German Catholic missionaries in Juye, in the province of Shangdong.

The defeat of Qing China by Meiji Japan in the war of 1894–5 unleashed another scramble for concessions by foreign powers in China. Shandong fell under the sphere of influence of imperial Germany. A latecomer to the global competition for colonies and power, the German empire pursued an especially aggressive foreign policy. Taking its cue from the British empire, which many saw in the eighteenth and nineteenth centuries as favoured by God as the instrument of global Protestant evangelization, as Stewart Brown has argued,[25] Kaiser Wilhelm II mobilized popular support at home for missionary fervour and implanted German Protestantism in the Holy

---

[24] Paul A. Cohen, *China and Christianity: The Missionary Movement and the Growth of Chinese Antiforeignism, 1860–1870* (Cambridge, MA, 1963), remains a good introduction to the formation of anti-Christianity in late nineteenth-century China.

[25] See in this volume, Stewart J. Brown, 'Providential Empire? The Established Church of England and the Nineteenth-Century British Empire in India', 225–59.

Land in 1898 with the construction of a German Lutheran church in Jerusalem during his visit. In its support for both Protestant and Catholic missions, imperial Germany differed from the Protestant identity of the British empire, although both shared the providential view of Christian imperialism. This sense of empire and missions was also shared by France of the Third Republic. Although the role of protector of Catholic missions overseas was undertaken by the Emperor Napoleon III in order to garner the support of French Catholics, this policy was continued under the Third Republic despite the change in constitution after 1871.[26] The late nineteenth century was the period of Christian imperialism par excellence.

The two murdered German missionaries had belonged to the Societas Verbum Dei, one of the many Catholic and Protestant missionary societies created in the nineteenth century for global evangelization. Their deaths in Juye turned out only to be the beginning of bloodshed. In the following years, anti-Christian and anti-Western militia organizations sprang up in northern China. Called Boxers, they targeted Westerners and Chinese Christians. Unable or unwilling to suppress them, the Qing government instead manipulated the Boxers for its own political ends. Rural attacks escalated into the siege of the foreign legation district in Beijing. A force of eight foreign powers consisting of Japanese, Russian, British, French, American, German, Austro-Hungarian and Italian troops (in order of strength) invaded Beijing. The imperial court fled to Xian. There were widespread looting and atrocities, and the Boxers were suppressed. In their anti-Christian campaign, the Boxers had killed 136 Protestant missionaries, 47 Catholic clerics, 30,000 Chinese Catholics, 2,000 Chinese Protestants, and several hundred Russian Orthodox Christians in Beijing and the northern provinces. It was the most bloody phase in the history of Christianity in China.[27]

One of the consequences of the Boxer Uprising was the eventual demise of the imperial regime in China. Seen as incompetent and powerless before a foreign onslaught, the Qing government failed to recover its authority after the debacle of 1900. Another effect of the violence was to prompt some soul-searching among the Christian missionaries themselves. In time, this would give greater voice

---

[26] See Young, *Ecclesiastical Colony*.
[27] For a summary of the *status quaestionis*, see Robert Bickers and R. G. Tiedemann, eds, *The Boxers, China, and the World* (Lanham, MD, 2007).

to those who advocated the indigenization of Christianity. If the Protestant and Catholic churches were to succeed, and if Chinese patriots were not to think of Christianity as arriving on the backs of gun shells, Christianity must become Chinese. More Chinese priests must be ordained, more Chinese ministers trained, more churches be built in Chinese style, and in time, the ecclesiastical leadership itself would become Chinese, and the mission would become an established church. In the 1920s and 1930s, changes were under-way. The Protestants established a network of universities, schools and hospitals, making substantial contributions to modernizing Re-publican China. While lagging behind in the educational field, the Catholics pushed for indigenization, ordaining more priests and the first group of Chinese bishops, policies implemented after the 1922 visit to China of Bishop Celso Costantini (1876–1958), who would later become a cardinal and secretary of the Congregation of the Propagation of Faith.[28]

Still the pace of change was not fast enough for many Chinese nationalists. The Anti-Christian movement of 1925–7 signalled that rising Chinese nationalism was also hostile to Christianity, which re-mained identified with Western imperialism. The rising left wing in Chinese republican politics was also hostile to Christianity, for the same reasons. Having survived the civil wars and the Japanese invasion relatively unscathed, the Chinese Christian churches would eventually succumb after the victory of the communists in the civil war that ended in 1950. The new regime, the People's Republic, em-bodied a secular, nationalist and anti-Christian force that expelled all Western missionaries and required the domestic churches to submit to its authority. This led to a schism in both the Catholic and Protes-tant camps. While many under communist direction joined the Patriotic Catholic Church or the Autonomous Protestant Church, others fled to Taiwan and Hong Kong, where they denounced the religious persecution in the People's Republic of China. The hostility between Christianity and Communist China would continue into the 1980s and beyond.

With the conversion of the Roman Emperor Constantine in the early fourth century, Christianity was firmly in the embrace of

---

[28] For the Catholic effort to build a Chinese Church with greater Chinese leadership and characteristics, see Hsin-fang Wu, 'The Transmission of Memories: Reprints, His-torical Studies, and Commemoration in the Jesuit Shanghai Mission, 1842–1949' (PhD dissertation, Pennsylvania State University, 2017), ch. 5.

empires. Whether it was the campaigns of Charlemagne against the pagan Saxons or the conquest of Mesoamerica by the Catholic monarchs of Spain, the spread of Christianity came to depend on imperial expansion. This was, nonetheless, not the only pattern of evangelization in the history of Christianity. The example of the Jesuit mission to Late Imperial China between the sixteenth and eighteenth centuries demonstrates that Christianity could accommodate to the political exigencies of non-Christian empires. The failure of that mission resulted not so much from the clash between Christianity and empire, but rather from the quarrels within the Catholic Church that subverted its global mission in the early modern world.

Providential Empire? The Established Church of England and the Nineteenth-Century British Empire in India

Stewart J. Brown*

University of Edinburgh

In the early nineteenth century, many in Britain believed that their conquests in India had a providential purpose, and that imperial Britain had been called by God to Christianize India through an alliance of Church and empire. In 1813, parliament not only opened India to missionary activity, but also provided India with an established Church, which was largely supported by Indian taxation and formed part of the established Church of England. Many hoped that this union of Church and empire would communicate to India the benefits of England's diocesan and parochial structures, with a settled pastorate, parish churches and schools, and a Christian gentry. As the century progressed, the established Church was steadily enlarged, with a growing number of bishoprics, churches, schools, colleges, missionaries and clergy. But it had only limited success in gaining converts, and many Indians viewed it as a form of colonization. From the 1870s, it was increasingly clear that imperial India would not become Christian. Some began reconceptualizing the providential purpose behind the Indian empire, suggesting that the purpose might be to promote dialogue and understanding between the religions of the East and West, or, through the selfless service of missionaries, to promote moral reform movements in Hinduism and Islam.

For many nineteenth-century British Christians, the rapid expansion of the British empire, and especially of British dominion over the vast subcontinent of South Asia, was inexplicable in worldly terms. Belief in the divine governance of the world led many to a belief that the British empire, like other great empires in the past, formed part of the providential plan for the world. The spread of British trade, the conquests by British arms, the migration of British settlers – all must reflect a higher purpose. 'In the course of Providence', noted

* School of Divinity, University of Edinburgh, New College, Mound Place, Edinburgh, EH1 2LX. E-mail: s.j.brown@ed.ac.uk.

Studies in Church History 54 (2018) 225–259   © Ecclesiastical History Society 2018
doi: 10.1017/stc.2017.19

the *Evangelical Magazine* in 1813, 'Britain is become mistress of the East, and possesses facilities for the purpose of propagating the gospel beyond any other nation'.[1] 'May we not assume', asked the London Missionary Society missionary to western India, William Clarkson, in 1851, 'that the East India Company has been God's servant, relatively to his gracious design of converting the Eastern world?'[2] 'I doubt not', observed the high church Anglican missionary to South India, Robert Caldwell, in 1857, 'that the rule of the English in India rests ... on the will of the Most High, the Supreme Ruler of the nations, who has raised up England, and confided race after race, and region after region to her care'.[3]

For some, the British empire was destined by God to be for the wider world what the ancient Roman empire had been for the Mediterranean world, providing networks of trade and communication, a common language, general peace and the protection of law, through which Christianity would spread. In the first age of Christianity, observed L. Norman Tucker of the Church Missionary Society in Canada in 1907, the gospel and Church 'were planted in an empire prepared by His Providence', and 'all the resources of the Roman Empire ... the military highways, the Greek language, the prevalence of law, the protection of authority, the unity and peace' were used for the spread of Christian truth. 'The counterpart of the Roman Empire of the first century', he added, 'is the British Empire'. As a sign of this, he observed, 'the 300,000,000 of India, while kept at peace by British authority and evangelised by Christian missionaries, are being gradually and insensibly won', and 'India will be converted to Christ by the combined forces of the Nation and the Church'.[4] India, many further believed, was the cradle of the civilizations of the East, and its conversion would lead inexorably to the conversion of the whole of Asia.

Recent literature on the British empire, and especially the impressive synthesis by John Darwin, has highlighted the provisional nature of the British empire, or, as Darwin describes it, the British

---

[1] 'Christianity in India', *Evangelical Magazine* 21 (1813), 172.
[2] William Clarkson, *India and the Gospel; or, An Empire for the Messiah*, 3rd edn (London, 1851), 291.
[3] Robert Caldwell, *Lectures on the Tinnevelly Missions* (London, 1857), 3.
[4] L. Norman Tucker, 'Canada (No. 1): The Church and the Empire', in J. Ellison and G. H. S. Ellison, eds, *Church and Empire: A Series of Essays on the Responsibilities of Empire* (London, 1907), 119–35, at 133.

world system.[5]   This nineteenth-century British world system, for Darwin, was a complex amalgamation of settlement colonies, sugar islands, trading outposts, coaling stations, crown colonies, dependencies, protectorates and spheres of influence; it was a 'project of an empire', which was never completed.   Many nineteenth-century British Christians would have shared this view of Britain's world system.   But for them, its vastness, diversity and extraordinary expansion indicated that it was not shaped by human hands and that its ultimate end was not what its human actors intended.   During the sixty years since the French Revolution, the evangelical Anglican bishop of Calcutta, Daniel Wilson, observed in 1849, Britain had been 'raised … to the possession of the most wonderful empire, and the widest influence which the world has ever seen, either in ancient or modern times'. 'And for what purpose?' he asked.   'Why has India been given to us, as it were by miracle?   Why are out Colonies extended over the universe?'[6]   For Wilson, the true purpose of the empire could only be discerned through faith.

This article explores the British providential discourse of empire during the long nineteenth century, with reference to the alliance of Church and empire in India.   In particular, it considers the idea prevalent among Christians that God had given Britain dominion over India for the purpose of converting its peoples to Christianity, and that the best means for achieving this purpose was an alliance of Church and empire, as expressed in the established Anglican Church. The article will build on the valuable work on the Anglican Church in India by such scholars as Robert Frykenberg, Rowan Strong, Jeffrey Cox, Penelope Carson, Daniel O'Connor, Andrew Atherstone, Bernard Palmer and M. E. Gibbs.[7]   In its conception of a providential purpose for Church and empire in India, the article follows the

---

[5] John Darwin, *The Empire Project: The Rise and Fall of the British World-System 1830–1970* (Cambridge, 2009).

[6] Daniel Wilson, *A Charge delivered to the Clergy of the Four Dioceses of Calcutta, Madras, Bombay and Colombo* (London, 1849), 10.

[7] Robert E. Frykenberg, 'Episcopal Establishment in India to 1914', in Rowan Strong, ed., *OHA*, 3: *Partisan Anglicanism and its Global Expansion, 1829–c.1914* (Oxford, 2017), 296–317; Rowan Strong, *Anglicanism and the British Empire c.1700–1850* (Oxford, 2007), 118–97; Jeffrey Cox, *Imperial Fault Lines: Christianity and Colonial Power in India, 1818–1940* (Stanford, CA, 2002); Penelope Carson, *The East India Company and Religion 1698–1858* (Woodbridge, 2012); Daniel O'Connor, *The Chaplains of the East India Company 1601–1858* (London, 2012); Andrew Atherstone, 'Introduction', in *The Journal of Bishop Daniel Wilson of Calcutta, 1845–1857*, ed. idem, CERS 21 (Woodbridge, 2015), xi–lii; Bernard Palmer, *Imperial Vineyard: The Anglican Church in*

approach of Anthony D. Smith, with his analysis of the idea that nations were 'sacred communions' and that as part of the general providence governing the world some nations were selected by God to be 'missionary peoples' for the global spread of divine truths.[8] The focus will be largely on the attitudes of the Anglican leadership, especially the Anglican bishops in India. It will show how the failure of the established Anglican Church to convert a large proportion of the Indian population to Christianity led to a waning confidence in the notion of a providential purpose for Church and empire in India. It will also suggest some ways in which this waning confidence may have affected broader British religious attitudes and beliefs.

Religious Awakenings and Overseas Missions: The Generation of 1790–1830

The modern British missionary movement and the modern British empire both emerged amid the extraordinary generation which lasted from 1790 to 1830. It was this generation that a former president of the Ecclesiastical History Society, W. R. Ward, described in his presidential address of 1970 as 'the most important single generation in the modern history not merely of English religion but of the whole Christian world'.[9] It was this generation that was shaken by the French Revolution and the Revolution's unprecedented assault on the institutional churches. This was the generation that experienced the sweeping movements of religious awakening which were linked with new movements of democratic nationalism and new notions about the capacities of the common people. This generation embraced heartfelt, emotive forms of piety, with emphasis on the evil of sin and personal conversion. This generation was troubled by apocalyptic visions of the impending end of the world, and by the signs and wonders that were the precursors of the end time. It was drawn

---

India under the Raj from the Mutiny to Partition (Lewes, 1999); M. E. Gibbs, *The Anglican Church in India 1600–1970* (Delhi, 1972).

[8] Anthony D. Smith, *Chosen Peoples: Sacred Sources of National Identity* (Oxford, 2003), 19–65, 95–130.

[9] W. R. Ward, 'The Religion of the People and the Problem of Control, 1790–1830', in G. J. Cuming and Derek Baker, eds, *Popular Belief and Practice*, SCH 8 (Cambridge, 1972), 237–58; reprinted in idem, *Faith and Faction* (London, 1993), 264–84, at 264.

to biblical prophecies and visions of the coming millennium.[10] 'That there is a time of peace, prosperity and purity awaiting all the nations of the earth', proclaimed the *Evangelical Review* in 1793, 'appears evident in the prophecies and promises in the sacred Scriptures'. 'From a serious attention to the signs of the times', it added, 'we may indulge the hope that this grand jubilee is at hand'.[11] The revolutionary and Napoleonic warfare also contributed to revived beliefs across Europe in elect nations, chosen peoples representing the divine will in history.

In Britain, many who embraced the intense religiosity of these decades joined Dissenting churches; the decades from 1790 to 1830 witnessed a phenomenal growth of Protestant Dissent in Britain. But many others remained within the established Churches – the United Church of England and Ireland and the Church of Scotland – which claimed to represent the religious identity and higher purpose of the United Kingdom. There were at this time major movements of reform and reawakening within the established Churches of the United Kingdom of Britain and Ireland, movements that were linked to nation-building, as I have argued elsewhere.[12] From about 1808, there were significant efforts to improve pastoral care, reduce pluralism and non-residence among the clergy, curb the abuses of patronage, build new churches and improve popular education. Bishops in England, Wales and Ireland became more regular in visiting the parishes within their dioceses, published lengthy visitation charges, and formed diocesan school-building, missionary and church-building societies. This formed what Arthur Burns described as a 'diocesan revival'.[13] The clergy on the whole became more effective parish ministers and were assisted by committed lay supporters; they were more zealous in visiting the poor and the infirm, distributing alms and establishing Sunday schools and day schools. From the late 1790s, the Church of Scotland conducted missions to the Highlands and Islands of Scotland, sending out a host of itinerant missionaries and building scores of churches and schools, aimed at

[10] Stewart J. Brown, 'Movements of Christian Awakening in Revolutionary Europe, 1790–1815', in idem and Timothy Tackett, eds, *CHC, 7: Enlightenment, Revolution and Reawakening: The Christian World, 1648–1815* (Cambridge, 2006), 575–95.

[11] Quoted in Andrew Porter, *Religion versus Empire: British Protestant Missionaries and Overseas Expansion, 1700–1914* (Manchester, 2004), 60.

[12] Stewart J. Brown, *The National Churches of England, Ireland, and Scotland 1801–1846* (Oxford, 2001).

[13] Arthur Burns, *The Diocesan Revival in the Church of England, c.1800–1870* (Oxford, 1999).

bringing Catholics, Episcopalians and the irreligious into Scotland's established Presbyterian Church. From about 1808, moreover, there were also growing efforts to convert the majority Irish Catholic population to Protestantism, and especially to the Protestantism of the established Church in Ireland, in part as a means of consolidating the Union of Great Britain and Ireland.

There were initiatives in overseas missions too. In 1792, the Baptist Missionary Society was formed, followed by the London Missionary Society in 1795, the Glasgow Missionary Society and the Edinburgh Missionary Society in 1796, the Church Missionary Society in 1799 and the Wesleyan Methodist Missionary Society in 1818. As Susan Thorne has shown, several thousand gathered in September 1796 at Woolwich to witness the departure of the first group of LMS missionaries for Tahiti; it marked for them a new epoch and they fully expected divine intervention in support of the venture.[14] In 1804, the British and Foreign Bible Society was founded in London and rapidly established local societies across Britain and Europe. Its aim was both simple and grandiose – to provide every inhabitant of the globe with a copy of the Bible, translated into their own language: this would hasten the evangelization of the world and the return of Christ in glory. The older missionary societies within the Church of England, the Society for Propagating the Gospel in Foreign Parts (SPG) and the Society for Promoting Christian Knowledge (SPCK), experienced new levels of public interest and commitment. British society was permeated by local branches of the national missionary societies. These branches developed networks through overlapping membership with anti-slavery societies and a host of charitable and home mission societies. They formed what scholars including Catherine Hall, Susan Thorne, Esther Breitenbach and Alison Twells have described as a philanthropic missionary public, largely middle-class and including women activists.[15] This public subscribed to missionary periodicals, absorbed missionary biographies, histories and

[14] Susan Thorne, *Congregational Missions and the Making of an Imperial Culture in Nineteenth-Century England* (Stanford, CA, 1999), 60.

[15] Catherine Hall, *Civilising Subjects: Metropole and Colony in the English Imagination 1830–1867* (Cambridge, 2002), 292–301; Thorne, *Congregational Missions*; eadem, 'Religion and the Empire at Home', in Catherine Hall and Sonya O. Rose, eds, *At Home with the Empire: Metropolitan Culture and the Imperial World* (Cambridge, 2006), 143–65; Esther Breitenbach, *Empire and Scottish Society: The Impact of Foreign Missions at Home,* c.*1790 to* c.*1914* (Edinburgh, 2009); Alison Twells, *The Civilising Mission and the English Middle Class, 1792–1850* (Basingstoke, 2009).

reports, as well as fictional stories about missionaries, attended missionary meetings and raised funds to support missionaries. Believing firmly in the providential direction of the world, they worked for more humane societies at home and overseas.

A few comments about providentialist thought are in order here. Most of those comprising the missionary public believed in a 'general' providential ordering of the world through gradual developments reflecting the natural laws of cause and effect. As part of this general providence, they believed, God singled out certain peoples to play pivotal roles in history, as had been shown by God's use of the people of Israel in the Old Testament. Alongside this general providence, some also believed there were also special acts of 'particular providence', manifested in sudden, intense, sometimes violent divine interventions in human affairs, such as the destruction of Napoleon's grand army in Russia in 1812.[16] As Andrew Porter has observed, 'it was not always easy to distinguish between the two modes of operation, nor was attention to Providence necessarily to be associated with a particular interest in apocalyptic and eschatological matters'.[17] Many, to be sure, were convinced by the upheavals of the French Revolution and Napoleonic Wars that the world was entering a new dispensation and that the millennium approached. But others, including most of the Anglican leadership, emphasized the actions of Providence in more gradual developments in human affairs, including improvements in manufactures, the growth of new technologies, the spread of commerce, the migrations of peoples and the expansion of empires. Regardless of the perspective, most British Christians holding providentialist beliefs saw themselves as a new chosen people charged with preserving divine truth and spreading it throughout the world. 'Latterly, indeed', observed the evangelical East India Company chaplain, Claudius Buchanan, in 1809, 'it should seem as if God had selected this nation, as formerly his chosen people, Israel, to preserve among men a knowledge of true religion'. 'Amidst the ruin or infidelity of other nations', he added, Britain had emerged as God's great missionary nation.[18]

[16] Boyd Hilton, *The Age of Atonement: The Influence of Evangelicalism on Social and Economic Thought 1785–1865* (Oxford, 1986), especially 13–17; David Fergusson, *The Providence of God: A Polyphonic Approach* (Cambridge, forthcoming), ch. 3.
[17] Porter, *Religion versus Empire*, 58–63 (quotation at 59).
[18] Claudius Buchanan, *The Star of the East; A Sermon preached in the Parish-Church of St James, Bristol*, 2nd edn (Greenock, 1809), 39, 41–2.

THE BEGINNINGS OF THE ESTABLISHED CHURCH IN INDIA

In 1813, the missionary public directed its attention to India, and the great work of converting the peoples of South Asia to Christianity. For many promoters of the India mission, Britain's conquest of India was only explicable in providential terms. The rapid extension of dominion over most of the South Asian subcontinent, representing about a fifth of the world's population and located thousands of miles away from the British Isles, otherwise seemed incomprehensible. Much of this military conquest had taken place between 1793 and 1815, when British public attention was focused on Europe and the armed struggle with revolutionary and Napoleonic France. As the reality of Britain's control over India became clear, there came a conviction that this control carried with it a higher religious responsibility. Before 1813, British missionary activity in India had been severely restricted. The eighteenth-century East India Company, the private trading company that governed India with support from the British state, had supported chaplains for its European officials, soldiers and traders, and it had quietly tolerated some missionary activity by its chaplains. From 1728, moreover, the SPCK provided financial support to German Lutheran missionaries in South India. However, the East India Company opposed opening its Indian territories to unrestricted missionary activity, believing, on the basis of strong evidence, that missionaries would antagonize the Hindu and Muslim populations, foment civil disorder and undermine the loyalty of its sepoy army. But from the late 1780s, there were growing calls from British Christians, including high church and evangelical Anglicans, for the opening of India to Christian missions.[19] In the lead-up to the renewal of the East India Company charter by parliament in 1813, the mission public, led by the Claphamite group of Anglican evangelicals, including William Wilberforce and John Venn, and with SPG and CMS support, campaigned vigorously for opening India to unrestricted missionary activity. Supporters of opening India to missions sent 895 petitions, with nearly half a million signatures, to parliament.[20] Significantly, there were also calls for the formation of an

[19] Strong, *Anglicanism and the British Empire*, 124–9; Penny Carson, 'The British Raj and the Awakening of the Evangelical Consciousness: The Ambiguities of Religious Establishment and Toleration, 1698–1833', in Brian Stanley, ed., *Christian Missions and the Enlightenment* (Grand Rapids, MI, 2001), 45–70, at 53–8.
[20] Carson, 'British Raj', 66–7.

established Church in India, calls which reflected the emerging state-supported reform movement within the British established Churches. 'The perpetuity of the Christian faith among Europeans in India, and the civilization of the natives,' observed Claudius Buchanan in 1805, 'appear to me to require … an Ecclesiastical Establishment'. 'Can any one believe', he added, 'that our Indian subjects are to remain for ever under *our* government involved in their present barbarism?'[21] At the renewal of the charter in 1813, parliament required the East India Company not only to open India to Christian missionaries, but also to use company revenues, derived in part from taxes on the people of India, to endow an established Anglican Church for India, with a bishop in Calcutta and archdeacons in Calcutta, Bombay and Madras. The formation of the Anglican establishment in India was controversial. It was to be supported by taxes levied on the Indian people, who did not want it, and many anticipated that this might well lead to unrest. (At this same time, parliament also created a modest establishment of three endowed Presbyterian chaplaincies in connection with the Church of Scotland.)[22] Because of strong opposition in some quarters to the idea of an established Church in India, the first bishop of Calcutta, Thomas Middleton, was quietly consecrated in Lambeth Palace Chapel in May 1814, the consecration sermon was not published (contrary to normal practice), and he arrived in India later that year with no fanfare. The authorities need not have been concerned. The general view among Indians, as Stephen Neill observed, was 'that the Company was at last resolved to follow its Hindu and Muslim predecessors in giving official recognition to the religion which it professed'.[23]

The fledgling Anglican establishment in India represented the belief that the empire, as Rowan Strong has observed, 'would now develop as an Anglican as well as a British one'.[24] Bishop Middleton was a high churchman, with a strong commitment to the alliance of Church and state, who firmly believed that India had 'been given

---

[21] Claudius Buchanan, *Memoir of the Expediency of an Ecclesiastical Establishment for British India*, 2nd edn (London, 1812; first publ. 1805), 3, 47.

[22] George Smith, *The Life of Alexander Duff*, 2 vols (London, 1879), 2: 36; Elizabeth G. K. Hewat, *Vision and Achievement, 1796–1956: A History of the Foreign Missions of the Churches united in the Church of Scotland* (London, 1960), 34–5.

[23] Stephen Neill, *A History of Christianity in India 1707–1858* (Cambridge, 1985), 262; John Kaye, *Christianity in India: An Historical Narrative* (London, 1859), 290–1.

[24] Strong, *Anglicanism and the British Empire*, 177.

by Providence to a distant island in the west' for the purpose of its conversion. Soon after his arrival, he began asserting his episcopal authority. 'We greatly err', he observed in a sermon in 1815, 'if we imagine that empire is conferred upon nations merely to gratify their avarice or their ambition'.[25] 'The day has at length arrived', he stressed in his charge that December, 'when the purest and most powerful of protestant churches is completely established in a vast region of Asia'.[26] Indeed, he insisted in 1819, 'in the revolution of ages, no event has apparently been more propitious to the interests of the Gospel than the acquisition, by a Christian state, of the sovereignty of Hindoostan'.[27] And at this great moment in history, he himself represented the alliance of Church and empire for this providential purpose. In his first episcopal tour, which lasted from December 1815 to December 1816, he travelled through much of India at government expense with a retinue of over three hundred chaplains, secretaries, servants and armed men. In his episcopal charge of 1821, he compared the prospects for Christianity in British India with those of early Christians in the Roman empire, noting with approbation how 'one of the most obvious differences is, that instead of our being here an obscure and persecuted people, we are the dominant power'.[28] He insisted that there was a need in India for an 'ecclesiastical polity' with the 'sanction and protection of the state'; and that the Anglican clergy in India should give 'the same attention to established order, which is generally expected at home'. His aim was that the whole of India would in time be organized into parishes, each with its parish church and incumbent clergyman, supported by churchwardens, 'as the parochial clergy are in England'.[29] The people of India, as subjects of the same imperial state, deserved the same benefits of religious instruction and pastoral care through the established Church as did the peoples of Britain and Ireland. Significantly, there was no effort to co-operate with the Roman Catholic Church, which had been introduced into India centuries earlier by the Portuguese and which in 1815 had seven bishops and 1,500 native clergy in South India

---

[25] Thomas F. Middleton, 'National Providence: A Sermon Preached at St John's Cathedral in Calcutta, on the 13th April, 1815', in *Sermons and Charges ... with Memoirs of his Life* (London, 1824), 39–56, quotation at 54.

[26] Thomas F. Middleton, 'Charge, Calcutta, December 1815', ibid. 185–248, at 189.

[27] Thomas F. Middleton, 'Charge of 1819', ibid. 213–30, at 213.

[28] Thomas F. Middleton, 'Charge, Calcutta, December 1821', ibid. 231–48, at 239.

[29] Middleton, 'Charge, Calcutta, December 1815', 193, 192, 191.

alone.[30] No, God had given Britain dominion in order to convert India to its Protestant religion.

Middleton viewed the Anglican missionaries, and especially those of the evangelical CMS, with suspicion. For him, the missionaries seemed to wander where they wished, without settled charges or episcopal authority. He insisted that Anglican missionaries must be licensed, and he remained cool towards them. He deprecated how the act of 1813 had allowed Dissenting missionaries to enter India; this had introduced 'sectarian schismatic sentiments', so that Indians encountered competing missionaries who 'agreed in nothing but in mutual accusations of error'.[31] His own best hopes for converting India lay in the Anglican Bishop's College, which he established in Calcutta with generous donations from the SPG, SPCK and also the CMS (which hoped that its donation might ease Middleton's distrust of their mission). The college was to educate young upper-caste Indians in Christian principles, train Indian converts to serve as catechists, promote the study of Indian languages and support the translation of the Scriptures and Christian theological works, all under the canopy of the established Church. It would combine 'into one [Anglican] system' the hitherto diverse efforts being made to 'advance the Christian cause'.[32] He laid the foundation stone in 1820, and Bishop's College was opened in 1824, two years after his death. In 1824, moreover, parliament passed an act permitting the bishop of Calcutta to ordain Indians (at this time mainly students of Bishop's College) as clergy of the established Church of England in India. For all these high hopes, however, Bishop's College was not a great success in its early years; there were only ten students in 1829, and fifteen in 1835.[33]

Indeed, despite the claims of the providential purpose for the Anglican Church establishment, its early years saw relatively few Indian converts. In 1824, Middleton's successor as bishop of Calcutta, Reginald Heber, lamented that the Church's adversaries 'taunt us' over 'the tardy progress of Christ's kingdom in the East'. For Heber, the slow progress resulted largely from a lack of public

---

[30] 'Church Missions', *Christian Remembrancer* 38 (October 1859), 377.
[31] Carson, *East India Company and Religion*, 155; [J. J. Blunt], 'Church in India', *Quarterly Review* 35 (1827), 450.
[32] Henry Kaye Bonney, 'Memoirs of the Life of Thomas Fanshaw Middleton', in Middleton, *Sermons and Charges*, v–cxiv, at lxxix.
[33] Neill, *Christianity in India 1707–1858*, 264–7.

support in England, where a 'general ignorance' prevailed concerning 'these important but distant territories'.[34] The established Church of England in India also encountered resistance from Indian communities. There was communal Hindu and Muslim violence directed against converts to Christianity, who were frequently declared to be legally 'dead' by communal leaders, their marriages dissolved and their property and inheritance rights forfeited. From the early 1820s, there were numerous incidents of church and school burnings, murders and death threats; these included violent attacks in 1827–8 directed against Shamar women converts to Christianity for seeking to cover their breasts.[35] As Penelope Carson has shown, officials of the Company state (the name often given to the hybrid regime of the East India Company and the British imperial state which governed much of India from 1765 to 1858) restricted the movement of missionaries after 1813 for reasons of public peace, while some company officials, among them Major-General Sir Thomas Munro of the Madras Presidency and Mountstuart Elphinstone, governor of the Bombay Presidency, were openly hostile to missionary activity. Some British military commanders, moreover, refused missionaries access to their sepoy soldiers and dismissed sepoy soldiers who converted to Christianity.[36]

The Company state's attitudes towards the established Church and Christian missions in India began to change in 1828 with the arrival of a new governor-general, Lord William Bentinck, a liberal Whig with evangelical sympathies. Although cautious about supporting missionaries, Bentinck was open about his own Christian faith. He also believed that the Company state had a duty to protect people of all faiths, including the Christian converts. In 1829–30, morally appalled by the practice and influenced by public protests in Britain, Bentinck outlawed *sati*, or the ritual burning alive of widows. The practice was largely restricted to the higher castes in parts of Bengal and among the Rajputs. Nonetheless, although *sati* had influential Hindu critics, the British abolition of *sati* was met with popular anger and viewed as unacceptable state interference in India's religion and

---

[34] Reginald Heber, *A Charge delivered to the Clergy of the Diocese of Calcutta* (London, 1827), 5.
[35] Carson, *East India Company and Religion*, 170–5.
[36] Ibid. 154, 158–70.

culture.[37] There was further such interference. In 1831 Bentinck's administration banned discrimination against employing Christian converts in government posts, and in 1832 it ended the operation of Hindu law by which Christian converts became outcastes and forfeited claims to heritable property. However, Bentinck also resisted Christian calls to end the company's involvement in the collection of the pilgrim tax at Hindu holy places, or the company's maintenance of Hindu temples. Nor was he an advocate of the established Church in India. 'One of the great objections to the introduction of an Episcopacy into India', he asserted to Daniel Wilson, bishop of Calcutta, in June 1834, 'is, that the greater the pomp and power and predominancy, you give to your own religion, the greater will be the distrust excited'.[38]

Despite Bentinck's misgivings about the established Church in India, there was now a growing respect among officials in the Company state for the work of its clergy, especially in the field of education, where church schools helped prepare upper-class Indian boys for company positions. The prospects for the alliance of Church and empire were brightening. In Britain, there was a recognition that India was far too large to be organized as one diocese under a single bishop and that overwork might well have contributed to the early deaths of the first four bishops of Calcutta. At the renewal of the East India Company charter in 1833, parliament agreed by large majorities to enlarge the established Church in India, creating new bishoprics of Madras and Bombay; the bishop of Calcutta now became metropolitan of the Church of England province of India.[39] The new bishoprics were to be supported from company revenues. In 1845, an additional bishopric of Colombo was created for the British crown colony of Ceylon; this became part of an enlarged Church of England province of India and Ceylon. From 1839, a newly formed Council of Education in India, based in Calcutta, began making grants-in-aid to both government and Christian schools, a practice which emulated the government's education policy in England. The India policy was confirmed in Sir Charles Wood's dispatch on education of 1854.

---

[37] John Rosselli, *Lord William Bentinck: The Making of a Liberal Imperialist 1774–1839* (London, 1974), 211–14.

[38] Carson, *East India Company and Religion*, 188; Rosselli, *Lord William Bentinck*, 212.

[39] *Hansard's Parliamentary Debates* (House of Commons), 17 July 1833, vol. 19, cols 797–807; 26 July 1833, vol. 20, cols 14–50; Carson, *East India Company and Religion*, 199.

The Indian grants-in-aid increased steadily from £30,000 in 1839 to £190,000 in 1852–3, with most of this money going to Christian schools. These schools were not exclusively Anglican, but by the 1850s most of them were, and the grants represented an additional state subsidy of the Church's evangelizing work. By 1853, Anglican and other missionary schools were educating 101,192 pupils, as opposed to 23,163 in government schools.[40]

In 1832, the Anglican establishment received forceful new leadership with the consecration of Daniel Wilson as bishop of Calcutta and (from 1833) metropolitan. Wilson was both an evangelical and a staunch Anglican churchman with high views of his episcopal authority. He believed that India should have an established Church similar to that in England, with a well-defined episcopal system, parish structures, regular services, pastoral care and a disciplined resident clergy. This Anglican establishment, he believed, was vital to the providential purpose of Britain's India empire. 'India', he maintained in his charge of 1838, 'presents a spectacle to the Christian world. It is the first instance of any of the Reformed Churches being established, after the Apostolical model, in the expanse of such an empire'. Indeed, he observed, 'Palestine in the heart of Western Asia was scarcely more calculated for a centre for the diffusion of the Gospel in the time of the Apostles than Hindostan in the heart of Eastern [Asia] is now'.[41] He insisted, by 1837 successfully, that the bishops should exercise clear authority over the missionaries supported by the CMS and other Anglican missionary societies, including their placement and discipline, while he acted to remove non-Anglican missionaries from employment by the church societies. This included the able, charismatic German Lutheran CMS missionary and scholar, Karl Rhenius, dismissed by Wilson in 1836.[42] Wilson further insisted that the chaplains maintained by the Company state must be regarded as under his authority as clergy of the established Church in India.

---

[40] Ian Copland. 'Christianity as an Arm of Empire: The Ambiguous Case of India under the Company, c.1813–1858', *HistJ* 49 (2006), 1025–54, at 1042, 1046.

[41] Daniel Wilson, *A Charge delivered to the Clergy of the Diocese of Calcutta, at the Visitation on Friday, July 6th 1838* (London, 1839), ix, 32.

[42] Hans Cnattingius, *Bishops and Societies: A Study of Anglican Colonial and Missionary Expansion 1698–1850* (London, 1952), 159–85; T. E. Yates, *Venn and Victorian Bishops Abroad: The Missionary Policies of Henry Venn and their Repercussions upon the Anglican Episcopate of the Colonial Period, 1841–1972* (Uppsala and London, 1978), 30–7; Robert E. Frykenberg. 'Episcopal Establishment in India to 1914', in Strong, ed., *OHA* 3, 303–6.

For Wilson, the established Church in India was an integral part of the established Church of England and Ireland, and had a vital role to play in consolidating British rule in India. The Indian established Church, he maintained in his charge of 1845, was part of 'the National Church of the Government, Nobles and People of our religious country, at home and abroad. It is the glory of our land; the main bulwark of Christianity in Europe and Asia'.[43] It represented the principle that the imperial state had a sacred responsibility to promote Christianity and to provide religious instruction and observances to all its subjects (especially the poor), alongside entire religious freedom for those who chose to remain outside the establishment. The same compelling arguments in favour of an established Church in Britain, he insisted, applied still more to 'the scattered flocks of Heathen India'.[44] Wilson brought the spirit of the English 'diocesan revival' to his diocese of Calcutta, establishing diocesan societies for infant schools (1833), church building (1834), the support of additional curates (1841) and the support of Scripture readers (1848), all aimed at mobilizing lay support and modelled on diocesan societies in England.[45] He claimed that 'our gentry all over India' were contributing money to building churches, just as the gentry were in England. As the influence of churches, schools and pastoral care spread, British India would become 'a second promised land'. This all pointed to 'the speedy winding up of the great scheme of Providence' in anticipation of Christ's return.[46] Between 1839 and 1847, the graceful Gothic St Paul's Cathedral, modelled on Norwich Cathedral and York Minster, and expressing in stone the 'apostolic commission' of its bishop, was erected in Calcutta.[47] The cathedral supported a model school for a thousand Indian children, a normal school for teacher training, and a number of missionary priests. By 1856, the three Anglican dioceses of India consisted of 326 clergy, including 146 CMS and SPG missionaries, and scores of churches

---

[43] Daniel Wilson, *A Farewell Charge delivered to the Clergy of the Diocese of Calcutta*, 2nd edn (London, 1845), 23.

[44] Ibid. 27.

[45] Atherstone, 'Introduction', xxii–xxiii.

[46] Wilson, *Farewell Charge*, 45.

[47] G. A. Bremner, *Imperial Gothic: Religious Architecture and High Anglican Culture in the British Empire, c.1840–1870* (New Haven, CT, 2013), 73–5.

had been built.[48] The Anglican missions had particular success in South India, in the region around Tirunelvēli. The second bishop of Madras, George Spencer, was impressed with the growing number of Christian villages, which he described as 'parishes'; in 1841 he insisted 'that the parochial system of the Church might be carried out as effectually in India as in England'.[49] In his charge of 1842, he noted that the number of Anglican clergy in the diocese had nearly doubled in the past four years, from thirty-one to sixty-one, while a new Madras Diocesan Institution, modelled on the Bishop's College in Calcutta, was training Indian clergy for South India.[50] In the diocese of Madras alone, thirty-six new churches were consecrated between 1837 and 1861.[51]

In Britain, India held a special place in the mind of the mission public. Between 1838 and 1873, half the missionary speakers at British provincial meetings of missionary societies had served in India.[52] There were, by the late 1850s, twenty-five Protestant missionary societies and organizations active in India.[53] The British missionary public was intrigued as well as appalled by lurid accounts of *sati*, of murderous gangs of *thugs* who allegedly followed the goddess Kali, of devotees hanging by hooks or throwing themselves under the Juggernaut cart, of dancing girls and licentious festivals at the temples, of female infanticide and human sacrifice, and of slavery and the forcible seclusion of women. In pious treatises, magazines and novels, missionaries were portrayed as liberating the peoples of India from idolatry and superstition, ending immoral practices and elevating the status of women, as well as spreading the gospel of eternal salvation. The Anglican establishment in India was engaged in a struggle against heathen darkness. 'In India Satan is indeed in his heaven', Wilson proclaimed in a sermon in 1846 while on furlough

---

[48] London, LPL, Tait Papers 194, fols 180–1, 'Minute of the Committee of the Church Missionary Society on the Question of "The Extension of the Episcopate" in India', 14 April 1856.

[49] George T. Spencer, *A Visitation Charge addressed to the Missionary Clergy of the Church of England in Tinnevelly and Travancore* (Madras, 1841), 14.

[50] George T. Spencer, *A Charge, delivered at his Second Triennial Visitation, in the Cathedral Church of St George, Madras, on All Saints' Day, 1842, and in St Peter's Church, Colombo, on January 27, 1843* (London, 1843), 24, 40–4.

[51] Frank Penny, *The Church in Madras*, 3 vols (London, 1904–22), 3: 34.

[52] Peter van der Veer, *Imperial Encounters: Religion and Modernity in India and Britain* (Princeton, NJ, 2001), 35.

[53] Edward Storrow, *India and Christian Missions* (London, 1859), 43.

in England. 'There he has reigned, almost from the Deluge, undisturbed until lately'.[54] India, insisted the CMS *Church Missionary Intelligencer* in 1855, 'is a land full of idols, from the dark chambers of imagery of whose temples the pure mind shrinks back with abhorrence – whose deities are stained with every vice – and where the foulest crimes are perpetrated in the name of religion'.[55] As India took an increasingly central place in the British empire – economically, militarily and strategically – Britain's responsibility before God for its Christian conversion and the fulfilment of the providential purpose grew all the more compelling.

The 'Mutiny' of 1857–8 and its Aftermath

In May 1857, north-central India was swept by a number of mutinies among the Indian sepoy soldiers, which quickly developed into a general uprising aimed at ending British rule and restoring the Mughal empire. There were widespread killings of European civilians, including missionaries and their families, as well as of Indian Christian converts. The rising was suppressed by British and loyal sepoy troops by July 1858, with thousands of Indian deaths, including hundreds of summary executions of suspected insurgents. The crown called for a 'day of national humiliation' on 7 October 1857, and special services were held in established churches and many Dissenting chapels across Britain. For the missionary public, the 'India Mutiny' was a divine call to Britain to redouble its efforts to Christianize India.[56] 'Who can doubt', asked Samuel Wilberforce, the high church bishop of Oxford, in an address in November 1857, 'that God has so dealt with us, in order that we may ... act, as we never yet have acted, with true Christian zeal and courage in the administration of our Eastern Empire?'[57] 'Not a few individuals, nor a mere band of enthusiasts', asserted the influential evangelical dean of Carlisle, Francis Close, in 1858, 'but the nation, with its royal mistress at its head, has publicly

---

[54] Quoted in Bob Tennant, *Corporate Holiness: Pulpit Preaching and the Church of England Missionary Societies, 1760–1870* (Oxford, 2013), 247.

[55] 'The Urgent Need of Increased Efforts on Behalf of India', *Church Missionary Intelligencer*, April 1855, 75–83, at 78.

[56] Brian Stanley, 'Christian Responses to the Indian Mutiny of 1857', in W. J. Sheils, ed., *The Church and War*, SCH 20 (Oxford, 1983), 277–89.

[57] Samuel Wilberforce, *Speeches on Missions*, ed. Henry Rowley (London, 1874), 106.

acknowledged that the late catastrophe, and the present difficulties in India, are judgements of God for our sins'.[58]

After the mutiny was suppressed, the British crown-in-parliament took over the governance of India from the East India Company; this was followed by massive legislative reconstruction, which one recent historian has termed 'the legalization of India'.[59] Significantly, however, this 'legislative revolution' did not include heeding the urgent appeals of the British missionary public to adopt a more aggressive policy of Christianization. In her royal proclamation of 1858, the Queen affirmed her own Christian faith, but her government disclaimed 'alike the right and desire to impose our convictions on any of our subjects'. That said, the imperial state in India did not become religiously neutral; it remained a Christian state which supported an established Church. There were no moves to disestablish and disendow the Anglican Church in India or to end the state grants-in-aid to missionary schools. 'It is not only our duty', the Whig prime minister, Lord Palmerston, assured a deputation on Indian education in 1859, 'but it is our interest to promote the diffusion of Christianity as far as possible throughout the whole length and breadth of India'.[60] In 1862, the state ceased collecting the pilgrim tax and helping to maintain Hindu holy places. The Anglican missionary societies increased their efforts. In the four years between 1857 and 1861, the number of CMS mission stations in India grew from 136 to 148, and the number of CMS missionaries increased from 218 to 258.[61] Anglican leaders continued to use providentialist language in speaking of the Church and empire in India. In his charge of 1863, Bishop Gell of Madras proclaimed that 'the chief purpose for which God has subjected India to England and sent us all hither' was 'that we might make known from North to South the glorious message of Salvation which God has made known to us'.[62] 'We have this charge to administer', Bishop Samuel Wilberforce asserted with regard to British India in 1867. 'It is given to us that we may bless India by Christianising it. If we refuse to do it, some other people will be

[58] Francis Close, *An Indian Retrospect; or What has Christian England done for Heathen India?* (London, 1858), 5.
[59] Jon Wilson, *India Conquered: Britain's Raj and the Chaos of Empire* (London, 2016), 292–317.
[60] Palmer, *Imperial Vineyard*, 18.
[61] Tennant, *Corporate Holiness*, 273.
[62] Frederick Gell, *A Charge delivered on the 23rd of April, 1863, at the Primary Visitation* (Madras, 1863), 17.

raised up to do the work of God there, and we shall be put down because we [refused to do it].'[63]

In the decades after the mutiny, the bishops continued working to Christianize India primarily through the diocesan structures of the established Church. The broad churchman, George Cotton, a protégé of the liberal Anglican Thomas Arnold, succeeded Wilson as bishop of Calcutta and metropolitan of India and Ceylon in 1858. Cotton was no less committed to the ideal of the established Church than his high church and evangelical predecessors; he promoted diocesan societies, including an additional curates society, a church building society and a district visiting society, and he worked to revive the Bishop's College.[64] He saw the diocesan and parochial structures of the established Church and the nurturing of Christian communities through a settled pastorate as key to the conversion of India. 'Our task', he insisted in 1859, 'is not to convert one man, but a whole nation to God'.[65] Following an episcopal visit to the region around Tirunelvēli early in 1864, Cotton wrote warmly to a friend of the parish system there. 'The whole country', he observed of the region, 'is now mapped into regular Christian districts, each furnished with a substantial church, parsonage and schools in the central village, and with small prayer-houses in the minor hamlets'. 'A thoroughly good simple vernacular education', he added, 'is given all over the country, and … in every parish there are short services morning and evening'. In playing fields around the schools, boys played cricket, while 'industry, order, cleanliness, domestic purity, improvement in worldly circumstances, are all conspicuous among the Tinnevelly Christians'.[66] The Anglican establishment was also ordaining a growing number of Indian clergy. In 1861, there were 27 Indian clerics in the diocese of Madras, a number which grew to 154 by 1896.[67] There were also large numbers of Indian lay catechists, who assisted the clergy. In 1868, John Thomas, the CMS

---

[63] Wilberforce, *Speeches on Missions*, 133.
[64] George Edward Lynch Cotton, *A Charge to the Clergy of the Diocese of Calcutta, at the Primary Visitation* (Cambridge, 1859), 34–104; idem, *A Charge to the Clergy of the Diocese and Province of Calcutta* (Calcutta, 1863), 4–31.
[65] Cotton, *Charge* (1859), 66.
[66] George Cotton to G. G. Bradley, 21 January 1864, in Sophia A. Cotton, *Memoir of George Edward Lynch Cotton, Bishop of Calcutta and Metropolitan* (London, 1871), 368–9.
[67] Gibbs, *Anglican Church in India*, 247–8; LPL, Tait Papers 194, fols 173–4, Frederick Gell, 'Statement sent to Sir H. L. Anderson on 1st April 1871, for submission to the Secretary of State for India'.

missionary at Mengnanapuram, South India, employed 52 Indian catechists, many of them leading worship in village congregations. About one in four of Thomas's catechists went on to receive Anglican ordination.[68] The missions had particular success among outcaste or lower caste communities, and among tribal peoples.

And yet for all the efforts of the established Church, and for all the faith in the empire's providential purpose, there was a worrying lack of progress in converting India. While the Church experienced success in the regions around Tirunelvēli and Chota Nagpur, this was not general. 'There has not', admitted Bishop Cotton in his charge of 1863, 'been any marked increase of missionary success'. The total number of Indian Protestant Christians in India, Burma and Ceylon, the bishops observed in a joint *Pastoral Letter* of 1863, fifty years after the formation of the established Church in India, was 213,182; however, this represented only 'perhaps about one in a thousand of the population'.[69] Hindu and Muslim communities continued to oppose missionary activity, often with violence. Far from being attracted to the established Church because of its connections to imperial power and authority, many Indians viewed an imperial established Church as a symbol of their subjection, and saw violence against converts as a justifiable form of resistance to colonial domination.[70] Indians often resented the missionary stations, with their comfortable bungalows, churches, schools, orchards, gardens and wells, which could be seen as outposts of 'missionary colonialism'.[71] As Peter van der Veer has argued, antagonism to Christianity became associated with later nineteenth-century expressions of Hindu nationalism, including claims of Aryan racial superiority, wrestling cults, body-building and 'muscular Hinduism'.[72] The local Hindu elites, warned Bishop Gell of Madras in March 1876, 'will oppress and cheat their Christian labourers; villagers still present every obstacle … against the purchase of land for Christian purposes; almost all will do all that lies in their

---

[68] Palmer, *Imperial Vineyard*, 61–2.
[69] Cotton, *Charge* (1863), 4; G. E. L. Cotton, Frederick Gell and John Harding, *A Pastoral Letter from the Indian Bishops to Members of the Church of England* (Calcutta, 1863), 7–8.
[70] Palmer, *Imperial Vineyard*, 68–85; Copland, 'Christianity as an Arm of Empire', 1049–50.
[71] Robert E. Frykenberg, *Christianity in India: From Beginnings to the Present* (Oxford, 2008), 234.
[72] Van der Veer, *Imperial Encounters*, chs 4, 6.

power to prevent a relative from being baptized'.[73] 'No one, till he comes to India', observed Bishop Cotton in 1863, 'can appreciate the greatness of the social sacrifices required from converts'.[74]

Also disturbing for proponents of imperial Christianity in India was the indifference or even hostility towards missionary activity among many British imperial officials. In the localities, British officials, isolated and responsible for governing vast non-Christian populations, could view Indian converts to Christianity, even to the Anglican Christianity of the established Church, as threats to public order. This was in part because the British government organized India, for administrative purposes, into Hindu, Muslim and Christian communities, each with its own system of laws rooted in traditional practices. As Gauri Viswanathan has shown, converts created difficulties for administrators, because they represented individual choice and insisted upon the individual's right to move freely between communities. Converts challenged the defined communal and caste identities on which local government was based.[75] In 1850, the imperial parliament in London passed the Caste Disabilities Removal Act, which provided a degree of protection of the personal property of converts. Daniel Wilson, as metropolitan of the established Church in India, had condemned caste distinctions in public worship as early as 1834.[76] However, British officials often opposed any church meddling with the caste system, and Hindu and Muslim families expected local civil courts to order the return of young adults who had converted to Christianity, so that family pressure could be exerted to secure their retractions. Bishop Gell of Madras complained in 1865 that an English high court judge had publicly denounced an Anglican clergyman for preaching against the caste system.[77] Such behaviour, Gell argued, was at odds with the state's maintenance of an established Church to create a Christian India. British officials in India, he insisted in his charge of 1863, must remember that theirs was a Christian government, and that 'the establishment of the kingdom of Christ among all its subjects [should be] its ultimate and far highest

---

[73] LPL, Tait Papers 226, fols 105–6, Frederick Gell to A. C. Tait, 11 March 1876.

[74] Cotton, *Charge* (1859), 65.

[75] Gauri Viswanathan, *Outside the Fold: Conversion, Modernity, and Belief* (Princeton, NJ, 1998), 75–117.

[76] Atherstone, 'Introduction', xxi; Robert E. Frykenberg, 'Christian Missions and the Raj', in Norman Etherington, ed., *Missions and Empire* (Oxford, 2005), 107–31, at 120.

[77] LPL, Tait Papers 84, fols 254–7, Frederick Gell to A. C. Tait, 28 April 1865.

object'.[78]   Another obstacle to Christ's kingdom in India was presented by British racist attitudes towards Indians, including Indian Christians.   Indian converts were denied burial rights in government cemeteries.[79]   As Andrew Porter has observed, 'the growth of nineteenth-century racial perspectives, so at odds with Christianity's egalitarianism, both distanced missions from empire and undermined the missionary enterprise'.[80] Many British residents would not employ Indian Christians as servants, claiming they were 'uppity' and untrustworthy.[81] Racism grew more pronounced in the second half of the nineteenth century, reinforced by the experiences of the mutiny and then by the influence of social Darwinism. When James Welldon arrived in 1898 as bishop of Calcutta and metropolitan, he later recalled, he had 'expected to see many dark faces in the Cathedral; but, except on rare or few occasions, I saw few or none at all'. 'It is not improbable', he added, 'that the European worshippers would have resented a strong native element in the congregation'.[82] The British 'claim of racial superiority', the bishop of Lahore later lamented in 1907, had created a 'tremendous ... gulf between ourselves and Indians in this great land'.[83]

RENEWAL MOVEMENTS IN THE INDIAN ESTABLISHED CHURCH

In November 1873, the Indian bishops met at Nagpur for the first synodical conference of the Anglican province of India and Ceylon. They made an urgent appeal to the archbishop and convocation of Canterbury, calling attention to what they perceived as an impending crisis in India. Their tone was far different from the earlier confident language of Providence, Church and empire. 'We would urge you', the Indian bishops exhorted, 'to consider that the season is critical. We are convinced that the future of India depends very much on what is done for it by the Church of England during the next few years'. The fabric of India's ancient civilization, they claimed, was

---

[78] Gell, *Charge* (1863), 14.
[79] Viswanathan, *Outside the Fold*, 112.
[80] Porter, *Religion versus Empire*, 283.
[81] Mary A. Procida, *Married to the Empire: Gender, Politics and Imperialism in India, 1883–1947* (Manchester, 2002), 90.
[82] J. E. C. Welldon, *Recollections and Reflections* (London, 1915), 237.
[83] George Alfred Lefroy, 'Our Indian Empire', in John Ellison and G. H. S. Walpole, eds, *Church and Empire: A Series of Essays on the Responsibilities of Empire* (London, 1907), 65–85, at 68.

unravelling. 'India, in the present century, is passing through a state of disintegration, and its habits and forms of life are subjected to influences which are affecting it seriously and fundamentally'. The forces of modernization – Western education, science, railways and commerce – were rapidly dissolving traditional beliefs, and carrying the people of India 'almost without a will, and as if by a tide of circumstances, from a past, to which their hearts cling with regret, to a future, which is still unknown and indiscernible'. Nor was there any reason to believe that all this would lead to a Christian India. The bishops continued:

> We should mislead you if we gave you to understand … that the conversion of India is as yet imminent. There is nothing which can at all warrant the opinion that the heart of the people has been largely touched, or that the conscience of the people has been affected seriously … . In fact, looking at the work of Missions on the broadest scale, and especially upon that of our own Mission, we must confess that, in many cases their condition is one rather of stagnation than of advance.

Rather than to Christianity, Western influences were drawing educated Indians towards 'a scientific Pantheism' or a 'debasing selfishness'.[84]

The response to this appeal was a renewed effort to enlarge the episcopate of the established Church in India. There had been a sense since the 1850s that the four dioceses in the province of India and Ceylon were far too large, both in territory and population, for effective episcopal supervision. The Church needed more bishops to revive its mission. The British parliament, now with a significant number of Catholic and Dissenting MPs, could no longer be expected to pass legislation to use Indian public funds to enlarge the established Church in India, as it had in 1833. However, political leaders did agree to permit the Church of England to enlarge its Indian episcopate using its own resources. To aid this process, parliament passed in 1874 the Colonial Clergy Act, which, among other provisions, confirmed the right of Indian bishops to consecrate

---

[84] LPL, Tait Papers 202, fols 4–10, Bishops of Calcutta, Madras and Bombay, 'To the Archbishops, the Bishops and the Clergy of the Province of Canterbury in Convocation Assembled', 17 November 1873; Tait Papers 194, fols 209–12, 'Minutes of Conference of the Bishops of the Province of India and Ceylon, held at Nagpur November 26th and 27th 1873'.

assistant or suffragan bishops. The British government further agreed that new bishoprics could be legally formed without a further act of parliament in those territories that had been conquered since the India Church Act of 1833, and also in Indian princely states not under direct British rule.[85]

In November 1875, A. C. Tait, the broad church archbishop of Canterbury, and a strong believer in the principle of an established Church, launched a public appeal in Britain to raise donations to endow new Indian bishoprics. Any legal obstacles to the creation of new bishoprics, he insisted, had now been removed, while the committee of the Colonial Bishoprics Fund promised to give substantial funds for the Indian bishoprics. The greatest gift that Christian Britain could bring to India, Tait insisted, would be 'to make their civilization Christian'. An enlarged episcopate would help organize Britain's Indian Empire 'into Christian communities, held together by a well-compacted, ecclesiastical Government, and united with our Church at Home by the profession of our common faith and the love of a common Lord'. Unless the Anglican establishment were strengthened for the work of Christianizing India, he warned, much of India would drift into an atheistic materialism, and this would have revolutionary consequences. For this reason, Tait observed, 'our wisest statesmen, who are best acquainted with India, now publicly acknowledge that the English Nation has no more useful or faithful servants than our Missionaries'.[86]

The coming years brought a remarkable extension of the Anglican episcopate in India. In 1877, the established Church in India consecrated two highly experienced missionaries as suffragan bishops – the high church linguist, Robert Caldwell of the SPG, and the evangelical educator, Edward Sargent of the CMS – to serve in South India. Then, in succeeding decades, new Anglican bishoprics were founded at Lahore (1877), Rangoon (1877), Travancore and Cochin (1879), Chota Nagpur (1890), Lucknow (1893), Tirunelvēli and Madura (1896) and Nagpur (1903).[87] The costs of endowing these new bishoprics were met by the Colonial Bishoprics Fund and by voluntary donations. For many Anglicans, the new bishops would be

---

[85] Julius Richter, *A History of Missions in India*, transl. S. H. Moore (New York, 1908), 273–5.
[86] LPL, Tait Papers 208, fols 281–4, A. C. Tait, 'Pastoral letter: New Indian Bishoprics and the Day of Intercession for the Mission', 15 November 1875.
[87] Gibb, *Anglican Church in India*, 278–96.

missionary bishops, on the model of the first Christian bishops, and they would revive the established Church as a missionary Church. 'The great missionary agency', insisted Reginald Copleston, high church bishop of Colombo (and later bishop of Calcutta and metropolitan) in 1879, 'is a living Church, united, organized, and ever spreading'; the Church would triumph through her 'internal vigour' and 'discipline'.[88] Impressive cathedrals were built at Lahore and at Allahabad, in the diocese of Lucknow. The synod of the province of India and Ceylon held in Calcutta in early 1883 was attended by nine bishops, and meetings of the episcopal synod now became regular events. Some exceptional bishops served the late nineteenth-century established Church in India. The evangelical Frederick Gell served for thirty-eight years as bishop of Madras, during which time the number of Protestants in the diocese rose from 65,000 in 1861 to 152,000 in 1896.[89] The first bishop of Lahore was the Oxford-educated CMS missionary and educator, Thomas Valpy French, who arrived in India in 1851, founded St John's College, Lahore, in 1870, and was known as the 'seven-tongued man' for his mastery of seven Indian languages.[90] French had a high view of his episcopal office, and viewed the Anglican Book of Common Prayer as the 'only wholesome representative of primitive catholic truth and order'.[91]

From the 1860s, moreover, single women missionaries brought new vigour to the Indian established Church. The India missions had long benefited from the work of missionary wives, who provided teaching, medical care and pastoral visiting. But now there came unmarried women, fervent in their sense of vocation, many of them trained at London's evangelical Mildmay Deaconess Institution or the high church SPG Deaconess House, Clapham. This growth reflected a larger trend within the British missionary movement, which would see women represent over half the CMS missionaries by 1899.[92]

---

[88] Reginald Stephen Copleston, *A Charge delivered at his Primary Visitation of the Diocese of Colombo* (Oxford, 1879), 23.
[89] Gibbs, *Anglican Church in India*, 247–8.
[90] Vivienne Stacey, 'The Legacy of Thomas Valpy French', *IBMR* 13 (1989), 22–7, at 24; for French's remarkable life, see Herbert Birks, *Life and Correspondence of Thomas Valpy French*, 2 vols (London, 1895).
[91] Ibid. 2: 151.
[92] Brian Stanley, *The Bible and the Flag: Protestant Missions and British Imperialism in the Nineteenth and Twentieth Centuries* (Leicester, 1990), 80; Jocelyn Murray, 'The Role of Women in the Church Missionary Society, 1799–1917', in Kevin Ward and Brian Stan-

Stewart J. Brown

As Jeffrey Cox has shown, the high church SPG sent over three hundred unmarried women missionaries to Delhi and Lahore alone in the century after 1850, more than six times the number of male missionaries sent to these cities during the same period.[93] Some of these women were members of high church Anglican sisterhoods, such as the Wantage Sisters and All Saints Sisters, who arrived in India in 1876. They lived disciplined communal lives in compounds, established schools and orphanages, and went into the surrounding communities for household visiting, teaching or medical service. Other single women served as evangelical Bible women. In the 1860s, Scottish Presbyterian women missionaries pioneered zenana work, aimed at reaching upper-class women who often lived in seclusion in their homes.[94] The work was taken up by the established Church in India, with a Church of England Zenana Missionary Society being formed in 1880. As Geraldine Forbes has shown, the zenana missions had only limited success, in part because the men who controlled access to the zenanas, while they might value women learning Western needlework and domestic skills, definitely did not want women converting to Christianity.[95] Nonetheless, in missionary literature the zenana missions became symbolic of work for the elevation of the status of Indian women, and through their zenana work, Anglican women missionaries were portrayed as having a special 'responsibility for non-Western women and children in an age of rising imperialistic fervor'. Anglican women who served as missionaries often embraced the notion of a providential empire bringing Christian civilization to India; according to Steven Maughan, they 'had a noticeable affinity for empire and its structures'.[96] The increasing presence of female missionaries contributed to what was becoming a distinctive

ley, eds, *The Church Mission Society and World Christianity, 1799–1999* (Grand Rapids, MI, 2000), 66–90, at 82, 89.
[93] Jeffrey Cox, *The British Missionary Enterprise since 1700* (New York, 2008), 188–95; Gibbs, *Anglican Church in India*, 301, 311–15.
[94] Hewat, *Vision and Achievement*, 75, 134–5; Lesley A. Orr MacDonald, *A Unique and Glorious Mission: Women and Presbyterianism in Scotland 1830–1930* (Edinburgh, 2000), 117–18.
[95] Geraldine H. Forbes, 'In Search of the "Pure Heathen": Missionary Women in Nineteenth-Century India', *Economic and Political Weekly* 21 no. 17 (26 April 1986), Review of Women's Studies, 2–8.
[96] Steven S. Maughan, *Mighty England Do Good: Culture, Faith, Empire and World in the Foreign Missions of the Church of England, 1850–1915* (Grand Rapids, MI, 2014), 228, 356.

aspect of the India missions from the 1870s, which placed greater emphasis on charity to the poor, visiting the sick and infirm, caring for orphans, teaching poor children and providing basic medical care, than on preaching or doctrinal instruction. These Anglican women missionaries were not ordained and were not to preach. Their ministry was about social service; they would spread Christianity through the example of selfless living. In their social work among the poor, they reflected the growing social gospel commitments of the Anglican Church in Britain.

Church leaders in India continued to appeal to the providential purpose of Church and empire. 'I do believe', asserted the bishop of Calcutta and metropolitan, Edward Johnson, in his charge of 1881, 'that England has been led or drawn into her present relations with this country by a force of circumstances ... which we must regard as mysterious and providential'. The work of Christianizing India, he continued, was 'given to us as a nation to do'.[97] Yet by the 1880s, such providentialist language was losing some of its power and conviction. The prospect of India's conversion seemed to move further and further into the distant future; the British empire in India was not being consolidated under established Christianity and the providential plan of empire appeared ever more problematic. At the current rate of Anglican Church growth, asserted Isaac Taylor in the London *Fortnightly Review* during October 1888, it would take 'nearly a hundred thousand years to convert India'.[98] As one author observed in 1873, it seemed 'that the Almighty is working out in India some great problem of His Divine will', and it was no longer clear that the solution would be a Christian India.[99]

New Interpretations of a Providential Empire

Increasingly, there was also doubt about the moral and civilizing influence of the empire in India. This included concern over the opium trade, by which opium produced in India was brought by British merchants, backed by British armed force, to China. Despite the

---

[97] Edward Ralph Johnson, *A Charge delivered by the ... Bishop of Calcutta [and] Metropolitan of India and Ceylon ... at his Primary Visitation* (Calcutta, 1881), 14.
[98] Isaac Taylor, 'The Great Missionary Failure', *Fortnightly Review* 44 (1888), 488–500, at 490.
[99] James Routledge, 'Our Present Position and Probable Future in India', *Macmillan's Magazine* 27 (1873), 529–43, at 543.

devastating human costs of the trade, an attempt in 1875 to convince the archbishop of Canterbury to express public support for the Anglo-Oriental Society for the Suppression of the Opium Trade was met by a rebuff.[100] Moreover, during the 1880s, the Anglican feminist reformer, Josephine Butler, helped expose Indian state involvement in prostitution.[101] Butler had played a leading role in the long public campaign from 1869 to 1886 to abolish the English Contagious Diseases Acts, which had forced suspected prostitutes to undergo invasive medical examinations for venereal disease and, if found to be infected, to undergo treatment. For the campaigners, the Contagious Diseases Acts meant the state licensing of prostitution and the institutionalization of an evil. Under public pressure parliament abolished these acts in 1886. By then, Butler and her supporters had turned their attention to the similar Contagious Diseases Acts in India, where their investigations into the licensing system revealed that Indian women, often young widows sold by their families, were being procured by the Indian government and pressured into lives of prostitution in the military cantonments. Through the state licensing of prostitution, Butler asserted in 1886, 'Indian women have been oppressed and outraged ... by a *Christian* nation'.[102] This 'legalised slavery to vice' in India, she wrote in 1887, 'is tending to bring hell upon earth in the face of all our missionary efforts to advance the kingdom of God'.[103] In its military cantonments, the imperial state was enslaving Indian women, while the established Church remained largely silent on the matter. At a large public meeting to protest the Contagious Diseases Acts in India held in May 1887 at London's Exeter Hall, there were no Anglican clergy among the speakers.[104] Under mounting public pressure, the Indian government did repeal the Indian Contagious Diseases Acts in 1888 and the 'Cantonment Rules' for the regulation of prostitution in 1895.

[100] LPL, Tait Papers 210, fols 96, 102–4, 106–7, 108–11, F. S. Turner to H. M. Spooner, 10 May 1875, Russell Gurney to A. C. Tait, [May 1875], Tait to [Turner?], 5 June [1875], Turner to Tait, 8 June 1875.
[101] Antoinette Burton, *Burdens of History: British Feminists, Indian Women, and Imperial Culture, 1865–1915* (Chapel Hill, NC, 1994), 127–69; Jane Jordan, *Josephine Butler* (London, 2001), 236–49; Jane Jordan and Ingrid Sharp, eds, *Josephine Butler and the Prostitution Campaigns*, 5: *The Queen's Daughters in India* (London, 2003); Porter, *Religion versus Empire*, 275.
[102] Burton, *Burdens of History*, 131.
[103] Josephine Butler, 'An Appeal to Missionaries', *The Sentinel* 9 (1887), 52–3, at 53.
[104] 'Exeter Hall on the Empire', *Pall Mall Gazette*, 21 May 1887, 11–12.

In the British Isles, meanwhile, many were being attracted to Eastern religions and ethical teachings. Interest in Eastern religions had emerged in the later seventeenth and eighteenth centuries with the British 'Orientalists', and it was revived in the 1870s and 1880s by the scholarship of F. Max Müller and the theosophical movement of Helena Blavatsky, Henry Steele Olcott and Annie Besant. Earlier condemnations of Hindu idolatry and Indian barbarism were giving way to new appreciations of the spirituality of the East, of the beauty of Hindu poetry and art, and of ancient wisdom teachings, mysterious Mahatmas and esoteric Buddhism. Annie Besant was a former Church of England vicar's wife, at one time an impassioned socialist, who had lost her faith in both Christ and socialism. She embraced theosophy through Blavatsky's influence, and in 1893 settled in India, where she adopted Indian dress, studied Sanskrit, founded the Central Hindu College in 1897 and became president of the Theosophical Society in 1907. She developed her own vision of the providential purpose behind the British empire. India, she observed in 1900, was 'a conquered nation, won by the sword, ruled by the sword'. But at the same time, India's ancient writings were now being translated into English, and through the British empire India's ancient wisdom was being spread throughout the world. 'Thus, while politically she is subject, her thought is beginning to dominate the whole of that Western civilisation.'[105] India under British occupation was spreading Indian spirituality, much as ancient Israel under Roman occupation had spread Christianity. While Bishop Middleton had maintained in 1821 that the connection of Christianity with the 'dominant power' in India was clear evidence of God's providential purpose, Besant was now suggesting that God's chosen peoples were in truth the conquered and the colonized of this world.

Some Anglicans were also reconceptualizing the providential purpose for Britain's Indian Empire. Perhaps that divine purpose might be, not the conversion of the East to Christianity, but rather the drawing together of the spirituality of East and West, contributing to ever higher and fuller revelations of divine truth. God might intend the empire to contribute to a distinctive religiosity that would represent a synthesis of the religions of East and West.[106] In an

---

[105] Annie Besant, *Ancient Ideals in Modern Life: Four Lectures delivered at … Benares, December 1900* (London, 1901), 9–10.
[106] Jeffrey Cox, *Imperial Fault Lines*, 39–40.

influential sermon given in 1872 at Cambridge, the regius professor of divinity, Brooke Foss Westcott, affirmed his belief in a providential role for Britain in India; however, he suggested that this role might be to promote dialogue between religious communities. 'God', Westcott argued of the British, 'has fitted us as a people and as a church … to be the interpreters of the East to the West, and of the West to the East, to be the witnesses and heralds of truth recognised as manifold'.[107] Late in 1873, F. Max Müller, professor of comparative philology at Oxford, gave an address at Westminster Abbey in which he spoke warmly of the growing emphasis on social service in the Christian missions in India. The result, Müller suggested, might not be individual conversions to Christianity, but rather the encouragement of ethical movements in Hinduism and Islam, so that through shared service to humanity all religions might be elevated.[108] As Rowan Strong has shown, such ideas infused the early India mission of the Anglo-Catholic Society of St John the Evangelist (the Cowley Fathers), a brotherhood founded in 1866 by Richard Benson. The Cowley missionary, Samuel O'Neill, travelled to India in 1874. Distancing himself from the established Church in India, O'Neill formed in 1880 a community in Indore, which included a simple ascetic life, a genuine effort to embrace Indian culture, and charitable work among lepers and the most destitute poor. It was a model followed by other Cowley missionaries.[109]

Similar ideas lay behind the formation of the Cambridge University Missionary Brotherhood in Delhi in 1877. The members of the brotherhood, including Edward Henry Bickersteth and George Alfred Lefroy, combined educational work and social service in the slums of Delhi. They distanced themselves from the power structures of the established Church, and sought to live as Indians and not as *sahibs*. 'I believe', wrote Lefroy in 1880, 'that our position as the ruling power puts a dead weight on the missionary enterprise which nothing but the direct grace of God can possibly enable us to lift'.[110] The brotherhood established St Stephen's College in 1882,

---

[107] Brooke Foss Westcott, 'The Universities in Relation to Missionary Work', in idem, *On some Points in the Religious Office of the Universities* (London, 1873), 25–44, at 28.
[108] F. Max Müller, 'Westminster Lecture on Missions', in idem, *Selected Essays on Language, Mythology and Religion*, 2 vols (London, 1881), 2: 46–86.
[109] Rowan Strong, 'Origins of Anglo-Catholic Missions: Fr Richard Benson and the Initial Missions of the Society of St John the Evangelist, 1869–1882', *JEH* 66 (2015), 90–115.
[110] H. H. Montgomery, *The Life and Letters of George Alfred Lefroy* (London, 1920), 20.

which affiliated with the new state University of the Punjab. In 1879, members of Oxford University, led by Anglo-Catholics, formed the Oxford University Missionary Brotherhood for work in Calcutta, which also combined educational work, social service and inter-religious dialogue. The Oxford group included Frederick Douglass, who arrived in Calcutta in 1892 and soon after established a mission station in Behala, where he lived simply in a modest hut and won local hearts, if not many converts, through decades of selfless charitable service.[111] In 1892, Trinity College Dublin established a missionary community in Chota Nagpur and in 1896 Westcott's sons, George and Foss, formed an SPG missionary brotherhood based in Cawnpore, a former centre of the mutiny and now a major industrial city; their aim was to explore the spirituality of East and West alongside engaging in Christian social activism.[112]

The purpose of the British empire, Brooke Foss Westcott, now bishop of Durham, insisted in November 1900, was to spread the 'spirit of England', 'the fulness of our highest aspirations' and the 'noblest in our character'. Moreover, there was a need now to atone for the past sins of the empire by sending out self-sacrificing 'brotherhoods of men' who 'will touch those among whom they work by the force of social devotion'.[113] (There was a personal note here: Westcott's youngest son, Basil, had died of cholera earlier that year while serving with the Cambridge Brotherhood in Delhi.) Within the brotherhoods, some embraced a fulfilment theology, believing that Hinduism and Islam possessed elements of divine truth, and that these faiths would be fulfilled as they also embraced Christian truths. 'We must go to India to learn as well as teach', insisted a member of the Delhi brotherhood in 1910, 'we must realise that India as well as the West ... has her contribution to bring to the full knowledge of Christ'.[114] But this emphasis by the missionary brotherhoods on interreligious dialogue could also seem overly intellectual, and was not without its critics.[115] The emphasis on dialogue, observed the former Anglican bishop of Sydney, Alfred Barry, in 1895, 'may

[111] Anon., *Father Douglas of Behala: By Some of his Friends* (London, 1952).
[112] Martin Maw, *Visions of India: Fulfilment Theology, the Aryan Race Theory and the Work of the British Protestant Missionaries in Victorian India* (Frankfurt am Main, 1990), 295–324.
[113] Brooke Foss Westcott, 'The Empire', in idem, *Lessons from Work* (London, 1901), 369–84, at 378–9.
[114] Quoted in Maw, *Visions of India*, 251.
[115] Cox, *Imperial Fault Lines*, 140; Maw, *Visions of India*, 320–4.

suggest the idea, only too congenial to the Hindu mind, that Christianity is only a philosophy to be intellectually learnt, or a morality which can be disassociated from its doctrines'.[116]

The End of the Established Church in India

The last decades of the nineteenth century witnessed significant growth in the numbers of Indian Christians. In 1871, there were, according to the official state census, 1,270,000 Indian Christians of all denominations, including Roman Catholics and Syrian Christians. By 1901, this number had increased to 2,776,000. Christianity was now growing at a rate faster than any other religion in India and faster than the population at large.[117] Between 1881 and 1891, the growth in Christian numbers was nearly 23%, compared to an overall population growth of 13%.[118] Yet these growing Christian numbers, while in some senses impressive, paled into insignificance when set against the total population of British India, which was nearly 300 million in 1901. The Christian population, moreover, was unevenly dispersed, with substantial Christian populations in south India around Tirunelvēli or in east India in the region of Chota Nagpur, but very few Christians in the north and north-west.

Further, the number of *Anglican* Indian Christians was only 492,752 in 1911; this was less than 20% of the Indian Christian population and less than 0.2% of the overall Indian population. Such numbers were disappointing after nearly a century of an Anglican established Church of India, representing that alliance of Church and empire which many had believed was to fulfil the providential purpose behind Britain's dominion in India. As both national identity and the independence movement in India grew in influence, the Anglican Church's links to the imperial state were no longer seen as a benefit, part of the providential plan for India; rather, they were becoming more and more a liability. The Church in Ceylon (which was not formally part of the Indian empire) had already been disestablished in 1881, and in Britain there were calls for the disestablishment of the Indian Church from the early 1880s.[119] At their synod

---

[116] Alfred Barry, *The Ecclesiastical Expansion of England in the Growth of the Anglican Communion* (London, 1895), 137–8.

[117] Copland, 'Christianity as an Arm of Empire', 1053; Palmer, *Imperial Vineyard*, 84–5.

[118] George Smith, *The Conversion of India* (London, 1893), 201.

[119] Louis George Mylne, *Charge of the Lord Bishop of Bombay, delivered to the Clergy of the Diocese* (Bombay, 1884), 2–4.

in 1908, the Anglican bishops in India began planning for disestablishment, including an end to state endowments and the creation
of an independent Anglican Church with its own synodical government. There was no political opposition to Indian disestablishment:
the imperial parliament in London passed the necessary legislation in
1927, and in 1930 the Church of India, Burma and Ceylon became
a self-governing church within the global Anglican Communion.[120]
Its role as symbol of the union of Church and empire and of the
providential purpose of the British empire in India was now ended.

Many, to be sure, continued into the twentieth century to speak
of a providential purpose for the British empire. Referring to the
empire in India in his episcopal charge of 1906, Bishop Lefroy of
Lahore insisted that it was 'Almighty God ... and He alone, Who
has called us to that extraordinary and unique position which we
occupy' and 'that it is to Him that we shall one day, as a nation, have
to give account'.[121] According to the *Report of Commission VII: Missions and Governments* of the World Missionary Conference of 1910
in Edinburgh, 'the Government of India is, in the opinion of most
Indian missionaries ... manifestly an agent of Divine Providence'.[122]
Some Anglicans, among them Bernard Wilson and the India-born
Bishop Henry Montgomery, continued to speak of a coming 'Church
of the British Empire' or of the Church of England as the 'Imperial
Church'.[123] Even Indian nationalists could refer to the empire as
part of a divine plan. John Darwin has observed how 'the "providential" nature of the British conquest of India was often invoked (with
no sense of irony) by those who attended the meetings of the Indian National Congress before 1914'.[124] Gerald Studdert-Kennedy
has noted how the British Israel movement, 'an explicitly imperialist
form of Christianity', with a providential view of the British empire,
motivated 'die-hard' defenders of the Raj during the 1920s and

[120] Palmer, *Imperial Vineyard*, 91–4.
[121] Montgomery, *Life and Letters of Lefroy*, 171.
[122] World Missionary Conference, *Report of Commission VII: Missions and Governments* (Edinburgh, 1910), 32.
[123] Bernard Wilson, 'The Church and the Empire', in H. Hensley Henson, ed., *Church Problems: A View of Modern Anglicanism* (London, 1900), 348–93, at 372, 393; Steven Maughan, 'An Archbishop for Greater Britain: Bishop Montgomery, Missionary Imperialism, and the SPG, 1897–1915', in Daniel O'Connor, ed., *Three Centuries of Mission: The United Society for the Propagation of the Gospel 1701–2000* (London, 2000), 358–70, at 362.
[124] John Darwin, *Unfinished Empire: The Global Expansion of Britain* (London, 2013), 296.

1930s.[125] But this language of providential empire had little meaning for the overwhelming majority of people in India. The number of Indians who viewed the British empire as an instrument of God's providence, Lefroy acknowledged in 1907, was 'infinitesimal'.[126]

CONCLUSION

This article has explored what many nineteenth-century British Christians believed was the providential purpose of British dominion in India, that of Christianizing the ancient and sophisticated civilization of India through the alliance of Church and empire. Its focus has been on the discourse of the Anglican leadership and the belief that India would best be Christianized through an established Church. That project inspired a considerable investment of resources and the efforts of numerous highly committed and able men and women, many of whom experienced broken health and shortened lives in return for their efforts. It had represented belief that the empire in India did not exist primarily to enhance Britain's material wealth and power, but had a higher religious and moral purpose. To be sure, the belief that the established Church in India was part of the providential plan for India's conversion was not shared by all nineteenth-century British Christians, those rejecting it including Protestant Dissenters, Roman Catholics and, as we have seen, many Anglo-Catholics. But for large numbers of committed Anglicans, including evangelical, high church and broad church bishops of the Indian establishment, the established Church in India was regarded as the means to bring the benefits of their own established religion to India, uniting Britain and India within one Church, with common diocesan and parochial structures, and providing the peoples of Britain and India with common patterns of doctrine and worship and shared moral and spiritual values. In sharing their established Church with India, many Anglicans, inspired by their own diocesan revival, believed that they were sharing the highest expression of their Christian civilization. Their efforts within the Indian established Church were not without some success. There were millions in India, and not only Christians, who benefited from what the

[125] Gerald Studdert-Kennedy, *Providence and the Raj: Imperial Mission and Missionary Imperialism* (London, 1998), 190–214; idem, *British Christians, Indian Nationalists and the Raj* (Oxford, 1991), 24.
[126] Lefroy, 'Our Indian Empire', 66.

Anglican established Church contributed, including churches, schools, colleges, printing presses and hospitals. However, it is also blatantly clear that the nineteenth-century alliance of Church and empire did not lead to a Christian India. It may well be, as Fryken-berg observed near the end of his magisterial history of Christianity in India, that 'Christian movements seem to have been most successful when least connected to dominion or empire'.[127] There was indeed something overly contractual in tone in much of the Anglican providentialist discourse, suggesting that God had elevated Britain among nations by giving it dominion in India, and in return Britain was to deliver the peoples of India to God by making them Christian.

That said, the failure of imperial India to become Christian would have seemed a mystery to the many nineteenth-century British Christians who had embraced the providential purpose of empire, and especially to W. R. Ward's 'great generation' of 1790 to 1830. It raised serious questions about the general providential ordering of history and the divine election of certain nations to fulfil the divine purpose – beliefs that could feed a cultural self-confidence, even arrogance, as well as inspire missionary effort. As we have seen, from the 1870s, despite the rising public enthusiasm for imperialism in Britain, some thinkers did seek to reconceptualize the providential purpose of the empire in India. Perhaps that purpose, they suggested, was to promote dialogue and mutual respect between the religions of East and West, or, perhaps, through the example of selfless service among missionaries, it was to encourage moral reform movements within Hinduism and Islam. Or perhaps, as Annie Besant argued, it was to spread the religious thought of the East to the West. There was another possibility. Perhaps the empire in India had no higher divine purpose; perhaps it had after all been simply a matter of British military conquest, economic domination and self-aggrandisement. The failure of the empire to Christianize India may have contributed to the waning British public faith, if not in Christianity, at least in a providential moral and spiritual purpose for their imperial state.

---

[127] Frykenberg, *Christianity in India*, 455.

Special Worship in the British Empire: From the Seventeenth to the Twentieth Centuries

Joseph Hardwick· and Philip Williamson*

Northumbria University; Durham University

Across the British empire, public worship was important for sustaining a sense of community and connectedness. This was most evident in special acts of worship, when the peoples of imperial territories, and sometimes of the whole empire, were asked at times of crisis and celebration to join together in special days or prayers of petition or thanksgiving to God. These occasions, ordered by a variety of civil and ecclesiastical authorities, were an enduring feature of all colonial societies from the seventeenth to the mid-twentieth centuries. Although these special acts of worship have considerable potential for deepening our understanding of various themes in the history of the British empire, they have yet to receive sustained analysis from scholars. This article is concerned with the fundamental task of considering why and how special prayers and days of fasting, humiliation, intercession and thanksgiving were appointed across the empire. By focusing on the causes of, and orders for, these occasions, it indicates reasons for the longevity of this practice, as well as its varied and changing purposes.

The British empire was linked in worship. Across the overseas colonies, protectorates, dominions and in India, churches of various denominations followed the weekly patterns of worship originating from the parent churches in Britain. The links were especially evident in *special* acts of worship. From the first settlements in North America during the early seventeenth century to the worldwide commonwealth and empire at the coronation of Queen Elizabeth in 1953, the peoples of particular overseas territories – or more strikingly still, those of the whole empire – were asked at times of exceptional crisis

* Joseph Hardwick: Faculty of Arts, Design and Social Sciences, University of Northumbria, Lipman Building Room 330, Newcastle upon Tyne, NE1 8ST. E-mail: joseph.hardwick@northumbria.ac.uk.
Philip Williamson: Department of History, University of Durham, 43 North Bailey, Durham, DH1 3EX. E-mail: p.a.williamson@durham.ac.uk.

Studies in Church History 54 (2018) 260–280   © Ecclesiastical History Society 2018
doi: 10.1017/stc.2017.14

or celebration to join together in prayer and praise to God. These acts of special worship took different forms. *Special prayers*, either of petition or thanksgiving, might be added to the usual church services. More often, *days of prayer* were 'set apart' on specified dates, for attendance at special services and sermons and for private devotions. During periods of anxiety or crisis, days of fasting, 'humiliation', intercession or national prayer were observed to implore God's intervention or to seek better understanding of the divine purposes.[1] At times of relief or celebration, days of thanksgiving were ordered to thank God for blessings received or for his guidance in the achievement of righteous aims. Until the late nineteenth century, these special days of prayer were normally ordered by governments, and were appointed for days in the middle of the week, requiring the closure of public offices and the stoppage of business and employment.

Special acts of worship might be *imperial* in one of several senses. Some special days or prayers initiated in Britain were ordered or recommended for observance throughout the empire, and later the commonwealth. Others were initiated by authorities in the overseas territories in order to associate their colonies or dominions with special worship that had been appointed in Britain, or to mark events that they regarded as having imperial significance. Councils, governors or churches in the colonies also ordered special worship for causes which were specific to their particular region.

Studies of these special acts of worship have considerable potential for deepening understanding of various themes in the religious, political and cultural history of empire. They provide a register of what the authorities in colonies considered, or judged that their peoples considered, to be matters of such exceptional importance as to require, and to be remediable by, divine intervention or guidance. They reveal how notions of collective sin and God's active providence persisted well into the twentieth century. They offer new perspectives on religious authority, on relationships between civil and ecclesiastical authorities, and on relations between different churches and faith groups. Studies of special days and prayers might also draw attention to varied senses of community, and to the sense of identification that

---

[1] A 'day of humiliation' was an alternative term for 'fast day', commonly used in government and church orders. The nomenclature of special days of worship changed over the centuries; for definitions, see the introductions to the three volumes of Philip Williamson et al., eds, *National Prayers: Special Worship since the Reformation*, CERS 20, 22 and forthcoming (Woodbridge, 2013–).

colonial peoples developed with their colonies, with new colonial nations and with the empire. They emphasize that among the elements that held together a heterogeneous empire were shared religious beliefs and emotional responses, a common monarchical culture and a language of British 'subjecthood'.[2]

Studies of these occasions might draw on a range of sources. The religious meanings that individuals attached to the great events marked by special worship can be found in devotional diaries and especially in the fast and thanksgiving sermons which have so far been the main means by which special worship has attracted historical attention.[3] The proclamations that appointed days of prayer and special services, as well as the forms of prayer issued for use in Anglican churches on these occasions, reveal much about changing conceptions of divine providence and of the higher purposes claimed for the empire. As the stated expectation was that all adult inhabitants should participate in these special acts of worship, newspaper reports of these occasions provide valuable indications of the extent of popular religious observances.

These are just some indications of an agenda for future research. The purpose of this article is the preliminary but fundamental task of outlining the patterns in the appointment and causes of acts of special worship across the empire.[4] It will establish the main chronological phases of this practice, consider the complications caused by religious pluralism, and direct attention to significant shifts that began during the late nineteenth century. It will also reflect upon the reasons for the longevity of the practice.

---

[2] Hannah Weiss Muller, 'Bonds of Belonging: Subjecthood and the British Empire', *JBS* 53 (2014), 29–58.

[3] Published sermons are a leading source for studies of religious and political ideas in colonial America and early modern Britain; these were commonly delivered on fast or thanksgiving days. For comments on the imperial visions and tensions in these sermons, see Nicholas Guyatt, *Providence and the Invention of the United States 1607–1876* (Cambridge, 2007), chs 1–3. For similar sermons in the nineteenth-century empire, see Joanna Cruickshank, 'The Sermon in the British Colonies', in Keith Francis and William Gibson, eds, *The Oxford Handbook of the British Sermon, 1689–1901* (Oxford, 2012), 513–29.

[4] Existing scholarship on imperial special worship focuses on particular colonies, rather than the empire as a whole: see Joseph Hardwick, 'Special Days of Worship and National Religion in the Australian Colonies, 1790–c.1914', *JICH* 45 (2017), 365–90; idem, 'Fasts, Thanksgivings and Senses of Community in Nineteenth-Century Canada and the British Empire', *Canadian Historical Review* 98 (2017), 675–703.

PHASES OF IMPERIAL SPECIAL WORSHIP

Special worship in the British empire can be divided into three phases: first, from the beginnings of colonial settlement in America to 1776; second, from the American Revolution through the period of the expanding 'second empire' (i.e. post-1783) in Asia, Australasia and Africa; and third, from the 1850s to decolonization in the 1950s.

The practice of observing fast and thanksgiving days was carried across the Atlantic by English settlers during the early seventeenth century. In the plantation colonies of Virginia and the West Indies, both special and annual fasts and thanksgivings were soon ordered for regional causes and, with the Church of England as the dominant church, from the 1660s the English annual religious commemorations (thanksgivings for the failure of the Gunpowder Plot on 5 November and for the restoration of the monarchy on 29 May, and a fast day marking Charles I's execution on 30 January) became official public observances.[5] Days of special worship also proliferated among the Puritan colonies of New England, with their keen sense of providential governance and freedom from the constraints of the crown and the Church of England, which also meant that they rejected the English anniversary commemorations. But by the time that royal government became established in the late seventeenth century, the New England colonies had their own entrenched customs of seasonal fast days early in the year and thanksgiving days in the autumn, as well as special days for exceptional events.[6] These customs later spread through the other North American colonies, with the days of prayer now ordered by the royal governors and councils.[7]

The first special worship across the whole empire was in 1688, when during June the Roman Catholic King James II ordered that

---

[5] George Maclaren Brydon, *Virginia's Mother Church* (Richmond, VA, 1947), 141, 176, 238–40, 434, 447, 461–2, 471–2; Nicholas M. Beasley, *Christian Ritual and the Creation of British Slave Societies, 1650–1780* (Athens, GA, 2009), 39, 48–51; Matthew Mulcahy, *Hurricanes and Society in the British Greater Caribbean 1624–1783* (Baltimore, MD, 2008), 38–9, 46–9, 56–7.

[6] See the large number of occasions recorded in William DeLoss Love, *The Fast and Thanksgiving Days of New England* (Boston, MA, 1895); Melissa Weinbrenner, 'Public Days in Massachusetts Bay, 1630–1685', *Historical Journal of Massachusetts* 26 (1998), 73–94.

[7] See the fast and thanksgiving proclamations included or reported in *Early American Imprints, Series I: Evans, 1639–1800* [digital resource], the printed records of the colonies published from the 1850s onwards, and the *Calendars of State Papers Colonial*. For publication details, see Williamson et al., eds, *National Prayers*, 2: xlv–li.

thanksgiving days for the birth of the Prince of Wales should be observed not only in England and Wales, Ireland and Scotland, but also in the nine colonies in America and the West Indies. Colonial governors duly proclaimed thanksgiving days once the orders reached them, for various dates from July to December. Even Congregational churches in New England obeyed the order, sharing the incongruity of Protestant churches thanking God for the birth of a Catholic heir to the throne.[8] From 1702 to 1706 the governors of what were now fourteen colonies similarly acted on orders to proclaim colonial versions of the thanksgiving days already arranged in Britain for the early military victories during the War of the Spanish Succession.[9]

Colonial observances of these orders from London, which enclosed copies of the English thanksgiving proclamation, were striking demonstrations of imperial authority, yet the issue of such orders did not become a settled practice. Numerous thanksgiving days were appointed in Britain between 1706 and 1759, but no orders were sent for colonial observances during this period, although they were resumed for the military victories of 1759 and the Peace of Paris in 1763.[10] Why imperial orders for thanksgivings were interrupted is unclear; but it may well be that governments in London, which received regular reports from each colony, understood that the colonial authorities would themselves order special worship to mark significant events in Britain. From the 1640s to the 1760s, assemblies, councils and governors in colonial America independently proclaimed special fast or thanksgiving days for such episodes as the Civil War, the Restoration, the Popish and Rye House plots, the 1688 revolution, the war of 1689–91 in Ireland and the Jacobite rebellions, as well as for campaigns against, victories over, and peace treaties with, other European powers. Sometimes these colonial proclamations were prompted by reports of British fasts or thanksgivings; just as often the colonial authorities acted simply on news of crises or

---

[8] See ibid. 1: 1688–EIr2, 1688–S2. Occasions are coded in the edition for ease of cross-reference: 1688–EIr2 is the second joint occasion for England & Wales (E) and Ireland (Ir) in 1688. Where an occasion refers to all three kingdoms, including Scotland (S), only a number is used, e.g. 1763–1. The *National Prayers* volumes include texts or summaries of the orders sent from London to colonial governors.

[9] Ibid. 2: 1702–EIr2, 1704–EIr2, 1705–EIr2, 1706–EIr1.

[10] Ibid. 2: 1759–2, 1763–1. For the first of these, the governor of New Hampshire even included the text of the English proclamation, complete with references to archbishops and bishops, as part of his own proclamation (see Fig. 1).

By His Excellency

BENNING WENTWORTH, *Efq*;

Captain-General, Governor and Commander in Chief, in and over His Majesty's
Province of New-Hampshire, in New-England.

IT having been His MAJESTY's Pleafure to fignify His Commands to Me, That His
Royal Proclamation for a Public Thankfgiving fhould be folemnized and kept in all
His Majefty's Colonies in *America*, particularly in thofe who are fo nearly interefted
in the happy Events, which gave Occafion for the Proclamation :

I have therefore thought fit to caufe His Majefty's faid Proclamation to be herewith
printed, and to appoint *Thurfday* the Thirteenth Day of *March* to be obferved and kept as a
Day of Public Thankfgiving throughout this Province ; and all Servile Labour is ftrictly
forbidden on faid Day.

Given at Portfmouth the Twenty-eighth Day of February, *One Thoufand Seven Hundred
and Sixty, and in the Thirty-third Year of His* Majefty's *Reign.*

B. WENTWORTH.

BY THE

K I N G.

A PROCLAMATION for a Public Thankfgiving.

GEORGE R.

WE do moft devoutly and thankfully acknowledge the great Goodnefs and Mercy
of Almighty GOD, who hath afforded Us his Protection and Affiftance in the
juft War, in which, for the common Safety of Our Realms, and for difappointing
the boundlefs Ambition of *France*, We are now engaged ; and hath given fuch
fignal Succefles to Our Arms, both by Sea and Land, particularly by the Defeat
of the *French* Army in *Canada*, and the Taking of *Quebec* ; and who hath moft feafonably
granted Us at this Time an uncommonly plentiful Harveft : And therefore, duly confidering
that fuch great and public Bleffings do call for public and folemn Acknowlegments, We have
thought fit, by and with the Advice of Our Privy Council, to iffue this our Royal Proclamation,
hereby appointing and commanding, That a General Thankfgiving to Almighty GOD, for
thefe His Mercies, be obferved throughout Our Kingdom of *England*, Dominion of *Wales*, and
Town of *Berwick* upon *Tweed*, upon *Thurfday* the Twenty-ninth Day of *November* next. And,
for the better and more religious and orderly folemnizing the fame, We have given Directions
to the Moft Reverend the Archbifhops, and the Right Reverend the Bifhops of *England*, to
compofe a Form of Prayer fuitable to this Occafion, to be ufed in all Churches and Chapels,
and other Places of public Worfhip, and to take Care for the timely difperfing thereof throughout
their refpective Diocefes. And We do ftrictly charge and command, That the faid public
Day of Thankfgiving be religioufly obferved by all Our loving Subjects, as they tender the Favour
of Almighty GOD, and upon Pain of fuffering fuch Punifhment as We may juftly inflict upon
all fuch as fhall contemn or neglect the Performance of fo religious and neceffary a Duty.

Given at Our Court at Kenfington, *the Twenty-third Day of* October, *One Thoufand
Seven Hundred and Fifty-nine, in the Thirty-third Year of Our Reign.*

GOD Save the KING.

PORTSMOUTH : Printed by Daniel Fowle.

Figure 1. Proclamation for a thanksgiving day by Benning Wentworth, governor
of New Hampshire, 28 February 1760, containing the English proclamation of 23
October 1759 for the military victories in Canada. Library of Congress, Printed
Ephemera Collection, portfolio 87, folder 9. Reproduced by permission of the
Library of Congress.

causes for celebration in Britain.[11] References to British events and
military campaigns and to the royal family were also regularly added

---

[11] For examples, see ibid. 2: cxlii–cxliii; Jonathan Hawkins, 'Imperial '45: The Jacobite
Rebellion in Transatlantic Context', *JICH* 24 (1996), 24–47.

to the fast and thanksgiving proclamations which they issued chiefly for causes that were specific to their own colony.[12]

From the texts of these proclamations and from the prayers and sermons heard on the fast and thanksgiving days, the inhabitants of the American colonies were encouraged to regard the British empire as a single spiritual body under divine providence.[13] Yet special worship could also become a means to claim divine sanction during disputes over imperial policies, as became evident with the American fasts and thanksgivings appointed during the Stamp Act crisis in 1765–6, and the fast days ordered by colonial assemblies, 'patriot' provincial congresses and then the Continental Congress after the Boston 'Tea Party' in 1774. During 1776 rival fast days were proclaimed by the Continental Congress for all the American colonies and by the British crown for the British Isles, in a competition for the favour of God as political disputes escalated into war.[14]

During the second phase, from 1776 to the 1850s, the appointment of special worship in the newer areas of British control in Canada, Australasia, India and Africa was left to governors and executives; the Colonial Office files for this period contain no imperial orders for thanksgivings. Colonial governments nevertheless tended to take their lead from reports of proclamations or acts of special worship in Britain, and to do so more regularly than had been the case earlier in colonial America. In the Canadian colonies from 1789 to 1816 the acts of special worship were, with few exceptions, repeats or anticipations of those arranged in Britain: special prayers during the illness of George III in 1788–9 and thanksgivings for his recovery, annual fast days during the wars with France from 1793 to 1815, and thanksgivings for peace treaties in 1802 and 1815–16. In Nova Scotia and the other Atlantic provinces, the governors' proclamations often stated explicitly that the purpose was 'to extend the effect' of the

---

[12] For example, *Early American Imprints I*, nos 141 (Massachusetts, 10 March 1668), 760 (New York, 27 February 1696), 1672 (Connecticut, 16 August 1714), 6361 (Massachusetts, 27 February 1750), 41468 (New Hampshire, 31 March 1764), 12734 (Connecticut, 16 October 1773).

[13] See comments on sermons in Guyatt, *Providence*, chs 1–2.

[14] John Berens, '"Good news from a far country": A Note on Divine Providence and the Stamp Act Crisis', *ChH* 45 (1976), 308–15; Philip Davidson, *Propaganda and the American Revolution 1763–1783* (Chapel Hill, NC, 1941), 92–6; Henry Ippel, 'Blow the Trumpet, Sanctify the Fast', *Huntington Library Quarterly* 44 (1980–1), 43–60; Williamson et al., eds, *National Prayers*, 2: cxliv–cxlv, 1776–1.

king's proclamations in Britain.[15] Similar patterns developed later in the Australian colonies and elsewhere.[16] In these ways, appointment of special worship matched the conservatism of British authorities in the early second empire; it may also have contributed to a broader policy that sought to align colonies with the social structure and values of the mother country.[17]

The appointment of Anglican bishops in the colonies from 1787 helped to connect colonial special worship with its British counterpart. As the first of these bishops, Charles Inglis of Nova Scotia and Jacob Mountain of Quebec, regarded the colonies as integral parts of the British nation and the Church of England, they routinely and successfully asked the governors of the Atlantic Canadian colonies and of Upper and Lower Canada to emulate British fasts and thanksgivings by the issue of proclamations for their own territories.[18] The Canadian bishops also initiated days of prayer for regional causes, notably during the cholera epidemics of the early 1830s.[19] Although Anglican monopoly over special worship collapsed after the 1830s, as the model of a single privileged religious establishment was abandoned in the colonial world,[20] governors continued to repeat British acts of worship. In 1842, even the news of thanksgiving prayers in Britain for a good harvest prompted proclamations of days of thanksgiving in Canadian Atlantic provinces.[21] Special prayers for the births of Queen Victoria's children and her escape from attempted 'assassinations' were marked in various overseas territories, and special days of prayer were also called in the colonies for the Irish famine, the

---

[15] Hardwick, 'Fasts, Thanksgivings and Senses of Community', 679–80.

[16] Hardwick, 'Special Days', 371.

[17] Christopher Bayly, *Imperial Meridian: The British Empire and the World, 1780–1830* (London, 1989), ch. 7.

[18] Ottawa, Library and Archives Canada [hereafter: LAC], MG23–C6/C–2227/3, fol. 30, Inglis to governors, 13 May 1799; Mountain in *The Correspondence of the Honourable Peter Russell*, 3, ed. E. A. Cruikshank and A. F. Hunter (Toronto, ON, 1936), 65, 111. For the conservatism of early Canadian Anglicanism, see Peter W. Williams, 'Anglicanism in North America and the Caribbean in the Nineteenth Century', in Rowan Strong, ed., *OHA*, 3: *Partisan Anglicanism and its Global Expansion, 1829–c.1914* (Oxford, 2017), 232–52, at 240.

[19] LAC, RG5–A1/C–6875/115, Bishop Stewart of Quebec to Lieutenant-Governor Colborne, 31 March 1832, fols 64739–41.

[20] Stewart J. Brown, 'Anglicanism in the British Empire, 1829–1910', in Strong, ed., *OHA* 3, 45–68, at 52–3.

[21] *Nova Scotian* [Halifax], 20, 27 October, 17 November 1842.

Crimean War, and the Indian 'Mutiny'.[22] Colonial observances of British acts of special worship were intended to remind colonists that they were British subjects, living in an extended British nation. Colonial proclamations addressed colonists as the 'loving subjects' of the crown, and preachers told churchgoers on imperial fast days that great calamities, like the famine and the 'Mutiny', resulted from the collective sins of a far-flung British people.[23] This imperial nation was a 'virtual' one, held together by ties of belief and sentiment and not by a formal political union, nor by an overarching imperial state that ordered worship in its territories.[24]

The third phase, from the 1850s to the 1950s, was marked by improvements in communication, and by more direct and frequent actions by authorities in the imperial centre to evoke colonial attachment to the empire. Until the mid-nineteenth century, colonial observances of British acts of special worship had taken place weeks later than the date of the observance in Britain. Now faster ships and the spread of telegraph cables made it possible for these occasions to be observed simultaneously in Britain and the colonies. The first arrangements to bind the empire in this way were made for royal events. In 1872 governors and churches in many territories spontaneously arranged thanksgiving days for the prince of Wales's recovery from illness.[25] For Queen Victoria's golden and diamond jubilees in 1887 and 1897, the Colonial Office took an active part, despatching copies of the English orders and forms of prayer to governors for their 'information', accurately assuming that governors and churches would act upon these by organizing public holidays and thanksgiving services. Messages from the queen were telegraphed to the governors for communication to their communities: in 1887 asking that her thanks to God should be expressed during the special services in the churches and chapels of the empire, in 1897 asking God to bless her 'beloved people'.[26] Similar arrangements were made to mark the funerals and

---

[22] See the commentaries in Williamson et al., eds, *National Prayers*, 2: 1840–1, 1840–2, 1841–1, 1847–2, 1854–1, 1855–1, 1856 –2, 1857–2.

[23] For examples of the language of subjecthood, see the proclamations in *Canada Gazette*, 7 April 1855, 7 November 1857. For the messages communicated on days of prayer, see Hardwick, 'Special Days', 372–9; idem, 'Fasts, Thanksgivings and Senses of Community', 683–6.

[24] Eliga Gould, 'A Virtual Nation: Greater Britain and the Imperial Legacy of the American Revolution', *AHR* 104 (1999), 476–89, at 485–9.

[25] Williamson et al., eds, *National Prayers*, 3: 1872–2.

[26] Ibid. 3: 1887–1, 1897–1.

coronations of sovereigns, and the thanksgivings for George V's recovery from illness in 1929 and for his silver jubilee in 1935. The Dominion and Colonial Offices sent the governors increasingly detailed information on the arrangements for these occasions.[27]

Still more urgent efforts to nurture imperial patriotism by acts of special worship were made in wartime. In February 1900, during the South African War, a day of intercession arranged by the Church of England was imitated by colonial bishops and some non-Anglican churches in the overseas empire.[28] During the First World War, a new type of 'national day of prayer' was created. These were initiated by consultation among the leaders of all the main churches in Britain (including the Roman Catholic Church), announced with the king's personal support, and then proclaimed or encouraged by governors in the colonies, dominions and India. By stages, this type of occasion became not only more ecumenical, but also still more 'imperial', with increased participation of the crown and government. Uniquely, for the peace treaty in July 1919 a single royal proclamation ordered religious thanksgivings for both the United Kingdom and the overseas empire (Fig. 2). During the Second World War, government ministers in London became directly involved, taking decisions on appointment of national days of prayer and asking governors to ensure that, wherever possible, religious services took place everywhere in the empire on the same day.[29]

All this demonstrates the importance of the monarchy and war for 'Greater Britain'. But special worship during this third phase also reveals the empire's centrifugal tendencies. Colonial governors in the 'second empire' had continued to appoint special days of prayer for regional causes, such as natural calamities,[30] emancipation from slavery in the West Indies,[31] and wars with indigenous peoples, notably

[27] Ibid. 3: 1901–1, 1902–2, 1910–1, 1911–1, 1929–1, 1935–2, 1936–1, 1937–1, 1952–1, 1953–1.
[28] For Canada, see Gordon Heath, *War with a Silver Lining: Canadian Protestant Churches and the South African War, 1899–1902* (Montreal, QC, 2009), 65–9. For services elsewhere, see *Sydney Morning Herald*, 12 February 1900; *Auckland Star*, 12 February 1900.
[29] Philip Williamson, 'National Days of Prayer: The Churches, the State and Public Worship in Britain, 1899–1957', *EHR* 128 (2013), 324–66, at 329–30, 333.
[30] See Hardwick, 'Special Days', 370–1.
[31] *Papers … in Explanation of the Measures … for giving Effect to the Abolition of Slavery, II*, in *Parliamentary Papers*, 1835 (278–II), [part A] 70, [part B], 21, 22, 24, 72–3, 220, 277.

No. 29.] ($azette $xtraordinary.) 35

THE SOUTH AUSTRALIAN

GOVERNMENT GAZETTE.

Published by Authority.

ALL PUBLIC ACTS appearing in this GAZETTE are to be considered official, and obeyed as such.

[REGISTERED AT THE GENERAL POST OFFICE, ADELAIDE, FOR TRANSMISSION BY POST AS A NEWSPAPER.]

ADELAIDE, FRIDAY, JULY 4, 1919.

PROCLAMATION BY HIS MAJESTY THE KING.

HIS Excellency the Governor directs the publication of the following Proclamation issued by His Majesty the King for general information. By command,

G.H., 42/1919. JOHN G. BICE, Chief Secretary.

By the King: A Proclamation, George R.I.

Whereas it has pleased Almighty God to bring to a close the late widespread and sanguinary war in which we were engaged against Germany and her Allies: We therefore, adoring the divine goodness and duly considering that the great and general blessings of peace do call for Public and Solemn acknowledgment, have thought fit, by and with the advice of our Privy Council, to issue this Our Royal Proclamation hereby appointing and commanding that a general thanksgiving to Almighty God for these his manifold and great mercies be observed throughout Our Dominions on Sunday the sixth day of July ; and for the better and more devout solemnization of the same we have given directions to the Most Reverend the Archbishops and the Right Reverend the Bishops of England to compose a form of prayer suitable to this occasion to be used in all Churches and Chapels and to take care for the timely dispersing of the same throughout their respective Dioceses ; and to the same end we do further advertise and exhort the General Assembly of the Church of Scotland, and all Spiritual Authorities and Ministers of Religion in their respective Churches, and other places of public worship throughout our United Kingdom of Great Britain and Ireland, and in all quarters of our Dominions beyond the seas, to take part as it may properly behove them to do in this great and common act of worship, and we do strictly charge and command that the said public day of thanksgiving be religiously observed by all as they tender the favor of Almighty God and have the sense of His benefit.

Given at Our Court at Buckingham Palace this first day of July in the year of Our Lord one thousand nine hundred and nineteen, and in the tenth year of Our Reign.

GOD SAVE THE KING ! ,

Adelaide: Printed and published by authority by R. E. E. Rogers, Government Printer, at the Government Printing Office, North Terrace.

Figure 2. Proclamation for the day of thanksgiving for the peace treaty of Versailles, 1919, to be observed throughout the empire, as printed in *The South Australian Government Gazette*, 4 July 1919. Reproduced by permission of the Government of South Australia.

in India and southern Africa.[32] But during the late nineteenth and early twentieth centuries the appointment of regional fast, humiliation or thanksgiving days multiplied in many parts of the empire. Canadian provinces regularly observed seasonal thanksgivings after 1859, and on twenty-three occasions between 1866 and 1914 Australian governments marked droughts by setting aside days of humiliation and thanksgiving.[33] Moreover, as the following section explains, an increasing number of these occasions came to be organized by churches rather than by governments.

THE EFFECTS OF RELIGIOUS PLURALISM

Until the mid-Victorian period, the orders issued by the crown for special worship in the British Isles assumed that everyone was a member of an established church. Instructions for services or prayers were addressed to the clergy of the Church of England, the Church of Ireland[34] and the Church of Scotland, although by the nineteenth century most other religious communities also observed these occasions, on their own terms.[35] The realities of religious pluralism were accepted much earlier in the colonies and in India. This was often inescapable. Some imperial territories had originally been settled by critics of or separatists from the established churches, and many contained populations of mixed religious and ethnic composition. From the seventeenth century, governors in several colonies in New England issued a distinctive style of proclamation. These were addressed in non-denominational terms to all 'ministers and people', and often consisted less of an order than an encouragement or exhortation to observe the fast or thanksgiving.[36] Elsewhere, in colonies where the Church of England was dominant, governors used the traditional language of English proclamations, with their assertions of

---

[32] See, for example, *Calcutta Gazette*, 20 June 1799; *Bombay Times*, 21 February 1846; Charles Gray, *Life of Robert Gray, Bishop of Cape Town*, 2 vols (London, 1876), 1: 163, 328; 2: 233.

[33] Peter Stevens, '"Righteousness exalteth the nation": Religion, Nationalism, and Thanksgiving Day in Ontario, 1859–1914', in Matthew Hayday and Raymond Blake, eds, *Celebrating Canada*, 1: *Holidays, National Days, and the Crafting of Identities* (Toronto, ON, 2016), 54–82; Hardwick, 'Special Days', appendix.

[34] From 1801 to 1871, the United Church of England and Ireland.

[35] Philip Williamson, 'State Prayers, Fasts and Thanksgivings: Public Worship in Britain 1830–1897', *P&P* 200 (2008), 121–74, at 161–2.

[36] See the examples in n. 12.

royal supremacy in matters of religion. Accordingly, proclamations in
the Canadian Atlantic colonies from the 1790s 'charged' and 'commanded' inhabitants to observe fasts and thanksgivings, with threats
of God's 'wrath and indignation' for non-observance.[37] This wording
suited a counter-revolutionary empire, and in some territories was
retained for a surprisingly long time,[38] but it became increasingly
outmoded as the empire came to include more peoples not of British
origin, and as religious toleration was widened in overseas territories.
The emergence of an atheistic revolutionary regime in France after
1789 may also have encouraged the adoption of more inclusive forms
of special worship. For fasts and thanksgivings in Upper and Lower
Canada from the 1790s, governors issued proclamations that embraced Catholics as well as Protestants.[39] The Catholic archbishops
of Quebec ordered special masses on these days, as did the Catholic
bishops in Ireland and the vicars-apostolic in England and Wales.[40]

Religious pluralism was belatedly acknowledged in Britain; the last
use of the traditional style of proclamation was in 1857.[41] The arrangements for the 1887 and 1897 jubilees were clearly intended to
appeal to all Christian communities across the empire. In India from
the 1850s governors-general had gone still further, issuing proclamations that were addressed simply to 'all loyal subjects', encompassing
not only the numerous missionary churches but also, by avoiding
Christian references, encouraging observances among the Indian religions.[42] Governments across the empire became more sensitive to
the varying beliefs and interests within their colonies. The development and extension of representative forms of government during the 1830s and 1840s prompted the replacement of orders for

[37] For a Nova Scotian example, see *Royal Gazette* [Halifax], 25 March 1794.
[38] For example, a Newfoundland proclamation of 18 May 1847 ordering a fast day for
9 June 1847: St John's, The Rooms Archives, Office of the Colonial Secretary Fonds,
Original Proclamations, Series GN 2.8.
[39] See Lower Canadian proclamations in *Report of the Public Archives for the Year 1921*
(Ottawa, ON, 1922), 58, 76–7, 93, 156, 169–70, 183, 187–8, 192–3.
[40] Henri Têtu and Charles-Octave Gagnon, eds, *Mandements, lettres pastorales et circu-
laires des évêques de Québec*, 2 (Quebec, 1888), 516–17, 531–3, 536–7, ibid. 3 (Quebec,
1888), 105–8, 111–14, 121–3, 123–4, 132–4. For Britain, see Williamson et al., eds,
National Prayers, 2: lxxxix–xc.
[41] Williamson, 'State Prayers', 161–3.
[42] See Williamson et al., eds, *National Prayers*, 2: 1857–2. Jewish communities usually
observed special occasions ordered by governments, and from the 1840s the chief rabbi in
London issued forms of prayer for the 'united congregations of the British Empire': ibid.
3: appendix.

special worship with official encouragement to observe these occasions. The clergy of New South Wales were 'invited' to hold divine services for an 1838 fast, and after 1850 Canadian governments would 'earnestly exhort' their inhabitants to observe days of prayer.[43] Given the increasing religious pluralism in areas of British settlement, governments were wary of privileging the Church of England, and from the late 1840s applications for special days of prayer that came from its clergy alone might be declined. In 1847, for example, the governor of the province of Canada refused to mark the Irish famine with a fast because the request was made without Roman Catholic support.[44]

Increasingly, government initiatives gave way to arrangements made by other authorities. In Ontario during the 1850s, town mayors ordered days of fasting and humiliation. Australian mayors did the same during times of drought.[45] More generally, churches either arranged special days of prayer or special prayers for their own denominations, or, more significantly, leaders of various local churches co-operated in organizing multi-denominational days of prayer, sometimes with the same effect as earlier orders by civil authorities. In 1872, for example, a thanksgiving day arranged by Montreal's Protestant churches resulted in the closure of businesses and offices.[46] The popularity of church-appointed days of prayer, even those appointed on weekdays, reveals much about the public authority wielded by institutional churches in the colonial world.[47]

For some churches, the practice of setting aside special days of prayer was an extension of their historical independence from the state: for example, in Presbyterian churches in Australia, synods appointed days for fasting or thanksgiving.[48] The appointment of these colonial Presbyterian occasions mirrored developments in Scotland, where from the 1820s more members of the Church of Scotland (as

---

[43] *Sydney Herald*, 19 October 1838; *Canada Gazette*, 22 December 1849.

[44] See correspondence in LAC, RG4–C1/H–2585/198/1267, 2387.

[45] Hamilton, Ontario, observed a fast after an 1857 railway disaster: *The Globe* [Toronto], 17 March 1857; for a drought that led to a municipal day of prayer in Australia, see *Warwick Examiner* [Queensland], 2 July 1881.

[46] *Montreal Gazette*, 15 November 1872.

[47] The confidence of the institutional churches in late Victorian Canada is described in Nancy Christie and Michael Gauvreau, eds, *The Christian Churches and Their Peoples, 1840–1965: A Social History of Religion in Canada* (Toronto, ON, 2010), 57–9.

[48] For example, a fast in eastern Australia during drought: *Sydney Morning Herald*, 11 November 1865.

well as the Free Church after the Disruption of 1843) came to insist that appointment of acts of worship was a matter for the Church itself, not the state. Anglicans, by contrast, were unfamiliar with days of prayer appointed on church authority alone. In England and Wales, the archbishops only began to make their own 'national' appointments of special worship, independently of the crown, during the 1870s.[49] By then, Anglican bishops in the colonies and in India had been issuing forms of prayer on their own authority for several decades. Moreover, by mid-century colonial bishops, among them John Strachan of Toronto, were arguing that they could appoint days of prayer in their own dioceses, as these were free from colonial government control and independent of the church at home.[50]

Although no count has yet been undertaken of the special days of worship appointed independently by churches across the empire, they appear to have multiplied after 1850. For Strachan and other Anglican bishops, such occasions were a means to stiffen denominational identities in a competitive religious environment. But often churches had no choice but to arrange their own occasions, as after 1850 governments were wary of appointing special days of prayer for many types of cause. To understand this shift, more comment is needed on how the causes of special worship changed over time.

CAUSES OF SPECIAL WORSHIP

Special days of prayer survived into the twentieth century because the colonial authorities continued to sanction, in some form, the doctrine of 'national providentialism'.[51] Everything in the human and natural worlds was believed to be subject to God's superintendence, and so the hand of God could be read in the fortunes and misfortunes of communities, nations and empires. God's dealings with ancient Israel showed how misbehaving 'nations' were punished for their 'national sins' by 'special providences', such as epidemics, storms and famines.[52] Belief in national providentialism took more positive

---

[49] Williamson, 'State Prayers', 164–6.
[50] Toronto, Archives of Ontario, Strachan Papers, F983–2/ MS35/12, Letterbook 1854–1862, fol. 61, Strachan to Mountain of Quebec, 26 March 1855. For colonial Anglican independence, see Brown, 'Anglicanism in the British Empire', 53–5, Rowan Strong, 'Anglicanism and the State', in idem, ed., *OHA* 3, 108–14; Williams, 'Anglicanism in North America', 241.
[51] The term is taken from Guyatt, *Providence*, 5.
[52] For the persistence of providential beliefs, see Williamson, 'State Prayers', 132–4.

forms too. Britain's victory over Napoleon and escape from revolution revived the idea that Britain had been providentially favoured to improve and Christianize the world.[53] Such themes remained important elements in the fasts and thanksgivings observed across imperial territories during the nineteenth century, but colonists also developed readings of divine providence that worked independently of the grander imperial narrative. Days of prayer set aside for regional occurrences nurtured the view that God treated colonial communities differently from those elsewhere.[54] Not every colonial community conceived of itself as distinctly 'favoured' or 'special',[55] but days of humiliation and thanksgiving called by colonies could deepen community attachments, as well as a sense of separation and distinctiveness.

Special worship was ordered for a variety of causes, although their range gradually shrank during the nineteenth century. In colonial America, proclamations for fasts and thanksgivings tended to gather several causes together: these could include regional causes relating to the particular colony and more general causes that also affected British subjects elsewhere or all inhabitants of a 'Protestant Christendom' that reached into continental Europe.[56] During the 'second empire' orders issued by colonial governors usually followed the English style of single or few causes. From 1789, royal occasions and war came to dominate empire-wide special worship. Few other causes outside particular colonies now attracted special worship, with the notable exception of the 'Mutiny' in 1857, and later support of relief funds during famines.[57]

After 1850 a larger number of special days or prayers in colonies were arranged for causes that related only to their particular regions. In the late nineteenth century, governments in Australia and South Africa responded to requests from church delegations by setting aside

---

[53] Rowan Strong, *Anglicanism and the British Empire, c.1700–1850* (Oxford, 2007), 60, 106–8, 125.

[54] For the Australian context, see Hardwick, 'Special Days', 376–8.

[55] For the concept of providential election in the Canadian context, see S. F. Wise, 'God's Peculiar Peoples', in A. B. McKillop and Paul Romney, eds, *God's Peculiar Peoples: Essays on Political Culture in Nineteenth-Century Canada* (Ottawa, ON, 1993), 19–43.

[56] See the examples in n. 12; see also Tony Claydon, *Europe and the Making of England, 1660–1760* (Cambridge, 2007), 168–71.

[57] Williamson et al., eds, *National Prayers*, 3: 1877–E, 1897–E. Congregational churches of Western Australia organized prayers for famine sufferers in 1900: *Southern Times* [Western Australia], 20 March 1900.

midweek days of prayer for drought, plague and cattle disease.[58] Elsewhere, however, the civil authorities became more hesitant. Some
requests were too controversial. Canadian governments, for instance,
refused requests for special thanksgiving prayers after the North-West
Rebellion of 1885. Other causes were too parochial. Until 1879
the Canadian Dominion government would not appoint a harvest
thanksgiving for the whole of Canada, because the crop yields were
unlikely to be good everywhere.[59] Colonial authorities were also increasingly alert to public opinion. The appointment of days of prayer
might be ignored; days might lead to levity rather than penitence and
humility; they might open up divisions in colonial societies. In late
nineteenth-century Australia requests for special days of prayer were
sometimes turned down, as state authorities feared that a proclamation would anger workers who would lose a day's wages.[60] Civil authorities in Canada increasingly left it to churches to appoint special
prayers and days of prayer for calamities, such as the 1885 smallpox
epidemic which killed 3,000 people in Montreal.[61] In Australia, the
ecumenical Evangelical Alliance and regional Councils of Churches
appointed days of prayer in times of drought and economic depres-
sion.[62]

While the civil authorities were attuned to the divisive potential
of special worship, churches and other colonial organizations were
free to appoint days of prayer that reflected their particular interests
and agendas. The range of causes of church-appointed special days
and prayers remained much broader than for state occasions, and
included famines, natural disasters, overseas missions and financial
crises. In the early twentieth century disenfranchised colonial communities organized special days of prayer as a means of protest. In
South Africa, 'Vigilance Associations', formed to defend and extend
the rights of Black and Coloured communities, organized days of
'humiliation and prayer' to petition God to 'deliver' them from their
'difficulties, oppressions and disabilities'. Circulars for these days of

[58] Special days of worship were called by Australian civil authorities in times of drought
in 1895, 1897, 1898, 1902, 1903, 1904 and 1912. An 1896 rinderpest outbreak and a
1912 drought prompted the appointment of days of humiliation in South Africa.
[59] Hardwick, 'Fasts, Thanksgivings and Senses of Community', 692–3.
[60] President of the Council of Churches to editor, *The Argus* [Melbourne], 16 May 1893.
[61] *Form of Thanksgiving to Almighty God for Deliverance from the Epidemic with which the
City of Montreal has lately been Visited* (n.pl., 1886).
[62] *South Australian Advertiser*, 14 May 1870; *Bowral Free Press* [New South Wales], 17
June 1893.

prayer appealed to all the oppressed 'sons of Africa', and suggested plans for prayer meetings. Blacks, Indians and Coloureds observed 31 May 1910 (the day the four South African colonies were brought into union) as a day of humiliation, mourning and prayer.[63] In these ways, special worship expressed the diverse and disparate nature of the empire.

Changes in the causes of special worship were not just a result of political developments. A decline in days of humiliation appointed for natural disasters reflected gradual shifts in religious belief. Such occasions became increasingly controversial as the old theology of fear gave way to a new religiosity that placed less emphasis on judgements, 'special providences' and a vengeful deity. Increasingly, God tended to be regarded as a benevolent figure who had created the human abilities to understand the operations of 'general providence' and take steps to avoid or remedy natural disasters. Developments in natural science also had an effect, particularly in relation to disease. As a greater range of occurrences were ascribed to a general providence that worked through natural laws, and as less scope was allowed to unpredictable special providences, the justification for days of religious humiliation for these causes was weakened.

The long history of special worship ordered by the British crown during natural disasters ended in 1866,[64] yet such occasions continued into the twentieth century in some parts of the empire. Australian states and the Union of South Africa appointed midweek days of prayer in times of drought and insect infestation during the 1920s.[65] In these places natural disasters were far-reaching and often had more serious effects than in Britain. However, here too there was an important change of emphasis, towards a stronger sense of human agency beyond acts of worship. For example, during the 1900 bubonic plague outbreak in New South Wales, congregations were asked to pray not for divine intervention, but that 'wisdom and insight' would be provided to 'experts', and that everyone would learn to live by 'the lessons taught by science'.[66] By the late

---

[63] *Izwi Labantu* [East London], 19 May 1908; *Indian Opinion* [Durban], 11 June 1910.
[64] Alasdair Raffe, 'Nature's Scourges: The Natural World and Special Prayers, Fasts and Thanksgivings, 1543–1866', in Peter Clarke and Tony Claydon, eds, *God's Bounty? The Churches and the Natural World*, SCH 46 (Woodbridge, 2010), 237–47.
[65] *Sydney Morning Herald*, 16 March 1923; for the South African occasion, see ibid., 29 July 1924.
[66] Ibid., 13 April 1900.

nineteenth century, the traditional idea, taken from the Old Testament, that judgements were visited on communities for their 'collective', 'accumulated' or 'national sins' was hard to maintain as colonial societies became more diverse, both ethnically and religiously. During droughts, Australian town dwellers wrote to newspapers saying they had no reason to observe days of humiliation because the visitation had been sent to punish sinful farmers, not innocent townspeople.[67]

The proliferation of days of prayer appointed for regional causes and the occasions observed by particular churches and communities indicate the growing strength of centrifugal tendencies in the empire. They also suggest the extent to which imperial inhabitants identified with regions, discrete communities and faith groups that, in the case of the episcopal churches, were now organized into metropoles, provinces and dioceses. Yet observances for these regional and sectional events continued to coexist with days of prayer or special prayers for more far-reaching purposes. These layers of imperial special worship demonstrate that the inhabitants of empire were capable of holding multiple identities and several loyalties simultaneously.[68]

THE PERSISTENCE OF IMPERIAL SPECIAL WORSHIP

Paradoxically, despite greater degrees of self-government, wider acceptance of religious diversity and the increased independence of the various churches, from the late nineteenth century to the coronation of 1953 acts of special worship organized in London for observance across the empire were more common than they had been during earlier periods. The imperial days of prayer of the late Victorian period possibly expressed in part the anxieties about empire and British geopolitical vulnerability that lay behind the contemporary appeals to a 'Greater Britain'.[69] Some late Victorian Anglican leaders assumed that the Church of England could be recast as an imperial church, with a special role in spreading an 'imperial Christianity' across the empire.[70] These ambitions were manifested in the more active role

[67] Ibid., 11, 12 February 1869; *The Australasian* [Melbourne], 22 April 1876.
[68] Phillip Buckner, '"Limited Identities" Revisited: Regionalism and Nationalism in Canadian History', *Acadiensis* 30 (2000), 4–15, at 12.
[69] Duncan Bell, *The Idea of Greater Britain: Empire and the Future of the World Order, 1860–1900* (Princeton, NJ, 2007), 35–40.
[70] Steven Maughan, 'Imperial Christianity? Bishop Montgomery and the Foreign Missions of the Church of England, 1895–1915', in Andrew Porter, ed., *The Imperial*

of the church in arranging imperial acts of special worship. Since the 1790s, some colonial bishops had borrowed the text of the special forms of prayer issued by the church in England for use in their own dioceses, using copies sent to them by the archbishop of Canterbury or the government printers.[71] For Victoria's golden jubilee in 1887, the arrangement became more centralized: not only did Archbishop Benson and the Society for Promoting Christian Knowledge distribute the English form to the colonial bishops, but the Colonial Office sent copies to the colonial governors. For Edward VII's coronation in 1902, Archbishop Temple composed and circulated a *Form and Order of Service Recommended for Use in the Churches of the Church of England throughout His Majesty's Empire.* The formulation in Temple's title turned out to be unique to this occasion, but it became usual for the chief occasions of special worship arranged by the church in England to be observed also by colonial dioceses, often using the services or particular prayers issued by the English archbishops. Other churches (including Scottish Presbyterian, the various Free Churches and Roman Catholic) organized their own services in response to calls for special prayer from London. Even more impressively, the national days of prayer organized during wartime by consultation among the leaders of the main British churches became imperial days of prayer, much assisted by the public support of successive kings.[72]

The sense of a unified and righteous empire under God remained strong. During the two world wars, this was because imperial peoples were drawn into the war effort, with great numbers of dominion, colonial and Indian troops serving in the imperial armed forces. The popularity of the royal occasions indicates that monarchy remained the empire's key integrative force. Indeed, the evidence from observances of special worship suggests that loyalty and attachment to

---

Horizons of British Protestant Missions, 1880–1914 (Grand Rapids, MI, 2003), 32–57; Brown, 'Anglicanism in the British Empire', 66–7. For Anglicanism's enduring association with empire in the twentieth century, see Matthew Grimley, 'The State, Nationalism, and Anglican Identities', in Jeremy Morris, ed., *OHA*, 4: *Global Western Anglicanism, c.1910–Present* (Oxford, 2017), 117–36, at 120, 128–9.
[71] Williamson et al., eds, *National Prayers*, 2: cxlvii, cxlviii.
[72] See commentaries and notices sent to the dominions and colonies for 1914–18 and 1939–45 in Williamson et al., eds, *National Prayers*, 3. Even the day of national prayer called by the king for July 1947 because of post-war crises in Britain was observed in parts of the commonwealth and empire: see ibid. 1947–1.

monarchy were intensified by distance.[73] For instance, for Victoria's jubilees colonies set aside thanksgiving *days* when only thanksgiving *services* had been ordered in Britain. Unlike other causes that had led to special worship in the past, royal occasions had broad appeal and appeared uncontroversial. For coronations and royal funerals, governments appointed civil holidays, and ministers of religion organized the religious observances. These occasions suggested that the empire was, as its advocates liked to think, an empire of voluntary action and religious liberty. Irish Catholics in Canada branded the 1887 jubilee for 'Evictoria' a 'mockery and a fraud',[74] but elsewhere royal occasions attracted observances from the varied colonial publics. The monarchy was an integrative force because the inhabitants of empire had varied reasons to identify with it, as a protector of indigenous communities, defender of Protestant liberties, focus for imperial unity, and symbol of Christian values in the struggles against paganism, barbarism, communism and fascism.

[73] Mark McKenna, 'Monarchy: From Reverence to Indifference', in Deryck Schreuder and Stuart Ward, eds, *Australia's Empire* (Oxford, 2008), 261–87, at 262.
[74] *True Witness and Catholic Chronicle* [Montreal], 15 June 1887.

Queen Adelaide and the Extension of Anglicanism in Malta

Nicholas Dixon*

Pembroke College, Cambridge

On a visit to Malta in 1838, Queen Adelaide expressed severe disappointment that the British colony did not possess a purpose-built Anglican place of worship. She determined to fund the building of one at her personal expense and within six years the grandiose neoclassical church of St Paul's, Valletta, was completed. This imposing structure occupied an ambiguous position in a colony where the British government was pledged to maintain Roman Catholicism. St Paul's was ostensibly intended for the existing Anglican population in Malta. However, the church was perceived by both evangelicals and Roman Catholics as a potential instrument of propagating Protestantism. In examining the basis for these perceptions, this article suggests that St Paul's was part of a larger effort, driven by high church clergy connected with the Society for Promoting Christian Knowledge (SPCK), to influence the Maltese towards greater sympathy with the Anglican tradition, while avoiding overt proselytizing. The concomitant establishment of the diocese of Gibraltar in 1842 was, it is argued, key to this enterprise. The analysis advanced here has important implications for our understanding of Anglicanism in an imperial context, the contribution of royal patronage to this process and the conflict between religious and governmental imperatives.

Close to the centre of the Maltese capital of Valletta there stands an imposing neoclassical church with an Ionic portico of six columns and a 210-foot tower crowned with a spire. Presenting a striking contrast with the large dome of the neighbouring Carmelite Church (rebuilt after the Second World War and completed in 1981), this tower occupies a prominent position on the city's skyline. Above the portico of the church is written in Latin: 'Queen Adelaide with a grateful heart dedicated this Collegiate Church to Almighty God

* Pembroke College, Cambridge, CB2 1RF. E-mail: nad43@cam.ac.uk.

Studies in Church History 54 (2018) 281–295   © Ecclesiastical History Society 2018
doi: 10.1017/stc.2017.15

1844'.[1] Consecrated to St Paul, this Anglican pro-cathedral has been more commonly known as 'Queen Adelaide's Church', after its royal benefactress. Why did King William IV's widow make such a bold statement of Anglicanism in an overwhelmingly Roman Catholic colony? The question has never been adequately answered. The standard explanation, expressed at length by Arthur Bonnici and Alan Keighley, is that Adelaide was simply providing for the needs of the English Protestant population of the island.[2] Yet contemporary observers saw the building of the church in more complex terms. As Robin Gill has noted in passing, there existed a definite perception that St Paul's was not simply an expatriate church, but also a means of propagating Protestantism.[3]

This perception was shared by two religious groups with widely divergent perspectives: evangelicals and Roman Catholics. The evangelical *Malta Times* stated after the consecration of St Paul's: 'it may be said that the public worship of the Church of England was never, with any good effects, celebrated in Malta until the 1st of November, 1844, from which day we hope we may date the rapid progress of the true faith in that island'.[4] Meanwhile, the Catholic periodical *The Tablet* complained that the Anglican bishop of Gibraltar had offended the Maltese by giving St Paul's the same dedication as the principal Catholic church in Valletta, and that 'the observant Maltese remark that his lordship … devotes his thoughts and time very particularly to laying schemes for proselytising themselves'.[5]

To what extent were such perceptions grounded in fact? This question relates to the wider historical debate about the extent to which Anglicans in general had a proselytizing mission in the period of the British Empire's expansion. Investigation affords important insights into the rationale, means and consequences of Anglican extension in an era of governmental ambivalence concerning support for religious exertion in the colonies. Furthermore, the building project's largely high church origin draws attention to the ways in which

---

[1] Alan Keighley, *Queen Adelaide's Church* (Trowbridge, 2000), 172; 'National Inventory of the Cultural Property of the Maltese Islands', entries 552, 556, online at: <http://www.culturalheritage.gov.mt>, accessed 27 August 2017.
[2] Arthur Bonnici, 'Thirty Years to Build a Protestant Church', *Melita Historica* 6 (1973), 183–91; Keighley, *Queen Adelaide's Church*, 1–44.
[3] Robin Gill, *Changing Worlds: Can the Church Respond?* (Edinburgh, 2002), 109.
[4] *Malta Times*, 31 December 1844, quoted in Gill, *Changing Worlds*, 109.
[5] *The Tablet*, 24 February 1844, 115.

Anglican extension had alternative modes to the evangelical archetypes typified by the Church Missionary Society (CMS) and the nondenominational British and Foreign Bible Society. These societies have generally been the focus of previous assessments of missionary activity in Malta. In *Imperial Meridian*, Christopher Bayly related Anglican missionary efforts to 'a growth of evangelical ideas within the established churches', arguing that a 'secondary aim' of evangelical missions was the conversion of Catholic and Orthodox Christians to Protestantism, with 'particular attention ... paid to Malta and the eastern Mediterranean'.[6]

More recent studies have broadened our understanding of Anglicans' imperial exploits. According to Rowan Strong, there was a consistent desire on the part of Anglicans, both evangelical and non-evangelical, to proselytize in the colonies, exemplified by the activities of the Society for the Propagation of the Gospel in Foreign Parts and the creation of the Colonial Bishoprics Fund.[7] Hilary Carey has argued that churches were involved in all stages of colonization, and that the Church of England's 'orthodox mainstream' took a renewed interest in colonial endeavours from the 1830s.[8] Joseph Hardwick has shown how the Colonial Bishoprics Fund was 'overwhelmingly associated with high churchmen and high church ecclesiology'.[9] Yet Malta, where debates concerning Anglican missionary activity and episcopacy were strikingly evident, has not yet been the object of any sustained enquiry. Historians have displayed a tendency to focus on settler colonies, while discussions of the place of Roman Catholicism in the British Empire have mostly revolved around Ireland and its diaspora.[10] Additionally, the role of royal patronage in promoting

---

[6] Christopher Bayly, *Imperial Meridian: The British Empire and the World, 1780–1830* (London, 1989), 136–7, 141–2; see also Frans Ciappara, *M. A. Vassalli: An Enlightened Maltese Reformer* (Santa Venera, Malta, 2014), 115–38; Gareth Atkins, 'William Jowett's *Christian Researches*: British Protestants and Religious Plurality in the Mediterranean, Syria and the Holy Land, 1815–30', in Charlotte Methuen, Andrew Spicer and John Wolffe, eds, *Christianity and Religious Pluralism*, SCH 51 (Cambridge, 2015), 216–31.

[7] Rowan Strong, *Anglicanism and the British Empire, c.1700–1850* (Oxford, 2007), especially 10–40, 198–221.

[8] Hilary Carey, *God's Empire: Religion and Colonialism in the British Empire, c.1801–1908* (Cambridge, 2011), 17, 65.

[9] Joseph Hardwick, *An Anglican British World: The Church of England and the Expansion of the Settler Empire, c.1790–1860* (Manchester, 2014), 125.

[10] See, for example, Colin Barr and Hilary Carey, eds, *Religion and Greater Ireland: Christianity and Irish Global Networks* (Montreal, QC, 2015).

Anglicanism abroad has received little attention.[11] This article aims to address these lacunae, and draws upon a wide range of neglected sources in London, Cambridge and Malta.

British sovereignty over Malta had been confirmed by the Treaty of Paris of 1814, since which time there had been a strong understanding that the British government would leave the rights and privileges of the Roman Catholic Church in Malta undisturbed. The support of the Maltese Catholic clergy had been of vital assistance in Britain's capture of the island from Napoleonic France in 1800 and in sustaining the subsequent occupation. Hence there was a firm desire on the part of the colonial authorities to avoid antagonizing the local clergy and the religious sensibilities of the Maltese.[12] Catholic bishops were accorded military honours by the British soldiers stationed in Malta, who also fired salutes and furnished guards of honour for Catholic feast days.[13] This attracted considerable Protestant censure, but an even greater focus of complaint was the lack of a proper Anglican place of worship. Church of England services were held in a dingy vault, formerly a kitchen, in the governor's palace, which could barely accommodate colonial functionaries, let alone the wider English community.[14]

From the mid-1820s, a steady stream of complaints regarding this situation was articulated. In January 1826, John Cleugh, the

[11] Missionary enterprises are largely absent from the most comprehensive study of modern royal charitable activity: Frank Prochaska, *Royal Bounty: The Making of a Welfare Monarchy* (New Haven, CT, 1995).

[12] Relations between the British Government and the Roman Catholic Church in Malta during this period are described in Harrison Smith, *Britain in Malta*, 2 vols (Malta, 1953), 1: 73–100; Adrianus Koster, *Prelates and Politicians in Malta: Changing Power-Balances between Church and State in a Mediterranean Island Fortress (1800–1976)* (Assen, 1984), 35–51; Joseph Bezzina, 'Church and State in an Island Colony', in Victor Mallia-Milanes, ed., *The British Colonial Experience, 1800–1964: The Impact on Maltese Society* (Msida, Malta, 1988), 47–78.

[13] See Thomas Atchison, *Some Particulars relative to the Co-operation Required of the British Troops in Malta, in the Superstitious Ceremonies of the Romish Church* (London, 1826); idem, *The Idolatrous Ceremonies of the Roman Catholic and Greek Churches at Malta, Corfu, and Zante, in which the Officers, Civil and Military, and Troops of the British Army are Commanded to Join* (London, 1830); London, LPL, Fulham Papers [hereafter: FP], Blomfield Papers 65, fols 182^r–183^r, John Le Mesurier to Charles Blomfield, 27 August 1829.

[14] LPL, FP, Blomfield Papers 65, fol. 178^r, John Le Mesurier to George Tomlinson, 24 June 1828. John Henry Newman lamented this state of affairs on a visit to Malta in 1833: Anne Mozley, ed., *Letters and Correspondence of John Henry Newman*, 2 vols (London, 1891), 1: 31.

government chaplain in Malta, wrote to Sir Frederick Bouverie, chief secretary to the government, that 'the respectability of our character as a nation, (to say nothing of the interest of our religion) is materially injured by the inadequacy & meanness of the present chamber; in a country where so much consequence is attached to externals'. Cleugh went on to state that Protestants desired 'an edifice that shall correspond with their important rank in the Island'.[15] The following month, Lord Hastings, the governor of Malta, wrote to the bishop of London, William Howley, of 'how desirable it would be to exhibit to the Maltese a more dignified stile of attention to the Duties of our Communion'.[16] However, the position had not changed by 1829, when John Le Mesurier, chaplain to the forces in Malta, wrote to the new bishop of London, Charles Blomfield, expressing the hope that the established Church in Malta would be placed on 'that respectable & efficient footing which even in a political view our national character demands'. He further remarked:

> ... it is the astonishment of every new comer not to find an English Church, & it is the lament of every right thinking person. Your Lordship must be well aware of the effect which externals have on the minds of the illiterate, & that in respect to the Soldier & the lower orders, inducements should be held out, & difficulties removed that they may be brought to perceive & feel the superiority of our National faith.

Referring to Anglican difficulties in other parts of the Mediterranean, Le Mesurier suggested the remedy of 'an Ecclesiastical head of talent & rank appointed to superintend & on the spot the concerns of our Mediterranean Church'.[17] Thus, by 1830, a strong argument for extending Anglicanism in Malta had taken shape, and had been brought to the attention of those in influential quarters. Its main premises were the importance of established religion to the national character, the necessity of an architectural manifestation of this and the potential for Malta to become an active focal point for an enlarged sphere of Anglican activity in the Mediterranean. Such a line of thought was made possible by Britain's naval dominance of the region and its rule of the Ionian Islands, which placed Malta at the

---

[15] Rabat, National Archives of Malta, CSG03/1048, John Cleugh to Frederick Bouverie, 9 January 1826.

[16] LPL, FP, Howley Papers 4, p. 522, Lord Hastings to William Howley, 13 February 1826.

[17] LPL, FP, Blomfield Papers 65, fol. 180, Le Mesurier to Blomfield, 12 March 1829.

centre of an emergent British Mediterranean empire stretching from Gibraltar to Kythira.[18]

The case was reiterated in extended fashion around 1835, in a pamphlet by the high church Winchester prebendary George Nott.[19] Nott was frequently resident in Italy, and his account of the state of Anglicanism in Malta suggests a detailed knowledge of local conditions, as well as an acquaintance with the views of Cleugh and Le Mesurier. He argued that the Maltese would not 'take umbrage at the English Government should they build a Church … for the sake of placing religious service among the English at Malta, on a footing of respectability similar to that on which their own is placed'.[20] On the contrary, the Maltese would see Anglicanism in a more favourable light if its worship were conducted in consecrated buildings.[21] The British Government's obligation to maintain Roman Catholicism among the Maltese did not require it to allow Anglicanism 'to remain in a state that tends to make it contemptible in their sight'.[22] If Malta were better provided with Anglican ministry, 'numerous would be the advantages we should gain, in a civil and political, as well as in a religious point of view'.[23] The Anglican clergy would inculcate spiritual and political orthodoxy, while a new church 'would facilitate the attendance not of the British only, but of various believers, of the Greek and other Christian communions, of whom there are a large number at Malta'.[24] Moreover, a 'superintending Minister' could be appointed to oversee all Mediterranean Anglican

---

[18] On this Mediterranean empire, see Bayly, *Imperial Meridian*, 102–4, 196–202; Robert Holland, *Blue-Water Empire: The British in the Mediterranean since 1800* (London, 2012).

[19] On Nott, see Stefano Villani, *George Frederick Nott (1768–1841). Un ecclesiastico Anglicano, tra teologia, letteratura, arte, archeologia, bibliofilia e collezionismo* (Rome, 2012).

[20] [George Frederick Nott], *General Statement respecting the Facility of Building a Church for the English at Malta* (Winchester, n.d.), 7. This pamphlet was printed with another entitled *General Statement of the Quantity of Ecclesiastical Duty to be Performed by the Two Chaplains at Malta* (Winchester, n.d.). On the rationale for dating these pamphlets to *c.*1835 and attributing them to Nott, see Villani, *Nott*, 869.

[21] [Nott], *General Statement respecting the Facility*, 8–11.

[22] Ibid. 12.

[23] Ibid. 13.

[24] Ibid. 13–15. A secondary concern of Nott's was to prevent a growth in Dissent: ibid. 14. A Methodist chapel was built in Valletta *c.*1824 but closed in 1843, its premises being taken over by the nascent Free Church of Scotland: G. A. Sim, 'Religious Liberty in Malta', in *Maintaining the Unity: Proceedings of the Eleventh International Conference and Diamond Jubilee Celebration of the Evangelical Alliance held in London, July 1907* (London, 1907), 205–16, at 208–9.

congregations.[25] 'If a free and brotherly intercommunion between all these congregations were effected', Nott asked, 'what means could be devised better adapted for the diffusion of Christian Knowledge, and the free circulation of the Scriptures, along the shores of the Mediterranean?' Accordingly, 'a more regular direction might be given to the exertions of the properly appointed Church Missionaries sent from England'.[26] Malta, in Nott's scheme, would be an important base for Anglican missionary activity.[27] Additionally, he believed that Anglican extension was emphatically justified by Malta's status as 'an integral part of the British empire, and one which an approaching crisis may prove to be ... indispensable towards the maintenance of our national greatness, and independence'.[28]

It seems that, indirectly, Nott's pamphlet finally accomplished the building of an Anglican church in Malta. A copy of it was transmitted to the Foreign Translation Committee of the Society for Promoting Christian Knowledge (SPCK), for whom Nott had worked on an Italian translation of the Book of Common Prayer.[29] More importantly, it appears to have found its way into the hands of Queen Adelaide, whose support for a variety of Anglican causes was generous and constant.[30] In widowhood, Adelaide aligned herself closely with the high church party within the Church of England, which dominated the SPCK increasingly and had a powerful advocate in William Howley, now archbishop of Canterbury and the society's president.[31] During a stay in Madeira in 1848, Adelaide was to take up the cause of the British chaplain there, Richard Lowe, who was threatened with dismissal by the foreign secretary, Lord Palmerston, after accusations

---

[25] [Nott], *General Statement respecting the Facility*, 15–16.
[26] Ibid. 16.
[27] Villani, *Nott*, 870–1.
[28] [Nott], *General Statement respecting the Facility*, 20.
[29] CUL, SPCK MS A16/1, 68, SPCK Foreign Translation Committee [hereafter: FTC] Minutes, 11 July 1836. SPCK material is cited by permission of the Syndics of Cambridge University Library.
[30] Prochaska, *Royal Bounty*, 55–60; Marilyn Thomas, 'Royal Charity and Queen Adelaide in Early Nineteenth-Century Britain', in Marilyn Button and Jessica Sheetz-Nguyen, eds, *Victorians and the Case for Charity: Essays on Responses to English Poverty by the State, the Church and the Literati* (Jefferson, NC, 2014), 42–57.
[31] James Pereiro, *'Ethos' and the Oxford Movement: At the Heart of Tractarianism* (Oxford, 2007), 17–25; Hardwick, *Anglican British World*, 110–14. 'High church' in this context does not generally denote Tractarianism, but rather an older high churchmanship of the kind described in Peter Nockles, *The Oxford Movement in Context: Anglican High Churchmanship, 1760–1857* (Cambridge, 1994).

of ritualism.[32] Robert Gray, bishop of Cape Town, observed after meeting Adelaide in Madeira that she was 'a capital Churchwoman ... and has told the Consul here that if the Chaplain is turned out and another thrust in without the Bishop's license, she will be very sorry, as it will prevent her attending church'.[33]

The queen dowager's commitment to high church activism had been equally evident a decade earlier. On a visit to Malta for health reasons in the winter of 1838, Adelaide had expressed severe dissatisfaction with the lack of an Anglican church in a fruitless appeal to Queen Victoria, before determining to erect one at her own expense.[34] The project moved apace: a site was granted by the government and the foundation stone of St Paul's was laid by Adelaide in March 1839.[35] Her rationale for this enterprise was expressed in a letter to Archbishop Howley of November 1840:

> I have received the most satisfactory report of the progress of the building of the Church which I have been enabled to erect at Malta and am naturally very anxious that it should become the Cathedral of a Bishopric. ... The peculiar position of the Island of Malta renders it adapted above all other for the Seat of a Bishopric & the spiritual Superintendence of the many Protestant Congregations scatter'd over Italy, the Levant & Gibraltar.

Adelaide proceeded to expand on her aims for this project:

> ... the assurance that 'both in a religious & political point of view it would be greatly to be desired, that the Maltese would take no umbrage, on the contrary it would give respectability and a higher & firmer footing both in Malta & throughout the Mediterranean if we

---

[32] W. M. Jacob, *The Making of the Anglican Church Worldwide* (London, 1997), 118; I am grateful to Dr Jacob for drawing this episode to my attention.

[33] Charles N. Gray, ed., *Life of Robert Gray, Bishop of Cape Town and Metropolitan of Africa* (London, 1883), 49. Adelaide also donated high church furnishings to St Michael's Church, Lewes: Jeremy Goring, *Burn Holy Fire: Religion in Lewes since the Reformation* (Cambridge, 2003), 124.

[34] Arthur Benson and Viscount Esher [Reginald Brett], eds, *The Letters of Queen Victoria: A Selection from Her Majesty's Correspondence between the Years 1837 and 1861*, 3 vols (London, 1908), 1: 138, Queen Adelaide to Queen Victoria, 13 December 1839. Adelaide expended around £20,000 on the church: Keighley, *Queen Adelaide's Church*, 25.

[35] Kew, TNA, CO 158/106, Bouverie to Lord Glenelg, 6 January 1839; Bouverie to Glenelg, 20 March 1839. For an account of the laying of the foundation stone, see *Morning Post*, 9 April 1839, 5.

had a Protestant bishop established' has encouraged me to request you will State these my anxious wishes to L[or]d J[ohn] Russell in order that the home Gov[ernmen]t may take into favorable consideration this important subject ... .[36]

It is apparent that in the quoted section Adelaide was directly paraphrasing Nott's opinions that the Maltese would not be offended by the building of an Anglican church, and that such a project would have numerous advantages.[37] That she was already thinking in these terms during her visit to Malta may be inferred from a letter of January 1839 from her chamberlain Earl Howe to Archbishop Howley, expressing the hope that the building of St Paul's would lead to 'the establishment of a Mediterranean Bishopric' which would 'give a dignity to our Church in the eyes of R[oman] Catholics & prevent their constant observation that a faith in which its votaries shew so little interest cannot be a true one!'[38]

By endorsing Nott's pamphlet, Queen Adelaide identified herself with the agenda of those who wished to make Malta a centre for the active extension of Anglicanism. Shortly before her visit, an attempt to build an Anglican church in Malta had been made by Christopher Schlienz of the CMS.[39] This had been obstructed by the governor, Sir Henry Bouverie, who expressed fears that:

> ... it would be extremely dangerous to allow of the building of a Church by the Church Missionary Society, unless ... that Church were put under the control of the Government so far as to prevent all attempts at conversion of the Maltese to the Protestant faith ... should any such attempts be made ... this Government would be plunged into endless difficulties.[40]

By contrast, Adelaide's proposal was, at least ostensibly, less ecclesiologically partisan; it was also more difficult to refuse on account of her status. In November 1844 her completed church was consecrated.[41]

---

[36] LPL, MS 1754, fols 5r–6r, Adelaide to Howley, 1 November 1840.
[37] See above, 286.
[38] LPL, MS 2185, fol. 145r, Earl Howe to Howley, 5 January 1839. Adelaide, in advocating a bishopric, went one stage further than Le Mesurier and Nott, who had only envisaged a 'superintending Minister'.
[39] Bonnici, 'Protestant Church', 187.
[40] TNA, CO 158/95, Bouverie to Glenelg, 16 March 1837.
[41] *Morning Post*, 4 December 1844, 5.

The church's neoclassical design was atypical for its period, and was deliberately intended to contrast with Roman Catholic places of worship.[42] Resisting suggestions to introduce more gilding, the architect William Scamp stated that 'the principle by which I have been guided, both to the interior and exterior' was '*Simplicity*'.[43] An allegorical statue of Faith donated by Earl Howe to the church was removed to the Garrison Library on the grounds that its appearance was too Catholic.[44]

The building of 'Queen Adelaide's Church' coincided with the establishment of a Mediterranean bishopric of the kind which Adelaide had called for, with the support of the newly established Colonial Bishoprics Fund. In 1841, Archbishop Howley had stated in a public meeting in aid of this fund that 'the proper seat' of a Mediterranean bishopric had 'been all but determined upon by the erection of a splendid church at Malta, at the expense of an illustrious lady … who was not more exalted in her rank and station than respected for her virtue and piety', but that '[t]he object was not proselytism'.[45] In one respect, however, the wishes of Adelaide and Howley were not fulfilled: to avoid offending the Catholic bishop of Malta, the new Anglican bishop assumed the title of bishop of Gibraltar and St Paul's was not made a cathedral. But, in effect, the plan was realized: the bishop of Gibraltar's main residence was in Valletta, and St Paul's functioned as a cathedral in all but name.[46]

In 1842, George Tomlinson was consecrated the first bishop of Gibraltar. A high churchman and former chaplain to Howley,

[42] On the dominance of the Gothic style in Anglican church architecture within the British Empire during the mid-nineteenth century, see G. A. Bremner, *Imperial Gothic: Religious Architecture and High Anglican Culture in the British Empire, c.1840–1870* (New Haven, CT, 2013). On the architecture of St Paul's, see Malcolm Borg, *British Colonial Architecture: Malta (1800–1900)* (Malta, 2001), 44–9; Conrad Thake, 'William Scamp: An Appraisal of his Architectural Drawings and Writings on St Paul's Pro-Cathedral, Valletta', *Treasures of Malta* 23 (2017), 12–24.
[43] William Scamp, Report and plans of St Paul's Anglican Cathedral, 28 March 1844, quoted in Thake, 'William Scamp', 20.
[44] *Gentleman's Magazine*, December 1844, 632.
[45] *Morning Post*, 28 April 1841, 3.
[46] Henry J. C. Knight, *The Diocese of Gibraltar: A Sketch of its History, Work and Tasks* (London, 1917), 41–2, 54–6. May Tomlinson, daughter of the first bishop of Gibraltar, referred to him as '1st. Bishop of Gibraltar & Malta': Cambridge, St John's College Biographical Archive, entry for George Tomlinson, May Tomlinson to Robert Forsyth-Scott, 25 November 1925. Cited by permission of the Master and Fellows of St John's College, Cambridge.

Tomlinson was a secretary of the SPCK, and had been heavily involved, alongside Schlienz and Nott, in furthering the efforts of its Foreign Translation Committee.[47] In his first charge to his clergy, delivered in St Paul's the month after its consecration, Bishop Tomlinson echoed Howley's denial of a proselytizing urge:

> I am desirous that you should act in the very reverse of that spirit which
> has shewn itself here and in other places, in making proselytes from us
> to the Church of Rome … We have not the least wish or desire to
> practice the arts of 'that cunning craftiness, whereby they lie in wait to
> deceive.'[48]

Yet, while eschewing overt proselytism, Tomlinson did take some steps that accorded with Nott's vision of Malta as a centre of Anglican missionary activity. Upon his arrival in Malta, he purchased the Valletta printing press of the CMS, who had recently abandoned their Maltese missionary post, for the SPCK's use.[49] In 1844, he admitted to Anglican orders Michael Angelo Camilleri, a Maltese Roman Catholic priest who had converted to Anglicanism.[50] Camilleri was a controversial figure among the Maltese, not least because he had eloped with a widow to Gibraltar and had been imprisoned for assaulting two legal officials in Valletta.[51] Tomlinson nonetheless championed him, commissioning him to translate the New Testament and the Book of Common Prayer into Maltese under the auspices of the SPCK, which printed these at its newly acquired Valletta press.[52] In 1847, when the translations were complete, Tomlinson stated with evident satisfaction that portions of the Bible were 'now,

---

[47] On Tomlinson, see Peter Allen, *The Cambridge Apostles: The Early Years* (Cambridge, 1978), 22–4. His role in the SPCK is recorded in George Tomlinson, *Report of a Journey to the Levant, addressed to His Grace the Archbishop of Canterbury, President of the Society for Promoting Christian Knowledge* (London, 1841), and throughout the FTC Minutes: CUL, SPCK MS A16/1–2. See also George Tomlinson, *A Letter to the Archbishop of Canterbury on the Approaching Tercentenary of the English Prayer Book, and of the Establishment of the Reformation in England* (London, 1848).
[48] George Tomlinson, *A Charge Delivered to the Clergy of the Diocese and Jurisdiction of Gibraltar, at the Visitation, held in the English Collegiate Church of St. Paul, Malta, December 28, 1844* (London, 1845), 33.
[49] CUL, SPCK MS A16/1, 220, FTC Minutes, 24 October 1842.
[50] *Morning Post*, 13 February 1845, 5.
[51] David Dandria, 'A 19th-Century Apostate Priest and Cause Célèbre', *Times of Malta*, 11 October 2015.
[52] CUL, SPCK MS A16/1, 299–300, 318–19, FTC Minutes, 11 March, 28 June 1844.

for the first time, presented to the people in their own language'.[53] Furthermore, Tomlinson lent his support as visitor to a Protestant college established in Malta in 1846, declaring it to be 'a Church of England institution' and 'a seminary of SOUND PROTESTANT INSTRUCTION ... where the *true* principles of our Reformers are understood and taught'.[54]

In such a context, the building of 'Queen Adelaide's Church' had unavoidable missionary overtones. Apparently undeterred by its high church origins, evangelicals claimed Adelaide's enterprise as their own. In a book dedication, S. S. Wilson of the CMS congratulated Adelaide for building 'a sacred fabric, which, in such a locality, may truly be styled a missionary church'.[55] The evangelical poet Harriet Burton presented Adelaide's gift as a powerful antidote to Roman ritual and Marian devotion. Recalling King William IV's deathbed prayer for the Church of England, she wrote:

And well by thee, Queen Adelaide, his prayer has been fulfill'd,
And laid the sole foundation stone, on which a man may build,
In Malta's rocky island, where at Error's gilded shrine
Bright robes, sweet incense, idol-pomps, and glimmering tapers shine;
Where holy saints are worshipp'd, – and the Virgin-mother paid,
Co-equal honours with her son, 'by whom all things were made.'
But blessed be the God of Truth, and blest that royal hand,
The instrument ordain'd by Him, to bless a Papal land![56]

---

[53] CUL, SPCK MS A16/2, 152, FTC Minutes, 3 July 1847. Tomlinson overlooked the earlier efforts of the Maltese professor Mikiel Anton Vassalli, who translated parts of the New Testament into Maltese for the CMS during the 1820s: Ciappara, *Vassalli*, 122–34.

[54] *Malta Times*, 6 April 1852, quoted in S. Mallia, 'The Malta Protestant College', *Melita Historica* 10 (1990), 257–82, at 260. Despite this episcopal sanction, the college was initially viewed with suspicion on account of its evangelical founders' failure to inform Tomlinson of their plans. See Blomfield's letters to Tomlinson from August 1844: LPL, FP, Blomfield Papers 41, fols 134–6, 156–8.

[55] S. S. Wilson, *A Narrative of the Greek Mission, or, Sixteen Years in Malta and Greece* (London, 1839), ii.

[56] H. E. Burton, 'Lines presented to Her Majesty the Queen Dowager on her return from Malta, May, 1839', in *Linda, or, the Festival: A Metrical Romance of Ancient Scinde, with Minor Poems* (London, 1845), 51–2. This collection was dedicated with permission to Queen Adelaide; cf. 'Sonnet: On Founding the First Protestant Church in the Island of Malta, by the Dowager Queen, Adelaide', *The Churchman*, June 1839, 200. On William IV's deathbed prayer, see [John Ryle Wood], *Some Recollections of the Last Days of His Late Majesty King William the Fourth* (London, 1837).

Such sentiments were repeated in evangelical periodicals. *The Harlequin*, printed in Valletta, welcomed the establishment of 'a Christian Protestant Church against a system of religion the most detestable the world ever saw!'[57] The *Church of England Magazine* exclaimed, 'who can say … how many souls may have been saved from the awfully false doctrines of popery, by the preaching of the truth of God in the protestant church thus given to the people of Malta by a protestant queen!'[58] The high church *Colonial Church Chronicle* took a more moderate line. Endorsing Bishop Tomlinson's avoidance of explicit missionary efforts, it expressed a hope that there would be a 'gradual awakening of the Maltese to a sense of the superstitions and absurdities which now disfigure their religious system … leading them gently to such a self-reformation, as … might make their church "a praise in the earth"'.[59]

However, Roman Catholics in Malta displayed little appetite for such 'self-reformation'. During her visit to the island, Adelaide had exhibited a cordial tolerance of Roman Catholicism, receiving and visiting Catholic clergy.[60] When her barge passed a procession carrying a statue of the Virgin Mary in the harbour of Bormla, it is recorded that, as a compliment to Adelaide, the image 'was brought to face Her Majesty … and she stopped to acknowledge this spontaneous expression by the waving of her hand'.[61] Yet Adelaide's plans for an Anglican church were highly concerning to the Catholic clergy. In February 1839, the papal secretary of state Cardinal Lambruschini told Archbishop Caruana of Malta that he could not be indifferent to the project, and advised him to take all necessary steps to impede its execution.[62] Maltese workmen had to receive papal dispensations to work on the building of St Paul's, and one local Catholic priest reportedly warned that an earthquake would result from the project.[63]

---

[57] *The Harlequin*, 21 March 1839, quoted in G. P. Badger, *Trial of J. Richardson, for an Alleged Libel against the Roman Catholic Religion* (Valletta, 1839), 8.
[58] *Church of England Magazine*, 3 January 1852, 6.
[59] *Colonial Church Chronicle and Missionary Journal*, October 1847, 126.
[60] Smith, *Britain in Malta*, 1: 86–7.
[61] Joseph Galea, 'An Unpublished Diary of Queen Adelaide's Visit to Malta in 1838', *Scientia* 29 (1963), 99–116, at 107–8.
[62] Floriana, Archdiocese of Malta Archives, Corrispondenza 1838/40, fol. 842, Cardinal Lambruschini to Archbishop Caruana, 12 February 1839; I am grateful to Fr Nicholas Doublet for supplying me with a copy of this letter.
[63] Emma Roberts, *Notes of an Overland Journey through France and Egypt to Bombay* (London, 1841), 65; *The Harlequin*, 27 June 1839, quoted in *The Era*, 21 July 1839, 513.

Louisianna Gibson, visiting Malta in 1842, recorded that when a comet appeared over Valletta, '[t]he Maltese declared that it hung over' St Paul's and 'foretold a judgement upon them for having allowed a Protestant Cathedral to be built'.[64]

After the completion, the building was viewed with suspicion and occasional hostility by the local population. In 1846, the square outside the church was the scene of disturbances after a sabbatarian governor, Sir Patrick Stuart, prohibited traditional carnival festivities from taking place on a Sunday. Some in the crowd masqueraded in the dress of Protestant clergy; others were heard to shout, 'To the Protestant church! let us pull it down!' Meanwhile, a service was in progress inside the church. The congregants, hearing an uproar, feared that the crowd would enter and attack them, but in the event the crowd moved on to the governor's palace.[65] However, manifestations of ill-feeling continued to be evident. Two years later, John Cleugh and the churchwardens of St Paul's informed the government that 'the walls and the premises of that Church are constantly defiled and defaced by evil disposed persons' and suggested that erecting iron railings would be the only possible solution.[66] State assistance in the face of such provocations was, however, not forthcoming, as Stuart's Roman Catholic successor as governor, Richard O'Ferrall, refused to use government revenues for this purpose.[67] O'Ferrall's decision was overturned by a later governor, Sir John Le Marchant, who in 1861 agreed to finance the placing of railings around the church.[68] Thus fenced off, the church reinforced its detachment from the Maltese population.

The subsequent history of 'Queen Adelaide's Church', in which it has served almost exclusively the English-speaking community in Malta, has concealed the circumstances attending its construction. St Paul's was intended by Adelaide, Nott and Tomlinson among others to be a focal point for the dissemination of Protestantism in Malta and across the Mediterranean. Disclaiming the overt proselytism practised by evangelical missionary societies, they nevertheless

---

[64] Winchester, Hampshire Record Office, DC/M5/5/1 part 2, 'Recollections of Louisianna Gibson, 1817–1899', 18.

[65] Henry Seddall, *Malta: Past and Present* (London, 1870), 240–4.

[66] National Archives of Malta, CSG03/1068, Cleugh et al. to William Sim, 19 October 1848.

[67] A. V. Laferla, *British Malta*, 2 vols (Malta, 1938–47), 1: 211.

[68] Keighley, *Queen Adelaide's Church*, 37–8.

attempted subtly to influence the Maltese towards a greater sympathy for the Anglican tradition. This was manifested in the grandiose architecture of St Paul's, the concomitant establishment of the bishopric of Gibraltar and the translation of the Bible and Prayer Book into Maltese. Their effort reveals much about the nature of Anglicanism within an imperial context during the mid-nineteenth century. Firstly, it underlines the centrality of missionary impulses within the upper echelons of the Church, and demonstrates that their implementation was not restricted to non-Christian colonies. Furthermore, it demonstrates the ways in which high church missionary activity, assisted by episcopal structures, could rival evangelical missions such as the CMS from the 1830s onwards. Queen Adelaide's involvement also shows the degree to which royal patronage continued to exercise a strong influence over ecclesiastical affairs, one that could overcome the conflicting imperatives of a pragmatically irenic governmental policy. That her wider ambitions for the advancement of Anglicanism in a Roman Catholic land were not fulfilled should not blind us to that intriguing moment in 1844 when Anglican hopes were fixed upon Valletta.

Claiming the Land: The Church Missionary Society and Architecture in the Arctic

Emily Turner*

University of Edinburgh

The Arctic has claimed much interest in both popular discourse and academic scholarship, most notably concerning the voyages of Sir John Franklin. However, the explorers of the British Navy were not the only representatives of imperial expansion in what is now the Canadian Arctic. During the second half of the nineteenth century, the Church Missionary Society (CMS), the evangelical missionary society of the Church of England, undertook a substantial programme of evangelism throughout the region, not just aiming to convert indigenous people, but also to claim the land for the British empire and establish a strong presence in the region as an integral aspect of the providential expansion of empire. This article contends that the CMS attempted to achieve those aims through the creation of permanent infrastructure which brought the region into the fold of empire in a way that exploration could not, as missionaries used buildings to transform the land and its inhabitants as part of the duty of empire and its agents towards all its inhabitants. In claiming the land for empire, architecture was not just a by-product of occupation but rather a vital and integral agent in securing northern territories for God and empire.

In 1820, the Church Missionary Society (CMS), the evangelical missionary society of the Church of England, entered North America, intent on disseminating Christianity throughout present-day northern and western Canada. By the end of the century, the organization had spread throughout the north-west, establishing missions and winning converts. However, the propagation of Christianity was not the only goal and preaching the word was not the only way in which the CMS achieved its mandate, which also included support of, and participation in, the expansion of the British empire, particularly through the promotion of British cultural and social norms. Although forwarding this agenda in a variety of ways, including

* 17/4 Teviot Place, Edinburgh, EH1 2QZ. E-mail: emily.turner@ed.ac.uk.

Studies in Church History 54 (2018) 296–313   © Ecclesiastical History Society 2018
doi: 10.1017/stc.2017.16

the transmission of religious beliefs and encouragement of British moral and domestic ideals, this article shows how the CMS used the built environment, the buildings and stations it erected throughout the Canadian north, as a central and integral aspect of its strategy. These structures were employed both practically and symbolically to convert indigenous people to Christianity and to assist in bestowing upon them one of the perceived great benefits of a benevolent and providential empire: civilization. Through both their usage and their visual appearance, the buildings erected by the CMS in northern Canada played a clear and acknowledged role in the organization's mission to convert and civilize non-Christian people and their landscape as part of the wider expansion of British culture, with the CMS acting as a de facto agent of empire through its building programme.

The CMS, its mission and its building programme cannot be understood outside the geographical context, which both affected its approach to evangelism and placed limitations on what missionaries were able to achieve, particularly with regard to building. In the nineteenth century, the Arctic, as both place and idea, was well ingrained in the British imagination and deeply romanticized.[1] An ill-defined geographic area, including both the Arctic and sub-Arctic, the north was a region characterized by its inhospitable environment and sheer vastness, stretching from the Arctic Ocean across the present-day Canadian territories and along Hudson's Bay.[2] With the exception of indigenous people, whose importance as occupiers was generally disregarded, the land was also unsettled. Initially viewed as the potential route to riches in the Orient, by the nineteenth century it had become an area where British exploration increased scientific and geographic understanding.[3] Here, British naval explorers took on the most challenging forces of nature at the very edge of the earth. Their successes demonstrated the sheer power of the British world by showing it could claim territory in any conditions through exploratory prowess, with the Arctic territories becoming a source of pride in national and imperial discourse.

---

[1] Janice Cavell, *Tracing the Connected Narrative: Arctic Exploration in British Print Culture, 1818–1860* (Toronto, ON, 2008), 28.
[2] Kenneth Coates, *Canada's Colonies: A History of the Yukon and Northwest Territories* (Toronto, ON, 1978), 32.
[3] Glyndwr Williams, *Arctic Labyrinth: The Quest for the Northwest Passage* (Berkeley, CA, 2010), 169–73.

The narrative of British Arctic exploration and its reception is well established in contemporary scholarship.[4] However, what is less clearly explored are its overtly Christian overtones. Arctic exploration was not explicitly directed to the conversion of indigenous people, although some explorers, including John Franklin, approached the CMS to this effect.[5] Nonetheless, Arctic exploration was subsumed within the mission of a Christian empire, indeed, of one that was often seen as providentially expanded through God's will, and the imbedded Christian discourse in some of the expeditions is hard to ignore. For example, the integration of Christianity into Franklin's expeditions is very clear. Deeply religious, Franklin ensured that Christian texts were carried on both his overland expeditions and promoted prayer and worship throughout; his crew was portrayed as devout and pious in the British press.[6] Both Franklin and surgeon John Richardson emphasized the importance of personal and collective faith in overcoming the difficulties of the Arctic in the pursuit of British imperial expansion.[7]

This Christian Arctic narrative fitted well with notions of a providentially expanded British empire where God saw fit to allow Britain to gain territory; possession of the Arctic, in particular, demonstrated Britain's exploratory prowess, spreading its sphere of influence under an explicitly Christian banner.[8] Explorers were presented as godly, pious men, exemplars of the notion of Christian manliness, expanding the bounds of empire through unimaginable suffering.[9] The idea that explorers survived and succeeded primarily through God's mercy

---

[4] See, for example, Pierre Berton, *Arctic Grail: The Quest for the Northwest Passage and the North Pole* (Toronto, ON, 1988); Robert David, *The Arctic in the British Imagination, 1818–1909* (Manchester, 2000).

[5] British naval captain Sir John Franklin is best known for his doomed 1845 expedition to find the North-West Passage, which resulted in his disappearance along with his men and ships. Franklin had previously led two overland Arctic expeditions in 1819–22 and 1823–5. It was on the latter that he encountered CMS missionary John West at Churchill. Birmingham, Cadbury Research Library, Church Missionary Society Archives [hereafter: CMSA], C/C1/M1, John West to CMS, 25 October 1823.

[6] Janice Cavell, 'Lady Lucy Berry and Evangelical Reading on the First Franklin Expedition', *Arctic* 63 (2010), 131–40, at 134–5; John Franklin, *Narrative of a Journey to the Shores of the Polar Sea, in the Years 1819, 20, 21 and 22* (London, 1823), 258.

[7] John Richardson, *Arctic Ordeal: The Journal of John Richardson, Surgeon-Naturalist with Franklin, 1820–1822*, ed. C. Stuart Houston (Kingston, ON, 1984), 148.

[8] *Illustrated London News*, 1 October 1859, 316.

[9] Cavell, 'Lady Lucy Berry', 132; Bernard Smith, *Imagining the Pacific in the Wake of the Cook Voyages* (New Haven, CT, 1982), 234.

further created an Arctic narrative intimately tied to a God-given empire. Even through disaster and failure, the Christian narrative continued, as the faithful hero faced a noble end in pursuit of a greater cause.

However, the CMS did not enter the Arctic through exploration. It was invited into the territory by the Hudson's Bay Company (HBC), the chartered company that controlled the North American fur trade until the late nineteenth century. From its inception at the end of the seventeenth century, the HBC held a monopoly over western North America and acted as the imperial agent there.[10] The company officially established a British presence in the region, but its rule was based on economic self-interest, not on larger imperial initiatives. The HBC was not interested in providential expansion, nor in the growing humanitarian concern for imperial populations during the early nineteenth century; it was often criticized for its lukewarm attachment to imperial ideals and poor treatment of indigenous people.[11] The HBC faced particularly harsh criticism for its role in Arctic exploration. The company had undertaken massive exploratory endeavours throughout northern Canada but made a great effort to keep its findings secret, afraid that its commercial interests could be compromised.[12] The HBC had also publicly refused to assist various Arctic expeditions in their missions, citing its lack of suitable resources.[13]

There were also concerns over the HBC's humanitarian record; the Christian public saw the company as having a duty to spread the blessings and benefits of Christianity and British civilization to local indigenous people and it was perceived, correctly, as not doing so.[14] Concerned over the backlash aimed at the East India Company during the renewal of its charter in 1813, and pressured by a number of

---

[10] John Galbraith, *The Hudson's Bay Company as an Imperial Factor, 1821–1869* (New York, 1977), 3.

[11] A. K. Isbister, *A Few Words on the Hudson's Bay Company* (London, 1846), 1; A. A. Den Otter, *Civilizing the Wilderness: Culture and Nature in Pre-Confederation Canada and Rupert's Land* (Edmonton, AB, 2012), 187.

[12] Adriana Craciun, *Writing Arctic Disaster: Authorship and Exploration* (Cambridge, 2016), 134–7; Theodore Karamanski, *The Fur Trade and Exploration: Opening the Far Northwest, 1821–1852* (Vancouver, BC, 1983), 10.

[13] Fergus Fleming, *Barrow's Boys* (London, 2001), 125.

[14] Stewart J. Brown, *Providence and Empire: Religion, Politics and Society in the United Kingdom, 1815–1914* (Harlow, 2008), 196; *Report of the Select Committee on Aboriginal Tribes* (London, 1837), 1–2.

prominent evangelicals on its board, the HBC administration responded in 1820 by inviting the CMS to establish a mission at Red River.[15] Ostensibly, this was intended as a mission for indigenous people, but in reality the HBC wanted the CMS to serve the retired HBC employees and their families living there, as a token Christian presence.[16] At the same time, the HBC allowed Roman Catholic priests from Quebec at Red River under the same assumption; these priests were subsequently replaced by a French religious order, the Oblates of Mary Immaculate (OMI), in 1845.[17]

Whatever the HBC's intention, the evangelism of indigenous people was the primary goal of both the CMS and the OMI.[18] Both had expanded beyond Red River by mid-century and continued to extend their operations, establishing missions throughout western and northern Canada. However, while all areas were seen as being worthy of evangelism, the north was the real prize and, by 1850, both organizations were poised to establish themselves in the Athabasca-Mackenzie and Yukon River watersheds and on the Hudson Bay coast.

The Arctic had been at the forefront of the missionary imagination since the early 1820s.[19] The successful evangelism of the north was consistently presented as the primary goal of both the CMS and the OMI. As a remote and inaccessible region, viewed by many as the very edge of empire, evangelism in that area was given clear mandate through Christ's commandment to spread the gospel to 'the uttermost parts of the earth' (Acts 1: 8 KJV). Designated 'the Ultima Thule … of Missionary Enterprise'[20] by William Carpenter Bompas, then Anglican bishop of Athabasca, who had been a CMS

[15] CMSA, C/C1/M1, Benjamin Harrison to CMS Committee, [1821]; Andrew Colvile to George Simpson, 11 March 1824, in Frederick Merk, ed., *Fur Trade and Empire: George Simpson's Journal, 1824–1825* (Oxford, 1931), 205; Penelope Carson, 'An Imperial Dilemma: The Propagation of Christianity in Early Colonial India', *JICH* 18 (1900), 169–90, at 179.
[16] Winnipeg, Archives of Manitoba, Hudson's Bay Company Archives [hereafter: HBCA], A.1/52, London Committee minutes, 13 October 1819.
[17] Raymond Huel, *Proclaiming the Gospel to the Indians and the Métis* (Edmonton, AB, 1996), 16–17.
[18] John Webster Grant, *The Moon of Wintertime: Missionaries and the Indians of Canada in Encounter since 1534* (Toronto, ON, 1984), 100.
[19] Joseph-Octave Plessis to Canadian clergy, 29 March 1818, in Grace Lee Nute, *Documents relating to the Northwest Missions, 1815–1827* (St Paul, MN, 1942), 39; CMSA, C/C1/M1, John West to HBC Secretary, 29 August 1823.
[20] William Bompas, *The Diocese of Mackenzie River* (London, 1888), 106.

missionary since 1865, success there represented, for missionaries, the great triumph of the Christian gospel in the furthest reaches of the globe.[21]

Both organizations entered the Athabasca-Mackenzie watershed in the 1850s and from there began what has been characterized by historian John Webster Grant as 'the race for the northern sea'.[22] Their initial period of expansion throughout the 1850s and 1860s resulted in the CMS and OMI competing for an audience amongst Canada's northern indigenous people.[23] It also resulted in the establishment and construction of mission stations as bases from which to work and to assert a presence in the region. Although these generally began as single structures from which all mission activities were performed, they gradually expanded to multi-building complexes containing houses, schools, churches and auxiliary buildings.[24]

For the CMS, the expansion of its northern operations was closely linked to the expansion and consolidation of Britain's sphere of influence in the far north. Christianity was often regarded as the forerunner of empire and, although explorers had already claimed the region, missionaries could establish themselves permanently and extend the benefits of empire to its inhabitants through programmes of conversion and civilization, making local people Christian citizens.[25] Furthermore, the CMS had developed an often fraught relationship with colonial authorities elsewhere due to their perceived bias against Christianity and humanitarian concerns.[26] But in the far north, while the CMS was at odds with the HBC, the company was consistently viewed as a poor imperial agent which failed to extend imperial benefits to non-Europeans; as a result, the CMS took on that role itself.[27] Unlike its commercial counterpart, the CMS provided a tangible representation of British morality and ideology that

[21] David Anderson, *The Gospel in the Regions Beyond* (London, 1874), 12.
[22] Grant, *Wintertime*, 96.
[23] Robert Choquette, *The Oblate Assault on Canada's Northwest* (Ottawa, ON, 1995), 126; Craig Mishler, 'Missionaries in Collision: Anglicans and Oblates among the Gwich'in, 1861–65', *Arctic* 43 (1990), 121–6, at 121.
[24] Joan Mackinnon, 'Oblate House Chapels in the Diocese of Athabasca-Mackenzie', *Western Oblate Studies* 2 (1992), 219–30.
[25] John Barker, 'Where the Missionary Frontier Ran Ahead of Empire', in Norman Etherington, ed., *Missions and Empire* (Oxford, 2005), 86–106, at 86; 'Recent Intelligence: North-West America', *Church Missionary Intelligencer* 1 (1849–50), 178.
[26] Brian Stanley, *The Bible and the Flag: Protestant Missions and British Imperialism in the Nineteenth and Twentieth Centuries* (Leicester, 1990), 98.
[27] David Anderson, *Britain's Answer to the Nations* (London, 1857), 10–11, 27–8.

coalesced with wider humanitarian concerns and supported the belief that the extension of Christianity was a vital aspect of the providential expansion of empire and a duty of its agents.[28]

Conflict between the agendas of the CMS and imperial expansion often arose, due to concerns over settlement and its impact on indigenous people, but this was not the case in the Arctic, where it was clear that settlement of the region was not a priority. The 1858 Select Committee Report on the HBC's position in the territory firmly established that settlement was neither expected nor encouraged.[29] When unexpected settlement did arise, in the 1886 Fortymile gold rush and the following Klondike strike, the CMS turned to governmental authorities, in this case the Canadian government, as natural allies in its aim of consolidating British influence and values in the face of commercial activity, demonstrating a belief in close ties between the missions of the Church and the colonial authorities of the wider British world.[30]

The imbedded Christian narrative of Arctic exploration also strengthened the CMS's commitment to its northern missions; David Anderson, the first bishop of Rupert's Land, was adamant as to the connections between the two endeavours and pushed for the CMS to enter the region, citing the need to bring the gospel to the edges of Britain's sphere of influence.[31] Anderson, while not a member of the CMS, shared the society's views on mission and its role in the expansion of empire. Members of the CMS, including secretary Henry Venn, also frequently discussed mission and exploration as interconnected aspects of the providential expansion of the British empire throughout the nineteenth century, including when they discussed the Arctic.[32] While God was seen as allowing Britain's sphere of influence to expand through the efforts of godly explorers, such as Franklin, it was the duty of missionaries to extend the benefits of Christianity to the inhabitants of newly opened territories. For missionaries, however, mission was the more important endeavour.

---

[28] Aborigines Protection Society, *Canada West and the Hudson's Bay Company* (London, 1836), i; W. K., 'The True Strength of Empires: A Lesson from History', *Church Missionary Intelligencer* 1 (1849–50), 51–2.

[29] *Report from the Select Committee on the Hudson's Bay Company* (London, 1857), 150–2.

[30] Ottawa, Library and Archives Canada, RG10, vol. 3906, file 105378, Bompas to Thomas Daly, 5 June 1894.

[31] Anderson, *Answer*, 19.

[32] Venn (1860), in Eugene Stock, *The History of the Church Missionary Society: Its Environment, its Men and its Work*, 4 vols (London, 1899), 2: 331.

For example, the Revd Arthur Lewis remarked: 'Arctic exploration seeks always to claim Christian sympathy … . The very heart of the nation becomes stirred with the exploits of Franklin, McClintock or Nansen. But these things … leave out of sight the greatest of all human projects, the evangelization of the heathen.'[33]

The CMS also saw itself as a representative of Britain in opposition to the French Catholic OMI, which was viewed as essentially foreign and exceedingly hostile, an opinion shared by some in the HBC.[34] The competition between these two organizations, although superficially denominational, ran deeper, reflecting the larger meta-narrative of British and French hostility, where Catholic priests represented French republican values; the OMI's ultramontane outlook placed them under increased suspicion due to their allegiance to papal authority which they clearly felt overrode national considerations.[35] Practice showed that the OMI were not hostile to British interests, but their identity as a French Catholic organization placed them firmly in opposition to the CMS, which believed itself to be the defender of British Protestant values and interests in the Arctic.

Missionary expansion ultimately resulted in the growth of mission stations throughout the north. These provided both practical and symbolic spaces for the CMS, playing a vital role in the dissemination of Christianity and the consolidation of British influence over the region. Buildings, for the CMS, fulfilled multiple roles in the missions, replicating British forms in a foreign landscape and, by extension, the religious and cultural ideology of the wider imperial project. At their most basic, these spaces provided necessary infrastructure for doing mission work.[36] Most evidently, churches were constructed for worship space, introducing people to the liturgical and theological norms of the Church of England. However, mission stations also contained other vital structures, including schools for education and catechism, basic medical facilities, a house for the missionary and agricultural buildings for subsistence. The mission was also a permanent Christian centre where indigenous people could gather

---

[33] Arthur Lewis, *The Life and Work of E. J. Peck* (New York, 1904), 315.

[34] Archives of Manitoba, MG12–E1, Bompas to Lt-Governor John Schultz, 3 June 1892; Glyndwr Williams, *London Correspondence Inward from Sir George Simpson* (London, 1973), 103.

[35] Martha McCarthy, *From the Great River to the Ends of the Earth: Oblates Missions to the Dene, 1847–1921* (Edmonton, AB, 1995), 53.

[36] CMSA, C/C1/O42/11, William Mason to the CMS, 11 September 1857.

to meet the missionary and be instructed in the CMS's message.[37] In remote missions with little contact and support from the outside world, these spaces were vital in ensuring the missionary's success and even survival.

However, these structures also served other purposes. Beyond their practical uses, they served to mark space, to inculcate British values and to differentiate the CMS from the HBC and the OMI, all of which served to strengthen Britain's claim to the land and its inhabitants. Most obviously, these structures demonstrated the CMS's presence, serving as a 'landmark of Christianity in a vast field of heathenism'.[38] The mission buildings, particularly churches, which were often stylistically distinctive and larger than many of the other buildings throughout northern Canada, were a clear indication that Christianity had arrived in the land, a function of architecture which missionaries consistently and explicitly recognized in a territory with limited permanent physical infrastructure. Bompas, for example, as bishop of Athabasca, was very clear that

> ... the house of God is the chief visible sign which we are still allowed to retain God's presence among us and I take it to be of great importance that the heathen should be reminded by this constant memorial before their eyes that the introduction of Christianity into their country is a reality and more than a mere tale.[39]

Bompas regarded architecture as a very tangible representations of the Church's evangelistic mission and encouraged his clergy to erect new buildings to assist in the permanent establishment of the CMS in the north and to solidify its presence there. The emphasis Bompas placed on marking the landscape through building was consistently reiterated, particularly by his fellow bishop, Anderson, who drew clear connections between buildings and Christianity's recognized presence.[40]

The presence of Christianity correlated directly to the presence of empire and, as a result, buildings were also able to demonstrate

---

[37] CMSA, C/C1/O39/31, William West Kirkby to the CMS, 18 June 1863.
[38] John West, *The Substance of a Journal during a Residence at the Red River Settlement* (London, 1824), 27.
[39] William Bompas, 'Address at the First Synod of the Diocese of Athabasca', in H. A. Cody, *An Apostle of the North: Memoirs of Bishop W. C. Bompas* (New York, 1908), 185.
[40] CMSA, C/C1/OE2/1/9, Anderson to Henry Venn, 9 August 1850.

imperial influence in the region. Anderson was very explicit in this recognition. In 1857, he addressed a meeting of the CMS in London:

> Ours is a country which has been opened so far that although we are not able to penetrate into the thousands and thousands of miles that are opened to our view, ... it is well for us to guard the lines .... . That line being strengthened, not with bulwarks of earth, but with church after church, so as to mark the British boundary from the Red River to Lake Winnipeg, stretching westwards as far as we are permitted to go.[41]

For Anderson, architecture played a definitive role in the demarcation of British territory and, in North America, it was the Church whose architecture answered that need. It was particularly important when placed in contrast with the buildings of the HBC.

Since its inception at the end of the seventeenth century, the HBC had developed a wide network of posts beginning on the Hudson Bay coast and eventually extending into the interior.[42] These posts contained vital buildings for the fur trade, including housing for employees, storage areas and work spaces. For the CMS, these buildings also represented the commercial proto-empire of the HBC and its poor moral influence on the country. As a result, the CMS attempted to separate itself from the HBC through its use of space. Although many CMS buildings were stylistically very similar to those of the company, the use of the Gothic Revival style, particularly in church building, denoted a clear material separation. This style, which was used in Britain and throughout its empire to communicate the presence of Britishness and of Christianity, reinforced the separateness of the CMS from its commercial counterparts and set it as an alternative, more benign British representative, one which it believed more fully represented the empire's greater purpose.[43]

In particular, the style of church buildings was connected to the CMS's role as a missionary arm of the established Church.[44] In the northern mission field where the only missionary organizations were

[41] Anderson, in Stock, *History*, 2: 322.
[42] Harold Innis, *The Fur Trade in Canada* (Toronto, ON, 1970), 119–20.
[43] G. A. Bremner, *Imperial Gothic: Religious Architecture and High Anglican Culture in the British Empire, c.1840–1870* (New Haven, CT, 2013), 200–4.
[44] T. E. Yates, *Venn and Victorian Bishops Abroad: The Missionary Policies of Henry Venn and their Repercussions upon the Anglican Episcopate of the Colonial Period, 1841–1972* (Uppsala and London, 1978), 98.

the English CMS and the French OMI, the Gothic style was seen by the CMS as reflecting the heritage of the Church of England and as enabling its liturgical traditions, allowing architecture to represent through style, historical association and ritual the established Church and its connection to the state. Part of the reason for this was that the Oblates often built in a Classical style which reflected church construction practice in French Canada; denominational differences in architectural style, therefore, were seen to reflect national differences, even though the Gothic style was pervasive across denominational boundaries and the CMS did not adhere to the style as dogmatically as, for example, its high Anglican counterparts elsewhere. It was also seen as particularly suited to worship because Gothic buildings were regarded as looking Christian and as reflecting the beliefs proclaimed within them. The CMS often expressed concern over the ability of northern architecture to fulfil the role of worship space in the local context, especially when faced with less than ideal circumstances for the erection of what it deemed to be English buildings. For example, when John Horden arrived at Moose Factory in 1851, there was already a church in place from an earlier, defunct Methodist mission; he was concerned that it did not allow for Anglican liturgy, nor did it reflect how a building of the established Church should look, noting that it was 'not much like that of a place of worship associated with the Church of England'.[45] His concerns were both liturgical and national, reflecting a need to articulate the CMS's wider mission through architectural forms. The Wesleyan church was replaced with a new Gothic building, completed in 1864 (Fig. 1).

To reinforce the dichotomy between them, the CMS also desired to distance itself physically from the HBC. The vast majority of CMS missions were constructed adjacent to HBC posts, where indigenous people gathered to trade; this made them easy to access.[46] However, the ultimate goal of the CMS was for a complete separation, to disentangle itself from the perceived moral corruptness of the post.[47] It found quickly that this was not realistic, owing to the difficulties in supplying the missions and the CMS's need for assistance from HBC personnel. The Revd Robert Hunt remarked: 'they [the HBC] could

[45] CMSA, C/C1/O33/17A, John Horden to Hector Strath, 1 September 1854.
[46] Huel, *Proclaiming*, 34–5.
[47] 'Metlakahtla and the North Pacific Mission', *Church Missionary Gleaner* 8 (1881), 109–20, at 113.

Figure 1. St. Thomas's Church, Moose Factory, 1856–64, completed 1884. Author's photograph.

probably disable you simply by letting you alone'.[48] His assessment was accurate; the CMS was unable to dissociate its missions from HBC posts, with the exception of Metlakatla in British Columbia and, to a lesser extent, Stanley Mission at Lac la Ronge.[49] Instead, the CMS attempted to create a physical separation through grouping its buildings as a distinctive unit away from the main HBC complexes (Fig. 2). Although a minor separation, it reinforced the differences between the two agencies through physical distance and created clear Christian spaces, where indigenous people could gather free of the influence of the HBC.[50]

Architecture also served to inculcate Christian values and, by extension, the perceived benefits of Christianity, to which many believed residents of British holdings had a right and that Britain's agents had a duty to extend. Mission stations, therefore, were areas where the theoretical benefits of the Christian world could be bestowed upon indigenous people. These included the direct benefit of Christian belief, taught through church and school.

[48] CMSA, C/C1/O34/66, Robert Hunt, Journal, August 1853.
[49] CMSA, C/C2/O8/63A, William Duncan to D. David, May 1875.
[50] CMSA, C/C1/O39/67, William West Kirkby, Journal, 9 June 1864.

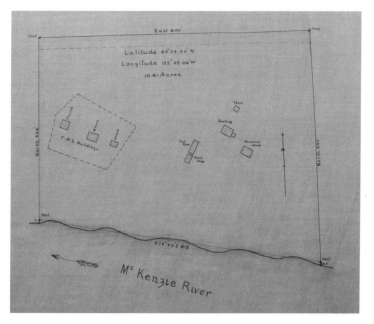

Figure 2. Plan of Fort Norman, Mackenzie River, Northwest Territories, [1898]. Winnipeg, Hudson's Bay Company Archives, G.1/315.

However, auxiliary to this were moral values and codes of behaviour and conduct known as 'civilization', which, in the words of Dandeson Coates (CMS secretary 1830–46), was 'intended to mean the moral and social improvement of a people'.[51] In a practical sense, 'civilization' involved the introduction of a sedentary, agricultural lifestyle to a non-sedentary culture and the creation of settlements where God could be worshipped and work could be done.[52]

These ideas could be implemented through the creation of a sedentary Christian population engaged in farming, which was seen as a manifestation of the need to engage in toil in order to satisfy God and demonstrate commitment to Christianity, in opposition to traditional indigenous life.[53] Architecturally, this translated into

[51] Dandeson Coates et al., *Christianity as a Means of Civilization* (London, 1837), 99.

[52] CMSA, C/C1/M1, William Cockran, Journal, 20 October 1820.

[53] Mark Francis, 'The "Civilizing" of Indigenous People in Nineteenth Century Canada', *Journal of World History* 9 (1998), 51–87, at 71.

Figure 3. Hay River, late nineteenth century. Toronto, Anglican Church of Canada General Synod Archives, P7559–73.

the construction of permanent houses, schools, worship spaces and agricultural establishments. In the southern part of the CMS mission in North America, model mission farms were set up in order to demonstrate to indigenous people the benefits of agriculture and Christianity and to assist in the transformation of their lifestyle to an idealized pastoral one, consistent with the CMS's general belief that it should bring the temporal benefits of empire to indigenous people alongside the spiritual ones.[54] Large-scale agriculture was not realistic for some northern missions where climate made it unfeasible, but in areas such as Hay River (Fig. 3), where the soil and climate could support limited crop development, these strategies were enacted quickly in order to promote the adoption of what was presented as the Christian world and its way of life. Erected as the initial aspect of agricultural settlements, missionaries thus saw buildings as directly bringing the benefits of Christian empire to their indigenous flock. William Mason at York Factory wrote in 1857: 'I trust when we get up our Church and School, the Station will be made a more extensive blessing to the heathen around us',[55] a very explicit recognition of the perceived role of buildings in the extension of the providential empire

[54] CMSA, C/C1/M2, Report on the State of Morality and Education at the Red River Settlement, 1835.
[55] CMSA, C/C1/O42/14, Mason to J. Myrie Holl, 12 September 1857.

and of its provision for its inhabitants, enacted through missionary agents.

Buildings not only demonstrated how Christians could and should live, but were understood as a tool of communication, both in their replication of British architectural forms and through their function. Edmund Peck at Little Whale River saw his new church, erected in 1879, in much this way. He wrote: 'You know how necessary it is to have a proper place wherein to worship God … . As the church will be visible to all, it will be a silent witness to God. The Eskimos will understand our desires for their welfare far better than if mere words were used.'[56]

Here too, the desires of which he spoke were for the transmission of Christianity itself and for civilization: effectively the complete re-ordering of indigenous life such that 'the Eskimos' might reap the benefits of belonging to a benevolent empire. Buildings inherently redefined space, reordering architectural norms towards European ones as opposed to indigenous ones. By extension, these buildings attempted to replace the temporal and spiritual world of northern communities through the activities that took place in them and the cultural associations of the structures themselves.

The CMS did not believe that these values could be transmitted or bestowed through HBC buildings, largely because the company's infrastructure encouraged an economic and social system oriented towards a more traditional trapping lifestyle with aims incompati-ble with those of the CMS.[57] The CMS and its buildings, there-fore, were the 'civilized' counterparts of the 'uncivilized' HBC, repre-senting a progressive and positive Christian empire. HBC buildings would simply not suffice as the infrastructure of empire because they were not 'civilized'. At Churchill, the Revd William West Kirkby explained that a church was:

> … much needed for the Indians and Esquimaux used to have to meet in one of the houses or fur stores, and my four months experience of this showed me how very undesirable it was. Fancy a little church at this, *the last place in the world*, for there is not another civilized dwelling between this and the North Pole.[58]

[56] CMSA, C/C1/O49/14, Edmund Peck to Henry Wright, 20 December 1879.
[57] CMSA, C/C1/O34/72, Robert Hunt, Report, 1853.
[58] William West Kirkby, 'Far away in the Cold', *The Net* (1874), 33–8, at 37.

However, the CMS did not only aim to separate itself from the HBC, but also from the OMI, thus reinforcing the British religion over that of France. It is telling that Protestantism and Catholicism were referred to respectively as the English and French religions, and the two organizations saw themselves in conflict across national as well as religious lines.[59] By building structures, the CMS claimed the land for Protestant Britain; concerned about Catholic construction projects, the CMS often felt compelled to build missions and expand existing ones specifically to counteract the OMI.[60] It also aimed to reinforce difference through style and detail, in the belief that architecture could influence character as well as liturgical and theological identity.[61] While both used the Gothic style, particularly for churches, they employed it differently. Whilst usually employing Classical forms, the OMI often used elaborate Gothic-style decoration consistent with contemporary Catholic visual culture, notably in the Church of Our Lady of Good Hope (Fig. 4). The CMS saw the OMI as demonstrating the excesses of popery; in contrast, its structures used Gothic detail in a simpler and more subdued manner, which it saw as representing a strong and stoic Protestantism, consistent with British worship and character.[62]

The CMS did not aim only to transform the north's indigenous people, but also its landscape. The north was seen in popular imagination as the ultimate wilderness, representing sin, danger and the unbridled forces of nature, reflected in the architecture of indigenous people.[63] In line with nineteenth-century assumptions that architecture was reflective of the people and society that built it, mission architecture represented the order of the wider British world, brought about through a positive administration, 'civilized' habits and Christianity, as opposed to 'wild' and 'heathen' indigenous buildings.[64]

---

[59] George Holmes, 31 December 1891, in *Extracts from the Annual Letters of Missionaries* (1892–3), 180–3, at 181; CMSA, C/C1/O35/58, James Hunter to Venn, 23 August 1858.

[60] Holmes, 29 December 1887, in *Annual Letters* (1887–8), 281–4, at 282.

[61] CMSA, C/C1/O39/78, Kirkby, Journal, 1 November 1873.

[62] CMSA, C/C1/O10/3, Bompas to Venn, 6 November 1865.

[63] George Stankey, 'Beyond the Campfire's Light: The Historical Roots of the Wilderness Concept', *Natural Resources Journal* 29 (1989), 9–24, at 10–11.

[64] See, for example, A. W. N. Pugin, *Contrasts, or a Parallel between the Noble Edifices of the Middle Ages and Corresponding Buildings of the Present Day* (London, 1836), 2; Susan Neylan, *The Heavens are Changing: Nineteenth-Century Protestant Missions and Tsimshian Christianity* (Montreal, QC, 2003), 236.

311

Figure 4. Church of Our Lady of Good Hope, Fort Good Hope, 1865–85. Author's photograph.

Therefore, the erection of buildings and, where possible, the plough-ing of fields could transform a landscape from one that was controlled by, and belonged to, the indigenous world to one administered and ordered by the British one. The transformation of the landscape through infrastructure development demarcated the land as British-controlled territory through the changing of its natural state and the kinds of infrastructure it supported.

The erection of buildings to serve this purpose was also under-taken in Arctic exploratory missions. Such buildings can be traced back as early as Martin Frobisher, the English Arctic explorer whose erection of a stone cottage on Kodlurnarn Island in 1578 was praised as a glowing reproduction of Elizabethan life.[65] Nineteenth-century expeditions over-wintering in the Arctic regularly erected buildings on the ice in an attempt to recreate Victorian life, including one dur-ing Edward Belcher's 1853–4 expedition named 'the Crystal Palace' after the London landmark.[66] Explorers also expressed a desire to

[65] George Best, *The Three Voyages of Martin Frobisher: In Search of a Passage to Cathaia and India by the North-west, A.D. 1576–8*, ed. Richard Collinson, Hakluyt Society 38 (London, 1867), 272.
[66] Edward Belcher, *The Last of the Arctic Voyages* (London, 1855), 64.

transform the landscape into something more closely related to those of Britain, or at least to find connections between them, such as in the direct comparison made by members of Franklin's 1819–22 Coppermine expedition between the Barren Lands north of Great Slave Lake and the English Lake District.[67] Despite their interest, however, exploratory missions did not have the permanence or the mandate to enact this transformation from the wild and indigenous world to the ordered and British one, but missionaries did, and they took control of the northern environment for God and empire through the erection of buildings and the ploughing of fields, which they believed would be both long-lasting and transformative.

Certainly this ideal was impossible to enact everywhere, especially in the High Arctic, where the landscape and environment effectively prevented large-scale building projects. Missionaries who worked there nevertheless looked to the ordered agricultural mission station as the ultimate goal, and constructed as much as was possible.[68] These actions were certainly impractical, but architecture was not simply about creating a space for mission work. In the Canadian north, it was embedded within a larger set of cultural values and the assumption that the erection of Christian structures could consolidate British imperial influence in the far north. Building on a constructed Christian narrative that painted the far north as a place where the heroic Christian, be he missionary or explorer, could claim the region for God and empire, mission stations could, in the words of Anderson, 'mark the British boundary' and lay claim to a land where settlers and larger administrative structures could not be transplanted. Blessed by a providential empire, it was the duty of Britain to bring the benefits of imperial rule to its citizens and, in the north, the CMS acted as its agent, using architecture to mark the land, to inculcate values and ideals and to transform the environment from a hostile, unknown territory into a firmly held British possession.

[67] Robert Hood, *To the Arctic by Canoe: The Journals and Paintings of Robert Hood*, ed. C. Stuart Houston (Montreal, QC, 1974), 145.
[68] CMSA, G1/C1/O/1909/73, Peck, Journal, 1909.

Anglican Emigrant Chaplaincy in the British Empire and Beyond, *c.*1840–1900

Rowan Strong*

Murdoch University

In the 1840s the Church of England, through the agency of the Society for the Propagation of the Gospel (SPG) and the Society for Promoting Christian Knowledge (SPCK), established an official chaplaincy to emigrants leaving from British ports. The chaplaincy lasted throughout the rest of the nineteenth century. It was revitalized in the 1880s under the direction of the SPCK in response to a surge in emigration from Britain to the colonies. This article examines the imperial attitudes of Anglicans involved in this chaplaincy network, focusing on those of the 1880s and 1890s, the period of high imperialism in Britain. It compares these late nineteenth-century outlooks with those of Anglicans in the emigrant chaplaincy of the 1840s, in order to discern changes and continuities in Anglican imperialism in nineteenth-century Britain. It finds that, in contrast to the imperialist attitudes prevalent in Britain during the late nineteenth century, Anglicans in this chaplaincy network focused more on the ecclesiastical and pastoral dimensions of their work. Indeed, pro-imperial attitudes, though present, were remarkably scarce. It was the Church much more than the empire which mattered to these Anglicans, notwithstanding their direct involvement with the British empire.

In December 1881, the archbishop of Canterbury sent to *The Times* and other newspapers a circular letter addressed to Anglicans about British emigration. Archibald Tait drew attention to the increase in the scale of emigration, with nearly 314,000 emigrants leaving British ports in the first nine months of that year, of whom nearly 160,000 were British subjects. Tait proposed 'that a systematic endeavour' should be made for 'the Christian welfare of the vast population which is continually passing westward from our shore' to the United States and to British colonies. He mentioned that this proposal was in accordance with the recommendations of the

* School of Arts, Murdoch University, South St, Perth, WA 6150, Australia. E-mail: R.Strong@murdoch.edu.au.

Studies in Church History 54 (2018) 314–327   © Ecclesiastical History Society 2018
doi: 10.1017/stc.2017.17

most recent Lambeth Conference (the second such pan-Anglican episcopal conference, which had taken place in 1878), and that a joint committee of the Society for the Propagation of the Gospel (SPG) and Society for Promoting Christian Knowledge (SPCK) had been formed with a view to implementing the conference's three proposals: to provide parish clergy with accurate information about emigration destinations, and particularly about their religious and educational resources; to publish cheap handbooks for emigrants about the colonies and the United States; and to make arrangements for the care of emigrants on their arrival, including the provision of commendatory letters from English clergy to their counterparts in the areas emigrants proposed to settle.[1]

As the circular stated, Tait was acting on recommendation 4 of the 1878 Lambeth Conference, which urged clergy to provide commendatory letters to emigrating parishioners. The recommendation concluded:

> And they consider it desirable that the clergy … should carefully instruct them as to the oneness of the Church in its apostolic constitution under its varying organisation and conditions … [they] suggest here the importance of impressing upon our people the extent and geographical distribution of our Churches, and of reminding them that there is now hardly any part of the world where members of our Communion may not find a Church one with their own in faith, order and worship.[2]

As the archbishop's letter intimated, it did not fall unheralded into appropriate Church of England circles, but was part of a revival of that Church's emigrant ministry at the start of the 1880s, a ministry which had begun in the late 1840s through the SPG and the SPCK. Since that beginning, emigrant ministry had been carried on continuously by the SPCK after the SPG relinquished its direct participation in the 1850s in favour of the slightly older society, although it

[1] 'The Church and Emigration', *The Times*, 22 December 1881, 6, online at: <http://www.gale.com/c/the-times-digital-archive>, accessed 7 July 2016.

[2] 'Recommendation 4: Union among the Churches of the Anglican Communion – Encyclical Letter 1.8: Of Commendatory Letters', online at the Anglican Communion website: <http://www.anglicancommunion.org/resources/document-library/lambeth-conference/1878/recommendation-4-union-among-the-churches-of-the-anglican-communion-encyclical-letter-18-of-commendatory-letters?author=Lambeth+Conference&year=1878>, accessed 7 July 2016.

Rowan Strong

continued to jointly fund this ministry. In June 1881, a combined committee of both societies had been formed to consider a draft of the archbishop's intended letter. The concern of the archbishop and the committee was that emigrants were leaving without adequate information about their colonial destinations, and particularly about the Church in those colonies. As a result they joined other denominations, or none. 'Many of the emigrants seem to leave without any information or advice as to the means of grace to be found in the country to which they are going, and are left to drift into whatever religious body may first offer itself to them in their new home, or perhaps to drift away from all religion.' The committee resolved to request that the SPCK provide up to £100 towards the expense of circulating the archbishop's letter.[3]

The lasting result of this 1880s Church of England initiative towards ministry for emigrants leaving Britain for settlement colonies of the British empire was the formation of an Emigration Committee by the SPCK, which took over the remnants of the earlier emigration work of the two societies and expanded it. The initial labour of the committee was the compiling and publication of handbooks for emigrants. However, the longer-term work was the oversight of a network of emigrant chaplains based in British and colonial ports; with other chaplains travelling on emigrant ships, either as emigrants themselves, or (on the shorter run across the Atlantic to Quebec) as British-based chaplains making repeated journeys. The network was overseen by a principal emigrant chaplain who was based in Liverpool, as the port with the largest scale of emigration. The Revd John Bridger was a member of the Emigration Committee and reported directly to it. The work clearly mattered to the Church, enough to invest considerable resources of organization and labour into it, without government funding. As a self-funded organization, the Anglican emigration chaplaincy stands in contrast to the characteristic synthesis of government-subsidized private bodies that Andrew Thompson finds so newly prominent in these decades.[4]

Anglican support for emigration into the British empire was a major undertaking by the Church of England which had grown from limited beginnings in the 1840s into a large-scale imperial network,

[3] Cambridge, CUL, SPCK MS A5, 466, SPCK Standing Committee, 13 June 1881.
[4] Andrew S. Thompson, *Imperial Britain: The Empire in British Politics c.1880–1932* (Harlow, 2000), 155–6.

316

supported by the highest level of its ecclesiastical structure and by one of its most central and well-regarded organizations. The SPCK had been founded in 1698, and by the nineteenth century its principal work was the publication of religious tracts and other religious works. It had a policy of theological moderation that brought it widespread appeal across the divisive Anglican theological spectrum. It also had a history of more direct engagement in foreign and colonial mission. In the eighteenth century the SPCK had been the funding and overseeing partner in the successful German Lutheran mission in southern India,[5] and since the 1840s it had maintained the emigrant ministry in Britain that was now being expanded.

This article seeks to assess the outlooks towards the British empire of the Anglicans directly engaged with it through the emigrant chaplaincy over the six decades of its nineteenth-century existence. Its purpose is to discover those characteristic themes of history – change and continuity – between the 1840s when the chaplaincy first came into existence, and the last two nineteenth-century decades, the period in Britain of high imperialism. For most historians, the Church of England, and its colonial offshoots, were unquestionably at the forefront of British imperialist sentiment and the export of British nationalism. Hilary Carey sees the SPCK as one of the first missionary organizations to infuse its pietistic language with that of nationalism.[6] J. C. D. Clark and Carl Bridenhaugh have seen an enthusiastically imperialist SPG in the eighteenth century; a view repeated for the same organization in the nineteenth century by James Greenlee and Charles Johnson.[7] Carey provides persuasive evidence that Anglican emigration societies in the late nineteenth century, particularly the Church Emigration Society (founded in 1886), propounded a thoroughly patriotic view of emigration as strengthening the Britishness of empire.[8] Other historians who see the emigration work of Anglicans or of the Church of England as the export of Britishness

---

[5] Robert Eric Frykenberg, *Christianity in India: From Beginnings to the Present* (Oxford, 2008), 145, 151, 154, 212–13, 215, 250.

[6] Hilary M. Carey, *God's Empire: Religion and Colonialism in the British World, c.1801–1908* (Cambridge, 2011), 58, 309–10.

[7] J. C. D. Clark, *Language of Liberty 1660–1832: Political Discourse and Social Dynamics in the Anglo-American World* (Cambridge, 1994), 173; Carl Bridenbaugh, *Mitre and Sceptre: Transatlantic Faiths, Ideas, Personalities, and Politics, 1689–1775* (New York, 1965); James G. Greenlee and Charles M. Johnson, *Good Citizens: British Missionaries and Imperial States, 1870–1914* (Montreal, QC, 1999), 149.

[8] Carey, *God's Empire*, 336–7.

or Englishness include Marjory Harper and Stephen Constantine.[9] John Darwin views the imperial transmission of a moral British culture as being the work of British clergy of all denominations, but particularly Anglicans, among settler and expatriate communities well into the twentieth century.[10] Most recently, the careful work of Joseph Hardwick has detailed some of the ways in which Anglican clergy and laity in settler colonies went about this business of creating a thoroughly British empire.[11]

This article does not seek to overturn this interpretation of Anglican engagement with the British empire as the export of British culture; the evidence, including that offered in some of my own work, is too obvious for that. However, I do want to suggest that these interpretations are too reductionist and monochrome, and that there is another, ecclesiastical, dimension to Anglican imperial engagement. An interpretation that seeks to highlight the importance of Christian belief and theology, including ecclesiology, as a major dimension for Christian engagement with the world has long put my work in the company of significant scholars who have made major contributions to the history of Christianity and the British Empire, including Brian Stanley, who began this theological revision of imperial historiography; Robert Frykenberg, who has argued for the inherent power of Christianity in South Asian history as a religion and not just as a vehicle for imperial power; and Hilary Carey and Andrew Porter.[12]

I have already undertaken assessments of the imperial viewpoints of the Anglicans involved with the emigrant chaplaincy from the 1840s to the 1870s, so the original aspect of this article is the contrast of that period with the 1880s and 1890s.[13] In those earlier studies it

---

[9] Marjory Harper and Stephen Constantine, *Migration and Empire* (Oxford, 2010), 33, 34, 226.
[10] John Darwin, 'Orphans of Empire', in Robert Bickers, ed., *Settlers and Expatriates* (Oxford, 2010), 329–45, at 339–40.
[11] Joseph Hardwick, *An Anglican British World: The Church of England and the Expansion of the Settler Empire, c.1790–1860* (Manchester, 2014).
[12] Brian Stanley, *The Bible and the Flag: Protestant Missions and British Imperialism in the Nineteenth and Twentieth Centuries* (Leicester, 1990); Frykenberg, *Christianity in India*; idem, ed., *Christians and Missionaries in India: Cross-Cultural Communication since 1500, with Special Reference to Caste, Conversion, and Colonialism* (Grand Rapids, MI, 2003); Andrew Porter, *Religion versus Empire? British Protestant Missionaries and Overseas Expansion, 1700–1914* (Manchester, 2004), 6, 10–11. For my own position, see Rowan Strong, *Anglicanism and the British Empire c.1700–1850* (Oxford, 2007), 283–94.
[13] Rowan Strong, 'Globalising British Christianity in the Nineteenth Century: The Imperial Anglican Emigrant Chaplaincy 1846–c.1910', *JICH* 43 (2014), 1–32; idem, 'Pau-

was found that the clergy directly involved in the emigrant chaplaincy were far more concerned with the extension of their church than with the empire. In this ecclesiastical focus they differed markedly from contemporary preachers, both Anglican and non-Anglican. British preachers in this period who did take up the subject of emigration portrayed the masses of steerage emigrants as potential constructors of colonial Britains, and therefore as glue for imperial loyalty; in other words, it was the preached promulgation of that imperial Britishness which the historians mentioned above have identified. In contrast, the emigrant chaplains funded by the SPG and SPCK in this earlier period viewed steerage emigrants simply as people in need, or as travelling Christians who, if they were ministered to with diligence by the church, would form, not an imperial bond but a Christian one, and a future global Christian or Anglican Christianity. It was planting Christianity or the Church of England in colonial settlements that mattered; empire was just a means to that end.

The question to be addressed in this article, therefore, is this: did the balance between Church and empire shift among these Anglicans in emigrant ministry during the decades of high imperialism? Did these Anglicans' sentiments move in favour of British imperialism during this later period? After all, the late Victorian and Edwardian decades are commonly regarded as the peak of imperial sentiment across the swathe of British classes. At one extreme, at a popular level, in the period of the South African War, were those imperialist sentiments we know as jingoism; in more political and intellectual circles, there were the proposals for a greater global imperial Britain associated with Joseph Chamberlain in the 1900s and tariff reform in the form of an imperial preference.[14]

In an earlier article, I pointed to an enthusiastic imperialism being expressed to the SPCK's Emigration Committee from its Anglican Canadian connections in the decades from 1880 to 1910. These included not just Anglican clergy but also Canadian women's organizations in which Anglicans were prominent.[15] The Canadian motif of Christianity, or the Church of England, being an agent for a

---

pers, Pilgrims, Progenitors: Religious Constructions of British Emigration from the 1840s to 1870s', *History* 100 (2015), 302–411.
[14] Richard Price, *An Imperial War and the British Working Class: Working-Class Attitudes and Reactions to the Boer War 1899–1902* (London, 1972), ch. 4; William L. Strauss, *Joseph Chamberlain and the Theory of Imperialism* (New York, 1971), 77–9, ch. 6.
[15] Strong, 'Globalising British Christianity', 20–1.

righteous empire had often been expressed negatively in the Anglican past in the form of anxieties about the debilitating effects of the colonial environment on settlers without adequate means of spiritual life. In this negative construction it was a viewpoint that went back to the beginning of deliberate Anglican engagement with the British empire. It had been frequently expressed by clergy and bishops preaching for the SPG since the beginning of the eighteenth century, and was reiterated in a series of sermons preached in England in the 1850s themed around the empire.[16] It was voiced again by the SPG in its report for 1838, in response to the sharp increase in emigrants to North America, and particularly Canada, in the 1830s: 'this country will be deeply sinful before God, if it permit the dependencies of the empire to grow up in practical atheism'.[17]

Women, including Anglican women, were perhaps particularly attracted to a Christian imperialism in this period because it was argued that this depended particularly upon females for its realization. From 1886 the SPCK worked with the British Women's Emigration Association (BWEA) to send parties of single women to the colonies, under the supervision of a matron, in what were known as 'protected parties'. The parties were organized, and the matrons selected, by the BWEA, and these matrons were paid by the SPCK. The groups were under the authority of a chaplain, if one was available for the voyage.[18] A Christian imperialism similar to that expressed to the SPCK by its Canadian contacts was also evident in the BWEA. That organization had been founded in 1884 as the United Englishwomen's Emigration Association, and was largely controlled by the Hon. Mrs Ellen Joyce of Winchester.[19] She had previously been involved in the emigration department of another female Anglican organization, the Girls' Friendly Society (GFS). Ellen Joyce regarded the safe migration of single women as a sacred duty for the promotion of a Christian empire. As the empire had a spiritual significance it required emigrants who were worthy of it. This spiritual task especially devolved on

[16] Strong, *Anglicanism and the British Empire*, 71–7; idem, 'The Church of England and the British Imperial State: Anglican Metropolitan Sermons of the 1850s', in Hilary M. Carey and John Gascoigne, eds, *Church and State in Old and New Worlds* (Leiden, 2011), 183–205, at 196.
[17] Quoted in Brian Stanley, 'Home Support for Overseas Missions in early Victorian Britain c.1838–1873' (PhD thesis, University of Cambridge, 1979), 81.
[18] CUL, SPCK MS A18/1, 82, SPCK Emigration Committee, 11 March 1886.
[19] Harper and Constantine, *Migration and Empire*, 226.

women as wives and mothers, or potentially so.[20] Female migration was understood by the BWEA as a means of securing the Christian identity of the empire by sending into its overseas territories worthy, moral and devout women who would be the progenitors of the next generations of upright Christian colonial populations.[21] This promulgation of Christian empire through the procreation of women had a eugenic dimension of suitability. Addressing the Winchester GFS, which Joyce described as 'the greatest Society for purity that exists', she told them, 'Emigration is just one of those things in which the doctrine of the "selection of the fittest" must be accepted, and this selection should come from the God-implanted instincts of adventure and enterprise.'[22]

In the period of a more widespread British pro-imperial sentiment during the late nineteenth century, it is thus apparent that a positive view of empire was shared by at least some Anglicans in their emigration network. Emigration of satisfactorily Christian emigrants, particularly women who would be influential as wives and mothers, was a means of linking Britain and her colonial territories, of enhancing the moral fibre of the empire, and of maintaining or boosting its British character. The empire would be held together by an emigrant British Christianity, whose moral framework looked remarkably like the values of the Victorian middle class, the section of British society from which the Anglicans in the emigrant ministry came. The agenda of making the empire more British, what Hardwick has called 'an Anglican British world', was certainly present in this emigrant project.

But was that export of Britishness in the persons of God-fearing Britons all there was to it? Was this Anglican project imperialist in the sense that it viewed the British empire uncritically as a jolly good thing? After all, British settler colonies remained the chaplaincy's major preoccupation, and these emigrant destinations would not have existed but for imperial conquest and acquisition.

In contrast to the explicit imperial sentiments expressed by Canadian Anglicans, and by Joyce and the BWEA that the chaplaincy network worked with, such overt and indiscriminate imperialism was

---

[20] Cecillie Swaisland, *Servants and Gentlewomen to the Golden Land: The Emigration of Single Women from Britain to Southern Africa, 1820–1939* (Providence, RI, 1993), 23–4.
[21] Ibid. 24.
[22] [Ellen Joyce], *Emigration: A Paper read at the GFS Winchester Diocesan Conference, Southampton, October 25th 1883* (London, 1884), 1–2.

not replicated in the official ecclesiastical base of the emigrant chaplaincy network or the official circles of the Church of England which supported it. We have already seen that the revival of this Anglican emigrant ministry was catalyzed by Archbishop Tait's response to the resolution of the 1878 Lambeth Conference. A decade later the third Lambeth Conference also paid some attention to British emigrants. The encyclical letter that the conference addressed to the churches of the Anglican Communion contained this section on emigration:

> In our emigrants we have a social link which binds the Churches of the British Islands to the Church of the United States, and to the Churches in the Colonies. No more pertinent question, therefore, could have been suggested for our deliberations than our duty towards this large body of our fellow Christians. It is especially incumbent upon the Church to follow them with the eye of sympathy at every point in their passage from their old home to their new, to exercise a watchful care over them, and to protect them from the dangers, moral and spiritual, which beset their path.[23]

Neither here, nor in the attached list of suggestions from the conference committee on the care of emigrants, nor in Tait's circular letter, was there any mention of empire. The suggestions were directed solely at practical ways in which emigrants could be ministered to at sea, and to encouraging colonial churches to do more for emigrants when they arrived.

In the Emigration Committee's records the only explicit mention of empire, other than that from the two Canadian sources already mentioned, comes in the annual report for 1898. Commenting on over 144,000 British travellers who left that previous year, among which the vast majority were emigrants, the report connected these migrating Britons with empire.

> If each proves himself a true Christian and a consistent Churchman, what a missionary effect his conduct will have! If the majority leave us unspeeded, drift across unshepherded, and arrive unwelcomed, what likelihood is there of that strengthening of the Colonies in moral fibre and true religion, which all true Imperialists must desire?[24]

---

[23] *Conference of Bishops of the Anglican Communion, holden at Lambeth Palace, in July 1888. Encyclical Letter from the Bishops, with the Resolutions and Reports*, Report 7: Care of Emigrants (London, 1888), 113.

[24] CUL, SPCK MS B2/1897–8, 479, SPCK Emigration Committee, July 1898.

Of course, in addition to these few explicit references to the British empire within the emigrant chaplaincy network and its official support, the imperial background to emigration was evidently taken for granted in this whole Anglican project by its attention to British colonies, colonies that would not have existed without imperial expansion by the British.

Nevertheless, the ongoing concern for British emigrants to the United States indicates that the Anglican emigration chaplaincy was not restricted to the empire. The SPCK had spent many years attempting to convince the Episcopal Church in the USA to establish an emigrant chaplaincy in New York, conscious of the myriad of migrants who went there. In March 1883 John Bridger reported to the SPCK Emigration Committee that the Episcopal Church had appointed a chaplain to emigrants in New York, Cornelius L. Twing; but he (Bridger) was having difficulty getting information from the said chaplain to include in the handbook for emigrants to the USA.[25] Clearly, this appointment was ineffective: in 1886 the Emigration Committee listed a number of local clergymen in Canada and the US who were prepared to act as immigrants' chaplains. This included clergy in Portland, Maine, Boston, Baltimore, Philadelphia, Chicago, Pittsburgh, San Francisco, St Paul (Minnesota) and Florida, but there was no mention of New York.[26] In March 1887 Bridger again reported to the committee that nothing about New York had yet been done by the Episcopal Church, and the committee agreed that the archbishop of Canterbury should be asked to raise the matter directly with the presiding bishop of the US Church.[27]

However, in the Emigration Committee's report to the SPCK in July 1887 there was a lengthy extract from the Revd Thomas Drumm, also a medical doctor, who had begun work in Castle Garden, New York. Castle Garden in Manhattan, a round sandstone fort, was the first New York immigration station, and predated Ellis Island as a disembarkation point for US immigrants from 1885 to 1890. Drumm signed cards of commendation to ongoing immigrants as the 'Port Chaplain, Protestant Episcopal Church'; he had offices at Room 227, 22 State Street, New York, and was still doing this work in 1891 when one family's migrant ancestor received such a card from

---

[25] CUL, SPCK MS B2/1882–3, 22, SPCK Emigration Committee, 15 March 1883.
[26] CUL, SPCK MS B2/1885–6, 27, SPCK Emigration Committee, 15 February 1886.
[27] CUL, SPCK MS B2/1886–7, 105, SPCK Emigration Committee, 17 March 1887.

him.[28] Drumm reported to the Emigration Committee that he had been in the work for three months and confined his efforts to seeking out Anglican immigrants. He had set a large sign in a conspicuous situation, advertising his name under the titles of 'Church of England, Church of Ireland, Protestant Episcopal Church of America'. Emigrants venturing towards the sign, he said, in self-deprecating humour, would find 'a little, elderly, clean-shaven, clerically dressed individual' waiting to greet them and provide them with letters of commendation and advice. He described Castle Garden as a 'dreary, desolate, uninviting spot', without any official help or accommodation 'at least for Protestants or Churchmen' (which suggests Catholics may have provided some assistance), and he believed his ministry was worthwhile. Drumm was an efficient and experienced pastor, having served as a parish priest in a number of congregations before taking up this work. He noted in his report that he was hoping to 'purchase or erection of a suitable emigrant lodging-house near the Garden. Our good Bishop's cathedral project may interfere a little with this object, but I hope to accomplish it'.[29]

Notwithstanding Drumm's good work, the New York chaplaincy was still a concern to the Emigration Committee in 1888. In that year they instructed their secretary to write to the bishop of New York and lay the urgency of the need for 'increasing the number of Emigrant Chaplains' before him.[30] So it appears that, although Drumm continued his work, the SPCK was concerned that one chaplain was insufficient for the number of Anglican immigrants flooding through New York.

The committee's minutes point to a proactive change in the institutional development of the New York emigrant chaplaincy occurring in 1898–9. In 1898 the Brotherhood of St Andrew was reported to be doing 'excellent work' in New York. This brotherhood is not mentioned in Peter Anson's classic work on Anglican religious communities in the nineteenth century, but may have been connected to the St Andrew's Waterside Mission, the Anglo-Catholic group which undertook ministry to seamen and emigrants in London.[31] The

[28] 'Family of Richard Perry Radcliffe, James Hegarty', online at: <http://rpradcliffe.com/886.htm>, accessed 17 January 2017.
[29] CUL, SPCK MS B2/1886–7, 17–18, SPCK Emigration Committee.
[30] CUL, SPCK MS B2/1888–9, 150, SPCK Emigration Committee, 1 November 1888.
[31] L. A. G. Strong, *Flying Angel: The Story of the Missions to Seamen* (London, 1956), 32; Maurice Rooke Kingsford, *The Mersey Mission to Seamen 1856–1956* (Abingdon, 1957),

following year the committee noted that a well-resourced mission to immigrants on Ellis Island had finally been established by the Episcopal Church, with offices at 20 Vesey Street in Manhattan.[32] This initiative, and that of the brotherhood, may have resulted from funding by Trinity Church in the city, as the SPCK Emigration Committee had mentioned the previous year that the church had now 'taken the matter in hand of looking after immigrants'.[33]

Returning to the imperial dimension of the SPCK emigrant work, the absence of explicit imperial references in the 1880s and 1890s is striking in an organization directly involved with imperial emigration, particularly in its meagre published material, which among its annual reports included those of the Emigration Committee. It could be expected that at a time of heightened and positive imperialist sentiment in these decades that mention of the British empire would have been a useful means of inculcating support among the public, whose culture was permeated with imperialism in these late Victorian decades.

The Canadian views quoted in the Emigration Committee minutes, and the solitary imperialist reference by that committee, do point to the presence of some Christian imperialism within Anglican emigrant ministry circles. But even more obviously present in these sources than this Christian imperialism was an unequivocal concern for the perpetuation and extension of a global Anglicanism by its British ecclesiastical leaders and their church agents. These leaders included both Anglican leaders, such as the archbishop of Canterbury and the bishops of the Anglican Communion assembled in the Lambeth Conferences during the 1870s and 1880s, and clergy and laity in the SPCK Standing and Emigration Committees. There was clearly anxiety at the 1878 Lambeth Conference to have parochial clergy emphasize to emigrating Anglicans the global extent of their Church: 'carefully instruct them as to the oneness of the Church in its apostolic constitution under its varying organisation and conditions'. Additionally, the recommendation ended with further attention to the global nature of Anglicanism to be impressed upon emigrants: 'the importance of impressing upon our people the extent and geographical distribution of our Churches, and of reminding them that

---

6; Peter F. Anson, *The Call of the Cloister: Religious Communities and Kindred Bodies in the Anglican Communion*, 2nd edn (London, 1964).

[32] CUL, SPCK MS B2/1899, 461, SPCK Emigration Committee, July 1899.

[33] CUL, SPCK MS B2/1896–7, 463, SPCK Emigration Committee, [July 1897].

there is now hardly any part of the world where members of our Communion may not find a Church one with their own in faith, order and worship'. This emphasis on the international nature of colonial and US Anglicanism probably arose from two causes. First, the development of these overseas churches under the growing impetus of voluntaryism throughout the nineteenth century, as delineated by Hardwick,[34] may have caused some emigrating members of the Church of England to question if it was still the same church in these places as that they knew in Britain. Due to their essentially voluntary composition, the colonial and US churches required more of their membership by way of monetary giving and commitment than did the Church of England. Colonial and US Anglican churches also introduced synods and other structures involving laymen in advance of the Church of England.[35] Second, the comparative isolation of settler communities outside the cities, and the difficulty of finding clergy for them, meant emigrants could find themselves in a parish or diocese whose churchmanship was less congenial than those they knew back home, with the consequent temptation to depart for a more attractive denomination, or for none. This was particularly problematic in these decades, with the intensity of party feeling amongst internal Anglican groupings.[36]

A concern for international Anglican connectedness was also at the heart of Archbishop Tait's 1882 circular letter: 'It has been proposed that a systematic endeavour should be made to establish more direct communication than at present commonly exists between the Church at home and the Church in our Colonies, and in America.' Equally obviously, the same ecclesiastical agenda of concern for the strengthening of global Anglican links and for denominational retention of emigrating Anglicans was present in the pronouncement on the subject at the 1888 Lambeth Conference. Such emigrants were a 'social link' between churches of the Anglican Communion, and by keeping a 'watchful care' over them on their emigrant journey they could be protected 'from the dangers moral and spiritual, which beset their path'. Anglican global unity was also a dimension

---

[34] Hardwick, *Anglican British World*, ch. 2.
[35] Rowan Strong, 'Anglicanism and the State in the Nineteenth Century', in idem, ed., *OHA*, 3: *Partisan Anglicanism and its Global Expansion, 1829–c.1914* (Oxford, 2017), 111–14.
[36] Strong, 'Introduction', 14–15.

of Ellen Joyce's emigration work, as she expressed in her address to the Winchester GFS:

> In fact, our Colonies offer good health, good wages, good land to all whom we can send to enjoy them; with schools, churches, clergy, bishops, to keep our brothers and sisters true to the one faith, which in every clime unites us in the family of the one God and Father of us all.[37]

The SPCK's emigrant chaplaincy network was not directly involved in the promotion of emigration, but in ministering to those who had already decided to make this life change as they travelled to their new homes. While there were dimensions of a Christian imperialism in the Anglican chaplaincy project by the end of the nineteenth century, there is also a remarkable consistency with the outlooks of those involved with its beginnings in the 1840s and 1850s. Anglican engagement with the British empire continued to be varied and nuanced. It included Anglicans at various levels of society and their church who saw the empire through rose-tinted spectacles as a good thing, and others who saw it as a divine vehicle for the perpetuation of the best of all cultures and societies, namely Britain and Britishness. However, Anglican outlooks and engagement with the British empire also contained a more predominant dimension of pastoral response to emigrants' needs, which was undergirded by a commitment to the expansion and unity of their church and Christian faith rather than to the British empire. Their theological and moral position is one that historians need to take more seriously as an authentic dimension of the dialectic between Christianity and empire in the nineteenth century. Such Christian sentiments and actions as those embodied in the Anglican emigrant ministry were not invariably some sort of cover for other political or cultural values. The leading Anglicans in the SPCK emigration chaplaincy network were far more concerned with the extension and future of their church than they were with their empire, or even with Britishness.

---

[37] Joyce, *Emigration*, 8.

Sisters and Brothers Abroad: Gender, Race, Empire and Anglican Missionary Reformism in Hawai'i and the Pacific, 1858–75

Steven S. Maughan*

The College of Idaho

British Anglo-Catholic and high church Anglicans promoted a new set of foreign missionary initiatives in the Pacific and South and East Africa in the 1860s. Theorizing new indigenizing models for mission inspired by Tractarian medievalism, the initiatives envisioned a different and better engagement with 'native' cultures. Despite setbacks, the continued use of Anglican sisters in Hawai'i and brothers in Melanesia, Africa and India created a potent new imaginative space for missionary endeavour, but one problematized by the uneven reach of empire: from contested, as in the Pacific, to normal and pervasive, as in India. Of particular relevance was the Sandwich Islands mission, invited by the Hawaiian crown, where Bishop T. N. Staley arrived in 1862, followed by Anglican missionary sisters in 1864. Immensely controversial in Britain and America, where among evangelicals in particular suspicion of 'popish' religious practice ran high, Anglo-Catholic methods and religious communities mobilized discussion, denunciation and reaction. Particularly in the contested imperial space of an independent indigenous monarchy, Anglo-Catholics criticized what they styled the cruel austerities of evangelical American 'puritanism' and the ambitions of American imperialists; in the process they catalyzed a reconceptualized imperial reformism with important implications for the shape of the late Victorian British empire.

In the 1860s and 1870s, British high church Anglicans (influenced and led by advanced Anglo-Catholics) launched a series of missionary initiatives in South and East Africa, India, Melanesia and Hawai'i, designed specifically to reorder the foreign missionary practice of the Church of England and challenge the dominance of evangelicals in the movement, both inside and outside of their communion. Fundamental to this programme was the arrival in Honolulu in November

* Department of History, The College of Idaho, Caldwell, ID 83605–4432, USA. E-mail: smaughan@collegeofidaho.edu.

Studies in Church History 54 (2018) 328–344   © Ecclesiastical History Society 2018
doi: 10.1017/stc.2017.18

1864 of three nuns vowed to the Society of the Most Holy Trinity (SMHT), the first of the revived Anglican female religious communities inspired by the Oxford Movement. They represented the first of a growing wave of English Anglican sisters and brothers to spread out into empire and world in the decades that followed. Theorizing new indigenizing models for mission inspired by the Tractarian thought associated with John Henry Newman, Edward Bouverie Pusey and John Keble, as well as a developing Anglo-Catholic holiness asceticism, the initiatives envisioned a different and better engagement with indigenous cultures, focusing on enculturated missions and community-based faith in contrast to evangelical emphases on individual conversion and cultural Westernization.

Central to the Anglo-Catholic initiatives were the newly revived religious communities in foreign missions: sisters and brothers in vowed religious life operating in emulation of the pre-Reformation ancient and medieval Church. Conceiving of themselves as employing methods for church expansion tested in the ancient era of the Roman empire, Anglo-Catholics believed themselves capable of founding and building enculturated churches that would outlast the governments and empires in which they operated. Despite setbacks in their first decade, the continued use of Anglican religious communities in India, Africa and the Sandwich Islands from the 1860s and into the twentieth century created a potent new imaginative space for missionary endeavour, but one made problematic by the uneven reach of the British empire: from formal and pervasive, as in India, to contested, as in the Pacific. Of particular relevance to the inauguration of the Anglo-Catholic missionary project was the Sandwich Islands mission, where the Anglo-Catholic bishop Thomas Nettleship Staley arrived in 1862. Anglo-Catholics and high church bishops, who shared a high valuation of the ordinances and historic authority of the Anglican priesthood, sought to extend the Anglican Church beyond the bounds of empire with independence from the British state. Immensely controversial in Britain and America, where among evangelicals suspicion of the supposedly 'popish' religious practice of Anglo-Catholics ran high, the Hawaiian mission mobilized discussion, denunciation and reaction. What difference did missions, that were limited in impact by their comparatively small numbers of converts and missionaries sent overseas, make to the missionary strategies employed in founding and growing churches in the late Victorian and Edwardian era of 'high empire'? Without doubt debates over

Anglo-Catholic missions catalyzed new and widely influential missionary methods as well as a reconceptualized imperial reformism that had important implications for the shape of late Victorian Anglicanism and the British empire.

The upholding in 1850 by the secular Judicial Committee of the Privy Council of the Gorham Judgment, in which the evangelical G. C. Gorham was instituted as vicar of Brampford Speke despite the proscription of his views on baptismal regeneration by the high church bishop of Exeter, Henry Philpotts, established a new era: 'low church' evangelicals were assured they would not be driven from the Church of England over doctrinal matters, while many high churchmen were subsequently determined to achieve its independence from what seemed ungodly secular control. As evangelical Anglicans underwrote the establishment of new dioceses in Hong Kong, Rupert's Land and Sierra Leone – all British dominions and thus unambiguously legal under British imperial crown authority – Anglo-Catholics and other high churchmen determined to move beyond the official sphere of the crown and thus of the imperial state. Thus the *Church Times*, the new, self-proclaimed newspaper champion of Anglo-Catholicism, featured in its inaugural issue in 1863 an article entitled 'Missionary Bishops' which advocated their use in a world of threats from the state. Fearing not only doctrinal interference but also disestablishment in England, high churchmen sought a means to safeguard and expand the Church by propagating independent Anglican religion throughout the world both within and beyond imperial bounds. Comparing the situation of the Church to that of the ancient Roman general Fabius Maximus in the face of Hannibal's victories, independent church expansion under the lead of the episcopate operated as an explicit strategy of persistence and defensive action.[1] This was to be carried out in particular areas, specifically those overseen by the few sitting overseas Anglo-Catholic bishops, in South and central Africa, Melanesia, India and Hawai'i.

Anglo-Catholic missionaries were determined to found their distinctive churches not only in empire, but also beyond it. Notably, when the sisters of the SMHT (also known popularly as the Devonport Sisters) arrived in Hawai'i, they were not entering a part of the existing British empire, but instead an independent indigenous kingdom, which was a contested, liminal area of Western rivalry and

---

[1] 'The New Missionary Bishops', *Church Times*, 7 February 1863.

indigenous struggle for independence. In this context the sisters worked consciously to create an independent enculturated church operating under the authority of, and at the invitation of, Hawaiian royalty. The Society of St John the Evangelist (SSJE, or Cowley Fathers), who provided the first overseas brotherhood missions in India in 1874, similarly (at least initially and in theory) operated on a model of enculturating Christianity within existing local communities, rather than insisting on the need to impose Western Christian cultures of restraint and respectability within a framework of imperial order and privilege.[2] By the end of the 1870s, the movement inaugurated by Anglo-Catholic women and men religious had had profound effects on missionary operations, if not directly in terms of numbers of missionaries. Most scholarship on British foreign missions, particularly in the second half of the nineteenth century, has focused on evangelicalism and Nonconformity; however, the expansion of high church Anglican missions, animated in large part by the aggressive experimentalism of its Anglo-Catholic wing, resulted in a response that was both reactive and stimulative, as the larger body of evangelical missionaries felt obliged to redouble their use of unmarried female missionaries, adopt a more positive attitude to the retention of non-Western cultural practices and the promotion of indigenous pastors within emerging 'native churches', and challenge the territorial expansion of high church missions throughout the world. In addition, it ushered in a transformative era of acceptability and influence for Christian missions in the British universities, as their educated Anglican supporters in Oxford and Cambridge redefined mission as a more 'gentlemanly' pursuit of educated, culturally sophisticated advocates and practitioners.[3]

Anglo-Catholic missionary plans operated on several controversial foundations: first, criticism of the personal conversionary focus of evangelical missions; second, greater willingness to accept indigenous cultural forms into the Church and its worship; third, introduction of a new missionary agency in the form of vowed sisters and brothers acting as missionary agents. Evangelicals saw each as a threat, as

---

[2] Rowan Strong, 'Origins of Anglo-Catholic Missions: Fr Richard Benson and the Initial Missions of the Society of St John the Evangelist, 1869–1882', *JEH* 66 (2015), 90–115.
[3] For discussion of this historiography, as well as more detail on the broad outlines of development in Anglo-Catholic foreign missions, see Steven S. Maughan, *Mighty England Do Good: Culture, Faith, Empire, and World in the Foreign Missions of the Church of England, 1850–1915* (Grand Rapids, MI, 2014), 11–15, 113–38, 194–205.

the subsequent controversies that arose over the Hawaiian mission show. In 1867 Priscilla Lydia Sellon, Mother Superior of the SMHT (1848–76), who was in her day one of England's most commanding and controversial religious women, appeared with three additional sisters in Honolulu, responding to an invitation from the Hawaiian royal family delivered by Queen Emma during her 1865 English tour. Sellon purchased land and established St Andrew's Priory as a base for the activity of her nuns in mission in Honolulu and Lahaina. The project had the public support of the Tractarian leaders, E. B. Pusey and John Keble, the latter preaching a sending sermon from his Hursley pulpit to these 'first mission sisters sent out by the English Church'. Comparing their coming endeavour with what he styled the historic English medieval parallel – the role of Queen (also St) Bertha in the conversion of sixth-century England – he observed to those assembled that '[t]he conversion of England began in some sort from a Queen; and in Hawaii [*sic*] He has raised up a Queen … [who] seeks her consolation in God, and in furthering the work of His Church'.[4] This resort to ancient historical precedent, tied so intimately to the Gothic revivalism and ritualist vogue animating the second generation of the Oxford Movement, pervaded what was coming to be called Anglo-Catholicism, creating a distinct set of goals for what was conceived of as a new kind of mission.[5]

Active Anglo-Catholic missions dated from the founding of the Universities' Mission to Central Africa (UMCA) in 1858 and the organization for high church expansion into the Pacific, first into Melanesia, as planned by Bishop Selwyn of New Zealand, and next into Hawai'i, both areas that extended beyond the bounds of the British empire. The Hawaiian royal invitation requested a clerical appointment to establish an episcopal church in the kingdom and was advocated by Bishop Wilberforce of Oxford, forwarded by the Hawaiian consul-general, Manley Hopkins, delivered directly to Queen Victoria, and relayed to the recently revived Convocation of the Church of England.[6] In Hawai'i, high church Anglican leaders were being asked more or less explicitly to produce an alternative

[4] 'Seed Time and Harvest: Sermon by the late Rev. John Keble', *Mission Life; or, Home and Foreign Mission Work* 1 (1866), 315.
[5] Thomas Jay Williams, *Priscilla Lydia Sellon, the Restorer after Three Centuries of the Religious Life in the English Church*, rev. edn (London, 1965), 229–30.
[6] [Thomas N. Staley], *Five Years' Church Work in the Kingdom of Hawaii* (London, 1868), 13–15.

missionary model which rejected a strategy that emphasized British imperial values and the expectation of European dominance, and which instead operated as a counterweight to the mission of the American Congregationalist evangelicals who had been in residence from the 1820s. In this, the Anglican mission and its use of female missionaries contrasted explicitly with the outlook of the dozens of American missionary wives who, as Patricia Grimshaw has shown, gloried in a confident assertion of the superiority of American society, spirituality and cultural forms.[7] By contrast, the Anglican mission would make use of recently revived Anglican sisterhoods, communities of single vowed women who would live in the midst of the Hawaiian children they instructed under the patronage of Hawaiian royalty as a mission agency directed to the creation of an autonomous indigenous church. Justifying the use of these 'popish' sisterhoods to English supporters, however, required emphasizing that they were not destructive of British notions of femininity or domestic order, especially when attempting to work with secretaries at the Society for the Propagation of the Gospel (which provided grants-in-aid) and its many missionaries of more traditional high church sympathies.[8]

In the 1840s, the Oxford Movement had reasserted the apostolic authority of the Church and raised the authority of ordination and particularly episcopacy to essential status, notably and explicitly above that of national or imperial authorities in church matters.[9] Lydia Sellon had a close connection to Pusey, leader of the older Tractarian generation, who served as her confessor and was a frequent visitor to her base in England at Ascot Priory; she was also in touch with the more radical younger ritualists of the age, such as Charles Lowder and Father Ignatius (Joseph Leycester Lyne). One of the pioneers of sisterhood work in Britain, Sellon was the first to found a daughter house abroad.[10] With a strong sense of mission to the poor developed through 'rescue' work with prostitutes, soup kitchens, charity schools

[7] Patricia Grimshaw, *Paths of Duty: American Missionary Wives in Nineteenth-Century Hawaii* (Honolulu, HI, 1989), xi, 154–6, 193–6.
[8] On alternative, indigenizing visions in Anglo-Catholic missions, see Geoffrey Rowell, *The Vision Glorious: Themes and Personalities of the Catholic Revival in Anglicanism* (Oxford, 1983), 177.
[9] Standish Meacham, *Lord Bishop: The Life of Samuel Wilberforce, 1805–1873* (Cambridge, MA, 1970), 175–6; C. Brad Faught, *The Oxford Movement: A Thematic History of the Tractarians and their Times* (University Park, PA, 2003), 30–1.
[10] Staley also extended invitations to the Clewer and East Grinstead sisters: Williams, *Sellon*, 216–19, 229.

and orphanages, Sellon was one of the pioneers of women's public charity work in Britain and the originator of the use of Anglican sisters in mission, but hers was hardly the only – or the most successful – of the new overseas foundations that flourished in the decades that followed.[11]

Tension between Anglo-Catholic sisterhoods and the episcopacy in England was the normal state of affairs, for unlike the Roman Catholic Church, Anglican bishops had far fewer institutional means to oversee or control religious communities.[12] Similar frictions rapidly emerged in the Hawaiian mission, and were exacerbated both by the personality conflicts that were so characteristic of so many mission fields (not to mention religious communities), and by the intense nationalistic and religious partisanship produced by the existence of an influential American Congregationalist mission forty years in residence and a large, successful Roman Catholic Church of some twenty years. Fiercely independent in her relations to external church authorities, and notoriously autocratic with regard to the internal dynamics and politics of the SMHT, Mother Lydia, while clearly ambitious to expand her religious model overseas, only agreed to enter the mission field with an explicit assurance of non-interference from Bishop Staley. For his part Staley, eager for support in his isolated location, proved far more willing than other bishops to accommodate the independence of an established women's community.[13] In support of the project, Queen Emma, a child of Hawaiian and English grandparents, as well as a devout and scrupulous Anglican, took decided action. Visiting England in 1865 to raise funds for an Anglican cathedral, Emma was shepherded on a round of visits to high church and Tractarian luminaries by Bishop Wilberforce and formed a friendship with John Keble, which led to a private audience at Ascot Priory with Mother Lydia. This in turn resulted in Emma's

---

[11] Sean Gill, '"The Power of Christian Ladyhood": Priscilla Lydia Sellon and the Creation of Anglican Sisterhoods', in Stuart Mews, ed., *Modern Religious Rebels: Presented to John Kent* (London, 1993), 144–65, at 147–8; Stewart J. Brown, *Providence and Empire: Religion, Politics and Society in the United Kingdom, 1815–1914* (Harlow, 2008), 171–3.

[12] Susan Mumm, '"A Peril to the Bench of Bishops": Sisterhoods and Episcopal Authority in the Church of England, 1845–1908', *JEH* 59 (2008), 62–78.

[13] Oxford, Pusey House, Ascot Priory papers, Ellen Mary Mason to Lydia Sellon, 10 November 1863.

lodging there four Hawaiian girls sent for an English education.[14] Noted as being 'of the Polynesian colour, nothing of the *negro* about them', these girls were presented as emissaries of dignified society capable of transformation under the educated leadership of upper-class ladies, a Polynesian version of Sellon's own model for the rehabilitation of urban Britain. The Anglo-Catholic periodical *Mission Life* proclaimed that race was not destiny, for by 'raising the social sentiments' to extinguish 'existing associations' – that is, licentious associations – such Hawaiian women would save their own people from extinction.[15] The charge to the sisterhood was explicitly to reject the supposed determinism of race, placing the fate of the Hawaiian people in what would become their own self-supporting systems of self-development. Indeed, the chief advocate of the mission, Manley Hopkins, made explicit that Hawaiian royal preferences for English Anglicanism had much to do with resentment in the royal family over racial insults, both gross and subtle, delivered at the hands of crass Americans, as well as the desire to strengthen Hawaiian political independence.[16]

While, like the UMCA's Zambezi expedition and the Melanesian mission, the Hawaiian experiment operated beyond the bounds of formal empire, it had the advantage of being initiated at the invitation of reigning indigenous royalty in Hawai'i. King Kamehameha IV and Queen Emma desired the founding of an Anglican Church for a variety of reasons, including a stated preference for the solemnity and dignity of Anglican services, particularly in comparison to the austerities of 'puritan' American Congregationalist worship. Moreover, their interest was supported by Anglicanism's known deference

---

[14] Ascot, Ascot Priory, 'The Hawaiian Mission of the Society of the Most Holy Trinity of Devonport (1864–1901)', typescript scrapbook; George S. Kanahele, *Emma: Hawai'i's Remarkable Queen: A Biography* (Honolulu, HI, 1999), 194–8, 219–20.

[15] 'The Hawaiian Mission', *Mission Life; or, Home and Foreign Mission Work* 6 (1869), 436–8, at 436; Katharine Shirley Thompson, *Queen Emma and the Bishop* (Honolulu, HI, 1987), 3–4. Nineteenth-century discourse on the fitness of races was extensive and focused particularly on the Pacific, given the propensity of Pacific islanders to succumb to introduced communicable disease – in Hawai'i, particularly venereal disease – which made the focus of missionary discourses on saving island cultures through transformation of social and moral patterns particularly resonant: Patrick Brantlinger, *Dark Vanishings: Discourse on the Extinction of Primitive Races, 1800–1930* (Ithaca, NY, 2003), 142, 150–9.

[16] 'Hawaiian Mission', *The Net Cast on Many Waters* 2 (1867), 65–73, at 70; Manley Hopkins, *Hawaii: The Past, Present, and Future of its Island-Kingdom* (London, 1862), 322–4.

to royalty, and also piqued by their knowledge that American merchant and planter interests designed to annex Hawai'i to the United States.[17] In this context, the SHMT's plans to establish both a boarding school for the creation of an educated Hawaiian female elite and a day school for 'more humble' classes, fitted local Hawaiian goals to international Anglo-Catholic ones.

Rapidly, however, the Hawaiian mission and its work began to unravel in a torrent of bad press. Staley sailed in August 1862 already dreaded by Congregationalist missionaries of the American Board of Commissioners for Foreign Missions (ABCFM); upon arrival he confirmed their fears by prohibiting Anglican clerical cooperation with any who denied the apostolic authority of Anglican sacraments. Publicized by the American Congregationalist missionaries, and ABCFM secretary Rufus Anderson, as a dangerous exponent of Anglo-Catholic ritual, 'papist' tyranny and British imperial ambition, Staley proved a lightning rod for a paranoia heightened by the American Civil War.[18]

The Hawaiian mission was particularly remarkable in its vision for an enculturated church with indigenous families reinforced in their resilience by an educated Hawaiian womanhood to be strengthened by the efforts of the sisters. Working in close cooperation with Queen Emma to establish boarding schools and multiply girls' education, the sisters, it was argued, would combat the decline of the Hawaiian people and their culture.[19] In the case of St Andrew's Priory and its girls' schools, the primary approach to mission generated out of the sisterhood experience, which was subsequently generalized in many high church missions, was guided by what Elizabeth Prevost has called an 'ideology of female protectionism'.[20] Anglo-Catholic supporters had argued from the 1850s that Anglican sisters were differentiated from Catholics by their public, charitable life; free from the isolation of the cloisters, they became (in Eleanor Frith's term) 'pseudonuns', whose liminal position as 'Sisters of Mercy' provided

---

[17] Ralph S. Kuykendall, 'Introduction of the Episcopal Church into the Hawaiian Islands', *Pacific Historical Review* 15 (1946), 133–46, at 135–6.
[18] Robert Louis Semes, 'Hawai'i's Holy War: English Bishop Staley, American Congregationalists, and the Hawaiian Monarchies, 1860–1870', *Hawaiian Journal of History* 34 (2000), 113–38.
[19] [Staley], *Hawaii*, 57–61; Kanahele, *Emma*, 155–6, 230–7.
[20] For the development of this model in 1870s Madagascar and Uganda, see Elizabeth E. Prevost, *The Communion of Women: Missions and Gender in Colonial Africa and the British Metropole* (Oxford, 2010), ch. 1.

them particular freedoms and a widening sphere for activity.[21] Nevertheless, Anglo-Catholics drew on Roman Catholic enculturated models of mission, often suggesting that Catholic missions were more successful than 'puritan' ones and that Anglicans needed to emulate the success of Catholics while neutralizing the dangerous 'tyranny' embedded in their supposedly authoritarian governance. They did this by rejecting the cloistering of nuns while at the same time often embracing a separatist model for the education of their young female charges, temporarily removing girls from the moral dangers presumed to exist in their own societies in order to transform them into agents of moral and spiritual change upon their return. In this, Anglo-Catholic sisterhoods embraced the community orientation of Catholic mission practice while denouncing the supposed metapolitics of Catholic spiritual and social authority. They also radically transgressed the predominant Victorian vision of home by constructing an alternative, all-female organization of publicly active women, while they embraced Victorian gender imperatives by insisting that sisterhoods were the most effective agency for educating girls, thereby strengthening the traditional Victorian Christian home. The vertiginous crossing of multiple spiritual, political and gender boundaries made Anglo-Catholic missions a particularly fertile ground for reimagining the approaches that might be taken towards engineering spiritual and cultural transformation in a particularly fluid era of imperial cultural formation.

Supported also by near universal mid-Victorian admiration for Florence Nightingale and roughly a hundred volunteer nursing sisters who served during the Crimean War, including several of Sellon's 'Sisters of Mercy', advocates for the Hawaiian mission played on their wartime popularity: the first two nuns sent to Hawai'i were veterans of the hospitals at Scutari and were defended against critics by reference to their earlier heroism.[22] Thus, despite overt evangelical hostility to Anglican religious orders, popular acceptance of the religious life and work of nuns grew; yet sisterhoods were actively disfavoured by the bishops because they proved resistant to episcopal attempts to manage them, a position modelled first by Sellon. Endorsing a larger legitimating ideology of home, at the same time sisterhoods

---

[21] Eleanor Joy Frith, 'Pseudonuns: Anglican Sisterhoods and the Politics of Victorian Identity' (PhD thesis, Queen's University, Kingston, ON, 2004), 64–7, 77–80.
[22] J. M. Ludlow, *Woman's Work in the Church: Historical Notes on Deaconesses and Sisterhoods* (London, 1866), vii–ix.

vigorously resisted assertions of the necessity of male governance. When appealing for sisters to undertake such work, bishops such as Webb of Grahamstown aimed at ensuring 'orthodoxy and continuity' as women carried English civilization to colonial homes.[23] Often, however, sisters treated such strictures with disdain, as exemplified by Emily Ayckbourn, Mother Superior of the Sisters of the Church, who in the course of considering a colonial mission stated that:

> [Webb's] ideas about … government (of sisterhoods by a father) are quite preposterous. Also his saying that it is for men to originate plans & women to carry them out. In real truth the only Sisterhoods (in [the] English Ch:) that have done well have been originated by women: and men have made such a mess of Religious Communities among themselves that it is absurd they should try to subject Sisterhoods now to their control.[24]

Because she shared this attitude Sellon eventually found herself at odds with Staley, her most Anglo-Catholic of bishops, who came to condemn independent female governance in the sisterhood he had earlier endorsed. Whilst continuing to praise the sisters' work, he denounced the principles of their rule as 'radically unsound, and mischievous in their result on human character' because of the way mothers superior were led to reject 'quiet subjection to authority', thus "'lording it over God's heritage"'.[25]

Perhaps even more radical than the development of a new Anglo-Catholic approach to acceptable forms of femininity and gendered mission was the Hawaiian mission's attitude toward indigenous masculinity. Rather than condemning traditional masculine behaviours, Staley instead insisted on tolerating 'heathen' customs such as the hula dance, Hawaiian men's sports such as surfboarding, and the political independence and leadership of Hawaiian royalty. In this way, Staley's 'Hawaiian Reformed Catholic Church' directly challenged American Congregationalist condemnation of Hawaiian traditional culture. The evangelical claim to have raised the morality of Hawaiians, he argued, was a sham because fetishizing the rote recitation of

---

[23] Allan Becher Webb, *Sisterhood Life and Woman's Work, in the Mission-Field of the Church* (London, 1883), 3, 54.
[24] Ham, Surrey, St Michael's Convent, CSC7, Emily Ayckbourn, Diary and House Book, 7 June 1884.
[25] T. N. Staley to John Jackson (bishop of London), 23 August 1871, in Henry Codman Potter, *Sisterhoods and Deaconesses: At Home and Abroad* (New York, 1873), 60–7.

Scripture had achieved little but 'a fearful amount of unreality and hypocrisy'. Suppressing traditional cultural expression denationalized Hawaiians shaped by eons into 'laughing children of the sun'; Staley argued that such approaches were also destructive in any modern civilization where 'the old Puritan principle, ... if carried out, would put an end to the athletic pursuits and recreations of every Christian country in Europe'.[26] Staley's position, shaped as it was by the English public school ethos of 'playing the game', continued to cast Hawaiians in the role of immature dependents; nevertheless, it also included members of the Hawaiian royalty in equal positions of leadership, creating greater space for cross-cultural Christian collaboration.

By the end of the decade, however, Staley's campaign against evangelical influence in Hawai'i had made only theoretical progress, and the end of the American Civil War saw a resurgence of American resistance to supposed English aggression.[27] In this context the sisterhood of the SMHT proved, in the end, to be the most successful of the Hawaiian mission enterprises, precisely because it was the most blameless. Staley had launched a self-proclaimed battle with evangelicalism, stating that in Hawai'i, 'this remote spot of the globe', his church aimed to fight 'the battle between modern Puritanism and primitive Catholicism'. But the death in November 1863 of King Kamehameha IV, the church's chief patron, had been a critical setback, which was compounded by Staley's failure to raise sufficient funds to build the medieval-style Gothic stone cathedral favoured by Queen Emma.[28] When Staley, his family finances strained to breaking point and facing continuous, extensive opposition from virtually all local Anglican clergy, relinquished the bishopric in 1870, he did so having lost the confidence of Queen Emma, denounced by her for what she saw as a disgraceful failure of leadership and a near-traitorous willingness to turn the mission over to the American Episcopal Church.[29] The original confluence of interests between

---

[26] T. N. Staley, *A Pastoral Address* (Honolulu, 1865), 13–14, 40–1.
[27] Henry Boyd Restarick, *Hawaii, 1778–1920, from the Viewpoint of a Bishop* (Honolulu, 1924), 68, 91–2.
[28] *Occasional Paper of the Hawaiian Church Mission (Sandwich Islands)* (London, 1865), 29–32.
[29] London, LPL, Tait Papers 170, fols 178–9, John Jackson to Tait (archbishop of Canterbury), 4 April 1870; ibid., fols 198–9, Manley Hopkins to Tait, 2 August 1870; Kanahele, *Emma*, 240–1.

queen and bishop, local Hawaiian and British Anglo-Catholic objects, which saw both aiming for independence, albeit for different institutions, had diverged in a way that exposed the importance of the mission as one element of a strategy designed by the Hawaiian royals to buttress indigenous governance in the face of aggressive American commercial power. However, despite Staley's withdrawal, Lydia Sellon proved unwilling to abandon the bonds she had forged with Emma and the mission of women religious she had created. Facing a diocese unable adequately to support itself and a demand from the archbishop of Canterbury for guaranteed financial support before a replacement bishop would be consecrated, Sellon underwrote the costs of creating an endowment for the diocese for five years. In this way she ensured that Staley would be replaced by Alfred Willis, also a bishop of advanced Anglo-Catholic sympathies, yet one who would have no right of visitation and thus limited episcopal control over her nuns.[30]

Proximate failure in the Hawaiian mission, however, did not mean a failure to influence or a failure to persist. Its troubles and the parallel disastrous failure in Bishop Mackenzie's Zambezi expedition for the UMCA quelled much early optimism. But they also fomented a critical moment of reinforcement for the central value of stubborn independency among Anglo-Catholics, exemplified in the blameless lives of women religious who were publicized as being as committed to the poor, the heathen and the downfallen as they were to their religious devotions. The subsequent history of the UMCA, with its continuous emphasis on forming enculturated African churches served by unsalaried vowed brothers, which became one of the inspirations for criticism of the high costs and European clerical lives of mainstream missionaries in the 1880s, is one indication of the dynamism of the Anglo-Catholic connection.[31] So too was the quiet work of the highly unworldly Bishop J. C. Patteson of Melanesia, who regularly denounced European violence and race prejudice, and who was killed on Nukapu Island in 1871 by islanders incensed over

[30] Andrew Forest Muir, 'Mother Lydia and the Support of the Hawaiian Mission', *Holy Cross Magazine* 62 (1951), 176–8.
[31] Andrew Porter, 'The Universities' Mission to Central Africa: Anglo-Catholicism and the Twentieth-Century Colonial Encounter', in Brian Stanley, ed., *Missions, Nationalism, and the End of Empire* (Grand Rapids, MI, 2003), 79–107; Thomas Prasch, 'Which God for Africa: The Islamic-Christian Missionary Debate in Late-Victorian England', *Victorian Studies* 33 (1989), 51–73.

European abductions for the Pacific labour trade. Patteson and the Melanesian mission provided a model of operation on different lines than those of conventional voluntary missions. Envisioning himself and his missionaries as educated professionals immune from the unrealistic enthusiasms of evangelicalism, Patteson and other Anglo-Catholic missionaries instead believed that under the guidance of a reverent, transcultural, historically malleable church, a solid foundation for indigenous Christianity could be built.[32] Patteson's widely publicized death was a turning point in Anglo-Catholic mission, inspiring a 'Day of Intercession for Foreign Missions' observed annually throughout the Church of England in honour of the 'martyr bishop of Melanesia'.[33] Anglo-Catholic and high church missions had a second phase of expansion in the 1870s: for example, the Wantage Sisters (Community of St Mary the Virgin, founded in 1848) and the All Saints Sisters of the Poor (founded in 1851) took up work in India in association with the Cowley Fathers, in Bombay [Mumbai] in 1874 and in Calcutta [Kolkata] in 1876, while sisterhoods also developed in South Africa under the direction of Bishop A. B. Webb, first in Bloemfontein (1874) and later in Grahamstown (1883), reinforced by the appointment in 1875 of the thirty-year-old R. S. Copleston as 'boy bishop' of Colombo, and the inauguration of the high church mission to Madagascar. Significantly, by then Anglo-Catholics had developed a missionary theory predicated explicitly on the idea of the spiritual equality of races in empire and classes in nation that assumed a common human intellectual, moral and religious potential. In this it mirrored core evangelical assumptions, but by contrast with these it rested on a professed respect for local traditions believed to make Anglo-Catholicism comparatively attractive to common people abroad and at home.[34]

As missionary sisterhoods and then brotherhoods spread, they reinforced a cultural trend that turned away from the defining missiological emphasis of the earlier Victorian period on atonement-based theology, which had focused on a simple binary choice

---

[32] J. C. Patteson to C. M. Yonge, 27 April 1864, in Charlotte M. Yonge, *Life of John Coleridge Patteson, Missionary Bishop of the Melanesian Islands*, 2 vols, 5th edn (London, 1884), 2: 93; Sara H. Sohmer, 'Christianity Without Civilization: Anglican Sources for an Alternative Nineteenth-Century Mission Methodology', *JRH* 18 (1994), 174–97.
[33] William Ewart Gladstone, 'Art. VI', review of Charlotte M. Yonge, *Life of John Coleridge Patteson, Missionary Bishop of the Melanesian Islands*, *Quarterly Review* 137 (1874), 458–92.
[34] Staley, *Pastoral Address*, 14.

(salvation or damnation), towards a wider embrace of human agency as critical to ameliorating the evils of the world, emulating an incarnate Christ and his earthly life.[35] Operating in mission fields lacking larger settler populations reinforced Anglo-Catholic missionaries' self-identification as visionary pioneers of a romantic antique Christianity, building what they imagined to be 'primitive' churches inspired by their reading of the earliest Church Fathers.[36] Such ideas reinforced in Anglicanism a willingness to accommodate indigenous culture and governance, attitudes later characteristic of renewed early twentieth-century interest in reformist theories of imperial trusteeship, and counter to the increasing advocacy by many mid-century commentators of deterministic race thinking stimulated by reactions to the Morant Bay uprising in 1865.[37] The strain of mid-Victorian thought that rejected deterministic race consciousness in favour of an enculturated 'civilizational approach' to understanding difference was reinforced by the growing influence, particularly in the universities, of strains of Anglo-Catholicism and an emerging orientalist historicism associated with the comparative religious scholarship of Anglicans such as Monier Monier-Williams and Friedrich Max Müller.[38] This comparative, historically informed approach to cultural difference continued to be widely insisted upon within the generally robust and extensive missionary culture of the mid-Victorian era, which demonstrated a resilient commitment to older forms of Christian universalism and environmental explanations for human behaviour, even in the face of emerging theories positing essentialist racial difference.[39]

Within the culture of advanced Anglo-Catholicism, sisterhoods operated as a particularly resonant element providing a gendered

---

[35] Boyd Hilton, *The Age of Atonement: The Influence of Evangelicalism on Social and Economic Thought, 1795–1865* (Oxford, 1988), 292–6.

[36] Jeffrey Cox, 'Independent English Women in Delhi and Lahore, 1860–1947', in R. W. Davis and R. J. Helmstadter, eds, *Religion and Irreligion in Victorian Society* (London, 1992), 166–84, at 166–8.

[37] Catherine Hall, *Civilising Subjects: Metropole and Colony in the English Imagination, 1830–1867* (Chicago, IL, 2002), 438–40.

[38] Peter Mandler, '"Race" and "Nation" in Mid-Victorian Thought', in Stefan Collini, Richard Whatmore and Brian Young, eds, *History, Religion, and Culture: British Intellectual History, 1750–1950* (Cambridge, 2000), 224–44, at 231–3; Paul Hedges, 'Post-Colonialism, Orientalism, and Understanding: Religious Studies and the Christian Missionary Imperative', *JRH* 32 (2008), 55–75.

[39] Alison Twells, *The Civilising Mission and the English Middle Class, 1792–1850: The 'Heathen' at Home and Overseas* (Basingstoke, 2009), 13–15, 174–5, 214–15.

metaphor for pious, godly independence, transferable to cultures regardless of race. In this way Anglo-Catholic women's activities abroad opened new patterns in missionary contact with non-Western peoples as Anglo-Catholics sought to rise above both nation and empire. In many areas – in India and South Africa in particular – Anglo-Catholics came to be deeply associated with British imperial agendas, and throughout non-Western lands white English women traded upon the prestige and position of race and nationality. Nevertheless, their ambition to encourage gendered solidarity and their desire for racial crossings that would strengthen indigenous peoples in the face of corrosive Western commercial interests and settler colonialism drove the actions of an incipient women's movement which was at odds with much sentiment in both English missionary circles and British popular culture in the 1860s. By the 1880s, sisterhoods were an established presence in the field, primarily in South Africa, India, Canada, Australia and New Zealand, but also in Persia, Korea and the United States.[40]

Anglo-Catholics challenged mid-century discourse on missions by proclaiming a superior model for missionary work. At the heart of this model was the figure of the Anglican nun fighting all obstacles and the odds set against her, in partnership with educated, culturally informed Anglo-Catholic priests set upon the task of transmitting the core traditions of Christianity supposedly traceable to the first centuries of Christian expansion. At the same time they encouraged the same kinds of cultural synthesis that, it was argued, had strengthened Christianity through a Hellenizing process in the second and third centuries of Christian growth. Despite the controversies swirling around them, Mother Lydia and Bishop Staley stood in Anglo-Catholic circles both as cautionary tale, for their excesses, and as inspiration, for their faithful efforts. By the 1870s British missions were settling into a new, late-century pattern, and the missionary movement – largely defined in the early nineteenth century by evangelical Nonconformist Congregationalists, Baptists and Methodists – was increasingly dominated by Anglican missions, both those of high churchmen and evangelicals, both camps using missions in their own contests for command of the Church of England itself.

---

[40] Susan Mumm, *Stolen Daughters, Virgin Mothers: Anglican Sisterhoods in Victorian Britain* (London, 1999), 129–30.

The story of Anglo-Catholic missions challenges prevalent ideas about the predominantly evangelical nature of foreign missions, and points to the complex ways that Christianity interacted with the 'worldly powers' of nations and empires to form ideas influential in the emergence of systems of imperial trusteeship and later of international humanitarianism in the twentieth century. In addition, an account of the ways that Anglo-Catholic missionary models challenged established evangelical missionary discourses about Westernization and the founding of missionary methods in the idealized Victorian family illuminates a debate that accelerated change in missionary practice. It resulted in both the normalization of women's missionary activity outside the bounds of missionary marriage and the expansion and professionalization of a university-based missionary culture. In this way, we can begin to see how Anglo-Catholic religious cultures, in addition to more thoroughly studied evangelical movements in the era, contributed to an expansion of women's public roles that presaged and ultimately supported women's enfranchisement. While it is tempting, then, to dismiss the Hawaiian mission as a failure, as evangelical controversialists and American interests in the Pacific did, the mission – using a metaphor so dear to mission supporters – sowed the seeds for future models of enculturated mission and expanded roles for women in the mission field, for Anglican Church independence from state and empire, and for the development of attitudes toward international and imperial reformism (outside England at least) along strongly humanitarian lines.

Ultramontane Efforts in the Ottoman Empire during the 1860s and 1870s

Mariam Kartashyan*

University of Bern

The attempts of Pope Pius IX to restrict the ecclesiastical rights of the Armenian Catholics with his bull Reversurus *(1867) led to the Armenian schism in 1871. A factor which was decisive for the development of the relationship between the Armenian Catholic Church and the Ottoman empire, under whose rule the Church existed, was the influence of other powers. This article analyses the background of this relationship and its significance for the Armenian schism. For this purpose, first, the ecclesiastical rights of the Armenian Catholic Church during the period before the publication of* Reversurus *and their relation to the internal policy of the Ottoman empire are outlined. Second, the influence of the domestic and foreign policy of the Ottoman state on its relationship with its Armenian Catholic subjects is elucidated. In this way, it is shown that the historical background of the Armenian Catholic Church and the internal political circumstances of the Ottoman empire were intertwined and shaped the relationship between the Armenian Catholics and the Ottoman state. Despite this, relations between the Ottoman empire, the Holy See and other European empires came to exercise a predominant influence, leading by the end of the 1870s to the Armenian Catholic Church's enforced acquiescence in ecclesiastical change.*

When he restricted the ecclesiastical rights of the Armenian Catholics in 1867, Pope Pius IX (1846–78) started a new Roman Catholic policy in the East. At first glance, the papal decision seemed to concern only the relationship between the Armenian Catholic Church and Rome. But the Armenian Catholic patriarchate and a large Armenian Catholic community were situated in the territories of the Ottoman empire.[1] Hence the papal decision was also closely intertwined with the domestic and foreign policy of the Ottoman state.

* Institut für Christkatholische Theologie, Länggassstrasse 51, CH-3000 Bern 9, Switzerland. E-mail: mariam.kartashyan@theol.unibe.ch.
[1] Since the Russo-Turkish War of 1828–9, Armenian territory had been split between the Ottoman and Russian empires. In the 1860s, there were about 27,000 Armenian Catholics in Constantinople and its surroundings, 8,000 in Syria, Mesopotamia and

Studies in Church History 54 (2018) 345–358   © Ecclesiastical History Society 2018
doi: 10.1017/stc.2017.13

This article begins by analysing the ecclesiastical rights of the Armenian Catholic Church. It then explores how these rights were related to the civil rights of the Ottoman Armenians, which helps to explain ecclesiastical changes in the East after 1867. Some light can then be shed on how papal policy moved the Armenian Catholic question from the ecclesiastical to the diplomatic level. This change in the relationship between the Holy See and the Armenian Catholics reveals ultramontane aspects to the policy of the Holy See as it engaged with the Ottoman empire.

THE ECCLESIASTICAL RIGHTS OF THE ARMENIAN CATHOLICS

The road by which the Armenian Catholics came into union with Rome was a long one. The Armenian Church, founded in 301, broke communion with the other Christian churches after the Council of Chalcedon in 451. During the following millennium, there were several attempts to bring the Armenian Church to accept the decisions of Chalcedon. The Council of Ferrara-Florence (1431–49) was one of the most remarkable of these, but its attempt to turn the Armenian Church into a uniate church, in communion with Rome but retaining its liturgy and traditions, failed. Finally, in 1742, the Chalcedonian minority of the Armenians officially came into union with Rome.[2]

Since the earliest attempts at union with Rome, the question of the ecclesiastical rights of the Eastern churches, including the Armenian Catholic Church, has been discussed several times. During the Council of Ferrara-Florence, Eugenius IV (1431–47) published the bull *Exultate Deo* regarding union with the Armenians.[3] This discussed the question of the *Filioque* clause, the doctrine of the two natures of Christ and the authority of the councils and the pope. In addition, it defined the theological changes and the revisions of sacramental doctrine which were deemed essential for the union. However, the bull made no reference to any abolition of the

---

Armenia Minor, 12–14,000 in Austria, 28,150 in Russia, and smaller communities in Italy and elsewhere: Joseph Hergenröther, 'Die Rechtsverhältnisse der verschiedenen Riten innerhalb der katholischen Kirche', *Archiv für katholisches Kirchenrecht* 7 (1862), 169–200, at 174.

[2] For this process, see Xačik Atanasean, *Vark̔ Abraham-Petros A. Arciwean kat̔oɫikosi* (Beirut, 1959), 183–96.

[3] *The General Councils of Latin Christendom from Constantinople IV (869/870) to Lateran V (1512–1517)*, CChr.COGD 2/ii, 1224–59.

ecclesiastical rights which formed part of the autonomous Armenian Church tradition.[4] Another bull, *Laetentur caeli*, published at the same council, aimed to end the East-West schism of 1054;[5] it tried to define the relationship between the Eastern rite communions and the Holy See, confirming the primacy of the pope as the successor of Christ but also affirming that the Eastern patriarchs should retain their rights and privileges. In 1566, Pius V (1566–72) published a bull in which he affirmed the distinctive features of the Oriental rites, but prohibited the mixing of different rites, characterizing this as a distortion of the ancient rite of the saints.[6] Following union between the Armenian Catholics and Rome in 1742, the Holy See remained open towards the ecclesiastical rights of the Armenian Catholic Church. An important document was the bull of Benedict XIV (1740–58), *Allatae sunt*,[7] which made clear that Rome's main purpose was the prohibition of the errors of Arius, Nestorius, Eutyches and other heretics in the Orient. At the same time, the pre-1054 Eastern rites should be preserved and respected, as previous popes had not wanted uniate churches to abandon their own rites and follow the Latin rite. Abolition of the Greek and other Eastern rites had never been Rome's aim.

The Holy See had not sought to restrict or change the ecclesiastical rights of the Armenians, and its tolerance was fundamental for the union. The Armenian Catholic Church was able to preserve its own election rules, regulations, hierarchy, administration, ecclesiastical language, liturgical formulations, ceremonies, celebrations

---

[4] This tradition goes back to the mother Church, the Armenian Apostolic Church, founded in 301. For more about it, see Tiran Nersoyan, *Armenian Church Historical Studies: Matters of Doctrine and Administration*, ed. and intro. Nerses Vrej Nersessian (New York, 1996).

[5] CChr.COGD 2/ii, 1212–18.

[6] Pius V, 'Revocatio facultatis quomodolibet concessae Graecis Latino ritu, & Latinis Graeco more celebrandi Missas, & divina Officia', 20 August 1566, in Aloysius Tomassetti et al., eds, *Bullarum diplomatum et privilegiorum sanctorum romanorum pontificum*, 27 vols (Turin, 1857–85), 7: 473–5.

[7] 'De ritibus Orientalium conservandis, de celebratione in eccl. alius ritus et Kalendario Gregoriano. Benedictus XIV, Allatae, 26. Julii 1755', in Theodor Granderath and Gerhard Schneemann, eds, *Acta et decreta sacrorum conciliorum recentiorum: Collectio Lacensis, Auctoribus presbyteris S. J. e domo B. V. M. sine labe conceptae ad Lacum*, 7 vols (Freiburg im Breisgau, 1870–90), 2: 534–7.

and other traditions.[8] These privileges included the distinction of
Eastern rites from the Latin rite, which made the union in some
senses incomplete. The real reason for Rome's toleration of the ecclesiastical rights of the Armenian Catholic Church is debatable, but it
seems clear that this was a strategy to accelerate the process of union.[9]
This became problematic over time. The Armenian patriarchs began
to exercise their prerogatives before being confirmed by the popes
through a *pallium*, and the Armenian Catholic Church tended to
allow movements, reforms and decisions that displeased the Holy
See.[10] The latter concluded that it did not have enough influence
over the Armenian Catholics and that the union of 1742 appeared as
yet incomplete. This was the background to the measures taken by
Pius IX to initiate a new reunification project in the East.

THE ARMENIAN CATHOLIC *MILLET* (1830) AND ITS ADMINISTRATION

The Holy See's new policy was decisive not only for the ecclesiastical rights of Armenian Catholics but also for their civil rights

---

[8] The preservation of the Armenian Church tradition was closely connected with the
national character of the Armenian Catholic Church: Boghos Levon Zekiyan, *L'Armenia
e gli armeni. Polis lacerata e patria spirituale: la sfida di una sopravvivenza* (Milano, 2000).
[9] The Roman Catholic church historian Klaus Unterburger explains the background of
this policy: While the Oriental churches believed that they could thus preserve their ecclesiology, Rome understood by 'privileges and rights' something which might be revoked by
the popes at any time: Klaus Unterburger, 'Internationalisierung als Bedrohungsszenarium des forcierten Ultramontanismus. Die Weichenstellungen an der päpstlichen Kurie
in den 1860er-Jahren und das Apostolische Schreiben *Reversurus*', *IKZ* 106 (2016), 236–
49, at 236–7.
[10] For example, there were moves towards union between the Armenian Catholics and
the Armenian Apostolic Church during the early nineteenth century (especially in 1810,
1817 and 1820): Vartan Artinian, *The Armenian Constitutional System in the Ottoman
Empire, 1839–1863: A Study of its Historical Development* (Istanbul, 1988), 34–6. The
Armenian Catholic patriarchate sometimes made decisions which provoked protest from
Rome, such as the decision in 1861 of Patriarch Grigor Pētros VIII (1844–66), to appoint the *abbas generalis* of the Armenian Catholic order of Antonians as archbishop of
the diocese of Antiochia. For Rome's countermeasures, see Bzommar, Les Archives du
Couvent Notre Dame de Bzommar [hereafter: BZ], Les Archives du Couvent d'Antonins
[hereafter: ACA], Box 6, Ṙapʿayēl Miasērean to an unknown recipient, 30 June 1866.
In addition, the Roman Catholic church historian Theodor Granderath suggested that
over the course of time the Oriental churches were growing increasingly autonomous,
and that the popes began to consider it their duty to change the mode of election and
so to limit the independence of these churches. In this interpretation, the Armenian
Catholic denial of the pope's rights to intervene in this question amounted to a denial
of his primacy: Theodor Granderath, *Geschichte des Vatikanischen Konzils*, ed. Konrad
Kirch, 3 vols (Freiburg im Breisgau, 1903–6), 2: 327.

in the Ottoman empire. The self-government of the Armenian Catholic Church and its independence from foreign powers was the foundation upon which the relationship between the Ottoman state and the Armenian Catholics was maintained. Since the formation of the Armenian Catholic *millet* (an officially recognized religious community in the Ottoman empire) in 1830/1, this relationship had not been beneficial for Rome.[11] Although the establishment of the Armenian Catholic *millet* secured the Church's identity and political status in the empire, changes were soon introduced by the state which altered the structure of the *millet* and lessened the scope for Roman influence on Armenian Catholics. Moreover, because of the feudal nature of Ottoman society, Ottoman Armenians had limited freedom and rights, which restricted their traditional religious practice.[12] However, in 1839, under the pressure of the European great powers, the Ottoman government started the *Tanẓīmāt* reforms.[13] Following the European model, these reforms aimed to improve the social situation of the oppressed classes. The edict *Gülhane Hatt-ı Şerîf* ('holy writing of Gülhane') issued in 1839 attempted to increase the security of the Ottoman subjects and guarantee their rights as well as to make the taxation system fairer.[14] A further edict in 1846 secured the properties and rights of the Ottoman population.[15] These reforms were deemed insufficiently effective, and after the Crimean war between the Ottoman, British, French and Russian empires (1853–6), which made the Ottoman empire more dependent upon the Western

[11] Kemal Beydilli, *II. Mahmud devri'nde katolik Ermeni cemāati v kilisesi'nin taninmasi (1830) / Recognition of the Armenian Catholic Community and the Church in the Reign of Mahmud II (1830)*, ed. Şinasi Tekin and Gönül Alpay Tekin, Sources of Oriental Languages and Literatures 27 (Cambridge, MA, 1995).

[12] The Ottoman empire was divided into different classes: the ruling class (Òsmani), servants of the sultan (Askerî) and subjects (Reâyâ); the Reâyâs had to pay high taxes, unlike the Askerîs: Suraiya Faroqhi, *Kultur und Alltag im osmanischen Reich. Vom Mittelalter bis zum Anfang des 20. Jahrhunderts*, 2nd edn (München, 2003), 72–3. In addition, the Ottoman government practised a theocratic system, in which the Armenians were treated as Gavurs (unbelievers): Kai Merten, *Untereinander, nicht nebeneinander. Das Zusammenleben religiöser und kultureller Gruppen im osmanischen Reich des 19. Jahrhunderts* (Berlin, 2014), 402.

[13] For more about the *Tanẓīmāt* reforms, see Dietrich Jung, 'Staatsbildung und Staatszerfall. Die osmanische Moderne und der europäische Staatenbildungsprozess', in Gabriele Clemens, ed., *Die Türkei und Europa* (Hamburg, 2007), 57–78.

[14] Ibid. 65.

[15] BZ, ACA, box 2, 'Harazat t'argmanut'iwn ardaradat patuirank'nerun, or Mēčlisi Ahk'eami Atliyēyin xorhərdacut'eambə grvec'an, ew Ark'ayakan hramanawn al hratarakvec'an', 18 February 1846.

powers, new reforms were undertaken. In 1856 the edict *Hatt-i Hümâyûn* ('the writing of the emperor') was published, which secured the autonomy and independent administration of the *millets* in the Ottoman empire.[16] Under the supervision of the Ottoman state, the Christian *millets* were allowed to manage their own financial and legal affairs, and no foreign power had any right to interfere in their affairs. This edict was based on the principle of religious freedom and benefited the Christian communities, including the Armenian Catholic *millet*.

Another important event was the publication of the Armenian National Constitution (*Ermeni Patrikliği Nizâmâtı*) in 1863.[17] The purpose of the constitution was to separate the religious and civil arenas, to diminish the influence of the Armenian patriarchate in civil affairs and to establish a more democratic civil order through national and civil assemblies. This constitution was originally addressed to members of the Armenian Apostolic community (*Ermeni Millet*), but the model was extended to Catholic Armenians (*Katholik Millet*). After the establishment of the Armenian Catholic archbishop's seat in Constantinople,[18] the Armenian Catholics in Constantinople and its surroundings had two heads. The first was the archbishop *primas*, who was responsible for religious affairs. The second was the *patrik* (civil head of the nation), who was appointed by the state in order to manage the civil affairs of the Armenian Catholics. In the provinces, the bishops[19] were the heads of the dioceses, administering both civil and religious affairs. In addition, from 1847 the Armenian Catholics had separate assemblies for the clergy (*Ruhani meclis*) and for the laity (*Cismani meclis*).[20] While the clergy assembly was mainly responsible for ecclesiastical questions, the general or national assembly functioned as the intermediary between the state and the Armenian

[16] BZ, ACA, box 2, 'T'argmanut'iwn kayserakan xat't'i hiwmayunin or 1856 p'etrvar 6in kardac'vec'aw barjragoyn duṙə'.
[17] H. F. B. Lynch, *Armenia: Travels and Studies*, 2 vols (London, 1901), 2: 446–67 (App. I).
[18] Despite the fact that in theory there was one Armenian Catholic Church with one patriarch, the archbishop *primas* was in fact more than an archbishop. Being appointed by the pope, he could act autonomously and was seen thus as another head alongside the patriarch. In addition to this, the fact that he had jurisdiction over the capital and its surroundings magnified his role.
[19] These bishops had some autonomy within their dioceses, but they stood under the immediate primacy of the patriarch.
[20] Hacik Rafi Gazer, 'Bibliographie', *IKZ* 106 (2016), 323–8, at 324.

Catholic nation, and was concerned with questions such as the administrative matters to do with the Armenian Catholic population, their rights, and the laws pertaining to them. Both assemblies were closely connected.

REVERSURUS (1867) AND ITS RELATION TO THE INTERNAL POLICY OF THE OTTOMAN EMPIRE

The democratic developments within the Armenian Catholic *millet* diminished the Church's administrative role. They therefore ran counter to Rome's ecclesio-political interests in the East and its wish to strengthen the influence of the papacy over Catholic Armenians; this would serve the project of the Holy See, which was to cement the union with the Eastern churches under Roman jurisdiction. The situation became more difficult because of the increasing autonomy of the Armenian Catholic Church.[21] In addition to this, there were similar problems also within other uniate churches.[22] Pius IX was the first pope to take serious action in this area through the bull *Reversurus*, which restricted the administrative autonomy of the Armenian Catholic Church.[23]

Before the publication of the bull, the head of the Armenian Catholic Church had been the patriarch, based in Bzommar, near Beirut. Besides the patriarchate, there were two administrative instruments, the synod of bishops and the patriarchal synod. Over time, the number of Armenian Catholics and of dioceses had grown, and in 1830 the seat of the archbishop *primas*, with jurisdiction in

[21] For instance, the abbot general of the Armenian Catholic order of Antonians received the right to hold office for life and to head the diocese of Antiochia without permission from Rome. These decisions, which were supported by the Armenian Catholic patriarch, met with protest from the Holy See: see Mariam Kartashyan, 'Das armenische Schisma, seine transnationalen Auswirkungen und seine Rolle für die Beziehungen zwischen Armeniern, Altkatholiken und Anglikanern, in den 1870er Jahren' (PhD Dissertation, University of Bern, 2016), 68–9. Beside the increasing autonomy, the relation to other non-Catholic Christian communities was another problem for the Holy See. Since the beginning of the nineteenth century there had been moves within the Ottoman empire to unite the Catholic and the Apostolic Armenians, which were criticized by the Holy See: ibid. 66–7; see also n. 10 above.
[22] For instance, the Melkite patriarch Gregory II Youssef (1864–97) complained of a lack of church discipline within the Eastern churches: Granderath, *Geschichte des Vatikanischen Konzils*, 1: 55. Granderath notes that the election of the bishops in the Eastern rites sometimes contravened the regulations governing the process: ibid. 2: 327.
[23] Granderath and Schneemann, eds, *Collectio Lacensis*, 2: 568–73.

Constantinople and its surroundings, had been established.[24] However, the patriarchate in Lebanon was more independent of Rome than was the archbishop *primas* in Constantinople: while the archbishop *primas* was chosen by the pope, the patriarch was elected by the synod of bishops. The bishops were elected by lower clergy and laymen. There was independence also in the administration of church property, which was under the control of the patriarchate. All this was changed by *Reversurus*. The two Armenian seats of Lebanon and Constantinople were united, with the seat of the patriarch being transferred to Constantinople.[25] A Latin-minded candidate, Anton Hasun (1809–84), was chosen as patriarch.[26] The election of his successor as patriarch, as well as the elections of the bishops, would depend on the decision of the pope. The patriarch was to be elected by the bishops alone, the lower clergy and laymen being excluded from the process. He could exercise his office only after his election had been confirmed by the pope. As for bishops, a list of three candidates would be sent to the pope. The pope had the right to choose one of them, but could also choose and confirm someone else as bishop. The property of the Church would be administered under the supervision of Rome. These administrative changes appeared to be a kind of reunification strategy on the jurisdictional level.

The context for this claim to power over the Armenian Catholic Church was the obvious failure of the efforts of Pius IX to strengthen his waning secular power through the apostolic constitution *Ineffabilis Deus*,[27] the encyclical *Quanta cura*[28] and the document attached to it, *Syllabus errorum*.[29] *Reversurus* was an important ecclesio-political step intended to increase the pope's power in the East and

---

[24] Aleksandr Palčean, *Patmutʻiwn katʻolikē vardapetutʻean i hays ew miutʻean nocʻa ənd hromēakan ekelecʻwoy i pʻlorentean siwnhodosi* (Vienna, 1878), 177.

[25] Because of the political importance of the capital, the transfer of the seat to Constantinople may be understood as a particular ecclesio-political strategy of Pius IX.

[26] Hasun tried to consolidate power, holding the office of *patrik* together with that of patriarch: Yovsēpʻ Askerean [Pōlos Pōynuēyrean], *Hasunean kalakʻakanutʻiwn: Eresun ew hing ameay patmutʻiwn Ger. Hasunean Anton vardapetin, skseal i kahanayutʻenēn minčʻ. čpatriarkʻutiwnn* (Tiflis [Tiblisi], 1868), 503–4.

[27] Pius IX, 'Litterae apostolicae de dogmatica definitione immaculatae conceptionis Virginis Deiparae', in *Corpus actorum RR. Pontificum, Pii X Pontificis Maximi acta*, 2 parts in 9 vols (Graz, 1971; first publ. 1857), 1/i: 597–619.

[28] Pius IX, 'Quanta cura', ibid., 1/iii: 687–700.

[29] Pius IX, 'Syllabus complectens praecipuos nostrae aetatis errores qui notantur in allocutionibus consistorialibus in encyclicis aliisque apostolicis litteris sanctissimi domini nostri Pii Papae IX', ibid. 701–17.

effectively to create the pope's own empire within the Ottoman empire. *Reversurus* would serve as a kind of model for *Pastor aeternus*, which asserted the pope's full and supreme power of jurisdiction over the whole Church, at the First Vatican Council (1869/70).[30] The publication of *Reversurus* was therefore an important step towards the promulgation of the dogma of papal infallibility.

The new ultramontane policy of the Holy See towards the East threatened to remove the autonomy of the Armenian Catholics, which, given their political situation in the Ottoman state, posed a real danger for their security. Living with restricted rights, the Armenian Catholics were about to lose the right to choose the patriarchs and bishops who would best meet their religious and social needs. The influential laymen, the 'notables', some of whom had high positions in government, would no longer exercise any influence in the Church's administration. All this led to considerable discontent amongst the Armenians, and, soon after the publication of the bull, a large proportion of Armenian Catholics protested.[31] However, the Holy See's new policy towards the Catholic Armenians was only a preliminary step, and *Reversurus* was intended to become a model for the other uniate Eastern churches; accordingly, protests soon followed from Catholic Chaldeans, Maronites, Melkites and Syrians.[32]

The escalating tensions were dangerous for the Ottoman empire's internal policy, especially given the administrative structure of the *millet*s. The election of church leaders and the administration of church property was to be managed by the patriarchate under the supervision of the state; it was a matter between the Ottoman empire and its subjects.[33] But in *Reversurus* the pope was claiming that his position was superior to that of the sultan. The Ottoman minister of war, Hüseyin Avni Paşa (1820–76), argued that the pope was seeking

[30] *The Oecumenical Councils of the Roman Catholic Church from Trent to Vatican II (1545–1965)*, CChr.COGD 3, 206–12.
[31] The main protagonists of this protest were the monks of the Order of Antonians.
[32] The reaction of the uniate Chaldeans, Maronites, Melkites and Syrians to this question will be described in my forthcoming article, 'Die Kirchenpolitik des römischen Stuhls während des Zusammenbruchs des Kirchenstaates (bis 1870)', *IKZ* 108 (2018). Jakub Osiecki shows that there were also protests against the pope's supreme jurisdictional power among Armenian Catholics in Artvin in the Russian empire, lasting until the beginning of the twentieth century: Jakub Osiecki, 'The Catholics of the Armenian Rite in Armenia and Georgia (1828–1909)', *IKZ* 106 (2016), 295–319.
[33] After election, the Armenian patriarch would be confirmed in office by the sultan through an official *berât* (licence): Claude Delaval Cobham, *The Patriarchs of Constantinople*, intro. Adrian Fortescue and H. T. F. Duckworth (Cambridge, 1911), 36–7.

to establish a new state within the Ottoman state.[34] Soon a schism among the Armenian Catholics, at the heart of which lay division between ultramontane and anti-ultramontane bishops, created another problem for the Ottoman government. The Armenian Catholic bishops were the intermediaries for the payment of taxes to the state, and the tax system was disrupted as, from the Ottoman point of view, the diocesan heads were divided between legal and illegal bishops.[35]

THE CHURCH POLICY OF THE HOLY SEE IN THE CONTEXT OF EUROPEAN DIPLOMACY

The ultramontane attempts of the Holy See in the East affected not only the domestic policy of the Ottoman empire, but also its foreign policy. The Western great powers realized that the situation created through *Reversurus* could result in increased Western influence in the East. Since the Treaty of Paris (1856), the Western powers had claimed the right to interfere as protectors on behalf of Ottoman Christians.[36] The eagerness of the Russian empire to act as their protector, with a view to expanding its territories, created competition and increased the motivation of the Western powers to assert their authority.[37] The political weakness of the Ottoman government and its apprehension in the face of the growth of Russian power forced it to take account of the position of the Western powers.

With all these forces at work, the Western powers had a clear interest in acting on the Armenian Catholic question. However, in the years following the publication of *Reversurus*, the Holy See did not receive much support from them.[38] While the Austrian government was trying to improve the position of the Holy See, as its protector in the Ottoman empire, the French government refrained from interfering. The Holy See initially tried to achieve a concordat with

---

[34] Anon., 'Constantinopel', *Deutscher Merkur* 5 (1874), 71.

[35] Gazer, 'Bibliographie', 326.

[36] Winfried Baumgart, 'Der Friede von Paris 1856. Studien zum Verhältnis von Kriegführung, Politik und Friedensbewahrung' (Habilitation dissertation, University of Bonn, 1970; publ. München, 1972).

[37] For more on this subject, see Dietrich Geyer, *Der russische Imperialismus. Studien über den Zusammenhang von innerer und auswärtiger Politik 1860–1914*, Kritische Studien zur Geschichtswissenschaft 27 (Göttingen, 1977).

[38] I have explained the reasons for this in much greater detail elsewhere: Mariam Kartashyan, 'Die Rolle der europäischen Imperialmächte für den Verlauf des armenischen Schismas (1871–1879/1881)', *IKZ* 106 (2016), 273–94, at 278–87.

the Ottoman state on its own, which failed. The consequences of all this were the rejection of *Reversurus* and the ban of the ultramontane patriarch Anton Hasun by the Ottoman state.[39] However, in 1871 an anti-ultramontane bishop, Yakob Pahtiarean (1800–83), was elected as patriarch, and in 1872 Yovhan Kʻiwbēlean (1820–1900) was elected as civil patriarch.[40] These events led to a schism between the Armenian Catholics and Rome.[41]

In 1873–4 the German government supported the anti-ultramontane Armenian Catholics, seeking to curb the influence of its political opponent in the East, France, which took on the role of protecting the interests of the Holy See in 1873.[42] The anti-ultramontane mood in Germany created favourable conditions for this interference: from 1871, the *Kulturkampf* was in process, and until 1876 liberals dominated the German government. In addition, the newly formed German Old Catholic Church, which had close relationships to the anti-ultramontane Armenians,[43] used its connections to influence the German government in favour of the anti-ultramontane Armenian Catholic party.[44]

Because of its diplomatic connection to Germany, in 1873 the Austrian government decided to retreat temporarily and not to act against the interests of the German government in the East.[45] The British empire also did not support papal interests: liberals dominated the British government until 1874, and several influential political and public figures, including prime minister W. E. Gladstone

---

[39] MałakʻIa Ōrmanean, *Azgapatum*, ed. Tigran Karapetean and Šahē Ačēmean, 3 vols + 1 register vol. (Ējmiacin, 2001–2), 3: 4962.

[40] BZ, ACA, box 23, portfolio 26, Pōłos Pōynuēyrean, "Ōragrutʻiwnk'"; box 174, portfolio Əntrutʻiwn Yakob Pahtiareani, Yovsēpʻ Šišmanean, [report about the elections], 12 February 1871; see also Ōrmanean, *Azgapatum*, 3: 4961.

[41] According to Herman Schwedt, the main reasons for the schism were the development of European Catholicism and the religious and social conflicts of the Armenian Catholic community in the Ottoman empire: Herman H. Schwedt, 'Weit hinten in der Türkei. Der Papst und das Schisma der armenischen Katholiken (1870–1888)', *IKZ* 106 (2016), 250–72, at 272.

[42] For more details about French and German interference, see Kartashyan, 'Die Rolle der europäischen Imperialmächte', 284–7.

[43] For more, see Kartashyan, 'Das armenische Schisma', 146–205.

[44] Unterburger shows that the internalization of the anti-ultramontane movements was seen as a threat in Rome: Unterburger, 'Internationalisierung als Bedrohungsszenarium', 248.

[45] Vienna, Österreichisches Staatsarchiv, Haus-, Hof- und Staatsarchiv, Gesandtschaftsarchiv Konstantinopel, box 288, portfolio 1, no. 18, Gyula Andrássy to Zichy zu Zich, 25 April 1874.

(1809–98) and the historian and publicist John Acton (1834–1902), had friendly relationships with Ignaz von Döllinger and the Old Catholic movement in Germany.[46]

However, from 1875 the political context in Europe began to change rapidly, strongly affecting the interests of the Western powers and the Ottoman empire.[47] The *Kulturkampf* in Germany weakened and subsided, and in 1876 the German chancellor, Otto von Bismarck (1815–98), began to cooperate with the conservatives.[48] By 1878, steps were being taken towards reconciliation between the German government and the Holy See. As for the British empire, the conservatives took power in 1874, and the new prime minister, Benjamin Disraeli (1804–81), who had good relations with the Ottoman state, was not interested in the success of anti-ultramontanism in the East. Given these circumstances, the Austrian and French governments were able to act effectively to support the interests of the Holy See, and soon British diplomats began to support these interests as well.[49]

Between 1875 and 1878, in the face of new conflicts between the Russian and Ottoman empires, the Eastern crisis escalated, and the Ottoman government became more dependent on the Western powers. This dependence arose because of an Ottoman economic crisis, but also from payments imposed by the Western powers, mainly by France and Britain.[50] Finally, the Ottoman political context changed when in 1876 Abdülhamid II (1842–1918) became sultan. The *Tanẓīmāt* reforms came to an end and the rights of Ottoman

---

[46] See Angela Berlis, 'Ignaz von Döllinger and the Anglicans', in Stewart J. Brown and Peter B. Nockles, eds, *The Oxford Movement: Europe and the Wider World 1830–1930* (Cambridge, 2012), 236–48, at 237.

[47] In a previous article, I analysed the reasons for the shift in Western policy. My aim was to show that the Western powers played a decisive role in the duration and conclusion of the Armenian schism: Kartashyan, 'Die Rolle der europäischen Imperialmächte', 287–92.

[48] Otto Pflanze, *Bismarck*, 2 vols (München 2008), 2: 51–4.

[49] See the complaint of the French chargé d'affaires in Constantinople: La Courneuve, Ministère des Affaires étrangères, Centre des Archives diplomatiques de La Courneuve, Correspondance politique Turquie, Mik. P 724, vol. 407, fols 258ᵛ–259ᵛ, Charles de Moüy to Louis Decazes, 31 January 1877.

[50] Berlin, Politisches Archiv, Auswärtiges Amt, Auswärtiges Amt des deutschen Reiches 1870–1945, 12409b, A 1090, 'Die türkischen Finanzen. Am Schlusse des Finanzjahres 1872/73', 13 March 1873.

Christians were curtailed.[51] As a result, the Holy See's church policy in the East gained a new political dimension. In order not to promote an anti-Western alliance amongst anti-ultramontane Armenian Catholics, all great powers agreed to the sixty-second article of the Treaty of Berlin (1878), which supported the hierarchical rights of the pope in Ottoman territories and declared France the only protector of the Uniate Catholics in the East.[52] Under pressure from the Ottoman government, the Armenian Catholic question was solved within a few years.[53] In 1879 the sultan published a *berât* confirming the appointment of the papal candidate, Anton Hasun, which officially ended the schism, and the anti-ultramontane Armenian Catholics had to abandon their previous position.[54] The situation of the other Eastern rite churches in the Ottoman empire was similar. Whilst the Maronites and other uniate churches gave ground relatively fast, the Chaldeans resisted Roman policy until about 1878. Like the Armenian Catholics, their protest ended under political pressure.[55]

CONCLUSION

In the 1860s and 1870s, the ultramontane policy promoted by Pius IX was part of the Holy See's reunification project in the East. The bull *Reversurus*, as a part of this project, was an attempt to influence the relationship between the Armenian Catholic Church and the Ottoman empire. Papal policy aimed at achieving supreme power for the pope in both ecclesiastical and civil fields, and for this reason it came into conflict both with the interests of the Armenian Catholics and with the domestic policy of the Ottoman state. During the

[51] He became known as the 'red sultan' for his oppression and massacres of Christians, especially Armenians, during his time in power: see, for example, S. V. Bedickian, *The Red Sultan's Soliloquy*, transl. Alice Stone Blackwell (Boston, MA, 1912).
[52] 'Der Berliner Vertrag von 1878. Faksimile aus dem Reichsgesetzblatt', in Imanuel Geiss, ed., *Der Berliner Kongress 1878. Protokolle und Materialien* (Boppard am Rhein, 1978), 369–407.
[53] Schwedt shows the role of the Holy See's flexible church policy, which developed a strategy of gradual action in order to solve the Armenian question. One important step was the challenge to the Armenian Catholic patriarch Hasun, whose strategy was one of the main reasons for the conflict, to retreat from his position in 1880: Schwedt, 'Weit hinten in der Türkei', 250–72, at 268–9.
[54] BZ, ACA, box 38, portfolio 19, Pōłos Pōynuēyrean, 'Tesutiwnk'.
[55] Kartashyan, 'Die Kirchenpolitik des römischen Stuhls', offers a fuller discussion.

1870s, the ecclesiastical and civil rights of the Armenian Catholics were upheld and strengthened by the Ottoman state.

However, the ultramontane policy of the Holy See also affected the foreign policy of the Ottoman state. By the end of the 1870s, the shifting political contexts of Eastern and Western Europe proved more influential than the internal policy of the Ottoman empire, and this allowed Roman ultramontanism to prevail, supported by the Western empires and their international diplomacy. By 1881, the Armenian schism had been concluded to the benefit of the Holy See and its protectors.

It is clear from this that the Holy See's church policy in the 1860s and the 1870s, which sought to bring about a particular form of ecclesiastical union on the jurisdictional level with the uniate churches of the East, also forced the ecclesiastical question of the relationship between the Holy See and the Eastern churches into the arena of international diplomacy. In the end this development provided support for Rome's ultramontanism, leading to the conclusion of the schism in the East and the restoration of the relationship between the Armenian Catholic Church and the Holy See. Neither the Armenian Catholic Church nor the Ottoman empire could resist the ultramontane policies of the Holy See when these were backed by the Western powers, demonstrating the strong interconnection between churches and empires, as well as their spheres of influence in the East and the West during the 1860s and 1870s. The fact that empires sometimes resolved ecclesiastical questions and in so doing demonstrated decisively their authority over churches, as in this case, shows the importance of looking at nineteenth-century church history from the perspective of the history of empires.

'Britishers and Protestants': Protestantism and Imperial British Identities in Britain, Canada and Australia from the 1880s to the 1920s

Géraldine Vaughan*

Université de Rouen / Institut Universitaire de France

This article explores the links between the assertion of British imperial identities and the anti-Catholic discourse and practices of a network of evangelical societies which existed and flourished in Britain and in the dominions from the halcyon days of the empire to the late 1920s. These bodies shared a broad evangelical definition of Protestantism and defended the notion that religious beliefs and their political implications formed the basis of a common British heritage and identity. Those who identified themselves as Britons in Britain and in the dominions brought forward arguments combining a mixture of pessimistic interpretations of British history since the passing of the Catholic Emancipation Act with anxieties about ongoing Irish Catholic immigration and an alleged global papist plot. They were convinced that Protestantism was key to all civil liberties enjoyed by Britons. Inspired by John Wolffe's pioneering work, the article examines constitutional, theologico-political and socio-national anti-Catholicism across Britain and its dominions.

In 1860, the French historian Ernest Renan wrote:

> … nearly all colonizing nations are Protestant. Because of its individual character, its simple means, its lesser need to be in communion with the rest of Christendom, Protestantism appears to be the perfect religion for the settler. With his Bible, the Englishman finds in the depth of Oceania the spiritual nourishment that the Roman Catholic

* 34 rue du Fardeau, 76000 Rouen, France. E-mail: geraldine.vaughan@univ-rouen.fr. This article was written during a period as a visiting fellow at the School of Divinity, Edinburgh University, which was generously funded by a Royal Society of Edinburgh / Caledonian Research Fund European Visiting Research Fellowship. I would like to thank Sir Tom Devine for his remarks on an earlier version of this article and also Patrick Vaughan for his comments.

Studies in Church History 54 (2018) 359–373
doi: 10.1017/stc.2017.20

cannot find without the official establishment of an episcopate and a priesthood.[1]

He might have added further that Protestantism provided settlers with a powerful means of attachment to the metropole. Renan's contemporary outlook on the spirit of British imperialism echoes one of the many connections between religion and empire which have since been explored by historians. In the past thirty years, the ties between empire and Protestantism have been studied according to its ideological, missionary and humanitarian facets. Linda Colley's 1992 opus showed how Protestantism had partly 'invented' Great Britain, while the conquest, possession and administration of a common empire held Britons together. The equation of Britishness, Protestantism and imperialism has since been revisited to highlight the diversity of Protestantism and the competing understandings of what it meant to be a Briton in the United Kingdom and its colonies.[2] However, historians such as John MacKenzie have demonstrated how the empire could provide an arena where members of the four nations could both express their different identities and come together as Britons.[3] By focusing on ultra-Protestant societies across Greater Britain, this article seeks to examine how some asserted a Protestant-British identity in a world which they saw as threatened by the aggressive competition of (Irish) Roman Catholicism and growing secularism. In line with the historiographical position adopted by Tony Claydon and Ian McBride, the purpose of this article is 'to redirect attention away

[1] 'Les nations colonisatrices sont presque toutes protestantes; le protestantisme, par sa tendance individuelle, la simplicité de ses moyens, son peu de besoin de communier avec le reste de la chrétienté, semble par excellence la religion du colon. Avec sa Bible, l'Anglais trouve au fond de l'Océanie l'aliment religieux que le catholique ne peut recevoir sans tout un établissement officiel d'évêques et de prêtres': Ernest Renan, 'De l'avenir religieux des sociétés modernes', *Revue des Deux Mondes* 29 (1860), 761–97, at 773.
[2] Linda Colley, *Britons: Forging the Nation 1707–1832* (New Haven, CT, 1992). For revision of the Colley thesis from historians focusing on the eighteenth and early nineteenth centuries, see Joseph Sramek, 'Rethinking Britishness: Religion and Debates about the "Nation" among Britons in Company India', *JBS* 54 (2015), 822–43; Hilary Carey, *God's Empire: Religion and Colonialism in the British World, c.1801–1908* (Cambridge, 2011).
[3] John M. MacKenzie, 'Essay and Reflection: On Scotland and the Empire', *International History Review* 15 (1993), 714–39; idem, 'Irish, Scottish, Welsh and English Worlds? A Four-Nation Approach to the History of the British Empire', *History Compass* 6 (2008), 1244–63.

from descriptions to aspirations ... [t]reating protestant nationhood ... as an anxious aspiration, rather than as a triumphal description'.[4]

In the 1880s, during the halcyon days of the British empire, a number of ultra-Protestant writers and organizations with imperial networks were anxious to assert the indissoluble link between an imperial Britishness and a Protestant identity.[5] Rather than exploring a specific church, this study concentrates on the anti-Catholic discourse and practices of a number of ultra-Protestant agencies active both in the metropole and across the empire. The Imperial Protestant Federation (IPF), founded by Walter Walsh in 1898, was instrumental in uniting a number of societies under the banner of empire and Protestantism.[6] Thus, amongst others, the Calvinistic Protestant Union (1888), the Scottish Protestant Alliance (1884) and the Women's Protestant Union (1891) in Britain, and the Protestant Protective Association in Canada (1890) and the Australian Protestant Defence Association (1902) in the dominions, together with Orange lodges across the British world, affiliated to the IPF. These bodies shared a broad evangelical definition of Protestantism which affirmed the supreme authority of the Bible, justification by faith alone, salvation through the unique sacrifice of Jesus Christ on the cross, and regeneration of believers through the action of the Holy Spirit. They also defended the notion that religious beliefs and their political implications formed the basis of a common British heritage and identity. John Wolffe's pioneering study has demonstrated how imperial networks of anti-Catholic societies had elaborated a common defence of

[4] Tony Claydon and Ian McBride, eds, *Protestantism and National Identity* (Cambridge, 1998), 26–7.
[5] The expression 'ultra-Protestant' appeared in the early 1840s (*OED*) and referred to people who put forward extreme views in religious matters. It was inspired by the French use of 'ultras' with reference to the ultra-royalists in early nineteenth-century France. In this article, the 'ultra-Protestant' militants are persons or groups who founded specific religious and/or politico-religious associations, who gave religious issues the highest priority in their *Weltanschauung* and who, arguing that there was an urgency to defend Protestantism, exercised pressure on political circles.
[6] Walter Walsh (1847–1912) was a militant evangelical Anglican journalist, essayist and writer, who launched the *Protestant Observer* in 1888. He was the author of the best-selling *The Secret History of the Oxford Movement* (London, 1898). The societies enrolled within the Imperial Protestant Federation were listed in several reports, such as *The Imperial Protestant Federation, Report for 1899–1900 and A History of the Formation and the Progress of the Federation, to which is appended Information regarding its 27 Federated Organisations* (London, 1900).

British values across the empire.[7] Those who identified themselves as Britons in Britain and in the dominions brought forward arguments combining a mixture of pessimistic interpretations of British history since the passing of the Catholic Emancipation Act with anxieties about ongoing Irish Catholic immigration and a so-called global papist plot. They were convinced that Protestantism was key to all civil liberties enjoyed by Britons.

This flourishing of ultra-Protestant societies must be set in a wider context of the ongoing Irish migrations to Britain and its empire, as well as the political turmoil manifested around the issue of Home Rule. Rates of Irish emigration since the 1840s had been impressive: by 1881, 5,400,000 people inhabited Ireland, while there were an estimated 3,680,000 living overseas.[8] In 1914, Catholics of Irish descent represented around 25% of the Australian population.[9] Nevertheless, the late Victorian and Edwardian eras were periods when Irish emigration rates were slowing down. Added to fears of an unending stream of Irish Catholic migrants to Britain and its dominions, political debates surrounding the possible advent of Home Rule in Ireland brought anguish to ultra-Protestant observers across the empire. In 1912, Robert Sellar, a staunch Protestant Scots-Canadian newspaper editor, addressed a warning to his compatriots in his *Ulster and Home Rule: A Canadian Parallel*: 'so long as Ireland is united to Britain they [the Protestants] are safe, but the moment the tie is cut and they pass under the government of a Home Rule legislature they will be, as a people, abandoned to their enemies'.[10]

In order to analyse the various forms of anti-Catholicism at work, the categorization adopted here will diverge slightly from Wolffe's typology.[11] An examination of the connection between religious principles and national identities, in the contemporary writings, journals,

---

[7] John Wolffe, 'Anti-Catholicism and the British Empire, 1815–1914', in Hilary Carey, ed., *Empires of Religion* (Basingstoke, 2008), 43–63. For a recent review of the historiography of anti-Catholicism in a comparative perspective, see Marjule Anne Drury, 'Anti-Catholicism in Germany, Britain and the US: A Review and Critique of Recent Scholarship', *ChH* 70 (2001), 98–131.

[8] Eric Richards, *Britannia's Children: Emigration from England, Scotland, Wales and Ireland since 1600* (London and New York, 2004), 214.

[9] Oliver P. Rafferty, 'The Catholic Church, Ireland and the British Empire, 1800–1921', *HR* 84 (2011), 288–309, at 291.

[10] Robert Sellar, *Ulster and Home Rule: A Canadian Parallel* (Belfast, 1912), 3.

[11] John Wolffe, 'Protestant-Catholic Divisions in Europe and the United States: An Historical and Comparative Perspective', *Politics, Religion and Ideology* 12 (2011), 241–56, at 250; see also idem, 'A Comparative Historical Categorisation of Anti-Catholicism',

newspapers and archives of these societies reveals three distinct forms of anti-Catholicism: constitutional, theologico-political and socio-national.

CONSTITUTIONAL ANTI-CATHOLICISM

Constitutional anti-Catholicism encapsulates all aspects of anti-Catholicism which were state-driven and operated within a legal framework to exclude Catholics from public and civic positions. No further anti-Catholic legislation was adopted in the United Kingdom after the enactment of the Ecclesiastical Titles Bill in 1851.[12] In fact, no *Kulturkampf* took place during mid- and late Victorian times.[13] Yet this did not prevent tensions from resurfacing around the 'true' allegiances of Roman Catholics and their loyalty as British subjects. Accordingly, the Imperial Protestant Federation (1898) prescribed in its revised constitution of May 1901:

> Article 7. To oppose all attempts to:
> a. Alter the Coronation Oath and the Declaration against Transubstantiation
> b. Open the Throne of England to a Romanist
> c. Repeal the Bill of Rights or the Act of Settlement
> d. Throw open the offices of Lord High Chancellor of England and Lord Lieutenant of Ireland to Roman Catholics.[14]

The article did not address any true political or social threat emanating from Roman Catholic milieux but demonstrated how members of the IPF were anxious to position themselves as the guarantors and protectors of the English constitution. Section (d) also confirmed their intention to maintain the political disabilities enshrined in the 1829 Roman Catholic Relief Act. In accordance with section (a), the Church Association and National Protestant League's first question to all candidates for the 1906 General Election was: 'Will you, if elected, resist every attempt to alter or abolish, either the King's Declaration now required by the Bill of Rights, or the Coronation

---

JRH 39 (2015), 182–202. Wolffe identifies four major categories of anti-Catholicism: constitutional-national, theological, socio-cultural and popular.
[12] This legislation was adopted in reaction to the restoration of the Roman Catholic hierarchy in England in 1850, but never enforced.
[13] Colin Barr, 'An Irish Dimension to a British Kulturkampf?', *JEH* 56 (2005), 473–95.
[14] *Report of the Council of the Imperial Protestant Federation for 1901–1902* (London, 1902), 29–34.

Oath?'[15] In 1910, the Church Association gathered over one million signatures from petitioners across the British dominions against any alteration of the King's Declaration.[16]

Safeguarding the restriction on Catholic processions prescribed in the 1829 Emancipation Act was key for ultra-Protestant societies. Section 26 of the act forbade Catholic liturgical processions with clergy in vestments. This section was often loosely interpreted by civil and judicial authorities in the late Victorian period, yet crises surrounding the public processions by Catholics resurfaced during the Edwardian era.[17] For instance, in September 1908, during the nineteenth International Eucharistic Congress, the planned procession of the blessed sacrament through the streets of Westminster sparked political turmoil. Ultra-Protestant societies and organizations put pressure on the police and the Liberal government to ban this demonstration of Roman Catholicism.[18] In the end, the Catholic authorities agreed to abandon the procession of the Holy Host, but the undiplomatic handling of the affair led to the resignation of Lord Ripon, a prominent Roman Catholic, as Lord Privy Seal.

Nearly a century after its adoption, parliamentary debates on the removal of major Catholic disabilities testified to the sensitivity of the subject. In December 1926, the Unionist Scottish MP McInnes Shaw argued that:

> In the West of Scotland we feel that not enough is known of this Bill, and the great deal of ill-feeling which has been aroused … … [T]here are a number of Orangemen in Scotland. They are a very gallant and law-abiding people, but they feel that there is more in this Bill than meets the eye, and for that reason more time should be given for Scotland to digest the proposals.[19]

After some debate, amendments to sections of the 1829 act were adopted by parliament and enforced in Scotland.

---

[15] London, BL, 3940.g.41, Untitled Church Association and National Protestant League pamphlet (London, 1906).
[16] W. Prescott Upton, *The King's Protestant Declaration: Why it must not be Altered*, Church Association Tract 404 (London, 1910).
[17] As shown by Ian Machin, there had been similar processions in 1898 and 1901 without legal prosecution: G. I. T. Machin, 'The Liberal Government and the Eucharistic Procession of 1908', *JEH* 34 (1993), 559–83, at 561.
[18] Ibid.; see also Carol A. Devlin, 'The Eucharistic Procession of 1908: The Dilemma of the Liberal Government', *ChH* 63 (1994), 407–35.
[19] *House of Commons Debates*, 3 December 1926, vol. 200 col. 1587.

In contrast, the constitutional position of Roman Catholics was more favourable in the dominions. In the Canadian colonies, the acquisition of French (Catholic) Quebec had led to the passing of the 1774 Quebec Act, which effectively granted freedom of religious practice. With the 1791 Constitutional Act, the legislative assemblies for Lower and Upper Canada permitted Catholics to vote and to become representatives. Legal and political toleration of Roman Catholics varied in each Canadian colony, but on the whole, it was in advance of the British Isles.[20] In the Australian colonies, the 1836 Church Act promulgated by Richard Bourke, the Irish Protestant governor of New South Wales, placed all Christian denominations on an equal footing. This legislation alarmed the Anglicans as it successfully disestablished the Church of England and 'seemed to question the essential link between Church and State which was the bedrock of the British Empire'.[21] Nevertheless, other state-related arguments were brandished by ultra-Protestant bodies, who persistently claimed, for instance, that Roman Catholics were over-represented in official occupations. Hence the Protestant Protective Association in Ontario, founded in the early 1890s, criticized the government because 25 per cent of civil servants were Roman Catholics, whereas their proportion in the general population was closer to 15 per cent.[22]

Another dimension of constitutional anti-Catholicism which emerged from the 1870s onwards centred on the related issues of education, secularization and the state's attitude towards denominational schools. The position of local and central colonial authorities regarding public support for schools varied significantly across the dominions. In Canada, the Manitoba Schools controversy in the 1890s illustrated the strong opposing views on the status of religious instruction in State schools. The Act to Establish a System of Education in the Province of Manitoba (1871) had put in place a system of separate Protestant and Catholic schools. Responding

---

[20] J. R. Miller, 'Anti-Catholicism in Canada: From the British Conquest to the Great War', in Terrence Murphy and Gerald Storz, eds, *Creed and Culture: The Place of English-Speaking Catholics in Canadian Society 1750–1930* (Montreal, QC, 1993), 25–48. The harshest legal attitude to Roman Catholics was to be found on Prince Edward Island, where Roman Catholics had to wait until 1830 before they had a right to vote and to hold public office.

[21] Peter Cunich, 'Archbishop Vaughan and the Empires of Religion in Colonial New South Wales', in Carey, ed., *Empires of Religion*, 137–60, at 145.

[22] *The Protestant Protective Association in Ontario: History and Principles of the Organization* (n.pl., 1894), 2.

to the pressure of ultra-Protestant and secularist lobbies in the early 1890s, Manitoba abolished state-supported denominational schools in 1891. This sparked a crisis which was partly resolved by the adoption of the 1896 act, which permitted half an hour of religious instruction in public schools.[23] Nevertheless, ultra-Protestant bodies usually aligned with secularists in asking for minimal or no support from the public authorities for Roman Catholic schools. Similarly, in New South Wales, the Australian Protestant Defence Association declared in its manifesto:

> Under the plea of 'freedom of instruction', Archbishop Kelly has publicly declared his intention to fight for State endowment of Roman Catholic schools. This unquestionably means State aid to religion, and as the control of Roman Catholic Schools is wholly in the hands of the priesthood who are under the direction of the Vatican in Rome, and as the teaching staff consists exclusively of members of so-called religious orders', it means State aid to the most undesirable elements in our community and not the most loyal. This would also involve the disruption of the present admirable system of public instruction.[24]

In the United Kingdom, in the 1920s, similar arguments were brought forward by ultra-Protestant bodies who protested against the 1918 Education (Scotland) Act, which had enabled Catholic schools to become part of the state system while remaining under Catholic clerical control. In its annual report for 1925–6, the Scottish Women's Protestant Union identified three great perils for Scottish society, one of which was the existence of the Roman Catholic schools.[25]

THEOLOGICO-POLITICAL ANTI-CATHOLICISM

This second type of anti-Catholicism encompasses the interconnection of theological and political concerns, particularly around the issues of power structures and authoritarianism. In the late nineteenth and early twentieth centuries, theologico-political anti-Catholicism was seen as contiguous with Reformation principles and in line with major evangelical values. Ultra-Protestant associations emphasized

---

[23] J. R. Miller, 'Anti-Catholic Thought in Victorian Canada', *Canadian Historical Review* 66 (1985), 474–94.
[24] Patrick O'Farrell, ed., *Documents in Australian Catholic History* (London, 1969), 181.
[25] *37th Scottish Women's Protestant Annual Report, 1925–1926* (n.pl., 1926), 1.

their anti-papal stance by combining theological rejection of Roman Catholicism with an abhorrence of the alleged tyrannical, freedom-destructive and imperialistic views of the Vatican. Classic religious 'errors' ascribed to Roman Catholics were 'transubstantiation, the Sacrifice of the Mass, Invocation of Saints, Purgatory, Prayers for the Dead, Auricular Confession, and Extreme Unction', along with alleged priestly domination, ignorance of the laity and the tyrannical powers of the papacy.[26] 'Provocations' by the Vatican energized the theological anti-Catholic discourse: thus the promulgation of papal infallibility in 1870 and the condemnation of mixed marriages contained in the *Ne Temere* decree of 1907[27] were presented as proofs of the Vatican's sectarian and political agenda. Ultra-Protestant societies thus connected religious and political dimensions in their writings and lectures.

These societies operated within imperial networks in different ways, and one efficient medium was the professional agitators whom they regularly invited to lecture throughout the British Empire.[28] For instance, Charles Chiniquy (1809–99), a former French-Canadian Catholic priest, who had joined the Presbyterian Church in 1860, spent the rest of his life lecturing against the 'Romish' Church in Scotland, Australasia and the United States.[29] Edith O'Gorman, a celebrated escaped nun, lectured across Britain in the early 1880s before travelling through Australasia from 1885 to 1888. In the thirty-fifth edition of her successful autobiography *Convent Life Unveiled* (first published in 1871), she wrote: 'The circulation of my books and thousands of lectures delivered have been the means of arousing the British public to the danger of Rome's aggressive encroachment on the rights of Free Speech, Free Press, and Liberty of Conscience'.[30]

The conviction that the Roman Church was profoundly anti-liberal led to the development of a discourse on the connection between the fight against Catholicism and the preservation of British

---

[26] 'Solemn Protestant League and Covenant for the British Empire', *Protestant Observer*, May 1902, 68.
[27] Wolffe, 'Protestant-Catholic Divisions', 191.
[28] Donald MacRaild, 'Transnationalising "Anti-Popery": Militant Protestant Preachers in the Nineteenth-Century Anglo-World', *JRH* 39 (2015), 224–43.
[29] *The Bulwark*, September 1892, 3; see also Paul Laverdure, 'Creating an Anti-Catholic Crusader: Charles Chiniquy', *JRH* 15 (1988), 94–108.
[30] Edith O'Gorman, *Convent Life Unveiled: Trials and Persecutions of Miss Edith O'Gorman, otherwise Sister Teresa de Chantal, the Escaped and Converted Nun*, 35th edn (Edinburgh, 1928), vi.

liberties across the United Kingdom and the dominions. It also prompted a progressive discourse contrary to the reactionary image ultra-Protestant societies sometimes conveyed. These associations were resolutely modern in their propaganda, in the prominent role women played in them and in their official discourse on the progress of Protestant societies. There was thus certainly a liberal and progressive flavour to the theological and political anti-Catholic discourse in Britain. This fits with what Michael Gross has demonstrated concerning the German *Kulturkampf*, which originated not in conservative but rather in liberal circles.[31] The indissoluble link between Protestantism and civil liberties was at the heart of this discourse and was insisted upon especially by colonists who were keen to remain loyal to their British roots. In 1912, the Orangemen of British Columbia sent a copy of an address to their brethren in Ireland, in which they stated: 'The Papacy hates Britain to-day as it hates no other nation on earth. This hate arises from the fact that Britons, as a people, insist on individual liberty'.[32]

SOCIO-NATIONAL ANTI-CATHOLICISM

In the third type of anti-Catholicism, ethnic prejudices and social considerations coalesced to form a xenophobic discourse which essentialized British identity. As the historian James Miller observed for Canada, 'in the late nineteenth century the emphasis on theological disputation gave way to a nationalistic preoccupation with the social and political implications of Catholicism'.[33] In this form, ultra-Protestant discourse stressed the socially progressive and modern aspect of Protestant Britishness, which was connected to ethnic stereotypes, over against the so-called reactionary character of Catholic nations. The common *Briton-ness* of metropolitans and colonists was supposed to rest on values of social and moral progress which had been fought for since the Reformation. As the Revd Robert F. Horton wrote in *England's Danger* (1899), the Protestant spirit 'since Descartes philosophized and Bacon opened the gates of

---

[31] Michael B. Gross, *The War against Catholicism: Liberalism and the Anti-Catholic Imagination in Nineteenth-Century Germany* (Ann Arbor, MI, 2004). There is scope for more research on this subject in connection with ultra-Protestant British associations.
[32] *Protestant Observer*, March 1912, 54.
[33] Miller, 'Anti-Catholicism in Canada', 25.

modern science, has made the progress of human mind'.[34] Thus Catholic countries and their inhabitants were described as backward and illiberal. National stereotypes of the Irish and the French associated the dominance of Catholicism with economic underdevelopment and archaic social structures. It was alleged that Catholic societies remained in a state of poverty partly because they needed to support numerous clergy through tithes and partly because of the superfluity of holy days on which no work was done. In Canada, the Scottish-born Methodist minister George Douglas (d. 1894) held similar views regarding Quebec, which was cited as a possible example of what could happen if French Catholics were not controlled:

> Take a million of the free men of your Ontario and contrast them with a million of our Franco-Canadians, and what is the commercial value of the one as contrasted with the other … . Because the intelligence of the one [Quebec] is stagnant and nil, while that of Ontario is aggressive, and hence the ever-increasing demand with the skilled power of supply.[35]

This view of Catholic backwardness was typical of the contemporary association of low moral standards with poverty; '[a]scribing poverty to laziness and, in turn, laziness to Catholicism evoked a sort of primordial note which few Protestants refrained from striking'.[36] The *Protestant Alliance Official Organ* drew its readers' attention to 'Protestantism as the bulwark of national independence and social freedom … Protestant nations have prospered and grown great, while those that have remained under the blighting influence of Popery have dwindled down and decayed.'[37] In ultra-Protestant discourse, the fear of national decay, which was heightened after the South African War (1899–1902) and various reports on the physical and moral disabilities of the working urban classes, became at times quite obsessive. In this display of anti-Catholicism, ethnic prejudices were mobilized to put forward a common British identity, with an insistence on the masculine and virile qualities of the Anglo-Saxon race. This also expressed itself in demonstrations of anti-clericalism, particularly directed against Anglo-Catholic priests

[34] R. F. Horton, *England's Danger* (London, 1899), 91.
[35] George Douglas, *Discourses and Addresses* (Toronto, ON, 1894), 304.
[36] Roberto Romani, *National Character and Public Spirit in Britain and France, 1750–1914* (Cambridge, 2006), 216.
[37] *Protestant Alliance Official Organ*, January 1898, 1.

in Anglican churches, who were ridiculed for their love of fancy vestments, incense and bells.[38] Caricatures of tonsured Anglo-Catholic priests could be found in the *Protestant Alliance Official Organ*. For example, in January 1900 a cartoon entitled 'Oil for Troubled Waters' featured two clergymen in a boat. The 'Strong Man', an evangelical minister, addressed a 'Little Man', saying: 'Why, your nonsense about incense, vestments, candles, chasubles, and tunicles has so troubled the waters, that we shall both go down unless you go overboard'.[39]

Amongst the anxieties expressed regarding loyalty to British identity, the fear of Irish domination was present in the colonies and regions where their migration had been significant. Thus promoters of the Australian Protestant Defence Association wrote in *The Watchman* in 1902: 'We are Britishers, and we have no desire that Australia should become a second Ireland, dominated by men who are never so happy as when they are in league with Britain's enemies'.[40] Thus anti-Catholicism acted as the best defence against the contamination of deleterious (worldwide) Irish and (Canadian) French influences. Also, within the colonial world, competition with French missionaries heightened a sense of urgency, in particular in connection with the indigenous inhabitants of Canada and on the Pacific islands. Accordingly, only imperial unity could act efficiently against papist influence, whether Irish or French, as the Canadian writer W. A. Armstrong asserted in the 1880s: '[i]f we British Canadians are to remain freemen, we must check the encroachments of the Romanists. To do so, there is in fact but one course open to us – the unity of the Empire.'[41] By asserting common British values, ultra-Protestant colonists were anxious to preserve what they considered as Anglo-Saxon values, that is, industriousness and progress. In turn, British associations in the United Kingdom relied on their colonial counterparts to maintain and preserve Britishness at home. In 1906, the Imperial Protestant Federation claimed to include 1.6 million members and 57 societies, of which a third were in the dominions.

After the First World War, there was a revival of this type of anti-Catholicism, both in Britain and in the dominions. Scotland was

---

[38] Hugh McLeod, 'Varieties of Anticlericalism in Later Victorian and Edwardian England', in Nigel Aston and Matthew Cragoe, eds, *Anticlericalism in Britain c.1500–1914* (Stroud, 2000), 198–220.

[39] *Protestant Alliance Official Organ,* January 1900, 295.

[40] *The Watchman* (Sydney), 1 February 1902, 4.

[41] [William R. Armstrong], *Essay on the Times: Canada, 1887* (n.pl., 1887), 23.

particularly affected by this resurgence. The campaign waged by the Kirk following the 1923 General Assembly Report on *The Menace of the Irish Race to our Scottish Nationality* targeted Scots-Irish Catholics for nativist and ecclesiastical reasons.[42] The offensive by the Kirk, which specifically claimed to be *ethnic*, because it targeted Irish nationals, and not religious, was set in a wider British and European context of mounting nationalisms. In Scotland as well as more generally in Britain, as convincingly demonstrated by R. M. Douglas, the 1916 rising and the Irish war of independence racialized attitudes to the Irish.[43] Douglas characterizes in this manner the racial prejudice which resurfaced against the Irish at the time of the partition of Ireland:

> With the withdrawal in 1921 of the Irish Free State from the United Kingdom … there seemed little advantage to be gained from continuing to proclaim the miscibility of British and Irish stocks. To the contrary, assertions of the racial incompatibility of the two peoples now served both to provide an explanation for Britain's failure to assimilate the Irish to Anglo-Saxon norms, and to assuage the wounded amour-propre of the nation whose identity Ireland had so brusquely repudiated. The 1920s thus witnessed the growth, to a degree unseen since the mid-1880s, of a tendency to characterize the Irish in racial – and usually derogatory – terms … .[44]

Douglas also argued that anti-Catholicism was not a component of the rise of anti-Irishness in Scotland. Yet, from the perspective of ultra-Protestant societies active in the 1920s, there was definitely a religious trigger to the socio-national rejection of Roman Catholics. It might be argued that there was in fact a combination of anti-Catholic and nationalistic concerns which sparked off some aggressive campaigns and demonstrations against Irish-born residents and people of Irish descent. The Scottish Protestant League, founded in 1920 by Alexander Ratcliffe, issued a leaflet entitled 'Who Fills our Prisons?' during the 1929 General Election Campaign:

---

[42] Stewart J. Brown, '"Outside the Covenant": The Scottish Presbyterian Churches and Irish Immigration, 1922–1938', *InR* 42 (1991), 19–45; David Ritchie, 'The Civil Magistrate: The Scottish Office and the anti-Irish Campaign, 1922–1929', *InR* 63 (2012), 48–76; Thomas M. Devine, *The Scottish Nation 1700–2000* (London, 2000), 498–9.
[43] R. M. Douglas, 'Anglo-Saxons and Attacotti: The Racialization of Irishness in Britain between the World Wars', *Ethnic and Racial Studies* 25 (2002), 40–63.
[44] Ibid. 43.

There is an immediate need for legislation to control the influx of Irish Roman Catholics, who are imported into this country to snatch the jobs from Protestants and to help the Romish Church Romanise the country ... for legislation to control the importation of undesirable Roman Catholic Irishmen, who are becoming a menace to the moral and spiritual welfare of the country and a heavy burden on the rates and taxes ...[45]

Ratcliffe's arguments were a typical nationalistic mixture of rejection on the grounds that Irish migrants were a labour-snatching, demoralizing and pauperized population.

The necessity of maintaining an imperial connection between anti-Catholic movements dwindled during the inter-war years. After the death of Walter Walsh in 1912, the IPF struggled to survive in the late 1910s and early 1920s.[46] But the slowing down of the IPF's activities was essentially due to mutations within the dynamics of anti-Catholicism. With its flexibility, the anti-Catholic stance had adapted to the various colonial contexts and could be mobilized for purely local purposes, with at times only a vague reference to a common British background. Outside the colonies, anti-Catholicism was a transatlantic movement which resurfaced in the United States within extremist associations such as the Klu Klux Klan.[47] Within the United Kingdom, the plasticity of anti-Catholic discourse and practice allowed it to be incorporated into rising nationalist discourses, especially in Scotland.

Conclusion

From the 1880s up to World War I, the imperial project of ultra-Protestant societies across the British world revolved around the maintenance of Protestantism and anti-Catholicism as the pillars of a common Britishness. Ultra-Protestant bodies were convinced they

---

[45] BL, 8142.i.14, Scottish Protestant League, *General Election Leaflet no. 7* (Falkirk, 1929).
[46] Wolffe, 'Anti-Catholicism and the British Empire', 567.
[47] See, for instance, John Higham, *Strangers in the Land: Patterns of American Nativism 1860–1925* (New Brunswick, NJ, 1955); Justin Nordstrom, *Danger on the Doorstep: Anti-Catholicism and American Print Culture in the Progressive Era* (Notre Dame, IN, 2006); Philip Jenkins, *The New Anti-Catholicism: The Last Acceptable Prejudice* (New York, 2003).

were fighting an enemy who had an imperial agenda, as Walter Walsh wrote in the IPF Report for 1899–1900:

> Rome knows that by weakening Protestantism in the British Empire she will paralyze it everywhere, and her emissaries are labouring day and night with this object in view. … We are face to face with a deadly foe, which will not be content to live with us on terms of equality …[48]

In some respects, these societies presented reactionary features, particularly with their determination to revert to a pre-1829 position and their exaltation of the virtues of an idealized Reformation past. Nonetheless, they were eager to appeal to the urban middle classes and presented a discourse which was meant to be liberal, modern and progressive. The leaders and organizers of these societies resorted to all modern means for the greater and faster propagation of their ideas – newspapers, pamphlets and books; women were actively employed in various capacities, and preachers were regularly invited to address the masses.

The plasticity and adaptability of anti-Catholicism was manifest in the progressive relinquishing of the imperial connections during the inter-war era. The three types of anti-Catholicism presented in this article (constitutional, theologico-political and socio-national) broadly corresponded to successive time periods, and the first two types were definitely losing ground by the late 1910s. By contrast, socio-national anti-Catholicism, which was particularly adaptable to different colonial and metropolitan contexts, thrived in the 1920s and early 1930s. In a context of rising European nationalism and successful racial theories, it could be mobilized to exclude the Irish from the nationalist project (Scotland, Australia) or to discard French influences (Canada). Further exploration is needed into the diminishing references to a common Britishness in ultra-Protestant bodies across the Commonwealth in the 1930s and into the links between the growth of secularization and the history of ultra-Protestant agencies in post-World War II societies.

---

[48] *The Imperial Protestant Federation, Report for 1899–1900* (London, 1900), 16.

Englishness, Empire and Nostalgia: A Heterodox Religious Community's Appeal in the Inter-War Years

Jane Shaw*

Stanford University

This article looks at the ways in which the Panacea Society – a heterodox, millenarian group based in Bedford during the inter-war years – spread its ideas: through personal, familial and shared belief networks across the British empire; by building new modes of attracting adherents, in partic- ular a global healing ministry; and by shipping its publications widely. It then examines how the society appealed to its (white) members in the em- pire in three ways: through its theology, which put Britain at the centre of the world; by presuming the necessity and existence of a 'Greater Britain' and the British empire, while in so many other quarters these entities were being questioned in the wake of World War I; and by a deliberately cultivated and nostalgic notion of 'Englishness'. The Panacea Society con- tinued and developed the idea of the British empire as providential at a time when the idea no longer held currency in most circles. The article draws on the rich resource of letters in the Panacea Society archive to contribute to an emerging area of scholarship on migrants' experience in the early twentieth-century British empire (especially the dominions) and their sense of identity, in this case both religious and British.

Walking in the grounds of the army residency in Lucknow, India, on Easter Sunday 1925, Lieut. C. E. Harold Dolphin of the Lin- colnshire Regiment found a little piece of the Union Jack flag that had fluttered to the ground after being torn off in the wind. He picked it up, feeling it to be of enormous significance, and sent it, along with a letter reporting on his spiritual progress, to the religious group to which he belonged, which was based in England.[1] The group was the Panacea Society, a millenarian community in Bedford, led by a woman named Octavia, their female messiah figure. She was

* Department of Religious Studies, Building 70, 450 Serra Mall, Stanford, CA 94305– 2165, USA. E-mail: janeshaw@stanford.edu.
[1] Bedford, Panacea Society Archives [hereafter: PS] F6.2/11, C. E. H. Dolphin to Miss Hilda Green, 3 May 1925.

Studies in Church History 54 (2018) 374–392   © Ecclesiastical History Society 2018
doi: 10.1017/stc.2017.21

delighted to receive the fragment of that Union Jack which had been flying in Lucknow and which had, appropriately, dropped through her letterbox in England on Empire Day, 24 May (Queen Victoria's birthday).[2]

The Panacea Society began in 1919 under the leadership of Mabel Barltrop in Bedford. There she created a community consisting of shared houses for members, mostly clustered on one street, a large garden and a chapel. Mrs Barltrop was a vicar's widow, who was identified by her followers as the daughter of God and the incarnation of the spiritual child of the early nineteenth-century prophet Joanna Southcott. Southcott had claimed in 1814 that she would give birth to such a messianic figure, 'Shiloh', but had died without (physically) doing so. Over the course of the nineteenth and early twentieth centuries, a number of other Southcottian prophets and movements emerged, of whom Mrs Barltrop was the last, creating a transnational millennial movement.[3] She was renamed Octavia by her followers and presided over a society whose members believed they would attain immortal life on earth through a tough spiritual practice known as 'overcoming': this entailed making themselves 'zero' by constantly confessing and working on their faults and failings. They eagerly anticipated the Second Coming of Jesus, and gave Britain a prominent place in the millennium, coming to believe that their own garden was the original Garden of Eden and therefore would be the site of Jesus's return.[4]

While there were (at any one time) between fifty-five and seventy resident members of the community at Bedford during the interwar years, there were also many hundreds of non-resident members. By 1934 (when Octavia died) there were 1,285 resident and non-resident members, and this number had risen to 1,978 by 1943. Of these, many had contact with the 'white settler countries' or dominions (Australia, New Zealand, Canada and South Africa), as well as

[2] Established in 1902 as a day to teach schoolchildren the importance of the British empire and their responsibilities to it, by the 1920s Empire Day was being questioned in some quarters: J. English, 'Empire Day in Britain, 1904–1958', *HistJ* 44 (2006), 247–76.
[3] For details of this movement, see Jane Shaw and Philip Lockley, *The History of a Modern Millennial Movement: The Southcottians* (London, 2017).
[4] On the Panacea Society, see Jane Shaw, *Octavia, Daughter of God: The Story of a Female Messiah and her Followers* (London and New Haven, CT, 2011). The Panacea Museum in Bedford tells the community's history and displays its rich material culture; see its website, at: <http://panaceatrust.org/the-panacea-museum/>.

parts of the British empire such as India, through family members who had emigrated; and about 20 per cent of them were living in a part of the British empire or a white settler country, had done so in the past, or did so for a period of their membership of the Panacea Society.[5]

In addition, tens of thousands of correspondents were part of the society's global healing ministry, which attracted about 132,000 correspondents from its inception in 1923 until its closure in the early twenty-first century, the main years of activity being between 1923 and 1939. The majority of these healing applicants came from the USA (39,055), but following closely behind was Jamaica (33,074) and then Britain itself (23,385); the dominions accounted for nearly 4,000 (Australia 1,597, Canada 1,353, New Zealand 662, South Africa 289), Ghana, the Gold Coast and British Togo for 2,863. Most countries that had some particular relationship to Britain were represented, even if only by smaller numbers of applicants (Hong Kong 2, Ceylon 30 and so on). The highest numbers from European countries were Finland (3,346) and France (3,030).[6]

The inter-war years saw many challenges to the British empire: while imperial troops had been essential to Britain's capacity to fight in World War I, in the wake of that war the 'everydayness' or 'taken-for-grantedness' of empire, as Catherine Hall and Sonya Rose express it, was being questioned, both at home and in parts of the empire.[7] But the Panacea Society retained an imperial mindset, drawing on a strong streak of nostalgia for a lost – or dying – sense of Britain and its place in the world. This meant that the society had a special appeal to many white Britons who lived in parts of the British empire, especially the dominions; it also reassured resident members back in the 'metropole' – Bedford, for them – that the old Britain with an intact empire still existed. There was a particular emphasis on a nostalgic notion of *Englishness*, which incorporated the imperial

---

[5] On migration to the dominions in this period, see Stephen Constantine, *Emigrants and Empire: British Settlement in the Dominions between the Wars* (Manchester, 1990).

[6] These figures were compiled by Alistair Lockhart of Cambridge University, and will be published in his forthcoming book on the Panacea Society's healing ministry.

[7] Catherine Hall and Sonya O. Rose, 'Introduction: Being At Home with the Empire', in eaedem, eds, *At Home with the Empire: Metropolitan Culture and the Imperial World* (Cambridge, 2006), 1–31, at 23. On the slow demolition of the imperial mindset in the twentieth century, see Andrew S. Thompson, 'Social Life and Cultural Representation: Empire in the Public Imagination', in idem, ed., *Britain's Experience of Empire in the Twentieth Century* (Oxford, 2012), 251–97.

mindset as 'natural'. As Alison Light puts it, this phenomenon is 'a conservative embracing of modernity, shaped by the experience of dislocation after the First World War'. It represented 'a more intimate and everyday species of conservatism which caught the public imagination between the wars and could itself recast the imperial, as well as the national, idea of Englishness'.[8]

This article looks at the ways in which the Panacea Society spread its ideas: through personal, familial and shared belief networks across the British empire; by building new modes of attracting adherents; and by shipping its books widely. It then examines how the society appealed to its (white) members in the empire in three ways: through its theology, which put Britain at the centre of the world; by presuming the necessity and existence of a 'Greater Britain' when in so many other quarters this was being questioned in the wake of World War I; and by a deliberately cultivated and nostalgic notion of 'Englishness'. (It should be noted that Britishness and Englishness were largely fused, and used interchangeably, in the society's literature; members came from all parts of the United Kingdom, although there was a particularly high proportion of women and men from England.)

The article draws on the rich resource of letters from migrants sent in to the Panacea Society in the 1920s and 1930s, and therefore contributes to what is, at present, a rather sparse field, namely, the British migrant experience in the inter-war years. As the historian of migration Stephen Constantine notes, such collections of letters are far more plentiful for the nineteenth century and 'only a few collections dating to the twentieth century are yet publicly available and fewest of all from English migrants'.[9] These letters, sent to the Panacea Society (an archive that has only recently been opened) especially relate senders' religious experiences and their sense of English (sometimes British) identity. [10]

---

[8] Alison Light, *Forever England: Femininity, Literature and Conservatism Between the Wars* (London, 1991), 11. On conservative modernity, see Alexandra Harris, *Romantic Moderns: English Writers, Artists and the Imagination from Virginia Woolf to John Piper* (London, 2010); Jed Esty, *A Shrinking Island: Modernism and National Culture in Modern England* (Princeton, NJ, 2003); Michael Saler, *The Avant-Garde in Interwar England: 'Medieval Modernism' and the London Underground* (Oxford, 1999).

[9] Stephen Constantine, '"Dear Grace … Love Maidie': Interpreting a Migrant's Letters from Australia, 1926–67', in Kent Fedorowich and Andrew S. Thompson, eds, *Empire, Migration and Identity in the British World* (Manchester, 2013), 192–213, at 193.

[10] On the opening of the Panacea Society archive, see Shaw, *Octavia*, ix–xiii; Shaw and Lockley, *History*, 2, 204–6.

Spreading Panacea Ideas

Migration was the primary way most Britons knew about the British empire: those who left and those who remained at home became part of 'a global chain of kith and kin'.[11] The Panaceans spread their ideas initially through their personal and familial networks, many of which extended into the British empire. Dolphin heard about it from his cousin, Mary Warry, an enthusiastic non-resident Panacean who lived in Somerset. He joined the society in 1924 while he was living in Surrey on the verge of entering the army, and visited Bedford before he sailed for India. Once he arrived in India, Harold Dolphin brought others in. Within two months of getting to Lucknow, he was writing to Octavia that he had explained Panacea ideas to a friend in the regiment, a dissatisfied Christian Scientist. A few months later, he had signed up two of his regiment colleagues, and a third was interested. As he wrote to Miss Hilda Green, who headed up the Panacea correspondence department, 'It is awfully jolly there being three of us & I do so want to make it four!!' However, Mr Hastie (one of the group) 'is worried by the wish to get home & enjoy himself before the coming of the Kingdom. I suppose this is an attack of Lucifer's and hope it will soon pass away.' Dolphin's letters track both his spiritual progress and his attempts to bring others into the Panacea Society. By 1928, he had become engaged to his colonel's daughter, a Miss Eileen Johnson, who was 'so enthusiastic' about the Panacea Society but could not read the books at home 'for fear of her parents', who did not agree with its beliefs. At their first opportunity, when he had leave, they visited Bedford together.[12] Such visits back to the 'Centre', when they were possible, were highly valued by non-resident members for the in-person interviews with Octavia, the worship according to the Book of Common Prayer in chapel, and the charm of tea parties, shared meals and conversations with fellow believers, all reassuring them in both form and content that the England they loved had not yet died.

Many at the very heart of the Panacea Society had strong familial or personal connections to parts of the British empire, not least

[11] Kent Federowich and Andrew S. Thompson, 'Mapping the Contours of the British World: Empire, Migration and Identity', in eidem, eds, *Empire*, 1–41, at 15. On migration, see also Marjory Harper and Stephen Constantine, *Migration and Empire* (Oxford, 2011).

[12] PS, F6.2/11, C. E. H. Dolphin to Octavia, 11 December 1924; C. E. H. Dolphin to Miss Hilda Green, 9 April 1925, 5 May, 1926, 27 July 1928.

Octavia, through her two surviving sons (a third had died in World War I): Ivan lived in Vancouver and Adrian in India, where he served as an officer in the army and had very definite views on the importance of the British empire, writing, 'The Hindus and the Mohammedans will never see eye to eye and it is for this reason that India belongs to the British Empire.'[13] Ivan had nothing to do with the society's beliefs, and Adrian later came to have deeply ambivalent and tortured feelings about his mother's religion, but in the early and mid-1920s he was an active member, who spread the word amongst his fellow army officers just as Dolphin did. In 1920, Captain Richard Maguire, who was at the Army Signal School, Kakul, Abbottabad, in India, wrote: 'Through Mr Barltrop who is now on a course at the school I got the wonderful news of the coming redemption of mankind.' His next letter, written in May 1921, demonstrates his efforts to tell others of his new conviction, but with little response, although one with whom he did have success was the twenty-one year old Lieut. D. M. Killingley, of the 17/37 Cavalry in Lucknow. After reading the books that Maguire had lent him, Killingley wrote to Bedford in June 1922: 'I am convinced that these writings are the truth, and I would like to know more about the whole thing.'[14]

Others back at the centre, in Bedford, who had strong personal connections to, or experiences of, the British empire included Mildred and William Hollingworth, who held key positions in the society as head of the healing ministry and head of the printing press respectively, and had been missionaries in Africa. Cyril Carew-Hunt, who had fought in World War I and attained the rank of major, had lived in Australia before the war and continued to have strong ties with his relatives there; he was the society's secretary and took on much of its general correspondence, especially after Octavia's death. Frances Wright, formerly a prominent Theosophist, and one of the wealthier members of the society, had lived in India. These leading members, at the centre of the society, set the tone with an imperial mindset, especially Octavia. She even dictated which newspapers members should read on these terms. In an editorial in *The Panacea*, the society's magazine, in 1934, she put the *Morning Post* at the top of the list because it was 'sound, loyal, independent and patriotic', especially on the monarchy and empire. The *Daily Express* was also

---

[13] PS, A3.5/8, Adrian Barltrop to Miss Mason, 19 May 1927.
[14] PS, F5.2/27, F6.3/10, Richard Maguire to the Panacea Society, 5 December 1920, 29 May 1921; F6.3/7, D. M. Killingley to the Panacea Society, 15 June 1922.

acceptable, for it was 'a strong champion in the cause of Empire and free trade within it'. The *Daily Telegraph* was to be commended for its general news, but it was not sound on the India question (home rule was anathema to the Panaceans) or the League of Nations (also despised). Unacceptable were the *News Chronicle* and *Daily Herald* for their liberal views, the latter being admiring of Gandhi and 'most impatient to give away India – and in fact, the whole Empire'.[15]

The Ricketts family – mother, son and daughter – were keen Panaceans and bridged England and different parts of the British empire. Thomas, known as Donald, was an undergraduate at Trinity College, Cambridge, when he became a member of the society in 1922. He graduated in the summer of 1923, and in 1924 he joined the Indian army, being posted to Rangoon in Burma; he often wrote pieces about Burma for *The Panacea*. His faith was strong and he encouraged his mother, Annie, to join the society; she visited Bedford to become a member in March 1925 before going on to Adelaide, Australia, to live with her daughter Ruth. Donald wrote to his mother that he expected that she and his sister would be 'the first to become "Panacea-ites" if the news has not already got there'.[16] They appear to have been independent of any other Panaceans in Australia, keeping all their links directly with the society or via Donald in Burma. Annie spent time with Donald in Rangoon, while Ruth remained in Adelaide until going to live permanently in Bedford in 1929. Donald visited Bedford often. In 1943, he was awarded the OBE for 'bravery and distinguished service in the evacuation of Burma', where he had become Deputy Director of Evacuation and Deputy Conservator of Forests.[17]

---

[15] 'Newspaper Opinion must not Determine our Opinion', *The Panacea* 11/126, 129–30. Issues of this magazine were not dated.

[16] PS, F6.3/19, Donald Ricketts to the Panacea Society, 25 March 1925.

[17] Information from A. C. Green, Assistant Archivist, Trinity College Library, Cambridge, 28 October 2009; *The Times*, 28 June 1924, 20 January 1943. The *London Gazette* reported of Ricketts's bravery in 1943: 'During the early stages of the evacuation of Rangoon, Mr Ricketts was in charge of the construction of all labour camps and welfare work in these camps. Later, when making arrangements at Mohnyin for housing and feeding evacuees, he was ordered, owing to the rapid Japanese advance, to start for India with his able-bodied refugees. Mr Ricketts[,] however, refused to leave behind any of the refugees in his charge and set out with a large number, including women, children and invalids. He led these overland 300 miles and was able to get more than 300 to safety. Mr Ricketts showed courage, determination and devotion to duty': online at: <http://www.angloburmeselibrary.com/extracts-from-the-london-gazette—awards-for-the-1942-evacuation.html>, accessed 15 July, 2016. See also Shaw, *Octavia*, ch. 7, for

The Panacea Society also spread its ideas through a transnational network of shared beliefs, of which it was already a part, throughout the dominions and the USA: in the nineteenth century Southcottian groups had spread to Canada, Australia, New Zealand and the USA.[18] The Panacea Society now appealed to some in those existing networks who saw in Octavia the fulfilment of Southcott's teachings. Joseph Gardner, who had been born in Coventry in England in 1836 and had married a Canadian woman from Lake Ontario, was, by 1920, living in Temperanceville, near Toronto. He wrote to Octavia about how he had come to Panacean beliefs through the society's published materials. When he received copies of Octavia's scripts (collections of the messages she believed she received daily from God) he sent them 'to Toronto for the believers there', a group of four with whom he met from time to time. Two of them, brothers William and George Martlett, had been down to Cleveland, Ohio, to see an American member, Mrs Florence Cullum, where 'they met with a cordial reception'. These were the kind of existing networks through which Octavia's ideas were spreading. At the age of eighty-four, Gardner declared that he would remain in Canada until 'I get word from the Lord to take my flight to the City of refuge in England which our heavenly Father [h]as graciously provided for the Church of the First Born beforehand – I have been very busy making preparations to leave the country, freeing myself from entanglement'.[19] The 'city of refuge' was, of course, Bedford, but Gardner never left Canada.

There was also an active group in Australia. Peter Rasmussen, the main distributor of Southcottian literature there, based in Sydney, travelled to England in 1922, quickly becoming Octavia's right-hand man and living the rest of his life in Bedford. But Octavia dissuaded most from turning up on her doorstep, and gave them tasks and duties in their own parts of the empire. Mrs Louise Coventry, who lived in the suburb of Newtown in Sydney, and had written at length to Octavia about her visionary experiences, was told 'Not to come here' but to prepare the way in Australia by selling books.[20] Mrs Coventry

---

a discussion of the sexual relationship that Donald Ricketts had with an American man, Edgar Peissart, at the Panacea Society in 1922–3, and the impact it had on community life.

[18] See Shaw and Lockley, *History*.

[19] PS, F6.3/10, Joseph Gardner to Octavia, 16 February, 7 May 1920.

[20] PS, F5.2/34, Louise Coventry to Octavia, 12 April 1923; Octavia to Louise Coventry, 26 June 1923.

Jane Shaw

remained in Australia, writing more letters back to Bedford between 1923 and 1925 than any other empire member. With her sister, Ellen Burke, she was at the centre of a group of Sydney Panaceans, including Alice West, a Mrs E. Hanley and Hans Anderson; the group had links to the existing Christian Israelite congregation, the Southcottian movement founded by John Wroe in the nineteenth century. In a late 1924 letter from Mrs Coventry, there is some insight into tensions within the small group, as Hans had begun to 'speak in ways I don't like of Octavia and Mrs Fox'. Ellen Burke also wrote often to Bedford, especially to seek advice about her trials with her Freemason husband, in July 1923 writing to ask if Octavia could explain to her husband that they must sleep in separate beds.[21] The Panaceans back in Bedford long acted as spiritual and moral directors to non-resident members and those taking the water for healing, creating an 'agony aunt' correspondence that stretched over many parts of the world, especially the British empire and white settler countries.

The Sydney group expanded, and by 1925, a Mrs Forscutt had joined and was providing a room for the Sydney Panaceans to meet in. They also had contact with a group in Melbourne, which centred on two sisters, Jemima Ramm and Elizabeth Summers, who had come to live in Australia in 1885; they had come from an old Southcottian family in England. Jemima Ramm kept in close touch with Rasmussen once he went to live in Bedford, and one letter indicates that she was arranging for her nephew, Arthur Loms, to bring a package with him from Bedford when he was sailing back to Australia, and that she was 'longing for the time to come when I shall be with you if the Lord permits it'.[22]

The Panaceans also spread their ideas through print. Certainly the society had plenty of books to sell – most of them by Octavia, who was highly prolific – and they shipped them efficiently around the empire. Many of the letters from empire members are about receiving and circulating the literature. An Anglican priest, Russell Payne, honorary canon of Calcutta Cathedral and chaplain of Kharagpur in West Bengal, found one of Octavia's books in Calcutta and was so taken with it that he became a member. A Canadian, Caroline D'Aguilar Henderson, wrote asking to become a member because she had read with profound interest Octavia's first book *Brushes with*

---

[21] Ibid., Ellen Burke to Octavia, 1 July 1923.
[22] PS, F5.2/27, Jemima Ramm to Peter Rasmussen, [December 1920].

382

the Bishops, which she had obtained in the public library in Victoria, British Columbia, where she lived. She noted 'I am writing from a far West city of the most Western Province of the Dominion of Canada so that you may know that the 'pulse' of these things is beating here.' She also enclosed a hymn that she had written, titled 'Glorious Advent'. She received a reply from the Panacea Society with details of her membership, appreciation for her hymn and the suggestion that she meet up with another Panacean, a Mr W. Richards in Vancouver. In her reply, Caroline Henderson gently pointed out that he was some distance away, a fact about the vastness of parts of the empire that those in the Bedford headquarters did not always realize: 'In reference to the address given of Mr. Richards I would say Vancouver is five hours journey by water from Victoria. It is the terminal city of the Canadian Pacific Railway on the Mainland.' However, she added: 'I shall write him and if I take a trip to Vancouver will try to see him.'[23]

Networks and literature could only do so much. In 1924, five years into the life of the community, the Panaceans developed a healing ministry that enabled them to become truly global. Octavia was declared to have healing powers, and these were transferred to water – used for drinking, bathing, topical treatments and protection – via little squares of linen, neatly cut up with pinking shears, upon which Octavia had breathed her divine breath, and which were then put into ordinary tap water. These could be sent anywhere by post, along with precise instructions for use. The healing proved popular both within Britain and abroad; by the time of Octavia's death in 1934, ten years after it had gone public, 32,742 people had applied for the healing; by 1943, 72, 806; and by the beginning of the twenty-first century the total number of correspondents since 1924 was just over 132,000.[24]

The Panacea Society deliberately targeted those in the empire in the earliest advertisements for the healing, which were placed in local newspapers such as the *Rangoon Gazette* in India, and invited people to write in stating all their complaints in as few words as possible. The society also advertised in Theosophist magazines such as the *Herald of the Star*, which had an international circulation, and these

---

[23] PS, F6.3/11, Caroline D'Aguilar Henderson to the Panacea Society, 7 July, 25 August 1920.
[24] These statistics are taken from Shaw, *Octavia*, ch. 8.

advertisements drew the first applications for the healing from Australia and New Zealand.

Once people signed up for the healing, they had to report quarterly. People responded enthusiastically, usually with details of their illness and to what extent they were now feeling better, but also sometimes relating surprising uses of the water, specific to their geographical contexts. Geraldine Bartrup from Upland Farm in North Shepstone, Natal, wrote to report that she had had an infestation of locusts and beat them away not only with police whistles and tins but also by sprinkling them with the blessed water – and the locusts had not returned. Archie Clark in Australia sprinkled his paddocks when he found his sheep dying from a sudden disease and all but one sheep recovered, while Miss Irving, also in Australia, sprinkled a bite she received from a poisonous redback spider and was fine.[25]

As the healing ministry grew – 4,339 people had applied by March 1926, two years after the healing had gone public – so the task of responding to all those letters became burdensome to the resident members working in the healing department in Bedford. They realized that they could not reply to each letter every quarter; this was distressing because they knew they were ministering to many across the globe. People wrote in about everything – their most intimate secrets, fears and problems as well as regular health complaints – for, as one man put it, 'You understand people.'[26] In addition, while the mail was essential to the healing ministry, it was also slow, coming and going by boat to distant parts of the empire. The solution was to select local, trusted Panaceans, whom they named the Towers, to head up satellite healing headquarters, gathering in and responding to the quarterly reports of the water-takers, as well as sending out the linen squares, and then simply sending a summary regularly to Bedford headquarters. All major parts of the British empire had such Towers except the British West Indies; those in the healing there always reported directly to Bedford. From time to time, brief reports from the Towers would appear in *The Panacea*. In 1930, reports appeared on the healing ministry on all five continents, but still the focus was on the empire. The writer noted: 'Our possession of India brings under the protection of our Society the continent of Asia,

---

[25] PS, F6.2/3, Geraldine Bartrup to Miss H. Green, 14 March 1932; S6.1/7, Elinor Partridge to the Panacea Healing Department, 4 November 1935.
[26] PS, F5.2/17, Joseph Taylor to Emily Goodwin at the Panacea Society, 11 September 1929.

where many faithful English people, as well as Hindus and other native races, are using the Healing treatment.' Many Panaceans in England had family members in India and the article went on to say: 'It is no small satisfaction to many who have relatives in India to remember that, at this difficult time, the protection by the Spirit and the Water, is available.' Of Africa, the reporter noted: 'In Africa, many difficulties are presented, owing to its vastness and very divided elements.' Again, the healing water would help: 'It is well to remember, when reading of political difficulties in S. Africa, that to have patients there taking the Water helps the whole colony.' National stereotypes were also reinforced. Americans were not always so keen on the healing because they 'like quick results, and "slow but sure" measures do not appeal to them'. By contrast, the Canadians, who had their own Tower, 'are easier people to deal with. Many settlers had not left the Motherland until they were grown up, and retain their sturdy English traits, not taking easily to a new idea, but steadily persevering when they have once started on the healing water.'[27] Some people who took the healing water became interested in the society's beliefs and joined. Others did not. But it was certainly one way in which the society continued to grow up to the early 1940s.

THE APPEAL OF THE PANACEA SOCIETY TO THOSE LIVING IN THE BRITISH EMPIRE

Many members of the Panacea Society reported that they were attracted to the promise of eternal life on earth, the spiritual practices which made their daily life more bearable, and the hope carried in the healing water. We may therefore presume that the Panacean core belief in immortality was what appealed to so many. But what would immortal life on this earth be like? The Panaceans put Britain at the heart of the world, and Bedford at the centre of the cosmos, and reflected this in their theology. They believed that Jesus would return to their corner of England, Bedford; and their idea of paradise was a tea party in their gardens, which, one day, Jesus would be enjoying with them. The *eschaton* was not so much about the end of the world as it was about a nostalgic version of the English and British imperial world. The Panaceans were intensely royalist and believed that their work meant that Britain – still, for them, ruler of a major

---

[27] 'Our Towers in Five Continents', *The Panacea* 7/76, 94–5.

empire – was 'the Motherland of the world because she is the country in which DIVINE RULE is beginning, slowly but surely, to operate'. And that divine rule was through 'H. M. King George V who is heir of the world, being descended from David, who was chosen by God to initiate the Royal line which sits on the Throne of Great Britain'.[28] In other words, when Jesus returned he would come to Bedford, and Britain would rule in the new Millennium.

Just at a moment when so many elements of the British empire were being questioned, the Panacea Society taught that such an empire, with Britain at its helm, still existed, would always exist, and was essential to God's great plan for the world. The Panaceans, conservative in their political views, intensely disliked the League of Nations and any form of internationalism, considering it threatening to the empire and therefore theologically damaging. In an editorial in *The Panacea* in 1931, internationalism was named as one of the factors hindering the Lord's coming, along with socialism, democracy, philanthropy, disarmament, and home rule for India.[29] Major Cyril Carew-Hunt (who had spent time living in Australia but not India), writing in *The Panacea* in 1930 on 'Our Troubles in India and some of the Causes', suggested that the people of India did not want 'the latest forms of Western democracy, for it makes no appeal to them and runs counter to all their traditions (which are many), their caste systems, and, indeed to their whole social structure'. Rather, 'Personal rule under the British official, or his own Rajah, is what appeals to the native of India.' He ended his article by reminding the reader that 'British engineers have built up a railway service of 40,000 miles and transformed huge areas of barren land into fertile tracts. British investments in India amount, at the least estimate, to 1,000,000,000 pounds, to which the country owes the development of its trade.'[30] In other words, the white man should be at the centre of this world; but through democracy, home rule for India and other popular movements, he was destroying that which he had built and which had made Britain great.[31]

---

[28] Mark Proctor [Octavia's male pen name, which she assumed when she wrote some articles, especially on political or church-related topics], 'Buy British', *The Panacea* 8/93, 198–9.

[29] Editorial, *The Panacea* 8/95, 242.

[30] Cyril Carew-Hunt, 'Our Troubles in India and some of the Causes: The Present Constitution', *The Panacea* 7/80, 180.

[31] For an analysis of this dynamic, see Bill Schwarz, *Memories of Empire*, 1: *The White Man's World* (Oxford, 2011).

In 1931, all Panacea members were instructed to 'Buy British' – a campaign inaugurated by the prince of Wales that year – which included not only goods made in Britain but also all dominion and colonial produce. Many members of the society joined the Tudor Rose League, an employer-sponsored, popular movement for protectionism to circumvent the free trade position of the British government. Octavia wrote to the head of that league, Rear Admiral Mark Kerr, in 1931:

> ... in days when Internationalism is becoming a positive religion, and the idea of a United States of Europe is projected with such amazing seriousness, it is very necessary that Great Britain should take her place as the premier power of the world, because she is the Divine Battle-Axe against all that opposes her destiny to govern a world redeemed from all distressing circumstances.[32]

She had written in *The Panacea*: 'Through the Panacea Society, there are enough people all over the world to begin to "Buy British" with a deep understanding of the Divine Purpose which is at the root of all present-day conditions.'[33]

Panaceans visited and celebrated the British empire exhibition at Wembley opened by George V on 23 April (St George's Day) 1924, where each of the colonies had their own pavilion. One member wrote an article about her visit in *The Panacea*: 'Men of every colour, of every race, creed and ideal, all salute the old flag with a sturdy, filial pride. Never has there been such a gathering of the nations. ... It is a pageant of Empire such as has never been seen before.' She refuted those critics who said that 'the British Empire had reached the top of its curve and will inevitably go down, down, down to the dogs', concluding that a nation that could produce such an exhibition 'has immortality at the back of it and will never die'. For the Panaceans, 'Britain's destiny was to become the New Jerusalem'.[34]

The Panaceans believed still in 'Greater Britain', a late Victorian idea that the 'white settler colonies' – Australia, New Zealand, Canada and parts of South Africa – formed a potential union with the United Kingdom, which would guarantee both British strength and a stable world. Developed especially by J. R. Seeley in the 1880s,

---

[32] PS, F2.4/33, Octavia to Mark Kerr, 29 November 1931.
[33] Proctor, 'Buy British', 20.
[34] F. S. Stuart, 'Wembley and After', *The Panacea* 1/4, 80–1.

this idea was being radically questioned by the 1920s, especially in Canada and South Africa.[35] But some still adhered to it, including at this time many in Australia and New Zealand, and a 1931 article in *The Panacea* by Mrs E. Stone, the Tower for Australia, reflected this. 'Australia is a very wonderful and beautiful country', she wrote. 'We have in our midst a sprinkling of all nations of the world, but Australians are essentially a British race, speaking the English tongue and holding fast to British traditions and customs, our laws being based on the British constitution.' The Aboriginal people were nowhere in this mindset: 'God gave to England the wonderful possession of Australia when Captain Cook first planted the Union Jack on April 28th, 1770.'[36]

A nostalgic and domestic version of 'Englishness', sitting at the heart of British imperial society, was cultivated. *The Panacea*, which was circulated to members in the empire, was full of articles that had titles such as 'Merrie England' (by Colonel Sullivan, MBE) and poems like 'God's England'. Short stories and serialized novels featured Trollopean cathedral closes, usually with a recalcitrant bishop or dean who would not accept Panacea teachings and a marginal cleric or clergy wife who saw the light. Visually, the magazine also provoked nostalgia, with reproductions of watercolours by painters who were at their height in the late nineteenth century, such as G. F. Nicholls, Sutton Palmer and Alfred Heaton Cooper, of rural scenes with country cottages and medieval churches, abbeys and gardens, conjuring up a supposed golden age, when everyone knew their place under the squire and was happy. (There were definitely no modernist landscapes by artists like John or Paul Nash in Panacea publications.) It was a nostalgic view reinforced by Stanley Baldwin, Octavia's favourite politician, in his address 'On England' to the Royal Society of St George in 1924, when he depicted a timeless, rural England in a rapidly changing, urbanized and suburbanized world.[37]

Central to this 'timeless' notion of England was a deep devotion to the Book of Common Prayer. Evening prayer was said every night

---

[35] J. R. Seeley, *The Expansion of England* (London, 1883). On this idea and its development, see Duncan Bell, *The Idea of Greater Britain: Empire and the Future of World Order, 1860–1900* (Princeton, NJ, 2007). On the attitudes of the dominions to it in the inter-war years, see John Darwin, *The Empire Project: The Rise and Fall of the British World System 1830–1970* (Cambridge, 2009), chs 8–9.
[36] E. Stone, 'Signs of the Times in Australia', *The Panacea* 7/82, 226.
[37] Stanley Baldwin, *On England* (London, 1926).

in the Panacea chapel in Bedford according to the Book of Common Prayer, the only addition being a third reading, the prophecy which Octavia sat down each afternoon to receive from the Lord by a process of automatic writing. Octavia also celebrated communion according to the Book of Common Prayer. This meant that worship had a deep familiarity to it, the only variations being the novelty of a woman officiating and presiding, and a new lesson each night – which they fervently believed was directly received from God. Not surprisingly, then, the Panaceans were deeply opposed to Prayer Book revision in 1927–8. On 12 June 1928, Octavia took the 'Deposited' (rewritten) Prayer Book to chapel along with the Book of Common Prayer, and threw the new book to the ground, stating: 'We shall use the old Prayer Book, as the Bishops have given permission to the people that they can do as they like about it.' She then took the 1662 book around to all the members gathered in the chapel and 'each put it to their lips in token of affection and devotion to it'. Two days later, when parliament voted on it, Octavia, Peter Rasmussen and two other members huddled around the wireless waiting for the decision to come through, and were delighted when the Commons rejected the revised Prayer Book by a majority of forty-six.[38]

All of this was appealing to the conservative middle classes, not least those white Britons who lived in the empire and longed for 'home', especially home as they remembered it, before the disruption of war and the new and unsettling forms of modern life, from talking pictures to short skirts to air travel to the demise of domestic servants to reliable birth control to ribbons of suburban housing. They wanted 'home' as they remembered it. An exchange in Virginia Woolf's *The Years* (1937) sums this up. Eleanor Pargiter comments on the 'Brand-new villas everywhere … . Little red villas along the road.' Her nephew North, just returned from Africa, replies: 'Yes, that's what strikes me, how you've spoilt England while I've been away.'[39]

Letters from members living in the empire often expressed their gratitude to the society for providing a link to 'home' as they remembered it. Mrs Ethel Scales was a member living in Kamloops, British Columbia, where her husband, John Scales, had a photog-

---

[38] Rachel J. Fox, *How we Built Jerusalem in England's Green and Pleasant Land, Part II* (Bedford, 1934), 68–9, 75–7.
[39] Virginia Woolf, *The Years* (Oxford, 2009; first publ. 1937), 357. Woolf's husband Leonard had been a colonial administrator in Ceylon and had returned home.

raphy studio, part of a network of Panaceans in British Columbia and Washington state; she wrote to Ellen Oliver, an early prominent member, to thank her for sending some photographs of the English countryside, which had touched off memories of the old country and her now deceased parents.

> I received your packet of Post Cards, it was truly thoughtful and kind of you to send them, it took me back to my old home, & a drive we had with my parents just before we came away, to Leith Hill – they both passed about 18 months ago, within 19 days of one another; they were 83 years – same day – same age & we celebrated their Golden Wedding in 1910 just before we left the old country. I'm telling you this just to show what a tender spot you touched in doing such a thoughtful deed.[40]

For Harold Dolphin, the arrival of any Panacea publications was a highlight: 'the brightest spot in the week is when the weekly scripts arrive, & the big monthly mail with *The Panacea*! How I look forward to them – they are just everything, & however busy one is, there is always time to read them.'[41]

The Panacea Society was the answer to any sense of alienation: a short story in *The Panacea* magazine, revealingly titled 'The Exile', told the story of an Englishman who was unable to get a cure for his cough when living in the Transvaal – until he heard about the healing water and, on taking it, felt for the first time in years that 'life was worth living'.[42]

Canon Russell Payne, the Anglican cleric from Calcutta, was one member who left 'the exile' of the empire and came to live in this nostalgic version of home. He and his wife Mary joined the society in 1928, and arrived in Bedford in April 1932. They had been longing to get back to England for some time, for they were 'very tired of the climate here, we have 9 months of heat, and would give anything for a cold climate', as Mrs Payne wrote.[43] By 1932, Canon Payne had drawn the wrath of the bishop of Calcutta for incorporating Panacea beliefs into his preaching and it was hard for him to continue working there. But what employment might a fifty-nine-year-old clergyman

[40] PS, F6.4/8, Ethel Scales to Ellen Oliver, 4 July 1919.
[41] PS, F6.2/11, Harold Dolphin to Octavia, 11 December 1924.
[42] *The Panacea* 2/21, 210.
[43] PS, F5.1/24, Mary Payne to Emily Goodwin, 28 October, 26 December 1928.

who had spent most of his career in India and embraced heterodox beliefs realistically find back in the Church of England? The Panacea Society was the means by which the Paynes could return to England, where they lived in a community house in return for their work, for they had few possessions and little wealth. Canon and Mrs Payne were the exception; the majority of Panacea members in the empire merely enjoyed this 'period piece' religion by correspondence, literature and the healing water. Far from England, they could believe that the Panacean version of home might just be reality.

CONCLUSION

In its heterodox theology, the Panacea Society was idiosyncratic and for that reason never attracted large numbers. But it was representative of another face of modernity to which historians are increasingly paying attention: the 'conservative modern'. It was therefore more symbolic of the culture, especially the preoccupations and concerns of a certain section of the middle classes, than it might at first glance appear. The British empire and all it stood for was an important part of those preoccupations and concerns, and the Panacea Society knew how to tap into the strong feelings that (nostalgic) ideas of England and the British empire evoked, and relate those feelings to its distinctive theology.

The Panaceans presented themselves as 'more Anglican' than the Church of England, believing that they were the true extension of the Church of England, which had taken a wrong turn by embracing liberal modernism; and they maintained a more consistently imperial outlook in their activities and beliefs than was prevalent or usual in the post World War I period. In particular, the society's theological outlook meant that the Panaceans retained a particular view of empire that had been ideologically important to the foundation of the British empire: Christian providentialism.[44] The British empire was seen as part of God's plan. This idea retained its hold in the nineteenth century and was, indeed, used to explain how this vast empire had come into being, given that it seemed inexplicable in

---

[44] For a discussion of this theological idea and its impact on the origins of, and rationale for, the British empire, see David Armitage, *The Ideological Origins of the British Empire* (Cambridge, 2000), especially ch. 3.

human or worldly terms.[45] However, by the twentieth century the idea of a providential empire was losing currency in most circles. The Panaceans kept it alive and gave it their own particular twist, by relating it to their theology of the Second Coming, which incorporated their ideas about Britain and its empire with remarkable geographic specificity and a certain heterodox quirkiness: Jesus would return to Bedford, their own community being the physical centre for *everything* that happened of metaphysical import. From Bedford, Jesus would conduct his divine rule, and thus Britain would rule in the new millennium. The British empire was therefore an essential and providential component of the *eschaton* as the Panaceans envisaged it.

The Panacea Society was remarkably effective at spreading its message through its networks, literature and advertising: its reach across the British empire from Bedford to migrants and others who regarded themselves as English (or British), however long they had been living away from the country, was significant. In its theology and politics, the society appealed to those who longed for a sense of 'Englishness' and an imperial Britain that were passing away in the wake of World War I. While there were others who welcomed that global shift towards a breaking apart of the empire and a move towards home rule, there were others who did not. The correspondence from white Panacea members and 'water-takers' living in the dominions and other parts of the British empire reveals attitudes towards 'home' that are rare in archives for this period, and suggest that a potentially fruitful area for further research on migrant experience is in correspondence of this sort. These letters explain the appeal of this heterodox religious group, not only with the conservative middle classes in Britain but also across the British empire. Read alongside the Panacea Society's literature, they reveal a picture of a transnational network that epitomized a 'conservative modern' mindset in the inter-war years, and the centrality of notions of empire to that mindset.

---

[45] See, in this volume, Stewart J. Brown, 'Providential Empire? The Established Church of England and the Nineteenth-Century British Empire in India', 225–59.

A Triangular Conflict: The Nyasaland Protectorate and Two Missions, 1915–33

David M. Thompson*

Fitzwilliam College, Cambridge

The idea that the churches became agents of empire through their mission-ary activity is very popular, but it is too simple. Established Churches, such as those of England and Scotland, could certainly be used by government, usually willingly; so could the Roman Catholic Church in the empires of other countries. But the position of the smaller churches, usually with no settler community behind them, was different. This study examines the effects of the Chilembwe Rising of 1915 on the British Churches of Christ mission in Nyasaland (modern Malawi). What is empire? The Colonial Office and the local administration might view a situation in different ways. Their decisions could thus divide native Christians from the UK, and even cause division in the UK church itself, as well as strengthening divisions on the mission field between different churches. Thus, even in the churches, imperial actions could foster the African desire for independence of empire.

For the last thirty years, historians have been pointing out the am-biguities of the relationship between Christian missions and the im-perial government.[1] To some extent this depended on whether the churches engaged in the missions were established or not, but it was also affected by rivalry between different missionary organizations. Colonial governments tried to maintain neutrality, not least where settler communities were small. The First World War put some of these relationships under pressure, particularly in Africa, where the borders between German and British colonies became a neglected

* Fitzwilliam College, Cambridge, CB3 0DG. E-mail: dmt3@cam.ac.uk.

[1] See Brian Stanley, *The Bible and the Flag: Protestant Missions and British Imperialism in the Nineteenth and Twentieth Centuries* (Leicester, 1990), especially 133–90; Andrew Porter, *Religion versus Empire? British Protestant Missionaries and Overseas Expansion, 1700–1914* (Manchester, 2004), especially 255–330; Jeffrey Cox, *The British Missionary Enterprise since 1700* (Abingdon and New York, 2010), especially 171–212.

Studies in Church History 54 (2018) 393–406   © Ecclesiastical History Society 2018
doi: 10.1017/stc.2017.22

front line. In extreme cases missionaries were interned or deported.[2] The brief but violent rising led by John Chilembwe in Malawi early in 1915 drew African support from several of the missions other than the dominant Church of Scotland, and led to the expulsion of all the missionaries from the Churches of Christ mission (among others) in the Nyasaland Protectorate.[3] This article explores the consequences of that expulsion for the African Churches of Christ in the period until the missionaries' return in 1929–31, and offers an explanation for what, for a mixture of financial and doctrinal reasons, became a permanent division.

The origins of the Churches of Christ mission in Malawi were quite recent (1908), and different from their other missions in Burma / Thailand and India. In the latter two there was plenty of territory without any other missions; the intention was also to establish 'industrial missions', where the local people would be able to work to increase their wealth, thereby avoiding a drain on UK funds. In southern Malawi the origin lay with the Church of Christ in Cape Town, established by British settlers, some of whose members moved north in the 1890s into the gold- and diamond-mining country, which became heavily dependent on immigrant labour from Zimbabwe and Malawi (as it still is). The leading missionary was George Hollis, a former South African policeman, originally from Australia, who had become disillusioned with British rule during the second South African War (1899–1902). He was attracted by the ideas of Joseph Booth, whose book, *Africa for the African*, caused controversy when published in 1897.[4] Booth was a religious chameleon, changing denominations frequently, but with Baptist roots. John Chilembwe was one of his first converts, and accompanied Booth to the United States in 1895, where he studied at the Baptist Lynchburg Academy (1897–1900). Booth had tried (unsuccessfully) to persuade the British Churches of Christ to begin an African mission in

---

[2] See the important article by M. Louise Pirouet, 'East African Christians and World War I', *JAH* 19 (1978), 117–30.
[3] The post-independence names will be used except in cases such as this one, where a specific institution of government is denoted.
[4] George Shepperson and Thomas Price, Independent *African: John Chilembwe and the Origins, Setting and Significance of the Nyasaland Native Rising of 1915* (Edinburgh, 1958), 7–123; see also John McCracken, *A History of Malawi, 1859–1966* (Woodbridge, 2012), 127–46; together with relevant background in idem, *Politics and Christianity in Malawi, 1875–1940* (Cambridge, 1977), 207–20; Harry Langworthy, *'Africa for the African': The Life of Joseph Booth* (Blantyre, 1996), 190–3.

1905–6, and in 1906 urged the annual meeting to use African evangelists, rather than government grants. He was rebuffed by the Foreign Missions Committee (FMC) because of the revolutionary implications of his ideas.[5] When the annual meeting changed its mind in 1908, it is not clear whether the FMC members were aware of the extent to which southern Malawi was a melting pot for different Christian groups.

Two other points should be made. Although Churches of Christ had resisted pre-millennial and adventist ideas since their institutional origins in the 1840s, they had not previously encountered Jehovah's Witnesses. The *Watch Tower* movement, as it was known in southern Africa, copied many of the Witnesses' teachings, without being institutionally connected. It was particularly strong in Malawi and had its own prophet, Eliot Kamwana. His message of 'regeneration, through baptism, leading to salvation at the millennium' was similar to Churches of Christ teaching on baptism for the remission of sins, although the latter never fixed a date for the millennium.[6] The Churches of Christ practice of baptizing only on confession of faith, often including converts from other churches, made them unpopular with other missions. Secondly, their polity, in which local elders presided at weekly celebrations of the Lord's supper, made it urgent for them to ordain local leaders, as well as to commission native evangelists.[7] According to their understanding of apostolic practice, the missionary's presence ceased to be necessary after the local church had been planted. Both these issues were important in the problems that followed 1915.

---

[5] The FMC stated: 'We do not find the Apostles organized the churches to secure that the Roman Government should restore its territories to former occupiers or interfere with such subjects': *Bible Advocate*, 30 March 1906, 203, cf. ibid., 17 August 1906, 517, 523; Langworthy, *Africa for the African*, 192–3. Although Booth claimed to be a member of a Church of Christ in Birmingham, no record of this has been found.

[6] McCracken, *Politics and Christianity*, 204. Kamwana predicted that Christ would take control of the world in October 1914: see John McCracken, ed., *Voices from the Chilembwe Rising* (Oxford, 2015), 27, 207–8. Discrimination against Jehovah's Witnesses continued even after independence in the 1960s: Klaus Fiedler, 'Power at the Receiving End: The Jehovah's Witnesses' Experience in One-Party Malawi', in Kenneth R. Ross, ed., *God, People and Power in Malawi: Democratization in Theological Perspective* (Blantyre, 1996), 149–76.

[7] For the importance of native evangelists elsewhere in East Africa, see the classic study by M. Louise Pirouet, *Black Evangelists: The Spread of Christianity in Uganda 1891–1914* (London, 1978).

The Malawi mission station of the British Churches of Christ in Namiwawa was just to the north of the Bruce estates, where the Chilembwe rising began; a group of several families regularly walked the thirty miles to the Namiwawa mission for Sunday service.[8] Those estates were effectively a law unto themselves: wages were low, with a proportion paid in kind; brutal physical punishment of workers was regular; schools and churches were banned.[9] In 1915 W. J. Livingstone, manager of the estates, was beheaded by Chilembwe, and his head used in a subsequent religious service led by Chilembwe.[10] Fifteen African members of the Churches of Christ, including several evangelists, were arrested on suspicion of being involved in the rising, and some were executed. Others were given prison sentences of varying lengths.

The most drastic result of the rising for Churches of Christ was the government's expulsion of all European missionaries from the territory, a process completed by 1916.[11] This did not eliminate the Churches of Christ in Malawi; it simply left Africans in charge, as at the Livingstonia Mission when missionaries volunteered to assist in the war effort. After the war, despite pressure placed on the Colonial Office by the FMC via government ministers and sympathetic MPs, the Churches of Christ were almost the last 'banned' mission to be readmitted, in 1928. Meanwhile the seeds for internal division had been sown.[12] The Colonial Office always referred the matter to the protectorate administration, where the churches were represented by the Church of England or the Church of Scotland, which had always resented proselytization by Churches of Christ.[13] However, in

[8] H. Philpott, 'Namiwawa Looking Back', *Our Missions Overseas*, no. 68 (October 1959), 5–6.

[9] McCracken, *History*, 130–2.

[10] Ibid. 140–1; McCracken regards the rising as a revolt against tangible injustice, rather than a proto-nationalist revolt.

[11] The way in which the British Churches of Christ mission became one of the scapegoats for that rising was first described in 1958 by Shepperson and Price, *Independent African*, 341–55.

[12] The Livingstonia missionaries who had been absent in the war also had difficulties in re-establishing their authority afterwards: McCracken, *History*, 156.

[13] Malawi had been settled by Scots, and in 1914 a significant number of members of the Executive Council were associated with the Church of Scotland mission. Institutional links are described by John McCracken, 'Church and State in Malawi: The Role of the Scottish Presbyterian Missions 1875–1965', in Holger Bernt Hansen and Michael Twaddle, eds, *Christian Missionaries & the State in the Third World* (Oxford and Athens, OH, 2002), 176–93, especially 181–2. Alexander Hetherwick, who served the Blantyre

1927, when the new chief secretary of the protectorate government, Alexander Rankin, was in London, FMC representatives met with him alone, and an agreement was reached.[14]

Rankin's permission for the missionaries to return was conditional on the mission joining the Federated Nyasaland Missions, in which white men had ultimate authority.[15] In October 1928 the FMC authorized the purchase of the Baptist Industrial Mission at Gowa, and applied to join the Federated Protestant Missions of Nyasaland.[16] It submitted a resolution to the 1929 annual conference, approving the resumption of work in Africa.[17] In January 1930 the Gowa property was secured, and in April the FMC received, or 'generally accepted', the constitution of the Federated Missions.[18]

The decision-making on each side in this story needs disentangling. In 1915 the governor acted partly under the Defence of the Realm Act and partly under the Nyasaland Defence Ordinance of 1914 in interning and subsequently expelling the Malawi missionaries.[19] There were questions in the House of Commons about the rising that brought it to the attention of the colonial secretary. In Malawi itself, the governor, many white settlers and their representatives in the Legislative Council, who keenly resented African claims to social equality with Europeans, believed that the root of the problems was the education of Africans in mission schools, where they were encouraged to read the Bible for themselves. There was even

---

Mission (1886–1928), was a friend of the governor in 1915, Sir Charles Bowring, and both were Freemasons, the latter having been grand master of the Nyasaland lodge. The influential Livingstonia Mission was associated with, but independent of, the (United) Free Church of Scotland before 1914, but by the 1920s was preparing for union with the Church of Scotland, to form the Church of Central Africa (Presbyterian) in 1924: Stanley, *Bible and Flag*, 126; Ian and Jane Linden, *Catholics, Peasants and Chewa Resistance in Nyasaland 1889–1939* (London, 1974), 90, 152.

[14] Sir Hector Duff, chief secretary (i.e. head of the colonial administration) at the time of the Chilembwe Rising, had been forced to retire from Africa because of ill-health.

[15] The Federated Protestant Missions of Nyasaland, formed in 1924, followed an earlier body established in 1904. One aim was to secure 'comity agreements' between missions in the same territory to ensure cooperation rather than competition. Their effectiveness in Malawi was weakened by the non-participation of the Roman Catholics and the (Anglican) Universities Mission to Central Africa. Marginal groups such as Seventh-Day Baptists, Churches of Christ and Jehovah's Witnesses were initially excluded.

[16] London, SOAS, Churches of Christ Missionary Records [hereafter: C/C Records], Publications, MCM Box 1, FMC Minutes, 21, 20 October 1928 (§§18–20).

[17] Resolutions 22 and 23, *Churches of Christ Year Book* (Birmingham, 1929), 176.

[18] SOAS, C/C records, MCM Box 2, FMC Minutes, 26, 15 June 1929.

[19] Shepperson and Price, *Independent African*, 333.

a motion (subsequently withdrawn) moved by David Livingstone's grandson, A. Livingstone Bruce, to ban native education altogether. This drew the Presbyterian missions into action, both Livingstonia and the Church of Scotland, which mobilized Arthur Steel Maitland's support at the Colonial Office. He ensured that their interests were protected: the smaller missions lacked this influence in high places.[20] After the war the Colonial Office gradually lost interest. The Phelps-Stokes Commission of 1924 recommended improvements in the standard envisaged for schools and the Legislative Council appointed a director of education in 1926, followed by the introduction of a system of government curricula and inspection (in which mission schools were included) a year later.[21] Thus 'empire' could mean London or Blantyre at different times. The educational changes explain why it was safe to change policy towards the Churches of Christ mission, because the changes ensured white control of schools. A new chief secretary was a great help.

On the Churches of Christ side, the primary actor was the FMC, with the support of other agencies such as the Anti-Slavery Society, so long as the scene of action was Westminster. This is reported, but not described, in the FMC's minutes and annual reports to the Churches of Christ conference. But, like the Seventh-Day Baptists and other smaller missions, they had no representatives in Nyasaland to plead their cause; almost inevitably they saw themselves as victims of the larger and older Presbyterian missions as much as the imperial government.

This should have marked a happy ending, but it did not. Soon after his arrival the first new missionary, Ernest Gray, made a preliminary visit to Namiwawa in May 1930, where he met Frederick Nkhonde and other leaders.[22] Nkhonde asked for an increase in the

---

[20] Ibid. 374.
[21] Ibid. 363; McCracken, *History*, 112, 143–4, 159–60. McCracken wrongly describes Churches of Christ as 'predominantly American-based'. There were no American Churches of Christ missionaries before 1939.
[22] Several of them had been imprisoned in 1915. The two key Africans were Frederick Nkhonde and Ronald Kaundo. Their prison sentences were eventually commuted, and they were released in 1918 and 1920 respectively, when they immediately resumed their positions of leadership. Significantly, Frederick's account of this meeting was sent via Hollis in Cape Town to William Kempster, who had been collecting funds for Malawi mission work since the early 1920s: see correspondence published in *Christian Advocate*, 22 August 1930, 530–1. Gray's letter of 9 July 1930 is at ibid. 531; the original is in SOAS, C/C records, Gray papers, PP1, Box A1, 'Papers relating to dispute with Frederick'.

teachers' salaries and a statement of his views on admission to communion. Gray had to refuse the first for lack of funds; on the second he said that Rankin had made the missionaries' return conditional on the mission joining the Federated Missions, which meant any member of those missions could receive communion. Nkhonde immediately wrote to his principal UK supporter, William Kempster, editor of the *Bible Advocate*,[23] accusing Gray of believing in open communion.[24] The exchange of letters implies that Nkhonde's question to Gray on communion had been Kempster's suggestion.

Nkhonde's letter was published in the *Bible Advocate* for August 1930, and led some churches to demand at the annual conference that Gray be recalled. The FMC received a letter from Gray at an emergency meeting, denying Nkhonde's account and indicating that he had subsequently told Nkhonde that 'he did not wish to interfere with the practice at Namiwawa whereby the unimmersed were excluded from fellowship'. This letter was read to the conference on its last day, and the conference passed a vote of confidence in Ernest Gray and the FMC by a large majority.[25]

In fact, Gray, who as a white man was trusted by the protectorate administration, had approached the Federated Missions as soon as he appreciated the strength of feeling at Namiwawa. The Federated Missions agreed that, because this was a matter of strong religious conviction, Churches of Christ need not join them; and they never did, until the Federated Missions became the Christian Council of Nyasaland in 1942, with a wider membership. Gray also made the policy at Gowa, which as a Baptist mission had admitted the unimmersed to communion, consistent with that at Namiwawa. The underlying issue was probably that after ten years in charge Nkhonde did not like a young white missionary telling him what to do. Gray appreciated Nkhonde's leadership of the Churches of Christ mission

---

[23] The *Bible Advocate* began publication as the *Apostolic Interpreter*. After 1920, the official name for the Churches' magazine changed from *Bible Advocate* to the *Christian Advocate*, and the *Apostolic Interpreter* took the name *Bible Advocate*; then it became the *Scripture Standard* in 1935.

[24] Among Churches of Christ 'open communion' meant the admission of those baptized as infants, as well as those baptized on confession of faith, whereas 'closed communion' meant the admission of those baptized on confession of faith only.

[25] SOAS, C/C records, MCM Box 2, FMC Minutes, 6 August 1930, 42; Resolution 35, *Churches of Christ Year Book* (Birmingham, 1930), 170.

during this period, and later became convinced that Nkhonde had been wrongly convicted of association with the uprising of 1915.[26]

A second problem concerned baptism preparation. Hollis's initial practice had been to baptize people on request, without giving them the instruction customary in the other missions. This led to Church of Scotland accusations of proselytism; more seriously it raised the question of the educational level of the Africans. Dr Hetherwick of the Church of Scotland told the commission of inquiry into the uprising that they would normally expect two years' instruction before baptism. Hollis seems to have changed his practice to require three to six months' instruction, but this was still significantly shorter than the preparation expected by other missions.[27] Gray's proposal for a catechumens' class, lasting at least a year, derived from his college training. It may also have revived African resentment at settlers' hostility to African education in 1915–16, especially for Nkhonde, who had originally belonged to the Church of Scotland mission (as had Tabu Chisiano, whom Gray appointed head teacher at Namiwawa in 1931).[28]

The final problem concerned the baptism of those under discipline from other missions. During a visit to the Church of Scotland mission, Gray learned from the missionary at Blantyre, the Revd J. F. Alexander,[29] that Frederick Nkhonde and Ronald Kaundo proposed to baptize three men under discipline from the Church of Scotland mission for marrying outside the church.[30] After an angry

---

[26] Ernest Gray, *The Early History of the Churches of Christ Missionary Work in Nyasaland, Central Africa, 1907–1930* (Cambridge, 1981), 21. Nkhonde is mentioned among Africans from the Churches of Christ mission in the 1915 commission of inquiry, but as Frederick Singani: McCracken, ed., *Chilembwe Voices*, 432, 441, 496, 613.

[27] Two years had been agreed as a minimum at the first Nyasaland Missionary Conference in 1900, before Churches of Christ arrived: McCracken, *Politics and Christianity*, 187. Hollis's change of policy was acknowledged by Henry Philpott, the third original Churches of Christ missionary, at the inquiry: McCracken, ed., *Chilembwe Voices*, 434–6.

[28] Evidence of Dr Hetherwick and Henry Philpott: McCracken, ed., *Chilembwe Voices*, 363–4, 428–31, 434–6. For Chisiano, see *Open Door*, May 1931, 9; he was a catechumen in a Church of Scotland school, but was baptized by Nkhonde in the Zomba district.

[29] James Alexander (educated at Dulwich College and the University of Edinburgh) was ordained as a missionary at Blantyre in 1908, became 'head' of the mission in 1934, retired in 1938 and died on 6 June 1941: McCracken, ed., *Chilembwe Voices*, 494; Church of Scotland, *Reports to Assembly* (Edinburgh, 1934), 654; ibid. 1938, 655; ibid. 1942, 342.

[30] What constituted marriage was also a contested area in the East African missions: McCracken, *Politics and Christianity*, 194–7; more generally, Adrian Hastings, *Christian Marriage in Africa* (London, 1973).

conversation, during which Gray tried to assure Alexander that he did not agree with this, Gray wrote an immediate letter to Kaundo. He saw him the following day and instructed him not to conduct the baptisms. Kaundo refused, because he did not wish to baptize some and not others. In a careful letter on 17 November 1931 to the chairman of the FMC, Gray described what had happened.[31] Noting that Namiwawa was in the middle of Church of Scotland territory, and that there were also schools or prayer houses belonging to the Roman Catholics, the Providence Industrial Mission (Chilembwe's original mission), the Zambesi Industrial Mission and the Seventh-Day Adventists, he observed that friction between the missions was easily caused.[32] All churches in the Federated Missions had agreed that Christians should not marry non-Christians in church. Gray inferred that the chief, whose son was one of those under discipline, had only invited the Namiwawa mission to build a prayer house in Chisupe to spite the Church of Scotland. The following Sunday Nkhonde baptized two men at Chisupe, once again illustrating his unwillingness to accept a white man's instructions.

The result was a showdown: the majority of elders at Namiwawa backed Nkhonde and only a minority backed Gray. He wondered whether to give up the work at Namiwawa completely, but did not wish to surrender to what he suspected were Kempster's schemes, since Gray feared that Kempster would then step in with alternative financial support. Gray forbade the church to celebrate communion until the dispute was resolved. The FMC backed Gray, and resolved that Nkhonde's letter of authorization to act as a pastor for the Churches of Christ Mission be returned, although there is no evidence that it ever was. Nkhonde, Kaundo and George Masangano left to form the 'African Church of Christ'.[33] After a failed attempt to bring about reconciliation in 1932, the FMC reported that it believed

---

[31] SOAS, C/C Records: PP 1, Box A1, 'Memorandum of Facts leading up to the Withdrawal of Ce F. Nkhonde and others from the Churches of Christ Mission, Namiwawa', E. Gray to L. Grinstead, 17 November 1931; E. Gray to Provincial Commissioner, Blantyre, 6 January 1932.

[32] Those belonging to the Federated Missions called Churches of Christ members *anthu akunja*, meaning 'the people outside Christianity': Gray to Grinstead, 17 November 1931.

[33] After Nkhonde's death, Masangano formed the 'African Church of God': 'The Stone-Campbell Movement in Africa since the 1920s', in D. Newell Williams, Douglas Allen Foster and Paul M. Blowers, eds, *The Stone-Campbell Movement: A Global History* (St Louis, MO, 2013), 311–43, at 324.

that the root cause of the troubles was 'a determination to be free at all costs from anything in the nature of European control'.[34]

Who was Nkhonde's correspondent, Kempster? William Kempster (1873–1943) worked for the Midland Railway and its successor the London, Midland and Scottish Railway at Kettering, Bristol, Nelson, Luton and Bedford.[35] He was a church member in Bristol and Nelson; but there was no Church of Christ congregation in Luton or Bedford, and he devoted his time to editing the *Bible Advocate*. Some of the conservative churches that supported that magazine sent money via its editor for the work in Malawi. Nkhonde's salary was paid from supporters in Canada, mainly UK emigrants, possibly originally mobilized by Albert Brown, an English minister who was the first minister of Fern Avenue Church of Christ, Toronto (1910–20). They saw direct support of the African leaders as an alternative after the expulsion of the UK missionaries.[36] As another channel for funds to Malawi, Kempster rapidly became a confidante of Nkhonde.

The *Bible Advocate*'s predecessor, the *Apostolic Interpreter*, opposed biblical criticism, which threatened the Churches of Christ claim to base every teaching and practice on the New Testament (as they understood it).[37] During the war it advocated absolute pacifism. It also opposed the 1917 union between the British Churches of Christ and the Christian Association – a small group of American-supported Churches of Christ that did admit unimmersed believers to communion – and the proposed establishment of a Bible training college.[38] When Overdale College, Birmingham, was founded

---

[34] *Churches of Christ Year Book* (Birmingham, 1933), 67.

[35] Kempster was appointed goods agent at Bedford in 1931, and became a member of the town and county councils and a magistrate: *Scripture Standard* 9 (1943), 73–4, 85. It is unclear whether he believed that the FMC was either necessary or desirable for missions overseas; he may well have adopted the anti-institutionalism typical of conservatives in the USA.

[36] Fern Avenue was an offshoot of Bathurst Street, the principal conservative Church of Christ in Toronto; such churches opposed missionary societies as unscriptural. After Brown's return to England in 1920, the Canadians offered to take over the Nyasaland mission, which the FMC rejected. Brown played a crucial role in the meeting with Rankin that secured the return of UK missionaries: Reuben Butchart, *The Disciples of Christ in Canada since 1830* (Toronto, ON, 1949), 531–3; *Christian Advocate* 11 (1931), 99, 115–16.

[37] For the change of name, see n. 23 above.

[38] Support came through the Foreign Christian Missions Society in Indianapolis, Indiana. For more on the union and the college, see David M. Thompson, *Let Sects and*

in 1920, its principal, William Robinson, and particularly the tutor in biblical theology, Joseph Smith, came under steady attack from the conservatives.[39] The mission in Malawi was drawn into this conflict.

In October 1930, Kempster asked the FMC to disclose their correspondence with the Nyasaland government about the resumption of the work there. The FMC refused, and passed three resolutions: the first reaffirmed the policy concerning admission to communion held by the British Churches of Christ, that only those baptized on confession of faith were to be admitted; the second affirmed that their interpretation of the conditions of the membership of the Churches of Christ's Namiwawa Mission in the Federation of Nyasaland Missions did not imply any alteration in communion practice (which was possibly misleading); and the third affirmed that the FMC was responsible to conference and would report to it, and therefore declined to submit copies of correspondence to any section of the churches. Finally, the FMC observed: 'it is detrimental to the best interests of the work to correspond with Native Christians in any of the fields, except through the missionary in charge'. The first and third of those resolutions were published in the *Christian Advocate*.[40]

Nothing of this ever appeared in the *Bible Advocate*'s (or later the *Scripture Standard*'s) description of the conflict. For it and its followers, the missionaries clearly wished to admit unimmersed people to communion; it ignored the scandal over baptizing someone under discipline, who subsequently committed adultery, and alleged that Gray supported infant baptism.[41]

Parties Fall: A Short History of the Association of Churches of Christ in Great Britain and Ireland (Birmingham, 1980), 83–5; 109–12, 129–34.

[39] Smith's early career was in the shipyards of the North-East; but from 1892, he had advocated treating higher criticism as a friend rather than an enemy: see a series of seven articles on 'The Higher Criticism', *Young Christian* 2 (1892), 104–6, 135–6, 158–60, 175–7, 224–6, 248–50, 270–1.

[40] SOAS, C/C Records, MCM Box 2, FMC Minutes, 11 October 1930, 43–4; *Christian Advocate*, 31 October 1930, 694; ibid., 20 February 1931, 119.

[41] Although Nkhonde died in 1935, the issue of admission to communion resurfaced after the Second World War, when the *Scripture Standard* published a letter from Ronald Kaundo, provoked by an exchange with Wilfred Georgeson at the Blackridge Church of Christ, while he was home on furlough. This restated the partial truths published in the new *Bible Advocate* in January 1931: *Scripture Standard*, Supplement, November 1945 (unpaginated), repeating the 1931 material.

Mary Bannister's diaries and letters explain what was going on.[42] She had been one of the original pre-1915 missionaries who were expelled. Bannister's diaries show that all the money she raised for Africa from visits to churches in the 1920s after her expulsion was sent through the FMC; hence the money raised by Kempster was separate, and probably went to Nkhonde directly. Nkhonde was in regular contact with her, urging her to return. He welcomed her in June 1928 at Gowa; later that month, when she was at Namiwawa,[43] and again in October, she had long conversations with Nkhonde and Kaundo, mostly at Gowa, which was a long day's journey north. Altogether there were half a dozen meetings with one or both. In October she remarked: 'How often I think that some of God's children hinder His purposes rather than help Him to work them out'.[44] Just over a year later she wrote that she had 'the stiffest fight I have ever had with them. I hope it will be the last'.[45] More surprisingly, Nkhonde came with Hetherwick (of the Church of Scotland) on 15 February 1930.[46] The content of her conversations is not given. Further conversations in May left Mary 'nearly heart-broken when they left'.[47] Finally, Nkhonde brought all the teachers with him in August, when she had not expected them to be 'so stubborn'.[48] She records no further meetings. Clearly Nkhonde wanted her support once she returned; he did not get it.

In a letter of 1931 to her relative, Clifford Slater, of the relatively conservative Burnley church, Bannister reported that Gray had the backing of all the missionaries including herself. In her opinion the letter written by Nkhonde to Kempster should never have been sent:

> You must remember that I have known Fred[k] nearly 20 years & I repeat, he has been put up to what he has done; in my own private opinion it is a boycott against the College <u>because</u> Mr Gray was trained there. The Saviour would condemn most mightily such methods &

[42] Mary Bannister's diaries, referred to by Shepperson, remained unlocated in the Edinburgh University Archives until they were catalogued in 2002 as MS 3211 and added to the online listing in 2011 without explanation of their context.
[43] Her report to the FMC is in *Open Door*, no. 64 (August/September 1928), 9–10.
[44] Edinburgh, UL, MS 3211, Mary Bannister, Diary, 17 October 1928.
[45] Ibid., 15–16 November 1929.
[46] Ibid., 15 February 1930.
[47] Ibid., 9 May 1930.
[48] Ibid., 9 August 1930.

they never will prosper. Mr Kempster asks you to do, what he would not do himself.[49]

She wrote more succinctly a year later to the Grays, 'I blame Mr Kempster for the whole trouble'.[50]

This story illustrates the interlocking of imperial and ecclesiastical conflicts. The 1920s were a turbulent decade for several missionary societies, as older missionaries encountered younger ones with more awareness of biblical criticism and a different approach to mission. All missionary activity was affected by the declining economic situation which led to financial problems.[51] For Churches of Christ, these problems were accentuated by a thirteen-year exclusion from the country, influenced by Presbyterian hostility. In many ways, the Malawi Churches of Christ under Nkhonde and Kaundo became an early example of an African-instituted church. The colonial administration's exclusion of white missionaries accelerated the African control they wished to avoid.

There is a final interesting twist. War alerted the administration to the importance of education, most of which was in the hands of mission schools. In 1927 all schools were taken over by the government, which required higher qualifications for teachers.[52] Mary Bannister lacked the qualifications to make the Gowa school eligible for a government grant, and so the Churches of Christ sent another male missionary, Wilfred Georgeson, a Cambridge PhD student of Ernest Rutherford in nuclear physics, to take charge of the Gowa school. Despite a decade of conflict, empire had its attractions, when coupled with money; and with white men once again in charge, the administration's attitude softened. Hetherwick retired. Georgeson became the favoured missionary, presumably because of his Cambridge education, and under him the Gowa school improved rapidly.

---

[49] SOAS, C/C Records, PP 2 (xiv), 3, Mary Bannister to Clifford Slater, 12 January 1931 (underlining in original).
[50] Ibid., PP 1, Box A1, 'Papers relating to Frederick', Mary Bannister to Mr and Mrs Gray, January 1932.
[51] The Bible Churchmen's Missionary Society was founded in the Church of England in 1922 to resist biblical criticism; Baptists experienced financial difficulties in the late 1920s; even Presbyterian missions steadfastly resisted cuts in expenditure of the kind that meant that Gray could not increase native teachers' salaries.
[52] McCracken, *History*, 159; Linden and Linden, *Catholics, Peasants and Chewa Resistance*, 149–60.

Gray, though unfairly maligned at the time, had a vision for the indigenization of mission in the early twentieth century. He studied as much as he could of the new Malawian history. Nevertheless, the systematic church government he introduced in Malawi was modelled on the British Churches of Christ, and subverted African hierarchies of authority focused on local chiefs.

The British Churches of Christ had been beguiled by Booth through Hollis into a missionary venture in Malawi which was more complex than the resources they had available. Their method of teaching 'the way of God more perfectly' (Acts 18: 26) was regarded as proselytism by the older churches. The latter were influential in the (nominated) Legislative Council, and the Chilembwe rising was an opportunity for discriminatory reprisals. Hollis was a pacifist, and therefore suspect in wartime; but any church with a primary emphasis on Scripture enabled its members to read the condemnations of economic exploitation in James 5. Such texts were not good news for estate managers or colonial administrators. The way forward was the improvement of schools, particularly with larger government grants.[53] A grant for Gowa school was an unexpected bonus from a previously suspicious colonial government. The divisive theological issues were real, but they were inflamed by intervention from a conservative minority in the UK with a different agenda. Thus, whereas the Presbyterian missions successfully encouraged the development of African leadership in the 1920s,[54] in the Churches of Christ mission the African trust in the new white missionaries after 1928 was poisoned by that conservative minority. The triangular conflict between the colonial administration, the dominant missions and those of the smaller denominations was worked out against the background of the different cultures, both secular and religious, in Africa and the UK. The course would have been difficult to navigate in calm waters; but in a storm the result was division.

---

[53] Hetherwick had scathingly pointed out to the commission of inquiry in 1915 that whereas the government grant in aid for schools per pupil in Cape Colony was 15s 9d, in Nyasaland it was 2d: McCracken, ed., *Chilembwe Voices*, 374.
[54] Andrew C. Ross, *Blantyre Mission and the Making of Modern Malawi* (Blantyre, 1996), 183–96; McCracken, *Politics and Christianity*, 221–36.

Social Anglicanism and Empire:
C. F. Andrews's Christian Socialism

Philip Lockley*

Cranmer Hall, Durham University

Charles Freer Andrews (1871–1940) was a close friend of Mohandas K. Gandhi and played a celebrated role in the Indian struggle for independence within the British empire. This article makes the case for understanding Andrews as a pioneering example of the evolution from nineteenth-century Christian Socialism to twentieth-century global 'social Anglicanism', as Andrews's career fits a form better recognized in later campaigners. The article draws attention to three beliefs or principles discernible in Andrews's life as a Christian Socialist in the 1890s: the incarnation as a doctrine revealing the brotherhood of humanity; the Church's need to recognize and minister to the poor; and the Church's call to send out its adherents to end 'social abuses' and achieve 'moral victories'. These three core Christian Socialist beliefs were applied in Andrews's thought and achievements during the second half of his life, in the colonial contexts of India, South Africa and Fiji. By comparing his thought and activity with perceptions of empire traceable among contemporary Anglican Christian Socialists, Andrews's colonial career is found to have enabled Anglican social thought to take on a global frame of reference, presaging proponents of an Anglican global social conscience later in the century.

Charles Freer Andrews is a name slipping from the contemporary Church's memory of significant twentieth-century Anglicans. He is still most easily remembered as Gandhi's closest Christian friend. Yet Andrews is a historical figure well worthy of study apart from Gandhi, as his significance is by no means subsumed within the reputation of the moral leader of Indian independence. In church history, Andrews has been recognized as a notable missionary thinker who developed influential ideas regarding Christian interchange with Eastern religions.[1] Less acknowledged is that Andrews was among the first to

---

* St Clement's Church, St Clement's Centre, Cross St, Oxford, OX4 1DA. E-mail: pjlockley@gmail.com.
[1] See especially Daniel O'Connor, *Gospel, Raj and Swaraj: The Missionary Years of C. F. Andrews 1904–14* (Frankfurt, 1990; since republished as *A Clear Star: C. F. Andrews and*

Studies in Church History 54 (2018) 407–421
doi: 10.1017/stc.2017.23

inhabit a mould of global Anglican social concern better recognized in later twentieth-century figures such as Trevor Huddleston in South Africa and Bishop Ronald O. Hall in Hong Kong.

This mould is known to have been derived from patterns of social thought, theology and campaigning originating in Victorian England and the urban conditions confronted by those Anglican thinkers commonly labelled Christian Socialists. In the post-1945 period, Huddleston and Hall took to their colonial (and post-colonial) contexts this theological inheritance from Frederick Denison Maurice, Brooke Foss Westcott, Charles Gore and others, and drew attention to how the Anglican social tradition was at work in non-Western settings.[2] After them came that more recent instance of the global Anglican social conscience, Archbishop Desmond Tutu.[3] Yet a generation or two before this, the early twentieth-century colonial career of C. F. Andrews had already demonstrated that this same Anglican social tradition had a global frame of reference. Andrews's career embodies the evolution from urban Christian Socialism to global social Anglicanism. The views of empire held by earlier and contemporary Christian Socialists in England did not actually guarantee this evolution. Rather, it was Andrews's personal experience of empire, as he witnessed colonialism in context, which led him to adapt and apply forms of Christian Socialist critique and campaigning across a more extensive imperial horizon.

REPUTATIONS: ANDREWS AND INDIA

Andrews was born in Newcastle-upon-Tyne in 1871 and died in Calcutta in 1940. From 1904, when he first set foot in India, to 1914, Andrews was a member of an Anglican religious order in Delhi, the Cambridge Brotherhood, and a missionary employed by the Society

---

India, 1904–1914 [New Delhi, 2005]); Kenneth Cracknell, *Justice, Courtesy and Love: Theologians and Missionaries encountering World Religions, 1846–1914* (London, 1995), 173–80.

[2] Moira M. W. Chan-Yeung, *The Practical Prophet: Bishop Ronald O. Hall of Hong Kong and his Legacies* (Hong Kong, 2015), 37–43; Piers McGrandle, *Trevor Huddleston: Turbulent Priest* (London, 2005), 21, 32–6. For the history of the colonial engagement of Huddleston's religious order, the Community of the Resurrection (founded by Charles Gore), see Alan Wilkinson, *The Community of the Resurrection: A Centenary History* (London, 1992), 229–30, 307–11.

[3] John Allen, *Rabble-Rouser for Peace: The Authorised Biography of Desmond Tutu* (New York, 2006).

for the Propagation of the Gospel (SPG), teaching at St Stephen's College, Delhi.[4] According to Andrews's most recent biographer, Daniel O'Connor, it was this first decade in India that essentially forged his future career.[5] During this time, Andrews came to reject the colonial mindset of regulated distance and detachment between European colonizers and the colonized. Instead, through close friendships with Indian Christians, then Indian Muslims and Hindus, Andrews developed views radically at odds with contemporary imperial culture.

Andrews's views included a strident rejection of the racist assumptions he recognized to be integral to Britain's empire system, and commitments both to what would now be called 'contextual theology' and to indigenous church leadership.[6] Andrews further advocated interreligious dialogue: his first two books written in India, missionary studies entitled *North India* (1908) and *The Renaissance in India* (1912), stressed the importance of inter-racial friendships for missionaries.[7] Andrews was not alone in such radicalism: other European missionaries demonstrated a similar resistance to the emergent racism of the late Victorian empire, while the Oxford philologist F. Max Müller had notably proposed greater dialogue with Hindus and Muslims as an approach to Christian mission in India back in the 1870s.[8] More distinctive among Anglicans though, was Andrews's Christian sympathy for Indian nationalism.[9] In time, he became

---

[4] Histories of the brotherhood and college include V. H. Stanton, *The Story of the Delhi Mission: the SPG and the Cambridge Mission to Delhi, 1852–1907* (London, 1908); Lillian Henderson, *The Cambridge Mission to Delhi* (London, 1931); Francis Monk, *A History of St Stephen's College, Delhi* (Calcutta, 1935); Constance Millington, *'Whether we be many or few': A History of the Cambridge / Delhi Brotherhood* (Bangalore, 1999); see also Daniel O'Connor, *Three Centuries of Mission: The United Society for the Propagation of the Gospel 1701–2000* (London, 2000).
[5] O'Connor, *Gospel, Raj and Swaraj*, 1–2.
[6] Daniel O'Connor, 'Gandhi, *Dinabandhu* and *Din-sevak*: Critical Solidarity from Two Anglican Missionaries', *Studies in History* 27 (2011), 111–29, at 113–14.
[7] C. F. Andrews, *North India* (London, 1908); idem, *The Renaissance in India: Its Missionary Aspect* (London, 1912); Cracknell, *Justice, Courtesy and Love*, 176–8.
[8] F. Max Müller, 'Westminster Lecture on Missions', *Selected Essays on Language, Mythology and Religion*, 2 vols (London, 1881), 2: 46–86. On missionary resistance to imperial racial thought, see Andrew Porter, *Religion versus Empire? British Protestant Missionaries and Overseas Expansion, 1700–1914* (Manchester, 2004), 282–315.
[9] Sarah Stockwell, 'Anglicanism in the Era of Decolonization', in Jeremy Morris, ed., *OHA*, 4: *Global Western Anglicanism, c.1910–Present* (Oxford, 2017), 160–85, at 166. Responses to Indian nationalism (and especially cultural nationalism) among Free Church missionaries varied: see Chandra Mallampalli, 'British Missions and Indian

convinced that the Indian independence movement was generating a 'new religious impulse' with great potential for a future synthesis of Hinduism and Christianity in the subcontinent.[10]

Andrews met Mohandas K. Gandhi after ten years' involvement in the Indian context. They were introduced in 1914 in South Africa, where Andrews had travelled at the behest of his friends in the Indian National Congress to research the conditions faced by south Asian workers and traders in the racially divided colonies, principally Natal.[11] Here Gandhi had been practising as a barrister since 1893, and had become a leading activist for Indian civil rights.[12] He campaigned particularly against mistreatment of Indian indentured labourers – migrants taken from Indian villages and shipped between British colonies, serving abusive contracts in some of the worst working conditions.[13]

Andrews had followed the Indian press coverage of Gandhi's campaign of non-violence and non-cooperation, and even wrote on his voyage before they met: 'I have a great happiness and blessing in store for me – to see Mohandas Gandhi … . My journey will be a pilgrimage to touch his feet'.[14] On arrival, Andrews did indeed touch Gandhi's feet on the dockside, a gesture which aroused apoplexy in the South African press. Their friendship was then forged as the pair toured indentured labour estates, then negotiated with the interior minister (later prime minister) General Jan Smuts.[15] Their collaboration has long been credited with securing the Indian Relief Act, which provided for the phased end of the indenture system in South Africa and the lifting of a punitive tax on South Asians.[16]

Nationalism, 1880–1908: Imitation and Autonomy in Calcutta and Madras', in Andrew Porter, ed., *The Imperial Horizons of British Protestant Missions, 1880–1914* (Grand Rapids, MI, 2003), 158–82.

[10] Andrews, *Renaissance*, 23.

[11] David Gracie, *Gandhi and Charlie: The Story of a Friendship* (Cambridge, MA, 1989), 25–6.

[12] Gandhi returned to India briefly in 1901–2. His own account of this period is given in M. K. Gandhi, *An Autobiography: The Story of my Experiments with Truth*, transl. Mahadev Desai (London, 2007; first publ. 1927–9); see also Judith M. Brown, *Gandhi: Prisoner of Hope* (New Haven, CT, 1989), 30–94.

[13] David Northrup, *Indentured Labor in the Age of Imperialism, 1834–1922* (Cambridge, 1995), 133–4.

[14] C. F. Andrews to Munshi Ram, 12 December 1913, quoted in Hugh Tinker, *The Ordeal of Love: C. F. Andrews and India* (Delhi, 1979), 79.

[15] C. F. Andrews, *What I Owe to Christ* (London, 1936), 119–26, 132–3.

[16] Revisionist studies now also emphasize the role of strikes and other campaigns more aggressive than Gandhi's non-violent approach in reforming and ending indenture in

During the remaining decades of their lives, Andrews and Gandhi maintained a deep personal bond through letters, visits and further travel, including to England in the 1930s, when Andrews was a key mediator in negotiations between Gandhi and the British government. The dynamic between them has dominated scholarly attention, as Andrews was one of Gandhi's few critical friends, unafraid to disagree with him, even arguing for Indian independence well before Gandhi was convinced himself.[17] In addition, Gandhi's lifelong interest in Christianity – or, more precisely, in Jesus and the New Testament – was shaped by their friendship. Gandhi could not dismiss Andrews's Christian practice and belief so contemptuously as that of most other Western Christians.[18] In recognition of their closeness and Andrews's wider fame as a Christian, for Indians 'C. F. A.' came to stand for 'Christ's Faithful Apostle'.[19]

Andrews was thirty-three years old when he arrived in India in 1904, a little under halfway through his life. The second half of Andrews's life has attracted by far the most interest from historians and biographers, and yet his Christian thought and experience were marked by greater continuity between his years before and after India – and Gandhi – than such notice implies. Concerns and principles traceable in Andrews's career as a Christian Socialist in 1890s England may be linked to his thought and achievements later. Even so, when this thought and activity is, in turn, set beside the varying perceptions of empire among Andrews's contemporary Anglican Christian Socialists, a significant difference can be discerned. Better known Christian Socialists of the time tended merely to lift their Christian moral horizon from urban England to celebrate or critique empire. Andrews, by contrast, applied campaigning principles and a theological perspective inherited from England to actual colonial contexts and conditions. As a result, this article makes a case for understanding Charles Freer Andrews as a pioneer who broke one mould of

---

South Africa: see Ashwin Desai and Goolam Vahed, *Inside Indian Indenture: A South African Story 1860–1914* (Cape Town, 2010), 399–419.

[17] Brown, *Gandhi*, 187, 217, 221, 251–9; Jad Adams, *Gandhi: Naked Ambition* (London, 2010), 136, 153, 206.

[18] Various quotations relating to Christians and Christianity are attributed to Gandhi, most of them unreliable in provenance, including 'you Christians are so unlike your Christ'. For Gandhi's sympathies towards, and rejection of, Christianity, see especially J. Jordens, *Gandhi's Religion: A Homespun Shawl* (Basingstoke, 1998), 45–7; Brown, *Gandhi*, 75–6.

[19] Eric J. Sharpe, 'The Legacy of C. F. Andrews', *IBMR* 9 (1985), 117–21, at 117.

nineteenth-century Christian Socialism yet recast himself in a related form, that of a twentieth-century global social Anglican, whose personal experience of empire shaped him as a witness and campaigner 'on the ground'. It is this distinctive pattern which recognizably fits the careers of later twentieth-century Anglicans such as Ronald Hall, Trevor Huddleston and Desmond Tutu.

THE MAKING OF A CHRISTIAN SOCIALIST

Space precludes all but a summary of Andrews's early biography. He was not born an Anglican, but grew up in the Catholic Apostolic Church, the millennialist body founded in the 1830s after Edward Irving's prophetic interpretations and his followers' claims to charismatic experiences.[20] Andrews's father was a minister in the church, first in Newcastle upon Tyne, then in Birmingham, so that Charles's upbringing involved immersion in the group's distinctive blend of elaborate high church liturgy with (as Andrews later described it) a 'strange, emotional atmosphere of prophesying and speaking with tongues and ecstasy in the Spirit'.[21] Both church and home reinforced a fairly reactionary brand of political conservatism, so that Andrews was raised to believe that 'Queen Victoria represented … God's anointed sovereign … and the vast British Empire in India was … the most glorious achievement of the Anglo-Saxon race'.[22] A day scholar at King Edward VI School, Birmingham, Andrews was given little opportunity to escape this context until university, when he secured a scholarship at Pembroke College, Cambridge.

In the months before his arrival in Cambridge in 1890, the teenage Andrews experienced an intense religious conversion, whereupon, he later wrote, 'my articulate life as a Christian began … Christ's presence became a daily experience … God in Christ had come to me in the night'.[23] Initially, Andrews responded to this inner conviction of God's love and forgiveness through more frequent attendance at his father's church; though he also found himself

---

[20] Andrews, *What I Owe*, 32–7. On Irving and the Catholic Apostolic Church respectively, see Tim Grass, *The Lord's Watchman: A Life of Edward Irving* (Milton Keynes, 2011); C. G. Flegg, *'Gathered Under Apostles': A Study of the Catholic Apostolic Church* (Oxford, 1992).
[21] C. F. Andrews, 'A Pilgrim's Progress', in Vergilius Ferm, ed., *Religion in Transition* (London, 1937), 60–89, at 64.
[22] Andrews, *What I Owe*, 30–1.
[23] Ibid. 42–3.

compelled to notice, as if for the first time, 'a slum quarter' next to the church. This was a place, Andrews wrote, 'where drunkenness and vice were forced upon the poor by their poverty itself, creating a vicious cycle'.[24] Andrews's spiritual autobiography continued: 'Never before had I even dreamt of visiting these homes or seeing these poor people. But now they were very dear to me for Christ's sake'. He recalled befriending several inhabitants of the slum, and 'would go from house to house … seeking to help them wherever occasions arose'.[25]

Commencing his studies in Cambridge in 1890, Andrews's piety was gradually drawn in an Anglican direction by the twin influences of his best friend, Basil Westcott, the youngest son of Brooke Foss Westcott, recently made bishop of Durham, and his tutor, the Revd Charles Prior, who happened also to be Bishop Westcott's son-in-law.[26] During the course of degrees in Classics and then Theology, Andrews broke with his millennialist past, and was confirmed in the Church of England, embracing the Anglo-Catholic devotion and so-cial concern closely associated with Westcott and other contributors to the recent volume *Lux Mundi*.[27]

Encouraged by Prior, Andrews spent extended periods at the Pembroke College mission and settlement house in Walworth, South London.[28] Here he reported discovering 'a joy which often carried me through the difficulties and doubts of college days. Life was simpler there; the suffering of the poor called out sympathy in return. Christ was near: I was consciously taking part in his service'.[29]

By 1895, Andrews had resolved to be ordained 'for college mission work among the poor', but first made use of Westcott family connections to become a lay worker in Durham diocese, living

---

[24] Ibid. 47.
[25] Ibid.
[26] Prior had married into the Westcott family. Like Andrews, B. F. Westcott had attended King Edward VI School, Birmingham, as had J. B. Lightfoot and Archbishop Edward Benson: Edward Norman, *Victorian Christian Socialists* (Cambridge, 1987), 163.
[27] Tinker, *Ordeal of Love*, 8–9; Charles Gore, ed., *Lux Mundi: A Series of Studies in the Religion of the Incarnation* (London, 1889).
[28] Cambridge colleges tended to establish settlements and missions south of the Thames, Oxford colleges in the East End. I am grateful to Bill Jacob for his insights on Oxbridge missions in Victorian London; see also Standish Meacham, *Toynbee Hall and Social Reform, 1880–1914: The Search for Community* (New Haven, CT, 1987); Lucinda Matthews-Jones, 'Oxford House Heads and their Performance of Religious Faith in East London, 1884–1900', *HistJ* 60 (2017), 721–44.
[29] Andrews, *What I Owe*, 57.

close to the Sunderland shipyards.[30] Andrews worked for St Peter's Church, Monkwearmouth, once one half of the Venerable Bede's twin monastery at Jarrow and Monkwearmouth. In the area surrounding St Peter's, Andrews remembered, 'poverty and stark hunger were widespread ... [and] little children were ill cared for and undernourished'.[31] Witnessing such 'cruel suffering', confirmed him as 'an out-and-out opponent of the capitalist system'.[32] Nonetheless, he wrote movingly of the transformation he witnessed when impoverished individuals were shown the love of Christ.[33] Ordained deacon in 1896, and priest the following year, Andrews returned to lead the Pembroke settlement in South London until 1899.

On the eve of moving to Sunderland, the twenty-three-year-old Andrews wrote a prize-winning essay, *The Relation of Christianity to the Conflict between Capital and Labour*. Published in 1896, the work has been passed over by most biographers, considered immature and of little consequence for his later career.[34] In it, he acknowledged his already extensive reading in 'the writings of F. D. Maurice' as well as those of Bishop Westcott.[35] Much of Andrews's argument is certainly derivative. However, three key principles are worth registering, for their resonances in his later life.

The first principle, derived from both Maurice and Westcott, is the assertion that the incarnation, particularly as presented in the Gospel of John, revealed the fatherhood of God and the brotherhood of humanity.[36] For Andrews, this theological principle should shape the Church's approach to capital and labour through an insistence on brotherhood as the foundation of society.[37] 'Human labour cannot be treated as a dead thing in the same way as cotton or coal', he observed; the relation between workers and employers cannot be ruled

---

[30] Ibid. 58.

[31] Ibid.

[32] Ibid. 61; Andrews, 'Reminiscences' *Modern Review*, February–March 1915, quoted in Benarsidas Chaturvedi and Marjorie Sykes, *Charles Freer Andrews: A Narrative* (London, 1949), 22.

[33] Andrews, *What I Owe*, 60.

[34] Tinker, *Ordeal of Love*, 9; O'Connor, *Clear Star*, 16–17.

[35] Andrews, *The Relation of Christianity to the Conflict between Capital and Labour* (London, 1896), [iii].

[36] Ibid. 48–50.

[37] Ibid. 87, 108.

by profits but by 'mutual good-will and self-sacrifice', the realization of brotherhood.[38]

Second, Andrews maintained that the Church needed to recognize and minister to a vast body of unskilled labour, 'the poorest of the poor', living precarious lives with 'bodies and minds stunted', a situation familiar to him from the 'coster-mongers and casual dock labourers' surrounding the Pembroke London mission.[39] He stated boldly: 'Christ is pleading here for the strong to help the weak. A Church which fails to go right down into the midst of the very poorest to bring help and succour is self-condemned'.[40]

Finally, for Andrews the Church was called to be a '"Prophet" of the State', her voice 'crying in the streets of the great city', sending forth Christ's followers 'to be a practical contrast to social abuses', and so march towards a 'moral victory'.[41] In doing so, the Church must be confident, he insisted, of a stronger 'motive power' than 'love of gain'. 'This stronger love, overcoming the love of gain and self', he identified as 'the constraining love of Christ, and its power is not theoretical, but has been practically proved stronger in every age'.[42]

> [T]hose, who have realised that constraining love, have been the most active ... the most energetic ... . [I]n the starving, the sick, the captive, the outcast of humanity, they see Christ pleading with them ... . They know that devotion can be stronger than greed ... . Again and again a stronger motive than self-interest has won the day, and the future will lend still ampler scope.[43]

In such words, Andrews articulated the Christian Socialist conviction that the exertion of moral influence and example, based on practical knowledge and the higher principle of love, would ultimately right the social 'wrongs' and 'abuses' of the age.

ANDREWS AND WESTCOTT

On advice from the Westcott family, Andrews left the Walworth settlement in 1899 to return to Cambridge, becoming vice-principal of

---

[38] Ibid. 67.
[39] Ibid. 68; idem, *What I Owe*, 65.
[40] Andrews, *Capital and Labour*, 68.
[41] Ibid. 106.
[42] Ibid. 108.
[43] Ibid. 108–9.

the Clergy Training School (now Westcott House), and soon after a fellow of Pembroke.[44] His move to India in 1904 also involved the Westcotts. Basil, Andrews's closest friend, had joined the Cambridge Brotherhood and taught at St Stephen's College, Delhi, before dying of cholera in 1900.[45] Andrews eventually decided he must 'take his place'.[46] This personal emotional pull was supplemented by the influence of Bishop Westcott himself, whose distinctive views on Christian mission in India Andrews learned at first hand.

Westcott considered India to be for the East what Greece was for the West: the great 'thinking nation', the source of its founding philosophy.[47] Like several contemporaries, Westcott dreamed of Delhi's becoming an Indian 'Alexandria', a place where Christianity would be translated into an Asian intellectual framework, 'for the fuller interpretation of the faith'.[48] A dimension of this enthusiasm was Westcott's interest in the mysticism of the Fourth Gospel. 'One of his great hopes', Andrews recollected from their conversations together, 'was that Indian thinkers would be able to interpret fully the Gospel of John'.[49]

Andrews's life in India, including the notable evolution in his beliefs there, followed a trajectory set by the formative influence of Westcott. The Gospel of John remained Andrews's anchoring text throughout his time in the East, where, he wrote, 'this Gospel has its true home in the hearts of men and is best understood'.[50] The

[44] Andrews, *What I Owe*, 70; Hugh Tinker, 'Andrews, Charles Freer (1871–1940)', *ODNB*, online edn (2004), at: <http://www.oxforddnb.com/view/article/38830>, accessed 9 April 2016.
[45] The Westcott brothers are discussed in Christian Littlefield, *Chosen Nations* (Minneapolis, MN, 2013), 45.
[46] Andrews, *What I Owe*, 72.
[47] Sharpe, 'Legacy', 118; O'Connor, *Clear Star*, 17–18.
[48] Brooke Foss Westcott, 'The Call of the English Nation and of the English Church', in idem, *Christian Aspects of Life* (London, 1897), 141–57, at 148. On the range of late nineteenth- and early twentieth-century thinkers who viewed India in this way, see Eric J. Sharpe, *Not to Destroy but to Fulfil: The Contribution of J. N. Farquhar to Protestant Missionary Thought in India before 1914* (Uppsala, 1965). Westcott's thought is also compared with other Anglican approaches to India in Stewart J. Brown, 'Anglicanism in the British Empire, 1829–1910', in Rowan Strong, ed., *OHA*, 3: *Partisan Anglicanism and its Global Expansion, 1829–c.1914* (Oxford, 2017), 45–68, at 56–61. See also Cracknell, *Justice, Courtesy and Love*, 60–71.
[49] Chaturvedi and Sykes, *Andrews*, 18. On the link between Westcott's fascination with the Fourth Gospel and his studies of the Church Fathers of Alexandria, see Michael Wheeler, *St John and the Victorians* (Cambridge, 2012), 62–3.
[50] C. F. Andrews, *Christ in the Silence* (London, 1933), 43.

principles of the incarnation and human brotherhood informed his view of almost every initiative he took, from his immersion of himself in the Indian community (not keeping his missionary distance) to his allying himself with the unifying movement of Indian nationalism, itself grounded, as he saw it, in the realization of brotherhood.[51]

Controversially, Andrews's efforts to formulate an indigenous Indian Christian theology, as Westcott had wished, led him to stray beyond the bounds of his mentor's orthodoxy for a significant period. This Andrews acknowledged by resigning from the SPG and the Church of England in 1914, although he resumed presiding and preaching in Anglican churches in the 1930s and found the resignation of his orders had never been formally accepted. Much of his theological reasoning was framed by the intention to 'widen' understandings of Christianity, to interact better with Hindu and Buddhist thought. Greek and Latin theology had too 'narrowly ... defined and confined the Faith', Andrews alleged.[52] The experiential and ethical dimensions of Christianity offered the terms most amenable for India to receive Christianity. 'To follow Christ', he insisted, was 'not the expression of an outward creed, but the learning of an inner life'.[53]

INDENTURE

Andrews shared this last reflection in a sermon in Lahore Cathedral, upon his return from South Africa in 1914. There, his experience investigating the conditions of indentured labourers had had a profound personal effect, building on the time spent earlier among the English poor. He informed his Lahore hearers: 'I have found Christ in strange, unlooked-for places, far beyond the boundary of sect or dogma ... . In South Africa, I found Christ's presence ... far more intimately ... in the Indian and Kaffir locations placed outside the cities of the Rand, than in those cities themselves built up of gold with all its fatal curse upon it.'[54] The white Christian West now worshipped 'Money and Race', while 'the meek and lowly Christ',

---

[51] O'Connor, *Clear Star*, 97, 137.
[52] C. F. Andrews, 'Preparatory Paper for World Missionary Conference 1909', quoted in O'Connor, *Gospel, Raj and Swaraj*, 286–7.
[53] C. F. Andrews, 'Sermon in Lahore Cathedral, May 1914', quoted in O'Connor, *Gospel, Raj and Swaraj*, 288. Richard Fox Young, ed., *India and the Indianness of Christianity* (Grand Rapids, MI, 2009), includes several essays which allow the thought of Andrews and Westcott on interreligious encounters to be set in wider perspective.
[54] Andrews, 'Sermon, May 1914', quoted in O'Connor, *Gospel, Raj and Swaraj*, 288.

he wrote elsewhere, was 'found and worshipped … amid the little groups of Indian passive resisters fresh from prison – Hindus almost all of them'.[55]

In 1915, Andrews resolved to build on achievements in South Africa by working to end indentured labour throughout the British empire. He was shocked by a Blue Book colonial report on conditions among Indian labourers in Fiji, an archipelago of islands with vast sugar plantations.[56] The statistics for suicides among indentured Indians there suggested the misery was even worse than Natal.[57] Stirred by a recurring vision of a beaten, cowering Indian labourer, whose face kept changing into the face of Christ, Andrews embarked for Fiji. He travelled via Australia, where he met with the prime minister and with executives of the Colonial Sugar Refining Company.[58] In Fiji, Andrews lived among the labourers, compiling a report on conditions at first hand. He drew particular attention to the plight of Indian women in labour camps: heavily outnumbered by men, they were routinely fought over, assaulted and abused. '[E]ach woman has to serve three males', he stated plainly; this was a 'moral evil' demanding response.[59]

His report sparked outrage in India, largely on account of the dishonour seen to be done to Indian women, and was accepted by the viceroy, Lord Hardinge. An Abolition Act was drawn up, but the Colonial Office delayed implementation to the extent that Andrews returned to Fiji in 1917 to compile yet more evidence in order to make the case for abolition irrefutable. His second report was controversial, yet effective: indentured labour was officially ended in the British empire on 1 January 1920.[60] This was a seismic reform 'almost equal to the abolition of slavery', one biographer has argued, and Andrews achieved it 'virtually on his own'.[61]

[55] C. F. Andrews to Rabindrinath Tagore, 11 February 1914, quoted in O'Connor, *Gospel, Raj and Swaraj*, 292.
[56] C. F. Andrews, *India and Britain: A Moral Challenge* (London, 1935), 122–3.
[57] Andrews, *What I Owe*, 145.
[58] Tinker, *Ordeal of Love*, 120–2.
[59] Andrews, *What I Owe*, 146; M. K. Gandhi, 'Speech at Ahmedabad Meeting', quoted in Gracie, *Gandhi and Charlie*, 49–50.
[60] On the reception of these reports, see K. L. Gillion, *Fiji's Indian Migrants: A History to the End of Indenture in 1920* (Melbourne, 1962), 177–87.
[61] Tinker, *Ordeal of Love*, 143. Before his biography of Andrews, Tinker authored a seminal study of indenture: *A New System of Slavery: The Export of Indian Labour Overseas, 1830–1920* (London, 1974). His assessment of Andrews's significance thus stemmed

Andrews's efforts on behalf of indentured labour won him the title in India *Dinabandhu* ('friend of the poor') by which he is still known.[62] This, and his manner of putting himself alongside the labourers, and seeing Christ in their midst, clearly demonstrates a continuity with his life with the poor in England. Strikingly, his campaign also followed the *modus operandi* of urban Christian Socialists: gathering statistics, gaining audiences with public and private authorities (frequently through Oxbridge and established Church connections), exerting moral pressure, demanding a 'moral evil' be ended and claiming the need for a 'moral victory'.[63]

CHRISTIAN SOCIALISTS AND EMPIRE

For all this apparent continuity in method and approach between the imperial and home contexts, C. F. Andrews's views on the British empire itself, as they evolved in India, South Africa, Fiji and elsewhere, departed in varying degrees from those of other Anglican Christian Socialists of his time.

This is perhaps most evident in relation to Brooke Foss Westcott's opinions on the empire. For Westcott, the British empire was a largely positive opportunity for the English nation and English Church to prepare 'the brotherhood of Christian nations'.[64] His perspective was notably that of someone with little if any first-hand experience of the empire outside Britain.[65] His thinking, most especially on India, was thus informed by his imagination, which drew upon his reading and hearing the accounts of acquaintances and family members. In an essay on 'Empire', Westcott wrote plainly of 'our race-obligations, especially in Africa and India', to spread the Christian message. He looked approvingly to a time 'when India will

---

from considerable knowledge of the subject. More recent historiography of indenture acknowledges the value of Tinker's overarching account of the system's ending, even though studies now prefer to highlight the diversity of indenture contexts and the agency of labourers themselves in redressing grievances and resisting the oppression of their conditions: see M. S. Hassankhan et al., eds, *Resistance and Indian Indenture Experience: Comparative Perspectives* (New Delhi, 2014).

[62] O'Connor, 'Gandhi, *Dinabandhu* and *Din-sevak*', 121.

[63] For campaigns featuring some or all of these techniques, see Norman, *Victorian Christian Socialists*.

[64] Westcott, 'Call of the English Nation', 147.

[65] Graham A. Patrick, 'Westcott, Brooke Foss (1825–1901)', *ODNB*, online edn (May 2006), at: <http://www.oxforddnb.com/view/article/36839>, accessed 13 February 2017.

finally be organised in distinct nations under our paramount power'.[66] In the same essay, he made clear his view of the Church as intimately bound up with empire, to the point of making the idea of empire almost 'holy'. Through the unceasing ministry of the Church, he wrote, 'each earthly Empire reaches its end in the largest ordered society of men; and in due time 'the kingdom' ... of the world becomes "the kingdom of our Lord and of His Christ"'.[67]

Westcott's acceptance of the fact of empire, and even enthusiasm for its opportunities, has been considered representative of 'an older generation' of Christian Socialists.[68] Certainly, F. D. Maurice's contemporary, J. M. Ludlow, held a similarly benign view of British imperial institutions.[69] But by the 1880s, a few younger members of the radical Guild of St Matthew were more willing to condemn colonialism, one declaring that its effect was to 'dram, drug and syphilise' native populations, particularly in Africa.[70] In time, 'Jingoism' and the Boer War provoked the indignation of Charles Gore and Henry Scott Holland, the leading Anglican Christian Socialists after Westcott. Their critiques nevertheless focused largely on imperial sins in South Africa: land-seizures from Boer famers, and – most notoriously – the placing of Boer families in newly invented concentration camps.[71] According to Peter Jones, Gore, Scott Holland and other Christian Socialists were influenced by John Hobson's theory of imperialism as a tool of capitalism.[72] War in South Africa, like other colonial exploits, looked suspiciously like the British state serving dubious capitalist concerns: securing mining interests, markets for manufactured goods, and yet more engineering projects to railway the world.

Once again, neither Gore nor Scott Holland, by this stage of their lives at least, had any real exposure to the reality of colonial

---

[66] B. F. Westcott, 'The Empire', in idem, *Lessons from Work* (London, 1901), 369–84, at 379.
[67] Ibid. 381–2.
[68] Peter Jones, *The Christian Socialist Revival 1877–1914: Religion, Class and Social Conscience in Late Victorian England* (Princeton, NJ, 1968).
[69] J. M. Ludlow, *Thoughts on the Policy of the Crown towards India* (London, 1859).
[70] *Christian Socialist* 4/40 (September 1886), 36.
[71] Jones, *Christian Socialist Revival*, 202–5.
[72] Ibid. 199–200; John Hobson, *Imperialism: A Study* (London, 1902).

contexts.[73] Empire, for them, was still encountered in newspapers, books and letters. It was thus, as for Westcott, imagined. Gore and Scott Holland certainly felt the empire's effects in urban Britain, in London and Birmingham, for instance. However, their moral horizon lifted principally to detect the extended arms of British militarism and capitalism as they reached out from its metropole. Without experiencing colonialism themselves, English Christian Socialists had little consciousness of how their moral critique and moral pressure might be applied there.

Andrews was different. Experiencing empire at first hand, he took concerns and principles common to the Anglican Christian Socialist tradition developed in an urban industrial setting, and applied them in colonial circumstances. Contrary to existing biographies, his extraordinary life and achievements may be seen clearly to be born of both the formative experience of becoming a Christian Socialist in the 1890s and his years in India. His significance in Anglican history, as distinguished from, say, the history of modern India, is therefore his creative realization of the imperial implications of Christian Socialist notions of human brotherhood, finding Christ amidst the poor and protesting moral and social wrongs. In the life of C. F. Andrews, empire reshaped Anglican social thought, giving it global purchase. In subsequent generations, Anglican campaigners against such evils as apartheid in South Africa or slum conditions in rapidly urbanizing Hong Kong likewise protested against moral and social wrongs on the basis of their own personal experience, witness and presence.[74] Significantly earlier, Andrews had shown how this Anglican social conscience reached not only within the parameters of the Church of England, from London to the north-east of England, but to India and Fiji; or, to put it another way, even to the ends of the earth.

---

[73] Gore toured India in the early 1930s: Alan Wilkinson, 'Gore, Charles (1853–1932)', *ODNB*, online edn (October 2008), at: <http://www.oxforddnb.com/view/article/33471>, accessed 13 February 2017.
[74] Chan-Yeung, *Practical Prophet*; McGrandle, *Huddleston*.